STRATEGIES FOR TEACHING
FIRST-YEAR COMPOSITION

Strategies for Teaching First-Year Composition

Edited by

DUANE ROEN
Arizona State University

VERONICA PANTOJA
Arizona State University

LAUREN YENA
Arizona State University

SUSAN K. MILLER
Mesa Community College

ERIC WAGGONER
Marshall University

National Council of Teachers of English
1111 W. Kenyon Road, Urbana, Illinois 61801-1096

Royalties from this book will be donated to the Conference on College Composition and Communication Scholars for the Dream Travel Award.

Staff Editor: Bonny Graham
Interior Design: Jenny Jensen Greenleaf
Cover Design: Pat Mayer

NCTE Stock Number: 47496-3050

Library of Congress Cataloging-in-Publication Data

Strategies for teaching first-year composition / edited by Duane Roen . . . [et al.].
    p. cm.
  Includes bibliographical references and index.
  ISBN 0-8141-4749-6 (pbk. : alk. paper)
    1. English language—Rhetoric—Study and teaching—United States.
  I. Roen, Duane H.
 PE1405.U6 S77 2002
 808'.042'071173—dc21
                                2001052109

To David Michael Benyo,
July 18, 1993–May 4, 2000,
who will continue to touch the lives of many

CONTENTS

Contents

Contents

Contents

Contents

Introduction

A collection on teaching first-year composition has the potential to serve several purposes, and we found that our purpose in compiling this collection continued to evolve as we gathered the ideas, suggestions, and experiences presented in the following chapters. In addition, editing this collection has caused us to reexamine our own responses as teachers and scholars to questions such as: Why teach writing at all? What is the place of writing in a university education? What will a collection such as this one add to a teaching assistant's or first-time teacher's preparation?

Unfortunately, students sometimes dread university writing courses. One reason may be that they often reduce the concept of writing to simple document production or the five-paragraph theme. Such popular and misleading conceptions of writing, however, can be displaced to reflect that writing is more than just producing a paper-based document—it can be a way for students to connect with their own ideas in ways perhaps not available to them before. Writing can provide a means for them to construct maps of their thinking, or outlines of their beliefs, and present them according to whatever rhetorical situation they may encounter.

Roger Gilles writes later in this collection that writing courses can serve the university by becoming places for "students to learn strategies explicitly designed to lead to a richly developed, sharply focused expression of ideas." Thus, teaching writing becomes increasingly important to the rest of the university community and to the student's life outside the university. For students, writing courses can become sites for practice in verbalizing their ideas and sharing thoughts with classmates.

When Veronica Pantoja asks herself the question, "Why do I teach writing in the first place?" she responds this way:

I think I was initially interested because I felt a need to help students understand that everyone can write and express his or her ideas—it just takes practice and work. Too many students believe that good writers are born that way and that they themselves can never be "good writers." I remember working with a student who felt he couldn't compose one paragraph describing a recent experience. I felt the student's helplessness and frustration as he struggled with all the ideas he wanted to include. We worked through his ideas until he constructed a few simple sentences that described his experience. He was astounded that he was actually able to convey his ideas. With his new confidence, he changed his text around and added a few more sentences until he was pleased with the result. I think that's what set me on my path toward graduate school—my desire to help students feel confident about the ways they could connect with others around them. I wanted to help erase that helplessness and frustration that comes from having something to say and feeling as if you cannot express it. I didn't want anyone to be silenced by a lack of skills (or apparent lack of skills) that could be learned through practice. And I believe that a student, once this confidence is gained, can apply what she has learned in her other course work and in the communities in which she lives. Especially for students who traditionally don't have access into the academic world and for whom the university and its language are unfamiliar, writing courses can provide the confidence to access other courses, other ideas. Because no student walks into a writing classroom without the ability to communicate and express his or her ideas, teachers of writing must learn to build on their students' knowledge and incorporate it into their own teaching to help students refine those abilities. They must guide students in effective, theoretically sound activities that will encourage their students to express ideas and construct text that is meaningful and inventive. This particular collection provides all teachers of writing with additional examples, models, and activities that will complement an experienced writing teacher's pedagogy and broaden a novice writing teacher's experience.

Writing instruction is integral to education, but particularly to a university education, for a number of reasons. As undergraduates, students who engage in writing as a critical practice have the opportunity to become more critical and persuasive readers, writers, and thinkers—skills that aid in their success, regardless of their particular field of study. This practice facilitates their ability to sift through and discern the value of various theories and ideas across the curriculum.

Some have argued in a similar vein that writing instruction is necessary preparation for students entering a marketplace in which employers continually voice the need for effective oral and written communicators. In keeping with this line of thinking, some contributors to this volume have addressed the role of technology-mediated writing instruction. Technological literacy has now become a widely accepted prerequisite for myriad employment opportunities and is swiftly becoming a key component of this preparedness; consequently, we must help students cultivate a deeper critical awareness of how this shift affects us all.

On a broader scale, we are able, through university-level writing courses, to illuminate the ideological and rhetorical structures within which students are implicated, thereby better equipping them with a critical apparatus they may use to effectively articulate their own concerns, as well as the goals and needs of their communities. These skills help extend the benefits of a well-designed and implemented writing curriculum beyond the classroom and the university into society at large.

Former students are some of the strongest advocates for teaching writing. At Arizona State University, for example, with an enrollment of 45,000, the Office of University Evaluation has collected survey data from almost all first-year students and most graduating seniors for more than a decade. That office has also collected similar information from alumni several years after graduation. The data from these three groups offer powerful arguments for teaching writing—as well as speaking, teamwork strategies, and technology skills. While incoming students moderately value writing, graduating seniors and alumni consistently rank writing as one of the most valuable proficiencies for life after college. Further, although students graduating from Arizona State University complete at least a two-course sequence of courses in writing, a high percentage of them wish they had participated in even more instruction in writing—as well as speaking, teamwork strategies, and technology skills.

The survey results from Arizona State University lead to another observation: too often, college and university faculty consider writing an academic enterprise—something done by people in academic settings for academic purposes. But the academic realm is only part of life, along with the professional, personal, and civic realms. For most of our students, the academic realm is much smaller than the personal and the professional realms. Given the varying proportions of these four realms, we can help students see the relevance of writing if we provide them opportunities to write in the realms that are most important to them while they are enrolled in our courses. We can give them opportunities to write to accomplish tasks in not only the academic realm but also the professional, civic, and professional realms of their lives. Shelly Whitfield, who teaches writing at Central Arizona College–Superstition Mountain Campus, answers the question "Why teach writing?" this way:

> Writing gives us that rare opportunity to come to terms with what we think and believe. Perhaps we are letting our ideas flow regarding a social issue or maybe we are carefully composing a love letter. No matter what writing act is taking place, when word and paper meet there is commitment. Why else are we asked—in several arenas of our life—to sign on the dotted line? Because writing—committing something to paper, whether it is your signature or an essay on civil rights—requires us to take some sort of responsibility.
>
> Teaching first-year composition gives me the rare opportunity to slow down long enough with a classroom of students to allow them to take responsibility for their writing. Through this forum, students can come to realize that writing is more than just being able to write effective essays for their future English and business professors. Writing is an extension of each and every one of my students. Writing takes on many shapes and forms, fulfilling many purposes depending on when and where they are asked to use it.
>
> Perhaps I drain the magic out of the composing process because I dispel the myth that only a few are born with the talent to become good writers. Instead I choose to infuse power in the act of writing, teaching my students that while writing may not be a magical process for them, it should be a liberating one. Uncovering new ideas through writing, seeing new beliefs staring back at them from the page, emptying the crevices of their brains on that seventh draft is a kind of liberation. And these actions can be applied to a critical paper on the sexism of Super Bowl commercials, or they can be applied to a narrative paper regarding the first day of school. No matter

what writing act is taking place, students are thinking and learning through writing. This is an exciting event to witness, especially when they realize that while they are writing to liberate themselves, they have the power to write to liberate others. First-year composition can be a beautiful thing and I am committed to that belief.

Before finishing the manuscript for this collection in early 2001, we posted the question "Why teach writing?" to the listserv for the Council of Writing Program Administrators (WPA-L@asu.edu). We include some of the responses here—with permission of those whom we quote:

Why Teach Writing? Well, I guess one reply would be "Why not?" But seriously, I teach writing because it not only helps students in other classes (besides English classes) but it also helps them hone thinking and analyzing skills as well as allowing them to investigate ideas and topics that they might not get in any other class. That and the fact that I'd be lousy at teaching math!

Brenda Tuberville, Texas Christian University

Why teach writing? Because the First Amendment says I can. Because revolution/change comes out of the ability to compose and express a vision, and I believe in people's right to shape policy by rising up and making change. Because language is power, written language is tangible power, and power should belong to the people.

Cynthia Jeney, Missouri Western State College

Why teach writing? Many major companies now don't care so much what an applicant's major is; they care whether the applicant can write well, speak well, and get along with other people.

David Reinheimer, Southeast Missouri State University

Why teach writing? I suppose I stumbled into teaching writing—I was teaching high school English (meaning mostly literature), and it didn't take too long to find out that through our writing the students and I got to know each other in ways that weren't possible in a teacher-teach, teacher-test, teacher-grade situation. One thing led to another, and that's why I teach writing. Of course one doesn't teach "just writing." That being said: it's simply a very useful thing to teach. Most of my students know that learning how to improve their writing abilities—even a bit here and there—is a good thing to do. Makes their lives richer, helps them understand things in ways they otherwise wouldn't have, contributes to their upward mobility. It's a sure winner.

Irvin Peckham, Louisiana State University

How could you not teach writing? Someone has to. Many of my students start the semester believing the ability to write is a talent they have to be born with, like a great artist or composer. However, though they might not feel inferior if they can't paint the Mona Lisa they do feel inferior when they don't have the skills to communicate effectively through their writing. Teaching them how to write, how to express themselves, how to get a grasp on the language and how to use it [to] their advantage, is, for me, a way of helping them gain a type of independence and freedom that they do not feel on day one of a new semester. Granted, I haven't done this for long and may become cynical and bitter after years of this, but I have never felt anything like the feeling I get when a student starts my class with no confidence, certain that they are just not a "writer," and leaves at the end of semester with certainty of their ability and knowledge that they can use throughout college and their career.

Jennifer Walker, Louisiana State University

Why teach writing? Just roll up the other answers into a big ball. It's helpful, meaningful, fascinating, powerful, all in ways that are something of our giant secret (though not for lack of trying to tell people about it). It makes me feel as if I'm at an edge of the known universe, moving outward. Even better, the main argument for teaching writing is the quality of the other people who are doing it, their even exaggerated display of great qualities: bravery, temperance, generosity, insight. In the bad times I look around and figure if these are the people doing this thing, there has to be something very right about it.

Keith Rhodes, Missouri Western State College

Why teach writing? It's my kind of social work and activism. Today's society ;-) is controlled by folks who can create, critique, and manipulate texts. Many of these texts are written ones, and by helping people learn and practice ways of creating, reading, critiquing, and revising writing, I believe I'm able to help people gain the skills that may help them participate more fully in the institutions and practices that shape much of the political and social environment.

Kurt Bouman, University of Pittsburgh

Why teaching writing? When I've heard this question before (sometimes in job interviews), often the implicit question is "Why would anyone with a PhD or scholarly interests ever find composition to [be] a worthy intellectual pursuit? How can you stand it?" One of the best responses I've heard was short and sweet and authentic, "Because that's where I find the real challenges."

Larry Beason, University of South Alabama

Why teach writing? Because some folks who have been silenced, who cannot say what they think, feel, mean, can write down what they would have said and give voice to what would re-main unsaid without writing.

Marcia Ribble, Michigan State University

Why teach writing? A few years back, when my son (now 8) was just starting kindergarten, we were talking about my work at the university:

"Writing?" he asked. "I can do that."

"Well," I replied, "it's a bit more complicated than that."

"Oh!" His eyes grew wide with interest. "Do you mean cursive?"

I've been lucky. Even as his sophistication about writing has grown, his interest for what lies ahead grows even faster.

Rolf Norgaard, University of Colorado at Boulder

Why teach writing? Because it matters.

Rebecca Moore Howard, Syracuse University

Why teach writing? Writing makes learning visible, and I like to see what I am working on.

Thomas Miller, University of Arizona

Why teach writing? Because a writing course is a place to work on all kinds of issues/problems/topics without having to be spe-cialists on those issues/problems/topics (see Plato spinning in his grave?)

Because being able to look at how writing changes (or doesn't) over time offers ways to talk about learning, cultural (re)production, and all the other things writing does that other venues/courses/media don't (or at least haven't yet)

   Because "good writing" is a trope in our culture that needs to be rethought, redefined, and sometimes subverted.

Seth Kahn, Syracuse University

Why teaching writing? My answer—especially in multi-disciplinary contexts—is that how people write, and how they learn to write, has fascinated me for the past 25 years in the way that the behavior of cells fascinates biologists, the study of other peoples fascinates anthropologists, etc. I really do just find it endlessly fascinating. So teaching writing is one extension of that fascination, and all the better when it seems like my involvement has effects that satisfy everyone involved.

Stephen North, University at Albany,
State University of New York

   There are also multiple answers to a related question: "What will this book add to TA preparation for teaching?" One feature of this collection is its wide-ranging scope of ideas centered on one common theme—writing instruction. The educational backgrounds, teaching experience, and future goals of composition TAs are increasingly diverse. At Arizona State University, for example, teaching assistants are earning degrees in disciplines such as linguistics, teaching English as a second language, creative writing, English education, literature, and rhetoric and composition. The ideas collected here reflect this variety of disciplinary approaches and provide flexible adaptations that may be suited to the strengths and interests of these different groups. With contributors who represent and speak from a number of perspectives, this text has a polyvocal quality that subverts tendencies toward totalizing narratives about what writing instruction is or should be. New teaching assistants and teachers will find not only chapters written by experienced teachers, but also chapters by instructors like themselves who are new to the classroom and who may share their more immediate concerns. And because writing instruction takes place in a variety of educational contexts, readers will find chapters and suggestions written by instructors who teach in community colleges, liberal arts colleges, state university systems, and research institutions.

Additionally, the chapters cover a broad range of topics, thereby enabling those who use the collection to focus on those issues most pertinent to the needs of their particular students and institutions. In this way, the text is more widely adaptable than those that take a more uniform approach.

New writing teachers typically confront a range of challenges before and during their first terms or semesters as classroom instructors. Often with little opportunity for critical reflection, they must craft effective responses to the following questions: What type of presence or ethos will I establish in the classroom? How do I develop and maintain a learning atmosphere that is productive and professional? How do I prepare a syllabus and daily writing assignments that will be substantive and dynamic? How can I be sure that those assignments meet the broad objectives of my institution? What philosophies and theories inform the pedagogical approaches I will select and use? How can I hone my own evolving philosophy of teaching? How can I help my students generate creative ideas for writing projects? Are there methods for responding to students' essays that will help foster a positive rapport and encourage revision? How can I be sure that the assessment strategies I use in my classroom will correlate with those used in parallel courses being taught at my university and elsewhere? To what extent will I focus on issues of grammar, style, or form in my assessment of students' writing? How do I teach my students to become responsible, skilled researchers? How will I incorporate the use of technology into students' writing and research assignments?

To varying degrees, this collection of essays is designed not only to provide the beginnings of possible answers to some of these crucial questions, but more important, to initiate the critical dialogue and reflection that are so often overlooked in the flurry of activity that accompanies the beginning of most teaching assignments. For this reason, Chapter 1 is devoted to discussions of the larger contexts for the teaching of writing at the university level. The focus then moves on to more specific questions such as syllabus design (Chapter 3), invention strategies (Chapter 7), and the teaching of research skills (Chapter 14).

Chapter 1, "Contexts for Teaching Writing," describes some of the contexts for teaching in colleges and universities. Because

it is often difficult for new teachers—and even experienced ones—
to know the contexts in which they will be teaching composition, this chapter includes discussions of how composition courses
are situated within composition programs, which have collective
expectations. In turn, departments and colleges that house composition programs have specific expectations for the ways in which
composition should serve those larger academic units. Beyond
that, universities often expect composition to fulfill institutional
goals for literacy. And, of course, universities answer to boards
of directors, boards of regents, and legislatures—all of which hold
additional expectations. Including perspectives of some highly
experienced teachers and administrators, this chapter describes
these multiple contexts and offers some productive strategies for
negotiating them. Given its contextualizing function, this chapter is probably the most crucial for anybody entering the classroom.

Chapter 2, "Seeing the Forest and the Trees of Curriculum,"
includes an outcomes statement drafted by composition scholars
from across the United States and officially endorsed by the Council of Writing Program Administrators. This document, the product of several years of debates about the goals of first-year
composition courses, may well serve as a cornerstone for curriculum for decades to come. Irv Peckham, one of the framers of
the statement, kicks off the chapter by discussing specific ways in
which teachers might enact these curricular goals. Other contributors then describe and explicate how curriculum can be
shaped for particular purposes and particular settings. This chapter also demonstrates the principle that instruction in any discipline and at any level must begin with goals. Of course, there are
many sources of instructional goals: an individual teacher's scholarly research, familiarity with instructional practices described
in professional books and journals, explicit and tacit agreements
among faculty in a program or department, university-wide general studies policies, professional organizations' endorsed practices, and sometimes accrediting agency guidelines. Regardless
of the source(s) of these goals and whether teachers are explicitly
setting them, teachers have them in mind as they plan what they
do in the classroom. Our purpose here is to encourage teachers
to think through goals explicitly instead of subconsciously al-

lowing the context in which they are teaching to shape what they do. Regularly discussing these goals with colleagues can help teachers more clearly see where they are going, why they are going where they're going, and how they can most effectively and efficiently get there.

The contributors in Chapter 3, "Constructing Syllabus Materials," build on the previous chapter by demonstrating how teachers can describe their course goals and activities to students. The syllabus is not just a contract with students; it is also a road map for them and for teachers. This chapter includes a sample syllabus and a course description. In the course description, Gregory Clark models possible ways for teachers to explain their courses to students. Students entering Clark's course know in detail what they are expected to learn and do during the semester. In the sample syllabus, Marvin Diogenes provides details for each unit and lesson in his course. His students also know what to expect each week as the semester progresses.

Chapter 4, "Constructing Effective Writing Assignments," suggests some strategies for constructing not only individual assignment prompts but also sequences of writing assignments. Among other things, the chapter includes assignments that permit students to explore professional, personal, and civic as well as academic topics of interest. Also included are some theoretical principles underpinning the prompts. Because of long-standing debates about the appropriateness of autobiographical assignments in first-year courses, Bonnie Kyburz presents a theoretical argument supporting such assignments.

Chapter 5, "Guiding Students to Construct Reflective Portfolios," includes sample assignment prompts to guide students as they construct portfolios for writing courses. Contributors to this chapter vividly illustrate how portfolios encourage students to see the value of a wide range of activities in composition courses, to think critically about their experiences with invention, revision, reading responses, peer responses to emerging texts, and the like. Unlike individual essays or final examinations, course portfolios offer students opportunities to demonstrate the full range of the skill and knowledge sets they have developed in a course.

In Chapter 6, "Strategies for Course Management," contributors discuss ongoing concerns such as maintaining classroom civility, orchestrating large- and small-group discussions, grading course work, promoting attendance, discouraging plagiarism, and constructing lesson plans. Although the topics in this chapter apply to courses across the disciplines, they certainly pertain to the day-to-day activities in composition courses. Effective course management requires some time and effort, but it is a necessary and high-yield investment.

Chapter 7, "Teaching Invention," includes general principles for teaching invention, as well as a variety of specific activities and strategies that help students generate material for writing. Several contributors illustrate invention strategies with samples from their students' work. David Sudol even describes how he practices invention alongside his students so that he can better empathize with them as they struggle to give shape to their thinking. Vicky Campo demonstrates the recursive nature of invention by showing how she uses it late in the composing process. Michael Murphy explains that teaching arrangement can be a form of invention; it should help students give shape to their verbal thinking, but it should never be a Procrustean bed. This chapter should help teachers guide their students as they make choices about arrangement, which can and should serve a range of rhetorical goals.

Chapter 8, "Orchestrating Peer-Response Activities," which includes strategies for constructing a fairly wide range of peer-response activities, is designed to help new teachers decide how to construct sequences of peer-response sessions so that teachers can, if they wish, use a different one each class meeting during a unit. Among other things, the chapter includes specific questions peers might answer early on when a writer is considering possible topics for writing. Other questions direct peers' attention to subsequent tasks that writers need to complete: generating ideas for developing the topic, selecting material from that which has been generated, organizing material in ways that help readers, and editing surface features of emerging texts. Contributors also offer suggestions for introducing peer-response activities, bringing them to closure, and encouraging writers to use peers' responses effectively as they revise.

Chapter 9, "Responding to In-Process Work to Promote Revision," focuses primarily on teachers' rather than peers' responses. While getting peers to do this work helps everyone in the classroom (writers, peers, teacher), contributors demonstrate that teachers can also effectively respond to in-process work. Generally, contributors suggest response strategies that encourage writers to take responsibility for their writing—as opposed to thinking that teachers are responsible. They also suggest strategies for responding efficiently. Among these suggestions—which contributors illustrate with sample drafts of student papers—are the following: asking questions that encourage writers to make decisions rather than telling them what to do, focusing on a few concerns rather than on everything that could be addressed, and addressing a concern once rather than every time it appears in an emerging text.

Chapter 9 also includes guidance for working with the campus writing center. These essays describe the kinds of services centers do and do not offer. Contributors explain how crucial it is for teachers and students to understand the functions of a writing center and to work with the writing center to fulfill those functions. Too often, teachers and students expect writing centers to fix problems with students' writing, especially surface features of their texts. The problem with that expectation, of course, is that fixing problems for students does not help students take responsibility for their own writing. Rather than fixing prose, writing center personnel help students develop strategies for reading their writing more critically, as well as strategies for all aspects of composing.

Chapter 10, "Responding to and Evaluating Polished Writing," offers strategies for responding to writing that students consider fully polished. The chapter is designed to help teachers decide when and how to encourage students to do yet one more round of revising content or editing surface features. It also should help teachers decide when enough is enough—when the exigencies of the semester don't permit another round or when the student can't muster the energy to revise and/or edit again. How can a teacher's comments help students understand what they have and have not accomplished with the project? How might students reflect on the project in the course portfolio? How can a teacher's comments help students understand the grades assigned to papers?

Although Chapter 11, "Teaching Writing with Technology," will not fully prepare teachers for teaching in electronic classrooms or for using electronic technologies in their teaching, it will help teachers begin to consider the choices they need to make about using such pedagogical/epistemological/literary tools. The chapter is designed to help teachers ask the following kinds of questions: How can I best prepare myself for using these tools in my teaching? How do such tools transform/modify/mediate/alter literate practices? How can I help students decide when and how to use current electronic technologies? How do electronic literacies change the nature of texts? When is an electronic classroom interaction better than, worse than, or the same as a face-to-face interaction or a pen-and-paper interaction?

Chapter 12, "Constructing a Teaching Portfolio," describes the possible contents of teaching portfolios: teaching philosophies, annotated syllabi, annotated assignment prompts, syntheses of course evaluations, supervisors' class visit reports, students' in-process papers with teacher's written responses, annotated lesson plans, and the like. Contributors discuss the functions of teaching portfolios for graduate students, tenure-track faculty, tenured faculty, and adjunct faculty. Included in the chapter are some sample materials from teachers. Teachers need to begin constructing teaching portfolios during the first year of teaching—not the year they apply for jobs, not the year they are considered for tenure. Beginning this work the first year of teaching helps teachers become the reflective practitioners Donald Schön describes in *Educating the Reflective Practitioner.*

Keith Rhodes opens Chapter 13, "Teaching Matters of Grammar, Usage, and Style," with a thoughtful analysis of some of the issues surrounding the teaching of grammar and usage. He offers a useful perspective that teachers of composition need to consider before they plan instruction. Following Rhodes's caution, several other contributors offer strategies for engaging students in constructing sentences to explore a range of syntactic options.

In Chapter 14, "Teaching Research Skills," contributors contextualize research within the academy and within composition courses. They describe strategies for helping students engage in a range of research activities: defining reasonable research topics and projects; making research relevant to students' academic, professional, personal, and civic interests; using the most effective research methodologies to answer the research question; finding, evaluating, incorporating, and documenting sources—including electronic sources.

As you begin reading, discussing, and using the chapters that follow, it will become immediately obvious that this book does not offer the one "right" way to teach writing, for there is no single right way. Instead, the many contributors to this collection offer multiple approaches, strategies, and activities for teaching writing, particularly in first-year courses. Each chapter showcases diverse means for achieving various goals in a writing classroom and provides theoretical explications for those means. We hope that the Bakhtinian polyphony of voices included in this collection will inspire you and your colleagues to discuss and construct additional approaches, strategies, and activities, as well as theories that inform them.

A number of different voices are represented in this eclectic mix, a multiplicity that reflects the diverse perspectives in the field. In the process of defining their own emerging teaching philosophies and approaches, new teachers would also do well to become aware of the larger, perpetual redefinition(s) of composition courses themselves. In the ever-changing landscape of university education, composition has alternatively been defined as a remedial course, a gatekeeping course, a service course, and so on.

When we asked Shelly Whitfield, who teaches at Central Arizona College–Superstition Mountain Campus, to read the manuscript of this book and to answer the question "Why would new teachers find this book helpful?" she offered this observation:

> As a new composition teacher, I am not only scrambling to find the most effective teaching methods, I am also establishing a belief system on which to build my teaching philosophy. So what happens? I head to the classroom, equipped with sound composition theories and a firmly rooted (and practiced) pedagogical style. I'm ready, right? Whoosh! My students have just disarmed one of my composition theories. It lies there lifeless in all its complexities, non-applicable to this particular bunch of people. But that is all right, I'll just activate my super-power

shield—the portfolio. That way I can catch and deflect any of their poor attempts at my writing activities and turn them into something useful, perhaps even promising. But wait . . . the semester ends and their portfolios are just as lifeless as the composition theory they succeeded in deactivating at the beginning of the term. I need help.

This book not only offers possible solutions to my immediate (somewhat fictionalized, but somewhat true) situation, but it also inspires me to reflect on other possible issues that I may confront in the composition classroom. For instance, I can go immediately to the portfolio chapter and compare how I chose to present and apply the portfolio to those instructors and scholars in this book. I can also begin to see and understand composition theory in action as I read the experiences of the many voices presented in this text. However, this book also uncovers some bigger, philosophical issues. Perhaps my difficulties as a new composition teacher do not stem from my teaching methods as much as from my teaching beliefs. Is my philosophy of teaching writing aligned with the school that has employed me? Do my expectations for English 101 even begin to consider my students' expectations?

This book becomes my "mentor on the shelf," ready to be asked most any composition/teaching question whether practical, theoretical, or historical, motivating me to look at teaching composition as a multi-dimensional and multi-faceted undertaking that has been shaped by many experiences and many people.

In 1975 Richard Ohmann and W. B. Coley edited for NCTE a collection of essays, all of which had appeared in *College English* from March 1967 to January 1975, the term of their editorship of that journal. In the preface to *Ideas for English 101: Teaching Writing in College,* Ohmann and Coley astutely note: "Not long after freshman English was invented, it began to draw the wrath of critics, reformers, and abolitionists in large numbers. It's a course nobody loves. But it endures" (v).

Early in the twenty-first century, first-year composition still endures—as it has since the late nineteenth century when it became a required course at Harvard. Many scholar-teachers, especially those who hold memberships in the Conference on College Composition and Communication (CCCC) and NCTE's special group on teaching English in the two-year college (TYCA), constantly strive to enhance the theoretical rigor and pedagogical effectiveness of first-year composition. This collection furthers that conversation.

Works Cited

Bakhtin, Mikhail. "Discourse in the Novel." 1975. *The Dialogic Imagination.* Ed. Michael Holquist. Trans. Caryl Emerson and Michael Holquist. Austin: U of Texas P, 1981. 259–422. (Original work published *as Voprosy literatury i estetiki,* Moscow, 1975)

Ohman, Richard, and W. B. Coley, eds. *Ideas for English 101: Teaching Writing in College.* Urbana, IL: NCTE, 1975.

Schön, Donald A. *Educating the Reflective Practitioner.* San Francisco: Jossey-Bass, 1991.

ACKNOWLEDGMENTS

Many people contributed to this collection. We thank the former and current chairs of Arizona State University's Department of English—Nancy Gutierrez and Dan Bivona, respectively—for financial and collegial support. All WPAs should be fortunate to work with such dedicated administrators and mentors. We also thank Gary Krahenbuhl, former dean of the College of Liberal Arts and Sciences, for helping to enhance the composition program at Arizona State University. Administrators in the Office of the Senior Vice President and Provost—Walter Harris, Tom Trotter, Kathy Church, Gail Hackett, Chuck Bantz, and Milt Glick—have provided leadership that has strengthened the composition program and the Center for Learning and Teaching Excellence, as well as many other units at Arizona State University.

Several scores of colleagues from across the United States have contributed to this collection. Their dedicated and inspired teaching, readily evident in every chapter of the volume, teaches us much about the profession. Collectively and individually, these insightful scholars demonstrate that students' learning is our most important priority.

Kurt Austin has been a steadfast, patient, and experienced guide throughout the process of editing this volume. He and the members of the NCTE Editorial Board have done much to enhance the usefulness of this collection to college and university composition teachers. We especially want to thank Bonny Graham, whose exceptional work, patience, and sense of humor made editing this collection a joy.

We thank Krissy Elwood, Demetria Baker, Amanda Sawyer, Susan Ledlow, Judy Grace, Laura Bush, Marguerite De Long, Shelly Whitfield, Josh Ackerman, and Janel White-Taylor for helping us with various portions of this project.

Acknowledgments

We are, of course, grateful to our students. They inspire, challenge, frustrate, complicate, and encourage us to improve our teaching.

To our friends and families, whose patience seems infinite, we offer infinite gratitude.

CHAPTER 1

CONTEXTS FOR TEACHING WRITING

Because it is often difficult for new teachers—and even experienced ones—to know the contexts in which they will be teaching composition, this chapter includes discussions of how composition courses are situated within composition programs, which have collective expectations. In turn, the departments and colleges that house composition programs have specific expectations for the ways in which composition should serve those larger academic units. Beyond that, universities often expect composition to fulfill institutional goals for literacy. And, of course, universities answer to boards of directors, boards of regents, and legislatures—all of which hold additional expectations. This chapter includes descriptions of the multiple contexts for teaching composition, along with some strategies for negotiating them.

The Departmental Perspective

ROGER GILLES

Grand Valley State University

*In addition to administrative work in several composition pro-
grams, Roger Gilles brings to this piece experience as chair of
an English department. Here he describes the multiple and
sometimes competing expectations for first-year composition
teachers.*

From its nineteenth-century beginnings, the composition course
in U.S. universities has typically been housed within the English
department. But it has not been the most welcome of lodgers.
Indeed, as Robert Connors has pointed out, the required first-
year English course was never intended to be a permanent addition to the curriculum; the idea was to get rid of it as soon as the
secondary schools started doing their jobs properly (7). Over a
century later, we are apparently still waiting.

Despite their nearly universal presence on campuses across
the country, composition courses continue to enjoy something
less than permanent status within many English departments. At
large universities, they are the courses most likely to be taught by
short-term graduate student faculty. At midsized universities like
mine, they are the courses most likely to be taught by part-time
adjunct faculty or non-tenure-track full-time faculty. The same is
true even at many small liberal arts colleges. We still seem to
operate on the assumption that one day, maybe one day real soon,
we'll no longer need any composition courses—so we'd better
not commit fully to them. And yet signs of serious commitment
are everywhere, from elaborate summer placement programs to
expensive computer classrooms and fully staffed writing centers.
Program directors spend lots of time and effort making sure that
short-term faculty are well prepared and well supported to get
the job done. Composition courses are clearly important to someone. As a department chair, I can think of several reasons why
composition programs are important, even crucial, to the English departments that house them.

Service Mission

To many, the first-year writing course is a "service course," and indeed the first courses in the nineteenth century were instituted at Harvard and other schools as a way to help "underprepared" students meet the lofty expectations of the college faculty. The course became known as a "fix-it" course with little or no intellectual content (see Berlin, for example). Its primary activities were grammar review and instruction in rigid forms of organization and development best known under the general heading of "the five-paragraph theme." Beginning in the early 1960s, however, teachers and scholars began to recognize the complex social and intellectual demands of effective writing—and effective writing instruction—and the service label was generally rejected in favor of the view that the first-year course was every bit as challenging and rewarding as other college courses and valuable enough in its own right to exist without the service function. There was no reason to limit composition to a role any different from other college courses.

Still, first-year writing programs continue to carry the service label, and many people still view first-year composition as a fix-it course. These labels bother many composition faculty because they seem to relegate composition to a marginal, "preacademic" status, and it appears that many non-English-department faculty and administrators value the composition course only insofar as it serves their rather shortsighted desire for error-free student writing. The service mission is an easy one for composition faculty to reject, but I'm afraid that our rejection only makes us look obstinate—or worse, obsolete.

People all over campus look to the English department to eliminate student writing problems. We should count ourselves lucky that they do. Yes, we know it is strictly impossible to "fix" student writing, but as the result of this mission we have the opportunity to contribute to the liberal education of nearly all college students nationwide. The further we get from even trying to fulfill this mission, the less important we become in the eyes of non-English-department faculty and administrators. Eventually they will look elsewhere to satisfy their demand. I can already imagine the TV commercials for private businesses promising perfect papers for any occasion: "Say, nice-looking essay, Bob!" "Thanks, Betty. It was easy: I took it to Komma King!" We may laugh now, but how will we feel when students take classes from komma kings rather than from teachers trained in the liberal arts discipline of rhetoric and composition?

As a department chair, I'd hate to see composition abandon its service mission. I think it's time we accept the service label and transform it into something positive and even noble. Service is not a bad thing. Clearly, however, our service needs to extend beyond helping non-English-department faculty avoid dealing with student errors in spelling and punctuation. Let's make sure we offer a legitimate and valuable service—something that serves our non-English-department colleagues, our institutions, and of course our students, not just as they move into other courses but also as they move on with their lives.

What is it that faculty outside of the English department really want from a composition program? When I ask faculty from around campus what they look for in a good student writer, I almost always hear "good grammar," but after I acknowledge this as one of the many signs of a good writer, I hear other qualities as well. All faculty love students whose writing is thoughtful, purposeful, and richly developed. Even in disciplines such as business and science, in which much of the writing aims for conciseness, faculty expect deep thought and reflection to go into the *preparation* of a piece of writing. The resulting spareness needs to be precise and insightful. And in all disciplines, many writing assignments call explicitly for reflection, analysis, interpretation, and theorizing. In first-year writing programs, these characteristics generally fall under the heading of "content" or "development" in the list of course goals or in the grading guidelines, and they are clearly among the most important characteristics we seek to develop in our students. These are goals of all college courses, naturally, but writing classes are one of the best places for students to learn strategies explicitly designed to lead to a richly developed, sharply focused expression of ideas. By focusing on such strategies, we are serving our students and our institutions quite well.

[handwritten margin note: ② well organized — organization as an expression of content]

Faculty also like writing that is <u>well organized</u>. At first this term calls up images of the five-paragraph theme, or some of the other set forms that dominated writing instruction for so long— the comparison/contrast essay, for example, with its ABAB, or for more adventurous students, AABB, format. Canned patterns of organization, such as the IMRAD format in the sciences, do have a place in academics, but the first-year writing course best serves its students and institutions by <u>focusing on organization as an expression of content</u>. Writers start <u>with purpose and audience</u> and then either <u>choose or develop a structure that suits their needs</u>. A good service course <u>will develop</u> in students the ability to make <u>decisions about organization that take</u> into account the relationship <u>between form,</u> content, and context. ⨉

[handwritten margin note: SO: start w/ purpose & audience & choose or develop a struct. that suits their needs]

Often, when faculty from across the disciplines call for good grammar, they refer not only to subject-verb agreement and the like, but also to what many faculty and students call the <u>"flow"</u> of a piece of writing. Everyone enjoys <u>smooth writing</u>. When faculty are bothered by a piece of writing, they often point to a few misspellings or grammatical errors as the explanation simply because they can't think of anything else to point to, when in fact the issue is stylistic rather than grammatical. Most beginning attempts at communication are <u>quite naturally marked by stiff or halting expression</u>. This is true of beginning pianists and beginning scientific writers. Like pianists, writers need practice, so that the physical act of writing becomes second nature and the expression of ideas becomes fluid and natural. Like good pianists, smooth writers let their individuality show even when they are writing within the strict conventions of a particular discipline or organization. The <u>key is regular,</u> informal practice at writing. The more, the better. Not all of this practice leads directly to finished writing, of course, but it helps writers produce better, smoother, more polished pieces of <u>finished writing</u> when they need to. Our service courses <u>should</u> provide students with the opportunity to *practice* the craft of writing.

[handwritten margin note: Key is regular, informal practice at writing]

English departments <u>need to share these</u> nongrammatical goals with all faculty and administrators. We need to publicize these goals on Web sites, in newsletters, and in our hallways. I suspect that if our first-year students routinely went on to produce writing that was <u>clearly focused, insightful, richly developed, smoothly</u>

[handwritten margin note: goal of writing]

expressed, and purposefully and sensibly organized, we wouldn't hear quite so many calls for "good grammar." Even so, however, those calls are unlikely ever to stop. Like it or not, the external perception of a writing program, and indeed of the department that houses that writing program, has everything to do with the spelling, grammar, punctuation, and mechanics of its students.

We must accept the charge to ensure that all successful students work effectively (not *perfectly,* which we know is impossible) with standard written English. This is not a prison sentence. Indeed, the ability to use standard written English effectively creates options for students; it gives them real freedom in choosing lives and careers. But we know from many years of research (see Hillocks, for example) that spending a lot of class time *teaching* the conventions of standard written English is an ineffective way to help students develop the ability to *use* standard written English. Instead, we need to do two things. First, we need to provide for students whatever developmental courses they need to succeed in first-year composition. Guided practice in writing is what developing students need most, and some students need more time to develop than others. We must provide the time and the interaction they need to develop their ability to use standard written English effectively.

But the number of developmental courses a student takes should not change the final goals of first-year composition. In the end, we need to insist that every student can produce writing that, among other things, adheres to the general conventions of spelling, grammar, and punctuation. Here is what I tell my students: the conventions can't be taught; they have to be *learned.* We can provide the resources—and there are plenty of them—that our students need to learn the conventions of standard written English. And perhaps most important of all, we can provide an academic culture in which those conventions are valued as important keys to success. If we discuss with our students our own reliance on the conventions and insist that all students develop a certain level of proficiency by the end of first-year composition, we will find that we are serving well both ourselves and our students. Again, this is not *all* we should do as teachers of first-year composition, but it is something we absolutely must do if we want to fulfill the service function that is expected of us.

Liberal Arts Mission

Although fulfilling this university-wide service function is crucial to the success of any department that houses a composition program, our nobler and ultimately far more important mission is to contribute to the liberal education of our students. In her presidential address at the 1998 meeting of the Council of Colleges of Arts and Sciences, Carolyn T. Adams argued that a liberal education must develop in students three abilities crucial to life in the twenty-first century:

1. Students must be able to make meaning from information. They must be able to access information and then to evaluate, interpret, and use that information to solve problems.

2. Students must know how to learn. They must become their own teachers.

3. Students must develop the capacity to see and understand the perspectives of people different from themselves. (2)

Seen in this light, composition is an ideal liberal arts course. And placed as it usually is in the first year of a student's college education, composition is ideally suited to introduce or reinforce these liberal habits of mind. Composition deals explicitly with strategies for accessing, evaluating, interpreting, and using information as students work with sources of various kinds. It highlights problem-solving abilities as students define and address rhetorical situations. It teaches students that no two situations are exactly alike and that all situations require original thinking and problem solving. And composition requires that students consider deeply the perceptions, beliefs, biases, and material conditions of their readers and their sources. Effective pieces of writing, from simple reports to complex arguments, demand that writers pay attention to these crucial components of a liberal education.

Of course, other college courses also develop these abilities, but any department that offers composition needs to highlight both within the university and out in the wider culture the important role that good writing instruction can play in developing these critical abilities simultaneously. To me, this is the most important reason to maintain composition as a universal requirement. It is, in the best sense of the term, a "skills course" that all first-year students need—not only for the rest of their college careers but also for the rest of their lives. The skills include grammar and punctuation, but they also include the foundational skills of democratic citizenship.

If we view the English department as a liberal arts department pursuing the three goals identified by Adams, we see how prominent the composition program should be in relation to other English department programs such as literary study, language study, and teacher preparation. All English department programs pursue the goals of the liberal arts, of course, but composition is the only one focused exclusively on the production of written texts. As Robert Scholes has pointed out, the primary work of an English department is to study texts of all kinds—their production (writing) and their reception (reading). The field of composition has been studying and theorizing about the production of texts for many decades now, and it's time that we place that work more centrally in the overall English department curriculum. This means both treating composition "service" courses with more respect and attention *and* developing more advanced rhetoric and composition courses for our English majors.

If we continue to relegate composition to a supporting role within the English department, we not only ignore the importance of the production of texts, but we also privilege the reception of literary texts over all others. Western culture at the turn of the twenty-first century is more textually based than ever, so English departments must recognize that our students need strategies for evaluating and interpreting the myriad nonfiction texts that all of us face on a daily basis, from newspaper articles and presidential addresses to Web sites and e-mail. The field I have been calling "composition" is, of course, most commonly called "rhetoric and composition," and the study of rhetoric has given the English department a solid foundation for resituating the study of rhetorical texts alongside the study of literary texts.

The successful English department of the twenty-first century will embrace its service role and work to prepare student writers both for the expectations of faculty across the disciplines and for the demands of democratic citizenship. The successful department will conceive of itself as a department of textual studies, with equal emphasis on the production and reception of texts, both literary and rhetorical.

Working Collaboratively

In the best sense, then, a composition program "serves" its students, the faculty throughout campus, the institution itself, and the larger democratic society. But a good composition program also serves the English profession by providing apprentice graduate students and many other faculty with an extremely valuable experience working with others within a coherent, goal-oriented program. Because composition programs are aware of their service mission, they tend to work harder than other English department programs to develop explicit course goals and consistent, effective pedagogical practices. Faculty who know how to work with and contribute to programmatic—rather than simply personal—teaching goals are invaluable to any department (and department chair).

Most composition programs stress a "we" attitude over an "I" attitude. As composition teachers, we need to understand the established goals of the program and respect the established expectations of the course. We must understand that we are part of a larger program. But we also need to work together to revise program goals and articulate those revisions to others—students, fellow faculty, administrators, and so on. Composition teachers often meet regularly in faculty groups, some designed for support, others for the sharing of ideas or for developing consistent grading standards. These kinds of activities simply don't happen often in other English department subfields. Have you ever heard of a medieval literature program that graded final portfolios in teams?

As a department chair, I find that many faculty hold a romantic notion about their work lives. They view themselves as solitary intellectual workers, beholden only to their subject matter and their personal muses. They have a difficult time seeing their work as a contribution to a larger program—a multiple-section course, a group of related courses, even a degree program. They interpret questions about their classes as threats, and they view any sort of shared expectations as violations of their academic freedom. And it's not just course-related matters they have trouble with. Many faculty bring such views to personnel work, curriculum development, and student affairs as well. Teamwork is often minimal.

I appreciate those faculty members—many with recent graduate school experience in large composition programs—who don't mind negotiating personal and programmatic goals. These faculty understand that communicating with others often brings about positive change for everyone involved. Teamwork comes more naturally to those who have worked in portfolio groups or attended weekly program meetings. I might even go so far as to suggest to job-seeking graduates that they include a description on their C.V. of their program-related experiences and contributions. This will signal to prospective department chairs that they are able and willing to participate fully in the important collaborative work of the department.

Works Cited

Adams, Carolyn T. "The Liberal Arts in a Culture of Careerism." *CCAS Newsletter* 20.1 (1999): 1–7.

Berlin, James A. *Writing Instruction in Nineteenth-Century American Colleges.* Carbondale: Southern Illinois UP, 1984.

Connors, Robert J. "The New Abolitionism: Toward a Historical Background." *Reconceiving Writing, Rethinking Writing Instruction.* Ed. Joseph Petraglia. Mahwah, NJ: Lawrence Erlbaum, 1995. 3–26.

Hillocks, George, Jr. *Research on Written Composition: New Directions for Teaching.* New York: NCRE/Urbana, IL: ERIC, 1986.

Scholes, Robert. *The Rise and Fall of English: Reconstructing English as a Discipline.* New Haven: Yale UP, 1998.

Composition, Community, and Curriculum: A Letter to New Composition Teachers

GEOFFREY CHASE
Northern Arizona University

Geoffrey Chase, like Elaine Maimon later in this chapter, offers a seasoned administrator's perspective on the work we do in composition classrooms. In addition to teaching composition and directing composition programs, he has served as chair of an English department, as well as dean of a university office.

When I began teaching writing more than twenty years ago as a graduate assistant in the Integrated Liberal Studies Program at the University of Wisconsin–Madison, I knew instinctively that teaching would be demanding, that it would require many different skills, and that I would have to move quickly just to keep ahead of my students. Consequently, I spent a lot of time preparing for class. I searched for ideas, exercises, and assignments that would "work." I had students freewrite, keep journals, write personal essays, respond to social issues, and analyze reading assignments. I borrowed ideas from other teaching assistants, read textbooks and articles searching for effective teaching strategies, and tried to balance what I was discovering about my students with what I thought they needed to learn. I came out of every class reflecting on what had just transpired and began thinking immediately about ideas for my next class. Immersed in the demands of juggling the myriad tasks involved in teaching, I took this experience day by day and week by week, and concentrated on making it to the end of the semester.

More recently, as a composition director working with many new and inexperienced teachers, I've come to believe that my focus on the day-to-day demands of teaching was not unique. Beginning teachers with whom I've worked deal with the anxiety that comes with teaching for the first time by paying attention to details, as I did. In the week leading up to the start of the semester, for example, they become increasingly focused on the upcoming week and ask questions that are direct, specific, and concrete: Should I use peer-response groups? What about freewriting? Should I require attendance? How much emphasis should I put on grammar and mechanics? What reading assignment will get students off on the right foot? How will I handle disruptive behavior? Should I penalize students for turning papers in late? And so on.

I take these questions seriously and try to provide the best answers I can, but often I find myself replying, "It depends." The answers to these questions, and to any other questions about teaching, depend first of all on the intended outcomes for the class and, second, on the relationship of our class to a larger curriculum. The choices we make as we give assignments and respond to student papers all depend on our theoretical understanding, whether or not it is articulated, of the broader curriculum and of the role that the class we are teaching plays in that curriculum. More specifically, our own teaching helps construct a sense of what it means to learn to write, to know how to write, and to write effectively in a range of rhetorical situations in relation to other courses students take. Consequently, composition teachers must think beyond the borders of their classes and about the broader set of expectations implied by any curriculum.

Thinking beyond the borders of my classroom did not come naturally to me when I started teaching. I taught in a kind of vacuum, I gave students exercises and assignments, and I responded to their papers following what seemed to me the best advice I could glean from books and articles on teaching writing that were appearing in the 1970s. I didn't give much thought to the ways in which the writing classes I was teaching related to other courses students were taking at the same time or that they would take later on. I didn't focus on other programs, curricula, or the larger goals of the institution.

All of this began to change for me when, still a graduate assistant, I was asked to teach technical writing in the college of engineering. My mentors in that program were very clear that we needed to teach students to do the kind of writing that other professors and future employers would expect of them. Rather than finding this restrictive, I found it freeing. I began to develop a general idea of what the specific goals of this technical writing class were. My notion of what it meant to be a better writer became clearer, and I began to see that helping students become better writers was a goal too broad and too vague. Without targets, or specific outcomes in mind, my lesson plans were a series of experiments loosely connected to each other.

As I developed a clearer notion of what it means to be a better writer, at least in terms of civil, mechanical, electrical, and industrial engineering, I began to choose texts, assignments, and classroom activities on the basis of how they would help me teach students to write more effectively *as engineers*. Students worked on projects in other classes, wrote reports on those projects for my class, revised the reports further, and then turned them in again for the class in which they were doing the project. Without realizing it at the time, I began to think of my teaching in terms of a larger curriculum. I began to think about the ways my course related to other courses and to look for activities and assignments that would draw on and reflect the work students were doing in other classes. I began to think about teaching writing in a much more comprehensive way, paying careful attention to the expectations others held for what I was doing in this course day by day, and developing a more connected, coherent vision of how my teaching contributed to the educational enterprise.

drawing on what's taught in other classes)

When I left graduate school, I was fortunate to get a position teaching in an interdisciplinary program with a well-defined four-year curriculum. This curriculum required all students to complete an intensive, two-year core requirement in the humanities, social sciences, and natural sciences, to take two methodology courses in their junior year, and to complete a year-long project, the major component of which was written in the senior year. Because this program was relatively small, I was able to teach the same students at all levels of the curriculum. Though I never followed one class for all four years, it was not unusual for me to see students in their first year and then again as juniors and seniors. Teaching in this curriculum with a small cohort of students greatly increased my understanding of curricula and appropriate developmental sequences. Because I knew what would be expected of students at all levels of the curriculum, I gave a good deal of thought to how my courses and the writing I taught fit into a larger context and contributed to an overall set of goals articulated by the institution.

Unlike the college of engineering in which I had taught as a graduate student, this interdisciplinary program was not designed to prepare students for specific and well-defined professional careers. It was aimed instead at giving students a broad liberal arts background that would enable them to pursue a variety of paths and objectives. Thus, I came to understand that even programs with diverse goals and very different students can be coherent and thoughtful, and move beyond being a collection of excellent courses. In *Lives on the Boundary,* Mike Rose notes that education is about relationships; he focuses primarily on the relationships teachers have with students and vice versa. I agree with Rose's assessment that relationships are at the heart of what teachers do, and would like to suggest that in addition to focusing on our relationships with students, we also need to think about the relationship the individual teacher has with colleagues who teach the courses that make up the broader curriculum.

One place to begin this examination of the curricular relationships among teachers in higher education is by focusing on the fact that composition is, first and foremost, a service course. Composition seeks to help students develop skills and abilities that will enable them to be more successful as they take courses in their academic programs. Composition thus concerns itself with a fundamentally important skill that is connected to nearly everything students do as they work toward a baccalaureate degree. It is critically important, then, that all composition teachers stop from time to time to consider the ends of the course they are teaching in relation to the ends suggested by the composition program as a whole, the general education or liberal studies program of which the composition program is most likely a part, and the major.

As inexperienced teachers take on their own classes for the first time and as they begin to develop their own pedagogical styles, they need to think beyond the immediate, short-term demands of getting through specific class periods to take an expansive view of the entire curriculum. In addition to asking questions about the details of teaching that inevitably arise from having a composition class for the first time, they also need to ask questions such as: What is the role of the composition class I am teaching in relation to the composition program as a whole? What will instructors who have my students next term expect them to be able to do on the first day? What is the relationship between the composition program and the students' general, basic, or liberal studies program? What are the overall aims of that program? What are the aims, goals, and learning outcomes expected for all students at this institution when they graduate?

Finding answers to these questions may not always be an easy task. Even in cases in which composition programs have clearly defined outcomes, teachers may find there is not much agreement about the relationship between the composition program and other components of the curriculum. That is, while everyone at a college or university may have definite expectations about what should be achieved by having students take composition, it is also likely that those expectations will vary enormously across the institution. One response to such a situation is to ignore the colleagues who don't understand the aims, goals, and complexities of trying to teach students to write more effectively in courses that represent only a small fraction of the curriculum. Another possibility is to respond by letting those outside of composition determine what students should learn in our classes.

It is critical, however, that all composition teachers, even those teaching for the first time, eschew these two options and focus instead on developing and understanding the relationships that constitute the curriculum. Teaching is fundamentally about community, about the relationships between individuals and the larger groups of which they are a part. In terms of composition, this means helping students write more effectively so that they become more fully contributing members of the communities in which they live and work. Being a teacher means working with other teachers to create more effective learning communities. At times we may decry the fragmentation that seems to characterize our world, and to lament our students' inabilities to make critical connections, to understand the relationship of the personal to the political, of individual action to global awareness, of individual freedom to responsibility to society. And yet many teachers, experienced and inexperienced alike, work with fragmented curricula built not around how faculty can work together to create coherent learning experiences for our students but around individual preference and our own specific, disciplinary training.

Being a teacher means working with other teachers. It means connecting what we do day by day to the outcomes for our own classes and for the curriculum as a whole. The goal for every inexperienced teacher should be to become a part of two communities: a community of scholars and a community of teachers. This can happen only if novice teachers and scholars consider seriously the ways they can learn from and help shape the broader arenas in which they work. When novice teachers hold their own classes, they need to look up from their daily experience from time to time to consider where they are in relation to a much broader community.

In a recent article on liberal education, William Cronon writes, "More than anything else, being an educated person means being able to see connections that allow one to make sense of the world and act within it in creative ways" (78). Paraphrasing Cronon, I would like to suggest that being a teacher means being able to make sense of the academic community and act within it in creative, productive ways. New teachers of composition would be wise to pay close attention to the expectations that others may hold for the students in composition classes. It is through an understanding of and an engagement with those expectations that we can become more fully contributing members of the teaching community. Teaching writing has the power to be an intellectually transformative experience, but transformation will occur only if we are prepared to engage our students on the one hand and to engage with our colleagues around issues of curriculum on the other.

Works Cited

Cronon, William. "Only Connect." *The American Scholar* 67.4 (1998): 73–80.

Rose, Mike. *Lives on the Boundary: The Struggles and Achievements of America's Underprepared.* New York: Free Press, 1989.

A Supervisor's Perspective

DAVID FRANKE
Syracuse University

David Franke offers some insights into how Syracuse University approaches TA training, seeking a balance between teaching the theories and the practices of composition instruction.

Dear composition teacher on the cusp of a new semester:

I remember well my first semester—sometimes I wish I could forget it as easily. My classroom policies seemed to teeter between terribly rigid and incredibly loose, sometimes in the same class in the same week. The focus was so often on reading, not writing, that I wonder if my students didn't check their registration cards to make sure they were enrolled in the right class. Not that I really taught reading anyway: I mostly just assigned it and figured they would sort it out. Often, they didn't. Keeping the focus on their writing has been a long struggle for me as a teacher (who received no formal training or practice in writing until my grad school practicum, which is not unusual). What I'd like to do here is mention some things that characterize the Writing Program at Syracuse University, where I learned to teach writing in a way that focuses on the student's development as a writer rather than on his or her appreciation of literature.

Even though you may be teaching in a program that differs from Syracuse's, my experiences may resonate with your own. At Syracuse we have up to thirty-six new teaching assistants in the fall of some years, and they are usually a disparate lot. Most tested out of any required composition courses and went on to become English department graduate students. They learned to write often by osmosis, at the hands of their highly literate parents and, usually, in good schools that stressed writing and reading (these claims are based on my experience with TAs here and are meant to be suggestive rather than definitive; my sense is that we have a lot of grad students from families in which one or both parents were academics or clergy of some type, but that's a guess. It would be interesting to research). Many TAs come to study literary theory, creative writing, or literature. Few come to study or teach composition, though that's changing slowly because we have a new composition doctoral program. I suspect, though, that we are a lot like most programs around the country. We share with everyone the problem of showing students how to picture themselves as academic writers who have a thing called a "writing process" connected to a hard-to-revise thing called the "draft."

Because our program is based neither on drilling students in "the basics," which would lead to a sequenced curriculum based on proceeding from the smallest units to the largest (from the sentence, to the paragraph, to the essay), nor on a romantic model (in which flashes of genius are fanned by the pages of great works of literature used as models), some of our new teachers have difficulty understanding just what is left. When we teach the practicum (part-time faculty team up with full-time faculty), we try to introduce TAs to the theories behind our practices, but to do so concretely. In other words, we avoid teaching a seminar in pure "composition theory" or reducing the semester to "teaching tips," disembodied hints and procedures about teaching. Of course, it's hard to keep a balance. Our goal is to produce in our students and teachers the ability to engage in reflective practice, by which I mean the ability to make decisions about how to enhance one's developing expertise. So we teach teachers how to reflect on themselves as teachers, and students learn how to reflect on themselves as writers.

Reflective practice means that one must make something and then look at it—simple as that. We teach incoming TAs how to get their students to make things (in writing) and then look at them. Therefore, in the list of teaching issues provided below you will see a lot of attention to writing processes that "make" (invention, discussion, reading, annotation) that are not rigidly separate from the reflection processes (revision, discussion, annotation, proofreading—even grades can and should be a moment in the reflective process). Furthermore, we view the writing process as an ongoing developmental performance unspooled over the course of a semester, which means that discrete writing tasks tied to a particular "faculty" of cognition (narration, description, exposition, etc.) are not the goal. Assignment sequences, in which students in one assignment make something that is taken up in another assignment, are our goal for teachers and for ourselves when we teach our own undergraduate classes—and the practicum. Our entire curriculum is based on the assumption that writers learn by doing and reflecting, so new TAs compose in a number of professional genres when they take our classes: they write syllabi, lesson plans, reflections on the semester, final papers, and short brainstorming pieces. Though they are usually pretty good at writing these pieces (so good they sometimes feel the practice isn't teaching them much), we insist. We believe that teachers can't teach writers how to enter a foreign maze of genres without first experiencing it themselves. Most writing teachers in most schools and colleges would probably agree that teachers are writers along with their students.

Still, these social/cognitive processes can't take place unless the teacher understands what assignments look like, how to structure a single class or an entire semester, or how to imagine the classroom as a community in which the teacher is a legitimate participant. In connection with this last point, we spend time talking about authority in the classroom. We try to have the teacher's authority come from her or his experience as a writer and familiarity with the writing process (not that all new teachers can "see" their writing process, having internalized it years before!). We try to focus on *writing* issues (grading as a problem for the teacher-as-writer; writing a syllabus as a writing challenge).

These concerns are drawn from a sophomore-level class in the practice of rhetoric. We try to teach new TAs to lead their classes not as "theory" classes (defining and contesting definitions of rhetoric), but as practica, places where writers employ rhetorical techniques and engage in rhetorical analysis. The goal of the class is not to promulgate rhetoric as grammar rules (as many handbooks use the term) or rhetoric as argument—and certainly not specious argument. The goal is to have students view their writing rhetorically, in terms of its effects and motives, and to be able to look at the writing of others in this light.

Following is a list of issues that often come up when we are teaching new instructors. You might find it familiar.

◆ Studio practices: finding specifics, abstracting, generalizing, thematizing, reflecting, linking or rejecting ideas (citing), inventing, collaborating, revising, reflecting, risking, claiming. What should this course teach? What other goals, besides institutional ones, do the student and teacher bring to it? What do you want students to know about? What do you want students to be able to do as writers when they leave the course?

◆ Authority issues: grading policy, grading individual papers, autonomy, general respect, even how to dress.

◆ Responding to papers in end comments, conferences, marginal comments, and workshops.

◆ Interpreting student texts. Also, how to actually read them when grading a large stack.

◆ Making texts part of the writing process: revision, invention, "publication" (reading aloud or assembling in a magazine), reflection, informal writing in class and before and after class.

◆ Stressing concrete practical matters: where to keep records, what to do with students with special needs, how to deal with student complaints, how to team teach, what to do in office hours.

◆ Creating communities in the writing classroom.

◆ Connecting reading and writing (setting up a reading, reflecting on it, writing out of it, annotating, citing and using "other thinkers" in a text).

◆ Creating a coherent semester (sequencing assignments, connecting reading and writing, establishing the topic of inquiry).

◆ Creating a coherent class meeting (beginning strategies, sustaining strategies, ending strategies).

◆ Introducing peer work and illustrating how to sustain, reflect on, and connect it to the ongoing writing assignment.

What practicum consultants can do:

◆ Aim discussions toward the paper (writing beforehand and afterward).

- Make the class a practice field for rhetorical practices, not a definition of rhetoric.

- Teach rhetoric as making (putting things together) and unmaking (analysis).

- Know how (and when) to teach grammar.

- Explore what role storytelling can have in making knowledge for teachers and students in a studio.

- Explore how creative writing and composition fit together for teachers.

A Cultural Perspective: Teaching Composition at a Historically Black University

TERESA M. REDD
Howard University

There are more than one hundred historically black colleges and universities in the United States. Having taught at one for eighteen years, Teresa Redd offers advice to composition teachers who have never experienced teaching in such a context.

So you've just arrived from Lily White University in Suburbia, USA, to teach first-year composition at Historically Black University in Inner City, USA. When you report for duty, the director of first-year composition thrusts an anthology of African American writing into your hands. But before you have a chance to explain that you have never taught African American literature, you realize that it's time for class. "How can I find Room 223 in Frederick Douglass Hall?" you ask. When you burst into Room 223, the students are talking to one another, some using a pronunciation, intonation, grammar, and vocabulary that make you feel like a foreigner. Flustered, you call the class to order and read aloud your roster, stumbling over the names: Lateisha, Warlesha, Jamal, Kaelie, Daud, Masirika, Tecia, Mahbleeta, Charnay, Tyneshia, Latoya, Shaneequa, and Jelani. Then, out of breath, you look at all of those black/brown/yellow/ivory faces and wonder, "What do I do now?"

Welcome to the world of HBCUs (Historically Black Colleges and Universities)! Below are some do's and don'ts that may help you appreciate the challenges and joys of teaching composition at an HBCU. In particular, these guidelines should prepare you for the cultural content of the curriculum and the linguistic heritage of the students.

Content Issues

1. *Let the content of your course reflect the historical mission of an HBCU.* An HBCU is not just a predominantly black school; it is an institution with a mission. For instance, Howard University strives to prepare African Americans and "other historically disenfranchised groups" for "leadership and service to our nation and the global community" (*HU-Facts* 6). Hence, our syllabus for first-year composition states, "It is the mission of the writing courses in the Department of English at Howard University to carry forward and transmit to you a liberating tradition in reading and writing skills. It is the purpose of these courses to make available to you the means of emulating these skills in your and the world's best interest" (1). Keep in mind that this is not just an administrative goal; many students come to HBCUs *because* of the institutions' historical commitment. So let that mission infuse your teaching.

What does this mean in the composition classroom? It means that you should remind students of the liberating power of literacy. You might discuss how Frederick Douglass, yet a slave, secretly taught himself to read and write, how he used those skills to become a free man, an abolitionist, a newspaper editor, and an international statesman. Or you might explain how Malcolm X, while imprisoned, found a new path in life within books, a path that led him to become a minister in the Nation of Islam and a spokesman for countless angry and disillusioned African Americans. It means that you might refer to the education of Thurgood Marshall (a Howard alumnus) whose legal arguments won the case of *Brown v. Board of Education* and later a seat on the Supreme Court. In other words, as you teach reading and writing, highlight the role of literacy in the African American struggle for freedom and equality. You don't need a degree in African American studies to offer this sort of perspective. Just add to your bedtime reading list books such as Frederick Douglass's *Narrative of the Life of Frederick Douglass,* Ida B. Wells-Barnett's *On Lynchings,* Malcolm X's *Autobiography,* and Richard Wright's *Black Boy.*

2. *Situate students within the intellectual and rhetorical tradition of African American writing.* Your students need to understand that they are not only the political, economic, and social beneficiaries of their ancestors' ability to read and write; they are also the cultural heirs of a rich and vibrant body of writing. That is why our syllabus opens with a poem by the African American poet Margaret Walker ("I Want to Write"), followed by these words: "The eloquence of the spoken word and writing—the art of language by line—are two of the most highly valued skills manifest in African-American culture" (1). The syllabus immediately links the culture of the academy to the students' culture, and so should you: help your students see themselves as writers. It is important, as Thomas Fox has argued, to work "against the separation of school literacy from the traditions of African American writing, against the notion that learning to write is learning to be white" (300). This philosophy also emerges in research on effective African American teachers. For instance, Michele Foster, Gloria Ladson-Billings, and Arnetha Ball and Ted Lardner attribute much of African American teachers' success to their ability to tie the culture of the school to the culture of the students' home or community.

Therefore, don't be surprised if you find that the assigned text for first-year composition at your HBCU is multicultural or even Afrocentric, i.e., a text that portrays Black people "as the subjects rather than the objects of education" (Asante 171–72). Ten years ago, our faculty adopted an Afrocentric reader for our first-semester writing course (English 002 *[A Syllabus]*). Since then, thousands of Howard students have read and written about essays written by/about Ishmael Reed, Ralph Ellison, Steven Biko, James Baldwin, Michael Eric Dyson, Gloria Naylor, Zora Neale Hurston, Stephen Carter, Martin Luther King Jr., and others. Did the Afrocentric reader fulfill our goals? During the 1991–92 academic year, we surveyed the 1,305 students who had completed English 002. Of those students, 911 filled out the questionnaire, responding as follows:

- ◆ 94 percent enjoyed reading about the Afrocentric issues, while 64 percent enjoyed writing about them.

- ◆ 89 percent thought more carefully about the black experience as a result of reading the essays; 79 percent did as a result of writing.

- ◆ 80 percent felt more positive about writing in general because they had read so many essays by black writers.

- ◆ 75 percent thought they had something worthwhile to say when writing about the Afrocentric issues, while only 6 percent said they did not. (Redd, "Afrocentric" 5–9)

Whether you choose an Afrocentric or a multicultural reader, these findings suggest that you or your department should consider choosing a reader that includes numerous selections by and about blacks. Among Afrocentric composition readers, two were compiled by professors at HBCUs, *Heritage* (Jarrett) and *Revelations* (Redd). You will find many more multicultural readers since most major publishers of anthologies now produce at least one. Another word of advice: as you discuss the readings in class, listen to your students. Think of them as cultural informants who might help you interpret the texts in startlingly new ways.

3. *Seek diverse audiences for students' writing.* While your students may broaden your understanding of some texts, as they respond to their readings you may find that class discussions of certain controversial topics become lopsided, even one-sided. In a composition classroom, such homogeneity of opinion can weaken class debates, peer review, and ultimately the revision process that the debates and reviews were designed to stimulate.

Here's a case in point: Year after year, my Howard composition students would write essays about racism, and year after year, when they discussed one another's drafts, the classroom sounded like an amen corner. Because they shared a history and a language, they seldom questioned what was expressed and often understood the unexpressed. Clearly, they needed a critical or uninformed audience to motivate them to supply missing explanations, stronger counterarguments, and more effective language. But I could not represent that audience because my students seemed to assume that any teacher (black or white) at an HBCU would be sympathetic toward their views on racism.

So what can a teacher do? Research suggests that many students will not adapt their writing to imaginary audiences (see Redd-Boyd and Slater). I would urge you instead to have students write and mail responses to editorial or letters-to-the-editor sections of newspapers, magazines, or journals that present the opposing views of real opponents. Better still, consider appropriating technology to reach challenging audiences. I solved the rhetorical problem for my students by arranging for white students in Bozeman, Montana, to e-mail critiques of my students' racism essays (Redd, "Accommodation" 141). Other teachers (e.g., Shamoon) have reported similar success with cross-cultural e-mail debates.

Linguistic Issues

4. *Learn about African American Vernacular English and discuss it with your class.* Many of your students will share not only a way of seeing the world but also a way of talking about it. Among friends or family, the majority of the students at an HBCU speak a variety of African American Vernacular English (AAVE), commonly known as Black English or Ebonics. So if you haven't done so already, learn about language variation, especially the history and nature of AAVE. Since the 1970s, linguists have demonstrated that AAVE is culturally rich and rule governed (see, for instance, Smitherman's classic *Talkin and Testifyin* and more recent books by Wolfram; Rickford and Rickford; and Baugh). Yet many English teachers are not familiar with this body of research.

In a recent survey of 983 secondary and college English teachers, the CCCC Language Policy Committee found that nearly one-third of the respondents had never taken a course in language diversity, although 96 percent agreed that "a college course in language diversity was necessary for anyone preparing to be a teacher today" (11).

Such a course is necessary because lack of knowledge about language variation can produce negative attitudes that hinder students' learning. For instance, in the landmark 1979 Black English Case *(Martin Luther King Jr. Elementary School Children v. Ann Arbor School District)*, the court ruled that the teachers' "negative attitudes toward the children's language [AAVE] led to negative expectations of the children which turned into self-fulfilling prophecies" (Smitherman, "What" 44).

But teachers aren't the only ones who lack sufficient knowledge about AAVE. Every semester I'm amazed to discover how little my students know about AAVE, even if they speak it. Let them know that AAVE and Standard English are "linguistically equal and the fact that they are not equal in society is a matter of society, not linguistics" (Gilyard 70).

Learning about AAVE can pay off in more ways than you might imagine. With a deeper understanding of AAVE, you can detect the logic behind some "errors" as students negotiate the rules of the written standard, Edited American English (EAE). Take my experience: One day after I wrote "two boys" on the blackboard, a student insisted that the plural -*s* suffix was unnecessary. Instead of merely correcting her, I pointed out that in AAVE and some West African languages, the number "two" is sufficient to indicate that there is more than one boy (Seymour 278). Although required in EAE, the -*s* is redundant. As a result of my explanation, the student saved face in front of the class while learning the standard rule.

As you expand your knowledge, you should realize that AAVE is a resource, not a deficit, so seize opportunities to encourage effective uses of AAVE in writing, including academic prose. For instance, AAVE rhetorical devices conveying sound, rhythm, and imagery are powerful tools for making compositions vivid and euphonious—instructing, entertaining, and moving an audience. Therefore, applaud the student who writes, "*Education* is the key, *family* is the key, *values* are the key to economic stability in the black community," instead of, "Education, family, and values are the key to economic stability in the black community" (Redd, "Untapped" 225). Or praise the student who sums up an argument with the line, "Affirmative Action is not giving handouts; it is giving a hand" (238). See Campbell and Troutman for other ways to help students exploit the rhythm and imagery of AAVE.

5. *Don't assume that your students' usage errors stem from dialect interference.* While learning more about AAVE is helpful, your study of AAVE will not reveal why many of your students struggle as they attempt to master EAE. Why? Here are three reasons: First, some of your students will not speak AAVE at all. Second, most of your students will be savvy "code-switchers" who can switch at will from AAVE to a standard variety of spoken English. At HBCUs such as Howard, only a minority will have difficulty switching from AAVE to Standard English in an academic context. Third, researchers have identified several obstacles to learning EAE but, contrary to popular belief, AAVE is *not* one of those obstacles (Hartwell 101; Morrow 156).

Instead, most AAVE speakers experience the same problem other composition students experience: unfamiliarity with the conventions of writing. When students are not certain about an aspect of the written code, they tend to omit inflectional suffixes (Whiteman 164) and to fall back on their oral resources (Hartwell 108). In the case of AAVE speakers, those oral resources include a nonstandard dialect. As a result, AAVE speakers may provide a dialectal form such as "two boy" or an interdialectical form such as "two mens" (i.e., what Morrow calls an approximation of EAE that students construct while learning EAE).

Regardless of their dialect, most first-year students—whether African American, European American, Hispanic American, or Asian American—are prone to make what Barbara Walvoord calls "performance-based" errors even when they know the rules of EAE (35). Therefore, ineffective proofreading strategies may account for some African American students' difficulties, regardless of whether they speak AAVE.

Like David Bartholomae, I have found that one helpful way to distinguish "performance-based" from "knowledge-based" errors is to ask students to read aloud their unmarked papers in my office. Look at the papers as they read aloud. If they correct the errors as they read (for instance, changing "my friend car" to "my friend's car"), they probably need better proofreading strategies, not more grammar exercises. If they *consciously* correct the errors, ask them about their proofreading process: did they take time to proofread each paper? If they proofread, did they proofread the hard copy? Did they proofread again after a time lapse? An answer of "no" to any of these questions is a starting point for your intervention. On the other hand, if they *unconsciously* correct the errors as they read to you, ask them to reread the "misread" passages. Show them how to slow down their eyes by tapping each word with a pen until they see what is actually on the paper. This approach can also help those AAVE speakers who unconsciously read aloud words in AAVE even though they have successfully written them in EAE.

Of course, while reading in your office, if a student reads the errors as they are written without acknowledging that they are errors, then the errors probably result from unfamiliarity with the conventions of EAE. A student who is an AAVE-dominant speaker may repeatedly substitute spoken (AAVE) forms for the unfamiliar ones. In that case, instead of marking up a paper filled with these AAVE patterns, I would recommend adopting the conference-centered approach that Arnetha Ball describes ("Evaluating"). You can assist your student better through a conference because you can learn more about the cultural context and intentions that produced the errors. A conference-centered approach may seem too time consuming if you have one hundred composition students, but remember that only a few of your students should require such help. Furthermore, after diagnosing the problem in your office, you can send the student to practice alone, with a tutor, or with a computer program such as Perfect Copy *(Perfect Copy Classic)*.

6. *Provide meaningful contexts in which students can master EAE.* Once you've completed your diagnosis, how can you reach the students you teach? The CCCC Language Policy Committee observes in *Students' Right to Their Own Language* that some African American students may resist learning EAE because "the

question of whether or not students will change their dialect involves their acceptance of a new—and possibly strange or hostile—set of cultural values" (6). Such resistance is less likely to occur at HBCUs than in compulsory primary and secondary schools, however, because most HBCU students are pursuing a career in the academic or professional worlds. Some of my students don't feel confident about using EAE, but virtually all of them wish to communicate effectively in those discourse communities, and they expect me to equip them for that task.

Therefore, you are more likely to encounter ineffective teaching strategies than resistant students at your HBCU. As Charles Coleman points out, sometimes our teaching *creates* problems. For instance, the common directive "a plural subject takes a plural verb" misleads students since the -s suffix marks plurality for nouns, not verbs (495).

So what strategies should you adopt? Teachers and researchers have recommended a variety of methods, but most supporting evidence has been anecdotal rather than empirical. Two noteworthy exceptions are Arnetha Ball's 1994 experiment and Hanni Taylor's Project Bidalectalism. Ball's study included a "worksheet-based, explicit instructional program" ("Language" 23): For instance, after the teacher contrasted the missing endings and -s endings in "Two boyS run_" and "One boy_ runS, "the students practiced adding -s to the right verb in paired sentences" (32). While this approach improved AAVE speakers' mastery of some EAE uses of the -s ending, Ball's study reveals that a "culturally sensitive literature-based approach" increased the students' control of other suffixes ("Language" 23, 43). For example, students improved their control of the plural -s after using nouns with this suffix to write a new conclusion for a story (34). Taylor achieved success as well by combining aspects of second-language (ESL) methodology with the reading of multicultural literature: students completed substitution, transformation, sentence-combining, and cloze exercises, but they also discussed, translated, and imitated literature written in different dialects.

Like Taylor, you can tap your knowledge of AAVE to contrast AAVE features (e.g., the uninflected verb in "She type") with EAE features that your students are struggling with in their papers (e.g., the *-s* suffix in "She types"). Both Ball's and Taylor's approaches, however, suggest that you should beware of isolated grammar drills. Whenever possible teach EAE in relevant contexts. For starters, you can engage students in writing for audiences who speak different dialects (Redd, "Untapped"), translating a passage from one dialect to another (Taylor), and noticing EAE conventions in the texts they are reading (Ball, "Language"). In this way, you can begin to move toward bidialectalism not only AAVE-dominant speakers but other HBCU students who speak nonstandard dialects.

Conclusion

If you feel overwhelmed by the preceding cautions and suggestions, don't be. Although teaching at an HBCU demands varied approaches, it does not require a complete overhaul of your graduate study or teaching methodology. Indeed, you will find that much of the pedagogy that works for Dick and Jane will work for Donnell and Jameela, too. As Jacquelyn Royster observes, "even though black students may be different from other students in a variety of ways, the process for educating them may be essentially the same as the process for students in general" (66). The real challenge is not how to teach African American students to write, "but how to teach any student to write" (Ramsey 78).[1]

Note

1. I would like to thank Dr. Karen Webb for her invaluable feedback on the first draft of this article.

Works Cited

Asante, Molefi Kete. "The Afrocentric Idea in Education." *Journal of Negro Education* 60 (1991): 170–80.

Ball, Arnetha F. "Evaluating the Writing of Culturally and Linguistically Diverse Students: The Case of the African American Vernacular English Speaker." *Evaluating Writing: The Role of Teachers' Knowledge about Text, Learning, and Culture.* Ed. Charles R. Cooper and Lee Odell. Urbana, IL: NCTE, 1998. 225–48.

———. "Language, Learning, and Linguistic Competence of African American Children: Torrey Revisited. *Linguistics and Education* 7 (1994): 23–46.

Ball, Arnetha, and Ted Lardner. "Dispositions toward Language: Teacher Constructs of Knowledge and the Ann Arbor Black English Case." *College Composition and Communication* 48 (1997): 469–85.

Bartholomae, David. "The Study of Error." *College Composition and Communication* 31 (1980): 253–69.

Baugh, John. *Out of the Mouths of Slaves: African American Language and Educational Malpractice.* Austin: U of Texas P, 1999.

Campbell, Kermit. "The 'Signifying Monkey' Revisited: Vernacular Discourse and African American Personal Narratives." *Journal of Advanced Composition* 14 (1994): 463–73.

Coleman, Charles. "Our Students Write with Accents: Oral Paradigms for ESD Students." *College Composition and Communication* 48 (1997): 486–500.

Conference on College Composition and Communication. *Students' Right to Their Own Language.* Spec. issue of *College Composition and Communication* 25 (1974).

Conference on College Composition and Communication Language Policy Committee. *Language Knowledge and Awareness Survey.* Final Research Report (January 2000). 20 Jan. 2001. <http://www.ncte.org/cccc>.

Douglass, Frederick. *Narrative of the Life of Frederick Douglass, an American Slave.* 1845. New York: New American Library, 1968.

Foster, Michele. "Effective Black Teachers: A Literature Review." *Teaching Diverse Populations: Formulating a Knowledge Base.* Ed. E. R. Hollins, J. E. King, and W. C. Hayman. Albany: SUNY P, 1994. 225–41.

Fox, Thomas. "Repositioning the Profession: Teaching Writing to African American Students." *Journal of Advanced Composition* 12 (1992): 291–303.

Gilyard, Keith. *Let's Flip the Script: An African American Discourse on Language, Literature and Learning.* Detroit: Wayne State UP, 1996.

Hartwell, Patrick. "Dialect Interference in Writing: A Critical View." *Research in the Teaching of English* 14 (1980): 101–18.

HU-Facts. <http://www.howard.edu/Hu-facts/factspg6.htm>.

Jarrett, Joyce M., Doreatha Drummond Mbalia, and Margaret Giles Lee, eds. *Heritage: African American Readings for Writing.* Upper Saddle River, NJ: Prentice-Hall, 1997.

Ladson-Billings, Gloria. "Who Will Teach Our Children? Preparing Teachers to Successfully Teach African American Students." *Teaching Diverse Populations: Formulating a Knowledge Base.* Ed. E. R. Hollins, J. E. King, and W. C. Hayman. Albany: SUNY P, 1994. 129–42.

Malcolm X, with Alex Haley. *The Autobiography of Malcolm X.* 1964. New York: Ballantine, 1973.

Morrow, Daniel. "Dialect Interference in Writing: Another Critical View." *Research in the Teaching of English* 19 (1985): 154–80.

Perfect Copy Classic. Diskette. Educational Edition, Version 2.02. North Tonawanda, NY: Logicus, copyright 1995–1997.

Ramsey, Paul A. "Teaching the Teachers to Teach Black-Dialect Writers." *Tapping Potential: English and Language Arts for the Black Learner.* Ed. Charlotte K. Brooks. Urbana, IL: NCTE, 1985. 176–81.

Redd, Teresa. "Accommodation and Resistance on (the Color) Line: Black Writers Meet White Artists on the Internet." *Electronic Communication Across the Curriculum.* Ed. Donna Reiss, Dickie Selfe, and Art Young. Urbana, IL: NCTE, 1998. 139–50.

———. "An Afrocentric Curriculum in a Composition Classroom." Paper presented at the Conference on College Composition and Communication Annual Convention, San Diego, 1993. ERIC doc. ED362898 (1993).

———, ed. *Revelations: An Anthology of Expository Essays by and about Blacks.* 3rd ed. Needham Heights, MA: Simon & Schuster, 1997.

———. "Untapped Resources: 'Styling' in Black Students' Writing for Black Audiences." *Composing Social Identity in Written Language.* Ed. D. Rubin. Hillsdale, NJ: Lawrence Erlbaum, 1995. 221–40.

Redd-Boyd, Teresa, and Wayne Slater. "The Effects of Audience Specification on Undergraduates' Attitudes, Strategies, and Writing." *Research in the Teaching of English* 23 (1989): 77–108.

Rickford, John R., and Russell J. Rickford. *Spoken Soul: The Story of Black English.* New York: Wiley, 2000.

Royster, Jacqueline Jones. "A New Lease on Writing." *Tapping Potential: English and Language Arts for the Black Learner.* Ed. Charlotte K. Brooks. Urbana, IL: NCTE, 1985. 159–67.

Seymour, Dorothy. "Black English." *Commonweal.* 1972. Rpt. in *About Language.* 2nd ed. Ed. William Roberts and Gregoire Turgeon. Boston: Houghton Mifflin, 1989. 274–82.

Shamoon, Linda K. "International E-mail Debate." *Electronic Communication Across the Curriculum.* Ed. Donna Reiss, Dickie Selfe, and Art Young. Urbana, IL: NCTE, 1998. 151–61.

Smitherman, Geneva. *Talkin and Testifyin: The Language of Black America.* Detroit: Wayne State UP, 1977.

———. "'What Go Round Come Round': *King* in Perspective." *Tapping Potential: English and Language Arts for the Black Learner.* Ed. Charlotte K. Brooks. Urbana, IL: NCTE, 1985. 41–62.

A Syllabus and Study Guide for Freshman English 002. Department of English, Howard University, August 2000.

Taylor, Hanni. *Standard English, Black English, and Bidialectalism: A Controversy.* New York: P. Lang, 1989.

Troutman, Denise. "Whose Voice Is It Anyway?": Marked Features in the Writing of Black English Speakers." *Writing in Multicultural Settings.* Ed. Carol Severino, Juan Guerra, and Johnnella Butler. New York: MLA, 1997. 27–39.

Walker, Margaret. "I Want to Write." *October Journey.* Detroit: Broadside, 1973. 30.

Walvoord, Barbara. *Helping Students Write Well: A Guide for Teachers in All Disciplines.* 2nd ed. New York: MLA, 1986.

Wells-Barnett, Ida. *On Lynchings: Southern Horrors, a Red Record, Mob Rule in New Orleans.* New York: Arno, 1969.

Whiteman, Marcia Farr. "Dialect Influence in Writing." *Variation in Writing: Functional and Linguistic-Cultural Differences.* Ed. Marcia Farr Whiteman. Hillsdale, NJ: Lawrence Erlbaum, 1981. 153–66.

Wolfram, Walt. *Dialects and American English*. Englewood Cliffs, NJ: Prentice-Hall/Center for Applied Linguistics, 1991.

Wright, Richard. *Black Boy: A Record of Childhood and Youth*. 1945. New York: Harper & Row, 1966.

An Experienced TA's Reflections on the TA Experience

JUDY COLLINS
Arizona State University

In the following essay, Judy Collins explores the transitions that new TAs experience in their first terms as classroom instructors. She also outlines the community-building practices that facilitate that transition.

Like all the graduate students in my TA training seminar, I wrote well enough when I entered the university as an undergraduate to waive the English 101 requirement. As a result, those of us admitted to the master's program in English who were awarded teaching assistantships in 1990 entered our classrooms for the first time without any experience of 101 from a student's perspective. Though I had tutored for two years in the writing center and received very good peer-tutor training, nothing can prepare a person to take the unaccustomed standing position in the classroom and pick up the chalk from its aluminum tray for the first time as a teacher.

And in the early weeks, it seemed that the minute details of classroom presence were the most troubling for all new TAs. We traded tales of surprising "firsts" in our shared offices just as all newcomers to complex activities share tales of initiation: stories of our minds going blank, an embarrassing inability to pronounce a word such as *door* in front of our class though we had long ago memorized our students' names. Strangely, nothing seemed more likely to reveal my identity as a first-time teacher to my class than the simple action of making uniform, well-aligned letters on the board.

We wanted to model ourselves after the teachers we had learned from who challenged us intellectually and initiated us into our chosen field of study and for whom writing was exciting; yet each day in our classrooms reminded us that there was much more to teaching than our personal knowledge of an area of English studies. It became clear that there were other kinds of knowledge involved than our knowledge of English language and literature.

What happens when graduate students enter composition in their new roles as teachers? Very likely they are also entering new roles as students in graduate school, which includes some of the most demanding reading and writing in cultural, political, literary, and language theory they have yet encountered. Like most graduate TAs, we were fortunate to have good preparation, professional mentoring, and weekly meetings. Our program director's door was never closed. At every turn, he reminded us as a group, and we reminded each other, that we were teaching process, not content. Yet the implications of that credo, which seemed so manageable in the abstract, are drawn intricately from the scholarship of the composition community, a complex community with different assumptions, theories, and praxis than any we had previously experienced.

We were all experienced members of creative writing and literary scholarship communities, but we gradually recognized that entering the community of writing teachers would require us to change. And teachers can change the way they think only by changing what they believe about what they know and how they know it (Bruffee x). Changing the way we teach is not easy. Learning to teach writing as a process is even less easy because what should work, or worked so well for us, doesn't work in the universal-requirement course of first-year composition. The assumptions we brought with us to composition were challenged daily by the context of first-year composition and the scholarship in the field, because both concern the production, not consumption, of texts. Composition is inherently interdisciplinary, a nexus of intersecting lines of inquiry such as rhetoric, sociolinguistics, language theory, education, writing research, and discourse analysis, all of which concern reading and writing within social processes.

As new TAs, we had been writing in specialized contexts for limited audiences for years. Though we were more comfortable in our new roles when we were reading student papers, we were also surprised at the tensions that emerged during grading sessions, when it became clear that consensus among us about good writing could not be assumed. We were responding to student texts as readers quite different from any reader who had served as our audience.

Our transition to the new context was incremental, in spite of our increasing familiarity with the theoretical issues raised in our reading *Encountering Student Texts: Interpretive Issues in Reading Student Writing* (Lawson), a collection prompted by the question, "How do writing teachers read student papers?" We had never intervened as facilitators/graders in the production of texts, and writing teachers read student papers differently than had the faculty who read our writing. We were also discovering that our students were not English majors and therefore not like us.

The kinds of problems we brought to our weekly TA meetings included the observations that sometimes our students didn't read the assigned essays and some may have nodded off during class, so the one classroom activity we were most familiar with— discussion—did not resemble the activity we remembered. We all embraced student-centered pedagogy, but many of our students were not rapt with attention, as we were in our student roles. Some students seemed not to enjoy writing either as self-expression or as anything of social value.

We were embarked on the process of becoming members of a new, unfamiliar community: teachers of writing. This membership began, much to our consternation at times, by engaging in the day-to-day practices of established members: facing a classroom of people different from ourselves, teaching processes, and encountering student texts. We were participating to some degree in the activities of fully participating members by reading theory and writing research, and by applying these readings to planning our writing assignment sequence, planning classroom activities, and managing classrooms. We were developing praxis.

Praxis translates knowledge into practical wisdom through the art of rhetoric (Swartz 553). Our knowledge came from reading Mina Shaughnessey, Mike Rose, Andrea Lunsford, James Moffett, James Britton, Frank D'Angelo, David Bartholomae, and Linda Flower and John Hayes, among others, during our course on teaching first-year composition. Our knowledge also came from our director of composition, who provided synopses of the intellectual history of composition, modeled process pedagogy, made challenging writing assignments, and served as an inspirational example of a professional teacher of writing. We also learned from each other.

We workshopped our writing assignments, graded and discussed papers together during meetings, observed each other's classrooms, and formed new friendships among other first-time teachers. We learned most from the small groups of three or four in a shared office where we could informally ask questions, complain, listen, offer sympathy and advice, seek help, brainstorm, trade inspiration, or translate the next assignment sequence into something theoretically consistent but more interesting. In small groups such as these, we tried out our ideas to integrate computer-mediated instruction. Gradually we gained enough classroom experience that daily classroom life became an additional source of knowledge.

As new teachers in a small program, we would also have found a collection such as *Strategies for Teaching First-Year Composition* an important resource. This book offers a window onto a broad range of theory and many years of experience in the classroom by collecting the exercises and teaching guides created by experienced teachers of writing. It is drawn from praxis—teachers' day-to-day activities framed by a guiding theory—and it answers the need we all felt as new teachers in composition for more exposure to what can happen in the classroom. For newcomers in the process of developing their own praxis, this book offers a diverse spectrum of theory and practice, and serves as another valuable resource for the teaching of first-year composition.

Works Cited

Bruffee, Kenneth A. *Collaborative Learning: Higher Education, Inter-dependence, and the Authority of Knowledge.* Baltimore: Johns Hopkins UP, 1993.

Lawson, Bruce, Susan Sterr Ryan, and W. Ross Winterowd, eds. *Encountering Student Texts: Interpretive Issues in Reading Student Writing.* Urbana, IL: NCTE, 1989.

Swartz, Omar. "Praxis." *Encyclopedia of Rhetoric and Composition: Communication from Ancient Times to the Information Age.* Ed. Theresa Enos. New York: Garland, 1996.

Writing and Learning to Write: A Modest Bit of History and Theory for Writing Students

DOUGLAS D. HESSE

Illinois State University

Although Doug Hesse ostensibly reflects on teaching composition at a particular kind of institution, he actually brings a special perspective to this historical/theoretical overview of work in the composition classrooms. He knows the field from a national perspective that few are privileged to have because he has served as editor of Writing Program Administration; *he also has served as president of the Council of Writing Program Administrators (WPA). His essay provides newcomers to the field with a history of major developments in writing pedagogy.*

We cannot promise a single, correct formula for writing, an algorithm guaranteed to produce success. There is none. There are many different strategies for various writing situations, and writers differ, too, in terms of the composing techniques that work for them. Learning to write better involves seriously trying a variety of processes and strategies in the context of specific writing tasks. Much that can be said about writing is very general: be well organized, analyze your audience's knowledge and beliefs, write prose that conforms to standards of correctness and clarity. All of this advice is true but helpful in only a limited sense. The real proof and practice come only when one engages specific strategies for, say, analyzing an audience, and only when one applies those strategies to specific writing situations.

Present-day writing courses have their roots in classical rhetoric. For several hundred years before Christ, students in Athens, Rome, and other centers of ancient civilization met with teachers to learn the arts of public discourse, primarily how to argue persuasively on matters under public deliberation. Aristotle, Isocrates, Quintilian, Cicero, and others all produced rhetorics, books of advice and strategies about how to produce effective speeches—speeches because oral presentations dominated written ones. This system of rhetorical education was adapted to writing and underwent numerous changes, modifications, and resurrections. Thus, rhetoric has been a key component of a university education for centuries. In fact, rhetoric and writing formerly held a much more central position in the U.S. college curriculum. Students at institutions such as Harvard in the 1860s could expect to take four years (or eight semesters) of public speaking and writing, in recognition of the fact that one learns to write with extensive practice and training over long periods of time. The one- or two-semester writing course requirement is a fairly recent development, established in the last part of the nineteenth century. (For a history of writing instruction, see James J. Murphy's *A Short History of Writing Instruction from Ancient Greece to Twentieth-Century America* or David R. Russell's *Writing in the Academic Disciplines, 1870–1990: A Curricular History*.)

Throughout much of the nineteenth and twentieth centuries, college writing courses bore a striking resemblance to one another. Instructors assigned topics or themes, and students handed in a completed paper, received a grade, perhaps a response, and another assignment. First-year writers in the early 1960s, for example, could expect to write a paper a week. Instruction about writing largely took the form of lectures about prose models or some stylistic, grammatical, or rhetorical feature, with occasional discussions about the content of some readings. Beyond this, students were on their own. They rarely received advice or input about their writing until after they turned in work to be graded.

By the mid-1960s, writing teachers, researchers, and theorists had increasingly begun to realize that there was a gap between this way of teaching writing and the way actual writers really worked, whether those writers were businesspeople, journalists, citizens with a complaint, or scholars. For actual writers, writing is a complex process that frequently extends over a period of time. It involves identifying and understanding a writing task, drafting, and revising. Writers frequently seek feedback during this process, talking with friends or co-workers, working with clients, editors, or bosses. It became clear that better writing instruction must include attention to the processes of writing. In other words, students would benefit from receiving input and advice about their writing during the process of completing a paper, not just after it. Teachers began teaching students strategies for "prewriting," "drafting," and "revising," and they began reading and commenting on drafts.

In the past twenty-five years, an extensive amount of research has been conducted on how people write and how writing should be taught. We now understand writing as a complex interaction of planning, writing, and revising, a process that rarely occurs in a linear fashion. Writers, for example, rarely complete their planning once and for all and then move on to writing, never to return to planning; instead, writers move back and forth among these processes. Writing processes are further profoundly influenced by the writer's experiences (life experiences, as well as reading and education) and circumstances, as well as by the different natures of different writing tasks. As a result, there are few universal truths and no simple formulas for all writers and writing tasks in all times and places.

If writing could be mastered by memorizing a few clear and simple rules, we at Illinois State University would certainly "give" students those rules. But there are no simple secrets. Learning to write is not like learning the dates of World War II. Writing abilities are acquired over time, through practice and feedback. Of course, there are some helpful strategies and advice that teachers can and will explain to students; after all, through scholarship and research we now know a good deal about writing. But even these strategies require practice before they are ingrained as part of a student's repertory of skills. Writing teachers are part coach, part critic, part expert practitioner. The writing classroom has far more in common with an artist's studio than it does with a lecture hall.

In general, writing is a process of constructing a text to achieve a desired effect within a specific group of readers. This characterization may sound straightforward: writers have something to say, have readers to whom they wish to say it, and know just what effect (actions or attitudes) they wish to produce. And sometimes writing actually works this way. But just as often it doesn't. Frequently, for example, the idea of "what" to say comes not from the writer but from the audience itself. A teacher assigns a paper, or an employer asks for a report, or a reader writes a letter to the newspaper that simply must be answered. In such cases, writers don't "fit" ideas they already have to an audience; rather, they generate ideas to accommodate an audience. Or, to cite another situation, sometimes writers have something to say and even something they want to happen as a result, but they have no sense of a specific audience or place of publication for this writing. The process of writing in this case becomes one of identifying an audience and shaping a text accordingly.

In truth, as a piece of writing evolves through several drafts, a sense of audience helps generate and change ideas, and newly emerging ideas alter the writer's sense of audience. Writers add and discard words, sentences, paragraphs, and entire ideas. They move concepts around. They substitute different words and ideas. They get fed up and start over. They change topics or approaches, knowing that the writing they've already done can be saved, perhaps, for some other writing situation. They ask for advice and feedback regularly. They put things aside and return to them later. They work on several projects simultaneously. They read critically and extensively.

A Further Note on Form and Formulas

At various points in our development as writers, we have all been taught forms or formulas for writing. It's important to realize, however, that while different writing situations have many things in common, no single formula is going to work for all writing situations. The world is far too complex always to be boiled down into some universal pattern of writing. High school students, for example, are frequently taught "the five-paragraph theme" (which may indeed have five paragraphs, or three, or twelve). Basically, this form consists of "tell them what you're going to tell them, make (usually) three points about it, and tell them what you told them." Certainly, there are writing situations in which an approach like this will work—some testing situations, for example. But in many other writing situations, the artificiality of the five-paragraph theme results in writing that warps the subject at hand. (Does every topic in the world really come in three parts—or in any number of predetermined parts, for that matter?) The five-paragraph theme assumes that topics are best handled by being partitioned into some fixed number of subtopics, preceded by a telegraphing thesis sentence and concluded by recitation of what the reader has just been told. College teachers often perceive a five-paragraph theme as substituting a formula for careful thought. In their haste to partition a topic into subtopics, writers often give no thought to the relation of those subtopics to one another. As a result, they don't build coherent papers whose parts have organic connections. What such writing might gain in organization and clarity for its readers it may lose in vitality and interest, at its worst suggesting that the writer really hasn't dealt with the topic at hand; instead, he or she has simply applied a formula.

The point is that while stock formulas are sometimes very helpful—and useful when that's the case—most often the writing situation is the best determinant for developing the form of a piece of writing. What a writer needs to do to be effective on a given topic with a given audience should always guide his or her sense of form. Of course, there is plenty of guidance available. One value of reading as a writer is to see how other authors writing to similar audiences on similar topics have organized their writing.

A good deal of writing takes the form of generalization and support. The writer has a progression of points he or she wants to make and includes support for each assertion, sometimes with one idea and its support in each paragraph. If this works well, readers feel as though they are being led in some meaningful progression, from one idea to the next. Other writings have a more reflective or narrative form, in which the writer seems to be led from one experience or idea to another less for logical reasons than for suggestive or aesthetic (artful) ones. Whatever the form, organizational design should be clear and natural for readers. Trying to outline a piece after it's written—or having peers try to do so—provides helpful feedback on organizational clarity.

English 101 students frequently report that they earned A's or B's in high school, believe they are good writers, and thus are frustrated at the difficulty or standards of English 101. What they need to keep in mind is that college writing puts demands on them they didn't have to address in high school. This is only natural. College biology, for example, covers different topics and ideas than does high school biology. If college writing courses were identical to those in high school, there wouldn't be a need for them.

What most distinguishes writing courses at Illinois State from most high school writing courses is that students regularly are asked to deal with argumentative nonfiction, perhaps reading several articles that take different positions on an issue. They are asked not only to summarize these readings but also to analyze and critique them. They have to be able to evaluate the qualities of arguments and defend positions for audiences that may be familiar with the background readings and have come to different conclusions. We find that students have a difficult time doing this. Any complex new task is difficult. We don't necessarily expect students to come to the university knowing how to do this well. But this new kind of writing is difficult for most students in the way that college-level calculus or a second language is difficult for them.

Works Cited

Murphy, James J. *A Short History of Writing Instruction from Ancient Greece to Twentieth-Century America*. Davis, CA: Hermagoras, 1990.

Russell, David R. *Writing in the Academic Disciplines, 1870–1990: A Curricular History*. Carbondale: Southern Illinois UP, 1991.

The Importance of Framing the Writing Classroom as a Space of Public Discourse

MICHAEL STANCLIFF
Arizona State University

Michael Stancliff's essay describes the public nature of writing in the democratic classroom and outlines strategies for dealing constructively with conflicts that public writing may cause.

In the front matter of all my syllabi, I include some statement about the "public nature" of classroom discussion and writing. The following is my most current rendition and is adapted from departmental syllabi here at Arizona State University:

> Please think of our class as a public forum. Throughout this semester, you will be expected to share your writing with others and to participate in class discussions. If there are things that you feel so strongly about you are unwilling to listen to alternative perspectives, I ask that you not write about these issues. Also, don't disclose any more about your personal life than you are comfortable with. Of course this does not mean that you should avoid addressing what is most important to you or that you should

act as if you have no opinion. I ask rather that you enter our classroom dialogue with an open mind, suspending judgment at least temporarily in the effort to share knowledge and create a space of mutual understanding. In this sense, the writing classroom is very much a microcosm of a democratic society. As citizens, we strive to maintain the balance between exercising our own freedoms without impinging on the rights of others. No doubt, we will share ideas, beliefs and preferences that will conflict. Ideally, we will disagree, challenge one another and learn from the experience. It is crucial that we strive to be considerate and respectful while being honest. If at any point during the semester you feel hurt, insulted or disrespected in any way, please bring it to my attention quickly so that we can address the matter. Don't let anger or frustration fester. Direct communication (via e-mail, a phone call or office visit) is the key to resolving such issues.

There are practical, pedagogical, and ethical reasons to include such a statement in your syllabus and to emphasize it as an active principle in your classroom. The question of public discourse is in fact where these different kinds of concerns converge. Your classrooms will be diverse, even if your eye registers demographic homogeneity. It is important to be proactive about the possibility of tensions that are a regrettable reality within diverse communities. There are also legal issues to be considered. Harassment does occur in the classroom, and it is our responsibility to help students avoid unthinking offenses and to resist a lapse into silence in the face of what is for them an unpleasant or upsetting interaction. It is important to remind students that their writing will be subject to a certain amount of scrutiny; often this does not become real to students until the day they bring their first rough draft to class. Suddenly, the very personal, or very polemical, essay they are working on no longer feels "safe."

Also, students must understand the responsibility of serious intellectual engagement with other perspectives; they should see this as the mark of a strong writer and a serious critical thinker and also, I would argue, as the primary activity of community building. You may well find that this disclaimer about the public nature of the classroom will become an important heuristic by which to explore the public issues that inevitably come up in composition classrooms. Finally, it is important to keep in mind that our most immediate institutional frame does not separate our classroom practices from a more inclusive network of cultural practices. I always make the effort to get students to consider the "company they keep" simply by posing a question or pursuing an issue. Where else in the world, I ask, are people concerned with these kinds of questions? The more clearly a classroom is framed within these larger contexts, the more engaged students will be. Certainly such classrooms offer richer and more dynamic opportunities to understand how rhetoric makes meaning.

"Black people tend to talk eubonics": Race and Curricular Diversity in Higher Education

AUSTIN JACKSON AND GENEVA SMITHERMAN
Michigan State University

As writing instruction has begun to include issues of diversity, teachers of writing are often called on to engage critical issues of diversity in their courses. Here, Austin Jackson and Geneva Smitherman offer advice, especially for TAs of color.

Black people tend to talk eubonics. . . . Like you in class, your tone of voice inflects back and forth so much that it takes away from the point of your lecture or question. . . .
Anonymous e-mail sent to a female African American TA teaching first-year composition (all-White classroom)

Teaching assistants in many university classrooms today are "strongly encouraged" to consider statements such as that above as "opportunities" to spark "critical" conversations related to the diversity content and goals of the course curriculum. For the

TA who is an African American (or other person of color), whose racial background makes her or him a part of the group under discussion, however, this pedagogical mandate poses an increasingly common but unaddressed problem. While our reflections here focus on race and racism, the aforementioned mandate extends to gender and sexism, ageism, homophobia, ableism, class elitism, and linguicism (bias and discrimination due to language).

It is useful to recall that social issues that came to the fore from previously marginalized groups became paramount in colleges and universities in the aftermath of the social transformation of the 1960s and 1970s. It was a transformation initiated by the Black Liberation Movement, to be sure, but it eventually affected all groups that had been marginalized and disempowered. In colleges and universities, this transformation resulted in two major changes relevant to our discussion. One was the restructuring of the curriculum to reflect the diversity of this country— hence the changes in curricula content and pedagogy, particularly in general education/required courses, such as first-year composition. Such courses now include texts and readings from African American, Latino, feminist, gay/lesbian, and other writers who had been excluded from these courses, as well as a pedagogical imperative to "interrogate," "investigate," "explore," and "create sensitivity" toward diversity. The second major change has been the diversification of faculty, staff, undergraduate and graduate students—and teaching assistants. Thus, along with women, gays/lesbians, and other previously outsider groups, TAs of color are now in composition and other required courses (although they are very much underrepresented).

> It seems to me that in an all around sense the blacks can't handle the English language, their freedom or even their lives!
> *From the same e-mail message quoted*
> *at the beginning of this essay*

The views of this student reflect the kinds of racial stereotypes and racialized attitudes that institutional curriculum reforms were designed to address. Some (many?) European American students bring such attitudes to the college classroom and impose these attitudes on classroom discussions about race. It is one thing for a European American TA to be confronted with this situation, but quite another for an African American TA. In fact, in the absence of guidelines or instructional tips, the African American TA is left floundering on his or her own to navigate the treacherous waters posed by such attitudes.

The strategies employed by TAs confronted with this dilemma sometimes work, sometimes don't, and sometimes achieve mixed results. One popular African American TA at a historically non-Black institution assigned an argumentative paper on reparations for enslavement. Students were required to use at least three sources, one of which had to be Frederick Douglass's *My Bondage and My Freedom*. One European American student expressed outrage that the class had to write about reparations for enslavement when there were no efforts underway to redress sexism and discrimination against women. The TA encouraged the class to explore and critically engage the issue of sex discrimination by talking about their personal experiences. This strategy took the onus off the TA and placed authority with the students and their experiences. During the heated discussion that ensued, several European American women students shared their personal and painful experiences with sexism. The TA refused to shy away from discussing their original topic—race (not possible, anyway, given the readings in the standard syllabus for this first-year composition class). She connected her female students' lived experiences with the subject of enslavement and reparations by illustrating how Douglass the abolitionist was also an ardent champion for women's rights and actively supported the women's suffrage movement. The students' conceptions of race and gender began to expand when they saw how the same oppressive forces were and still are at work in the struggle for equal rights for both African Americans and women. (Although this strategy worked with the class, the same student who was the catalyst for this successful class discussion filed a formal complaint of racism against the TA.)

In another instance, involving a different African American TA at a different historically non-Black institution, the strategy of interrogating, exploring, and so forth was effective with the majority of the class, but also resulted in a lone dissident voice who lodged a formal complaint. The students were reading poetry by Langston Hughes, part of the standard syllabus in this particular required first-year course. One student said that Hughes's poetry was unworthy of study because it "was written in Ebonics." The TA capitalized on this opportunity to launch a class discussion about language attitudes and their impact on social judgments and decisions about speakers. Anecdotes and ideas from his students (White as well as a few students of color) clearly illustrated the linguicism in our society and the relationship between linguicism and race. Apparently, not all students appreciated the enlightenment that emerged from that discussion. One student sent a letter to this TA's administrative supervisor, indicating that the TA was "unprofessional" and that the class discussion about Ebonics was "irrelevant" (despite the fact that the discussion was in the context of analyzing African American poetry written in Ebonics). Further, this student wrote that the TA was a "racist" who was "out to make white people feel bad about themselves."

> They [Blacks] don't know how to be considerate of feelings, they don't know how to send a point across w/out getting all hyped up, and they don't know how to talk. Maybe, just maybe, I've gotten my luck w/ all the "dumb" or nasty blacks, but what are the chances of that happening. Could you please give me your point of view as to why I seem to be meeting only these kind of people? Or maybe why a majority of the minority is this way? Thank-you for your time.
>
> E-mail from the anonymous student quoted earlier

The above statement relates to yet a third instance in which an African American TA dealt with race in the context of a first-year composition course. In this case, the student chose to critique the Black communication style as inappropriate, reflecting incompetence: the TA's "tone [is distracting because it] inflects back and forth," "the blacks can't handle the English language," they make their points in a style that is "all hyped up." As it turns out, this particular TA is from the hood in a large urban metropolis. This is her viewpoint on her linguistic style: "Language is a reflection of who I am, and I don't try to cover it up. I use it not only for the benefit of my Black students, but also for my white students. They need to see that other ways of speaking besides their own can be used to communicate intelligent thought." Interestingly enough, this clash between African American and European American linguistic practices and communication norms was addressed over two decades ago by sociolinguists. Kochman, for instance, using his college classrooms in Chicago, conducted an extensive study of "black and white styles in conflict." He states:

> The black mode . . . is high-keyed, animated, interpersonal, and confrontational. The white mode . . . is relatively low-keyed, dispassionate, impersonal, and nonchallenging. The first is characteristic of involvement; it is heated, loud, and generates affect. The second is characteristic of detachment and is cool, quiet, and without affect. (18)

The TA in this situation was easily able to determine the identity of her "anonymous" student and sought to critically engage the student in further discussions about race through e-mail. Their dialogue continued through several e-mail conversations in which she challenged the student to defend his assertions and generated a productive conversation. Remarkably, after the class was over (grades turned in), this student thanked her for the conversations and said that he had a different perspective on Black people and their language and culture.

Waaaaaaay back when one of the authors of this essay (Smitherman) was teaching first-year composition, she never had to deal with the kinds of contradictions and conflicts that African American TAs are confronted with in today's higher education classrooms, not because there was less racial conflict in those days, but because the standard syllabus was filled with texts by DWM's (gloss: dead White males), implemented with a sterile, lifeless pedagogy that completely excluded topics dealing with race, gender, class, sexual orientation, and the like. Obviously, we are in no way calling for a return to those "good old days." Rather, we are calling attention to an unintended and unaddressed consequence of diversification in the curriculum and in institutional policies in historically non-Black colleges and universities. The mandated pedagogical strategy in first-year composition and other university-wide required courses staffed by English TAs—

critical dialogue, interrogation, exploration, and investigation of diversity issues such as race—has the potential for creating conflict and contradiction for African American TAs, whose numbers higher education policies seek to increase. It is an issue that universities, eager to flaunt their commitment to diversity, need to be about the business of addressing.

Work Cited

Kochman, Thomas. *Black and White Styles in Conflict.* Chicago: U of Chicago P, 1981.

Rhetorical Situations and Assignment Sheets

DAVID SUDOL
Arizona State University

David Sudol, who has taught first-year composition for several decades, offers some strategies for helping students make the transition from the context of the high school English classroom to the college composition course.

I like to spend some time at the start of my English 101 classes discussing the difference between high school and college composition. In fact, on the first day of class—after we conduct introductions and review the syllabus—I ask the students to freewrite on the term *composition* and then to compare and contrast high school and college composition. We start the second day discussing what they've written.

During this discussion, I try to clear up any misconceptions the students may have about composition. For instance, I tell them that not every essay has to have five paragraphs (introduction, three body paragraphs, and a conclusion) and that it's okay to write in the first person and to use contractions. And, believe it or not, it's acceptable to begin a sentence with a conjunction.

More important, I use this discussion to explain that college composition—indeed all composition—is concerned with effective communication. Borrowing liberally from Erika Lindemann (11–21), I present a minilecture on rhetorical situations. First I introduce the communication triangle (writer, reader, subject, message); then I complicate it. I talk about the writer's persona—who he or she wants to be in the essay, what voice or ethos to project. Next I talk about how the writer has to analyze the reader's interests and needs, and not just assume the audience will understand. When discussing subject and message, I point out different purposes for writing—to inform, instruct, persuade, entertain—depending on what the writer wants to accomplish. I also note the importance of organization and arrangement; and I stress that form follows function, not a formula. I do, however, concede that certain kinds of writing are conventional (e.g., a lab report or a résumé). Next I talk about language: diction, syntax, tone, and style. I also touch on form (essay, letter, memo, etc.) and format (double-spaced, wide margins, twelve-point type, etc.). Finally I explain context, the environment or milieu of the writing (e.g., school, family, work).

The point of my talk isn't to intimidate or overwhelm my students—to show them that college is much harder than high school. On the contrary, I want to make them knowledgeable. In essence, I want them to learn that college composition means more than writing papers. It involves considering all the elements of a rhetorical situation and making choices that will ultimately result in good essays—effective communication. To reinforce the importance of this lesson, I include rhetorical situations in my assignment sheets.

Work Cited

Lindemann, Erika. *A Rhetoric for Writing Teachers*. 3rd ed. New York: Oxford UP, 1995.

Meeting of Narratives, Meeting of Minds: WPAs, TAs, and Transferring Independence

RACHELLE M. SMITH AND DOUGLAS DOWNS
Emporia State University

Rachelle Smith and Douglas Downs demonstrate how new and experienced teachers can work together effectively to make the transition to university teaching less stressful.

We are interested in the dynamics of what happens between experienced writing instructors and beginning teachers of writing within the confines of a university writing program. Specifically, how are composition pedagogies transferred from writing program administrators, who have the responsibility to train novice graduate teaching assistants, to first-year TAs? Our goal is to help illuminate the process whereby novice instructors move from directly supervised teaching to independence in the design and construction of writing assignments. This difficult process is rarely discussed because it is so sensitive an issue. How do experienced writing teachers train peers rather than merely supervise employees?

We attempt to show how this process occurs by juxtaposing narratives from both an experienced and successful TA and the WPA who taught him. This pairing of experiences reveals gaps between the message and its reception, between the intentions of the WPA and the actual responses of the TA. By forcing novice TAs to think about the writing process and to invent for themselves ways to teach their students specific composing strategies, the WPA establishes the means by which TAs can continue to improve their teaching pedagogies on their own. Through reading our narratives, we have concluded that TAs are initially resistant to this kind of training because they lack the perspective, the teaching experience, necessary to embrace it. Beginning TAs seem to think that the WPA's approach makes the process more difficult than necessary. Many wonder why the WPA doesn't simply tell them what to do instead of forcing them to make their own plans. Only after experiencing firsthand the realities of teaching without direct supervision do TAs recognize the wisdom of the WPA's approach. Only after looking at both of our narratives did we find confirmation of the process as a whole. We learned that the approach is effective but that we need to understand that it is natural, even necessary, for graduate teaching assistants to be initially resistant to designing their own writing assignments.

We begin with Rachelle Smith's narrative detailing how she goes about training new TAs and her feelings regarding the process.

Rachelle's Narrative

The moment I realized the significance of my new appointment as director of first-year composition was not when I got the call from the chair offering me the job, nor was it the welcoming dinner given by colleagues or the brand new computer shining in my new office. Reality hit when I walked into my first meeting with the new group of graduate teaching assistants. Suddenly, I realized that those familiar looks of confusion and mild panic that I was used to seeing on the faces of my peers in graduate school were no longer directed at someone else. These new TAs were looking at me for help. At that moment, everything I had ever read about composition, every class I had ever taught, took on a very different meaning. Sure, I knew I was a good teacher of writing. Now the question was, could I help teach anyone else how to do it?

Since the advent of the writing-as-a-process movement, those who teach writing in college have struggled to match theory with day-to-day classroom practice. It is far simpler to recognize the necessity of breaking the act of composing into constituent parts, or stages, than it is to determine how to teach those stages. Much of the research done in composition studies over the last twenty-five years is an attempt to understand these stages, and much progress has been made. Yet those of us responsible for overseeing the training of TAs in composition programs across the country know that for each new graduate teaching assistant we must start over again at the beginning.

It is just this process that I wish to examine in this essay. How do experienced teachers, scholars, and administrators respond to the needs of novice writing instructors? How do we all prepare not just our composition students, but ourselves, for the rigors of constant reinvention? How can experienced teachers help graduate students deal with the normal, expected, resistance TAs have to the process of learning how to teach? How do we all avoid complacency?

I find myself constantly repeating to TAs the same piece of advice over and over: "What can you have your students do in class to practice the kind of writing you require them to produce in their papers?" The question seems simple, almost obvious, when you think about it. Of course teachers of writing should have students practice the kind of writing they will be evaluated on later. No TA I have ever supervised has questioned the validity of this concept. Something happens, however, between the concept and its implementation. Even experienced TAs find their teaching notes lack such opportunities for students to learn to write. Why? The answer lies, I believe, in the process itself, in how TAs must do their other work.

In *Subject to Change*, Christine Farris reminds us that the average experience of being a TA naturally predisposes one to resist the application of composition theories. Most TAs enter graduate programs having just completed undergraduate degrees in English, where the majority of courses offered remains in literature and literary criticism. If they think at all about how they will go about teaching first-year composition prior to the start of the year, they probably imagine some course that fits their own experience. But there is little in the average TA's own educational experience to help prepare him or her to teach writing. Few undergraduates, even those who major in English, receive much instruction in how to write, despite the fact that composition studies itself began in the late 1960s. Most TAs have no idea how to begin to plan their courses. Since most of their education was spent in analyzing texts, many novice TAs fill class time with reading and commenting on texts found in composition textbooks, leaving little or no time for actual practice in composing. Even experienced writing teachers sometimes lose sight of the need to provide students with opportunities to practice the features of specific writing assignments, especially when designing new units. This is the single most difficult task teachers of writing must learn in order to provide students with competent instruction in composition. Recognizing this, I designed the following handout [summarized below], which I have used for a number of years now with new TAs during the summer workshop.

This handout is useful to new TAs in a number of ways. Using one kind of writing assignment, the personal narrative, it breaks down the stages of composition for the novice instructor. It is as important for new TAs to recognize the need for revision as it is to provide students with opportunities to practice the kinds of writing tasks necessary to complete the writing assignment. The personal narrative is perhaps the most familiar genre of writing for most TAs since it shares so many of the features of fiction. Description and dialogue, for example, do help make personal narratives successful, just as they do for fiction. Breaking the task into parts in this manner allows TAs to see more clearly why it is important to have students practice writing description and dialogue for a personal narrative writing assignment. This handout also serves as a reminder for TAs of the issues discussed during the summer workshop by summarizing the stages of the writing process using such a familiar example. It is designed to serve as a guide for subsequent lesson plans when TAs must construct their own exercises for different types of writing assignments, such as argument.

As useful as this handout, and the approach to teaching writing that it represents, is for novice writing instructors, it nonetheless asks for a rather sophisticated analysis of different kinds of writing. TAs must, in subsequent writing units, ask themselves, what are the constituent features of the texts students are asked to produce, and then isolate those features into individual writing exercises. This is asking a lot of experienced writing instructors, let alone novice TAs. Nonetheless, this ability is crucial to the continuing development of a writing teacher's pedagogy.

Doug's Narrative

Well. I have now come so far on this writing project as to select double line spacing. And if all goes well enough for this piece to ever see get a professional edit, that feature will eventually disappear anyway. How often do my students feel like this when they sit down to write an "explaining concepts" paper or a "letter to the editor"?

That wasn't a question I even thought to ask when I showed up for my first presemester seminar on teaching composition. A highly decorated graduate of an English program with a writing specialty, I knew how to write and I knew how writing was taught. It had been at least four years since I'd met a writing assignment with anything less than total confidence and about that long since I'd last seen writing taught badly. In fact, my writing classes were staffed by excellent faculty—I'd somehow managed to miss those teaching assistants lurking in Comp I and Comp II, and only faculty who cared about writing as craft taught my upper-level writing courses. They were so good at what they did that I didn't even notice what they were doing. If I recall correctly, it was Peter Elbow who said in *Writing without Teachers* that good writers should not be allowed to teach writing because they don't understand the problems less-skilled writers encounter. I have learned how true that is.

After our first half-hour of get-to-know-you chatter, Rachelle tugged her fresh-faced TAs into reality with two questions. The first was, "What was your first-year comp experience like?" Many of us were disturbed to find we couldn't remember it all that clearly. Others dredged up memories of current-traditional literature-based composition courses radically unlike those Rachelle masterminded at ESU. The second question was worse: "How will you teach your students how to write their 'Remembered Event' narrative?" Well . . . don't you just . . . *teach* it? I suppose I had some vague plans, of course, of finding a perfect model text, analyzing the hell out of it, and then turning to my students to say, "Now you try it."

Nice try. Before our wondering eyes, Rachelle unveiled her

grand scheme, whereby we would slice the required piece of writing into its constituent features (for a narrative, we might ask specifically for a meaningful and suspenseful piece that uses dialogue and colorful, descriptive writing) and have students practice those *features,* instead of merely teaching *form.* It looked good on the white board, but I left that day with the impression that I was not the only skeptic among us. After all, this *complicated* things. Why make it so difficult? *I* was never taught "features" of my writing assignments. My teachers just . . . taught. But instead of figuring out how to practice narratives, I and my fellow TAs were left scratching our heads. How do you practice dialogue? Our troubles, it seemed, were merely multiplied by this approach.

This regression of the problem turned out to be, in fact, a lifesaver—for the teachers and for the students. The features approach does have its benefits. Perhaps most important, it helped us TAs keep one mantra at the forefront of our plans: "Practice the parts and then try to build the whole. Practice the parts." Rachelle was fond of repeating before lesson planning sessions the principle that "you should be able to tell how what you're doing in your classroom at any given moment will help students produce the writing you want." The features approach is perhaps the surest way to meet that standard.

The features approach is also valuable in that it serves as a guide or template for new teachers. The "chunking" of an assignment into smaller parts creates more questions for a teacher, but they're smaller questions. Instead of "How will I teach the letter-to-the-editor?" the question becomes, "How will I teach tone?" Eating is an apt analogy. Only the biggest of mouths could consume an entire salmon filet at once; normal people cut it up to consume it.

In addition, I have seen TAs fall back on the features approach as a sort of autopilot for their teaching. Combined with a manual that lists specific criteria for each standard assignment, teaching features can make lesson planning a very simple process. The TA has only to decide in what order to teach and practice the criteria, or features, of the assignment at hand. For a TA with an unusually crowded schedule (which, oddly enough, seems to be most of us), relying on a sort of premade road map that tells us *what* to teach, without ordering us *how* to teach it, is a wonderful backup system.

The features approach is as much a helping hand for students as it is for inexperienced teachers. It removes an element of threat from the process of writing an assignment. Unlike in my own (delightfully) broad first-year comp assignments ("pick a topic and write five pages about it"), my students need have no fear of doing the wrong thing. The same road map that guides the teachers in what to teach guides the writers in what to write. Uncertainty and a fair amount of fear caused by the danger of failure are removed from the process simultaneously.

We TAs were largely sold on the features approach to teaching after that first narrative assignment, for which it worked well. Narratives, after all, are made up of a number of discrete, entertaining, and easily teachable elements such as descriptive language, figures of speech, dialogue, suspense, and storytelling presentation.

As I continued to teach different assignments, however, including concept-based informative papers, position papers, persuasive papers, research papers, bibliographies, and analysis papers, I began to realize that practicing features was becoming less and less helpful. The criteria for each assignment became vaguer (what does "appropriate tone for your audience" *mean?*) as the number of successful approaches a writer could take to a paper multiplied. For instance, it's much less useful to practice the "feature" of organization than to practice dialogue. The latter always follows the same rules, and its mechanics and principles can be distilled to four or five basic ideas. I believe, on the other hand, that the number of ways to effectively organize a paper is roughly equal to the total number of papers ever written. "It just depends" is not a particularly helpful answer to the students who have trouble with this feature, because unlike dialogue it is not something you can pop in or take out at will. Neither are sound reasoning, appropriate tone, or opposing viewpoints. These are not "features" of the paper; they *are* the paper.

This realization was at first a source of frustration, but after a while I thought it might be a sign of a maturing teacher, one who had moved beyond the autopilot. On some assignments, and for some features of writing such as source integration or definitions, practicing features continues to work well. But for the reasons mentioned earlier, as well as for two others, I do not rely on the practicing-features approach as much as I did at the beginning of my teaching career.

I rely on it less now because I focus more on teaching broader issues of writing that are applicable to many different assignments or types of papers. I'm more interested in teaching the principles underlying good organization (e.g., fulfilling reader predictions) than in trying to cover five different organizational patterns (e.g., cause/effect, chronological, compare/contrast, etc.). It's the "teach a person to fish" argument: I don't want them to learn how to write this particular paper so much as I want them to learn how to successfully complete any writing task they might encounter. I've found that if a feature is clearly enough defined to make practice truly possible, then it's rarely broadly applicable to other writing projects, and vice versa.

Second, I've found that in many cases practicing narrow features takes too much creative drive out of the students' hands. In a truly nonthreatening, nonpunishing environment, I've seen students do just fine, indeed thrive, on writing assignments from general instructions where the features of a form are not practiced in class. (For instance, "create a list of outstanding sources in a particular field." We do not practice the features of such writing; instead, we work on the intellectual challenge of deciding what sources should go on the list.) In fact, the creativity and initiative students manifest in such circumstances usually surprises me. The road map, the carefully delineated and practiced features, can be as numbing for students as it is easy for teachers. It removes a step of problem solving that students are forced to take in all their other classes and certainly after graduation. Requests for reports rarely come with criteria sheets and formatting directions attached. I hasten to add, however, that I do not at all mind removing that problem-solving step for Comp I students. Just as the features approach benefits newer teachers more than more experienced ones, so this approach is more a necessity for newer college students than advanced students. Only my Comp II students see assignments not taught by practicing features.

Because I am going on for a Ph.D. in comp/rhetoric with the hopes of teaching comp or even holding a WPA position in the future, Rachelle has challenged me to speculate on what place the practicing-features approach might find in my own TA program. My experience to this point has taught me to value the practicing-features approach variably. I can't imagine, now, being a new teacher without that strategy—just as, before I was a teacher, I had no vision whatsoever of what teaching would actually require. Even with more experience and a growing sense of the terrain of teaching writing, there are still times when I won't enter a classroom without that map.

Though my critique of the approach Rachelle has shown us is firm, for the time being at least, I'm sure that I too would teach that approach to TAs of my own. Its limitations for experienced teachers and students do not offset its value for new teachers and new or even intimidated first-year students. Like any other method of teaching composition, the features approach is neither a magic potion nor a cure-all. But it surely has a place on the shelf of any writing "coach," and I think new TAs should keep it as close at hand as their hard-used bottles of aspirin.

Conclusion

Having read our narratives side by side, we confirmed what we both believed prior to starting this project: the process whereby novice writing instructors gain independence and skill is difficult yet doable. By reading our paired narratives, we discovered the gaps that existed between what the WPA intended to communicate and what the TA understood.

The major miscommunication we discovered relates to Rachelle's desire to teach her new TAs how to analyze genres of writing, what Doug calls "features" of writing. It was only through reading these narratives that we discovered this gap. What Rachelle thought was clear in terms of the need for analysis, Doug proved was not clearly communicated. In his narrative, "organization" becomes a "feature" of writing, something that Rachelle would never identify as a constituent part of a specific genre of writing. A traditional persuasive essay, for example, includes a logical argument structure of claim, reasons, and evidence. But this is not equivalent to "organization" as Doug understood "features" to mean. A subtle distinction, it nonetheless affected Doug's understanding of how one goes about designing writing assignments.

We believe more dialogue such as this would greatly enhance the training of graduate teaching assistants. The process will always be difficult. TAs will continue to resist learning composition pedagogies, just as WPAs will continue to fail to communicate effectively. As long as both parties are aware of this natural tension, they can make it a productive one.

Works Cited

Elbow, Peter. *Writing without Teachers*. London: Oxford UP, 1973.

Farris, Christine. *Subject to Change: New Composition Instructors' Theory and Practice*. Cresskill, NJ: Hampton, 1996.

Students as Audience

RUTH OVERMAN FISCHER
George Mason University

Ruth Fischer offers some keen insights into the ways in which students shape the context in which we teach. Too often, we forget the effects of the Bakhtinian heteroglossia of any classroom.

An important concern for writers is an awareness of audience. Such an awareness is also important for teachers of writing, especially in first-year composition (FYC). And as teachers of FYC, we are in a unique position to get to know our students because of FYC's tendency toward smaller class sizes and more interactive pedagogies. Taking the time to get to know our students at the beginning of the term is time well spent.

The whole person/student learns. This axiom recognizes the importance of attending to the multiple aspects of our students, the affective/emotional and social as well as the cognitive/ intellectual. Students enter our FYC classes with their own individual histories and their own narratives of who they are as learners, writers, and human beings. These narratives play a major part in how they see themselves in our classrooms. A student, for example, who has been told that he or she cannot write brings that schema to the class.

In addition, learning styles and personality types differ among students and play a role in how our students approach the reading/writing/thinking work we ask them to do in our classes. Asking students to take a learning-styles inventory and a personality inventory such as the Myers-Briggs Type Indicator, and then reflect in writing on how they can apply the results to themselves as writers/learners, helps both you as teacher and them as students obtain a sense of who they are. Check with your career services or counseling services office to see what instruments are available for students on your campus.

Students also need to feel comfortable in our classrooms even as we challenge them with intellectually rigorous assignments. It's easy to overlook the affective/emotional piece of the puzzle that constructs each of our students. At the same time, it's not always easy to figure out ways to encourage students to greatness without totally stressing them out.

Along with teaching writing and all that entails, we can help students enter the postsecondary educational culture. Not only does our awareness of this acculturation process help us understand how our students write and how we can help them write better, but it also gives our students a better chance for survival in the new culture.

Learning to write is a developmental process and so too is learning the college/university culture. Regardless of the number of college prep courses they have taken, most first-year students do not begin college as college students but as extended high school seniors. They bring with them the strategies that worked well in high school but are not usually as successful in college. For example, many think they will be able to complete assignments, especially writing assignments, at the last minute—"I write better under pressure," some will say. They may assume they can turn assignments in late without penalty, because their high school teachers were happy to get work, late or not. Or they may expect that effort will be a direct factor in the grade they receive—"I did the assignment. How come I only got a C?" you might hear. Throughout high school, they may have been able to get tolerable grades by just listening in class without reading or rereading and studying assignments. And many have come to rely on teachers to remind them of overdue work.

These assumptions accompany them to your class, along with possible clashes of expectations. You see your class as an opportunity for them to develop as writers; they may see it as a required course that highlights the fact that they did not learn to write in high school. You see revision as a part of the ongoing development of a paper; they see it as surface editing. You may expect them to put in three hours of study time for each hour in class; they may be spending their time trying to find new friends and negotiate the campus social scene and, if yours is a commuter campus, trying to find a parking spot.

Clashes may also occur over differing expectations about what constitutes allowable topics in the classroom. If your purpose is to get students to look at controversial issues, especially those that might conflict with the worldview in which they have been raised, they may respond with resistance and knee-jerk clichés. And if you ask them to interrogate their position, you may hear, "Well, that's my opinion and it's just as good as anyone else's!" You may find them running headlong toward closure even as you want them to consider an issue from multiple perspectives.

An additional factor in your relationship with your students is your aura of authority as a teaching assistant. If you are only a few years older than your students, you may be reluctant to position yourself as the one "in charge." And yet you are the one ultimately responsible for the way the course syllabus is implemented and the way your students' writing is assessed. And so the extent to which you claim your authority either works to support or to undermine what goes on in the classroom.

This authority need not be heavy-handed or loudly proclaimed. I have found that first-year students are usually apprehensive as it is about being in a college classroom for the first time. Your authority, however, can find articulation in your syllabus by the way you have set up your course and delineated your expectations. Although students might whine at the beginning of the course about how hard they are having to work, many find their hard work a source of pride at the end of the course, especially if they perceive that their writing has improved.

Keep your expectations high, state them clearly in your syllabus and course assignments, provide scaffolding and support in reaching these expectations, and try not to take perceived student resistance or immaturity personally. Hold them accountable as candidly and impartially as you can and with as much patience and good humor as you need.

Of course, these steps I've described depend somewhat on your local context. And even within one class setting not all students will have all these assumptions. But if you allow for their possibility, you can save yourself from being blindsided.

Memo from a Provost

ELAINE P. MAIMON

Arizona State University West

This memo from Elaine Maimon offers a perspective that reflects her experience as a high-level administrator and provides new TAs with a broader view of their role at the university. She's taught much composition in her career, and she's served composition programs in other ways. From her current position as chief academic officer on her campus, she observes the following:

To: First-Year TAs
From: Elaine P. Maimon, Provost, Arizona State University
        West
Re: The Big Picture

Your work as a writing instructor is fundamental to students' success at the university. Whether or not your composition program officially introduces writing across the curriculum, you more than anyone else will map the university for your students. For many students, yours may be the only small class during their first, formative year of college. You may be the first person to whom students turn for advice. It will be in your classroom, through collaborative learning, that students will form intellectual bonds with classmates. Through talking, reading, writing, and revising, students will discover their own voices in the ongoing conversation of educated women and men.

Now, you may be thinking, all that sounds rather grand for the status and pay you receive as a TA. Here are a few points to remember to help you sustain your morale and perspective:

1. Remember that your work as a TA is an apprenticeship. Learn as much as possible from the composition director, other professors, fellow graduate students, and, most important, the undergraduates in your classes. At the same time, it is important to give yourself a timetable to *complete* the apprenticeship—and your Ph.D.

2. Adopt the stance of a teacher-researcher. Pose systematic questions about writing and how it is learned, and conduct in-class research projects. Incorporate this research into your agenda for graduate study. Present papers at professional meetings and publish your results. As an apprentice, practice the integration of research and teaching—an integration that should be natural for writing teachers. This habit of mind will sustain your sanity as you work to complete your Ph.D. on time, and will establish momentum toward a balanced life in the academy.

3. Do not readily believe the sad stories about the job market. Excellent writing teacher-researchers will find jobs, especially if you have also developed an institutional perspective.

4. Gain an institutional perspective by welcoming opportunities for administrative experience. Assisting the writing pro-

gram director will give you insight into how the university works. This experience will also provide another important tool for a future job search.

5. Integrate teaching, research, and administrative experience. You may be wondering how you are supposed to teach, publish, help with administration, and still complete your apprenticeship before retirement. Again, integration is the answer. Much of what you do should serve at least two purposes: e.g., teaching an assignment that is part of your research agenda; helping with scheduling to understand enrollment patterns; fulfilling assignments in graduate courses with an eye toward the dissertation or publication.

6. Consider the idea that the senior administration of your university is not the enemy. The president and provost may not be models for the evil corporate types in the *Dilbert* comic strip. Sometimes your composition director may even have influence with the provost or president because of an authentic leadership commitment to the teaching of writing.

In general, when you consider the big picture at your university, I would advise a suspension of disbelief. Resist taking an us/them attitude (unless something happens that warrants it). You may even be at an institution where the dean, provost, or president is a former TA who remembers the significance of what you do.

CHAPTER 2

SEEING THE FOREST AND THE TREES OF CURRICULUM

C ontributors to this chapter use various lenses—from fairly wide-angle to very narrow-angle—to examine curricula in first-year composition. The chapter begins with Irv Peckham's description of an outcomes statement developed by composition scholars from across the country. Because the outcomes statement has generated much interest at national conventions and on organizational listservs, it has become an important document for focusing discussions of how we enact curriculum through pedagogy.

Teaching in an Idealized Outcomes-Based First-Year Writing Program

IRVIN PECKHAM
Louisiana State University

One of the framers of the outcomes statement, Irv Peckham provides commentary that reflects insights he has gained through scores of conversations with other scholar-teachers.

I have been working for over three years with a protean group of postsecondary writing teachers to arrive at some sort of agreement on what we consider to be desirable outcomes for first-year writing students. I am using the word *outcomes* here under protest, for I don't like the word—in my own mind, I translate it into the kinds of skills and knowledge that I would like first-year students to have. Compromise has been, however, the hallmark of our search for a commonly agreed-on set of outcomes, and so I refer to them as outcomes in this essay. I suppose that part of being linguistically alive is being able to compromise on words.

We have posted a draft of what is now called the Outcomes Statement at http://www.mwsc.edu/~outcomes.[1] The statement outlines defensible outcomes for first-year writing; however, I like to think of the outcomes in a format simpler than that of the official version. Accordingly, and with all due apologies to my outcomes colleagues, I refer in this essay to a simpler version that I wrote in a wickedly uncollaborative gesture after our last workshop. Although I may be straining the goodwill of my friends, I excuse myself by thinking that I am working within the spirit of our original goal, which was to agree on a set of outcomes that we could present nationally for others to either use verbatim or to adapt to their local situations. For the moment, this essay is my local situation.

My purpose is to describe the kind of first-year writing program that would support these outcomes and a way of assessing how well students have achieved them. The writing program I describe is imaginary. I began this essay with the intention of describing the program that I and my colleagues designed (well, plagiarized) at the University of Nebraska at Omaha, but I soon found myself imagining it as more effective than it is—as I frequently imagine my teaching as better than it is. So I have mixed with my description of our program elements with what I think a good first-year writing program should be. As I was imagining my idealized program, I also thought about "the problem of first-year writing"—that is, my ideal began to break down in my head as I matched it with my experience. So I also include in this description a discussion of "the problem" with some reflections on the possibility of new directions.

When I describe a way of assessing how well students have met the desired outcomes, I am describing my use of portfolios to evaluate student achievement in my courses. This leads to a sidebar discussion of ways to respond to student writing, which in turn brings up the knotty issue of grades. I try to avoid the debate on whether one should grade student writing, but that question will always be in the background of the portfolio discussion. There are three issues involved in this problem: (1) responding to student writing, (2) assessing student achievement, and (3) grading. It's easy to confuse these. Although I acknowledge their intersections, I do my best to tease them apart, very much as I tease them apart in my practice.

The Outcomes Statement

Following is a simplified version of the Outcomes Statement. It is available under Drafts at the URL cited earlier, and I present it as it appears on the Web page. I admit to some ambiguity in my claim that "the following document is the result of the collective effort of writing teachers from a variety of colleges and universities." Many of the words and all of the ideas are the result of that collaboration. I did do some significant editing, and I want to make it clear that my collaborative friends do not have to share any blame for the version I have reproduced here. I also need to note that the original statement carries a warning that I have ignored. It says, "*We strongly discourage any use or attribution of the following language that does not take great care to represent it accurately.*" I did try to represent it accurately, but I'm the kind of person who can't be trusted with someone else's words. I'm looking forward to a time in this new millennium when our conceptions of whose words are whose are forever warped by electronic appropriation.

I had two audiences in mind when I wrote the simplified version of the Outcomes Statement: other members of my department and area high school teachers. I basically wanted to make the Outcomes Statement shorter and avoid any college compositionist words. I thought high school writing teachers might resist outcomes such as the following: "To use the media, including especially computerized media, commonly used in communicative transactions." If I were going to rewrite that, I would have said, "To write with computers," but this would have been simplifying quite a few other things that I know were behind the original statement. I ended up removing that particular statement (mostly because I supported a move to insert a section on computer and writing skills).

The original statement—as it appeared before revisions and adoption by the WPA—had quite a long introduction that was particularly academic in its attempt to hedge on the use of these outcomes. It carefully delineated the difference between standards and outcomes and pointed out that we were not trying to create benchmarks, which I think are useful only for political campaigns. The original statement was also careful to warn readers that the document was written for other professional writing teachers and in their language. Thus, the original statement said, "Among such readers, terms such as 'rhetorical,' 'genre,' and 'text' convey a rich and specific understanding." But with many readers, a "text" might mean something one buys in a bookstore.

So in general, here are the ways I changed the original statement:

1. deleted most of the preface

2. inserted a forecast

3. changed discipline-specific words

4. collapsed series of related statements into single statements

5. deleted sections that described what teachers in other disciplines could do to support these outcomes.

Thus, my apologia. Below is my simplified version that I will use as a basis for this essay.

Outcomes Statement for First-Year Writing
[Revised: 7/18/98]

[This draft is a simplified version of the statement presented to the WPA Executive Committee on 7/17/98. The purpose of this draft is to have a statement to use in workshops with teachers or a general public who may not have specialized knowledge in rhetoric and composition. The official statement can be read at http://www.mwsc.edu/~outcomes.]

The following document is the result of the collective effort of writing teachers from a variety of colleges and universities. These teachers worked together to agree on what students should know and be able to do at the end of first-year writing courses at the college level. The writers of this document have functioned as an ad hoc committee of the national organization of Writing Program Administrators. The document is currently in a draft stage and is awaiting final responses and revisions before formal endorsement by the Writing Program Administrators Executive Committee.

The knowledge and skills are divided into four categories.

1. **Rhetorical knowledge:** this covers the kinds of things students need to know about the writing situation, such as who the readers are and what kind of information they may be expecting from the text.

2. **General reading, writing, and thinking skills:** this covers general reading, writing, and thinking skills students must have to meet the demands of different kinds of writing situations.

3. **Processes:** this covers the processes students need to follow to produce successful texts.

4. **Conventions:** this covers specific conventions, such as spelling and punctuation, that readers will expect the students to control.

The document provides *only* general descriptions of what students need to know and be able to do. It does not define standards or precise levels of ability. These have been left for specific institutions to define and assess.

Rhetorical Knowledge

By the end of their first-year writing courses, students should

- ◆ be able to focus on a specific purpose;
- ◆ be able to anticipate the needs of different kinds of readers;
- ◆ be able to recognize the differences among kinds of writing situations;
- ◆ be able to use the conventions of format, organization, and language appropriate to specific writing situations;
- ◆ understand what makes writing types (like a book review, a project proposal, or a research report) different.

General Reading, Writing, and Thinking Skills

By the end of their first-year writing courses, students should

- ◆ be able to use writing to record, explore, organize, and communicate;
- ◆ be able to find, evaluate, analyze, and synthesize appropriate primary and secondary sources in order to meet the demands of different kinds of writing situations;
- ◆ understand the general relationships among language, knowledge, and power.

Processes

By the end of their first-year writing courses, students should know how to use

- multiple drafts to improve their texts;

- strategies like brainstorming, outlining, and focused freewriting in all stages of the writing process;

- generating, organizing, revising, and editing strategies that are appropriate to the specific writing situation;

- effective collaborative strategies to investigate, write, revise, and edit.

Conventions

By the end of their first-year writing courses, students should

- control general conventions of spelling, grammar, and punctuation expected in standard written English;

- be able to document primary and secondary sources appropriately;

- know how to check for conventions about which they are uncertain;

- understand that different conventions are appropriate for different kinds of writing situations.

Writing Program Description

Most of the teachers to whom I have shown these outcomes have agreed that they represent the kinds of things students at the end of a first-year writing course should know and be able to do. It is important to note—as did the original framers of the outcomes constitution—that these outcomes do not specify level of knowledge or skill. It would obviously be silly to try to establish a benchmark for the level at which a student knows, for example, "what makes writing types (like a book review, a project proposal, or a research report) different," or at what level a student should be able to use "generating, organizing, revising, and editing strategies appropriate to the specific writing situation." To establish seriously defensible benchmarks, we have to find the kinds of things we can count—and that simply isn't the game we're playing when we teach writing. We can also establish benchmarks of a sort by using essays or portfolios that represent achievement at a particular level, say 1 though 5, but we should be wary of ascribing either objectivity or accuracy to this kind of assessment. We can, however, get a picture of student achievement—getting this kind of picture is the purpose of the portfolios I describe in the second part of this essay.

Journals

My idea of journals is broad: they could be daily entries in spiral-bound notebooks, group journals on a newsgroup listserv or Web bulletin board, or e-mail entries sent to the teacher at the end of each class period. Journals can be as counterproductive as the five-paragraph essay, but used well they will help students meet several of the outcomes. My students write in journals at least once a week. I almost always have students write outside of class, although there are effective ways of using them in class. Perhaps the most effective in-class use is to devote five to ten minutes at the end of each period to an entry in which the students write their responses to what happened in class. These responses could include issues left unresolved or a critique of the day. A good way of responding to these student reflections is to take notes on what the students wrote and then begin the next class period with a summary and discussion of the issues broached in the journals.

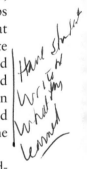

Other uses of the journal include reflective responses to reading assignments or summaries of what students are doing with their writing projects. The reflective responses to reading assignments do not have to be complicated: I ask students to tell me what the reading was about, what they liked about it, what they didn't, what kind of claims have been made that they didn't agree with, whether there's anything from the reading they are wondering about or would like to discuss in class, and anything else for the good of the order. Journal entries about writing could be progress reports that also function as a place in which students can write about their problems or successes with writing. I am particularly interested in what students are learning (or not learning) about writing, mostly because I take the stance of teacher-as-researcher, and journals are one of my primary sources of information.

Particularly in the case of the reflections on reading, these kinds of journal entries are most useful if the teacher can have the entries turned in on e-mail before the class period in which the reading selection is to be discussed. The teacher can scan these entries and respond with a quick reply or by taking notes and summarizing at the beginning of class what the students have written. These summaries can then be used as a point of departure for the discussion of the reading.

guidelines

There is, of course, a good deal to say about journal entries, but here I offer only a couple of summary remarks: First, journals should be responded to in some way on a regular basis. They are most effective when teachers use them as a place for dialogue with the students. The dialogue on the teacher's part doesn't have to be an extensive written response. It can even be an oral response. Journals have worked best for me when I use them as a place to find out what is happening in the class *from the students' points of view*. Journals do not work when students interpret them as busywork (probably because they are). Teachers need to have clear reasons for having students write in journals—and the reason should be better than the old one about frequency leading to fluency.

Here are the outcomes that *effective* journal writing supports. Under **Rhetorical Knowledge,** students should

- be able to recognize the differences among kinds of writing situations;
- understand what makes writing types (like a book review, a project proposal, or a research report) different.

Under **General Reading, Writing, and Thinking Skills,** students should

- be able to use writing to explore.

Under **Processes,** students should know how to use

♦ strategies like brainstorming, outlining, and focused freewriting in all stages of the writing process.

And under **Conventions**, students should

♦ understand that different conventions are appropriate for different kinds of writing situations.

Students who have never or rarely written in journals quickly learn something about the differences among kinds of writing situations: writing in a journal presents a different rhetorical situation than writing a position essay that the writer will publish for the rest of the class. Even the rhetorical situation of writing a journal entry that will be read only by the teacher is different from the situation of writing an entry that will be read by the rest of the class. A journal entry in which writers reflect on some of these differences in writing situations can be moments of discovery and can lead to further class discussion and exploration. Such an exploration helps students achieve the second outcome listed earlier: they learn something about "what makes writing types . . . different." Part of what makes writing types different is different conventions. Most students coming in to my classes think that a common set of conventions apply to all writing situations. One journal entry (and subsequent discussion) in which they reflect on the differences between journal conventions and formal business letter conventions disabuses them of the notion of monolithic writing conventions. The use or prohibition of first person within different writing situations is one of the more obvious examples of differences in conventions. I like to point out that Chester Burnett would have sounded pretty silly singing, "I am not going down that dirt road by myself" rather than, "I ain't goin' down dirt road by myself." The former may have been good grammar but it's bad blues.

Finally, by writing in their journals about their ideas and about their writing, students learn how to use writing to explore. There will always be students, particularly in first-year composition, who write in journals as if they were brushing their teeth—and these students will never learn the exploratory function of writing—but most students eventually find themselves thinking about something through their writing that they had never thought about before. Perhaps because I am a diary addict myself, I think that students who have never internalized the exploratory function of writing have missed the fundamental lesson. Once they have caught the exploratory function, it's a small step to use journals to brainstorm, outline, and freewrite. Almost all of my serious writing begins in my diary. That's where I get my ideas, where I outline, and where I write about my progress and what's getting in my way. The trick is to move outward—and that is the purpose of learning how to write in different genres.

Writing Types—or Genres

It seems quite clear that if we intend to teach our students anything about rhetorical knowledge, they should learn how to respond in writing to different writing situations. We certainly don't want them to think that all writing is what James Britton et al. called "dummy run" writing (writing to the teacher to show him or her that you know how to write) (104), the "research paper" (this could be dummy run writing or writing to tell the teacher what he or she already knows in order to prove that you know it, too), or the five-paragraph essay in one of its various guises. To respond appropriately to different writing situations, one needs to know how to write in different genres. This seems to be a basic piece of knowledge about writing.

There is quite a history to the question of whether we should teach students how to write "in" genres; the discussion has come to be known as "the genre debate" (see Reid). The genre debate is rife with ideological positions that pit individual expression against traditional discourse, and is somewhat muddled with concepts of form and function as working independently (Peckham, "Yin and Yang"). Writing teachers who resist any kind of instruction based on genres worry about the insipid writing that comes from following formulas, as if writing were a fill-in-the-dots activity. Their concerns are serious. At its worst, this kind of writing instruction was based on the five-paragraph model; at only a slightly lower level of generalization, it was based on the modes of writing generally attributed to Alexander Bain:

description, narration, exposition, and argumentation (with poetry—i.e., creative writing—being his fifth type).[2]

With its focus on individual expression, the sixties were perhaps the nadir of genre-based instruction. The latter part of the
sixties and early seventies ushered in a more informed sense of
what genres are and how they function. A plethora of genre theories were floating around, but the three Jameses (Moffett, Britton,
and Kinneavey) developed perhaps the best-known theories, introducing a new note of respectability to genre-based instruction. The other high-water marks were in 1981 and 1986, which
saw, respectively, the translations of M. M. Bakhtin's *The Dialogic Imagination* and "The Problem of Speech Genres." Walter
Beale's *A Pragmatic Theory of Rhetoric,* a sophisticated analysis
of genre functions, deserves special mention. With a developing
awareness of the importance of workplace writing and writing in
disciplines, writing specialists in the 1990s made genres one of
the main features of writing instruction, theory, and research.
Current theory and research on genres have featured a few concepts worth noting here:

1. Genres are concepts only; they do not have, as Richard Larson
   has noted, an "objective existence" (207), although writers and
   readers frequently act as if they do. The same is true of laws.

2. Genres (as concepts) exist at different levels of generalization
   (argumentative writing is more general than literary criticism,
   legal briefs, or unsolicited recommendations).

3. Genres are not reducible to textual features alone; they are
   intersubjective. They are inextricably a part of rhetorical situations that include such things as readers, writers, medium, and
   previous discourses.

4. One is always writing *in* genres, even when one is trying to escape them.

5. Genres are mutable. Trying to freeze genres is like trying to freeze
   words.

The Outcomes Statement reflects the importance of genre
functions in writing. The outcomes described in **Rhetorical Knowledge** point out that writers have to learn how to adapt their texts
to different writing situations, within which are embedded readers'

genre expectations—that is, a reader of grant proposals expects a writer to follow a conventional grant proposal format. As genres affect how texts are read, they also affect how texts are written—one might say that genres have both hermeneutic and heuristic functions. Good writers know how to use a variety of available genre structures to generate ideas and text. Similarly, good readers know how to read in different genres. These are basic literacy skills.

A Genre-Based Program

In order to meet the outcomes described under **Rhetorical Knowledge,** students need to do more than learn how to write in a generic form such as the so-called academic essay, with the single audience of the teacher and the single purpose of proving that the writer has mastered the genre (which uninformed teachers think of as "writing"). This kind of single-genre program seems to be hopelessly stalled in a historical allegiance to "the essay," as it came to be known in literature studies.

In order to encourage some kind of rhetorical knowledge, a first-year writing program will have students writing in a variety of genres, to different readers, and with different purposes. The rationale here is that writers learn about a concept through comparing and contrasting. They learn about the concept of audience by writing to different audiences. If they are writing always to the same audience, that audience is naturalized and becomes synonymous with audience in general. So it is with such things as register and organization—two of the more concrete features of genres.

There seem, however, to be serious limitations to the variety of rhetorical situations possible in first-year writing courses. Still, teachers can set as one of their goals the creation of rhetorical situations that will feature different genres, audiences, and purposes. We have already seen how the journal can be one genre with a particular audience and purpose that would be quite different from writing, say, a music review for one's classmates, for the school newspaper, for a zine magazine, or for publication on

DO This

a class Web page. As teachers have moved into computer-based classrooms, the possibilities for different rhetorical situations have increased dramatically. In computer-based instruction, teachers can easily distribute each student's text to the full class for review or reader response. Texts can be sent to other classes in the same university, to different universities, or to different countries. No teacher has to be reduced to having all essays handed in to him or her to be graded—which to my mind represents one of the most impoverished writing situations imaginable.

If students write in response to different kinds of rhetorical situations, they will meet not only the outcomes described under **Rhetorical Knowledge,** but they will also meet several of the outcomes under **General Reading, Writing, and Thinking Skills.** If students write in different genres that require different kinds of information, they will learn how to interweave with their own writing information derived from interviews, observations, and reports of other people's investigations. They should learn how to compare information gathered from brochures, tabloids, general newspapers, and professional journals. They should also learn how to evaluate the different kinds of power that information has for different audiences when coming from different sources. Naive students (and probably quite a few naive teachers) think information that comes from academic research, for example, has more power in all situations than does information that comes from anecdotes. A little research in business communication (see Anderson) quickly turns this notion on its head.

Research Sources

Students could easily analyze differences in power and source of information after writing a report that might be featured in a school newspaper and another report that could appear in a discipline-specific journal (see Fahnestock). If students were to analyze the citation conventions for these different kinds of writing, they could learn not only what the conventions are but also why one set of citation standards would not be appropriate for all kinds of writing situations. Thus, they would learn more about

Citation

1. the differences in different kinds of writing situations;

2. how to find, evaluate, analyze, and synthesize primary and secondary sources in response to different kinds of writing situations; and

3. the general relationships among language, knowledge, and power.

Students would simultaneously work toward meeting the outcomes listed under **Conventions**. They would learn more about the conventions of what is (mis)called standard written English—what it is and when it is appropriate. They will also learn how to document appropriately. With good instruction, they should learn how to check for conventions about which they are uncertain. In a technologically sophisticated classroom, students should learn how to discover these conventions on the Web.

There seems to be no end to the genres teachers could have their students write in—as long as teachers are able to think carefully about whether the students are meeting goals that seem legitimate for a first-year writing program, such as the ones described in the Outcomes Statement. Students can write e-mail, hypertext documents of instructions, job application letters, personal essays, memoirs, profiles, interpretations of poems, empirical research reports. If students play the field a bit, they learn that there *is* a field rather than a few square yards of belletristic turf.

We have constructed in our first-year program a sequence of genres based on Moffett's theory of information processing: the movement is from genres in which the information comes from observation, to those from memory (observations processed by time), to those from interviews (replays, so to speak, of others' memories), to those from others' research (based on others' observations, interviews, memories, and research). The sources of information are telescoped, as it were, within each other so that one kind of information source includes the more immediate and concrete (closer to the event *happening*, Moffett would say), so that a profile of a person, based primarily on an interview, would include notes taken while observing and from memories of other observations while conducting the interview. These genres lead to empirical research reports and various kinds of argumentative and/or persuasive genres (reviews, evaluations, position papers, literary interpretations, familiar essays, and so on). At the very least, when the students' attention is focused on how the information is abstracted from reality, they gain a critical awareness of what passes for information and proof. They also gain a critical

[handwritten: genre sequence]

awareness of how they process information and construct arguments.

This kind of genre sequence has become well known in the past twenty years. I think Axelrod and Cooper ushered it in with *The St. Martin's Guide to Writing,* one of the more popular rhetorics in college writing instruction. Since then quite a few rhetorics have reproduced in various fashions this kind of genre sequence. I reproduce it here as only one example of how teachers can use genre-based instruction to support most of the outcomes in the Outcomes Statement. I can imagine other sequences, or even a set of unsequenced writing tasks in different genres, that do the same thing. I have lately begun to think we should turn to a closer analysis of workplace writing and recreate as much as possible the conditions and genre expectations that students will meet in their professional lives. This line of thinking admittedly leads to vocationalism, which is anathema to writing teachers nourished on the liberal arts. But perhaps our allegiance to the liberal arts is part of the problem with first-year writing.

[handwritten right margin: Be careful to avoid vocationalism]

I want to offer in addition a final reflection on the problem with first-year writing programs. Regardless of the genres in which we have our students write, the central problem is usually student interest. In essence, many students don't believe that what we are teaching them has anything to do with their lives—which include their plans for professional achievement. I don't think we have seriously investigated the possibility that they are right—not that writing won't be important to their lives, but that the kinds of writing we are teaching may not be important. As I write this, I hear a chorus of writing teachers protesting that we are also teaching them how to think critically. I have been in too many department meetings to take this claim seriously.

[handwritten right margin: Critical - student interest. The kinds of writing we're teaching not important to their lives]

These things I know about teaching writing: When students are impelled by the writing situation (Britton et al.), they write and learn better than when they are uninterested in the subject and task. When students are engaged in "dummy run" writing, the game is pretty much over. I also know that students have more fun learning together than in isolation. And they (or at least those who don't get A's) hate having grades hanging over them as they write.

[handwritten: 2 Things: (1) when impelled by writing, they learn better (2) Better in groups than isolation]

Responding to Student Writing

Traditionally, teachers respond to student writing by making in-text corrections and comments, writing summary comments, and signifying the whole with a grade. The arguments about whether teachers should grade any or all student writing are more or less legend (see Peckham, "Beyond Grades"; Zak and Weaver), so I will bypass them here and point out that if a teacher assigns grades only in response to portfolios, then they have more room to respond to student writing as a reader rather than as a grader. This kind of response situation offers three advantages worth mentioning here:

1. The teacher becomes a reader, not *the* reader. Of course, students will always be aware of the hyper-importance of the teacher's response, but the nongrading stance allows the teacher to shift the focus so that there is at least some importance attached to the opinions of the student's peers (which is, after all, the rhetorical situation of most of our writing).

2. Teachers find themselves responding differently, and I would argue more productively, when they are responding as readers rather than graders. The productivity is both a consequence of the different quality of the response and students' reaction to it—students actually read the responses. I need to add one additional benefit that at least I have found true: I sincerely enjoy reading what my students write. My students and I are engaging in a communicative act. We are in fact celebrating language.

3. The objective reality of grades loses some of its oppressive factuality. Certainly grades are always lurking in the background, but teachers can do quite a bit to unlurk them without making them be *the business* of what's really going on in the classroom. My business and my delight is teaching the very particular students who come into my classes a little bit about writing. I am primarily and almost exclusively interested in effective ways of helping them with their writing.

The one thing I do know about my own teaching practice: the more I can erase the concern about grades in my classroom, the more I and my students are able to get down to the important business of working on our writing. It's simply a question of focus. Using portfolios has been my way of doing this.

Following are the kind of portfolio instructions I give to my classes.

English 115
Final Portfolio

Put on a disk if convenient. I have given file names. If you put this in a folder, all parts (files) should be clearly labeled. **SASE!** If you want only the response and grade, I will mail these to you via e-mail. [**put your email address on the outside of the portfolio or on the disk**] If you would like to have me return your disk or your hardcopy folder, please put it in an envelope and include sufficient stamps.

1. **Selected Journals (seljn.doc):** Selected journal entries that you think represent your best reflections on the readings, your writing processes, or class activities. This should be only two or three entries.
2. **Memo Journals (memjrn.doc):** A memo regarding those journals. Why did you choose these? What of yourself do you see in those entries?
3. **Favorite Essay (favess.doc):** Pick one of the four essays that we wrote—the one that you like best. You can make any changes you would like to: I will be reading it again.
4. **Favorite Essay Reflection (favrefl.doc):** Just tell me what you liked about this essay, why it was your favorite. You can also tell me about some things you are still unsure of or things that you think should be different.
5. **Process (process.doc):** Include the first and last draft of one of

your essays. If you choose to make this the essay that is also your favorite essay, just indicate that—you do not need to give me two copies of the last draft of your favorite essay.

6. **Memo Process (memproc.doc):** Look carefully at the two copies of the essay that you have chosen to represent the process of your writing. Write me a memo in which you describe the differences between the two drafts and why you made some of the changes that you did.

7. **Ten Things Learned (tenlrnd.doc):** List and comment on ten (or more) things that you learned in this class about writing. I am looking for what were the most important things that you learned. I would like to know why these are important to you.

8. **Miscellaneous (misc.doc):** Anything else that pops into your head. This category is not required.

9. **Self-Evaluation (self.doc):** This is entirely optional. If you would like, you can give me some guidance on things to consider when I evaluate your portfolio and performance in the class. If you will review my syllabus, you will see that my criteria are simple: attendance and conscientious completion of all assignments. If you wish to suggest the grade that you feel you have earned, please do so.

10. **Permission to Publish:** I give Irvin Peckham permission to publish my writing for English 115, fall 1998, in whole or in part. I do (not) give him permission to attach my name. [Cross off the "not" if it's okay to use your name; don't sign this if you don't want me to ever use your writing.]

Signed: _____

———————

I should add here that I do not wait until the end of the semester to let the students in on what grades they are headed for. We have at least one conference in midsemester during which their progress in the course is one of the subjects we cover. In addition, I let the students know that they can come into my office at any time to talk about their progress and/or go over any of their essays if they want to know how I would grade it—if I had to grade it.

By the time students turn in the portfolio, I have a pretty good idea of the grade (which is usually either an A or a B—and the difference is not hard to tell)[3] I'm going to give the student before I read the portfolio, but there are always several students on the cusp; the portfolio is their chance to present themselves and re-present what they have achieved and learned in the class. In a good many instances, students who I thought would earn B's have convinced me (sometimes inadvertently) that they deserved A's. When students include self-evaluations and suggest the grade they think they deserve, I take their suggestions seriously, but I do not feel bound to concede to their judgment—and I tell them this when we talk about what I want them to put in the portfolio.

But there is a more important reason than grades to have students construct a portfolio at the semester's end. The portfolio is the vehicle for our last communication—at least insofar as our English 115 connection is concerned. It is the time for them to wrap their learning into a textual representation and say something to me about it. The end of the semester is the chance for me to read this representation and send a response. As frequently as not, the grade is incidental—it's what we say to each other that really counts, and I suspect that's my final lesson in English 115. You will perhaps call me an idealist, but I enjoy my teaching.

Notes

1. To find the officially adopted version of the WPA Outcomes Statement, please visit the WPA Web site, http://wpacouncil.org, which includes a link to the statements.

2. The history of the modes begins before Bain. The modes seemed to have been in common circulation as early as 1776 when George Campbell made them the basis of his rhetoric. One could trace them back further to Cicero, who wrote about the different purposes of discourse as being to please, to persuade, and to instruct. It is worth noting that Bain found his modes to be an unsatisfactory classifying system—he dropped them from his post-1866 rhetorics, or at least he mentioned them only in passing rather than using them as an organizing principle. The modes took off again in the 1920s when publishers found them to be a nifty way of organizing textbooks (see Peckham, *Necessary*).

3. I need to be defensive here: I can imagine all the rigor people wagging their fingers. Rather than engage in a full-court defense, I will say that the few students to whom I would give C's, D's, and F's show early on their disinclination to take the course seriously. I talk to them as soon as this disinclination shows itself and suggest that they try the course some other time, when they are ready to commit to it.

Works Cited

Anderson, Paul V. *Technical Communication: A Reader-Centered Approach.* 4th ed. Fort Worth, TX: Harcourt Brace College Publishers, 1998.

Axelrod, Rise B., and Charles R. Cooper. *The St. Martin's Guide to Writing.* New York: St. Martin's Press, 1985.

Bain, Alexander. *English Composition and Rhetoric.* New York: D. Appleton, 1866.

Bakhtin, M. M. *The Dialogic Imagination.* Ed. Michael Holquist. Trans. Caryl Emerson and Michael Holquist. Austin: U of Texas P, 1981.

———. "The Problem of Speech Genres." *Mikhail Bakhtin: Speech Genres and Other Late Essays.* Ed. Vern W. McGee. Trans. Caryl Emerson and Michael Holquist. Austin: U of Texas P, 1986. 60–102.

Beale, Walter H. *A Pragmatic Theory of Rhetoric.* Carbondale: Southern Illinois UP, 1987.

Britton, James, et al. *The Development of Writing Abilities (11–18).* London: Macmillan Education/Urbana, IL: NCTE, 1979.

Campbell, George. *The Philosophy of Rhetoric. The Rhetoric of Blair, Campbell, and Whately.* Ed. James L. Golden and Edward P. J. Corbett. New York: Holt, Rinehart, and Winston, 1968.

Cicero, Marcus Tullius. *De Oratore. Cicero on Oratory and Orators.* Trans. J. S. Watson. Carbondale: Southern Illinois UP, 1970.

Fahnestock, Jeanne. "Accommodating Science: The Rhetorical Life of Scientific Facts." *Written Communication* 3 (1986): 275–96.

Kinneavy, James L. *A Theory of Discourse: The Aims of Discourse.* Englewood Cliffs, NJ: Prentice-Hall, 1971.

Larson, Richard. "Classifying Discourse: Limitations and Alternatives." *Essays on Classical Rhetoric and Modern Discourse.* Ed. Robert J.

Connors, Lisa S. Ede, and Andrea A. Lunsford. Carbondale: U of Illinois P, 1984. 203–14.

Moffett, James. *Teaching the Universe of Discourse.* Boston: Houghton Mifflin, 1968.

Peckham, Irvin. "Beyond Grades." *Composition Studies/Freshman English News* 21.2 (1993): 16-31.

———. "The Necessary Illusion of Genres: An Argument for the Importance of Genres in Composition Studies." Diss. U. of California, San Diego, 1991.

———. "The Yin and Yang of Genres." *Genre and Writing: Issues, Arguments, Alternatives.* Ed. Hans Ostrom and Wendy Bishop. Portsmouth, NH: Boynton/Cook-Heinemann, 1997. 37–44.

Reid, Ian, ed. *The Place of Genre in Learning: Current Debates.* Geelong, Victoria, Australia: Deakin University, 1987.

Zak, Frances, and Christopher Weaver. *The Theory and Practice of Grading Writing: Problems and Possibilities.* Albany: State U of New York P, 1998.

Constructing Bridges between High School and College Writing

MARGUERITE HELMERS

University of Wisconsin Oshkosh

As Marguerite Helmers explains, first-year composition is an especially transitional site for many first-year students in their adjustment to the college environment. She describes how the Odyssey program developed at the University of Wisconsin addresses the transition and retention of these students.

In 1994 the University of Wisconsin Oshkosh initiated a summer reading program for all students arriving from high school. Naming it the "common intellectual experience," and later simplifying that title to "Odyssey," the university intended to stress the importance of building common bonds through intellectual achievement. As the years progressed, the common intellectual experience came to be a part of the Department of English's composition program. As the writing program administrator, I was required to answer to the vice chancellor of the university and the dean of students, who both supervised and funded the new student orientation program. In addition to carrying out its own goals, the goals of the wider university general education program, and the expectations for literacy in the culture at large, the composition program was responsible for a very specific task: building a social and intellectual bridge from high school to college. In the end, the resulting reading program was celebrated by the university and the board of regents as a successful, energetic program.

The first common intellectual experience reading selection was chosen by a committee of representatives from various departments across the university working in association with the provost and vice chancellor. At that point, the common reading existed as a summer reading program. The next year (1995) the composition program was brought in to reinforce the goals of the common intellectual experience. The provost and the dean of the College of Letters and Science wanted the classroom community and the graded assignments it provided to build intellectual bonds and bridge the gap between academic pursuits and social friendships. An unexpected benefit to the Department of English, however, was that the composition program gained more status by associating itself with the general education goals of the university in a highly publicized program. This meant that the program was no longer a "ghetto," but moved into a position of centrality to the university's mission. The English department was ceded the authority to speak about appropriate texts for all entering students and became a powerful body for arguing about pedagogy.

Since then the English department has worked seriously and continuously with the reading selections that have become part of the new student orientation program. Integrating the reading selection into a writing course is not without pedagogical challenges: concerns about retention at the university have caused the administration to stress the importance of the first six weeks of a first-year student's semester. During this time, new students need to be emotionally and intellectually captured in order to ensure that they remain in school beyond their first year—and the common intellectual experience has been marked as an integral part of these efforts. As at many schools, retention of first-year students is a serious issue for us; we lose approximately 29 percent of the entering students between the first and second years of college. Essentially, the use of Odyssey as a retention vehicle and the emphasis on the first six weeks of class place the composition program directly in the service of the administration, so that its retention goals become the primary object for the first weeks of the class. The benefits to the program, however, are that the composition course is seen as an essential socializing course for all students; rather than discourage students from taking the course, advisors and administrators extol its pivotal role in the life of the student.

Our job as instructors is not to foster appreciation through lecture but to encourage questioning through discussion, research, and writing. I have often thought of the common text as an announcement of university and programmatic values. Writing programs are often the largest server of the general education, first-year population on campuses. They come under direct scrutiny by administrators, regents, legislators, and the public because they are engaged in the work of "literacy," a kind of public education in the basics of expository prose, argumentation, and syntactic skill. Ethically, any composition program must represent the discipline at large and represent itself to the wider disciplinary community. It must have a salient coherence that demonstrates that all students are receiving a theoretically relevant, common course of instruction despite differences in instructors. The Odyssey reading selection actually enables the composition program to have cohesiveness, thus facilitating program articulation to a wider community. Since our first-year composition program does not use a common rhetoric or reader, the shared experience of the Odyssey book and the attendance at a theatrical performance enable us to strengthen the bonds between the university's general education goals and first-year composition. For two years, the program has employed a Web site to make the goals of the program available to a larger audience of students, parents, faculty, and administrators. Titled *Einstein's Web*, http://www.english.uwosh.edu/einstein, the site is housed on the English department server and maintained by members of the department. It thus becomes part of a collection of university documents that describes the goals of university programs. Beyond that, *Einstein's Web* is a visible, viable, usable publicity tool for the composition program because it doesn't deal only with issues of "composition," but instead engages the students in positioning themselves within a program and the virtual, global universe.

Teaching Writing as a Process

DAVIDA CHARNEY

Pennsylvania State University

In this essay from the Penn State University Composition Program Handbook, Davida Charney outlines some of the advantages and limitations of process-based approaches to writing instruction.

The idea of teaching writing as a process starts from one or two simple premises:

- ◆ that there are many different ways to get from a blank piece of paper to an effective text; and

- ◆ that people can benefit from reflecting on how they go about writing and from comparing their processes to those of peers and more experienced writers.

A great deal of research on reading and writing processes over the past twenty years—including observational studies of what children and adults do as they write—supports these premises. When we teach students to think of writing as a process, we are trying to make them more aware of the activities involved in writing, to increase their repertoire of strategies and activities, and to recognize situations in which some strategies may be helpful and others counterproductive.

Compared to other skills, writing is unusual in that more experienced writers tend to invest greater time and effort than do inexperienced ones. Usually, practicing a skill over and over makes it more "automatic," reducing the time and effort needed to execute the skill successfully. But in the case of academic writing, this kind of automaticity is largely confined to the physical techniques of handwriting or typing. Few writing situations are so formulaic that they become completely automatic. As a result, some people who do significant amounts of writing report that they find it difficult—especially in situations where much is at stake. Some are dissatisfied with how they write, assuming that there must be a better way, a more efficient way. Others value the effort of rethinking and revising because of the pleasure they get when an idea or phrase finally clicks. (See, for example, case studies of highly published academics by Jane Rymer and the personal account by Howard Becker.) It is important for students to know that writing is often hard work—that they are not necessarily doing anything wrong and are not deficient in some essential gift or genius if words do not flow immediately or easily from their fingers.

Even though academic writing is seldom easy and even though there is no one right way to write, some approaches are more reliable than others. Some students who have serious problems writing are relying on overly rigid processes or ones that focus attention on low-level concerns at inappropriate times. In some cases, nothing is wrong with the approaches themselves except that they have been transformed from helpful hints (or heuristics) into what Mike Rose has called "rigid rules." Here are some strategies common to first-year students:

♦ Some students adopt a "perfect first draft strategy," believing that the text must emerge grammatically and in order from first sentence to last. They paralyze themselves agonizing over the first sentence or paragraph. Then they pull an all-nighter before the paper is due—they find that if they are tired and desperate enough, sometimes the muse appears and several pages spill out. Because the text finally "flows easily," it must be good.

◆ Other students strain to make their texts conform to some ideal-ized structure ("the five-paragraph theme"?), leaving out ideas that don't fit and adding filler if they don't have three examples.

◆ Some students treat the texts they read as absolutely authorita-tive and their own role as merely compiling and reporting on received wisdom. If they find conflicting accounts in their read-ing, they artificially harmonize them rather than engaging in in-terpretation or critique (see case studies by Christina Haas and Jennie Nelson.) When asked to defend a position to an audience that might disagree with them, they find it difficult to establish shared values or to treat alternative values as legitimate (see Janice Hays and Kathleen Brandt).

Observations of writers have led researchers (e.g., Carl Bereiter and Marlene Scardamalia; Linda Flower et al.) to sketch models of writing processes that include components such as planning, drafting, evaluating, and revising but that do not connect these components in any prescribed order. Experienced writers' pro-cesses seem to be recursive; drafting can lead to more planning, as can revising. However, different writers prefer different start-ing points and different ways of proceeding—some spew and re-vise, some gradually expand lists and outlines, some write the easiest part first. Most experienced writers spend some time plan-ning before writing out drafts with connected prose. They think about the rhetorical situation early and at many points while writing. In deciding how to go about writing the text and what to include, they also reflect on their previous experience with similar texts and make provisional decisions about what writing strategies to use. They are more willing to reconsider their strat-egies, their plans, and their texts along the way. They seek feed-back at various points, some talking out their ideas in the early planning process, others waiting to show a fairly complete draft to others.

The benefits of flexible strategies that focus on generating plans and ideas have been supported not only by observing their frequent use by successful experienced writers but also by some formal studies. For example, Shawn Glynn and his colleagues found that students who were asked to write a complete draft in order in grammatical sentences produced many fewer ideas than students who were free to write as they liked. Even having a chance to revise didn't allow them to catch up—students tend to delete ideas in revision and add very few new ones. Other studies suggest that students benefit from reflecting on their strategies and practicing others.

Many of the techniques for making assignments in this handbook incorporate strategies for promoting thoughtful engagement in writing processes. Planning is encouraged through topic proposals and workshops. An early start gives students time to engage in extended invention and reconceptualization, which are also encouraged through reviews of partial and complete drafts. Some instructors discuss and demonstrate a variety of inventional strategies, such as freewriting, brainstorming, and concept mapping. Revision is encouraged through multiple drafts, peer-review workshops, and opportunities to revise graded papers. Many instructors find ways to encourage students to reflect on their writing processes. Some ask students to comment on the effectiveness of the processes they use in a workshop or in a cover sheet to a draft. Others ask students to compare the process demands of writing in different rhetorical situations (e.g., e-mail, a résumé, and a policy evaluation).

In recent years, the idea of talking about writing processes in class has been challenged in some quarters. Some scholars argue that generalizations about writing processes are too far removed from real-world practice, inevitably turn into rigid rules, or create paralyzing self-consciousness. Those who support research and instruction in writing processes argue that formulating, reflecting on, and pushing against the generalizations is a way of improving one's skill and one's critical thinking. The most appropriate form of instruction in this area is also a matter of debate—whether instructors should describe and demonstrate various writing strategies or whether students should arrive at their own through reflection or observation of themselves or others. It is clear that not everything that is learned was explicitly taught—and that not everything that is expounded is learned. But it is also clear that teaching and learning can be productively intermingled. Explicit generalizations that describe how people go about a process successfully need not be prescriptive or nor-

[margin annotations: have students reflect on their strategies; planning thru topic proposal & workshops; inventional strategies]

mative. Examining what we do in the context of what others do helps us question whether our approach is as good as it could be and when other approaches might be useful.

Works Cited

Becker, Howard S. *Writing for Social Scientists: How to Start and Finish Your Thesis, Book, or Article.* Chicago: U of Chicago P, 1986.

Bereiter, Carl, and Marlene Scardamalia. *The Psychology of Written Composition.* Hillsdale, NJ: Erlbaum, 1987.

Flower, Linda, et al. "Detection, Diagnosis, and the Strategies of Revision." *College Composition and Communication* 37 (1986): 16–55.

Glynn, Shawn, Bruce Britton, Denise Muth, and Nukhet Dogan. "Writing and Revising Persuasive Documents: Cognitive Demands." *Journal of Educational Psychology* 74 (1982): 557–67.

Haas, Christina. "Learning to Read Biology: One Student's Rhetorical Development in College." *Written Communication* 11 (1994): 43–84.

Hays, Janice, and Kathleen Brandt. "Socio-Cognitive Development and Students' Performance on Audience-Centered Argumentative Writing." *Constructing Rhetorical Education.* Ed. Marie Secor and Davida Charney. Carbondale: Southern Illinois UP, 1992. 202–29.

Nelson, Jennie. "This Was an Easy Assignment: Examining How Students Interpret Academic Writing Tasks." *Research in the Teaching of English* 24 (1990): 362–96.

Rose, Mike. "Rigid Rules, Inflexible Plans, and the Stifling of Language: A Cognitivist Analysis of Writer's Block." *College Composition and Communication* 31 (1980): 389–400.

Rymer, Jane. "Scientific Composing Processes: How Eminent Scientists Write Journal Articles." *Advances in Writing Research, Vol. 2, Writing in Academic Disciplines.* Ed. David Jolliffe. Norwood, NJ: Ablex, 1988.

CHAPTER 3

CONSTRUCTING SYLLABUS MATERIALS

This chapter begins with a memo from Victor Villanueva describing common goals and assumptions that writing teachers should consider before preparing their courses. The chapter also includes a course description and a sample syllabus. The course description, constructed by Greg Clark, provides a useful model for teachers who wish to explain to students the goals of a course in language that students can understand. He explains how reading and writing can function in a first-year composition course to help learners understand their reasons for using language. Rather than assuming that students cannot understand the theories that underpin our instruction, Clark knows that explaining our practices to students will help them engage with those practices with greater purpose, commitment, and awareness. The sample syllabus, constructed by Marvin Diogenes, demonstrates some of the details that help students move through the course—unit to unit, week to week, class meeting to class meeting.

On Syllabi

VICTOR VILLANUEVA
Washington State University

*In this memo to English 101 teachers, Victor Villanueva pro-
vides some guidelines about writing instruction and how these
guidelines can be implemented in a syllabus.*

MEMORANDUM

TO: All teachers of English 101
FROM: Victor Villanueva
DATE: 31 February PME (the PostModernEra)
RE: On Syllabi

It's time to get back into the classroom. So before (or as) you
begin to formulate your courses, there are some things I want to
lay out.

Common Goals

From Erika Lindemann *(A Rhetoric for Writing Teachers)*: "All
writing courses share a common goal: giving students enough
guided practice in composing that they become more fluent, effective writers at the end of the course than they were at the
beginning." To that, I'd add the goal of giving students enough
sustained critique to have them come away with a greater understanding of what they need to consider as they continue to develop as writers. You won't turn most C writers into A writers in
fifteen weeks (which is not to say a C *student* can't become an A
student in that time). But you can point the way to becoming an
A writer. It takes time to become a writer. We are not here to
teach students How-To-Think. They do that. Or they'd be in
intensive care. And though we might want to show them other
ways of thinking about ideological matters, the best we can do is
present the matters for their consideration and require the conventions for polemics and dialectics. In other words, civility isn't

as much an issue as academic conventions for presenting views and substantiating them.

Common Assumptions

We have common goals. We need to have common assumptions, if the students taking 101 are to have broadly similar experiences, whatever their particular sections. Here are the assumptions I find most important:

1. Writing is ontological (decidedly human); it is epistemological (a way of learning); it is ideological (tied to ways of seeing the world and its peoples and social systems). As such, writing becomes a medium for self-reflection, self-expression, and—most important—communication. Writing is a means of coming to know for both writer and reader, and as such it is rhetorical (as in someone saying something to someone within certain contexts, which is the essence of the rhetorical triangle).

2. Learning to write requires writing (and *judicious* feedback). Writing is a craft that can aspire to (and can sometimes achieve) art. As a craft, it can be learned, and it can be honed. Writing practice, then, must be the major emphasis of a writing course. Writers should have opportunities for writing in the classroom. There should be room for some writing that is explicitly from experience, since this becomes a way of discovering the underlying ideological assumptions of the writer, underlying assumptions forming the foundation for effective academic critique. Although student writers need, as soon as possible, to develop an understanding of and fluency in academic discourse (exposition and argumentation), the academic should not be the only genre required in a course. Limiting writing to the academic can be stultifying to those who already believe writing to be boring or the special gift of the gifted.

3. The codes, registers, and dialects of academic discourse are simply that: codes, registers, and dialects. "Proper" usage

and grammar are matters of propriety and good manners, as important as not eating mashed potatoes with fingers at a restaurant, but not matters of the inherently right and wrong. Grammar instruction (even when necessary) is not writing instruction. Grading must not be based on an error count.

4. Grading is based on a Platonic sense that we know good texts when we see them. This is every bit as subjective as students accuse it of being. A teacher must establish his or her criteria and subjective quirks from the outset and remain consistent.

The Books

More pragmatic matters we had all best hold in common: the books. Use them. There will never be a required book that will be liked by all who are required to teach from it. Volatile texts are intended to be volatile. Forget "multiculturalism," which might be the goal some decades down the road but isn't what we're working with right now. Our books that demonstrate the lives and ideas of people different from ourselves and many of our students are not to be "appreciated" but to be *engaged,* wrestled with. Our classrooms can be comfortable environments, but the issues might not be at all comfortable. That's fine. No change comes from complicity. And if you are yourself uncomfortable with the book or feel that you don't know enough about the material contained in the book, that too is fine. Authority concerns keeping the course moving, not knowing most about writing, or about racism, or about classicism, or about gender, or about any of the many other issues that should arise in an active classroom.

The Syllabus

◆ Underscore that this is a writing course, with plenty of writing and revising, a course in which discussions on matters read should flow from what's been written by the students (whereas a literature course would do the opposite—discussion first, then writing). This is a studio-type course, where the central mode of work is by discussion of works in progress.

◆ Divide the course into thirds:
one-third to writing, based on or connected to the personal
one-third to analysis and interpretation of reading
one-third to revision and convention

◆ Consider using a portfolio grading method. Here's my shtick on portfolios:

> **The Portfolio**—*Everything* you write for this class must be gathered in a folder, which comprises your class portfolio. Make two copies of everything you produce—one for me, one for your portfolio. Don't keep your copy on disk. Too many papers disappear mysteriously on disk. So if I have a copy, you have a copy in a folder. Comments you receive from your three-person peer group are to be signed by the person commenting and submitted in your portfolio. At times, you will be asked to proofread something from your portfolio; when I do, copy the copyedited version, so that I have one copy and you have one. Again—*everything* you write for this class goes in a folder: your portfolio. I will call for it at least three times in the semester with very little warning.
>
> As well, one essay from that portfolio will be submitted to an English Department Portfolio reading during midsemester. The English Department Portfolio serves two purposes: (1) a chance to hear from another reader; and (2) a dry run of sorts for the University Portfolio you will have to submit as you approach 63 credit hours.

Other Considerations

You need to include a statement on plagiarism and accommodation of disabilities on your syllabus. The old saw that plagiarism is theft goes to intent, yet there is such a thing (and it's commonplace) as unintentional plagiarism. And there is the possibility of confusing the matter by encouraging collaboration. Plagiarism is both the grand taboo and the grand contradiction for those of us who teach writing as social construction. So for now, it's better to err on the side of the overly cautious. If, for instance, a peer-group member provides a certain wording, have students acknowledge the source (e.g., "In the words of my partner, Joan Smith, . . . ").

Some student will inevitably feel compelled to defend sexism (either along gender lines or along sexual preference lines), or to defend racism, or to defend ethnocentrism. Inform students from the outset where they are: an environment that doesn't seek to censor but which does have a low tolerance for any form of bigotry.

Okay. Take a deep breath. Relax. Read this all again tomorrow. Construct your syllabus.

Work Cited

Lindemann, Erika. *A Rhetoric for Writing Teachers*. 3rd ed. New York: Oxford UP, 1995.

Departmental Syllabus: Experience in Writing

GREGORY CLARK
Brigham Young University

In this course description, Gregory Clark provides context for his course, Experience in Writing. Framing his course with the assumption that texts function like conversational speech, Clark asserts that written texts have social consequences.

Experience in Writing is a writing course that locates the practices of writing and reading explicitly within the discourse of a rhetorical community. In doing so, it defines writing as an act of responsive assertion, and reading as an act of critical response; and it locates both in the context of a process of communicative exchange, or discourse, in which people address together, over time, a shared question, problem, or project.

By locating writing and reading in the discourse of a rhetorical community, Experience in Writing assumes that texts function similarly to conversational speech. That is, the course treats writing as functionally similar to speaking and reading as functionally similar to listening, when speaking and listening occur in the context of an ongoing and purposeful communicative exchange. Given this functional context:

◆ Written texts are understood as actions more than objects. That is, they are treated as acts of human relationship rather than as transcriptions of information only. As such, they are produced and used as social means more than as cognitive ends.

◆ Written texts are understood to function as turns taken in the larger context of a communicative exchange.

◆ Reading is understood as an act similar to listening, with listening understood as an active process that entails the reception, interpretation, and evaluation of a statement and also serves as a prompt and preparation for response.

◆ Writing is understood as an act of communicative response, with response understood as an assertion that is prompted by prior assertions to which it is inherently accountable. As such, writing functions communicatively to refute, or modify, or affirm, or extend in some way prior assertions of others.

Within this functional context of communicative exchange, written texts are understood as taking the form of particular human relationships that have social consequences. In this sense, form is not so much a matter of an aesthetic order as it is a matter of pragmatic action taken in response to communicative acts of others who are engaged together in a particular textual exchange that addresses matters of shared concern. If the assertions that constitute this textual exchange are published in some way, the broader participation this enables makes this exchange a *public* discourse. There are general forms of response that keep a discourse going, and each functions as a kind of relationship between writer and reader. In Experience in Writing, students practice six of these functional genres of writing within the context of a public discourse selected by the instructor:

1. Locating or identifying in a particular discourse a question, problem, or need shared by its participants. In other words, stating a shared problem.

2. Examining or exploring a statement of a shared problem in the terms of interests and issues that sustain that discourse. In other words, analyzing critically a problem statement.

3. Evaluating or reinterpreting a problem statement in response to that critical analysis. In other words, modifying a problem statement.

4. Responding to a problem statement by proposing a shared belief, value, or action.

5. Modifying the proposal of another.

6. Evaluating the consequences of a proposal.

Particular content for the course will vary widely across sections, depending on the preference of the instructor. The common ground of all sections is student reading and writing that embeds these discursive genres in the discourse of some sort of rhetorical community.

Theory: Writing and Reading in the Context of Community

The purpose of general education at this university is "to help students think clearly, communicate effectively, understand important ideas in their own cultural tradition as well as that of others, and establish clear standards of intellectual integrity" (*Brigham Young University Bulletin* xii). Experience in Writing is designed to provide capable students with a first-year writing course that serves each of these purposes directly by locating the literate practices of thinking, communicating, and knowing within a cooperative project in which people are engaged together. In doing so, it treats writing and reading as social actions that take the form of interpersonal relationships, and it treats writers and readers as cooperating people who are inherently accountable to each other. To explain this design, I describe the conceptual frame of the course, the rhetoric that follows from those concepts, and the notion of public discourse that is central to it.

Concepts

Two metaphors provide the conceptual frame for this course:

1. The metaphor of community is used in the course to describe the social context in which writing and reading have a communicative function. Conceptually, it suggests that writing and reading are to be understood as social actions more than as individual skills, and that they function as social means more than as individual ends. Specifically, the concept that a community is the context in which writing and reading have their communicative function locates a person's writing and reading practices within a collaborative project that is maintained and advanced through communication among people with whom that person is communicating. The function of writing and reading in that context is to enable those people to work together to accomplish something beyond that communication itself.

2. The metaphor of conversation is used to describe the kind of social interaction within which communication functions. Conceptually, it suggests that when people write they do so in response to others just as one person's talk in a conversation is in response to what others have said or done, and it suggests that when people read they do so to understand, evaluate, and prepare to respond to another in much the same way that a person engaged in conversation actively listens. Indeed, it suggests that as speaking and listening are interdependent acts in conversation—listening is a preparation for speaking and speaking is a completion of listening—writing and reading are also interdependent. Further, just as a conversation enacts relationships and not just an exchange of information, writing and reading also enact interpersonal relationships.

A single, unifying concept for the course emerges from these two conceptual metaphors. If writing and reading are understood to be located in the context of a community of people working together to meet needs and fulfill purposes they share, and if writing and reading are understood to function in that context as turns taken in an ongoing exchange that involves people not only in communicating ideas but also in developing and maintaining relationships, these seemingly separate skills of assertion (writing) and interpretation (reading) must be understood as interdependent parts of the act of response. People write as response: they write to someone else in the context of some kind of relationship and prompted by some kind of prior communication. But people also read as response: they interpret and evaluate the writings of others in order to prepare and support some sort of assertion that eventually follows. In Experience in Writing, writing and reading are understood as interwoven in the act of response, an act that is inherently embedded in a textualized conversational exchange in which each text draws on resources provided by texts that have preceded it and in which that text in turn provides resources that prompt the texts that follow.

Teaching the Concepts

The Experience in Writing course needs to begin with the kind of conceptual exploration of writing and reading that is suggested by the metaphors of community and conversation as the context in which writing and reading have a social function, and by the notion that this function can be understood finally as the act of response. The purpose of this exploration is to bring students through a kind of paradigm shift in the way they think about writing and reading—a shift from writing and reading as skills that individuals develop and master in order to produce their own texts that appropriate knowledge and credentials for themselves, to writing and reading as individual contributions made to inherently collaborative processes of knowledge and action that meet shared needs and fulfill shared purposes. This can be done using:

1. **Theoretical discussion:** These concepts and their consequences can and should be presented for class discussion.

The major difficulty with a theoretical discussion of these ideas is their abstraction. But a discussion that persistently illustrates these concepts with common and accessible examples, oral or written exercises, or role-play can make them accessible for students and enable students to begin to shift their understanding of writing and reading from personal performance to genuinely communicative and thus collaborative action. Careful theoretical discussion will be required throughout the course to keep students from slipping back into prior conceptions of writing and reading. This discussion will be most effective if integrated into the course work in the form of explanatory examples or exercises that are frequent, brief, accessible, and theoretically descriptive.

2. **Cases:** The library research and six major papers required by Experience in Writing are designed to locate student writing and reading within a particular public discourse that is ongoing both inside and outside the classroom. This discourse provides the class with an extended case in which these concepts of writing and reading as the discourse of community are fully enacted. Multiple cases that are simpler and more familiar than this one—examples of common textual conversations, really—can be introduced early in the course and referred to throughout to clarify and exemplify this conceptual discussion. Such cases—oral or written—might be found or invented by the instructor, found or invented by students or student groups, or even invented and examined collectively by the class in an open discussion. And that kind of discussion, tracked or transcribed, can be used to exemplify immediately to students the concepts of community as context for communication, conversation as its structure, and response as the function of individual participation.

Rhetoric

I use the term *rhetoric* here to describe conventions and principles that order and organize writing and reading within the discourse of community. The five-paragraph theme as traditionally taught in first-year writing courses enacts a rhetoric—a set of conventions and principles that order and organize the discourse of that community. And in that community, that theme has a communicative function: it communicates to the instructor the extent to which the writer has learned to perform the writing and reading skills it is the purpose of that course to teach. That is not, however, the communicative function of most texts that are written and read outside that classroom; that is not the rhetoric students use if they are to write and read successfully in other courses in the university, or in communicative situations outside it. Experience in Writing is designed to provide students with instruction and practice in a rhetoric that is more genuinely communicative, more broadly useful, more widely practiced: the rhetoric of a discourse of community.

When the term *rhetoric* is used as I am using it here, it describes the forms of communication that are conventional in a particular social situation. In doing so, it can also be used to prescribe principles for shaping and presenting information, but those principles are not universal. The forms of communication prompted by those principles are the genres of discourse that organize communication in that setting. In designing this course, I have tried to present a rhetoric that describes the general conventions of communicative practices that students will find in the university as well as in the public culture (institutional communities of all kinds—business, government, and so forth) that universities like this one are established to serve. To do that, I have designed writing assignments that require students to practice six general genres of the discourse of community, any of which may need to be adapted to the particulars of a given discourse.

In terms of communicative function, genres are best understood as forms of action and social relation rather than as forms of text. They are best understood as conventional ways that people organize their work together on a common project. This notion of genre is central to the rhetoric taught in Experience in Writing, and it is likely, again, to require of students a paradigm shift. Having learned to understand the texts they write and read as artifacts rather than as actions, and having learned to understand the information presented in texts as a person's property rather than as a community's project, students tend to understand genres as textual objects. But if writing and reading are individual actions that contribute to an ongoing project shared by members of a community, and if those actions are organized within that project in ways that connect them as elements of a communicative exchange, then textual genres must be understood as functions, as conventions of work and relationship.

The writing assignments in the course present students with six genres of communicative collaboration. Each prescribes a general content and structure, but that content and structure are determined together by the kind of relationship between writer and reader that they enact. Kenneth Burke's definition of textual form describes their essential interconnection: the form of a text is constituted in the act of establishing a reader's expectations of what is to come in that text and then in fulfilling those expectations. That is, texts are meaningful when they prompt in readers the questions and concerns and purposes that these texts proceed to answer and address and satisfy (31, 124, 146). In terms of the concept that writing and reading are together elements of the social act of response, a text responds to needs shared by writer and readers by providing readers with ideas and information that might meet those needs in a way that prompts readers to become writers in response. Individual texts are meaningful and effective when they prompt and meet a sequence of expectations that serve a purpose that their writers and readers share. Genres are constituted of those sequences that enable communicating people to establish conventional collaborating relationships. They do that by functioning in a way that prompts readers to anticipate writing and writers to anticipate reading—to anticipate exchanging roles in the communicative project of ongoing and, ideally, cooperative response.

Teaching the Rhetoric

Experience in Writing needs to introduce students to this rhetoric early on, as a part of the paradigm shift from writing and reading texts for their own sake to writing and reading as participation in the discourse of community. Students have learned to understand genres as textual containers of information that have more or less arbitrary forms. These forms involve not only the organizational structure of those containers, but also rules of language and presentation. This perception of genres comes about because students have learned to write and to read texts as objects rather than as actions, as commodities rather than as relationships.

In this class, they need to learn that genres are forms of social interaction, of cooperative relationship—that within any genre the content communicated and the textual structure that communicates it are inherently inseparable because the text transcribes an active relationship between people. The interaction of writer and reader through texts takes the shape of an exchange of assertions and responses, questions and answers, problems and solutions. Even conventional rules of usage inscribe social relationships: they enact the communicative codes of a community in such a way that deviations identify the boundaries of its members' common ground. And, like genre, conventional usage is a matter of both content (the meaning of a word) and structure (its form), with the two understood as inseparable because they inscribe together an element of the relationships that constitute a community's common values, beliefs, knowledge, purposes, and actions.

This rhetoric can be taught using:

1. **Theoretical discussion:** Again, the students can and must examine these ideas conceptually. Again, they will need to have these concepts made concrete in discussion through examples and exercises, both oral and written. The principles of this rhetoric will need to be taught throughout the course in ways that integrate these concepts into the students' ongoing experiences of rhetorical practice so that they can use what they learn to communicate successfully in a variety of discursive situations.

2. **Cases:** Again, one way to make these ideas concrete is through minicases. Instructors and students can develop a

variety of exemplifying situations in which these notions of genre as social action and relationship, of textual content and structure as interdependent and inseparable, of textual conventions as matters of cooperation and shared identity, can be clarified and examined.

Public Discourse

What these concepts and this rhetoric of writing and reading describe is public discourse. Most people understand *public discourse* as a term that describes the more or less official communication of politics or law. The purpose of Experience in Writing is to introduce students to the idea that almost all of the writing and reading they do is public discourse, because almost all of it functions in some way to enable broad participation through texts in the project of responding to the problems and needs of a community. Public discourse, then, is the discourse—the communicative exchange—of collaborative action. That collaboration —and the community engaged in it—can vary in scope: it can address the concerns of a planet or a nation, an institution or an organization, an interest group or a profession or a classroom. To the extent that people use communication as a means of working together to meet needs and fulfill purposes they share, their writing and reading functions as public discourse. That makes writing and reading acts of citizenship.

Writing and reading are acts of citizenship when they contribute to and are held accountable to the purposes and the projects of a community. When writers write to others proposing beliefs and actions that are to be shared, and when readers read what others have written to judge and respond to the shared beliefs and actions proposed there, writing and reading enact citizenship in a community.

The purpose of Experience in Writing is to involve students in writing and reading that functions within this kind of purposeful, collaborative exchange. To do that, the course must make students conscious of writing and reading in the context of two kinds of communities.

The first community—the smaller, tangible, immediate one—is the class itself. All writing and reading in Experience in Writing needs to function within a collaborative communicative project that is maintained by the students themselves, a project in which they need to write and read in ways that are accountable to each other and to purposes they share if they are to do well in the course. The required coursework needs to be structured in such a way that its successful completion requires students to communicate cooperatively with each other. That is, to write and read successfully in Experience in Writing, students must write and read with other students because they need to share what they learn. The course is designed to make individual success dependent on the collaboration and cooperation of genuine communication.

The second community—the larger, abstract one—is represented by the discourse, or case, the instructor selects that provides the context for student writing and reading. This case must constitute an ongoing textual discourse that is maintained by a community of people within which members of the class can locate their own concerns and interests. Their project is to initiate and develop a textualized conversation between themselves that engages this discourse, that allows them to address the interests and issues they find pertinent in the discursive exchange of that larger, public community. They will access that discourse through collaborative library research, extracting from what they find there a set of texts they can use to represent that discourse in the classroom. The writing assignments enable them to begin to develop their own exchange in response to it. Students in Experience in Writing need not directly address the people whose writing they gather from the library; rather, they need to bring the discourse of that larger community into the immediate community of their classroom.

Each instructor of a course section chooses the particular public discourse she or he wants students to bring into the class. Students work together to locate elements of that discourse in the university library and to extract from them a set of texts that represents that discourse. Then they can begin a process of responding to that discourse using six interconnected genres of cooperative discursive exchange, writing and reading together toward the goal of addressing the issues of common concern they find there. One syllabus, for example, represents a section of Experience in Writing that locates student writing and reading within a discourse on Glen Canyon in southern Utah. This is an example of a particular public discourse that addresses questions regarding the development and preservation of public lands in the United States, questions especially pertinent to people who live, whether temporarily or permanently, in this region of the country. In entering that discourse through the course work of Experience in Writing, students join a community that is larger than the class, though only members of their class will actually read and respond to their contributions. Their common project is to work together in a communicative exchange to understand and effectively address matters of common concern they find in that discourse in a way that promotes their individual and collective success in the class.

Teaching Public Discourse

Essentially, instructors of Experience in Writing teach writing and reading as public discourse, as I have broadly defined the term. The notion of "discourse" involves the process of exchange: writing and reading functioning together as interconnected responses. The notion of "public" involves the context of an open community: communication functioning as collaborative work toward the solution of shared problems.

Works Cited

Brigham Young University Bulletin. 1994–1995 Undergraduate Catalog. Provo: Brigham Young University, 1994.

Burke, Kenneth. *Counter-statement.* Berkeley: U of California P, 1968.

An Honors Course in First-Year Composition: Classical Rhetoric and Contemporary Writing

MARVIN DIOGENES
Stanford University

Marvin Diogenes provides a complete syllabus that illustrates how detailed a syllabus needs to be for students to understand how their daily responsibilities are integrated into the broad objectives of the semester-long course.

The honors composition sequence at the University of Arizona has included materials from classical rhetoric for almost twenty years. While rhetorical concepts are prominent in all the composition program courses, the honors courses foreground the classical sources of the rhetorical tradition and invite students to analyze how classical ideas have evolved over time in response to changing cultural circumstances. When using these materials with first-year students who have not encountered Plato or Aristotle before, one challenge is to make them accessible and relevant despite the unfamiliar structure and language of the texts. The course design featured here, titled "Classical Rhetoric and Contemporary Writing," begins with Gorgias, Plato, and Aristotle but soon brings these classical voices into dialogue with contemporary writers and topical issues.

I have included the overview of the course; the daily syllabus, including reading assignments and journal response questions; the four major writing assignments; peer review worksheets; criteria for evaluation; and the final exam study guide.

English 103h—Course Description and Syllabus

Instructor: Marvin Diogenes

COURSE OVERVIEW

Socrates: Well, then, to me, Gorgias, rhetoric seems not to be an artistic pursuit at all, but that of a shrewd, courageous spirit which is naturally clever at dealing with men; and I call the chief part of it flattery.

—From *Gorgias,* Plato

Rhetoric may be defined as the faculty of observing in any given case the available means of persuasion.

—From *Rhetoric,* Aristotle

English 103h is a reading and writing course that focuses on the nature and practice of rhetoric, beginning with classical texts by Plato and Aristotle and proceeding to contemporary ideas about rhetoric collected in the anthology *Living Languages.* We will develop a dialectic, a mutual questioning, between past and present, assessing the usefulness of classical definitions and categories while analyzing how rhetoric has evolved parallel to technological advances in the professions and society as a whole, the rise of mass media, and expanded access to education in democratic societies.

Although rhetoric will provide the thematic focus for the course, the course assignments will emphasize critical reading, analysis, and synthesis of varied perspectives (including your own). As several of the required texts are translated from classical sources, we will develop strategies for reading with a sense of historical context, taking into account the cultural circumstances in which the writers produced their work. As Plato and Aristotle situated rhetoric primarily in the public spheres of politics and law, we will explore how these classical categories inform writing in those contemporary contexts while also exploring the role of rhetoric in personal, academic, and professional contexts. In other words, in your portfolio responses and essays you will analyze classical definitions and taxonomies of rhetoric in relation to your own writing at the university and in other areas of your experience.

REQUIRED TEXTS

Aristotle, *The Rhetoric and Poetics of Aristotle.* New York: Modern Library, 1984.

Buffington, Nancy, Marvin Diogenes, and Clyde Moneyhun, editors, *Living Languages: Contexts for Reading and Writing.* Upper Saddle River: Prentice-Hall, 1997.

Church, Lori, Barbara Heifferon, and Sarah Prineas, editors, *A Student's Guide to First-Year Composition,* 19th edition. Edina: Burgess Publishing, 1998.

Plato, *Gorgias,* translated with an introduction by W. C. Helmbold. Indianapolis: Bobbs-Merrill, 1952.

ESSAYS AND MAJOR ASSIGNMENTS

You will write a three- to five-page typed, double-spaced essay that responds to Gorgias's "Encomium on Helen," which will be distributed on the first day of class. This response will push you to explore your attitudes toward language and rhetoric as you enter the university. This first essay, which I will respond to but not assign a grade to, will be useful to you for the rest of the semester as you continue to explore the nature and practice of rhetoric.

You will keep a portfolio of responses to the assigned readings; these responses should lead you into the more formal essay assignments by generating ideas and areas for further exploration. Plan to respond to all assigned readings in your portfolio. Sometimes I will give you a specific question to consider in your response; other times you will determine the focus of the response, guided by your essay topics. Portfolio entries must be typed.

You will write three major essays of five to eight typed, double-spaced pages. All essays will be written through a process involving multiple drafts, peer response, and response from the instructor.

You will write an in-class final exam that serves as a capstone assignment for the course as a whole. While there will be a lot of in-class writing practice, only the final exam will be graded.

You will receive an assignment sheet for each major essay that fully describes what you are expected to do and the criteria that will be used to evaluate your work. The general criteria of the Composition Program for the areas of content, organization, expression, and mechanics and usage are described in prose and chart form in Chapter 4 of the *Student's Guide* (pp. 65–71). Chapter 4 as a whole is a thorough exploration of the program's grading standards and the multiple factors that affect the evaluation of writing at the university level.

COURSE OUTLINE AND DAILY SYLLABUS

08/25 Introduction to the course. Discussion of major requirements and first essay, a close reading of and response to Gorgias's "Encomium on Helen."

08/27 For class: Begin working on response to Plato's *Gorgias*; read LeGuin's "Bryn Mawr Commencement Address" in *LL*, pp. 15–28. Write in response to questions 1 and 4 in "Working beyond the Text," p. 29. Discussion of language and rhetoric.

09/01 Response paper to "Encomium on Helen" due (prepared according to guidelines above); for class: begin reading *Gorgias*, pp. 3–26.

09/03 For class: continue reading *Gorgias*, pp. 27–49; read Jung's "The Pleasures of Remembrance" in *LL*, pp. 9–14. Question: In what ways can an essay like Jung's enact a dialectical inquiry?

09/08 For class: continue reading *Gorgias*, pp. 49–107. Question: How does Plato continue to develop his ideas throughout the dialogue? What strategies does he use along with the dialectical method of questioning?

09/10 For class: begin reading *Rhetoric*, pp. v–xx (Corbett's introduction), pp. 3–18 (Roberts's summary), and Book I, pp. 19–34. Question: What seems familiar in Aristotle's categories? What seems useful?

09/15 For class: continue reading *Rhetoric,* pp. 34–90; in *LL,* read Anzaldua's "How to Tame a Wild Tongue," pp. 29–39. Question: How does Anzaldua's essay complement and complicate Aristotle's view of rhetoric?

09/17 For class: continue reading *Rhetoric,* pp. 128–164; draft of Essay 1 due (prepared according to guidelines above).

09/22 For class: continue reading *Rhetoric,* pp. 199–218; in *LL,* read Hoffman's "Exile," pp. 72–79, and Rodriguez's "Aria," pp. 98–108. Question: How do Hoffman and Rodriguez use narrative as a persuasive strategy?

09/24 Revision workshop.

09/29 Revision workshop; discussion of evaluation criteria for Essay 1.

10/01 Introduction to Essay 2: The Rhetoric of _____ Assignment; discussion of Brad Wallace's "I Want My MTV" and "Whacking Day" episode of *The Simpsons.*

10/06 Revision of Essay 1 due (with commentary, drafts, and peer review sheets); for class: in *LL,* read Ullman's "Getting Close to the Machine," pp. 240–244, and Miller's "Deride and Conquer," pp. 307–315. Question: How do Ullman's and Miller's analyses illuminate the purposes beyond the surface purposes of the rhetoric of computer programming and television?

10/08 Discussion of academic and professional rhetoric; for class: read, in *LL,* Witherspoon's "This Pen for Hire," pp. 173–182, and Tannen's "Women and Men Talking on the Job," pp. 227–239. Question: How do Tannen's strategies differ from Witherspoon's? Are you reading writing like Tannen's in other courses?

10/13 Discussion of professional and scientific rhetoric; for class: read, in *LL,* White's "The Invisible Discourse of Law," pp. 246–256, and Martin's "The Egg and the Sperm," pp. 263–278. Question: What are the features of the rhetorics of the other subjects you're studying this semester? What are the special topics and lines of proof in these fields?

10/15 Library visit: using SABIO and the Internet to research rhetoric (class will meet in library computer classrooms, Section 8 in Main Library A315, Section 11 in Science-Engineering Library 311); for class: read, in *LL,* Rapping's "Needed: A Radical Recovery," pp. 282–289, and Sontag's "On AIDS," pp. 290–297. Question: What are the features of cultural commentary?

10/20 Draft of Essay 2 due; for class: bring extra copy of Essay 2 for peer review workshop.

10/22 Peer review workshop.

10/27 Oral presentations of Essay 2 research projects.

10/29 Oral presentations of Essay 2 research projects.

11/03 Oral presentations of Essay 2 research projects.

11/05 Peer review workshop.

11/10 Final draft of Essay 2 due; introduction to Essay 3, The Rhetoric of Personal Exploration. Make a list of several important events in your life, big and small; then list the people, settings, and sequence of events that were part of these experiences. Draft a one-paragraph mini-essay describing the experience and its meaning.

11/12 For class: in *LL,* read Sommers's "I Stand Here Writing," pp. 370–376, and Lockett, "How I Started Writing Poetry," pp. 347–351; scene/specification exercise.

11/17 For class: in *LL,* read Mosle's "Writing Down Secrets," pp. 332–345, and Gluck's "The Education of the Poet," pp. 352–363; reportage and meditation as modes of narrative writing; associative thinking/metaphor exercise.

11/19 For class: in *LL,* read Rich's "Anger and Tenderness," pp. 377–385; defining the self/identity in relation to the maxims and common values of the culture.

11/24 Peer review workshop; portfolio responses for Essay 3 due.

11/26 No class—Thanksgiving Holiday.

12/01 Peer review workshop.

12/03 Final draft of Essay 3 due; distribution of reading for final exam—Jim Corder's "Argument as Emergence, Rhetoric as Love."

12/08 Final exam preparation.

12/11 Final exam—8:00–10:00 a.m.

Essay Assignment—Close Reading of and Response to Gorgias's "Encomium on Helen"

In this speech, Gorgias defends Helen's actions by developing the premise that language is powerful—as powerful as physical force, as powerful as a drug. To what extent do you agree with Gorgias's claims about language? In your essay, provide both a close reading of Gorgias's speech and a detailed, well-supported answer to the question above. You may draw on personal experiences with language along with observations of language at work in your culture to develop your essay. Your essay should be three to five typed, double-spaced pages (750–1250 words) and include a Works Cited page listing Gorgias's "Encomium on Helen" and any other texts you cite in your response. In completing this assignment, aim to fulfill two main purposes: (1) read Gorgias's speech closely and critically in order to write a thorough summary integrated into your essay; and (2) explore your attitudes toward language and rhetoric, using Gorgias's claims as a catalyst, as a starting point for your work in this course.

DUE DATE: Tuesday, September 1

Process and Strategies: Begin exploring your attitudes toward language and rhetoric by writing about your experiences with language. When did you realize the importance of language in your life? Do you recall any experiences that illustrate the power of language? When you observe the world around you, what role do you see language playing? Does language seem powerful in the wider culture?

Gorgias uses one major example in his speech, the historical case of Helen's abduction. He assumes his audience is familiar with the facts of that case; in your essay, you will likely need to provide more context than Gorgias does in developing your examples.

Essay 1—Close Reading/Application of Plato and Aristotle

DUE DATES: September 17 (draft and portfolio responses to Le Guin, Jung, Anzaldua, Plato, and Aristotle);
October 1 (revision and commentary on writing process)

Format: Follow guidelines for manuscript preparation in the syllabus. Prepare Works Cited page and include internal page references according to MLA format.

Length: final version should be five to eight typed, double-spaced pages (1250–2000 words).

As we've discussed in class, writing can be used to demonstrate learning and also as a mode of inquiry and exploration. This essay assignment requires writing in both modes. While I describe these two aspects of the assignment separately below, you do not have to structure your essay in this manner. Indeed, consider how to interweave demonstration and exploration as you work your way through the assignment.

Demonstration Task: In your essay, show that you understand Plato and Aristotle's definitions of rhetoric, including the contexts in which rhetoric is used and the purposes they believe rhetoric serves. In demonstrating your understanding of their ideas about rhetoric, you will likely illuminate the important differences between their views and consider whether their views can be reconciled.

Application/Inquiry/Exploration Task: In your essay, apply your understanding of Plato and Aristotle to contemporary instances of rhetoric, which may include your own use of rhetoric as well as manifestations of rhetoric that you observe in your culture. In applying Plato and Aristotle's ideas to contemporary contexts, be sure to be specific and analytical in your development of examples. For instance, if you explore the role of rhetoric in advertising, provide specific examples of advertisements and analyze the rhetorical strategies at work and the purposes these strategies serve. If you explore the role of rhetoric in politics, provide specific examples of political speeches and written discourse in order to analyze closely the techniques of persuasion employed. I add the terms "inquiry" and "exploration" to this task because I want to encourage you to be inventive and creative in developing your essay. While Plato and Aristotle provide the foundation for the inquiry, you might find in your exploration that their ideas must be further developed, translated, updated, even transformed to be useful to you. (In other words, while Plato and Aristotle's views of rhetoric can help us think about such contemporary phenomena as radio, television, electronic journalism, and the Internet, we may have to reformulate or extend their categories to understand and analyze the rhetorical features of these forms of communication.)

———————

Peer Review Sheet—Close Reading/Application
of Plato and Aristotle

Writer's Name:_____   Reader's Name:_____

On 9/24 and 9/29, class time will be devoted to peer review; each day you will work with a different classmate, so be sure to have a clean copy of your essay-in-progress with you on both days. Remember that these peer reviews are designed to be deliberative, not ceremonial; although you may wish to praise and blame each other's writing, try to focus your written comments and oral discussion on a future course of action that will improve the essays. To this end, try to be specific and constructive in your responses. At the end of each class, give this sheet with your written comments on it to the writer. You may also write on the back of this sheet.

1. Describe the demonstration component of the essay. How effectively does the writer demonstrate an understanding of Plato's and Aristotle's views of rhetoric? How clearly does

the writer show the important differences in their views? What other elements of their views do you think the writer should consider addressing in the essay?

2. Describe the application component of the essay. How effectively does the writer apply Plato's and Aristotle's views of rhetoric to contemporary contexts? Are these contexts primarily personal, political, cultural? Are the examples offered relevant and well developed? Are the enthymemes/statements persuasively presented, with sufficient clarity and development of reasoning?

3. What are the major strategies used by the writer in the essay? How effectively does the writer use these strategies (analogy, narrative, example based on past fact, example based on invented fact, maxim, enthymeme)? Which parts of the essay should be developed further? Should the demonstration and application components of the essay be integrated more fully?

Evaluation Criteria for Essay 1

The *Student's Guide* includes a complete overview and explanation of the grading standards of the Composition Program. Review Chapter 4, particularly pp. 65–71, to understand the program's expectations in the areas of content, organization, expression, and mechanics and usage.

To supplement these general criteria, each essay assignment lays out more specific requirements for the particular essay being written. In the case of Essay 1, these criteria derive from the assignment sheet itself and from the questions on the peer review sheet.

Quality of Demonstration: how effectively the writer demonstrates an understanding of Plato's and Aristotle's views of rhetoric. While your essay cannot exhaustively cover all of their ideas and categories, you need to do more than summarize and paraphrase their ideas in a superficial manner. Average or weaker essays will simply assert generalizations about their views ("Plato is an idealist seeking truth while Aristotle is a pragmatist concerned with being effective") without working closely with terms, definitions, chains of related ideas, and even contradictions in their systems. Stronger essays will cite the texts consistently to illuminate major elements of Plato's and Aristotle's views, exploring beyond the general level of paraphrase.

Quality of Application: how effectively the writer applies Plato's and Aristotle's views to contemporary contexts. This requires well-developed examples and illustrations that show rhetoric at work in our lives and in the culture that surrounds us. Average or weaker essays will simply point to or mention instances of rhetoric ("Rhetoric is clearly an important element of advertising") without providing close readings of specific examples that utilize Plato's and Aristotle's terms and categories. Stronger essays will provide well-developed examples and in-depth analyses using Plato's and Aristotle's views as critical tools.

Quality of Presentation: how effectively the writer uses a variety of strategies to develop ideas and engage the reader's attention. This does not mean that you should overload your essay with too many elements (lists of examples, strings of long quotations, series of narratives), but that you should use close reading, analysis, illustration, analogy, and narrative example in ways that build on and reinforce each other. Your essay should be unified in its thematic exploration of rhetoric while it varies in strategy to illuminate Plato, Aristotle, and contemporary uses of rhetoric.

Documentation Format: You should use MLA guidelines for parenthetical page references and for the Works Cited page. Finally, you should proofread your revision carefully to avoid typographical errors and other careless mistakes.

Please see me if you have any questions about these criteria.

Essay Two—The Rhetoric of [blank] Assignment

DUE DATES: October 20 (draft and portfolio responses to readings in *LL*);
November 5 (revision, commentary, and peer review sheets)

Format: MLA format for Works Cited page and internal citations; read Chapter 3, "The Process of Research," in the *Student's Guide*, pp. 37–60, for advice on research and incorporating source material into your essay.

Length: Final revised version should be six to ten typed, double-spaced pages (1500–2500 words), with at least four to six sources.

In this essay, you will explore, through research, the rhetoric of some specific aspect of contemporary culture. Your initial task is to choose a subject that interests you and that can be studied and analyzed from a rhetorical perspective. You may choose to write about the rhetoric of an academic field (history, economics, literature, biology), a profession (law, business, medicine, computer programming), an element of popular culture (*The Simpsons, Star Trek,* MTV, *Sportscenter, The Oprah Winfrey Show*), a major figure (Martin Luther King Jr., Bill Clinton), a topical issue (the budget deficit, health care, educational reform), or any other aspect of culture you believe has a rhetorical dimension. You will meet with me between October 8 and October 13 to discuss your subject for Essay 2; bring a one-page proposal to the conference outlining your subject and the questions you wish to explore.

Questions to Consider for Essay Two:
—What is the rhetorical dimension of your subject?
—What is the purpose of this rhetoric? Does the purpose align clearly with classical categories (deliberative, forensic, ceremonial), or must you develop a new, or hybrid, or multilayered category to explain the rhetoric of your subject?
—What are the common forms of this rhetoric? Spoken? Written? Visual images coupled with printed or spoken words? Words coupled with music?

—What are the common appeals of this rhetoric? Do these appeals align with classical categories (emotional, ethical, logical), or must you develop new, hybrid, or multilayered categories?
—What is the medium of this rhetoric? What is the relationship of technology to the transmission of this rhetoric?
—Does this rhetoric utilize the common topics described by Aristotle?
—What are the special topics associated with this rhetoric? In other words, what kinds of knowledge and/or training are particular to this rhetoric?

We will meet in the library on October 15 to learn about the university library's SABIO system and develop research strategies for this assignment, including the use of the Internet. In this essay, you will use both primary and secondary sources. Primary sources are examples of the rhetoric of your subject (political speeches, legal documents, textbooks, newspaper editorials, scripts of television shows, transcripts of talk shows), while secondary sources are commentaries and analyses that explicitly address this rhetoric. Many of the readings in *Living Languages* provide examples of secondary sources, including White on the rhetoric of the law, Tannen on the rhetoric of interpersonal communication in business, and Sontag on the rhetoric of AIDS.

You must provide photocopies of all printed source materials you use for this essay. This is a required part of this assignment, and your essay will not be accepted if not accompanied by photocopies of your sources.

Oral Presentations: Another aspect of this assignment will be an oral presentation of your research on October 27, October 29, or November 3. Your purpose in these presentations will be to teach the class something about the rhetoric of your subject through analysis of primary source materials. You may wish to put together a panel of related presentations with your classmates if your subjects are similar.

———————

Peer Review Sheet—The Rhetoric of _____ Assignment

Writer's Name:_____   Reader's Name:_____

On 10/20, 10/22, and then again on 11/5, class time will be devoted to peer review; be sure to bring a clean copy of your essay-in-progress to exchange with a partner. Remember the deliberative purpose of peer review: we are aiming at improvement of the essays, not praise or blame. Also remember that you can work with peers outside of class; for an assignment like this, which likely will involve multiple drafts, this strategy can be very helpful as your essay develops. Give this sheet with your written comments on it to your peer at the end of the class session.

1. How does the writer define/describe the rhetorical dimension of the subject? What is the persuasive purpose of this rhetoric? Is the purpose multilayered, with a commonly acknowledged surface purpose (for instance, entertainment) accompanied by other deliberative or ideological purposes?
2. How does the writer define/describe/analyze the common forms of this rhetoric? If relevant, how does the writer discuss the rhetorical elements beyond the verbal, such as music or visual image? How does the writer describe/analyze the medium of the rhetoric, including the role of technology in its transmission?
3. Does the writer provide sufficient examples of the rhetoric from primary sources? Are the examples analyzed closely in order to illuminate the rhetoric at work? How does the writer define/describe/analyze the common appeals of this rhetoric? How does the writer illuminate the common and special topics of this rhetoric, including special knowledge and training particular to this rhetoric?
4. Does the writer effectively utilize secondary sources to provide commentary about and analysis of the primary source material?

Evaluation Criteria for Essay 2

As before, the *Student's Guide* (Chapter 4) includes a complete overview and explanation of the grading standards of the Composition Program, focusing on expectations in the areas of content, organization, expression, and mechanics. The more specific criteria for Essay 2 are described below, derived from the assignment sheet and the peer review sheet.

Quality of Definition/Description of the Rhetorical Dimension of the Subject: how effectively the writer defines/describes the persuasive purpose of the rhetoric that provides the focus of the essay. This criterion is particularly important for subjects that are not commonly understood as utilizing rhetorical/persuasive strategies (music, film, television, other forms of entertainment or everyday communication).

Quality of Definition/Description of the Forms of the Rhetoric: how effectively the writer defines/describes the rhetorical elements at work, including the verbal (speeches, lyrics, written documents) and visual (video and film images, dramatic presentations, other forms of performance or spectacle).

Quality of Analysis of Primary Source Materials: how effectively the writer analyzes a sufficient range of examples of the rhetoric that provides the focus of the essay. This criterion emphasizes close reading of primary texts, including analysis of rhetorical appeals, common topics, special topics, and lines of proof.

Quality of Use of Secondary Sources: how effectively the writer cites/quotes from a sufficient range (popular, academic) of secondary sources to provide context (historical, cultural), commentary, and analysis.

Documentation Format: you should use MLA guidelines for parenthetical page references and for the Works Cited page. As stated in the assignment sheet, you must provide photocopies of all the printed source materials, primary and secondary, you use in this essay. Your essay will not be accepted if it is not accompanied by photocopies of your sources. (Certainly, you do not have to photocopy entire books or long journal articles, but you are required to photocopy relevant sections you use in your essay. See me if you have questions about this.) Finally, you should proofread your revision carefully to avoid typographical errors and other careless mistakes.

Essay Three—The Rhetoric of Personal Exploration

DUE DATES: November 19 (by this date you should have a complete draft of Essay 3 to discuss with me in conference); November 24 (portfolio responses due for Sommers, Lockett, Mosle, Gluck, and Rich); December 3 (revision, commentary on writing process, and peer review sheets)

Format: Follow guidelines for manuscript preparation in syllabus.

Length: Final version should be 6 to 8 typed, double-spaced pages (1500–2000 words).

Just as writing can be used as a mode of inquiry and exploration for academic purposes, writing can be used to explore and increase understanding of personal experience. One of the most famous quotations attributed to Socrates is, "The unexamined life is not worth living." For many, the human capacity to reflect on, learn from, and teach with personal experience is an essential element of being fully human. This essay assignment requires you both to present your experience in narrative form and to reflect on the meaning of the experience. From a rhetorical perspective, your purpose is most likely in the realm of "identification" rather than traditional persuasion; however, you will be persuading your readers to pay attention to your narrative and to reflect its meaning along with you. This form of identification does not come easily or automatically.

Narration Task: In your essay, you should aim to present/ dramatize your experience coherently and vividly, using narrative strategies such as character development, dialogue, description of setting, and figurative language. You will also need to decide on the scope and the pace of your narrative, which involves careful selection of what to include and what to emphasize.

Inquiry/Reflection Task: As we've noted in a variety of narrative essays we've read this semester, writers generally don't describe events from their lives in a linear, uninterrupted manner. Writers of narrative interweave commentary, reflection, interpretation, and sometimes direct statements of the meaning of their experiences. In your essay, you will need to decide how direct and explicit to be; to some degree, events can speak for themselves through careful development and arrangement, but in most cases you will need to balance narration and reflection carefully.

Peer Review Sheet—The Rhetoric of Personal Exploration

On November 24 and December 1, class time will be devoted to peer reviews of Essay 3. The questions below are derived from the assignment sheet, and you should also consider these questions as describing the evaluation criteria for this essay. As always, remember the deliberative purpose of peer review.

1. How effectively does the writer narrate the central story or the constellation of events in the essay? How well does the writer describe and develop such elements as people (characters), dialogue, and settings? How effectively does the writer utilize metaphors and figurative language?

2. How effectively is the narrative structured? Do parts of the narrative seem rushed or underdeveloped? How do the parts of the narrative work in relation to each other? Does the structure depend more on a central story or on a constellation of related events?

3. How effectively does the writer interweave reflection, commentary, interpretation, and/or assertion with the narrative? Do the events speak for themselves through careful development and arrangement, or does the essay require more explicit reflection to explore and develop the meaning? In other words, does the writer balance reportage and meditation effectively?

Final Examination Study Guide

Date/Time: Friday, December 11, 8:00–10:00 a.m.
Location: Education 240
Materials: Large-size bluebook, pens, Corder essay, notes/outlines (to be turned in with your essay at the end of the final examination period)

The final examination for this course includes summarizing and analyzing a reading, Jim Corder's "Argument as Emergence, Rhetoric as Love," which will be distributed in class on Thursday, December 3. Read Corder's essay carefully. Read it more than once. Annotate it, marking key passages and sections that seem confusing or unclear. In class on December 8, you will have the opportunity to discuss the essay with your peers. Composition Program guidelines preclude me from leading that discussion, so come to class prepared with questions and comments related to the reading. I recommend writing a complete portfolio response as part of your preparation for the final; you are allowed to bring such notes and commentary to the exam. Here are some questions to consider before class on December 8:

1. How does Corder define rhetoric?

2. How does Corder's definition differ from those offered by Plato and Aristotle?

3. How do Corder's ideas about rhetoric and language relate to those of other writers we've read this semester?

4. How does Corder incorporate the psychological theories of Carl Rogers into his discussion of rhetoric?

5. What is Corder's sense of the role of narrative in rhetoric? How does he expand the definition of narrative in developing his ideas about rhetoric?

6. If the key term in Plato's rhetoric is "truth," and in Aristotle's "persuasion," what is the key term in Corder's rhetoric?

7. What in Corder's essay seems most relevant to contemporary culture's use of rhetoric?

8. To what specific rhetorical situations can you most fruitfully apply Corder's ideas about rhetoric?

9. What specific guidelines does Corder offer for the application of his rhetoric?

Your final examination essay should do three things:

1. Summarize Corder's essay, providing a clear analysis of his views of rhetoric.

2. Develop your own definition of rhetoric, incorporating elements from Corder and other readings from the course (and adding any other elements you believe are important).

3. Apply your definition of rhetoric to one or more specific situations or cases, showing its usefulness as an analytical tool and as a guide to the effective use of language.

While your essay should complete all three of these tasks, you do not have to do them in this order or necessarily separate them from each other. You may wish to integrate the tasks in ways we've discussed this semester.

CHAPTER 4

CONSTRUCTING EFFECTIVE WRITING ASSIGNMENTS

This chapter offers some strategies, along with examples, for constructing not only individual assignment prompts but also sequences of writing assignments. As you contemplate the assignments included in this chapter, notice how they encourage students to approach writing tasks with some flexibility—to link the writing to their individual interests.

The last three essays of this chapter include a variety of writing-to-learn strategies and assignments, many of which can be used in writing-intensive courses in other disciplines as well as in composition courses. In general, these activities can serve to focus students' attention on understanding and personalizing course content. For each, consider how you might revise the assignment to encourage students to explore not only academic interests but also professional, personal, or civic ones.

Sequencing Writing Projects in Any Composition Class

From the Penn State University Composition Program Handbook

The following excerpt from the Penn State University Composition Program Handbook provides an overview of how writing assignments can be structured and sequenced to encourage engagement with all aspects of the writing process.

For each writing project in your course, whether you are teaching ENGL 015, ENGL 030, or ENGL 202, try to follow the general sequence of activities sketched out below. This procedure teaches students ways to plan throughout the process of a given writing project, makes students more aware of various activities that constitute the writing process, and provides them with excellent opportunities to consult with others about their work in progress.

The Overall Writing Assignment

Explain in class the nature of the project (sometimes using an example and, almost always, some full-class activity that gets all students involved in doing the particular sort of project you are assigning). Be sure the assignment involves subject, aim, genre, and audience. Then lead students through an invention activity to get each person thinking about his or her own project (usually involving a particular heuristic and speculative writing, followed by informal consultation with others). It usually makes sense to put assignments in writing but to avoid the overspecification that can lead students to write a fill-in-the-blanks response.

Topic Proposals

Topic proposals are informal plans that can serve writers in two ways: as tools for sorting out their ideas and planning, and as ways of consulting with others to get suggestions.

Proposals can be informal, as they often are in ENGL 015 ("In an essay, I want to persuade readers of King's 'Letter from Birmingham Jail' that King establishes ethos in several different ways"), or more formal, as they often are in ENGL 202 courses ("The Athletic Department would like to know whether men's basketball fans prefer games to start at 7:30 or 8:00. Thus, they assigned me to study the question and to write a recommendation report with an answer. The report will enable them to decide when to schedule games this winter"). In either case, proposals probably should contain the following:

proposals

- what you want to say (a hypothesis) or what issues you will try to resolve,

- for whom,

- for what purpose, and

- in what form or genre.

When students are in doubt about what to do for a given writing project, encourage them to sketch out a couple of proposals and talk over possibilities with others. Also encourage them to revise their plans as they work through a project.

If you have time, at least once before the proposals are handed in try to give students a chance to consult with each other (in groups of three or four). After they consult, allow them time (even just a few minutes in class) to revise their proposals before handing them in for your suggestions and approval. For the sake of encouraging good writing habits and discouraging academic dishonesty, it is probably best not to accept a paper unless the student has gained your permission to do it by means of a written proposal.

Rough Draft Workshop(s)

To encourage good writing habits, show students you care deeply about rough drafts. Suggestions for conducting writing workshops are described in a later section.

Final Self-Assessment and Reading

On the day the final writing is due, have writers do another self-assessment, using questions similar to those used for the rough draft assessment while adding a comment on the whole process (e.g., noting major changes from the draft to the final paper, commenting on the reasons for these changes, identifying a major problem encountered when writing the paper and how it was solved, commenting on a particular strategy they tried to use). Have students hand in their proposals, drafts, self-assessments, and reader responses. Again, do not grade papers handed in without a proposal and a rough draft.

Evaluation of Student Work

Read your students' papers carefully and return them in a timely way, annotated with praise and suggestions for improvement in appropriate areas. Suggestions for commenting are described in a later section. Grading standard policy sheets are included at the end of the handbook.

Further Reading

Elbow, Peter. *Writing without Teachers*. New York: Oxford UP, 1973.

Nelson, Jennie. "This Was an Easy Assignment: Examining How Students Interpret Academic Writing Tasks." *Research in the Teaching of English* 24 (1990): 362–96.

Autobiography: The Rhetorical Efficacy of Self-Reflection/ Articulation

BONNIE LENORE KYBURZ
Utah Valley State College

Bonnie Kyburz offers an argument for constructing autobiographical assignments in composition courses. Sometimes teachers consider students' autobiographical writing as less intellectually rigorous than other forms of discourse, but Kyburz counters that view with convincing theoretical perspectives.

In envisioning the impact of autobiographical writing on my life and work, I've seen Donald Murray's textual reminder: "All writing is autobiography" (66). I have always imagined that Murray is correct, and if he is—and I think that he is—then we must consider the potential power of exploring with students the nature of autobiography.

I believe that autobiography may be especially crucial to students' development as writers. Yet autobiography is often maligned as self-indulgent, as naively willing to privilege outmoded notions of subjectivity, as unproductively "expressive" in the rigidly codified Berlinian taxonomy (Berlin, "Rhetoric," *Rhetorics*). Perhaps the most daunting for autobiographical practices in composition has been the postmodern critique of subjectivity. Yet, despite postmodernist assaults on the notion of the subject and notions of individual agency, Murray's contention continues to make sense in light of our understanding that all writing emerges from writers unable to escape who they are at the historical moment of articulation, unable to disengage themselves from an infinite variety of ideological influences that determine them as unique, however socially constructed and capable of change. Thus, all writing "speaks" of and from a complex and multivocal "source" or "self," however problematic.

For autobiography critic James Olney,

> tracing an autobiographical text back from manifestation to source, one sees it recede into a fine and finer point, and there, where it disappears into its own center, is the spiritual mind of man, a great shape-maker impelled forever to find order in himself and to give it to the universe. (17)

Olney underscores the notion of the writer as capable of creating order from chaos. Murray seems to agree with Olney, and his agreement resonates in his endorsement of autobiography for writing courses in which students learn to "make meaning through language" (67).

For Murray, making meaning through language clarifies, to himself and to his audience, the ways in which his "voice is the product of Scottish genes and a Yankee environment, of Baptist sermons and the newspaper city room, of *all the language I have heard and spoken*" (67; emphasis added). This understanding of the ways in which subjectivity is shaped, and "individuality" is attenuated, by the language(s) we are born into and the cultures we inhabit, is derived from critical engagement with processes of articulating "the self," through language, at a particular historical moment, in a particular cultural situation. Such knowledge may be critical for students as they work through their student roles to gain rhetorical skills and some sense of the power of those skills; such knowledge may be capable of encouraging students to see themselves as capable agents rather than as submissive clones or members of an oppressed class of individuals in the community of the intellectual elite.

Autobiographical writing processes may also embody possibilities for critical consciousness that may be important for students' intellectual, public, and personal well-being. As bell hooks suggests, autobiographical writing may be important for the synthesis of theory and practice, particularly in terms of theorizing that is capable of catalyzing Freirean processes of conscientization (processes through which we gain critical consciousness): "When our lived experience of theorizing is fundamentally linked to processes of self-recovery, of collective liberation, no gap exists between theory and practice" (61).

My theorizing on autobiography is shaped in various ways by Murray, hooks, and other important voices, among them Mike Rose, Peter Elbow, John Trimbur, and Kurt Spellmeyer; it would take a lifetime to explain the infinite ways in which such voices have bolstered my imagination as I have worked in the classroom. Synthesizing these voices is not wholly possible in these pages. But let me suggest what such a synthesis allows me to theorize: it allows me to consider autobiographical practices as capable of catalyzing for students—in ways unseen and objectively unverifiable—a belief in the power of language, to see how they've been shaped by culture and ideologies once considered essentially ineffectual in light of "autonomy" and "American individualism." In this way, autobiography renders the "autonomous self" highly problematic, underscoring postmodern critiques on subjectivity in the process of exploring personal experiences in writing. I consider the work of self-reflection and conscientization to be delicately and importantly symbiotic, and for this reason, I find that autobiographical writing processes are intensely useful for students of first-year composition.

As I reflect on the ways in which autobiography has informed my theoretical and pedagogical orientations, I recall student writing that is rhetorically powerful; I recall processes that have been challenging, pleasurable, exciting, and capable of encouraging students to learn essential rhetorical concepts early in their college careers. In particular, I recall autobiography as capable of promoting students' awareness of the need for an engaging thesis—explicitly or implicitly articulated—which is both supported by reasons and evidence, and rendered problematic as a means of exploring further the rigid meanings and myths they might ordinarily assign to writing produced in institutional contexts.

If autobiographical writing is promoted as engaging, pleasurable, and rhetorical, student writers are likely to find studies in rhetoric less daunting than they might if we begin by teaching Latinate terms and phrases that serve not to invite students to "invent the university" or to truly "make meaning" but to alienate them and to render their creative and intellectual strengths impotent or invalid. Instead, teaching autobiography not as genre but as rhetorical strategy, we may encourage students to think about their experiences and the world(s) that shapes them. By breaking the natural "boundaries" of genre thinking, and by encouraging critical engagement not only with the self but also with the complex ways in which the self is shaped by and responds to the world, we disavow the notion of autobiography as exclusively expressionistic in Berlinian terms. We work instead within the social constructionist rubric that includes "self" and "world." We desegregate two key literacy myths that Shirley K. Rose identifies as "autonomy" and "participation" (4). S. Rose notes that "because autonomy and participation suggest opposite poles of experience . . . writers' representations imply that the two myths contradict one another and that an individual must make a choice between them," but that the two myths are actually reconciled in many key autobiographies, among them those of Malcolm X, Richard Rodriguez, and Maxine Hong Kingston (4). S. Rose suggests that autobiographical writing may reconcile myths of autonomy and participation, confirming what hooks sees as a process of conscientization that occurs as we work critically through processes of self-articulation.

In addition to bridging personal and public lives through autobiography (where Phillip Lopate is especially effective), which renders the "autonomous self" problematic, autobiographical writing may promote students' awareness of the nature of the theses they've learned about (usually in high school), those theses that are often unimaginative and dualistic, those that have a clear "counterpoint" and are thus unproblematic in a comprehensive sense. Through autobiography, for instance, they may learn that claims and assertions must be supported and that the support they choose is determined by the rhetorical context. I like to teach autobiographical strategies in the context of artistic proofs—as powerful imagistic language, metaphors and similes, thick description and detail that may be particularly useful to writers who seek to use Aristotelian appeals to ethos, pathos, and logos, whatever their aim. In this way, autobiographical strategies may promote student writing that is more engaging and imaginative even as it advances clearly articulated arguments that are appropriate for the college level.

Over the years, I've thought carefully about the ways in which autobiographical writing is particularly useful for first-year students, who generally have very specific notions about what "college writing" is. In my experience, many first-year students carry with them a notion of college writing as cut-and-paste arguments, arguments that are unimaginatively dyadic, lifeless, and passive. Such works can be considered the product of what Richard Miller calls a "pedagogy of obedience" (41), or of what Freire derides as the "banking" model (54), in which, as bell hooks notes, "pleasure" and "excitement" are missing lest a teacher make it his or her mission to "transgress" such staid traditions of academic "order" in favor of a truly liberating pedagogy (7).

In short, I've come to see that autobiographical writing is rhetorical, and that autobiography can be useful, pedagogically, in many important ways, including these:

1. Autobiographical writing can be used strategically to deconstruct familiar pedagogies with which students are at ease, compliant with, and complacent about.

2. Autobiographical writing may be used to generate hybrid pedagogies that incorporate rhetorical sophistication, critical cultural and personal inquiry, and playfulness. Autobiography may be used as part of what Richard Miller calls a "pedagogy of exploration," forcing on students the burden of critical thinking at a time when the familiar makes transitions easier and recognizing that "exploration," with its postcolonial connotative value, also implies a kind of "contamination," the kind students encounter when writing on demand in institutionalized settings (Miller 51). Students may explore the politics of literacy, thus encouraging their ability to problematize who they are and who they may become in the context of a particular historical and cultural moment.

3. Autobiographical writing is capable of assisting students as they unwittingly discover ways to argue effectively, even passionately, in the context of their own interests, which are not prescribed. In this way, autobiography may encourage students to understand the power of rhetoric in their personal, academic, and civic lives as they come to understand ways in which they are constructed by and connected to the social contexts in which they live.

For these reasons, and many others, autobiographical writing processes are capable of encouraging students to develop critical consciousness through self-recovery and social participation. Such work encourages students to engage in both reflection and action as they work through their often submissive positions as students, as the educationally oppressed. In this way, such work encourages students to heed Freire when he passionately suggests that "we cannot enter the struggle as objects in order to later become subjects" (qtd. in hooks 46).

Works Cited

Berlin, James A. "Rhetoric and Ideology in the Writing Class." *College English* 50 (1988): 477–94.

————. *Rhetorics, Poetics, and Cultures: Refiguring College English Studies.* Ed. Steven North. Urbana, IL: NCTE, 1996.

Elbow, Peter. *Writing with Power.* New York: Oxford UP, 1981.

Freire, Paulo. *Pedagogy of the Oppressed.* New York: Herder, 1970.

hooks, bell. *Teaching to Transgress: Education as the Practice of Freedom.* New York: Routledge, 1994.

Lopate, Phillip. *The Art of the Personal Essay: An Anthology from the Classical Era to the Present.* New York: Anchor, 1994.

Miller, Richard E. "What Does It Mean to Learn? William Bennett, the Educational Testing Service, and a Praxis of the Sublime." *Journal of Composition Theory* 16 (1996): 41–60.

Murray, Donald. "All Writing Is Autobiography." *College Composition and Communication* 42 (1991): 66–74.

Olney, James. *Metaphors of Self: The Meaning of Autobiography.* Princeton: Princeton UP, 1972.

Rose, Mike. *Lives on the Boundary: The Struggles and Achievements of America's Underprepared.* New York: Free, 1989.

Rose, Shirley K. "Metaphors and Myths of Cross-Cultural Literacy: Autobiographical Narratives by Maxine Hong-Kingston, Richard Rodriguez, and Malcolm X." *Melus* 14 (1987): 3–15.

Spellmeyer, Kurt. *Common Ground: Dialogue, Understanding, and the Teaching of Composition.* Englewood Cliffs, NJ: Prentice-Hall, 1993.

Trimbur, John. "Literacy and the Discourse of Crisis. *The Politics of Writing Instruction: Postsecondary.* Gen. Ed. Charles I. Schuster. Ed. Richard Bullock and John Trimbur. Portsmouth, NJ: Boynton/ Cook, 1991.

Deliberative Writing

FROM THE GRADUATE TEACHING ASSISTANT HANDBOOK
AT MICHIGAN TECHNOLOGICAL UNIVERSITY
(http://www.hu.mtu.edu/~mmcooper/gtahandbook/deliberative.html)

The following material discusses the role of deliberative writing in a first-year composition curriculum and provides examples of viable topics for deliberative essays.

You may find this material useful not only as you describe deliberative writing in your syllabus, but also as you construct specific writing assignments focusing on deliberative writing.

Deliberative Writing

All first-year writing courses at Michigan Tech teach deliberative writing. Deliberative writing addresses an issue of concern to the writer and to the writer's community and attempts to develop a useful position on the issue, a position that serves as a good ground for action or a better resolution of problems. In deliberative writing, the writer considers thoughtfully others' ideas and positions, trying to understand the reasons others hold these ideas and positions, and considering whether they can be adopted or adapted to form part of the writer's position.

In developing and arguing for a useful position on an issue, deliberative writing does not rely on common sense. Common sense, or what most people believe to be true, may or may not be true. Deliberative writing often explores whether or not what seems to be common sense is really true. Deliberative writing always relies on evidence to support a position—people's real experiences, recorded history, observations, the results of research.

In writing deliberatively on an issue, you offer evidence and reasons for your position because other people will not automatically agree with you, and you want to find the most reasonable position because how the issue is resolved matters to you and to others.

Many students have learned to support their own opinions or preferences in essays but not to consider issues about which there are serious differences of opinion. In defining an issue to write about, they need to be helped to find an issue that has serious consequences in our society and that people hold different opinions on.

Examples

NOT: The history of the Internet. (This is a topic, not even an issue.)

NOT: The Internet offers a world of possibilities. (Who would disagree?)

YES: The Internet is improving the workplace by allowing people to work at home and by stimulating the growth of small businesses in remote areas.

NOT: Alternative music is better than mainstream music. (This is a simple preference; whether you like one kind of music or another has no serious consequences.)

NOT: When mainstream music producers take over popular alternative bands, they destroy their individuality. (Better, but still more an observation; why does this matter?)

YES: The music business only promotes music that has broad appeal, thus restricting the variety of music available. (Restricting choice of music is an issue that has broad cultural consequences.)

Another way to look at a position is that it is an answer to the question readers ask on reading a lot of information: "So what?" or "How does this affect my life?" Obviously, in order to consider the various possible positions on an issue and to develop a useful position of their own, students need to consult and refer to a broad array of sources of information on the issue. But the information and ideas they draw from sources are used to help them understand the issue, develop a position on it, and offer evidence to support their position. Deliberative writing is not the same as writing a research paper.

purpose 1

The purpose of deliberative writing is to find reasonable resolutions to issues of concern, not just to report information.

The readings students do in the textbook for the class are one source of ideas and information, but in all first-year writing classes students should also be asked to find sources beyond their textbooks. Many will turn first to the Internet, which can supply lots of good information on some issues but might not be so useful on other issues. In addition to the Internet, students should be encouraged to use *library* sources, particularly newspaper, magazine, and journal articles, government documents, and archival information. Movies, television, their friends, their parents and other relatives, and other faculty at Michigan Tech can also be good sources of information, depending on the issue they are addressing.

Rhetorical Analysis: Terms of Contention

ANDY CROCKETT
Pima Community College

Andy Crockett's essay demonstrates the importance of exploring the definitions of key terms in building arguments, and provides sample assignments that encourage engagement with the defining process.

By rhetorically analyzing key terms in controversial issues, students learn the multiple contexts that shape and finally define these issues. A key or pivotal term serves as a doorway to greater understanding of the issue, so that when students have conducted a thorough rhetorical analysis of a key term, they can appreciate the complexity of an issue and shape a personal stance. As a result, students grow in metacognitive ability and gain currency in intellectual culture.

Likewise, learning the flexible and contextual nature of words helps students appreciate the role of rhetoric in democracy. As Bakhtin tells us, language is both centripetal and centrifugal: unifying and diversifying, self-identical and self-different. Thus, for students, citizens, or senators to engage in meaningful debate, they must agree on the meaning of key terms; their language must be centripetal, shared. But the centrifugal property of language, the tendency of words to reflect and deflect one another and thus to multiply meaning, forces students to recognize that meanings are social, complex, and ever evolving. (Burke's idea that communication happens in the tension between identification and division, sameness and difference, speaks to the same phenomenon.) Thus, the aforementioned debate can and often does turn in on itself, making the very definitions of words the ultimate "stakes."

The abortion rights conflict, for instance, returns again and again to the meaning of life—when does it begin? Is dependent or developing life truly viable or human? (Is a fetus dependent?) Should mere mortals defer to science or to religion when making this determination? And what does it mean to put one's faith in science or religion? As the structural linguistics of Ferdinand de Saussure showed us, life means something because it is not death, though students might feel most alive when plunging off a bridge at the end of a bungee cord. In other words, life accrues meaning from the related "terms" clustered around it: survival, work, play, health, quality, vital signs, faith, consciousness, and so on. The controversial ethicist Peter Singer (known for jump-starting the animal rights movement when he claimed that a healthy chimpanzee is more deserving of life than a vegetative or otherwise profoundly disabled human) bases much of his utilitarian ethics on notions of awareness and consciousness.

As I write, the country and the world wrestle with reconfigurations of the terms *competition* and *monopoly* within the realms of finance and telecommunications. When banks and brokerage firms merge as a result of deregulation, do we get more or less competition? When Disney weds AT&T, do consumers have more options at their disposal, or do they live more at the mercy of these conglomerates? Another instance is Bill Gates's Microsoft-Internet Explorer package. Defenders argue that Gates has played by the rules of the market and won; others argue that the ends don't justify the means when the tactics are "unethical." At any rate, in order to take a meaningful stand on this issue, one must contend with the terms *free market, fairness,* and *justice,* not to mention *success* and *ethics.*

The recent debate over how best to handle an impeached president teemed with power words and often zoomed in on them, turning the dispute into a metaconflict over interpretation. What combatants quickly found, of course, is that meaning is contextual and that interpretations are inflected by one's values and experiences. They may also find that they are mistaken as to a word's denotative meaning. *Impeach,* for example, despite its iambic kick, is a lower house hearing, not removal, not even a trial. Likewise, by learning a term's history or etymology, students gain historical perspective. *The American Heritage Dictionary* tells us that nothing hobbles a president so much as impeachment, and there is an etymological as well as procedural reason for this. The word *impeach* can be traced back through Anglo-Norman *empecher* to Late Latin *impedicere,* "to catch, entangle," from Latin *pedica,* "fetter for the ankle, snare." Thus, we find that Middle English *empechen,* the ancestor of our word, means such things as "to cause to get stuck fast," "hinder or impede," "interfere with," and "criticize unfavorably." A legal sense of *empechen* is first recorded in 1384. This sense, which had previously developed in Old French, was "to accuse, bring charges against." A further development of the sense had specific reference to Parliament and its formal accusation of treason or other high crimes, a process that the United States borrowed from the British. Although we have used it rarely at the federal level, impeachment stands as the ultimate snare for those who would take advantage of the public trust.

During impeachment hearings in the House, people argued about what the founders of the Constitution intended as the proper threshold for impeachment. Many have argued, however, that Madison, Hamilton, and others were deliberately vague about the criteria for impeachment, or at least for removal, leaving that all-important interpretation up to officials engaged in actual democratic debate, thus underscoring the connection between meaning and practice, words and situations. Because the dictionary fails to clarify meaning (and meaningful action), members of Congress and citizens made analogies between Clinton's situation and others in which impeachment was considered. Hamilton himself was threatened with impeachment for paying hush money to the husband of the woman with whom he had an affair. Hamilton, however, confessed publicly, and he was not "persecuted" by an independent prosecutor or partisan politicians. Federal judges have been impeached for perjury, but should judges and their work be viewed in a different context? Is a perjurer a liar in any case, and does a Senate trial set a dangerous precedent for the office of president? The linguistic possibilities are endless.

Lesson

Students read two essays representing opposing viewpoints on an issue. First, they write a summary of each essay, defining its central argument or thesis and its major supporting points. Second, working in small groups they compare summaries. This can be enlightening, for what is obvious or salient to one student may not be to another. It is also valuable to have students characterize the persona of the essay and the tone of voice, supporting their claims with concrete textual evidence. Again, what may sound ironic to one student may ring utterly sincere to another. Students can begin to reconcile the differences in what they "hear" by considering the baggage (conditioning, beliefs, experiences, values) they bring to their reading experience.

Next, students select a key term to study contextually. (This can be done individually, in pairs, or in small groups. The benefit of additional people working with the same term is that the potential facets they can unveil increase exponentially, leading them to related terms.) Their task is multifold: One, using a college dictionary, they write down the denotative definitions of a term. Two, consulting a thesaurus, they investigate the term's connotative meanings. Three, using the definitions they have found and the essays themselves, they identify related terms (including antonyms). The main term and its related terms form a word cluster. (For instance, *law* would be clustered with *code, rule, convention, custom, agreement, folkway, principle,* etc., as well as *crime,* perhaps *anarchy,* and so forth. It could also be subclassified into constitutional law, case law, statutory law.) Four, students consult the *Oxford English Dictionary* to gain a historical perspective of their chosen term (they should photocopy that page of the *OED* and bring it to class). Five, in light of their exploration, students return to the articles they are reading and write a new précis.

Student Writing

1. Working alone or with others, students create a taxonomy from their cluster of related terms. The taxonomy must address denotative, connotative, and contextual (i.e., the present and how the past informs the present) meanings. This taxonomy can be portrayed as a tree with branches and historical "roots," or it can be a map with illustrations, road signs, streets, arrows, perhaps geographical barriers, and of course inhabitants. It will probably be organized by categories such as legal, moral, ethical, and constitutional, if not tribal and political. Students present the taxonomy to the class and report what they've learned and how their opinions have changed.

2. Students write a rhetorical analysis of the role their key term—and its family of related terms—plays in the issue. Thus, they will analyze how the various players in the issue use the term, including the conditions or threshold for agreement and the sparks for disagreement. The purpose of the rhetorical analysis is to teach their classmates, their teacher, and themselves not simply the meaning of the term but also the meaning of the issue.

3. Finally, students write a formal argument employing what they have learned. They may take a stand on the general issue or argue for an interpretation of their key term. At any rate, the key terms will focus the students' essays.

Works Cited

Bakhtin, Mikhail. *The Dialogic Imagination.* Ed. Michael Holquist. Trans. Caryl Emerson and Michael Holquist. Austin: U of Texas P, 1981. (Original work published as *Voprosy literatury i estetiki,* Moscow, 1975.)

Burke, Kenneth. *A Grammar of Motives.* Englewood Cliffs, NJ: Prentice-Hall, 1945.

de Saussure, Ferdinand. *Course in General Linguistics.* Ed. Charles Bally and Albert Sechehaye. Trans. Wade Baskin. New York: Philosophical Library, 1959.

Singer, Peter. *Animal Liberation.* New York: Avon, 1977.

Assignment Prompt

EDWARD A. KEARNS
University of Northern Colorado

Edward Kearns describes a novel assignment that requires students to critically examine issues raised by newspapers published on their birthdays.

Assignment

Students examine newspapers published on the day of their birth (or their parents' or grandparents' births)—or newsmagazines printed during that week—then write a three- to five-page essay. The source provides ample material; the task is to make sense of it: to establish a unifying theme or perspective. Simply reporting on various stories, editorials, ads, and so forth won't do; raw data of any kind is meaningless without a point of view or underlying structure that establishes relationships and meaning.

Of course, students will want teachers to supply examples of unifying themes, and certainly we can do that, but insisting that the students simply examine the raw material to "see what it suggests" leads to brainstorming/inventing and to the discovery that doing research without prior frames of reference is in itself inventive and stimulating. Creativity in any art often amounts simply to juxtaposing forms or materials in uncommon ways—hence, for example, metaphors such as "pearl of blood" or "blue roses." Simultaneously, the analysis and synthesis required offers an exercise in inductive reasoning.

If students have trouble, however, teachers can suggest comparing today's prices or clothing styles to "back then," or ask, "What does advertising tell us about people's tastes, behavior, or interests twenty years ago?"; "What do movies and television shows (or bestsellers, or pop music) tell us about _____ (fill in 'values,' 'taste,' 'censorship,' etc.)"; "Where did _____ (a piece of legislation, an event, a trend) lead?"

The assignment provides a bridge from personal narratives to formal exposition, to research, and to writing with sources—while retaining the motivational value of personal writing. Such research might be used, for example, to contextualize personal memories. It requires students to work with categorical (rather than chronological) organizational structures and leads to longer, more complicated expository tasks such as writing papers about entire decades, developments in various fields, shifting values, pop culture trends, and so on. It can even lead back to narrative and fiction since story writers commonly conduct such research to create atmosphere and verisimilitude for their stories.

Profile Assignment

SARAH T. DUERDEN, JEANNE GARLAND, AND
CHRISTINE EVERHART HELFERS
Arizona State University

Duerden, Garland, and Helfers outline a series of assignments that expand the scope of profile projects by asking students to make connections between their professional or academic interests and their writing.

Rationale for the Assignment

Because the profile genre requires students to integrate their observations and field research into a paper, it is a useful and enjoyable assignment that can lead naturally into assignments requiring integration of research. The profile can also be used to help students begin to think about their careers and the professions they would like to enter. Although this may seem premature for first-year students, with the increasing pressure to complete a degree in four years, students benefit from investigating career choices early on.

This profile assignment, developed by the three of us, asks engineering students to discover what engineers really do in their professions. We developed this assignment in response to the number of engineering students who realize at some point in their degree programs that engineering involves much more than good math and science skills. Nevertheless, many students are advised to enter engineering because they excelled in these subjects in high school. They have less understanding of the additional oral and written communication skills, teamwork skills, and creative skills they will need to develop. Therefore, our profile assignment asks students to interview a professional engineer, attend a presentation by another professional engineer, and integrate that material into a profile that shows high school students what the engineering profession involves.

critical to assg [handwritten]

The assignment is presented to students as a problem they can solve through a piece of writing. We find this approach useful with engineering students since members of their profession often regard themselves as problem solvers; however, we have also used this terminology with nonengineers to encourage students to see that we usually write for a purpose rather than just because a teacher has asked us to do so. Their task is outlined in the solution. They must write a profile of an engineer they have interviewed, but they must also incorporate material from a presentation and material from a book on engineering. In this way, students learn to synthesize multiple sources, a task which allows us to discuss the question of validity of sources. The assignment sheet also identifies the purpose and audience for the piece of writing. In all of our early assignments, we give students a specific purpose and audience; as the semester progresses, we remove this scaffold and ask students to create their own audiences and purposes. Thus, our early assignments also act as models for students as they learn to create their own rhetorical situations for their writing. Finally, the assignment identifies the constraints within which the students must write. Again, we deliberately employ this term because it is one they work with in engineering. As the semester progresses, we also remove this scaffold so that by the end of the semester, students develop their own constraint lists—constraints the rhetorical situations have created.

Having students complete this assignment is beneficial in many ways. By writing the profile, students discover for themselves—from the mouths of "real engineers"—what working as a professional involves. They identify the skills they will need to develop during their university careers. If they focus solely on developing outstanding math and science skills and neglect teamwork, communication, and creative skills, they will find themselves ill prepared for the workplace. Students also learn to incorporate quotations in a natural way because they are quoting their interviewee and other sources to support the interviewee's claims about the profession. We have found that this approach helps students make the transition from assignments that focus on themselves to assignments that focus on issues outside their personal experience.

[Handwritten margin notes: "write for a purpose + synthes", "assignment purpose audience | then ask them to create purpose and", "what they learn"]

[Handwritten margin numbers: 1, 3, 4]

We later revised this assignment for use with non-engineering students. This time, we asked them to interview someone in a profession they had themselves worked in or one they hoped to work in. We also asked them to find supporting material on the Web or by using Career Services. A second option was based on an essay that argues that part-time jobs teach students few useful skills. Since most students have worked in part-time jobs in high school or currently work while they are in college, we felt they would have easy access to someone they could interview.

This version of the assignment proved successful. Some students interviewed relatives who worked in professions they wanted to enter, and so the assignment allowed them to discover more about their potential future careers. Others interviewed friends who held part-time positions, and several found that although they thought they would prove that part-time jobs are a positive benefit to students, their observations and subsequent profiles showed otherwise. They saw the problems their peers experienced juggling work schedules, schoolwork, family duties, and social lives.

Invention Activities

With both engineering and non-engineering students, we do a number of activities to help them think about whom they might interview. Once the students have decided on subjects, they can work on a list of questions they want to ask. Again, we often practice this in class by using ourselves (teachers) as professional interviewees and asking students to design questions for us. Then we give them invention sheets to fill in for the presentation and for the interview. (Both are appended at the end of this assignment.) Students may use the invention sheets to arrange the materials and use the tables to further organize those materials.

The Assignment for Engineers

PROBLEM #2: WRITING A PROFILE
First Draft Due: Friday, October 2
Second Draft Due: Monday, October 5
Polished Draft due: Friday, October 9

Situation

You are one of several student representatives for the first-year engineering program. You have just met with the dean of engineering and the president of the university. At the meeting, the dean and the president discussed the low retention rate in engineering. After the first year, almost 30 percent of the students change majors. The dean and the president asked you to review a questionnaire distributed to students who left engineering at the end of last year. One response stands out. Many of these students said they changed majors because engineering is not what they thought it would be. In fact, many felt they had been poorly advised in high school, where advisors had often recommended engineering as a career because the student was good at math and science. However, upon entering the university, many have found that engineering requires a number of skills, including communication skills and teamwork skills. At the next meeting, you explain this to the president and the dean, and they ask you to help them come up with a solution that will help future engineering students.

Solution

You and the other representatives decide to write profiles of a particular type of engineer that will be distributed to high school students considering a career in engineering. These individual profiles of a mechanical engineer, a civil engineer, an electrical engineer, and so on will be assembled and given to high school students so that they can gain a more realistic view of engineering before they begin their university careers. Therefore, your assignment is to profile a particular engineer.

Base your writing on an interview with a professional engineer you know, or a senior engineering student about to graduate, or an engineering professor. (Of course you can interview relatives.) In addition, draw on the material that Joe Circello presented and on Chapter 2 of James L. Adams's *Flying Buttresses, Entropy, and O-Rings: The World of an Engineer* (Cambridge: Harvard UP, 1991) in which Adams defines engineering. Adams begins with dictionary definitions, though these do not prove to be very useful. He then discusses misconceptions people have about engineering, the variety of professionals who classify themselves as engineers, the kind of work they do, the range of knowledge engineers must possess, and various definitions and descriptions applied to engineering.

Your Purpose

Your purpose in this paper is to inform potential engineering students about the kinds of work typically done by a specific professional engineer, his or her allocation of time for various tasks and activities, and so on.

Your Audience

Your readers are high school students who know little about what professional engineers do but who are considering engineering as a career because they are good at math and science.

CONSTRAINTS:

♦ You must interview and use quotes from a professional engineer, a senior engineering student, or an engineering professor in this profile.

♦ You should also use material from Joe Circello's presentation and material from Adams as further support for your profile.

♦ When you quote or paraphrase your interviewee or Joe Circello, you must make it clear that this is their idea. Thus, you should use signal phrases in your sentences such as "According to Joe Circello" or "Joe Circello explains." Make sure that you explain their expertise the first time you mention these people in your profile. Also note that you should use the present tense: "Circello explains," not "Circello explained."

◆ When you are relying on Adams, make sure you identify the ideas that belong to him by using signal phrases such as "According to Adams" or "James Adams explains that." Again, initially explain Adams's expertise to your readers. You must follow quotations or paraphrases with in-text parenthetical citations (the page number[s] in parentheses) as we discussed in class. Also, see the *St. Martin's Guide to Writing,* pages 595–605. Again, remember to use the present tense: "Adams says," not "Adams said."

◆ You must include a copy of your interview questions with your paper.

◆ You must write for your audience. Since they are high school students, you may have to define unfamiliar terms and give examples and comparisons.

◆ You will need a thesis in your introduction. In your textbook, this is called a "dominant impression." All paragraphs in your essay must support that thesis. There should be an obvious order to your paragraphs, and each paragraph should develop only one idea.

◆ You can choose to organize your profile topically or chronologically (a day in the life of). See page 140–142 of your textbook for details.

Format

◆ Length: 4 to 5 typed pages or 1000–1250 words, double-spaced with one-inch margins. Include your name, our names, and the class time in the top right-hand corner of the first page. Number pages, please. Page 1 is always counted but it is not numbered on your work, so you must suppress that number on the first page. Give your work a title that is not in caps and is centered on your first page, and begin typing your essay one double space below your title.

◆ Include a separate alphabetized works cited page.

◆ See page 628 of your textbook for a sample works cited

page. See page 605 for how to cite the book by Adams. See page 612 for how to cite a personal interview. Use the following format to cite Joe Circello's presentation:

Circello, Joe. Presentation. Foundation Coalition Program. Arizona State University, Tempe. 23 Sept., 1998.

Assignment Revised for Students Other Than Engineers

(Much of the instructional information in this adaptation of the assignment echoes the first; in such cases, repetitive text has been omitted.)

WRITING A PROFILE
Due Dates (same)

With your polished draft, you must submit the following materials:

1. All invention work
2. All drafts
3. All peer review work
4. Interview notes
5. Article from print or Web sources
6. Reflection on writing to be written in class on Wednesday, October 7 (see page 152 of *St. Martin's Guide to Writing* for the prompt)

Format
Length: 4–5 TYPED PAGES OR 1000–1250 WORDS
Spacing: double-spaced with one-inch margins
Number pages: Put your name and page number on each page.
Title: Give your work a title that is not in caps and is centered on

your first page, and begin typing your essay one double space below your title.

Option One

Choose a profession that you believe people have mistaken notions about. It may be one that you would like to enter, or one that you have already worked in, or one that a relative works in. You will find sources about professions by going to Career Development in Career Services (3rd floor of the Student Services Building). You may also use the Web. I have found the following Web site especially helpful: http://www.jobprofiles.com/.

You can also search the library indexes of magazines for profiles of careers.

Situation

As a member of the Professional Organization of (add the profession here), you have just attended a conference in which you and your colleagues discussed the low numbers of new graduates entering your profession. One member of the conference presented a survey showing that a number of high school students interviewed about your profession either had mistaken notions about the profession or knew little about it. (Remember how David Noonan tries to correct mistaken notions about surgeons and their attitudes in his profile.)

Solution

Write a profile of this professional that could be distributed to high school students considering a career in this profession. This would allow these students to gain a more realistic view of the profession before they begin their university careers. Base your writing on an interview with a professional you know in that field, or a senior student about to graduate and work in that profession who has done an internship. (Of course you can interview relatives.) In addition, you will need to find an article that describes that profession. You should include this material with your paper when you hand it in for grading.

Your Purpose

Your purpose in this paper is to inform potential students about various aspects of this professional's workload, including how he or she typically works and on what time frame, the nature and variety of tasks completed, the skills he or she needs, and so on.

Your Audience

Your readers are high school students who know little about what professionals in this field do but who are considering this as a career.

CONSTRAINTS:

◆ You must interview a professional for this profile and quote extensively from that source in your paper.

◆ You should also use material from another source such as a print article or material from the World Wide Web. You must include copies of these sources with your paper.

◆ When you quote or paraphrase your interviewee, you must make it clear that this is their idea. [Omitted here are the rules for paraphrasing cited in the earlier assignment sheet.]

◆ You must include a copy of your interview notes with your paper.

◆ When you are relying on other sources, make sure you identify the ideas that belong to that author by using signal phrases such as "According to Adams" or "James Adams explains that." [Omitted here are the rules for using quotes cited in the earlier assignment sheet.]

◆ You must write for your audience. Since they are high school students, you may have to define unfamiliar terms and give examples and comparisons.

◆ You will need a thesis in your introduction. [Again, students are instructed to consult the *St. Martin's Guide*.]

◆ You can choose to organize your profile topically or chronologically (a day in the life of). See pages 140–142 of *St. Martin's Guide to Writing* for details.

Option Two

Many educators believe that part-time jobs do little to teach high school students useful skills. In fact, many believe that such jobs harm students because they take away time students need to spend on their studies. Read "Working at McDonald's" (*St. Martin's Guide to Writing*, pp. 299–300) for an example of someone who feels that part-time jobs in high school are a waste of time.

Situation

Imagine that the PTA of the local high school you attended read this article and is now considering asking students not to work part time.

Solution

If you agree with the premise of the article on McDonald's, write a profile of someone you know who does a part-time job, showing how that job is not teaching the student useful skills. If you disagree with the premise of the article, write a profile of someone who does a part-time job showing how that job teaches students useful skills.

Your Purpose

To persuade the PTA that they should support the ban on part-time jobs or to persuade them that they should not support the ban.

Your Audience

Your readers are parents of high school students.

CONSTRAINTS:

◆ You must interview a student who holds a part-time job and quote that person extensively.

- You should also use the article "Working at McDonalds."

- When you quote or paraphrase your interviewee, you must make it clear that this is their idea. [Again, rules for paraphrasing are typically reiterated here.]

- You must include a copy of your interview notes with your paper.

- When you are relying on other sources, make sure you identify the ideas that belong to that author by using signal phrases such as "According to Adams" or "James Adams explains that."

- You must write for your audience. You may need to explain and give examples for this audience.

- You will need a thesis in your introduction. [Include instructions on paragraph and essay organization from earlier instructions.]

- You can choose to organize your profile topically or chronologically (a day in the life of). See page 140–142 of the *St. Martin's Guide to Writing* for details.

Observation Notes for Profile

Prior to class, answer the following questions:

- What do I already know about engineers?

- What words do I associate with them?

- What kinds of work do I think they do?

- What skills do I think they have to possess?

- What skills are less important to them?

- What do I expect to discover?

- What would surprise me?

- What do most people think about engineers?

- What would most people be surprised to discover?

How do my views of engineers differ from most people's views?
Observation Notes for Profile

During or immediately after class, fill out the following:

- Name, Company, Position

- Years of work/overview of career

- Physical appearance

- Key points discussed

- Least surprising

- Most surprising

- Dominant impression

- Quotation or paraphrase

Invention Sheet for Writing a Profile

You have now gathered a lot of information. Use this invention sheet to help you begin to sort out and organize that information.

- What is my purpose in this profile?

- Who are my readers and what must I do to meet their needs in this profile?

- What have I learned about a professional engineer that I found surprising or new?

- Does that differ from what most people think, and if so, how?

- ◆ Could I turn that into a thesis?

- ◆ How would I describe this person professionally?

- ◆ How would I describe this person physically?

- ◆ Should I organize my material topically? If I organize topically, what topics should I focus on?

- ◆ Which source deals with each topic?

- ◆ If I organize chronologically (a day in the life of), when do I begin? What events or actions do I describe? Should I include a description of the workplace?

- ◆ What source will help me support my description of a particular event or action?

- ◆ Should I begin this profile with a striking image or vivid scene, an interesting fact, an anecdote, a question, or a piece of dialogue?

- ◆ Should I close this profile with a new image, an anecdote, a piece of dialogue, an interesting fact, or should I use the one that I began with?

- ◆ How can I restate my thesis without repeating the same words I used in the introduction?

Picture Exchange: Sharing Images and Ideas in First-Year Composition

DONNA REISS
Tidewater Community College

Donna Reiss's assignment links students' interests with their writing in a uniquely personal way.

Originally developed as a way to engage first-year students in the writing process at the beginning of the term and to build a learning community by introducing busy commuter students to their classmates, a picture exchange has become the foundation of our semester, establishing writing-editing partnerships, electronic communication exchanges, and attention to detail that I hope will continue throughout the term. I assume that all students have a picture they care about and that the task of describing their own picture will be less unsettling than other personal topics would be as a first piece of writing that will be shared with strangers. I ask that they select an image that is already part of their personal collections to ensure that they really do know and care about both the image and the content depicted. This exchange fosters the kind of active learning recommended by Marilla D. Svinicki in which students "make connections between what they know and what they are learning" (31).

Because students write these descriptions as letters to classmates with copies to me, they usually think about audience even before that concept is introduced in class. The letter is a familiar form, encouraged as a genre for academic writing by Elbow, Fulwiler, Reiss, and Young, among others. Because students attempt to distinguish between their own and their classmates' objective descriptions of the images and their subjective interpretations or explanations, they are practicing skills they will further hone as they read and respond to the essays in their textbooks, subsequent peer papers on general topics, and the sources they locate for their required research paper.

Depending on how often we can access a computer-networked classroom, we do some elements of the picture exchange in class and others asynchronously between classes. Now that my students also develop electronic portfolios, future students will scan their images and incorporate revisions of their accompanying letters into Web pages.

> **Step 1**: Each student selects a picture and makes two copies, one for a classmate and one for me. They also compose a 300- to 500-word letter to their classmate in which they describe the image in objective, concrete language and explain the importance of the image and their reason for selecting it.

Step 2: Before reading the partner's letter, students view the classmate's picture and write a 150- to 200-word letter to that classmate describing the partner's image in objective, concrete language and explaining what feelings the image evokes and why they think the image is important to the classmate.

Step 3: The partners exchange their step 2 letters. Each student writes a short note thanking the classmate for his or her thoughts on the picture and identifying specific points that were interesting and ways in which their perceptions about the image were similar and different.

Step 4: The students meet, each reading the partner's original step 1 letter and the partner's response. They compare the descriptions and reactions. Together, they write a letter to the entire class in which they highlight similar and differing reactions to the pictures and discuss the reasons. This letter is published and distributed to the class. If time permits, each pair also makes a brief oral presentation to the class.

Students usually bring pictures of their family or friends, sometimes including themselves, sometimes not. Because we live in a community that annually hosts the East Coast surfing championships, pictures of surfing or bodyboarding are also typical choices. One student, for example, brought a picture of himself standing on a reef overlooking a beach in Puerto Rico, where he had mastered a particularly challenging wave, and described the setting as a reminder of the exhilaration of that achievement as well as a memory of the colors and feel of the water. His respondent was a woman who did not surf herself but as a lifelong resident of Virginia Beach was familiar enough with the equipment, a surfboard, and our own sandy, reefless beach to discern that the setting was a distant beach and that the person who selected the picture probably had a passion for beaches as well as for the sport.

The picture-letter exchange demonstrates to students that many writers and scholars work and learn together rather than in isolation, as emphasized by Ede and Lunsford in *Singular Texts/ Plural Authors: Perspectives on Collaborative Writing*. Their casual writing exchanges help novice writers connect with their classmates and prepare them for later peer-response groups as they share writing first in a nonthreatening but meaningful way.

Works Cited

Ede, Lisa, and Andrea Lunsford. *Singular Texts/Plural Authors: Perspectives on Collaborative Writing*. Carbondale: Southern Illinois UP, 1990.

Elbow, Peter. "High Stakes and Low Stakes in Writing." *New Directions for Teaching and Learning* 69 (1997): 5–13.

Fulwiler, Toby. "Writing Back and Forth: Class Letters." *New Directions for Teaching and Learning* 69 (1997): 15–25.

Reiss, Donna. "Epistolary Pedagogy and Electronic Mail: Online Letters for Learning Literature." *Learning Literature in an Era of Change: Innovations in Teaching*. Ed. Dona J. Hickey and Donna Reiss. Sterling, VA: Stylus2000.

Svinicki, Marilla D. "Practical Implications of Cognitive Theories." *College Teaching: From Theory to Practice*. Ed. Robert J. Menges and Marilla D. Svinicki. New Directions for Teaching and Learning 45. San Francisco: Jossey-Bass, 1991. 27–37.

Young, Art. "Mentoring, Modeling, Monitoring, Motivating: Response to Students' Ungraded Writing as Academic Conversation." *New Directions for Teaching and Learning* 69 (1997): 27–39.

Reflecting on Journal Writing

LISA EDE
Oregon State University

The following assignment prompt is designed to encourage students to reflect on a range of course material. As Lisa Ede notes, the prompt also serves as "a mechanism for having students evaluate their own journals. It was originally developed by Lex Runciman (now at Linfield College in Oregon) when he was WIC director at OSU. I have used it in first-year writing and literature courses, as well as advanced courses. It's wonderfully efficient for teachers. I can move through a journal that a student has preevaluated very quickly. More important, though, it engages students in self-reflection and self-assessment. I've found over the years that students are almost always accurate in their self-assessment; if anything, I often have to raise the grade they've given themselves."

Journal

Purpose and Logistics

The journal has one primary purpose: to encourage you to inter-act more deeply (and also more enjoyably) with the texts we are reading. Your entries should be more controlled than freewrites—simply free-associating or writing whatever random thoughts come to mind is not acceptable—but they are in no sense mini-essays. You do not need to come to conclusions in your journal entries, nor do you have to attend to the formal and logical con-straints characteristic of essays. Rather, the entries are designed to provide an opportunity for you to speculate freely, and even playfully, without having to feel sure of your outcome. Your en-tries can take many forms. A successful entry might explore a question or topic by considering a relevant example or by work-ing through an analogy. You might draw on your own experi-ence to consider the implications of an idea, or you might make a list of all the questions or issues that a particular topic, quota-tion, or question raises. Just about anything goes as long as it indicates real intellectual engagement.

Most often, I will provide prompts for journal entries. Though my prompts will obviously guide and constrain your response, you nevertheless have great freedom in how you address the question(s) or issue(s) it raises. A prompt might cause one stu-dent to reflect on her personal experiences, while another might address the prompt in a more theoretical or historical vein. As I have said already, but will repeat for emphasis, what I'm looking for is engagement with the texts we are reading.

I will read your entries and return them to you. Please keep your entries in a folder for resubmission during and at the end of the term. (Be sure to print and save all online postings as well.) If at the start of the term you have any concerns about your journal entries, I'll be happy to review them with you.

For print journal entries, please date all entries and write the topic, question, or quotation to which it is a response at the top of the page. (If the quotation is lengthy, feel free to write a brief summary of it.) Your entries may be handwritten or typed.

Evaluation

Journal entries will be evaluated on three criteria: commitment, ambition, and engagement. Style is a consideration only to the extent that your ability to manipulate language influences your ability to articulate complex and engaging ideas. The focus in the journal is your ability to engage in critical thinking.

I will collect your journals around midterm time and at the end of the quarter. On both occasions, when you hand in your journals you will include an evaluation based on the criteria listed above. (See the evaluation sheet, which includes descriptions of A, B, and C journals.) As part of this evaluation, you'll write two or three sentences to explain your ratings and then indicate an overall grade. I'll review your journals and your evaluation, and I'll use the same criteria to guide my feedback to you and to arrive at your journal grade at the end of the term.

Journal Evaluation Sheet

A Journals

Commitment: The writer turns in all journal entries (unless he or she has an excused absence). Entries may vary in length, but they regularly go on for enough time to reflect and accommodate extended thought.

Ambition: Journal entries regularly try to consider issues or pose questions which engage the writer but for which the writer may have no ready answer. The writer is willing to speculate and to try to make connections between this course and his or her experience. The writer is not afraid to address complex—and even paradoxical and contradictory—ideas.

Engagement: The writer is clearly using the journal entries to "push" his or her understanding of the text or question in particular and of the course material in general.

B Journals

Commitment: The writer turns in all but one or two journal entries. The entries often reflect and accommodate extended thought, but at times they seem merely to summarize or in an unengaged way to comment on the topic.

Ambition: Journal entries often try to speculate about issues and questions and to make connections between the course and the writer's experience. But a number of entries discuss conclusions and/or summarize or respond in an unfocused way to the topic. The writer is also less comfortable with tension, dissonance, and paradox and tries to resolve or "iron out" complexity.

Engagement: The writer sometimes uses journal entries to "push" his or her understanding of the text or question in particular and of the course material in general; a number of entries, however, seem formulaic or completed merely to fulfill the assignment.

C Journals

Commitment: The writer fails to turn in three or more journal entries.

Ambition: The journal entries seem cursory, the result of coercion rather than interest. There is little or no effort to speculate, to reach for more than obvious conclusions, or to connect with the writer's own experience.

Engagement: The writer rarely if ever uses journal entries to deepen, much less "push," his or her understanding of the text or question in particular and of the course material in general.

Journal Evaluation Sheet

Name_____   Date_____

Evaluation of COMMITMENT
    Grade
    Reasons:

Evaluation of AMBITION
    Grade
    Reasons:

Evaluation of ENGAGEMENT
    Grade
    Reasons:

Overall grade

Role-Playing as a Writing-to-Learn Activity

MARY M. SALIBRICI
Syracuse University

Mary Salibrici's role-playing assignments encourage students to explore how writing is shaped by authorial identity and context.

As part of a writing course that emphasizes the rhetorical nature of language, I have designed a sequence of role-playing assignments that function as write-to-learn activities. Such writing tasks work effectively as learning exercises since, building from Emig, I have found that they relate to students' "evolutionary development of thought, steadily and graphically visible and available throughout as a record of a journey, from jottings and notes to full discursive formations" (129). Completing this assignment sequence, in other words, provides students with an opportunity to invent perspectives with words and thus deepen their understanding of the basic rhetorical premise of the course—that is, what you write is governed by who you are, why you are writing, to whom, and at what cost. Additionally, they are more fully prepared for subsequent formal essay assignments that ask for critical analysis of various rhetorical features of a text. The write-to-learn activities prepare students to think deeply about the rhetorical nature of writing as they invent a persona and try to write convincingly in the role of a particular author.

Specifically, I have used such role-playing writing assignments for a six-week unit that focuses on the trial and subsequent execution of Julius and Ethel Rosenberg and culminates in a mock trial that applies the rhetorical principles under investigation through an integration of reading, writing, speaking, and listening activities. For the first two weeks of the unit, students read a variety of pieces representing different interpretations of the case, including excerpts from a defense attorney's bestselling book, a novelist's fictional rendition, feminist perspectives about Ethel, the Rosenbergs' son's interpretation of events, articles from the *New York Times,* and editorials from the *Daily Worker,* to name a few. Complete texts from which the excerpts are taken, along with additional readings that are described in an annotated bibliography, are placed on library reserve for further student reading and research.

The first role-playing exercise is assigned after students read excerpts from Nizer's *The Implosion Conspiracy* (1973) and Radosh and Milton's *The Rosenberg File* (1983). They have begun to form preliminary impressions of the people and events involved in the case and often have strong opinions about the Rosenbergs' guilt or innocence. After completing these readings,

I ask students to provide a two-page general summary of the case as they understand it so far; however, there's a twist to my request because they must adopt a particular persona as they write. The options are as follows:

- ♦ Write as if you are a reporter for the *New York Times* putting together a news summary to run on the front page shortly before the Rosenberg's scheduled execution in 1953.

- ♦ Write as if you are submitting a text to your twentieth-century American history professor as part of a take-home final exam.

- ♦ Write as if you believe the Rosenbergs to be innocent (or guilty) but your magazine editor has asked you to prepare a neutral summary of the case to be run in a For Your Information column.

The options are hypothetical, of course, but each one asks for a particular spin that students will have to convey, with the take-home exam persona being the most familiar. Interestingly, most students choose the unfamiliar stances of newspaper reporter or magazine writer. We then share the written texts as a class, discussing the nuances of word choice, style, and tone as representative of specific personas. We discuss whether they have been effective in making their roles come alive in writing and how they accomplished such an effect. Through specific language choices, they have invented the way a particular author might approach a particular task. These write-to-learn inventions result in a deeper appreciation for the way language works and a more personalized understanding of the various interpretations that can be made about the Rosenbergs' story.

The next role-playing exercise asks students to write in an even more specific way. Having read further about the case at this point, students have begun to develop a fuller understanding of the various people and events central to the case. There are several layers to the next exercise, because students are asked to share what they are reading and writing in small groups that will ultimately parallel their working groups for the mock trial. They are actually working on reading-to-learn and writing-to-learn activities as this exercise proceeds.

First, I ask students to join a small group that fits a perspective of particular interest to them, perhaps the point of view of the defense, the prosecution, scientists and historians, or reporters covering the case. We continue our assigned readings, but students are expected to read further on their own, perhaps utilizing materials on library reserve, so that they can familiarize themselves with the role of a specific person represented by their small group. For the writing portion of this exercise, I ask students to assume the voice of one individual involved in the case and represented by their group and to choose a format in which to play that person's role in writing. They may choose, for example, to portray the Rosenbergs' defense attorney and write an opening statement to the jury, or they may choose to portray Ethel Rosenberg through a witness affidavit. I ask that they adhere to the historical facts as closely as possible; in other words, they should not fictionalize material if they are trying to portray an actual historical person.

As students gather in their small groups, they share material they have gained from the readings and work on short presentations they can make to the entire class about the specific individuals they represent. I also ask students to meet me for short "reading conferences" so that before they actually write their pieces we can cover what they have learned and any questions that may arise. As we proceed through this role-playing exercise, I supplement the class readings by presenting film documentaries and artistic renditions of the Rosenberg case. Throughout this experience, students are taking notes and jotting down ideas that relate to the individuals they want to represent in writing. I also share an actual witness affidavit form, and we read excerpts from the opening statements used at the trial in 1951.

All of these writing and reading preparations help students discover and invent approaches for our class production of a mock trial, in which we give the Rosenbergs a second chance to defend themselves. Additionally, such writing-to-learn activities provide students with a more sophisticated understanding of the way rhetoric works in language, thus preparing them for the more complex and formal essay assignments that are required before the unit concludes. Just before the mock trial begins, for instance, students are asked to complete a critical essay that presents their analyses of the rhetorical choices made by particular authors we have studied. They can either compare and contrast the rhetorical choices made by two different authors in order to argue that one is more effective at making a case, or they can do a more expository essay that simply explains the way rhetoric operates in a particular text and for a particular author. At the close of the unit, after students have watched each other produce the many dramatic facets of a mock trial, including newspaper coverage and literary representations, I ask them to write a critical essay that explains their current understanding of some aspect of the case. The various write-to-learn activities, which have served to complicate their understanding of how language works rhetorically, prove useful to this final endeavor since most students now realize that a simple argument about guilt or innocence is the least interesting approach.

Such write-to-learn activities can be very useful, especially for composition courses with inquiry topics that revolve around the rhetorical nature of language. A class that looks closely at different historical and political events such as the Lindbergh kidnapping, the Vietnam War, or even Generation X, could model the kind of activities I have presented here. Several current anthologies would also well serve the type of approach that asks students to read and reflect on the way a single event or issue can lend itself to a multitude of interpretations. Bizzell and Herzberg's *Negotiating Difference* (1996) and Selzer's *Conversations* (1997), for example, appear suitable for such purposes because they represent topics of inquiry through a diverse range of contrastive readings.

Works Cited

Bizzell, Patricia, and Bruce Herzberg. *Negotiating Difference: Cultural Case Studies for Composition.* New York: Bedford, 1996.

Emig, Janet. "Writing as a Mode of Learning." *The Web of Meaning: Essays on Writing, Teaching, Learning, and Thinking.* Ed. Dixie Goswami and Maureen Butler. Upper Montclair, NJ: Boynton/Cook, 1983. 122–31.

Nizer, Louis. *The Implosion Conspiracy.* Garden City, NY: Doubleday, 1973.

Radosh, Ronald, and Joyce Milton. *The Rosenberg File: The Search for the Truth.* New York: Vintage, 1983.

Selzer, Jack. *Conversations: Readings for Writings.* 3rd ed. Boston: Allyn and Bacon, 1997.

Writing-to-Learn Prompts

EDITH M. BAKER

Bradley University

Edith Baker's writing prompts, like Mary Salibrici's role-playing exercises, ask students to explore issues from various writers' perspectives, and also require them to engage in critical thinking, such as the synthesis and analysis of complex ideas raised by their reading of American authors.

These writing-to-learn strategies for a beginning American writers course are based on Peter Elbow's philosophy that students need to write often and freely, without fear of evaluation or restriction. Britton's belief that writing allows for "shaping at the point of utterance" is the foundation for these writing to learn prompts. Their purpose is to foster fluency as they encourage students to probe critical questions about the content of American literature. Central to the design of the one-semester course is the philosophy that by developing students as American writers themselves, they will wrestle with some of the same concerns that other American writers have debated.

All voices will create a conversation on similar topics, such as the individual's relationship to society or the rugged individual's confrontation with nature. Thus, the first prompts listed below are open-ended and attempt to engage the self (Polanyi) before engaging the students in written texts. A variety of forms, from poems to autobiography, are also encouraged. Later, students can read what other American writers have said about similar issues, concerns, values, or beliefs. These prompts move from more open-ended protocols to more focused freewriting; the final examples attempt to challenge students to make connections and demonstrate mastery of course content.

Open-Ended Freewriting Topics

1. Discuss your favorite novel by an American writer. Why do you like the book? Do you remember anything about characters or themes?

2. The SAT II examination is now being marketed as a way for students to "achieve the American dream." Define the American dream. What are some of the personal characteristics that historically have distinguished Americans? What is your personal interpretation of the American dream? What do you hope happens to you in your lifetime? (After students write on this topic, a good activity is to read Martin Luther King Jr.'s "I Have a Dream" speech.)

3. Sometime before midterm, write freely on the most important things you have learned in this American writers course. Try to mention specific authors or texts.

4. Situate yourself in a place outdoors. Concentrate on your surroundings and begin to describe what you see around you. Give many details of your observations. Imagine you are Thoreau at Walden Pond and are walking the fence posts and being "an inspector of snow storms." Where do your musings take you? Allow time to immerse yourself in nature for at least forty-five minutes, and write down your thoughts in a stream-of-consciousness manner.

5. The instructor will provide selected passages from Thoreau's *Walden*. Read these before going into nature and see what thoughts emerge as you ponder your surroundings in a favorite place.

6. Freewrite on any topic of your choice, remembering that you are an American writer, too. You might want to try to imitate the style of Paine or the topics of concern for Bradstreet. If you were Ben Franklin, what would your eleven attributes of a de-

cent human be? (Remember, he added humility after his first list of ten!)

Because I prefer discussions with students who have read the material, some prompts simply require condensation of reading assignments due at class time. I might ask students to summarize a short story or an introductory chapter of Puritan history, for example. I have found that mentioning specifics, such as character development, tone, mood, conflict, plot development, symbolism, style, and theme, gives students more schema to trigger their thinking.

Modeling an author's style is another possibility for a writing-to-learn prompt. When reading Thoreau, students might copy ten sentences from his essays or *Walden* and discuss his writing style. This same technique of imitation is offered in the option to write a poem or chapter from their autobiography in the manner of Bradstreet, Cabeza de Vaca, Franklin, or Equiano. Likewise, one in-class prompt for a freewriting exercise asks students to write the first sentence of their autobiography. I challenge them to think about how they would define themselves. I read some beginnings from other autobiographies and ask students to identify what defines their lives. Is it a value or a belief? Knowing they will not be graded, students can freely reflect on these questions.

After the more open-ended prompts and imitation of models, I suggest focused freewritings. These prompts challenge students to make connections between the texts, define important concepts, and trace themes throughout U.S. history such as the idea of westering, the concept of the frontier, different responses to nature, and the evolution of the Puritan work ethic. These log entries are writing-to-learn activities that help students master major concepts of the course.

During the first class sessions, I present many ideas on a continuum and note that during the course of the semester we will be tracing the evolution of these ideas. I also tell students that their final examination will consist of taking one of these ideas and tracing the issue, value, concept, or belief through at least six writers and at least three centuries, developing their own thesis about the evolution of this concept. Student writings thus serve as invention activities, in the manner of Aristotle, throughout the course. These prompts require thinking skills of comparison/contrast, definition, and synthesis.

Text-Based Writing Prompts That Require Specific References to Readings

1. Discuss major characteristics of eighteenth-century writings: styles, topics, authors, concerns, voice, tone, etc. Develop your own theory about this period in American literature.

2. Read the works or transcriptions of Native American cultures: oral chants, writings, creation myths, songs, and rituals. Ponder the role of oral literature in American literature and the influence of Native American thought on our world today.

3. Summarize the similarities and differences in Hawthorne's text "Rappaccini's Daughter" and the PBS video of the same story. Note themes, style, symbolism, plot, and character development, as well as other points.

4. Write out succinctly Poe's theory of the "unity of effect" (handout). Apply this concept either to Crane's "The Open Boat" or Gilman's "The Yellow Wallpaper."

5. Having read some short stories by modern writers, what do you think has happened to Poe's theory of the unity of effect? Include specific references to at least three writers.

6. Discuss at least three authors' responses to nature. Compare and/or contrast topics, approaches, styles, concerns. Cite specific passages. Develop your own theory about the evolution of writers' concerns about nature.

7. Compare and/or contrast images (portraits) of women or men in at least three works of literature. How do you see roles of characters evolving?

8. Read one of the plays in the text by O'Neill or Tennessee Williams and discuss character development and themes.

9. Rent some of the recent movies based on the works of Henry James, such as *The Portrait of a Lady* or *The Wings of a Dove,* and discuss how the issues in the movie relate to the topics we are discussing in class.

10. Consider the idea of God as different authors have written about their relationship to a metaphysical or supernatural world. Men-

tion some of these writers and discuss how individuals' responses to "something greater than themselves" have changed over time. Cite specific authors and texts.

Works Cited

Britton, James, "Shaping at the Point of Utterance. *Reinventing the Rhetorical Tradition.* Ed. Aviva Freedman and Ian Pringle. Conway, AR: L&S Books, U of Central Arkansas (for Canadian Council of Teachers of English).

Elbow, Peter. *Writing with Power: Techniques for Mastering the Writing Process.* New York: Oxford UP, 1981.

Polanyi, Michael. *Personal Knowledge: Towards a Post-Critical Philosophy.* Chicago: U of Chicago P, 1958.

CHAPTER 5

GUIDING STUDENTS TO CONSTRUCT REFLECTIVE PORTFOLIOS

This chapter includes guidance to help students as they construct portfolios for writing courses. Contributors to this chapter explain how portfolios encourage students to see the value of the many activities they do in composition courses. That is, students think critically about their experiences with invention, revision, reading responses, peer responses to emerging texts, and the like.

A Writing Portfolio Assignment

PHYLLIS MENTZELL RYDER
George Washington University

Phyllis Ryder's assignment requires students to compose persuasive reflection essays that encourage them to trace their evolution as writers over the course of an academic term.

I used the following portfolio assignment in a composition course that incorporated multiple assignments in which students were to reflect on their own writing, their writing goals, and their achievements; all of this reflection built up to the final portfolio assignment, laid out below. The course itself demanded a variety of writing assignments, from an "intertextual essay" (in which students had to revise their essays several times, each time incorporating material from other classmates' work), to a somewhat ethnographic investigation and analysis of a discourse community, to an argument. They wrote short essays based on assignments in Sharon Crowley's *Ancient Rhetorics for Contemporary Students;* in these assignments, they experimented with various tropes and with shifting rhetorical situations. The following is a sample from the handout I give my students.

The Final Portfolio (a general overview)

Your final portfolio represents your work in the most advanced general writing course at the university. Be aware that your reader (maybe only me, maybe all instructors for English 306) will be looking at between twenty to sixty portfolios, so yours should be as concise and efficient as possible. Consider the following general guidelines as you compile your portfolio.

Contents
Persuasive Reflection
  You should use this 3- to 10-page essay to reflect on the writing you have done over the semester and to persuade your read-

ers that the portfolio demonstrates your learning and achievement in this course. In this piece, you should refer to the other selections in your portfolio and help your reader recognize how they serve to document your persuasive reflection. Realize that your readers may not look at any additional documents unless you refer to those documents in this reflection. (I'll hand out more specifics about this essay later.)

Formal Pieces

At least one of the three major projects, with all drafts attached. If a piece has been revised since it was turned in, be sure to include the original submission as well.

Additional Selections from this Semester

Include other samples of your writing which help to support your persuasive reflection. These might be excerpts from your journals, some of your short essay assignments, samples from your own self-reviews or your peer-reviews of others' work, sections of your in-class notes, etc.

Other Selections

You may wish to include selections from your initial portfolio (the one where you described your writing as you entered this class) or other pieces to which you refer in your persuasive essay to give background on your writing self.

Organization

You should arrange your portfolio in a way that effectively supports the major points of your persuasive reflection and that facilitates your readers' understanding of the collection of work.

More Specifics about the Persuasive Reflection Essay (PR)

Your Persuasive Reflection (PR) is the place for you to reflect on the writing you have done over the semester and to persuade your readers that the portfolio demonstrates your learning and achievement in this course. Because we all begin writing courses with different questions and concerns, and because we all learn different things about ourselves and our writing, the main focus of your portfolio and your PR will be specific to your development

—you must decide what you see as your main areas of development over the semester, and then you must persuade your readers (me and other English 306 teachers who may read this portfolio) of two things: first, that the progress you've achieved is a significant aspect of your development as a writer, and second, that you have achieved this through your work this semester. You should refer to the Sharon Crowley textbook and to our class discussions as support for the first part of this argument. You should refer to specific writing you've done in the course—whether journal entries, short essays, or any of the longer projects—as support for the second part of the argument.

The PR is the most important part of your portfolio because it is the guide your readers will use to navigate the rest of the portfolio. In your PR, you will persuade your readers that they should understand the other materials in the portfolio. For example, you might include in your portfolio some sections of early work that you now see as flawed and some later work in which you have significantly improved on those areas of your writing. In your PR, you can explain to your readers that they should see the relationship among those pieces of writing, and you can convince them through your own reflections on your writing that you understand your writing well and can see the developments in your work. Without the PR, they will not know that you see one piece as flawed and the other as good, and they will not know why you included them.

Keep in mind that your readers will have up to sixty portfolios to read. Therefore, you need to make sure your whole portfolio—the PR and the accompanying supporting work—is well organized.

Some Thoughts on How to Get Started

To prepare to assemble your portfolio and your reflective persuasive essay, take notes about your overall changes (either in writing or in thinking) in this course as you review your work in the following areas:

- Look through your journals and notice what writing experiments you did, which were successful in your opinion, and whether you were able to transfer any of them into essays.

- Look through your analyses of your processes of writing essays (Short Essays 1, 6, and 8) and note the patterns and the differences—has your approach to writing changed?

- Look through your self-evaluation sheets and notice any changes in how you answered various sections (especially purpose, strengths, and risks): Has your approach to writing changed? Have you discovered some strategies for certain situations; which do, or do not, work in the situations? What factors contributed to the different levels of success in your essays?

- Look over your initial portfolio and consider how you would define yourself as a "writer" now.

- Skim through Crowley and jot down the concepts you feel are most important; explain how you have or have not incorporated these concepts into your writing and why.

How might you classify or categorize the changes you see? Which of the many things you've written for this class will you draw on to demonstrate your attempts? Successes? Current understandings of what didn't work so well?

Work Cited

Crowley, Sharon. *Ancient Rhetorics for Contemporary Students*. New York: Macmillan, 1994.

Portfolio Requirements for Writing and Discourse

C. BETH BURCH

State University of New York at Binghamton

Beth Burch's assignment illustrates how to structure a first-year composition course around a portfolio approach for the assessment of student writing.

Your portfolio is the record of your writing process, your writing accomplishments, and your thoughts about writing for this semester. Your primary goals for this course are to learn about yourself as a writer, to become a stronger writer, and to create a portfolio that presents your writing strengths and documents your growth as a writer. My goal is to help you in these endeavors.

Criteria for Assessment

Near the end of the course when I assess your portfolio for a grade, I will consider your growth and change (as evidenced by your portfolio); the quality of individual papers; the breadth of writing experience (illustrated by the choices you made for the portfolio); the amount of work you have done (signified by the number of significant drafts); and the level of reflection and understanding realized in your writing processes. I am looking for excellent writing, self-awareness, and professional presentation.

My assessment of your portfolio will be the final of several assessments of your work throughout the semester. Your writers' group will assess your writing. Outsiders may assess your writing. And you will have a chance not only to assess yourself but also to help create the rubric or assessment instrument I will use with your portfolio.

Your Concern about Feedback and Response

Although you will not receive a formal grade on your writing until the end of the semester, along the way you will get lots of advice for revision from your writers' group and from me—and from writers outside our class as well. You will be asked to turn in your working portfolio for a "dry run" at midterm and to have a portfolio conference with me then. If you would like a sense of the grade that you are earning, you may on any two occasions during the semester ask for an oral, nonbinding, "as is" grade on a draft.

What to Put in Your Portfolio

Be prepared to include these items in your final portfolio at the end of the semester:

- *Table of contents.* The table of contents should provide an overview of the contents of the entire portfolio and help readers find specific pieces of writing. Don't forget the page numbers!

- *Several pieces written specifically for this course (with drafts).* Toward the end of the semester, the class will work together to create a rubric for assessing portfolios and in the process determine how many major pieces will go into the portfolio. In the meantime, though, you must turn in drafts of all assigned pieces. It is possible that your portfolio may contain (besides these major pieces) a free-choice piece, so you might be thinking about writing that you have done or are doing outside this class as a possible component of the final portfolio. If, for instance, you write a poem or short story during the semester, you may include that in your portfolio if the class decides to allow a free-choice piece.

You'll probably want most of your portfolio pieces to represent your best work. You may, however, consider including a piece that has not developed as you hoped, along with writers' group work and an analysis of your writing process on that particular piece. Regardless of whether you have a "best work" portfolio or a mixed portfolio, you must include dated drafts.

- *Reflective analysis, including an introductory piece* that describes the contents of the portfolio and your rationale for its arrangement. This introductory piece must be self-reflective; it should articulate what you learned from assembling the portfolio and what you know about yourself as a writer. You should determine the best way to include self-assessment and reflection in other places throughout the portfolio as well.

- *Acknowledgments page,* wherein you list people who assisted you in any way with your writing. This may include friends, roommates, writing center tutors, parents, former teachers, librarians, etc.

- *Other pieces that you consider appropriate* (comments from reviewers or readers, index, art, etc.): these are optional.

Due Date

Throughout the semester, we will have due dates for drafts of pieces and for writers' group review; members of your writing group and I expect your drafts to be ready on time. Your completed portfolio is due in my office on Friday, December 15, by 4:30 P.M. You may then retrieve your portfolio and confer with me about it on Thursday, December 21, or Friday, December 22, or next semester. Call for an appointment, please.

We'll talk about compiling the portfolio throughout the semester, but don't hesitate to ask any time about aspects of this project that confuse or trouble you.

The Importance of Student Portfolio Presentations in Composition Courses

LISA CAHILL
Arizona State University

In this essay, Lisa Cahill provides a rationale for the use of portfolios that considers her students' investment in their evolution as writers, and teachers' investment in stressing shared reflections on that evolution.

Karen Mills-Courts and Minda Rae Amiran discuss the metacognitive benefits of portfolios in the context of the General College Program (GCP) at State University of New York College at Fredonia. They decided to implement portfolios after a program assessment revealed that their "students were not approaching their own learning consciously enough and were operating much too often on unexamined basic assumptions about both the learning process and the content involved in that process" (102). In making this decision, the college recognized portfolios as being an effective way for students to "think about their own thinking" (102) by encouraging students to use or practice what they learn and to write about what they learn.

Mills-Courts and Amiran's explanation of how portfolios are used across their campus points to the student-centered benefits of using portfolios. Often the benefits tend to be transferable regardless of the subject or the course for which they are used. The common denominator in portfolio creation, regardless of the subject or course, is writing. The authors point to the fact that writing "can encourage students to analyze and synthesize their thinking" (105) and can also increase students' sense of ownership, not only in terms of the work produced but also in terms of their own development and education. Portfolios are a good way to provide students with a sense of symmetry between courses; they provide an additional exigency for students to designate goals—goals that can be achieved in the next semester or in the following years. Additionally, portfolios allow teachers to "see with clarity the effects of their efforts in the classroom" (107). In this way, portfolios also provide teachers with a sense of symmetry between the courses they teach; they give teachers a chance to theorize their practices and to make adjustments both for their own sake and for the sake of their students.

As teachers we decided to reflect on our portfolio practices in the context of our composition classes for two reasons: (1) to evaluate our implementation of portfolios and (2) to share the processes we asked our students to engage in. When students are given the responsibility and freedom of choosing materials for portfolio inclusion (even when basic guidelines are provided) and are asked to provide a rationale for their choices (both inclusions *and* exclusions), they can reflect on macro issues that transcend the immediate context of the course. In the case of composition courses, portfolios give students the chance to identify and examine their writing strengths while also providing them with a forum for setting goals that will continue to develop their writing capabilities. Students can also confront their writing processes and see firsthand the benefits attached to process work—invention, drafting, peer review—when they look at the bulk of writing they have produced in one semester. Often these lessons are more powerful and last longer when students make the discoveries on their own and are then asked to (a) organize materials chronologically, topically, thematically, etc.; (b) create a table of contents, an overall portfolio design, and commentaries that preview or explain what appears in each section of the portfolio; and (c) compose a cover letter to reflect their achievements, frustrations, challenges, and goals for writing done in the class and, often most important, for writing yet to be done in their academic, professional, civic, and personal lives.

Portfolios provide a place for students to think about the writing they have done and will do; they also provide them with a chance to think about the way they think about writing. This is not a form of circular thinking. Rather, it is a reflective opportunity and an important step in "develop[ing] students' metacognitive skills, one that would help them achieve an awareness of how they 'do' intellectual work" (102).

Portfolios developed over the course of one semester can also provide students with an immediate sense of pride and accomplishment. At the same time, teachers can enhance their own metacognitive awareness of their teaching and their portfolio practices by experimenting with the portfolio genre.

I began teaching composition at Northern Arizona University where midterm and final portfolios were built into the curriculum of its composition program. The only stipulation the program made was that both midterm and final portfolios be read and evaluated by a group of three to four teaching assistants. This process did not necessarily require students to prepare and turn in anything more than a physical representation of their work—including a cover letter, drafts, peer-review responses, and final versions of papers. There was room in my classroom schedule to have enabled students to share and discuss their work with their peers and with me, but at the time I was not aware of the underlying necessity for facilitating such an activity. I enjoyed meeting with my teaching colleagues to review our students' portfolios because it further developed and strengthened our sense of community. The group evaluation process also provided me opportunities to see ways that both my colleagues *and* their students handled assignments differently than my students and I did.

When I began teaching composition at Arizona State University, final portfolios were required but midterm portfolios were not. Although the composition program did not require its teaching assistants to engage in group evaluations of their students' portfolios, this did not lessen the program's ability to foster a strong community among teaching assistants or to provide for collaborative opportunities. My teaching benefited tremendously from collaborative sessions with my teaching colleagues, and I began to realize that my students needed the same opportunity. One of my colleagues, Mary Stone, had also taught at Northern Arizona University, and she encouraged me to make midterm portfolios a part of my composition classes. Additionally, she provided me with a description of the writing portfolio, which I in turn adapted and made available to my own students. She shared her belief in the importance of having students step back from their work in the middle of the semester in order to forecast ways of enhancing their strengths and achieving new goals. Mary was conducting individual midterm portfolio conferences during which students engaged in a reflective discussion of their work with her—a discussion supplemented with a visual presentation of their work to date.

I took her advice, and the results were wonderful. Students met with me for one fifteen- to twenty-minute session and were responsible for setting the course of our discussion; they also had to direct my reading and understanding of their portfolios. For the visual portion of their presentation, I asked students to organize their materials to make a statement about their writing process and their growth as writers. Based on our composition program's requirements, I asked them to include the following materials:

- table of contents
- cover letter
- in-class assignments, homework assignments, writing log entries, and other reflections on their writing
- final versions of essays including selected invention work, drafting, feedback, and revision plans
- commentary on each piece or group of materials in the portfolio
- one-page, single-spaced revision plan for one essay discussing how they would revise it if they had the opportunity to do so again

For the oral portion of their presentation, I encouraged students to make notes to guide their discussions. Students highlighted the ideas in their cover letters, explained the rationale behind the organization of their materials, and elaborated on their writing goals for the course and beyond the course. I provided students with the following concepts to consider during their presentations:

- Show that you are ready to move on to other writing situations (show your effort, growth, and seriousness).

◆ Reflect on differences and similarities in writing genres, invention, peer review, drafting, and the writing process.

◆ Show your conception of portfolio as its own genre (e.g., it has its own purpose and forms of organization).

◆ Demonstrate another level of audience awareness.

During these one-to-one meetings, I saw a new level of engagement and interest in a majority of my students. They had an opportunity to talk about what they found most useful in the course and about components that were not necessarily working for them. Yet they were quick to supply me with suggestions and ideas. I in turn had the chance to compliment them on good work and pose personalized writing questions. It was a learning experience for the students and most definitely for me.

Based on the success of the midterm portfolio conferences, I wanted to do something just as effective for students' final portfolio projects. I decided to expand my students' audience beyond that of just the student and myself. This time I wanted students to know what all of their classmates had accomplished and thought during the semester. To do this, we met during our hour-and-fifty-minute final exam period and worked in small and large groups. I divided students into three groups of six, each with one of the following three questions to discuss for ten to twelve minutes:

◆ You have worked with four definitive genres: remembered event, remembered person, academic profile, and explaining a concept. Each has its own unique features. In general, how would you characterize the portfolio as a genre? What are its attributes?

◆ How would you characterize your portfolio according to the following writer-reader-based prose continuum? (See Flower.)

Writer-based prose ⟵──────────⟶ Reader-based prose

◆ What would potential audiences learn about you based on the topics you chose to write about in each essay and, in particular, on how you specifically rendered your subject (i.e., in what light)?

These questions were designed to encourage students to think beyond the scope of our classroom and to reflect on the significance of the writing they had done over the fifteen-week period. Following their small-group discussions, each group took its turn at the front of the room, each group member presenting his or her work to the class as a whole. Each group of six students had approximately twenty minutes to present. The same midterm portfolio guidelines were in effect. After each group member highlighted portions of his or her portfolio and discussed goals and growth, the group presented its responses to its question.

What I discovered was students' genuine interest in hearing what their peers had to say and in seeing what they had produced. This large-scale exchange made it possible for students to validate some of their own practices and also to learn some new methods they could adapt. My students had worked in small groups for class discussions and in pairs for peer review throughout the semester, but we had never really engaged in such a complete and integrated discussion. They were most respectful to one another during individual presentations, and the spirit of collaboration during the group discussions was strong. The portfolio presentations not only made students aware of the amount of work and progress they had made, but the presentations also made students more aware of their peers. I am currently working on new ways to encourage student collaboration and interaction during and after portfolio construction in an effort to expand students' notions of audience and genre.

Works Cited

Flower, Linda. "Writer-Based Prose: A Cognitive Basis for Problems in Writing." *College English* 41 (1979): 19–37.

Mills-Courts, Karen, and Minda Rae Amiran. "Metacognition and the Use of Portfolios." *Portfolios: Process and Product.* Ed. Pat Belanoff and Marcia Dickson. Portsmouth: Boynton/Cook, 1991. 101–12.

Group Portfolio Presentations

ROCHELLE RODRIGO BLANCHARD, AMY D'ANTONIO,
AND LISA CAHILL
Arizona State University

These authors have collaborated on developing methods for conducting group portfolio presentations that require students to reflect on and demonstrate the skills and concepts they have acquired in their composition classes.

The Idea

This portfolio assignment is different from most because the students present their work to a panel of five other students and two instructors. During a fifty-minute period, each instructor is responsible for the evaluation of three student portfolios, and each of the six students is responsible for a five-minute presentation of his or her portfolio. This leaves the entire group twenty minutes to discuss all the students' portfolios. Some instructors require their students to pass out copies of their cover letters. Other instructors require the students to pass out copies of their table of contents.

Logistics

At first it might appear that the administrative logistics for this type of a conference project would be difficult; we promise, they are not. We first used our regular classrooms as meeting locations, figuring that each classroom was large enough to hold two groups for each session. For example, Lutfi and Amy, plus Shelley and Lillian, met with three students from each instructor's class in Lutfi's classroom during his usual class hour (if it did not conflict with any of their schedules). The difficulty was that we ran out of classroom space. At this point, we needed to request rooms during the hours that none of the instructors taught.

Each instructor had approximately forty-four students. Because each instructor was responsible for three students during every fifty-minute session, each instructor would have to meet for fifteen fifty-minute sessions. Since, however, we all had under the forty-four-student maximum, ultimately we needed only fourteen fifty-minute sessions per instructor. We conducted the presentation sessions over a three-day period, meeting a total of six times on both a Monday and a Wednesday and twice on the intervening Tuesday. All of us taught on Mondays, Wednesdays, and Fridays, which meant that most of the students wanted to meet only on one of those days.

Amy D'Antonio's Portfolio Assignment Prompt for English 101

(Amy D'Antonio's assignment draws heavily on the writing outcomes that Irv Peckham describes in Chapter 2.)

Over the course of this semester, you will develop a variety of important skills. The portfolio is your opportunity to concretely demonstrate your mastery of those skills. Because only some skills will be evident in any given project you complete for the course, you need to provide a sampling of all your work in this course to demonstrate what you've accomplished as a reader, writer, thinker, and learner. In general, the portfolio provides you an opportunity to illustrate how you make informed choices as a writer.

Portfolio Overview

The portfolio project for this semester has two components: First, an introduction that discusses your changes (and, we hope, your growth) as a writer over the course of the semester. The idea here is to both explore and demonstrate in what specific ways you have further developed your reading, writing, and thinking skills as you "wrote your way" through this class. Second, the portfolio project asks you to compose a revision plan—how you'd go about revising one of the writing projects you constructed during the semester. Keep in mind that you do not do the actual revision; rather, you discuss what you would do if you had the chance to revise the project.

Please include the final version of the text with my comments and then, attached to these, a detailed discussion of how you are seeing the paper differently and how you would go about revising it now.

Be sure to comment on audience, purpose, goals, and so on for the essay and provide specific examples of the changes you'd like to make.

The Project

To complete the portfolio for this course, you will need to save your written work throughout the semester—invention work, drafts of projects, "final" versions of projects, postcomposing reflections on each project, writing folder entries, written peer responses, and the like. You do not, however, need to submit all of your written work in the portfolio. Rather, submit only whatever you consider necessary to demonstrate your accomplishments as a writer. You also need to submit an introduction in which you explain what you've chosen to include in the portfolio and what each item in the portfolio demonstrates. For this portion of your introduction, you need to be as detailed as possible, using examples from your writing projects to illustrate your growth as a writer—what you've learned from the invention, peer review, and other activities, and from the final "production" of each writing project. Your introduction should also include a paragraph or two in which you look to the future, commenting on how you plan to use your rhetorical knowledge and composing skills in your academic, professional, personal, and/or civic lives. Your revision plan should include examples and details of specific changes you'd make in the composition if you were to revise it.

Using Your Writing Folder for This Project

Your writing folder is a crucial tool for constructing your portfolio. First, you will want to skim it cover to cover to find excerpts demonstrating particular kinds of knowledge and skills that you've acquired in the course. Second, you should carefully read each of the postcomposing reflections you wrote when you submitted each of the course projects during the semester. Third, as you have done all semester, you will want to use the writing folder to reflect informally on the portfolio project as it emerges. You might want to set up a special section of the writing folder with a heading something like "Ideas for the Portfolio."

Expectations

To construct an effective portfolio, you need to make wise choices as you select written work to illustrate what you've learned and accomplished in this course. To do that, you need to listen carefully to your peers, who can help you decide which pieces of your written work best represent you as a writer, reader, thinker, and learner. While we expect you to have taken steps toward developing as a writer, some of those steps will be smaller than others. It's unreasonable to expect that all of your strides have been big. Learning to write effectively is a lifelong journey. By the end of this semester, you will have made a small portion of that journey. Help us see what that portion has been like by explaining in detail what you've gleaned through constructing your writing projects throughout the semester.

Oral Presentation

To prepare your five-minute oral presentation, you should determine which portions of your introduction best summarize your progress as a writer, reader, thinker, and learner. Bring eight copies of your table of contents with you so that each member of your audience can follow along with the examples you use to support the claims of progress you make in your introduction. Be sure that each component of your portfolio is labeled in accordance with the name you give that piece in the introduction. Be prepared to answer any questions the audience might pose regarding your portfolio. I expect you to respond thoughtfully to other students' presentations, so bring a notebook and a pen to jot down any questions or comments that arise as each student presents. Remember, you are presenting to your audience your best work, the work of which you are most proud. A carefully prepared presentation that includes both an eloquent verbal summary and a neatly organized and clearly labeled professional presentation of materials will influence your audience to your advantage.

To begin assembling your portfolio and drafting your portfolio introduction, consider each of the following possible areas of progress. For those areas in which you have made progress, locate a place in your written work that clearly demonstrates that progress. Places to look include your invention work, rough drafts, final drafts, revision plans, writing folder entries, peer reviews, and any other written material you have generated for this class. The more areas of progress you present convincingly, the more easily you will be able to persuade your audience that you have carefully evaluated your own work and that, therefore, your portfolio is well done. Remember, you are not limited to discussing only the areas of progress listed here. Any skill you have developed over the course of this class is appropriate for inclusion in the portfolio.

RHETORICAL KNOWLEDGE

- ◆ Focus on a purpose.

- ◆ Recognize and write to a specified audience.

- ◆ Recognize differences in communicative situations and respond appropriately to those different situations.

- ◆ Use conventions of format, structure, and language appropriate to the purpose of the texts you write.

- ◆ Adopt appropriate voice, tone, and level of formality.

- ◆ Have a sense of what genres are and how they differ.

- ◆ Know that different genres have different rhetorical purposes.

- ◆ Write in several different genres.

- ◆ Acquire the ability to treat the same information in multiple formats.

- Learn the main features of writing in particular fields.

- Learn the main uses of writing in particular fields.

- Learn the expectations of readers of writing in particular fields.

CRITICAL THINKING, READING, AND WRITING

- Use writing and reading for inquiry, learning, thinking, and communicating.

- Learn the steps necessary to carry out a writing assignment or task, including locating, evaluating, analyzing, and synthesizing appropriate primary and secondary sources.

- Investigate, report, and document existing knowledge, as well as knowledge you develop yourself.

- Understand the relationships between language, knowledge, culture, history, and politics, and how different forms of language enter into these relationships in different ways.

- Learn the uses of writing as a thinking method as well as a communicative performance.

- Learn the interactions between critical thinking, critical reading, and writing.

- Learn the relationships between language, knowledge, culture, history, and politics in particular disciplines and cultures.

PROCESSES

- Be aware that it usually takes multiple drafts to create and complete a successful text.

- Understand that writing is an ongoing process that permits writers to use later invention and rethinking to improve all aspects of what they are writing.

- Develop strategies for generating, revising, editing, and

proofreading texts as appropriate within the development of a specific text.

♦ Understand the collaborative and social aspects of writing processes.

♦ Learn to critique your own and others' writing.

♦ Learn to balance the advantages of relying on others with the responsibility of doing your part.

♦ Use a variety of media, including standard computerized media in particular, in ways that permit you to make your writing acceptable to a wide variety of readers.

♦ Learn to build final results in stages.

♦ Learn to review work in progress in collaborative peer groups for purposes other than editing.

♦ Learn to save extensive editing until invention and development work have been completed.

♦ Learn to use the media, including computerized media in particular, commonly used to engage in communicative transactions in particular fields.

KNOWLEDGE OF CONVENTIONS

♦ Develop knowledge of genre conventions ranging from structure and paragraphing to tone and mechanics.

♦ Aquire knowledge and conventions for different kinds of writing and occasions for writing.

♦ Pactice appropriate means of documenting the knowledge you incorporate into your texts.

♦ Control such surface features as syntax, grammar, punctuation, and spelling.

♦ Learn the ways in which particular disciplines differ from others in conventions of usage and documentation.

♦ Learn how better outcomes in conventions can be achieved.

◆ Learn the main conventions that are valued by writers in particular fields, especially conventions of specialized vocabulary, format, and documentation.

CHAPTER 6

STRATEGIES FOR COURSE MANAGEMENT

This chapter includes perspectives on concerns that inevitably arise in any college or university classroom. The contributors offer strategies for maintaining classroom civility, orchestrating small- and large-group discussions, and discouraging plagiarism. Drawing on their own years of experience in the classroom, the mentors in this chapter approach these topics with sensitivity to the needs of teachers and students alike.

Fostering Classroom Civility

Lynn Langer Meeks, Joyce Kinkead, Keith VanBezooyen,
and Erin Edwards
Utah State University

*Holding students accountable to policies for classroom con-
duct can be a difficult yet crucial aspect of effective teaching.
Here, the authors describe strategies they have developed for
designing and enforcing such policies.*

The issue of classroom civility increasingly receives attention
nationwide (e.g., May 1, 1998, *Chronicle of Higher Education*
letters to the editor; Amada's *Coping with the Disruptive Student*) as faculty complain about students reading the campus
newspaper or answering cell phones during class. Many faculty
went to college during the days of in loco parentis and rebelled
against that approach; however, some institutions have found
they must reclaim the classroom, besieged by a small group of
students who affect the overall learning environment. "University Plans Remedial Work in Manners" proclaims an April 14,
1995, *Chronicle* headline as Washington State University com-
bats "rampant rudeness" (Monaghan). Conrad Kottak of the
University of Michigan cites "teleconditioning" (10) as one reason why a student felt empowered to say to him, "Gimme five,
Connie, baby."

Rather than returning to the concept of the university as parent, we prefer to ground our discussions of classroom civility in
the idea that the university is, in part, accountable for preparing
responsible citizens. Disruptive students tend to see themselves
as individuals with rights or—as they frequently voice—custom-
ers who have paid the freight. We want our students to acquire
"the democratic virtues of honesty, tolerance, empathy, generosity, teamwork, and social responsibility" (Astin B1).

In our reform of general education, for instance, we penned
a philosophy statement that defined goals for developing "citizen-
scholars." In addition to formulating a curricular program that fostered those goals, we found that we needed to articulate explicitly to students what the expectations are for civility in the classroom,
laying out the rights and responsibilities of both students and

instructor that build on the institution's Student Code. Civility in cyberspace—an extension of the classroom—is also a growing concern. Earlier, the Writing Program had penned a plagiarism statement that students must sign for each assignment—again as the result of increased instances of academic dishonesty.

Because first-year English is often a gateway class for students, a document on "Student-Instructor Expectations" has been developed by Writing Program Director Dr. Lynn Meeks and a committee of graduate teaching instructors. The committee consisted of two first-year, first-semester graduate instructors, Erin Edwards and Keith VanBezooyen. Edwards and VanBezooyen developed the first draft of the document, "Student-Instructor Expectations: Toward a Civil and Productive English Classroom Environment," based on their experiences with student incivility and VanBezooyen's extensive background in counseling.

VanBezooyen used his experience as a counselor to ground "Student-Instructor Expectations" on the work of William Glasser. Drawing on Glasser's philosophy explained in *The Quality School* and *Choice Theory in the Classroom,* VanBezooyen felt that rather than a "rule rich" document full of "thou shalt nots," our civility document should contain as few rules as possible. He explained that Glasser's philosophy is one of problem solving, which emphasizes responsibility, rather than an adversarial relationship, which emphasizes blame. With that in mind, he and Edwards set down to work. Writing along with them were Meeks, Associate Dean Joyce Kinkead, and two assistant directors of writing who reviewed drafts of the document.

First, Edwards and VanBezooyen informally surveyed the first- and second-year graduate instructors for suggestions on what should be in the document. The survey found that there was no real consensus. Some wanted very strict rules; others wanted total control over their classrooms and no departmental policy, no matter how benign. Edwards and VanBezooyen were at first hard-pressed to develop a document that would give some instructors something hard and fast to fall back on while accommodating those who wanted to run the classroom their own way. The committee's vision, however, was of a document that contained the language of invitation, conciliation, and mutually shared responsibility for classroom management.

Several months of work, discussion, revising, and reviewing by the original authors and the graduate instructors in the English department resulted in the document reprinted below. The opening text, consisting of sections on "Student-Instructor Partnership," "What Students Can Expect from the Instructor," "What Instructors Can Expect from Students," and "Behaviors That Promote Success and Quality Work," prefaces a more punitive-sounding section titled "English Department and University Policies Regarding Nonproductive Behavior." This section lists the instructor's options in dealing with uncivil behavior that persists or cannot be solved using Glasser's model. We found this a helpful compromise between those who had lobbied for a rule-based document and those who preferred a more invitational and conciliatory document, or none at all.

The document has been printed in the English 1010 Handbook, which every 1010 student is expected to purchase. Accompanying this document is the form "Addendum/Handbook Awareness." Some graduate instructors ask their students to sign and initial this form to indicate that they have read and understand the handbook. Other graduate instructors give their students "quizzes" over the handbook to encourage them to read and review it.

As a department and college, we feel strongly that we need to set expectations not only for students but also for the instructors, and to make clear to students that everyone is responsible for a smoothly running, productive classroom. We hope that our document and our modeling of appropriate civil behavior will show students that a good learning environment is the result of a partnership between students and teacher.

Student-Instructor Expectations: Toward a Civil and Productive English Classroom Environment

Student-Instructor Partnership

Much of the work instructors and students do will be in class; therefore the student-instructor partnership is central to a positive learning environment. Both the instructor and the student are responsible for maintaining a classroom atmosphere where courtesy and goodwill prevail. This means that instructors and students are kind, listen to what others have to say, and do not "put others down," or show disrespect. In some classes, instruction and communication carry over to cyberspace (e.g., e-mail, Internet); the same expectations for behavior extend to that learning environment.

Students and instructors can maintain a positive learning environment by constantly working to improve the quality of interpersonal relationships. If at any time the student or teacher feels that the relationship needs improvement, he or she should approach the problem appropriately, by saying something like, "It seems that there is a problem here. I would like to talk to you and see if you agree." The university expects that participation in collaborative class management will contribute to students' development as citizen-scholars.

What Students Can Expect from the Instructor

There are many things instructors can do to help set a positive tone for the classroom:

- Respect and show courtesy for students regardless of their gender, race, religion, or sexual orientation.
- Offer assistance to students when needed.
- Listen attentively when students "have the floor."
- Listen to suggestions for improving the classroom environment.
- Arrive on time and prepared.
- Inform students of changes in the syllabus.
- Work on solving problems if they arise.

What Instructors Can Expect from Students

There are many ways in which students help set a positive tone for the classroom:

- Respect and show courtesy to classmates and the instructor regardless of gender, race, religion, or sexual orientation.

- Ask for assistance when needed.

- Listen attentively when another student or the instructor "has the floor."

- Listen to suggestions for improving the classroom environment.

- Arrive on time and prepared.

- Make note of changes in the syllabus.

- Work on solving problems if they arise.

Behaviors That Promote Success and Quality Work

Students who succeed and produce quality work in English 1010, as well as other university classes,

- read the 1010 Handbook (syllabus) and the instructor's addendum thoroughly.

- complete assigned homework on time.

- read the assignments carefully and critically.

- participate in discussions about readings.

- complete written assignments before due dates to compensate for possible technical difficulties.

- participate in peer reviews.

- offer collaborative assistance to others.

- respond respectfully to instructor and classmates.

- show consideration and respect for students who are different in gender, race, religion, or sexual orientation.

- come to class on time and with a positive attitude.

- attend to and write down the instructor's in-class statements about assignments.

English Department and University Policies Regarding Nonproductive Behavior

The following behaviors are considered violations of University Standards as prohibited by *The Code of Policies and Procedures for Students at Utah State University* (1993), Article V, Section 3: "Obstructing or disrupting instruction, research, administration, meetings, processions, or other University activities including its public service functions on or off campus, or authorized non-university activities on University premises. This includes aiding, abetting, or encouraging another person to engage in such activity. . . .

"Wrongfully inflicting physical or mental duress, harm, or abuse upon another person, including but not limited to verbal abuse, threats and intimidation, sexual violence, arson, and murder" (10–11).

If an instructor finds that a student's behavior obstructs or disrupts classroom instruction or out-of-class conferences, the instructor may:

- Give an oral warning.

- Request a conference with the student.

- Give a written warning.

- Request a mediator.

- Ask the student to complete a behavior contract.

- Refer the student to the Counseling Center.

- Ask the student to meet with the University Discipline Officer.

- Ask the student to meet with the Vice President of Student Services.

These methods will be used as the instructor sees fit, bearing in mind that the goal during a dispute is a quick, fair, and amicable resolution of the difficulty whenever possible.

Addendum/Handbook Awareness

Your instructor may ask you to initial, sign, and turn in this form:

_____ I have read and understand the class addendum.

_____ I understand that I must arrive in class on time.

_____ I understand that attendance in this class is part of my grade and I will make every attempt to come to class.

_____ I realize that this class requires daily reading and writing assignments, and I am committed to doing my homework.

_____ I understand that participating in class is part of my grade. I understand that means working in groups and volunteering responses to questions asked in class, as well as appropriate contributions to discussions.

_____ I know that I am responsible for assignments as outlined in the English 1010 Handbook and in-class statements made by my instructor regarding assignments and the due dates.

_____ I understand that when I have specific questions regarding my grades or participation, it is my responsibility to discuss them with my instructor outside of class.

_____ I understand that it is not acceptable to disrupt or obstruct instruction in the classroom with inappropriate behavior such as talking when the instructor or other students are talking.

_____ I understand that a good learning environment is the result of a partnership between the instructor and the student, and I am willing to make an effort to make that partnership a positive one.

_____ I understand that I must show courtesy during conferences with my instructor.

Signed: _____

Print Name: _____

Instructor's Name: _____

Date: _____

Works Cited

Amada, Gerald. *Coping with the Disruptive Student: A Practical Model.* Asheville, NC: College Administration Publications, 1994.

Astin, Alexander. "What Higher Education Can Do in the Cause of Citizenship." *Chronicle of Higher Education* 6 Oct. 1995: B1–B2.

DeWitt, Robert C. Letter. *Chronicle of Higher Education* 1 May 1998: B8.

Glasser, William. *Choice Theory in the Classroom.* New York: HarperPerennial, 1988.

———. *The Quality School: Managing Students without Coercion.* New York: HarperPerennial, 1998.

Hunt, Tamara L. Letter. *Chronicle of Higher Education* 1 May 1998: B8.

Koodin, Jeffrey F. Letter. *Chronicle of Higher Education* 1 May 1998: B8.

Kottak, Conrad Phillip. "Teaching in the Post Modern Classroom." *General Anthropology* 1 (1994): 10–11.

Minner, Sam. Letter. *Chronicle of Higher Education* 1 May 1998: B7.

Monaghan, Peter. "University Plans Remedial Work in Manners." *Chronicle of Higher Education* 14 April 1995: A39.

Parker, Kate Horsely. Letter. *Chronicle of Higher Education* 1 May 1998: B7–B8.

Romesburg, H. Charles. Letter. *Chronicle of Higher Education* 1 May 1998: B8.

Stone, Marta E. Letter. *Chronicle of Higher Education* 1 May 1998: B7.

Course Management Guidelines

REBECCA MOORE HOWARD
Syracuse University

Rebecca Howard developed the following course management guidelines while serving as director of composition at Texas Christian University. These guidelines are full of useful, sound practices for establishing expectations for students.

General Principle: When in Doubt, Err on the Student's Side

Grading

Keep your grading policy as simple as possible.
Include your grading policy, in all its detail, in your syllabus.
Turn your course grades in on schedule.

Attendance

Proposed revision of our common attendance policy: "*Attendance:* In English 1803, 1833, and 2803, only official university absences are excused. Students in English 1803, 1833, and 2803 who accumulate three weeks' unexcused absences will automatically fail the course." Official university absences are posted on a list on the bulletin board in 314 Reed.

Make clear to your students at the beginning of the semester—and remind them occasionally during it—that you do not excuse absences; instead, your grading policy accounts for a few of the unavoidable absences that many people encounter from time to time. Thus, they should not cut class, because later in the semester they may have an illness or emergency that takes them over your absence maximum, and they will not be "excused" for these unavoidable absences, except in the most extreme circumstances.

As students approach an F for their workshop grade, send them a warning letter. When students miss three weeks of classes and earn an F for their workshop grade (and hence for the course),

1. Send them a letter that says, "Your absence from English [course and section] on [date] brings your total number of unexcused absences to [number] for the term. According to English department policy, these accumulated absences give you an automatic F for the course."

2. At the same time, send copies of your letter to the director of composition, the chair of English, and the dean of campus life.

When students have earned an F for your course, they still have the right to attend it—unless they are disruptive.

You may also reduce students' grades for absences under the three-week maximum.

Consider alternatives to attendance grade reductions. An in-class writing policy such as the following can accomplish similar work: "On fourteen class days, class will begin with a twenty-minute in-class journal assignment. At the end of the twenty minutes, all journals will be handed in. Your ten best grades will count toward the calculation of your course grade." If these journals constitute an appreciable part of the course grade and if you administer in-class journals on unannounced days at the beginning of the class period, accepting only those journal entries that are handed in when you announce that time is up, your students have a powerful incentive to prepare for class, to come to class, and to arrive on time. If you drop their lowest grades (including the zeros for the days on which they are absent), you don't have to get into the business of excusing absences. (You are, however, required to allow students with official university absences to make up the work.)

Include your attendance policy, in all its detail, in your syllabus.

Think very hard about tardy policies before you implement them.

Syllabus

Distribute your syllabus, containing grading and attendance policies, on the first day of class. Do not modify or add to your grading policy or your attendance policy during the semester.

Assignments

If you give assignments that require students to interview people, make sure the students clearly identify their task and purpose to the people they are interviewing. A written statement, which you previewed and the students give to interviewees, is a good idea.

Require drafts to be attached to papers submitted for a grade.

Require a second copy of students' final drafts submitted for a grade, and keep the second copy in your files.

Textuality

In writing workshops, patchwriting is not classified as plagiarism unless you have some reason to believe that the student is intentionally trying to deceive you:

> *Patchwriting:* When following the language of a source text, students are expected to use fresh words and fresh sentence structures. (See handbook section 49b2.) Inadequate paraphrase customarily results in a lowered grade for the paper and may also result in a required ungraded revision.

Teach students how not to plagiarize—how to cite, how to quote, how to paraphrase, how to summarize.

When you receive student work that is submitted for a grade and that is of questionable authorship,

1. Do not return the paper to the student. Return papers to the rest of the class when you've finished them. Tell the student that you have questions about the paper and get his or her campus address, e-mail, and phone number. Tell the student that you will get in touch with him or her very quickly to arrange a conference.

2. Read the plagiarism policies in the student handbook and the faculty handbook.

3. Make an appointment to talk with the director of composition (sign up on the green "administrative" signup sheet outside the 314B door). When you come to the appointment, bring a copy of the student's work. If it appears to be copied from another source, bring a copy of that source, too. Highlight the similar passages in both texts.

4. Once you and the director of composition have decided on the best course of action, make an appointment to talk with the student. A department faculty member must be at the meeting; do not meet with a student alone to talk about issues of questionable authorship. The director of composition is available as a third party for such conversations; you can sign up for a time on the green "administrative" sheet for you and the student to meet with the director.

5. After you and the student have met with the director of composition, make a final decision about what you are going to do with the paper in question. Write a letter to the student stating your decision and the reasons for it. Include with the letter a copy of the paper in question and the source text. At the same time, send a copy of your letter (with its enclosures) to the director of composition, the chair of the department, the dean of AddRan College of Arts and Sciences, the dean of campus life, and the dean of the student's college (if it is not AddRan).

Conferences and Class Meetings

Hold individual conferences with your students at least twice each term. Schedule these conferences during class time and office hours and whatever additional hours are necessary. A good formula for how many class hours you allocate for a round of individual conferences is six to seven minutes of class time per student. Thus, for a class of twenty-five students, three hours' worth of class meetings (plus additional scheduled hours) should be allocated. For a class of twenty students, allocate two hours of class time for each round of conferences.

For the conferences, fifteen minutes per student should be plenty of time. Make sure that the students know in advance what to expect and how to prepare for the conference.

Never cancel class meetings.

When you cannot teach your class, make arrangements for a proctor or substitute, following departmental guidelines.

Prepare a writing lesson that you could teach at a moment's notice to a classroom of strangers—in case you're called on as a substitute for a sick colleague.

Never let a class go early. When a day's lesson concludes early, turn the class to other matters:

1. Before the term begins, prepare several fifteen-minute minilessons that you can teach at the end of a class that concludes early.

2. Whenever you're grading papers, make overhead projections of papers (with students' names removed) that illustrate principles that many class members need to learn.

3. Have your students bring their handbooks to class every day.

With these materials on hand, you're always ready to use the entire class period productively.

Give a final exam in your course, or an in-class final essay. Give your final exam at the scheduled time.

Students' Behavior

If students are disruptive in class or abusive, harassing, or threatening toward you, talk immediately with the director of composition or the department chair—even if the student is just making you feel vaguely uneasy.

Facilitating Class Discussion

MARGARET M. LYDAY
Pennsylvania State University

In the following article from the Penn State University Composition Program Handbook, Margaret Lyday describes some general guidelines she has developed that facilitate productive and dynamic class discussions.

Discussion is one of the primary ways to move students from passive to active learners. While passive learners focus primarily on information recall, active learners are able to apply concepts to different contexts and to analyze and evaluate new results.

Although discussion, by its very nature, involves more student voices than does a lecture or a question-and-answer format, it follows many of the same principles of planning and emphasis as the other teaching methods.

Two items are essential for a productive discussion:

1. The teacher must have a goal, a desired outcome.

2. The students must have enough "raw material" information, from previous experience, reading, or prior class presentation, to make some analytic and evaluative conclusions.

One of the main goals of all English 202 classes, for instance, is to make students aware of complex audiences and provide them with the skills to write successfully for these audiences. The transmittal or cover letter—an introduction to a report, proposal, or essay—and a résumé or vita all have a primary purpose: to present information in a way that argues for its importance and acceptance, often within a competitive environment. A teacher who is trying to develop students' abilities to identify audience and interest can build a discussion around two or three core questions: Who are the likely readers? What are their primary concerns and interests? How does the form support the audience's goals?

Thus, instead of lecturing to students about the differences between academic audiences (who favor longer paragraphs and cover letters and tend to read essays from beginning to end) and professional audiences (who respond to short paragraphs and letters and often read only sections of reports and proposals), teachers can lead students to a discovery of this crucial rhetorical insight, one that will prove valuable throughout a lifetime of writing.

But how do we get students to risk sharing ideas in our classes? Certainly we have to create an environment that students consider safe. Fortunately, most of us know strategies for supporting and reassuring students and engaging them in discussion:

◆ Call on students by name.

◆ Use their insights as the basis for the next question or point.

◆ List comments on the board.

◆ Summarize the major points of the discussion with their examples.

◆ Ask for questions or reactions to students' comments.

◆ Give students time to think of responses.

Most students learn successful discussion patterns early in the course. A teacher, like a coach or a director, must be willing to wait, sometimes as long as a minute, for the first brave student to venture a response. Most students are all too happy to let the teacher take over the discussion, and we should simply refuse to supply the pat answer. Sometimes, providing questions for students to write about before class or during the first few minutes of class gives them a head start. Another strategy that is particularly helpful at the beginning of the semester is to group students in twos or threes to share their individual answers and then have someone give the group report. Listing important ideas from each group and then asking for examples or exceptions often will prompt individuals to ask questions of other students and elaborate on their own experiences.

Students need to learn that seldom does one answer or model fit every situation and that a successful writer in any environment is one who can present and support a point in a way that engages and excites the audience. Discussions, then, can develop active learning and critical thinking skills, skills we all need in order to write successfully in ever-changing life situations.

Following are some helpful sources on class discussion. An excellent review of methods and potential outcomes of discussion can be found in the collection edited by Diane Enerson and Kathy Plank, which contains an interview with English professor John Moore, a university teaching award winner at Penn State.

Further Reading

Davis, Barbara Gross. "Leading a Discussion" and "Encouraging Student Participation in Discussion." *Tools for Teaching*. San Francisco: Jossey-Bass, 1993. 63–74, 75–81.

McKeachie, Wilbert. "Organizing Effective Discussions." *Teaching Tips: Strategies, Research, and Theory for College and University Teachers*. 9th ed. Lexington, MA: D. C. Heath, 1994. 31–52.

"Teaching Discussion." *The Penn State Teacher.* Ed. Diane Enerson and Kathy Plank. University Park: The Pennsylvania State University Instructional Development Program, 1996. 42–56.

A Structure for a Successful Class Session

David A. Jolliffe
(with the help of Madeline Hunter and Judy Fox)
DePaul University

David Joliffe outlines some general guidelines for setting a productive tone for class discussions and keeping students engaged in course concepts and goals.

Begin the class by doing something that focuses the students' attention on the intellectual substance that will follow in the next hour, ninety minutes, or three hours Write a pithy quotation or challenging question on the board and ask students to write for three minutes silently about it. Solve a quick, illustrative problem and pose another one. Plan to use the material you generate later in the session. Do anything *except* class business.

Let students know your sense of the purpose of the class session—what you hope they will learn in the next hour, ninety minutes, or three hours—and provide them with an overview of what you and they will be doing during the session.

Take care of any business—announcements, distribution of assignment sheets, and so on. Do anything businesslike here *except* return graded papers. Do that at the end of the class session, unless you intend to teach about the work they have done in the papers.

(Note: Next two items are interchangeable.)

Explain, illustrate, or demonstrate the material, idea, technique, or strategy you want students to learn in the class session. Provide specific examples from the readings, observations, or experiments.

Ask students to extend your explanation, illustration, or demonstration of the material, idea, technique, or strategy with an explanation, illustration, or demonstration of their own, either individually or in groups. Give them feedback (i.e., assessment) on their work while it is in progress. Coach them to provide specific examples from the readings, observations, or experiments.

Assign students, again either individually or in groups, to work on additional explanations, illustrations, or demonstrations on their own. In common parlance, this is called homework.

Close the class. Do something, or have students do something, that will pull together most of what you and they have done for the past hour, ninety minutes, or three hours. Let them know what you expect them to do before you see them again.

A Strategy for Student-Led Writing and Discussion

JULIE ROBINSON
Colorado State University

Encouraging students to take an active role in leading classroom discussions about writing is one way to increase their accountability for their own learning. Julie Robinson here explains an assignment she has designed to accomplish this goal.

This easily adaptable lesson features in-class presentations that make use of student-centered instruction, discussion, and evaluation and end with one-to-one conferencing. I conceived this idea as I searched for ways to have daily in-class writing without overburdening myself with paperwork. Before teaching at the university level, I worked in the public schools, and this experience taught me that when papers stack up, everyone in class suffers. I also believe that asking students to construct their own writing prompts adds new perspectives to the class.

This lesson begins with each student assigned to a particular day. On their day, students are responsible for leading the class discussion on the assigned reading and designing a ten-minute in-class writing assignment. The writing assignment takes into account the major essays we are working on, where we are in the writing process, and the assigned reading. We complete the writing assignment in class and give our copies to the student. (I too complete the assignment and offer feedback to the student.) The student has one week to grade the writing and meet me in my office to discuss the presentation. I then read, record, and return the papers to the class.

Many versions of this assignment exist on our campus. Another teacher, Christina Francis, has students give their assignment in advance, lead a discussion, and have the class respond to the discussion as homework. Jeff Ritchie worries about shy students without public speaking experience. He has students work in pairs and meets with students prior to the day of their lesson to discuss ideas for the writing prompt and class discussion. Assigning partners also gives students a chance to do an in-class presentation twice in a semester. To adapt this project to my computer-assisted classes, I altered the assignment so that students e-mail their assignments to one another and copy me.

In-class Presentation

Objective

The purpose of this assignment is twofold. The first is to read the assigned essay and apply that reading to the writing you are doing for the course. The second is to play the role of teacher by constructing and grading a ten-minute writing assignment designed to assist the class in writing the assigned essays.

This assignment gives you the opportunity to get up in front of the class and direct us to look at the reading homework in order to help us write our major essays. The directions you give should be clear, appropriate for a ten-minute time limit, and make us think about how the reading applies to the major essays we are writing for the class.

You will continue the role of teacher by grading each essay. For every essay, you should ask yourself, "Is this essay what I'm looking for?" and base the grade on how you answer that question.

Your last responsibility is to meet with me during my office hours to discuss your in-class presentation. Before coming to my office, all papers must be graded. Bring the graded papers with you to my office within one week of your presentation. This means that if you give your presentation on a Tuesday, you need to meet with me before the following Tuesday.

Presentation grades will be based on:

♦ Professional appearance and demeanor during presentation.

♦ Use of excerpt or entire assigned reading homework as a base for your presentation.

♦ Reflection of outline explained in class during presentation:

    I. Introduce what you find significant about the reading.

    II. Explain what the reading has to do with the major writing assignment we are working on in class (invention, drafting, revising, editing).

    III. Clearly tell us what you want us to do.

♦ Conscientious grading.

♦ Meeting with me in my office within one week after presentation.

E-mail Adaptations for the In-class Presentation

This adaptation uses the same instructions, with a few adjustments:

> Students must post their discussion questions to our class listserv twenty-four hours before their presentations.
>
> When grading the essays, students must reply to each through e-mail and be sure to "cc:" me. Each response should be two to three sentences in length.
>
> Students must complete a worksheet before meeting with me in my office with the graded papers.

Grades amount to 10 percent of the final grade and will reflect:

- ◆ Professional appearance and demeanor during presentation.
- ◆ Use of reading homework during presentation. Students should plan on quoting excerpts directly from the text to aid in their lessons.
- ◆ In-class writing assignment assists students with major essay we are currently writing for the class. If we are working on drafting our Arguing a Position paper, for example, lessons should have us working on our draft for that paper.
- ◆ Students clearly tell us what they want us to do, both orally and in their e-mail directions.
- ◆ Conscientious grading/responding.
- ◆ Meeting with me in my office to discuss assignment.
- ◆ Students working together may plan one lesson together or plan two separate lessons and give us a choice between the two. If they plan one lesson, they must make it a two-part lesson and expect the class to write for fifteen minutes, participating in each aspect of the assignment. Both students must speak in front of the class, grade papers, and meet with me in my office together for one combined appointment.

Students must complete the following sheet and bring this mini-essay with them when they meet with me in my office with the graded papers. They must start this worksheet while the class writes essays based on their in-class presentations, and address the attached questions.

———————

IN-CLASS PRESENTATION

YOUR NAME:_____

DATE:_____

YOUR PRESENTATION IS BASED ON THE ESSAY CALLED:

_____

PP._____

I PLAN TO MEET WITH JULIE (CIRCLE ONE):

WEDNESDAY/THURSDAY/APPOINTMENT

1. Describe what worried you most while preparing your in-class presentation:
2. How do you think your presentation went? Why?
3. Write an essay that would earn an A based on your assignment (you may use the back of this page):

Strategies for Discouraging Plagiarism

DEIRDRE MAHONEY
Arizona State University

In the following essay, Deirdre Mahoney briefly outlines some of the strategies she finds successful in dealing with plagiarism.

Plagiarism basically comes in two forms: students inadvertently do not acknowledge sources properly, and students turn in a paper they have lifted entirely from another source (e.g., a friend in another section of composition, an Internet Web site that "houses" sample student papers).

First, let's talk about the "accidental" type of plagiarism that occurs when a student paraphrases a source and does not realize that he or she is required to acknowledge that the idea or words originated with another writer. I have found it useful to talk throughout the semester about the types of improper "borrowing" that may occur. It is not enough to simply ask students to read the section in their texts on plagiarism or mention plagiarism in the course syllabus the first day of class; rather, ongoing conversations about appropriate documentation are necessary throughout the semester. By thoroughly explaining to students why and how plagiarism occurs and by providing strategies for avoiding plagiarism, teachers create a comfortable classroom environment where students are well informed and feel safe asking for guidance in the construction of their texts.

In my experience, teachers who assign projects or essays that require the completion of prewriting activities and multiple drafts, and who remain involved with their students' work throughout the writing processes, experience very few cases of overt plagiarism. Yet it still can and does happen. If you suspect a paper has been overtly plagiarized, it's best to meet with your composition director or other supervisor to ascertain how to proceed. Generally speaking, teachers should *not* accuse a student of plagiarizing a paper, even if they have proof; rather, the teacher should ask the student to describe his or her writing process and to talk about the subject matter of the paper. Students who turn in papers they did not write typically have *not* studied the writing well enough to engage in a knowledgeable conversation about the paper. In this scenario, students often realize their work is in question and thus reveal the transgression.

Ultimately, I highly recommend including a policy in your course syllabus stating that teachers do not read final essays unaccompanied by invention work and early drafts of the assignment.

Working with Groups

FROM THE MICHIGAN TECHNOLOGICAL UNIVERSITY WEB PAGE

This excerpt helps provide beginning instructors with guidelines that ensure successful use of collaborative group assignments (http://www.hu.mtu.edu/~mmcooper/gtahandbook/groups.html).

Having students work in discussion or peer-response groups in class has several benefits. Students who are too shy to speak in a whole-class discussion may be able to participate in small-group discussions. In both discussion groups and peer-response groups, they learn how to work together to develop ideas and arguments and to revise their writing. And they can learn a lot about writing strategies from each other. Of course, students need help in developing strategies for working together effectively in groups.

Setting Up Groups

You can set up stable groups that meet throughout the term or semester to discuss readings and ideas and to respond to each other's work, or you can set up different groups each time—it depends on how you have arranged your course and what kinds of work you expect them to do.

Set up groups of three to four students. Fewer than three reduces the possible interaction, whereas larger groups tend to become less productive.

You can allow students to help choose groups by asking them to pair off with someone they want to work with and then putting pairs together. It can be valuable to mix students of different backgrounds in groups. But students who are distinctly in a minority in the class already—blacks, women, international students—may be more comfortable in groups together.

Don't automatically spread around "minority" students one to a group. Have students introduce themselves to each other in groups, and, especially if they are in stable groups, have them exchange phone numbers and e-mail addresses.

Pay attention to how well groups are working together. If you have stable groups, be open to adjusting them if a group is having serious problems, and give students a way to respond to you individually and confidentially about how well the groups are working (through midterm evaluations or via e-mail, for example).

Guidelines for Working with Groups

Before having students work in groups for the first time, discuss with them how to work in groups, including why it's important for all members of the group to participate and how to work together to make sure the group functions well and gets its work done.

Discuss with students the different kinds of productive roles people can play in groups—facilitator, idea person, evaluator, mediator, synthesizer—and that not everyone has to participate in the same way all the time.

Always give groups specific tasks to accomplish: questions to write group answers to, lists to make, experiments to perform, drafts to read and comment on. Make sure they understand the task and its purpose before they break into groups.

Effective groups have specific tasks to accomplish and know what the purpose of each task is.

For peer responses, provide worksheets that explain what they should focus on and why, and that give them specific questions to answer. The worksheets should be clearly linked to the purposes and work specified in the assignment and should encourage students to provide writers with constructive feedback for improvement.

Schedule time for groups to report to the rest of the class on what they've come up with.

Ask groups to appoint one member as facilitator for each meeting.

Encourage students to take turns being "secretary."

Keep track of how groups are working and whether they need help from you in getting started or when they get stuck or have questions. If they are writing something as a group, read their first effort and give them some feedback that helps them develop more complex ideas.

If students come to peer-response sessions unprepared, work with them to make sure they still participate in the group work: if they don't have copies of their draft, send them to the photocopier; if they have only a handwritten couple of paragraphs, ask group members to at least respond to that; if they have no draft, have them respond to other members' drafts anyway.

Periodically ask groups to assess their own productivity and progress.

Discussing Time Commitments with Students

DEIRDRE MAHONEY
Arizona State University

Explaining the amount of time and effort a course will require can be essential in helping students succeed. Here, Deirdre Mahoney discusses her experiences with this issue.

Students enrolled in university composition courses for the first time typically do not understand the need to devote many hours of study and writing time *outside* of regularly scheduled class time. Additionally, they may not realize initially that composition courses require students to engage in a tremendous amount of writing, rewriting, and yet more rewriting. Telling students they should plan to spend two to three hours outside of class for every hour in class may not suffice, for they might be thinking, "I've heard this before and breezed through my high school classes."

Rather than insisting that composition classes are highly time intensive and leave it at that, I demonstrate to students how they should plan to proceed through the semester, suggesting that their time spent outside of class may occur in ways they might not consider initially. I tell students, for example, that drafting an essay always takes much more time than a writer expects, and therefore they should expect their time at the computer to be at least double what they allow initially for drafting essays—especially if they run into computer problems.

I encourage students to spend at least one hour a week working with a tutor at the university Writing Center. I also encourage students to visit me often during office hours for additional feedback on their work in progress, especially early in the invention process when they are considering subject matter for their writing. I assign peer review responses wherein students complete typed, in-depth written critiques of their peers' work in progress outside of regularly scheduled class time. Additionally, I encourage students to meet outside of class in small groups (in addition to the in-class peer-review time) to continue to critique, edit, and polish one another's work.

I cite these examples early in the semester to reinforce to students how the time commitment and activity in a composition class probably differs from the requirements of their other college classes or from their past experiences.

CHAPTER 7

TEACHING INVENTION

This chapter includes a range of common invention strategies and activities.

Teaching Invention

Arizona State University

Sharon Crowley shares her knowledge of diverse rhetorical approaches to the process of invention and illustrates how those approaches may be used to help composition students develop their own invention strategies. From the Penn State University Composition Program Handbook.

Invention can be defined as the practice of looking for the arguments that are available in a given situation. Invention is both energized and constrained by rhetorical situations. A writer or speaker begins looking for arguments because some situation needs to be addressed. Careful and sustained attention to invention, however, will turn up many more arguments than can be used in a given situation. In ancient rhetoric, invention included consideration of the rhetor's ethos, his or her relation to the audience and to the issue under discussion; the audience's relation to the issue; and the place and time (including a history of previous discussion) in which the issue has become important. Considerations of the issue itself will yield arguments as well. All of these are "places" in which to look for arguments.

Invention is perhaps the most difficult part of rhetoric to teach. Novice writers are generally unaware that professional writing is a product of many drafts. Modern students typically do not understand that good arguments much be searched for—that finding arguments appropriate to a given situation is hard intellectual work. Nor do they see the need to produce more arguments than they plan to use on a given assignment. Indeed, students typically use arrangement as their sole means of invention, thinking in terms of composing an introduction, a thesis statement, proofs, and a conclusion—in that order.

Ancient teachers insisted that students who were preparing to speak or write should construct all the arguments available in a given situation, even though they might use only one or two. These teachers thought that the search for useful and effective arguments was good intellectual practice. They also pointed out that good arguments can be transferred from one composing occasion to another with only a little modification to fit the situation.

Here are some questions that may help students begin the process of invention:

◆ Questions about audience. Who is my audience? What is their attitude about the issue I am addressing? What do they know about the issue? Can I change their position on this issue? Can they be made to examine what they know more precisely or from a new perspective? What new information would be useful or interesting to them, and why?

◆ Questions about ethos. How do members of my audience regard me as a member of their community? What is my reputation with them? Is there anything about my public persona, such as my relative youth, that will influence their reception of my position?

◆ Questions about issues. Why is the issue I am addressing important in the community to which I am about to speak or write? What is the history of this issue? Why has it come up for discussion at this time? What, exactly, is my position on this issue? How does that position differ from the position taken by my audience?

These questions are drawn from the rhetorical situation itself. But there are as many means of invention as there are composers. Invention may occur haphazardly (people sometimes have flashes of invention in the middle of the night, or while they are doing something unrelated to composing). Invention can also be stimulated through use of a system. Invention systems include several fairly complicated approaches derived from ancient rhetorical theory such as stasis, the topics, and Aristotle's contributions of enthymeme, example, sign, and maxim. Complex modern systems of invention include Stephen Toulmin's claim/warrant/data model; Young, Becker, and Pike's tagmemic system; and a model derived from Kenneth Burke's "pentad" of motives.

In his discussion of invention, Aristotle proposes a series of "topics" (*topoi* or "places") in which arguments in support of a thesis can be discovered. In most handbooks, the classical topics have evolved into the "modes" of expository writing, although in fact the modes are more precisely aids to invention than methods of arrangement. We can use the *topoi* to encourage students to look at a subject from a particular perspective, frequently leading to the discovery of details that, without a point of departure, they might overlook. The writer who goes beyond the most obvious similarities between two objects to make comparisons at increasingly specific levels, for example, will discover details about both objects that might not be obvious if they were considered separately. Considering these specific details leads in turn to the discovery of general principles of similarity and difference that organize the final product, an arrangement of details based on comparison.

Kenneth Burke's "dramatistic pentad" is a deceptively simple yet potentially powerful system that helps writers analyze the complex relationships always at work in any situation or problem. The pentad is made up of five concepts: act, scene, agent, agency, and purpose. While the pentad applies most obviously to specific human actions, it can be applied at increasingly more abstract or concrete levels, with different connections or "ratios" between the five concepts, to produce a detailed analysis of, say, the ecosystem of a forest or the organization of a university. The pentad, because it is abstract, may be difficult for students at first, but its range of usefulness makes it an interesting guide to the invention process.

We should introduce formal invention procedures into our courses in several ways. We might include a general discussion of invention early in the term to establish its importance and place in the writing process. Later we might ask students to experiment with different systems of invention (brainstorming, topical questions, the pentad, systems for audience analysis, etc.) to discover the particular power of each. We should follow up on that start, however, whenever we assign a paper, discussing what kinds of probing a new subject might require and what method of invention might be most fruitful. And we should probably discuss the continued importance of invention in composing and revision: a paragraph in need of details or a paper with no clear point or a confused sense of audience or argument signals that the writer should stop, step back for a moment, and reconsider the questions about the subject, audience, genre, and intention with which the whole process began.

Works Cited

Burke, Kenneth. *A Grammar of Motives.* New York: Prentice-Hall, 1945.

Toulmin, Stephen. *The Uses of Argument.* Cambridge: Cambridge UP, 1958.

Young, Richard, Alton Becker, and Kenneth Pike. *Rhetoric: Discovery and Change.* New York: Harcourt, Brace & World, 1970.

Invention Activity

THERESA ENOS
University of Arizona

Heightening students' awareness of the roles that voice, ethos, and context play in shaping their writing is the goal of the invention activity Theresa Enos has adapted for her teaching.

Both the rich fascination of and the "problem" with pulling out invention exercises from our teaching storehouses, especially those of us who have been teaching writing for a very long time, is remembering what's "original," what's been modified to fit individual pedagogy, and what's known as "lore" (a particular classroom strategy we hear a colleague talking about, ask for the written strategy to try, and most likely modify to fit our own teaching style). I do not remember what, if anything, I "invented" from the exercise I describe below and what I got from one colleague or several. I'm reminded of one of Erika Lindemann's "stimuli perception" examples, one she used in an invention workshop back in the 1970s. The point was that the decisions we make about what to select and what patterns to impose on them are based largely on what we already know. Erika pointed out the fact that we are all familiar with a deck of cards, and then she asked each of us to try to sketch on a piece of paper the five of hearts from memory. Predictably, none of us got it right, at least on the first try. Is it that we just can't remember what we've seen so many times? No, it's that we don't just perceive stimuli— we impose patterns on stimuli; we compose them. (For examples of Lindemann's approach to invention, see *A Rhetoric for Writing Teachers*.)

I'm also reminded in presenting an invention strategy, one that has worked well in my classes over the years, that we don't seem to do much anymore with classical proofs or topics, perhaps because of the shifts in assumptions about the world from classical to modern rhetorics. Or perhaps in our increasingly postmodern pedagogy, we simply have internalized all the Aristotelian philosophy so that it "seems" absent. But there are still issues of development and arrangement; there are still issues of voice and presence, even in the postmodern classroom. (We theorize about subject positions, but in our writing classrooms, voice and ethos are still being considered.) In shaping the voice exercise described below, I tried to apply what I believe are appropriate criteria for inventive strategies:

- structuring it so that students can use the strategy for a wide variety of writing situations

- seeing that it has a clear sequence of operations that characterize effective invention strategies

- making it generative, engaging the writer in a matrix of insight— visualizing, analogizing, classifying, defining, rearranging, and dividing

I use the exercise for illustrative purposes—that is, before beginning to work on voice and ethos and on adapting language in a particular context for a particular purpose.

What I hope this exercise does is expand the problem-solving approach by first having students work toward understanding how writing gets written, the Berthoffian approach to thinking through observation, then formulating something about the object, and then articulating it (see especially Ann E. Berthoff's *Forming, Thinking, Writing*). The students are self-reflexively comparing and then learning that perception depends on presuppositions and on remembering, anticipating, and working out one's purpose.

The exercise: The students form themselves into groups of three, preferably, and choose one of a group of like objects that the teacher has brought to class (e.g., a collection of fruits and/or vegetables). For instance, one group might choose a carrot; another group, a banana; another group, a kiwi; and so on. Each of the three students in a group is asked to choose a role and a particular type of discourse that reflect a recognition of a rhetorical situation and a conscious choice of language. The students write out their roles and discourses. One student in the group that chose the carrot might take on the "writer's" role and write a diary entry from the carrot's point of view about being grown for human consumption. Another student might emphasize the "subject" by writing an objective, encyclopedic description of the carrot. Another student might aim for the "audience" by writing a commercial for the carrot grower's association. Shared with the rest of the class, each group's collection illustrates the aim of different kinds of discourse and the rhetorical choices reflected by voice.

Works Cited

Berthoff, Ann E., with James Stephens. *Forming, Thinking, Writing.* 2nd ed. Portsmouth, NH: Boynton/Cook, 1988.

Lindemann, Erika. *A Rhetoric for Writing Teachers.* 3rd ed. New York: Oxford UP, 1995.

Invention as a Strategy of Revision

ROBERTA A. BINKLEY
University of Tennessee at Chattanooga

Roberta Binkley provides a history of the role of revision in composition studies, from current-traditional through postprocess pedagogy. She also includes some concrete sugges-

tions for encouraging students to move past surface editing into deep revision of the content and arrangement of their writing.

We fall in love with our own prose. I know I do; certainly my students do. The problem with this romantic attachment is that we become reluctant to change anything. But frequently in first drafts it isn't until the last paragraph that the whole idea for the piece becomes clear and maybe finally expressed. So I often ask my students to do the following with their first draft:

- Take your final paragraph and move it to the top.

- Cut your original introductory paragraph.

- Now rearrange, cut, and add; do everything to make sense of that new beginning.

- Last, write a new conclusion that not only summarizes what you've written, but also opens up the significance of this essay for both you and the reader.

After students have gone through this exercise, I ask them to compare the two drafts and to write me a letter explaining how they're going to revise their third, and perhaps final, draft. If there's time, it's also important to have students exchange both drafts with their peers, discuss the differences between the two drafts, and exchange a written evaluation of their peer's two drafts before they write their own letter explaining the changes they plan for their third draft. Then they see how these changes are working for other students as well as in their own work.

Another variation of this exercise in invention and rewriting is Donald Murray's suggestion in *The Craft of Revision:*

- Write down at the bottom of a page what you want the reader to think and feel after reading your draft.

- Pick a starting point in the material that is as close to the end as possible while including all the information the reader needs to arrive at the conclusion you have written down at the bottom of the page.

♦ Note the three to five pieces of information the reader needs, in sequence, to arrive at your ending (111).

The obvious purpose of these exercises is to encourage deep revision. Most students know all about editing and sentence-level revision. They don't know about deep revision, the kind of revision that forces them to rethink their essay.

Theory

The history of revision theory in U.S. composition studies explains a great deal about approaches to revision used in the classroom. In her book *Towards Knowledge in Writing*, Jill Fitzgerald reviews the shifting conceptions of writing and revision since 1950.

Revision and Current-Traditional Pedagogy

Fitzgerald notes that the traditional view of revision for centuries has been editing. In this view, writers make changes only at the word and sentence level (36). Polishing becomes the key to this "final" stage of writing. Teachers read on the level of error correction, hence the "red pen" syndrome. The pedagogical principles of current-traditionalism characterize this view.

Revision and the teaching of it, in this schema of traditional pedagogy, are closely connected with a view of knowledge as transmission, "in which one 'found and structured' information or content and then transcribed it into words" (36). Fitzgerald argues that such a view is "'positivistic' in that knowledge is posited as located in the world, static, unchanging, composed of facts, is 'truth,' and it exists independently of the learner" (6).

Revision and Process Pedagogy

The next phase in the history of composition came about as a result of early research in the field of composition during the 1960s. This research emphasized "scientific" research, reflecting the general pattern of direction in the social sciences. It was this research that helped stimulate the concept and pedagogy of writing as process.

The process model of composition—in which the writer progressively goes through the stages of composing: invention, drafting, and revision—evolved during the 1970s and 1980s. The process model of composing in practice frequently becomes a model of writing taught as a compartmentalized phenomenon. Each stage is strictly adhered to and followed in sequence. The robotic application of the steps of composing ignores the complexities of cognition. It tends to concentrate on problem solving. Revision, in this model, becomes the end process, with the result that it is practiced more as editing than true rewriting.

Revision and Postprocess Pedagogy

It is this last model, revision as a socially interactive process, as discussed in the recent work of Nancy Welch, Donna Qualley, and Donald Murray in particular, that interests me. It is, as Nancy Welch articulates in her recent book, *Getting Restless,* a delicate dance between social constructivism and expressionism, not as an either/or process, nor as a process of linguistic or social correction, but as a way of continually looking at the formative and shifting relationship of self in society. These authors talk about revising for the purpose of reaching an audience and communicating with readers, revision that tends to be more than surface editing—it is content directed. At its best, it also becomes a social/interactive process, an opening up of meaning, a suspending of conclusion, and a way of arriving at a self-reflective stance. Welch begins her book, for example, with the comment, "I seek to recognize how concepts—socially shared ideas about the world—very much underwrite seemingly loose, associative, and underprocessed narratives" (2) She goes on to explain that revision, as it is taught and practiced, has become a way of achieving clarity and conclusions in socially acceptable ways. Welch questions this concept and asserts:

> "In this book I consider that an ethical practice of revision begins
> with drawing out those concepts [socially shared ideas about the

world], not to make them clearer and more consistent, but to question them, try to glimpse the future they may be in service of making—and the futures they may eclipse. (2)

Works Cited

Fitzgerald, Jill. *Towards Knowledge in Writing: Illustrations from Revision Studies.* New York: Springer-Verlag, 1992.

Murray, Donald M. *Crafting a Life in Essay, Story, Poem.* Portsmouth, NH: Boynton/Cook, 1996.

———. *The Craft of Revision.* 3rd ed. New York: Harcourt Brace, 1998.

Qualley, Donna. *Turn of Thought: Teaching Composition as Reflexive Inquiry.* Portsmouth, NH: Boynton/Cook, 1997.

Welch, Nancy. *Getting Restless: Rethinking Revision in Writing Instruction.* Portsmouth, NH: Boynton/Cook, 1997.

A Model for Invention

DAVID SUDOL

Arizona State University

David Sudol's activity helps students generate and explore ideas for essay topics by combining Aristotle's common topics and ancient modes of discourse with freewriting exercises.

According to Donald Graves, "Children suggest that when adults write, the words flow, arrive 'Shazam!' on the page. Like the Tablets, words are dictated to us from on high; we only hold the pen and a mysterious force dictates stories, poems, and letters. The better the writer, the less the struggle" (43). While college students are by no means children, they too have a hard time understanding how writing works. In fact, they often have particular difficulty selecting essay topics. I'm not sure why, although I suspect they're used to having teachers just give them topics. In any event, to help my students learn not only to generate topics but also to explore them, I spend lots of time in every writing class I teach—from First-Year Composition to Writing about Literature—on invention. And, following Graves's lead, I model my own invention process by writing along with my students and sharing my work.

Usually, I like to spend at least two class periods on invention. On the first day of a new essay, after reading through the assignment sheet, we do activities to generate topics. In the following class period, we do different activities to explore potential topics. The activities I use are numerous and are drawn from many sources: Lindemann's *A Rhetoric for Writing Teachers,* Connors and Glenn's *The St. Martin's Guide to Teaching Writing,* Murray's *The Craft of Revision* (which also has lots on invention), Elbow's *Writing with Power,* and Kirby and Liner's *Inside Out.* I also use first-year composition textbooks with good chapters on invention, such as Axelrod and Cooper's *The St. Martin's Guide to Writing.* I even use an old copy of Elizabeth Cowan's *Writing: Brief Edition.*

What do I use? I try to select activities that are interesting, helpful, and suitable to the sort of essay the students are composing. If they're writing a first-person narrative on a significant experience, for example, I may ask them to do lots of free- or focused freewriting. If, by contrast, they're writing on a concept and are having difficulty deciding what they already know or want to say, I may ask them to do some looping. Often, however, I rely on my professional judgment: I choose whatever works for me and assume it will work for them as well. I also like to mix up the activities so the students don't get bored and they learn that there are many ways to generate and explore topics. Rather than letting them sit around waiting for divine intervention before they can write, I offer them a box full of rhetorical tools.

Most important, I always do the invention writing along with my students. I find these activities lots of fun. I'm always surprised by the stuff that flows from my mind, through my pencil, onto the page. It's also useful to share my writing with the students—and for them to share their work with each other. They see me not only as their instructor but also as a fellow writer, struggling with the same problems. (I also think they're more willing to do the activities because I'm working along with them and not just staring out the window.) Moreover, they see how other classmates respond and often get new ideas in the process. In fact, many return to a previous activity after a student has shared his or her response. In some ways, this sharing is like a whole-class brainstorming session, in which everybody benefits from everybody else's ideas.

Another benefit is that within two class periods, students produce lots of text. It's not unusual, for example, for them to end up with ten to twelve pages of invention writing. Although they still may not know for sure what to write about, they have lots of raw material to draw from.

To make what I've presented so far more concrete, let me present a specific case. Last week in my Writing Reflective Essays class we began our third paper, a Montaigne- like essay on a general topic about which students have a genuine interest or curiosity and with which they have personal experience. After we reviewed the assignment sheet, I asked the class to get out some paper and, first, jot down whatever topics came to mind. Because the first response is often the best one—the most obvious, the most natural—I think this is a good starting point. Next, I asked them to produce a series of "thing" lists. Since the essay is essentially their reflections on some "thing," this seemed a logical approach. In particular, they responded to these prompts: Things I love (to do); things I hate (to do); things I feel strongly about; things I'm curious about; things I'm confused about; things I know lots about. After completing this activity, we shared a few responses, just to see what the class was thinking; then we moved on to the next activity: personal attributes. This time I asked them to jot down any unusual interests or hobbies, any special abilities or skills, and any distinguishing features or characteristics. Sharing some of these, I learned that one student makes balloon animals and another does stand-up comedy on weekends. We also had a lively discussion about tattoos. Finally, I asked them to log all their activities in a typical day and then in a typical weekend. I asked that they pay special attention to those things that seem quite ordinary but—on reflection—are actually pretty interesting. For the following class, I asked that they simply be receptive to everything around them, noting whatever caught their attention and interest.

When we met for the next class period, I wanted them to start exploring topics more thoroughly. I thought about using several activities but decided on a modified form of cubing or heuristics (using Aristotle's common topics). In fact, I used the old modes of discourse—description, narration, exposition, and argumentation—to get the class to view their topics from different angles, which is key in this sort of essay. Before starting, however, I asked them to review the long lists they'd made during the previous class period and to choose one topic for each of these categories: (1) the most outrageous or off-the-wall, (2) the most fun, (3) the most appealing to general readers, and (4) the most personally meaningful.

When the students had four potential topics (some had only two or three because the most fun was also the most off-the-wall or the most personally meaningful), we began to write. (In one class I wrote on "Turning 50"; in the other class I wrote on "Not Being Handy.") First I asked them to describe their topics: "Try to show what you see when you imagine your topic. Give lots of visual details, but also think about your other senses—touch, taste, sound, and smell." Next I asked them to make a list of all the stories they could tell about their topic, or if they had only one story in which to sketch out the different parts.

I broke exposition down into illustration; definition; comparison and contrast; analogy; classification and division; and analysis of causes, effects, and processes. For illustration, I asked the students to look through their lists of stories and choose their favorites. Then I asked them to freewrite on those stories, fleshing them out with as many examples and details as possible. When the students wrote formal definitions of their topics, several commented that they were able to focus better and had a clearer sense of purpose. Most of the students had no difficulty making comparisons or contrasts to their topic (which also helped to clarify focus and purpose), but some had trouble thinking of analogies. Others, however, really enjoyed playing with figurative language.

(Having Richard Reeves's essay "Breaking Down," in which he compares his own middle-age health problems to an old car breaking down, was certainly helpful.) Likewise, some students had difficulty putting their topic into categories, but others noted that this strategy could help them organize their essays. Although analyzing the causes of their topics confused some, no one had any problem enumerating effects—minor and major, short and long term. Process analysis was productive for some topics, but not for all. Finally, we argued for and against our topics, making a list of pros and cons.

At the end of the period, I surveyed the class to see how the invention activities had gone. Lots of students had topics and material to work with and, from what I could tell, were excited about writing. Some were still searching, but I was confident they had acquired the tools needed both to generate and to explore other topics successfully.

My Invention Writing on "Not Being Handy"

I. Description: What do I see when I imagine my topic? I see my toolbox, which is actually a beat-up cardboard apple box, with one side hanging loose. I see tools salvaged from my father's vast collection, castaways, secondhand tools, discards, stuff he should have thrown away but gave to me instead. A vice grip big enough to loosen sewer pipes, pre–World War II screwdrivers, a metric socket set, a torque wrench that does God knows what, a hundred-foot tape measure that I never use because if I pull out the tape I'll never be able to get it back into the case. A prehistoric saber saw so mean looking that I'm afraid to touch it. I also see myself getting sick to my stomach when something breaks. I imagine myself stranded in the desert, lost and helpless. I see my wife, standing at my side offering words of encouragement but not doing any work herself. I see myself attempting to hammer a nail, missing, banging my thumb. I hear myself cursing. I feel my thumb throbbing and my head pounding. I taste the sweat dripping from my forehead. I smell body odor, a by-product of anger. I see myself slumped on the couch, disgusted.

II. Narration: These are the stories that come immediately to mind:

- Spending six hours trying to assemble a fertilizer spreader. Putting it all together except for this turning thing that keeps the fertilizer flowing. Finally, as a last resort, supergluing the stupid turning thing on.

- Just last week, trying to fix a broken doorbell (when it woke us up by ringing incessantly at 3:00 A.M.).

- Attempting to fix a leaky faucet, ripping the faucet off the sink, paying a plumber over $200 to fix the damage I'd done.

- Attempting to rewire a lamp.

- Attempting to put a dimmer switch in our dining room.

- Attempting to fix a sticking closet door at my mother's house. Taking the door off and planing one side. Putting the door back on only to realize I'd planed the wrong side.

- Attempting to make miter cuts on some molding for our kitchen. Moving the refrigerator over to cover up the gap between the molding and the cabinet.

- Attempting to remove a stuck oil filter, scraping half the skin off my wrist.

- Attempting to put a new vent on an electric drier, slicing my index finger to the bone.

III. Exposition:

A. Illustration: Just last week, at about 3:00 A.M., my wife and I were rudely awakened by the incessant ringing of the doorbell. I bolted from bed as soon as I heard the noise and turned to my wife, who had turned away from me and covered her head with a pillow. "Peg," I said, "get up. Someone's at the door." Slowly, she opened her eyes, focused them on the alarm clock next to her, and said incredulously, "It's 3:00 A.M." By then I realized that the doorbell wasn't actually ringing; it was making a loud buzzing-humming sound. I quickly surmised that there was probably a short in the bell, and that I'd have to get up and fix it, or at least try. "Peg," I said, "get up. We need to fix the doorbell." She gave me a look that said, "Oh, no, not another household repair," then staggered out of bed. We made our way into the hall and looked up at the bell housing, which was buzzing-humming even louder now. Since it was ten feet off the floor, we needed to get the stepladder from the garage. Slowly, I climbed to the top rung, holding on to the wall while trying to cover my ears at the same time. I took off the cover and confronted a mass of multicolored wires and a wildly vibrating piece of metal. Holding the ladder steady, Peg looked up and asked, "What do you see?" I shrugged my shoulders. Slowly, I climbed down and went outside to examine the ringer. I unscrewed it from the wall and pulled out the wires, but the bell kept ringing. Peg got a flashlight, went around the side of the house to the circuit breaker, and pulled the switch that was connected to the doorbell. The noise finally stopped. She came back in, gave me a look of disgust (although I'm sure she'd deny that), and said, "I'll call a handyman in the morning." We went back to bed, but I didn't sleep. I just lay on my back and stared at the ceiling, suffering yet again the silent ignominy of the unhandy.

    B. Definition: Not being handy means not being able to do simple household repairs or projects such as rewiring a lamp or replacing a washer in a leaky faucet. It means a lack of skill, a lack of confidence, and a lack of success. It also means a lack of respect from the majority of men who are naturally handy and take simple household repairs or projects for granted. I hate to say it, but I'm afraid not being handy means being unmanly.

    C. Comparison and Contrast: The most obvious contrast that comes to mind is between me and my father, who was a terrific handyman. My father handled all the household repairs; I usually end up hiring someone to do even minor jobs like fixing a running toilet. He approached repairs calmly; my first instinct is to panic and curse. He assessed the problem rationally; I start taking things apart. He made a plan; I pray for an easy solution. He laid out his tools; I grab a hammer or screwdriver (no matter what the problem is). He worked methodically; I work spastically, jabbing and poking at every moving part. He took his time; I constantly look at my watch, thinking about what I could be doing instead. He was patient; I'm jittery, anxious as hell. He approached unexpected problems calmly, dispassionately; I reel with deep-stomach dread and more cursing. After finishing the repair, he cleaned up his mess and neatly put all his tools away in their proper place; I leave everything behind for my wife to clean up or else toss all my tools into my toolbox (the broken cardboard apple box).

D. Analogy: I am to household repairs what a surgeon wearing mittens and a blindfold is to a quadruple bypass. Trying to explain a household problem to a salesperson at a hardware store is like trying to speak Arabic or Mandarin Chinese; I'm in a foreign country and don't have the language to express myself.

E. Classification and Division: I could probably classify and divide my topic chronologically by the stages of my life: childhood, adolescence (especially trying to do repairs on my first car), and adulthood (subdivided into my twenties, thirties, and forties). Or maybe I could classify by degrees of difficulty: easy projects that I screwed up, moderately hard projects that I screwed up, hard projects that I screwed up. (If I'm honest, though, I have to admit that I've never really tried a hard project like tiling a kitchen floor or putting on an addition to a house.) Probably the best categories would be types of repairs: electrical, plumbing, carpentry, mechanical. . . .

F. Analysis:

1. Of Causes: I'm not sure why I'm not handy. Partly I think I was born that way—without any talent for practical work. (That's probably why I became an English teacher.) Even as a kid I remember being unable to put together model airplanes. Big gobs of glue, crinkled decals, leftover parts. I was totally incompetent. I felt stupid, foolish, so it's no surprise that whenever I approached a project I lacked confidence. I knew I couldn't do it, so why try? Plus, when I think about how handy my dad was, as were all my uncles and most of my cousins (two of whom became engineers), I felt ashamed. Instead of doing something about it and becoming handy—which seemed futile—I avoided household projects altogether, or if I couldn't avoid them I did them with a fatalistic attitude.

2. Of Effects: The effects of being unhandy are numerous. There are lots of things around our house that never get fixed: nail holes that need a spackle patch; cracks in the stucco that need some kind of stucco patch; a noisy ceiling fan whose incessant click, click, click I've come to ignore; a dripping faucet whose incessant drip, drip, drip I continue to ignore; a constantly running toilet; squeaky doors. The list goes on. Personally, the effects are mixed emotions. On the one hand, I'm embarrassed that I can't do these simple repairs. I'm ashamed (although that may be too strong a word). I'm irked. I'm also irritated that my wife can't do the repairs. I'm annoyed that I have to call a handyman to do what any average man should do himself. In fact, I tend to disappear whenever a handyman shows up. Rather than deal with him or try to save face by saying I already tried to tighten the faucet chain—or some such gibberish—I volunteer to buy groceries and let my wife deal with him. On the other hand, I constantly tell myself that it's no big deal to be handy. I didn't get a Ph.D. so I could fix toilets. I have lots of other skills. Still, I have this nagging sense of inadequacy.

    3. Of Processes: The only process I can think of is the one I follow whenever I try to fix something, but I already explained that earlier when I compared my father's process to my own. Only one more thing to add: when I've gotten so frustrated or I've screwed things up so badly, I go to the kitchen and pour myself a scotch while my wife looks up the phone number of the nearest plumber, electrician, carpenter. . . .

IV. Argumentation: So what are the pros of being handy? Not having to pay exorbitant fees to tradespeople to do simple work. Not having to live with a lot of broken stuff. More self-confidence. Pride in knowing that I can take care of my house. The respect of my male family members. What about the cons? Who cares whether or not I can do plumbing? Is it such a big deal? Isn't it more important that I can read and write and teach? Aren't those more important skills? Don't I have better things to do with my time and money than wander the aisles of Home Depot looking for left-handed socket screwdrivers? Isn't it better to use the extra space in my garage for bookcases instead of a workbench and a seven-tiered toolbox? Won't I be calmer overall—and probably live longer—if I don't try to install a new outlet on the patio?

Works Cited

Axelrod, Rise B., and Charles R. Cooper. *The St. Martin's Guide to Writing*. 5th ed. New York: St. Martin's, 1997.

Connors, Robert, and Cheryl Glenn. *The St. Martin's Guide to Teaching Writing*. 2nd ed. New York: St. Martin's, 1992.

Cowan, Elizabeth. *Writing: Brief Edition*. Glenview, IL: Scott, Foresman, 1982.

Elbow, Peter. *Writing with Power: Techniques for Mastering the Writing Process*. New York: Oxford UP, 1981.

Graves, Donald H. *Writing: Teachers and Children at Work*. Exeter, NH: Heinemann, 1983.

Kirby, Dan, and Tom Liner, with Ruth Vinz. *Inside Out: Developmental Strategies for Teaching Writing*. 2nd ed. Portsmouth, NH: Boynton/Cook, 1988.

Lindemann, Erika. *A Rhetoric for Writing Teachers*. 3rd ed. New York: Oxford UP, 1995.

Murray, Donald M. *The Craft of Revision*. 3rd ed. Fort Worth: Harcourt Brace, 1998.

Reeves, Richard. "Breaking Down." *New York Times Magazine* 15 Jan. 1984: 44.

To Whom It Might Actually Concern: Letter Writing as Invention in First-Year Composition

LENORE L. BRADY

Arizona State University

Lenore Brady's letter-writing activity activates a heightened sense of audience and purpose for students' writing.

Not too far into my first semester of teaching first-year composition I began to feel frustrated with what we call the "polished draft" of any assigned essay my students handed in. For the most part, the polished drafts lacked focus and clarity, and were audience-ambiguous. Over the course of that same semester, as part of a series of weekly homework assignments, I engaged my students in a series of letter-writing activities; one focused on letter writing as a persuasive/explanatory/positioning act in which students drafted a letter to a parent or significant person in their lives explaining why the student was doing something that was in opposition to the recipient's ideological stance—for example, why the student had decided to drop out of school. The second letter-writing activity was assigned in conjunction with their final essay assignment of the semester—proposing a solution. This assignment consisted of two letters. The first articulated to a specific person or department on campus a specific problem the student had encountered in the campus community and proposed a solution to that problem. The second letter was a fictional response to the first letter from the person or department to whom it was originally sent, indicating the validity, usefulness, or practicality of the proposed solution. What I noticed about these letters was that they seemed to enable the students to write clearer, more focused essays that included many elements of argument. The students felt in control of the essay/subject matter—it did not control them. In short, the letters were like invention activities for the polished drafts of the solutions essay. The following semester, I used the same assignments but with a sharper eye toward their usefulness as heuristic or invention activities.

Following is the actual two-letter solution assignment, the one I feel had the most positive effect on the students' writing.

A Call for Action

Think about campus issues which affect you either on a daily basis or in the course of your academic career here at ASU, such as residential policies, parking arrangements, library or computer services, academic advisement, disability services, to name just a few. Determine the particular problem you have on campus and propose a solution for it.

This assignment will be in two parts:

First, you will draft a letter to the appropriate person or department here at ASU, articulating your problem in detail and proposing a solution for it.

Second, you will write a fictional response from that individual or department explaining why he or she is accepting or rejecting your proposed solution. You are to assume that your letter will actually be sent, so make sure that the issues and solutions are real.

The letters and their responses were peer reviewed in groups of three, then discussed as a whole-group activity. This collaboration with peers allowed for critical input on multiple levels: the adequate articulation of the existence of the problem, the usefulness of the solution, and the practical application of the solution for a specific audience.

The letters work as a form of invention because the letter format unfolds the essay, in a sense. The letter is an authentic conceptual and textual communication between writer-thinker and audience; it's a social act, not an isolated one. The structure of the assignment reflects the social nature of writing—the "I" interacting with the community. When the student writer composes the letter, he or she anticipates a response. The audience response, even though fictional in this case, reshapes, re-views, and perhaps even reinvents the original idea, which in turn clarifies the composition of the essay. (The closure of the response letter actually reopens thought processes and reinvents the solution.) These external and internal influences on the compositions support the view of invention as social, as stated by Karen Burke LeFevre:

> Invention often occurs through the socially learned process of an internal dialogue with an imagined other, and the invention process is enabled by an internal social construct of an audience, which supplies premises and structures of beliefs that guide the writer. (2)

Work Cited

LeFevre, Karen Burke. *Invention as a Social Act*. Carbondale: Southern Illinois UP, 1987.

Invention Activity Late in the Writing Process

VICKY CAMPO

Arizona State University

Disrupting linear notions of sequenced steps in the writing process, Vicky Campo illustrates why she uses invention activities with students after they have brainstormed and generated particular topics.

When students write narrative, they often want to *tell* their story rather than *show* the sequence of action. They leave out important elements such as setting and dialogue; they have trouble coming up with concrete details and sensory images. And so they need help bringing the story to life. Erika Lindemann points out that "at least initially, students need guidance in generating *useful* details, and enough of them to permit discarding those that seem irrelevant" (108). That seems to be precisely the issue—helping students generate details they can and will use.

Composition textbooks address this issue by encouraging invention strategies such as brainstorming and clustering early in the writing process so that students will have plenty of raw material to draw from. I agree with that practice. I think it's an essential step for getting the process started. Once the drafting begins, however, the brainstorming often stops, and this can be counterproductive. As most of us know from experience, the writing process is rarely linear. It is recursive. In the words of Erika

Lindemann, it is "like the forward motion of the wheel, its leading edge breaking new ground but then doubling back on itself" (24). Writing is a process like sculpting. We shape and mold, then we step away and reflect on what we have, then we move forward to shape and mold again, going back over, redefining.

We may agree that writing is a recursive process, but what guides the process? Linda Flower and John R. Hayes assert that although the recursive nature of writing makes it seem chaotic and disorganized, writing is really a goal-directed process. All writers are guided by a set of self-imposed goals. Inexperienced writers, those who might benefit most from a list of concrete details, "frequently depend on very abstract undeveloped top-level goals" (335) to guide their writing. These goals can prevent students from focusing on detailed writing. Students may be more concerned with appealing to a broad audience, for example, rather than a specific one. Or they may be focused on letting readers form their own conclusions; thus, they purposely leave the writing vague. During the composing process, they will repeatedly return to these higher-level goals, even when these goals are harder to negotiate. As a result, many of the details generated in those early brainstorming activities never make their way into an actual draft of the paper.

Flower and Hayes point out, however, that many people "rapidly forget many of their local working goals once these goals have been satisfied" (335). It might be beneficial to students, then, to do some brainstorming activities in the final stages of the writing process in order to generate details to slip into an essay that is essentially complete. At this stage, students have either satisfied or abandoned other more abstract goals, and they can turn their attention to fine-tuning their writing.

I used one brainstorming activity last semester that worked particularly well for an assignment that asked students to write about a significant person in their lives. The activity came from a fiction workshop I once took, and I introduced it after students had already workshopped one draft of their paper with their peers; therefore, they felt fairly confident about their drafts. I turned off the lights in the classroom so the students would relax. Because of the arrangement of the room, they were all facing away from each other toward their computer monitors, so there were few distractions. The first prompt I gave was this: "Imagine it is early in the morning. You're just waking up from a sound sleep. You're groggy, hazy, but you vaguely remember a dream you had about your remembered person. What is that dream?"

I spoke softly, wanting them in a dreamlike state themselves so they could tap into emotions about that person that they might not otherwise be aware of. A dream could be anything they wanted it to be, and I hoped that writing it would bring them into emotional proximity with their person without forcing them to confess to any emotions directly. Here is the dream that one student, Laura Czarzasty, recorded:

> It was more of a nightmare than a dream. Loosely based on an event from my childhood it was practically as scary in real life as it had been in the dream. In the dream I was seven again. She sat in the passenger seat her hands clutching her purse on her lap. We had just pulled into the driveway of my school. Children ran yelling and shouting around the car. Girls with pigtails, boys with brightly colored shirts. A steady stream of orange, yellow, green, blue ran steadily past the windows. The heat in the car was unbearable. My grandmother leaned forward and turned on the air.
>
> "There that's better," she said, false teeth already chattering. I looked at her arm to see it covered with goose bumps. They started out the small size that goose bumps generally are. But they didn't stop there. They kept growing until my grandmother's arms were grotesquely misshapen. I reached for the door to find it locked. It was getting colder in the car. Snow started to blow from the vents, flakes melting on our faces and sticking in her close cut silver hair. Outside the children had melted into a quickly flowing blur. Their cheerful shouts had morphed into sounds of terror and pain.

There is plenty of detail in Laura's dream. Even before this brainstorming activity, Laura used detail well, but writing this dream generated ideas that made her essay even stronger. She actually used a revised version of this dream in her final draft.

Next, I asked the class to imagine themselves in a scene with their remembered person. I told them, "Go back to the moment in time when the scene actually took place. Now look around you. What physical items surround you?"

Laura's list included a bulletin board, prayers on the board, breakfast dishes in the sink, a coffee pot, and a place mat with fish on it. Then I asked, "What sounds do you hear?" to which Laura responded with the following: a dripping of water in the sink, the hum of the fridge, distant shouts of kids playing, and a lawn mower. When I asked what smells students could remember, Laura generated: old coffee, vanilla air freshener, and medicine. And when I asked what gestures the person made, she wrote: pushes her glasses up her nose, wrinkles face up, squints, hands on hips, arms folded, hands shaking, closes eyes. Finally, when I asked students to record the sights they recalled, these were Laura's recollections: sliding glass door, parking lot, cars, small farm behind large wall, dimly lit rooms, houseplants, and books scattered around.

At this point, I asked students to write a new scene, one that had not yet appeared in their papers. The following is Laura's added scene:

Her breath smelled of old coffee. Her dentures yellow with the sludge in her mug. She sat at the table, absurdly decorated with tropical fish placemats.

"Morning Nana," I ventured timidly from the hall.

"You want some breakfast dear?" It was the first time since I arrived that she hadn't called me either by my name, or the offensive title, Girl.

I accepted and she stood, stretched like a cat. I was surprised to see that she was still so flexible. She smiled mildly at me from behind her chair. I was starting to think that there might be some hope here after all. Despite all the horrible things she had done to my mother, despite my childhood fear of her, we might be able to have the grandmother/granddaughter [relationship] that neither of us had ever experienced.

"I thought you could help me with the shopping today."

While this scene never made its way into Laura's final essay, some of the images in the scene did. In fact, Laura's lists generated a number of useful images. The final version of her essay appears below.

Nana

Her brown eyes were fixed on me as I walked down the ramp. She raised her arm to wave from where she stood, making no effort to meet me. I hardly recognized the woman in front of me. Our heights had reached the same plane as she had shrunk and I had grown since I'd seen her last. I practically took all five feet of her in with a glance. The awkward hellos in the terminal made me quite aware of how long it had been since I had seen this woman, my Nana.

"How was the flight? Did they feed you?" Nana asked in the squawking voice I remembered.

"Um, no. They didn't. But the flight was OK," I offered, unsure of what she wanted to hear.

"Well, the baggage claim is over there," Nana motioned. "Go get your bags and I'll bring the car around." She turned and walked away. The loose change in her purse jingled, creating a sound that was at odds with her walk. It wasn't exactly shuffling, or broken, but it was slower than the quarters and pennies made it sound.

I gathered my bags and struggled out to the curb, where she stood waiting. Together we wrestled my bags into the trunk. Nana could barely see over the steering wheel as she drove. She craned her neck like a turtle, and didn't move much faster than one.

The ride to her apartment lagged on in silence, and I wondered why Nana had agreed to let me stay with her these two weeks. After four years of no contact from her I was shocked by the sudden about face. There had been no birthday telephone calls, or even Christmas cards. I had been given four years to forget she existed and nearly no time at all to get used to the idea of living with her for two weeks.

The last time I had seen her had been Christmas Eve when I was ten. It had been an angry holiday. The kind that becomes hushed family legend. That night Nana had laid everything on the line. Her feelings of resentment toward my mother, the years of withheld hostilities. During the shouting match that had drowned out the caroling neighbors my mother endured her mother's accusations. Having locked myself in the den I couldn't be sure of all that was said. At times the screaming was loud enough to filter through the walls.

"You can not hold me responsible for Dad's death!" My mother's booming voice shook the ornaments on the tree. "He had cancer, Mom. He was going to die whether I spent that time with him or not. At least I tried to make his final time here bearable."

"Not at all what you did for your brother though," Nana answered coldly. "You never could give him the help he needed. You were always wrapped up in your own selfish concerns!"

It didn't matter that the people they were talking about had been my mother's father and brother. Nana was too consumed by her own rage, guilt, and sadness to see my mother's pain. As my mom pulled out of the driveway to spend Christmas Eve in a hotel, I caught my last glimpses of Nana standing on the porch, hands on her hips.

"Well, here we are!" A forced cheerful voice at my side exclaimed. I looked up, jolted out of my thoughts. I was surprised to see that we were parked at Nana's.

Her apartment was a jungle of houseplants. The rooms were kept cool and dark. She led me down a narrow hallway to the guestroom.

"You must be starving," she announced my hunger more than she asked me about it. "Help me fix dinner." Within seconds of entering the kitchen I was aware how differently she moved. As if a physical change had occurred as we crossed the threshold. Her wrinkled brown hands didn't shake as she handled ingredients. She stooped in front of the refrigerator with no complaints of her knees or back. I was surprised to see that she was still so flexible. Nana mastered cooking at a young age, and while every other aspect of her youth slipped away, this one trait remained. She juggled the simmering foods, moving swiftly and surely. I almost expected her to toss tortillas in the air and catch them in her skillet. Here in the kitchen she was in control. I didn't help so much as watch in awe.

As she neared the end of her culinary spectacular she sent me to set the table. On the wall of the dinning room I noticed a bulletin board. It was covered in scraps of paper, her tiny scrawling on all of them. Some were merely grocery lists, but others had thankful statements, almost prayers written on them. "Thank God for my health. With all that I have put this body through it is holding up delightfully." "Thank God for my grandchildren, all of them, even those whose minds have been poisoned against me." There was an AA pamphlet held up with a green thumbtack. I knew through the gossip line of my aunts that it had been a long time since Nana had consumed so much as one glass of wine with dinner. I pulled the pamphlet down and opened it. The steps of the program were listed. Number one: take things one day at a time. Number four: apologize to someone. Number six: forgive someone, and so on. It occurred to me that these were the mottoes that Nana now employed. The little steps had become the pace of her life. But it seemed to me that those who needed the apologies went without, and that those she never once let down were drowning in apologies belonging to others.

"What are you looking at, girl?" Nana's voice from behind caused me to jump.

"Oh nothing. I was just . . ." I hastily put the pamphlet back. "I was just looking," I concluded lamely.

She regarded me for a moment from where she stood, her hands lost in oven mitts. Then a smile split her face, displaying her flawless dentures. "At least you are an inquisitive girl. Get the rest of the food, we're ready to eat." I practically danced into the kitchen. I began to think these two weeks might be bearable. We just needed a little time to warm up to each other. Sitting at the table we talked of inconsequential things. How I liked my new high school, the errands Nana needed to run the next day. It was banal, but it thrilled me. After so long with no grandmotherly influence I was basking in it. Then she turned the conversation in a direction I wasn't as pleased with.

"How's your father doing, Laura?"

"Oh good, he's all moved into his new apartment. I think he likes it—"

"Your father is a good man. The best thing that ever happened to that mother of yours. She was a fool to let him go. A really dumb move." Nana proclaimed around a mouthful of refried beans. I just sat there silent. How could she say such things about my mother to me? She had just started to seem like a human being to me, then this.

"Don't you think so? Huh?" My wounded silence didn't satisfy her. "Girl, I asked you a question."

First she insulted my mother, then she compounded her error by reverting back to calling me "girl." I suddenly was more tired than I had realized.

"Goodnight Nana. I'll see you in the morning," I stood. "I don't think she's a dumb fool." I whispered it to myself in the hallway.

* * *

I sat in the driver's seat; this was odd because I was only six in the dream. Nana sat next to me. We were parked in front of my elementary school. There were children running past the car, calling to each other, a steady stream of reds, greens, blues, and yellows. Nana sat waiting for me to give her a good-bye kiss. But I couldn't. The reptilian aspects of her skin were too frightening. The car was running impatiently. Her sunken eyes regarded me from behind her glasses. She leaned over so I could kiss her cheek, but I backed as far away as I could in the confines of the car. Outside the children ran past the car so quickly that their bright colors blurred together. An old smell affronted me. The laughing shouts now sounded like those of pain and terror.

I awoke with a start, surprised to find myself dreaming of an event that had taken place so long ago. The real aspects of the incident, together with the chilling images in the dreamscape, had shaken me. I took a few deep breaths while recalling the time I refused to kiss my grandmother as a child. I'd forgotten about that morning in the car. It'd been locked away in that dusty part of memory where the things one is least proud of go.

Swinging my legs out of bed I stretched, then started down the hall. The wall space in the hall was crowded with pictures. I stopped to look at them. They were all of my uncle, David. The hallway had become a timeline documenting his life. My mother and three aunts were not anywhere among the pictures yellowed with age. There was David as a chubby toddler, seven-year-old David at Easter, David in a Little League uniform. Not one of Nana's four daughters held a place in the photographic tribute to her son.

There was a break in the timeline. I could find no pictures from the time David was seventeen to about twenty-three. I knew this to be a hint of another family legend. Those were the years in David's life that the alcoholism had nearly destroyed him.

I lifted one of the school pictures off the wall. Something fell out of the frame. It was another picture, older with bent edges. It was a picture of a young man eternally frozen in the act of lifting a young woman up off her feet. The man is handsome in an old fashioned way. The woman is my Nana, the man the grandfather I never met. They are smiling with joy that won't last. Several years after the picture is taken the marriage will lose its impulsiveness; the rapture that was in the picture will fade. The man will die of cancer, spending his last days in a stark hospital with his youngest daughter, instead of the wife with the pretty smile that dissolved along with her kindness and their love.

The shuffling sound of slippers on carpet brought me out of my thoughts. Before I could slip the old picture back into the frame, Nana appeared at the end of the hall. Clad in a robe, she held an empty coffee cup in her weathered hands. The stink of coffee residue floated down the narrow hall to me. She pushed her glasses up on her nose.

"What is that?" The grating voice had a sharp edge to it. I tried to slip the photo where it had come from, but her bony hand was on mine. She glanced at it, her eyes not seeming to focus. "This is nothing that concerns you! Nothing at all!" Nana yanked the picture from me and ripped it in half.

"Where are the pictures of my mother and her sisters?" She stopped walking away from me.

"What?" Her back was to me.

"Don't you have any pictures of your girls I could look at?"

"If I had anything else I wanted to share with you I would, you nosey thing!" Her knuckles went white on the handle of her mug. "You ask stupid questions. I should never have agreed to this. You're too damn much like your mother!"

"Why don't you love her? David wasn't her responsibility. And he's better now. All my mom did was love her father. Why are you so mad at her?"

Color appeared on her cheeks, not the uneven splotches of blush she usually wore, but the marks of rage.

"You can't leave them alone can you? Why do you hate the men I love? What gives you the right? Girl, you weren't even alive during most of this. It concerns you not at all. Ignorant bitches, you and your mother both!" She spat these words out as she let the mug fly. It hit the large picture I had just rehung. The glass portion of the frame shattered and fell, along with any illusion I still held about building a relationship with my Nana.

Within the day I was back where it all had started, the airport. The crowds seemed like the kind one usually only sees on TV. They bustled about, cheerful, and excited, as I stood in line alone, a melancholy looking adolescent.

I was sorry for the pain that my grandmother endured, and I was even sorrier that she wouldn't let anyone get close enough to help her with it. Instead she only let people get close enough for her to share the misery, then send them packing, as she so literally did with me.

"Hey miss!" The man behind the counter shouted, breaking up my thoughts. "You wanna check that baggage?" A small sad smile flitted over my mouth. As I struggled my suitcase onto the scale it dawned on me that I had more baggage than I knew what to do with. "Yeah," I thought to myself. "I sure do, both the luggage I had brought, as well as the new baggage Nana was sending home with me."

Admittedly, Laura came to this assignment with a good eye for detail, but this exercise works even for students who are less proficient with concrete images. In the final portfolio, a number of students commented that this was one of the most helpful exercises of the semester.

Works Cited

Flower, Linda, and John R. Hayes. "A Cognitive Process Theory of Writing." *Instructor's Resource Manual, The St. Martin's Guide to Writing.* Ed. Rise B. Axelrod, Charles R. Cooper, and Alison M. Warriner. 4th ed. New York: St. Martin's, 1994. 327–39.

Lindemann, Erika. *A Rhetoric for Writing Teachers.* 3rd ed. New York: Oxford UP, 1995.

Writing Exercise—Connections

SUSAN J. ALLSPAW

Arizona State University

Susan Allspaw's assignment asks students to consider a photograph from various perspectives—the subject's, the photographer's, and their own—as a vehicle for learning about the layers of framing and interpreting that occur around images and other texts.

There is a delicate balance between being an observer and transferring those observations into writing. The emotions and reactions experienced by the subjects are very personal; basically, the cameraperson or writer is an unwanted observer. Writing takes some of the power of the writer and transfers it to the subjects—they control the scene because they create it. But the writer also controls how the scene is presented for others to experience when the immediate actions of the subjects are finished. The writer should be under the control of the subjects, and he or she should want to please the subjects and present the scene exactly the way it was witnessed. The emotions of the observer will undoubtedly infiltrate the scene and might not even be similar to those of others who view the same scene. Someone else might interpret the scene in an entirely different light, one that isn't what the subjects had intended. It is difficult to determine who has the most power—the subjects or the writer.

I use the following exercise when my students are writing personal narrative:

Connections: A Perspective Exercise

Find a picture with more than two people in it—this can be a snapshot, a picture from a book or magazine, anything—and write about the people in it. Write about their physical attributes, what they look like (who they look like—"this man had the stature of a politician, but his clothes told me he was a janitor . . ."), as well as your speculations on what their behavioral attributes could be—are they cranky, stubborn, scared, naive; what would they do in certain situations?

Now write about what their relationships to each other are—if one is in the foreground and another is in the background, why are they separated like that? If one has his or her face half turned, why is that? Do they know of each other's existence? What would happen if they did (or didn't)? Is there one person who dominates the picture? Is that person aware that his or her picture is being taken?

Next, consider the relationship of the photographer—what does he or she have to do with the people in the photo? What does he or she know about the placement of these people? Has the photographer manipulated these people in any way?

Finally, consider that you are involved with all of these relationships by holding the photo and looking at it. How have the people in the photo manipulated or affected you? How has the photographer manipulated or affected you? Have you in any way affected the people in the photo? How? Involve yourself in this process of relating.

One last thing: consider this process transposed onto writing, with you as the author taking the place of the photographer and somehow affecting people at both ends, as participants and as viewers. What does this position do to your sense of power? How does it affect your sense of "doing it right"? What fears does this position raise? Will people at either end realize these fears?

This exercise shows students a number of things, but most important, it gives them perspective. Oftentimes students will write about an event, experience, or person without thinking about how they are positioning themselves—as participant, observer, or even observer's observer. This exercise allows them to see how many different vantage points there are, and how, depending on this perspective, readers can have very different interpretations of their writing.

Second, this exercise demonstrates the importance of reader consideration. Beginning writers often don't think about audience (beyond the teacher), or about another person or group of people reading their work. As students consider how they place themselves within a narrative, they must also place their reader and envision the work from that distanced perspective. In the photograph exercise, students must consider the photographer's point of view as well as the perspective of the person viewing the photograph.

I like to depict for students this concentric circle of involvement, with the people in the picture as the smallest, central circle; the photographer as the next, outer circle; and the viewer as the outermost circle, all overlapping and including one another. It is also important that they see how the writer or photographer has affected both the participants and the viewers in some way.

In the past, my students have reacted positively to this exercise because when they're writing they're not aware of its intended purpose until the end. By taking the quick and often unconsidered action of studying a photograph, they become involved with it, as well as with all of the people involved in the making of the photograph.

Following is one student response to the exercise:

Connections: A Perspective Exercise
Elizabeth Shimkus

They sit together closely on the wooden bench fighting the anxiety and both trying to maintain an aura of calmness. They make petty conversation—it only breaks the silence intermittently. The ticket is folded inside his right pocket—already bought, paid for, and decided on months ago. The bag rests on the bench beside him; carefully packed and settled; the other major possessions shipped days before. This moment had always seemed so far off—countless flips of the calendar pages away.

Their hands rest folded half-heartedly—her fingers laced throughout his, trying desperately to hold on like before. His do not reach full closure and instead seem to rest more on his leg for support instead of holding the hand that has supported him all this time. Their hands are wet with the cold dewiness of sweat—the tell-tale sign of the nervousness they are both trying so hard to fight and hide. His look of defeated dejection—a blank stare off on the distance. She looks at him pleadingly. His posture reflects the same defeat his eyes reveal. Slouched, sliding forward on the bench, his foot bends to the ground instead of its usual strong, upright position. She looks upwards to his face—the same pleading look of a child to the parent who has rejected the plea for the new toy. She can't make him stay and she can't go. She knows there is nothing more to say but instead tries to say it all, knowing she can't change his mind and knowing that the clock silently ticks off the minutes until his departure. He listens and can't respond—it's all been said countless times before; the tears shed, the sides argued and the pleas made.

The photographer apparently captures the couple without their knowing it. I can assume this only because neither one of them is directly looking at the camera and both seem so absorbed in the other that they don't appear to notice anyone that might be watching them. The photographer has nothing to do with the photo—if anything he is a rude intruder on a very private and personal moment. If I were one of these two I would be pretty upset at his prying and spying.

These two people have made me very sad. I can only imagine how hurt she feels and how hopeless life must seem to her at this point in time. It's a decision he had to make; he had to go to wherever he's going to for whatever reason. It is the grueling battle between being true to yourself and doing what is really important to you as an individual but also balancing those priorities with your relationships with others. It is also accepting the fact that sometimes those goals do not always match up with those relationships. She looks at him with such sadness and hopelessness. She is begging him not to leave—without saying it in so many words. Her eyes tell her story of knowing he has to go to be true to himself—but wanting him to stay and be true to her. He wants to go to fulfill what he's been working for during those four years in college. The time has finally come for him to reap the rewards of his hard work. But sadly those rewards come with the sacrifice he must make in leaving her behind. They say it's going to be okay, that they'll call every day and that it won't be for that long. But they both know it will be longer than they think, the phone calls will get expensive, and it's hard always wondering what the other person is doing. It won't be the same.

Exploring Topics: Rationale for a Class Exercise

MICHAEL STANCLIFF
Arizona State University

Michael Stancliff emphasizes the role of questions in generating ideas and describes a simple assignment that utilizes student-generated questions to guide class activities and writing.

Whenever possible I let my students choose their own topics. It is my experience that when students can pursue issues in which they are truly invested, many will commit to doing their "best" work and commit also to the vital discussion of what constitutes "good writing" in a given situation. This aspect of my pedagogy was reinforced this year as I piloted a departmental syllabus organized around *The Allyn and Bacon Guide to Writing* by John Ramage and John Bean. Ramage and Bean, following the work of Paulo Freire, see writing largely as an act of posing questions, of "problematizing." They stress that successful writing projects begin with a question that comes from the writer's life experience, one in which she or he has a personal stake as an individual and/or a member of a community. I encouraged students, when choosing topics for an exploratory research project adapted from the *Allyn and Bacon Guide,* to make lists of questions that truly interested them, questions to which their life experience led them. I was happy in all my classes to find a majority of students who seemed excited by the upcoming project.

Of course, this excitement engendered its own problems, the most marked being a certain stubbornness of perspective. The stubbornness often results in an unwillingness to consider alternative perspectives. Some students, when writing about things they care about, have difficulty getting beyond their initial view, what they've been raised to believe, prevalent media images, and so on. Sometimes it's not stubbornness so much as what Erving Goffman calls "frame lock." Each of us has a set of terms and concepts, provided for us by our cultures, histories, families and other institutions, by which we understand our lives. What seems like an important question for one person is invisible to the next, or at least radically different in perceived importance and meaning. For years now I've used Peter Elbow's suggestion to have students freewrite their gut reactions to their chosen topic, their biases, their "first thoughts," and all the clichés that come to mind. Once this is on paper, I find, some powerful discussion can begin. Where do these perspectives come from? Or in the language of Louis Althusser, what institutional or cultural narratives have interpolated us?

Tweaking the Elbow exercise a bit, I do a group exercise designed to brainstorm a range of perspectives in the space of one class meeting. I do this at the beginning of a writing project, just after students have finalized their focus. Here are the steps I follow:

1. Make sure the class is sitting in a circle.

2. Have each student write her or his topic or question at the top of a sheet of paper.

3. Pass the topic sheets clockwise or counterclockwise.

4. Ask students to write down their gut reactions to each topic, cliché s that come to mind, related questions, etc.

The exercise is over when each student's paper comes back around. I have gotten overwhelmingly positive feedback from students regarding this assignment. Several students have said that the feedback allowed them to consider aspects of their topic or question that they "never would have thought of." Certainly, those of us teaching exploratory and persuasive writing would do well to promote such thinking as a way to encourage "writing as thinking" and effective counterargument.

Works Cited

Althusser, Louis. *Lenin and Philosophy, and Other Essays.* London: New Left Books, 1971

Elbow, Peter. *Writing with Power: Techniques for Mastering the Writing Process.* New York: Oxford UP, 1981.

Freire, Paulo. *Pedagogy of the Oppressed.* New York: Continuum, 1993.

Goffman, Erving. *Frame Analysis: An Essay on the Organization of Experience.* Cambridge: Harvard UP, 1974.

Ramage, John D., and John C. Bean. *The Allyn and Bacon Guide to Writing.* Boston: Allyn and Bacon, 1997.

Teaching "Organization": Transition Moments, Cueing Systems, and Modes of Coherence

Michael Murphy
Oswego State University

Using complete short student papers, Michael Murphy discusses overall structural concerns to highlight how teaching organization can be more than just thinking about form.

Of course, it's been out of fashion almost since the dawn of process theory in the early 1970s—at a moment when expressivist sentiment against mechanical "themewriting" (Coles) in grammar-and-style-oriented "Engfish" courses (Macrorie) ran high—to talk too openly about teaching organization patterns and strategies in student writing. Indeed, organization—or worse, "arrangement"—is now so fraught with associations with roman numeral outlines, underlined topic sentences, the prescriptiveness of the five-paragraph theme (Baker), and a general product orientation that many teachers of writing have dismissed it altogether as a simple concern of surface correctness, or even as a vaguely sinister mode of intellectual surveillance and coercion. At the very least, strategies for teaching student writers how to cluster and sequence text in coherent wholes are seldom any longer considered a topic for serious pedagogical discussion. Talk deeply through a student writer's ideas at some remove from textual particulars, this line of thinking usually goes, and the skills needed for connecting discussions will emerge for that student naturally, organically.

Almost inarguably, this approach is most useful when working with students who show a certain level of native fluency and rhetorical sophistication, students who have some at least intuitive sense of available rhetorical shapes and patterns. The following paper, written by sophomore Emma Ansah in a survey of modern Western literature and culture at Oswego State University in upstate New York, offers a good example. The assignment was to relate one of the themes identified in the course as characteristically "Western" to some artifact outside the course, whether a book, a consumer object, a film, or some experience in one's own life. Emma chose to relate the Christian notion of original sin and human imperfection to the sense of guilt she associated with organized religion as she was growing up.

Memoir: Guilt and Christianity
Emma Ansah

Guilt is a feeling of responsibility for wrongdoing. It is being aware of or suffering from guilt. Society, laws, religion, and culture play major roles in our lives. Guilt is derived from these in so many fashions. Religion is one of the strongest reasons for guilt. The reason I say this is because it has impacted the way I live my life.

Growing up in a Christian home, I was taught to live by certain rules bestowed in the Bible. I know when I broke some of them I felt a tremendous amount of guilt. Sometimes I think I did because I knew what I was doing wrong. But the question is what is right or wrong? Not everyone believes the same things are right and wrong, but I feel when you feel guilt you have the conviction to differentiate right or wrong.

Throughout the years I've learned that everything I was taught wasn't exactly true. Now I've learned to make my own decisions. Most of the guilt I experienced as a child is irrelevant to me now. For example, I remember my cousin went to Catholic school. This school system instilled in small children that they were going to hell if they wore short skirts, had a boyfriend or wore red nail polish. Being a Christian girl in a public school I saw things completely different from everyone at school. It was as though I was in another world. I didn't wear the short skirts, nail polish or have a boyfriend, because I was going to hell. This is how guilt was instilled in me. At times I would put on the short skirts, nail polish and feel as though I was committing some kind of sin.

Throughout high school I didn't get involved with associating myself with boys for the simple fact that it was giving in to the flesh. Now that I have a boyfriend, it is difficult at times for me, because those beliefs are still alive in me. I can say now that all these beliefs do not affect me as much as they used to, but some of them come up once in a while.

Vanity is was what all these things were, and we weren't suppose to give in to the flesh because it was sin. This completely relates to "Parker's Back" when he was giving in to the attention of other women and tattoos. He was giving into the flesh. I remember growing up how I'd been tempted to give in to the flesh, and I would be guilty for days. At times I felt guilt if I was giving in to material things, and it isn't easy.

College is where I feel the most guilt, because I can do whatever I want without being supervised. It isn't that I'm doing the wrong things, but at home it seems as though I follow a script, and here I'm making my own script. I struggle with guilt because I want to do what is right, but at times I don't know what is right or wrong. Now I tend to go with the way I feel, but I pay a price for that everytime I deviate from the bible.

In the book of Genesis, "The Garden of Eden," the guilt portrayed there is a good example of how people behave in general. Eve knew she shouldn't have eaten of the fruit, and Adam her husband partook of eating the fruit also, and they both felt guilt when they were caught. As soon as God called their names in the garden, they knew they had done wrong. However, while they were eating of the fruit they didn't think what they were doing was wrong, but somewhere in the back of their minds they knew it was wrong. When you are given rules to abide by, and you break them you don't have to be arrested to feel guilt, it naturally appears.

In a Christian upbringing, everyone in your neighborhood is watching you. I remember my mom always told me "If I don't see you, God sees you." This remark stays with me up till this day. It strikes me when I'm doing something that I am supposedly not to be doing, I feel so burdened with guilt. You never feel guilt till you are usually caught doing something wrong or you know what you're doing is wrong. Where there are laws to abide by, there will be guilt.

Guilt can be positive from a different perspective. It can benefit you in making the right decisions at times. I know if I hadn't felt guilt at times, I would have made some mistakes in my life that I couldn't turn back on. I believe guilt keeps you on your feet at times. For example, I get lazy sometimes, and I don't want to go to class or study, but guilt makes you feel horrible and then I find myself doing what I have to do. Guilt causes humans to act in mysterious ways. I know this by what I've observed in my life and others.

The guilt I've experienced growing up felt very burdensome and negative at times. From the day I was born I was a born-again Christian. As a child I didn't understand all the rules, so I felt guilt all the time. Now that I am getting older, I see it from a different angle, because I understand what I am doing and what I believe in. Guilt I believe is insecurities and misunderstanding. When you believe in what you do, and there is no doubt that what you are doing is wrong, guilt plays no role in your life.

I believe guilt is instilled in us from a very young age on purpose. What better time to do it, when your mind is fresh, and you have no idea of the outside world. If I didn't feel guilt I would have done plenty of things that would not better my future. If you are incapable of feeling guilt of any wrongdoing, you are the most dangerous person on the face of the earth. Guilt helps us make judgments which work out for our own good. Whether you are religious or not you feel guilt because of what and how you view the world.

In my life I would have to say my religious beliefs, culture, and society has given a broad picture of what is right or wrong. I would only feel guilt due to the laws and traditions I have been accustomed to my whole life. Guilt had been a warning for me, and a way of God telling me if I was going in the right or wrong direction. It is my job to take heed to these signals, and use the mind that he has given me to figure out what I have to do. He gave us free-will, but guilt keeps us in a straight line.

Of course, there are a number of awkward constructions ("Guilt . . . is being aware of or suffering from guilt") and even a few simple mechanical errors here to which a composition teacher might well call attention. But Emma seems to me a relatively accomplished writer, someone not prone to such mistakes—who could easily correct them if they were pointed out to her—since she doesn't make them systematically. So I am inclined to think of these "errors" as what David Bartholomae calls "markers in the development of a writer" (Wiley 475), passages in which Emma is struggling with difficult ideas and therefore her language is under stress. In fact, I'd be tempted to respond to "errors" of organization here—the paper's repetition of key ideas, its feeling of tentativeness and even aimlessness, and most of all its inconsistencies of position—as evidence of a similar kind of struggle. It's as if Emma is trying—somewhat heroically—to write her way out of a discursive box: she wants to critique the Christian notion of guilt and its function in her life, but each time she invokes its familiar language, it overpowers and suffocates her critique, enlisting her attention in projects of its own. Her discussion of outgrowing adolescent prohibitions against "giving in to the flesh" becomes a discourse (though never quite a sermon) on "vanity," and her cynicism about the psychological "price" paid for "deviat[ions]" from Bible ethics somehow metamorphoses into a sympathetic retelling of the Eden story. Guilt, which one "only feel[s] . . . due to the laws and traditions," she ends up affirming by the paper's end—despite where she started—as something that "keeps us in line." Indeed, one can hardly avoid seeing Emma's inadvertent failure to clean up the extra verb in the sentence

"Vanity is was what all these things were" as a manifestation of this sort of Manichaean tug-of-war enacted during the middle of the essay, through which she essentially reverses her position on guilt from paragraph to paragraph—from seeing guilt as oppressive, to seeing it as potentially benevolent, and back again. Once invoked, the language of Christian judgment is impossible to resist and seeps into each of her discussions.

So what to do with a writer such as Emma, confronted with an intellectual problem she can't quite find the language to articulate? Rather than prescribing an outline or detailing the paper's formal shortcomings, I'd try to push Emma gently toward that language by initiating a dialogue that might build to a few key content-centered questions: What exactly would she like to say about guilt? Could she elaborate on what she means by "making [her] own decisions," by some guilt being "irrelevant to her now," and especially by defining guilt early in her essay as "the conviction to differentiate right or wrong"? And how does this sit with her later contention that "guilt can be positive from a different perspective" by "keep[ing] you on your feet"? If she wants to take a mixed position on the effects of guilt, how can she *name* the forms, functions, or aspects of guilt she sees as positive in order to distinguish them from the oppressive forms, functions, or aspects of guilt she experienced as an adolescent? Does she mean to make a distinction between matters of *conscience* and matters of simple *fear* or *shame*? Between guilt's *personal effects* and *social function*? Again, what David Bartholomae observes about one student writer at the level of the sentence seems to me to apply on a higher level for Emma: her work "fall[s] apart not because [she] lacked the necessary syntax to glue the pieces together but because [s]he lacked the full statement within which these key works were already operating" (Wiley 475–76). Emma needs more than anything else to be prodded toward a discovery of this sort of "full statement."

At the same time, however, I would also argue that this sort of oblique questioning alone might not be a fruitful approach with many writers who do not share Emma's native skills. I believe that supplying the connective tissue that ties together and shapes individual discussions in an extended piece of discourse is one of the most genuinely difficult cognitive tasks for developing writers to perform, and that different strategies for constructing this tissue are a matter of textual convention *to which many students simply may not have had great access in their individual histories as readers or conversants.* Indeed, preparing these pieces of connective tissue presents a relatively daunting intellectual challenge for most writers, necessarily requiring a higher degree of conceptual abstraction than other passages since they are the moments when ideas are named and when the often complicated relationships between those ideas, still submerged for many writers working on early drafts, finally require articulation. Though they can be understood in a mechanical, surface-level spirit, then— my students, for example, often talk about what they call "flow" rather than what I prefer to think of as "coherence"—transition moments are by nature the textual sites of intense intellectual work. If we accept that language is a kind of *equipment for thinking,* a way not simply to communicate but to generate and refine ideas—or, in Anne Berthoff's influential echo of I. A. Richards, an "instrument of knowing" (*Making of Meaning*, 85), a "means of seeing and articulating relationships" (25)[1]—then it is difficult to imagine that acquiring a sophisticated and pliable language in which to construct transition moments in texts is not an especially fundamental intellectual skill. And, of course, this is not a difficulty limited to novice writers: articulating the relationships between a given text's individual discussions becomes increasingly difficult as those discussions themselves become more complex. To "organize" a text is not simply to tidy it up; it is to wrestle with its concepts and their significance for readers in a deep and immediate way.

Intending to emphasize the generative potential of form, though understanding form in much more foundationalist, even scientistic, terms, some composition studies scholars have recommended offering student writers a comprehensive set of standing models or templates through which to develop and elaborate ideas. In addition to James Kinneavy's widely implemented scheme of four basic "aims" of discourse (referential, persuasive, literary, and expressive), made increasingly static when practiced (against Kinneavy's strong insistences) as "modes" in what's become known as the "current-traditional" approach to teaching writing, Frank D'Angelo's *A Conceptual Theory of Rhetoric*

(1975) described eighteen different basic conceptual paradigms for student emulation. The calls made by others, such as Mina Shaughnessy and Patricia Bizzell, for "a taxonomy of academic discourse" compiled through consultation with "our colleagues in other college departments" (Bizzell 37) resulted in the writing-across-the-curriculum movement's focused studies of disciplinarily defined genres and its commitment to the utility of teaching them. (See Charles Bazerman's *Shaping Written Knowledge* [1988] for one important study of science writing, for example.)

Many others, however, would object—and *have* objected—that this sort of modeling of taxonomized forms necessarily offers a limited range of artificial conceptual patterns that grossly simplifies the formal complexity of real discourse, encourages a superficial preoccupation with style, and discourages the purposeful and creative manipulation of form. Instead of supplying relatively static models for students, they recommend cultivating the general cognitive skills students use to give shape to their ideas, as well as a certain self-awareness about the effect of language-embedded forms on perception, interpretation, and articulation. Berthoff, for example, suggests one simple, practical method for cultivating meaningful focus and cohesion in student writing without encouraging students to make incidental, facile, or artificial surface connections between discussions (that is, to demand "coherence" instead of "flow"): ask students to outline *after* rather than *before* drafting. The idea here is to get student writers to crystallize their ideas without repressing or short-circuiting the messy but fertile dialectical process through which ideas are generated and refined—to use form as a way to *name* but not to *simplify.* More generally, Berthoff advises, at all costs avoid institutionalizing a rigid and static prewriting/writing/rewriting model of composing in course activities:

> Composing is not a process like playing a game of tennis or cooking a meal; there are no hard and fast rules, and it does not proceed in one direction—in a straightforward manner. Composing is not a linear process, though what it creates has linear form. That's why it's easy to mistake the methods appropriate to teaching the product as being equally appropriate to teaching the process. Thus conventional textbooks describe a sequence in which

you "get" your idea; develop it by means of the appropriate rhetorical strategies; outline the hierarchical order in which comparisons, allusions, definitions, examples are to be presented; and then write it up. The final stage of composition, then, is going over the paper to "catch" any errors. But nobody writes this way—not even the authors of conventional textbooks. (*Making of Meaning*, 20)

Meaningful form can emerge only from real thinking, Berthoff would say, while only superficial dogma and cliché emerge from the narrow imposition of formulas. Writers should articulate useful connections between significant ideas in transition moments, not smooth over incidental and artificial connections. Many teachers try to accomplish this by prescribing "clustering" techniques, such as provisionally gathering ideas in groups on individual sticky notes and then shifting them around to begin articulating connections between them and experimenting with different ways to sequence them. Others, following Berthoff's vision of composing as a recursive, continual process of forming, testing, writing, and reforming, encourage multiple, successive, provisional, shifting outlines. Outline not early, we might suggest to students, but often and in multiple ways.

Of course, though complex, the process of articulating connections comes to seem a kind of second nature to those writers steeped (like most instructors) in academic (and, more broadly speaking, *Western*) assumptions about text, which place a high premium on linearity and supporting evidence—to those writers, that is, who we tend to regard somewhat chauvinistically as "fluent" or even "literate" in most U.S. colleges and universities. Academics are much more comfortable dealing in abstractions than most nonacademic writers. But we should remember that the process of sequencing ideas and abstracting the connections between them is by no means a *natural* cognitive act—not all text is linear, particularly in non-Western cultures[2]—and students from "nontraditional" sociocultural backgrounds working at a variety of levels of cognitive sophistication often find this process particularly difficult. What we tend to recognize as textual coherence may not only be cognitively challenging for many students but also culturally distant and unfamiliar. So while we may well trouble over the ethical dilemmas associated with immersing students in culturally specific (and even socially empowered) ways of knowing,[3] many students will find the very concept of linear or sequential coherence alien and even irrational without some explanation. Indeed, though the language of remediation often implies a cognitivist understanding of differences in student skill levels, the belief implicit in most composition curricula that literacy skills can be taught suggests that they are more learned than natural. And for better or for worse, in most writing programs the ability to connect large ideas is often taken to define one of the key differences between the work done in standard courses and that done in remedial courses: "remedial" writers are restricted to work at the level of the sentence and paragraph; others push beyond.

While struggling to cultivate the sort of dynamism and recursivity of process that Berthoff sees as so important to writing-as-thinking, then, I also often present examples of student writing in class in order to begin talking explicitly about idea sequencing and the specific conceptual functions of transition moments in texts, as well as to begin providing models of different transition strategies. The paper reprinted below, written by a first-year student in a required first-year composition course at Oswego State, has been particularly useful for me. Kiera's transition sentences (since, indeed, she *does* write what we can recognize easily as transition *sentences*) crisply accomplish exactly what we expect such sentences to accomplish in academic discourse: they declare the focus of a new paragraph or section, name its relationship to the preceding discussion, and make the necessity of the new discussion clear in the context of the paper's general conceptual momentum. She invokes the conventionalized cueing language of academic discourse with great fluency and authority, using "furthermores" and "stills" expertly in order to negotiate deftly between some fairly substantial and complex ideas. Student readers are of course struck immediately by this authority and fluency of language—the "smoothness" of its "flow"—but their discussion almost always settles finally on how much *work* these cues do for her. She is not simply setting things tidily in place, they point out, but also *actively developing her ideas.*

The Language of Illness
Kiera Wooley

In the sterile environment of the psychiatric hospital there exists a special vocabulary that serves to further dehumanize and depersonalize the environment for the patients. Similar to medical hospitals, the language used in this environment is a mixture of acronyms and medical terminology, heavily sprinkled with the psychobabble popular in today's society. In order to function in this milieu, it is necessary for the patient to adopt this vocabulary, for it defines the nature of his or her hospitalization and provides for a sense of identity within the group. This form of communication allows the patient to separate himself from the painful nature of his visit, which, in many ways is helpful. Still, it is my contention that ultimately this vocabulary becomes destructive in the time after treatment, because this language changes the structure of the individual's thoughts, and causes him to view others in the same detached manner in which he has learned to view himself.

An excellent example of this is a typical statement that is meant to serve as an introduction in such a milieu. "Hi, my name is Taryn, and I'm here for ideation, DTS/O, PTSD, BPD, and ED. I'm on GO, so if you need anything, just ask." Translated, this means that Taryn considers suicide on a regular basis, is a danger to herself and others, has post-traumatic stress disorder, borderline personality disorder, and an eating disorder, a common diagnosis in these institutions. Furthermore, she only needs to be seen by a staff member every half-hour due to her elevated GO status. The language is consistent with these hospitals, and it is very common to introduce yourself to a new patient with one's diagnosis and life story. In fact, in many institutions, such as Four Winds Saratoga, it [is] a requirement that you do so. With this philosophy, the patient begins to identify himself with his disease, and no longer views himself as an individual with interests, talents, and goals. Furthermore, anyone that is introduced to Taryn, for example, doesn't think of Taryn as a person but as someone with a laundry list of problems of a serious nature.

In addition to these problems that occur within the hospital setting, further complications arise when the patient is thrust back into the "real world" after living in a protected reality for what is usually an extended period of time. Since the patient has adopted this new language that forms the basis of his communication, he must readjust to his normal speech patterns in order to deal with his environment in a functional manner. Even though this "code-switching," as it is called in linguistics, is usually simple, it is not so simple to relearn how to think. While it would be perfectly acceptable in the hospital to discuss the nature of one's mental illness, and patients are in fact encouraged to do so regularly, it is different when the patient returns to society. Discussion of one's problems is taboo in a society that is obsessed with the quick fix and denial as the solution to every problem. So the patient is then faced with the task of readjusting to an environment that is unsupportive and scornfully critical as well as generally ignorant about the problems facing today's mentally ill. Suddenly it is unacceptable to be what the patient has learned in the hospital he is: a disease, a diagnosis, a therapeutic problem to be unraveled.

Herein lies the central conflict. Now that the patient has accepted that he is first and foremost a psychiatric patient and a human being only second, what then does he do when he re-enters a society that wouldn't know the definition of PTSD if it was written on their foreheads? It has been my experience that he usually withdraws, sees himself as a societal outcast that must cling to a label to be worthwhile. An occasional slip of the tongue reveals him for what he defines himself to be, the diagnosis. The knowledge that he has gained as a patient becomes useless in his "new" environment, because no one else is equipped with the knowledge or the language used to express it. He finds himself alone, wearing a mask of normalcy and coating his words so as not to frighten anyone with the dark side of life. The openness he enjoyed in the hospital, the immediate kinship he found with the others who were there is now gone, an[d] no one can even understand his thinking anymore as it is shaped by language that is restricted to the select few who have been forced to learn it.

I conclude, then, that the experience of psychiatric hospitalization is worthwhile only while one is hospitalized, for the process of learning new methods of communication and self-identification is useful only within the milieu in which it is taught. Once outside, the language is as useful as conversational Latin, for all the results it produces. Furthermore, the very nature of the sterility of this language is isolating. While alternate methods of communication can be useful, in this case it is ultimately destructive to the individual in the sense that the result is not communication, but isolation. Communication should bond individuals, not divide them.

But if "expressivists" have seen a narrow pedagogical focus on organization in student writing as cultivating a mechanical, stifling, intellectually empty formalism, others have worried about its potentially prescriptive nature—in particular, that it might suggest to impressionable student writers that all effective discourse follows certain generic and universal principles of coherence. Indeed, though it doesn't subscribe to Sheridan Baker's formula exactly, it's hard not to notice that Kiera's paper *is* five paragraphs long, or that its language is self-consciously academic. It would be not only a disabling lie but also a great disservice— even an act of fairly crude intellectual imperialism—to suggest to students that this is the *only* viable way to make sense, the *only* legitimate form of textual coherence. Still, I would argue that teaching form by no means necessitates ordaining or seeming to ordain any single universalized Form, and in fact that a close attention to organizational patterns and strategies actually offers a powerful way—maybe the only way—to begin to suggest differences between *modes* or *styles of coherence*. The manipulation of standing formal conventions is simply the way meanings get made, and forms will not go away if we pretend they don't exist, refusing to acknowledge them because they seem confining. The trick, of course, is to avoid being either narrow or prescriptive about them.

In my own classroom, this means, among other things, trying to define the parameters of what counts as organization as broadly as possible, even while accepting a certain unavoidable level of cultural bias, as I have suggested. Most readers they will encounter, I tell students in an attempt to qualify my generalization, will expect finished transactional texts (1) to set themselves up to be experienced sequentially, (2) to integrate some number of discrete but related discussions within some single, overriding purpose, and (3) to either fulfill or subvert some conventionalized and legible system for indicating the relevance of those individual discussions. But within these general parameters, I encourage students to take up whatever forms seem to them compelling and effective in the context of a given audience and project. In fact, this even becomes the basis of one paper I routinely assign in introductory writing courses: identify some prose voice you find compelling, use it as a stylistic model for a short piece of your own on any topic you like, and prepare a short preface for this piece describing the specific formal qualities you found compelling in the model, as well as why you found them appropriate for your project. This relativism of form also means adopting a pluralized vocabulary for formal qualities: it is more than paying simple lip service, I think, to speak regularly in class, as I have here, of relative "modes" of coherence, of multiple "cueing systems" legible for different audiences in different contexts, and of transition "moments" rather than transition "sentences" (in the hope that I will avoid raising the specter of some narrow and universalized textbook model from writing courses past).

But perhaps most important for me, avoiding formal prescriptiveness while teaching "organization" means offering a range of different prose models based in recognizably different coherence patterns. The paper reprinted below, by a Syracuse University junior in an advanced writing course on creative nonfiction, does much to press my pluralized vocabulary of form into service for students. It has been particularly effective for me because—given that it clearly doesn't cohere in the way Kiera's does, for example, following the general conventions of acceptable academic language—many student readers insist at first that it's simple chaos, that it *has* no organization. Only on closer and more systematic inspection does its relatively subtle and unusual organizational logic and system of reader cues become apparent to those students. Only after some discussion do they recognize the rhythm of its short chapters alternating between present-tense descriptions and interpretive glosses, its coordinating repetition of ritualized dialogue, and its slow, careful development and qualification of a central critique. This raises some key questions for those students: *What are the implicit rules of this cueing system? What is its organizing logic? Where does this form come from? Who exactly is this text's imagined audience? Why do they think like this and not in other ways?*

Untitled
David Coffey

Walking in all I could think about was Michael Keaton in his movie about breaking drug addiction, *Clean and Sober*. Would it be like the movie? I had images of everyone smoking cigarettes, biting their nails, fidgeting in their seats and healing their souls. Would everyone be depressed, nervous, defeated? Would it be like the stereotype everyone thinks of?

"Hi, I'm Bill, and I'm an alcoholic."

"Hi, Bill."

"Well, I haven't had a drink in four months."

Everyone smiles, "Good Bill."

"I'm taking it day by day and everyday I feel better and stronger."

"Good, Bill."

AA, Alcoholics Anonymous. The Ten or Twelve or Fifteen Step Program, all on the lower level of Crouse-Irving Hospital. Sitting around, drinking coffee, eight or nine in a room that doesn't seat more than twenty-five or thirty. A room about the size of two school buses with an open space at one end. This allows them to set up a table on which is placed a coffee machine and an assortment of pamphlets. Here we are, a block from a college campus, in a world that somehow doesn't seem to fit.

Suddenly they start shuffling in. This is it, the real patients, the real cases, the ones straight from detox. Bathrobes, slippers, hair uncombed, these people don't look healthy. These are people on the verge of something.

"Hello, my name is Mike, and I'm a cross-addicted alcoholic."

"Hi, Mike."

Michael has been to jail, the city jail, the state jail. He's been locked up a long time, even got drunk and high in jail. You couldn't keep Mike away from alcohol. Mike's been sent away to the mental hospital for a few years, was out on the street for a couple more.

Mike's open and public baring of his soul brings to mind the afternoon talk shows and the question they usually raise in my mind, why are these people telling us this? People willing to tell their worst sins and failures to anyone who will listen. These are the types of secrets that help to display why they allow for anonymity in church confessional booths. Despite this, and almost embarrassingly so, the members of AA are willing to tell these secrets in public with seemingly no sense of apprehension. And, just as anyone can turn on Oprah and hear about some housewives affairs, anyone can walk off the street and into an AA meeting and listen to Michael's drunken perversions. The only difference being that Mike doesn't get his fifteen minutes of fame.

Andrew has been in drug raids with his bike gang. He's been shot and he's shot people. When he lost his job and when his wife, his brothers, and his parents wouldn't speak to him he decided that it was time to get help. Now, instead of running drug raids with his bike gang, he delivers toys to sick kids. When he gets mad at his supervisor at work, instead of "beating the crap out of him," he gets down on his knees and prays. I've never formally met Andrew.

"Hi, I'm Andrew, and I'm a drug addict, a cocaine addict, and an alcoholic."

"Hi, Andrew"

Just about every American knows the story of the televangelists. Jimmy Swaggart, Jim Bakker, Tammy Faye

Bakker taking the American public for everything they can get their hands on and then winding up in a motel with a soon-to-be-famous prostitute. All this comes out in the papers and a month later you see them on the TV, eyes overflowed with tears. The images seem all too clear. Jimmy Swaggart with his choir behind him, his hands raised to heaven, uncontrollably crying, tears streaming down his face. Or Tammy Faye with her overdone mascara running down her cheeks. All the while claiming the reasons for their actions were the temptations of evil and, in some cases, the Devil himself.

You can't help but get the same feeling of empty remorse and self-righteousness from the members of AA. People who seem to have screwed up their lives so badly, and many times the lives of those around them, that they have to come back week after week and put on this big display in order to avoid their own guilt. Do they come to AA and talk about the evils of alcohol and alcoholism as a disease in order to avoid facing up to what they have done? I've seen a lot of drunk assholes in my life, I've even been a drunk asshole a few times myself. It's almost as if the members of AA don't want to admit that they were idiots so it becomes easier to come to these meetings, talk about their "disease," and claim they have no power over their own lives. Somehow claim that they're grown adults with no control. Among some members there even appears a type of arrogance. They are better than others because they once messed up so bad, and now they're able to show up for work in the morning. "We were so bad that now that we're O.K., were somehow more O.K. than you."

"Hello, my name is Terry, and I'm an alcoholic and a drug addict." Terry is wearing the bathrobe and slippers of the detox unit.

"Hello, Terry."

"I've been on drugs for over ten years and it's time for me to get off. My whole life's been messed up and I just want to try and put it all back together. They want to take my kid away which is probably right 'cause I can't take care of her like this. I want to feed her and not spend all my money on dope. I don't want to end up a doped up whore."

Terry is starting to quiver now, her eyes are filled with tears. The man in front, who looks like my neighbor's dad, gets up for a cup of coffee and offers to the person next to him, she declines.

Terry regains, and out of nowhere states "I just hate those intellectual drunks."

Just about everyone at this meeting is either in the detox unit at Crouse-Irving or were formerly in the unit. They return to remind themselves of where they were once at, what they once looked like. Everyone here has been so low that none of these stories seem to faze them. People admitting that they've shot and stabbed people, that they've spent money on drugs that they could have used to feed their kids, that they've beaten their ex-wives and, in one case, have thrown her out of a second story window. No matter how bad the crime all they can say is that we've all made mistakes, take it day by day.

In spite of all the apparent emptiness all one has to do is look at Terry with her uncombed hair and hospital gown, crying in the corner and losing her grip on her sanity, then picture her kid at home, and think maybe, for some of these people, there is no other way.

"Hello, I'm Henry and I'm an alcoholic."
"Hello, Henry."
Hank either beat his wife and kids daily or drank away his house and family business, who knows? He'll just have to take it day by day.

Though I seldom discuss Kiera's and David's papers at the same time in my courses, the discussion of each is almost always informed by comparison to the other. As students wrestle with the two papers' different organizing principles and modes of development, though, the key pedagogical move becomes finding the right moment to focus their attention back on their own writing. I always assign these student examples on days when my students have also brought drafts of their own to class, and I always try to use this discussion as a way for them to interrogate those drafts. After students have done a close, silent reading of their work, and with a discussion of these papers fresh in their minds, I ask students to identify at least two significant moments of transition in their own papers. What ideas are they moving between? What are the relationships between those ideas? What language do they use to name or signal those relationships to readers? I like to think that this activity ends not only in more sharply conceived individual texts, but also in an enhanced ability to think about textual form in ways that are neither narrow and mechanical nor essentialist and prescriptive.

Notes

1. Though she herself seems to connect the term as it's been invoked by many teachers with a kind of surface tidiness, no responsible discussion of "organization" in student writing could fail to mention Berthoff's influential work, which articulates an especially dynamic and complex notion of form—in fact, by and large equating the writing act with what she calls "forming." See *The Making of Meaning* and *Forming, Thinking, Writing* for further elaboration of Berthoff's complex representation of the dialectical relationship between internalized forms and externalized thoughts.

2. See Xiao Ming Li's *"Good Writing" in Cross-Cultural Context* for a careful description of the effect of cultural difference on preferred coherence patterns, especially in terms of characteristically "Eastern" and "Western" assumptions about coherent text.

3. Patricia Bizzell's *Academic Discourse and Critical Consciousness* almost certainly represents the best, most thorough, and most sustained exploration of these dilemmas in composition theory.

Works Cited

Baker, Sheridan. *The Complete Stylist*. New York: Crowell, 1966.

Bartholomae, David. "Inventing the University." Rpt. in *Composition in Four Keys: Inquiring into the Field: Art, Nature, Science, Poli-*

tics. Ed. Mark Wiley, Barbara Gleason, and Louise Wetherbee Phelps. Mountain View, CA: Mayfield, 1996.

Bazerman, Charles. *Shaping Written Knowledge: The Genre and Activity of the Experimental Article in Science*. Madison: U of Wisconsin P, 1988.

Berthoff, Anne E. *The Making of Meaning: Metaphors, Models, and Maxims for Writing Teachers*. Montclair, NJ: Boynton/Cook, 1981.

Berthoff, Anne E., with James Stephens. *Forming, Thinking, Writing: The Composing Imagination*. 2nd ed. Portsmouth, NH: Boynton/Cook, 1988.

Bizzell, Patricia. *Academic Discourse and Critical Consciousness*. Pittsburgh: U of Pittsburgh P, 1992.

Coles, William E. Jr. *The Plural "I": The Teaching of Writing*. New York: Holt, Rinehart, and Winston, 1978.

D'Angelo, Frank J. *A Conceptual Theory of Rhetoric*. Cambridge: Winthrop, 1975.

Kinneavy, James. *A Theory of Discourse*. Englewood Cliffs, NJ: Prentice-Hall, 1971.

Li, Xiao Ming. *"Good Writing" in Cross-Cultural Context*. Albany: SUNY P, 1996.

Macrorie, Ken. *Uptaught*. New York: Hayden, 1970.

CHAPTER 8

ORCHESTRATING PEER-RESPONSE ACTIVITIES

This chapter includes strategies for constructing specific peer-response activities. It is also designed to help new teachers decide how to construct sequences of peer-response sessions so that teachers can, if they wish, use a different one each class meeting during a unit. The chapter includes specific kinds of questions that peers might answer early on when a writer is considering possible topics for writing. Other questions focus peers' attention on subsequent tasks that writers need to complete: generating ideas for developing the topic, selecting material from that which has been generated, organizing material in ways that help readers, editing surface features of emerging texts, and the like. Further, the chapter offers suggestions for introducing peer-response activities, bringing them to closure, and encouraging writers to use peer responses effectively.

Approaches to Productive Peer Review

FIONA PATON

State University of New York at New Paltz

Fiona Paton provides some background and guidelines for constructing peer-review assignments.

This essay aims to present a concise discussion of the main procedural and theoretical issues associated with peer-review workshops in the college classroom. Although these guidelines are broadly applicable to all academic levels and disciplines, I have developed them within the context of a required, one-semester writing course of around twenty-four first-year students, and this is the context in which I imagine them being used. The advice I offer here has evolved gradually over the course of my own teaching and represents much trial and error, throughout which I have drawn constantly on the ideas of students and colleagues as well as published theorists. Hence, I make no claims to originality. My goal here has not been to develop a new approach to peer review, but rather to present the most useful advice in a form that can be reviewed and consulted easily. In short, this is the sort of introduction to peer review that I would like to have had when I began to teach composition. The essay is divided into three parts intended to reflect the normal sequence of events in a typical writing course: Introducing Peer Review, Setting Up Peer Review, and Maintaining Peer Review. This discussion is followed by a list of basic guidelines that summarizes the key principles of effective peer review.

Introducing Peer Review

One of my own early mistakes was to launch into peer review with few preliminaries, believing that the students would automatically accept its importance and benefits. They, however, were often less than enthused, viewing the process as busywork with no tangible benefits. Many anticipated receiving superficial or misinformed comments from their peers while at the same time suspecting themselves of the same inadequacies. And anyway, since it was the teacher who was going to grade the writing, what was the point of getting your classmates' advice, which was usually wrong anyway?

Therefore, one of the most necessary elements of productive peer review is to establish a positive but realistic attitude toward the process. Openly acknowledge that it is not a magical process that will automatically result in a better paper. Present peer review as an activity that, when taken seriously and practiced regularly, develops skills that are essential to successful writing, whether in your class or any other. For writers, peer review develops an awareness of writing as a process of drafting and revising, which can significantly reduce anxiety. It offers practice in reworking finished discourse, something that inexperienced writers are notoriously loath to do. And it develops a more concrete sense of audience and the valuable insight that language does not always do what its author intended. For readers, peer review provides training in critical analysis and the application of the same principles they need to master in their own writing. Peer review exposes students to a variety of forms and techniques, and helps them to develop a sense of what works and what doesn't (Harris 371). Furthermore, peer review fosters important interpersonal skills: the ability to listen respectfully, to voice opinions openly, to offer advice tactfully, and to negotiate between different points of view.

Here I find it helpful to give students a brief overview of the pedagogical rationale behind group work, partly to move them beyond the negative association with busywork and partly to emphasize that group work is a skill that needs to be learned like any other. Using Bruffee, I point out that teamwork is now the norm in business and industry, and that employers routinely complain that college graduates are not only too dependent and passive, but are also competitive rather than cooperative in the workplace (Bruffee, *Collaborative Learning* xii). Collaboration also results in better learning while in college because the process of verbal negotiation encourages the application rather than the storing of knowledge. And it can be empowering in its demonstration that knowledge is socially constructed by communities that negotiate their way toward consensus (Bruffee, *Collaborative Learning* xiv). Students can begin to see themselves as generating rather than passively receiving knowledge in their discussions of each other's writing. Productive collaboration does not necessarily happen spontaneously, however, and students should be aware that even in peer review they need to consciously work on skills such as validating individual input, rephrasing ideas, clarifying questions, reading nonverbal cues, and using disagreement productively. A handout summarizing such skills encourages students to take group skills seriously.

At this point, it is important to reassure your students about their roles as peer reviewers. They are not expected to "play teacher," but rather to respond as supportive and interested peers who, while not expert writers, are literate and educated and quite capable of offering constructive criticism. Reassure them also about their roles as writers—they do not necessarily have to implement all the suggestions they receive, for while some may be useful, others may not. But emphasize that part of the value of peer review lies in learning to assess the choices open to them as writers and in developing a conscious awareness of why they make certain choices. To conclude this preliminary discussion, give your students the chance to openly voice their questions and concerns.

Finally, before the first peer-review session, take them through the process itself by running a practice session using a sample student paper. This is an important step, and time should be made for it because it allows you to model the process for the students and coach them on appropriate feedback before they begin to work with each other. You may have particular strategies you want them to use, such as using a straight line to mark sentences that seem unclear, a wavy line for sentences that are especially effective, noting questions in the margin, or circling potential grammar problems. Be aware, however, that most first-year students will approach peer review as a proofreading exercise and will tend to remain on the level of correcting spelling and punctuation simply because this is the most obvious and least risky type of feedback to give. Hence, during this first practice workshop emphasize the difference between revising, editing, and proofreading, and focus the students on substantive revision issues such as focus, audience, development, and coherence. This is an important first step in their transition from writer-based to reader-based prose. Also, coach them in the appropriate wording of suggestions. Ask them to consider the difference between *criticism* and *feedback* (Spear 131). When working with a past student paper, it can be instructive to have them generate examples of insensitive, vague, or misdirected comments, just to clarify the difference between constructive and unconstructive comments. Remind them of the importance of praise. End by having the students restate in their own words the criteria for effective peer review. At this point, your students should be ready to carry out peer review for real.

Setting Up Peer Review

Of course, before even setting foot in the classroom you will have had to make a number of important procedural decisions regarding what students bring to peer review, what they do during peer review, and the extent to which they are held accountable for peer review. Careful advance planning and specific instructions can avoid the kind of frustration and ambiguity that lowers student morale, so be prepared to explain exactly what is expected and why, and provide a printed handout that students can refer to later.

First of all, I avoid the phrase "rough draft workshop" because "rough draft," to most first-year students, means a page of barely legible notes hastily scribbled during the chemistry lecture preceding your class. Productive peer review requires a typed and *completed* draft representing the student's best effort to that point. Remember, however, that lack of confidence is often behind a student's reluctance to produce a completed draft for review; completed drafts, after all, can be evaluated in a way that rough notes cannot. Offering to work with students even before a review session may help them come to class more confidently prepared. In any case, encourage a sense of professionalism toward peer review, and do not absent yourself from the process. I usually leave the class alone for the first ten minutes; then I return and circulate unobtrusively, sitting in on discussions, reading a page here and there, and generally demonstrating active interest in their discussions of writing. This may seem to run counter to the idea of the student-centered classroom, and many composition theorists maintain that peer review sessions should provide an unauthoritative space for students to take control of their own writing without the hovering presence of the teacher (Wiener 57). A class that is based on graded writing assignments, however, can never elide (and shouldn't pretend to) the authority of the teacher, and students generally appreciate your involvement and interest in the review process.

Ideally, peer review should be a process of active learning that leads the students toward greater independence as writers and thinkers. But they need a great deal of structure to begin with, and they need to be pushed beyond noncommittal comments such as, "I really liked your paper, but I'm not the one grading it." Response sheets with questions or prompts are a good way of focusing students while helping them internalize the principles you are trying to teach. Response sheets can take several forms. The least productive are checklists that employ the same basic criteria each time ("Is there an introduction?" "Is there a thesis statement?"). Apart from being boring to work with, such checklists usually consist of yes or no questions that invite simple yes or no answers. I have found it more productive to tailor response sheets to the demands of the assignment at hand. This gives you the chance to restate your own criteria for the assignment and focus the students on the principles they are currently learning, thus showing that peer review is a progressive rather than a repetitive activity. Initially, I limit questions to no more than five. After the first two sessions, I encourage students to bring in a few questions of their own based on their specific concerns with that paper. At the same time, I increase the number of prompts I provide but ask that students select only the ones that seem most relevant to their paper. This allows for a degree of flexibility—students are not restricted to only the areas you have identified, and as they become more independent, they take more control of the review process by themselves choosing what their peers will comment on. Of course, this is by no means the only way to structure peer review. Peter Elbow's method generates both objective and subjective responses through

criterion- and reader-based questions. Bruffee distinguishes between descriptive, evaluative, and substantive reviews, and requires students to draft and revise peer-review essays that are
then graded. (For an excellent summary of these two approaches,
see Holt.)

I have found that groups of three work best for peer review.
Students need more than one response to their writing, but any
more than two tends to be counterproductive—the students get
tired and their comments become superficial. I also switch the
groups around for each workshop so that by the end of the semester each student will have worked with every other student.
This runs counter to much collaborative theory, for groups do
take time to settle down and develop the trust and commitment
necessary for maximum productivity (Johnson and Johnson 119).
And, it has been argued, this spirit of trust and commitment is
especially important in peer review, when students can feel threatened by the evaluative process (Lindemann 185). I have found,
however, that when the same students always work together for
peer review, they can fall into roles that are not necessarily enabling. All writers naturally feel most comfortable with readers
who affirm rather than question their favored rhetorical strategies, and when peer-review groups become comfortable cliques,
it is often at the expense of innovation and growth. In addition,
the less able writer may become dependent on a more accomplished peer and get stuck in the role of advice taker rather than
advice giver. This can lead to frustration and resentment on both
sides. By grouping students solely according to who has not yet
worked together, I try to communicate that everyone has something to learn from everyone else. I avoid organizing peer-review
groups in terms of ability, race, or gender because students quickly
perceive a teacher's underlying agenda, and they can become
uncomfortable with what they see as their symbolic status. For
full-scale research projects, these are important considerations
and should be discussed openly with the students before groups
are even formed. (For a good introduction to these issues, see
Fox.) But in peer review, I try for a genuine sense of community
within the class as a whole.

Once students are in their groups, remember to give them
sufficient time to respond fully to each other's work. This can be

problematic if you invite students to read their papers aloud, for this is more time consuming, and three peer reviews cannot realistically take place within a fifty-minute class (which is standard in many universities). Bruffee insists that the sharing of papers should always take place orally because this helps students develop an ear for rhythm and fluency while increasing their sense of control over and responsibility for their writing. He also rightly points out that reading aloud fosters a sense of community (*Short Course* 149). Students do not always read well, however, and trying to follow one voice in the midst of seven others can be frustrating for the listeners. It is also often difficult to critique a paper that has been heard only once. A reader, on the other hand, can pause, reread, and make notes as he or she goes along. Having said this, I am very much committed to the idea of the writing classroom as a community of supportive and interested peers, and hence I always try to leave time at the end of class for the verbal sharing of responses within groups and the verbal sharing of writing with the class as a whole. Rather than have students read their entire papers, I ask everyone to choose something good from a paper to share with the class. This can be the idea itself, a particularly effective paragraph, a few lines of dialogue, or even the title. Sharing good writing at the end of class, even if just for a few minutes, brings the slightly chaotic process of workshopping to effective closure and encourages students to feel positive about the drafting process.

In an ideal world, our students would always be enthusiastic about peer-review sessions, would always come prepared, and would always give it their best shot. But unfortunately, peer review is often the first thing to give in a student's busy schedule, so I have learned to make my students accountable for both preparation and participation. First of all, a finished paper is not accepted without a previous draft and written feedback from someone in the class. If a student has to miss a workshop, then he or she has the opportunity to make this up outside of class with the cooperation of a classmate. Most accept this as fair, but the knowledge that they will have to arrange an alternative peer review on their own time is a great incentive to come to class. Second, I evaluate students' written responses in terms of the effort they put into the process. This usually takes the form of check, check plus, or check minus and counts for 10 percent of the final grade. This system has proved manageable and effective for me. Bruffee, as noted earlier, has a much more elaborate system that requires students to draft and revise peer-review essays that are then formally graded, and while I respect his approach, I find that it takes too much time away from other activities. Peer review, I feel, should be integral to a writing course, but not the entire course.

Maintaining Peer Review

Be aware that maintaining peer review as an effective classroom practice requires consistent effort from the instructor and the students throughout the semester. Once the students have done a couple of draft workshops, their responses can become a bit habitual—they've become comfortable talking about one or two things, or they've learned some of the instructor's catchphrases, and they begin to trot them out without a great deal of thought. This is why it's important to tailor the prompts to the individual assignment; instead of working their way through the same set of standardized criteria, the students are evaluating each other's papers in light of the demands of that particular assignment. Of course, basic principles underlying academic discourse will be repeated from one assignment to another, but the review sessions themselves should not seem like rote exercises. Create different response sheets for each assignment, and, as discussed earlier, ask the students to formulate their own questions so that their own perspectives become part of the learning experience.

In order to keep students focused on peer review as a process of active learning, I ask them to keep a brief log of each session. This log consists of two entries, one from the writer's and one from the reader's perspective. As the writer, each student reflects on what was or was not helpful in the session. As the reader, each student considers what he or she has learned or had reaffirmed by reading the other two papers. These logs, along with the peer-review comments and draft, are turned in with the final draft.

Sometimes these are worth anonymously sharing—particularly positive reflections on good feedback and new insights. I also make a point of sharing good peer-review comments with the class in order to constantly reinforce what is meant by constructive feedback. Praising and encouraging students in their reviewing as well as their writing is crucial, for they are often equally anxious about both activities. It can also be constructive to ask for their feedback several times throughout the semester in the form of anonymous written comments and to make any necessary changes based on that input.

I have recently experimented with another dimension of peer review, which I have dubbed "reconvening." It has often seemed to me that an important final step of the process is missing: students get together, offer each other feedback, go off and revise their drafts, and turn them in, but never know whether their input was helpful to their peers. Nor need they ever feel any particular sense of responsibility, because their comments disappear with the paper and are never heard of again. This missing step seems to me to deny peer reviewers a valuable learning opportunity, because they never get to see whether their comments agreed with or diverged from those of the instructor. Developing a more analytical, readerly perspective is part of what students should achieve through peer review; as it is, however, they never find out whether their comments were on or wide of the mark. Reconvening brings students together in the same groups when the papers are returned so that comments can be shared and compared. Of course, this works best in a portfolio-based course in which separate grades are not assigned to each paper, for most students will not initially feel inclined to share their grades with their classmates. Even when grades are assigned, however, these need not be disclosed; instructor and peer comments can simply be summarized. Is this too threatening for first-year students to deal with? Perhaps, and I have received mixed responses from my own students. But it seems worth experimenting with as a means of closing the current gap in the circuit of writing, responding, and rewriting.

Guidelines for Peer Review Workshops

◆ Call it "peer review," not "rough draft workshop." Require students to bring a complete typed draft to class. Peer review is more productive if the readers are not frustrated by illegible or incomplete drafts.

◆ Talk about peer review before the first session. Students invariably have some misconceptions and resistances, usually based on lack of confidence and their reluctance to "play teacher." Be honest about what peer review can achieve and what you expect from them.

◆ Model the process in class before doing it for real. Using a past student paper, have students critique it in groups using your questions. Show them the level of specificity you're after. Talk about appropriate ways of wording criticism. Emphasize the importance of praise.

◆ Hold peer-review workshops the class before the final draft is due. Students sometimes complain about lack of time to revise, but remember that they ought to have a complete (not rough) draft ready for peer review. If major rewriting is required, students can request an extension.

◆ Groups of three work best, giving students two responses to their work. Responding to more than two papers is exhausting for the students.

◆ Having two sets of comments on one peer-review sheet is convenient, but this can encourage the second reader to simply restate the first responses. You might put your questions on a transparency, or supply two comment sheets per student.

◆ For the first few sessions, provide a small number of specific questions that clearly highlight the criteria you have established for that assignment. For instance, "Comment on the use of concrete examples. How do they support the thesis? Which is most effective, and why?" Later, you can allow them to choose from a variety of prompts and also have them generate their own questions based on the specifics of their own papers. This leads them gradually toward greater independence.

◆ Don't ask simple yes or no questions such as, "Does the paper have a clear focus?" If you do, the students will give simple yes or no answers.

◆ Make the paper, not the writer, the focus of attention in your questions.

◆ Change the groups around for each session. Otherwise, students get stuck in certain roles and can become either dependent or resentful. The security of working with the same people every time is not worth the pedagogical disadvantages. Should you deliberately put certain people together? You can, but everyone should have the chance to work with everyone else. Make the process seem random. Don't let students think you have labeled them in terms of most or least proficient.

◆ Make the students accountable for peer review in some concrete way. At the very least, it should be part of their class participation grade. A check, check plus, or check minus is a simple method of evaluating their effort. Make peer review a required part of the process by accepting only papers accompanied by a previous draft and peer-review comments. If you take the process seriously, your students will be more inclined to.

◆ Show the students that you read their comments. Share some good responses in class, and explain why they're good. Keep them anonymous and no one need feel threatened. Praise is a great incentive, and students need to know what they are doing right.

◆ I usually leave the room for a short time during peer review, just to give the students the sense that this is their class time. When I return, I unobtrusively join a few groups, reading whatever pages are available and writing comments in the margins. I feel that this creates a more positive atmosphere—I am involved in the workshop rather than sitting behind the desk reading.

◆ Finally, peer review should not be conducted in silence. If a community atmosphere is to be fostered, students need to talk to each other. Leave at least ten minutes at the end of the session for students to discuss and clarify their responses. Encourage a relaxed atmosphere.

Works Cited

Bruffee, Kenneth A. *Collaborative Learning: Higher Education, Inter-dependence, and the Authority of Knowledge.* 2nd ed. Baltimore: Johns Hopkins UP, 1999.

———. *A Short Course in Writing: Composition, Collaborative Learning, and Constructive Reading.* 4th ed. New York: HarperCollins, 1993.

Elbow, Peter. *Writing with Power: Techniques for Mastering the Writing Process.* 2nd ed. New YorhÙ Oxford UP, 1998.

Fox, Thomas. "Race and Gender in Collaborative Learning." *Writing With: New Directions in Collaborative Teaching, Learning, and Research.* Ed. Sally B. Reagan, Thomas Fox, and David Bleich. Albany: SUNY P, 1994. 111–22.

Harris, Muriel. "Collaboration Is Not Collaboration Is Not Collaboration: Writing Center Tutorials vs. Peer Response Groups." *College Composition and Communication* 43 (1992): 369–83.

Holt, Mara. "The Value of Written Peer Criticism." *College Composition and Communication* 43 (1992): 384–92.

Johnson, David W., and Frank P. Johnson. *Joining Together: Group Theory and Group Skills.* 5th ed. Boston: Allyn and Bacon, 1994.

Lindemann, Erika. *A Rhetoric for Writing Teachers.* 2nd ed. New York: Oxford UP, 1987.

Spear, Karen. *Sharing Writing: Peer Response Groups in English Classes.* Portsmouth, NH: Boynton/Cook, 1988.

Wiener, Harvey. "Collaborative Learning in the Classroom: A Guide to Evaluation." *College English* 48 (1986): 52–61.

Reflection on Peer-Review Practices

LISA CAHILL
Arizona State University

Moving away from peer-review workshops that emphasize detailed reading heuristics, Lisa Cahill explains her current, less formally structured approach to these activities.

My Teaching Background

At this writing, I have been teaching composition for three years, but when I began teaching composition I was not necessarily a proponent for *or* an opponent of peer review. Initially, work in the classroom was primarily informed by my understanding of the critical reading process. I tried to incorporate peer review, rather unsuccessfully, in the first course that I taught, because I did not really understand how to facilitate a productive review session. My first composition teaching experience metamorphosed into a writing-across-the-curriculum (WAC) partnership at Northern Arizona University between the English department and the School of Forestry. This experience helped me see ways that the peer-review process could function differently and more productively. During this time, I recognized a need to know more about the social, academic, and personal exigencies for writing.

My WAC experiences taught me a great deal about the value and logistics of peer review and collaborative writing experiences. The students with whom I consulted were regularly engaging in discussions of their work with their classmates; they trusted one another as credible readers and as responsible, careful, and knowledgeable reviewers. Sharing a discipline enabled them to bypass some of the obstacles that often confront students in first-year composition courses. The students in forestry were part of an established discourse community that provided them with certain advantages over students in first-year comp. Forestry students shared a language, a methodology, and an understanding of acceptable discursive forms. Students in my composition class had different disciplinary affiliations and experiences, and different reasons for participating in peer review.

Students in first-year composition courses bring a variety of writing experiences to the table. Some are familiar with peer review, while some have had fewer opportunities to carefully critique others' work, provide specific suggestions, and illustrate their concerns with examples from their peers' texts. Another very human factor tends to compound this difference of experience—a protocol of politeness that tends to impede an honest exchange of ideas. Understandably, some students are somewhat leery about pointing out "weaknesses" in their peers' work, while others may feel overwhelmed at not merely having to discover specific ways to strengthen the paper but also having to pose questions that will encourage a productive peer-review meeting. While peer review may seem like a simple exercise in building a sense of classroom community and in applying critical reading skills, it really is a more complex endeavor for students.

Likewise, peer review can be a complex endeavor for instructors who want to successfully implement it in their classrooms. In the fall of my first semester at Arizona State University, I taught English 101. My approach to peer review was predicated on one major goal—helping students learn how to recognize and respond in detail to the "right" questions during peer-review meetings. What was not fully clear to me at the time was the fact that there are not necessarily "right" or "wrong" questions. Questions for peer review are really only guided by one principle—the fact that writers' texts as well as their rhetorical goals vary from text to text and from situation to situation. Therefore, peer-review questions are contingent on the context of the writing assignment; different writing tasks call for new sets of questions. Instead of challenging students to write their own questions for peer review *and* to negotiate their concerns and responses with one another, I took responsibility for creating the questions to be used at different stages of the peer-review process. For each paper, I also prepared long peer-review response sheets derived from the criteria appearing in our text, *The St. Martin's Guide to Writing*.

The Theory behind My New Practices

In 1985, Faigley argued for the social perspective in studying nonacademic writing; however, applying this perspective in the composition classroom is just as important. With the rise of social constructivism that followed soon after, compositionists began to realize the necessity of looking beyond the visible signs offered by a text to deeper issues of ideology and discourse communities' conventions—writers' reasons for making certain choices about content, organization, and style. Faigley's social perspective acknowledges the textual and individual perspectives that focus on genre-specific conventions, writers' perceptions of tasks, and writers' applications of strategies. The social perspective takes off in an important direction, however, a direction that is important when peer review is present in the composition classroom. Faigley's advocacy for researchers to "study how individual acts of communication define, organize, and maintain social groups" (235) is a task just as crucial for both teachers and students. James Berlin supported the notion of teachers as researchers, and it is time also to encourage our students to be researchers—to reflect on their practices and goals as well as the real and potential impact of their communications.

I am now working to make the peer-review process more than a series of questions that function in the textual vein—analysis of the way that stylistic and rhetorical figures are used. I want my students to "view written texts not as detached objects possessing meaning on their own, but as links in communicative chains, with their meaning emerging from their relationships to previous texts and the present context" (Faigley 235). To expand their notions of audience, purpose, context, and argumentation, students need to reflect on the traditions out of which their papers may come. In my English 102 class, for example, my students write the following series of essays: justifying an evaluation, taking a position, speculating about causes, and proposing solutions. I encourage them to think beyond their classmates and me as their only interested readers. I ask them to identify communities that are or have been realistically affected by the issues they write about and to investigate the histories of controversies and solutions surrounding that issue.

In doing so, the peer-review stages have to be altered. During group brainstorming sessions, I encourage students to invent a general list of questions related to the genre in which they are writing. Then students work in pairs and trios to work through different stages of the writing process. I ask them to set their own agendas, and I also encourage them to use peer review for more than the reading of a draft or polished document. Students will discuss the range of topics and positions under consideration, the communities related to these topics, possible counterarguments they may encounter, potential organizational structures, implications of their arguments, and previous progress made on these issues. All of this constitutes my response to Lester Faigley's 1985 call.

Rather than having my students begin peer review one week before the final draft is due, I integrate the process at the beginning of each unit. I want students to talk about their reasons for choosing to include particular subjects, positions, and evidence in their texts. In Lee Odell's ethnographic study of supervisors and administrative analysts who evaluated proposed legislation, he suggests that students "could benefit from discussion throughout the composing process" (277). Furthermore, Odell warns that teaching students fixed sets of analytic procedures designed to elicit ideas and reader responses may not necessarily be the best approach. His concern is that "in trying to reduce cognitive complexity we unwittingly increase it" (276). The sets of questions I posed to students for the four genres in English 101 were, for the most part, productive. They were only productive, however, in that moment and may not have translated beyond the scope of each assignment. Furthermore, these predetermined questions may have limited students to a certain degree. Odell is justified in asserting that "the writer must also be able to translate those terms [from heuristics or analytic procedures] into specific strategies or questions that will enable him or her to investigate a particular subject matter" (276).

Peer-review practices need to make students self-sufficient and capable of reading and writing in a variety of contexts and able to respond to a variety of rhetorical situations—be they civic, personal, professional, or academic. I have come to understand the composition classroom as a testing ground for students' professional, civic, personal, and academic endeavors. The classroom is a site for practicing heuristics, taking communicative risks, and participating in social efforts to create and interpret meaning. Peer review is one way to provide students with the chance to "practice the interpersonal skills that will enable them to function effectively in a dialogue or group discussion" (Odell 278). Allowing them to generate questions, direct their own meetings, and negotiate tensions are important precursors for their roles outside of the classroom.

Reflecting on Past Practices

My original intentions were good ones; I wanted students to assist their peers in writing cogent papers of which they could be proud. But the means I used to achieve my goals were not necessarily the best. Throughout the semester, I provided students with lengthy worksheets that asked them to answer open-ended questions that required more than a yes or no response. Rather than gradually weaning students away from canned or prepackaged questions and making them responsible for devising the questions as a class and as partners, I continued to use the worksheets. I discovered that, as readers, students were spending more time in quiet, individual contact with the paper than in discussion. They could not look up long enough to really *talk* to the writer; they felt compelled to answer all the questions and then return their responses to the writer. In turn, as writers, the students had to individually confer with the written responses instead of talking to their readers.

Because my approach to peer review in the composition classroom was to supply students with the "right" kinds of questions—questions that I took sole responsibility for creating and distributing—my students had a difficult time taking responsibility for directing the reading of their papers. I put students in pairs and gave them a twenty- to thirty-minute time slot during which to work. I provided them with very general directions: talk to one another, share concerns, help direct your partner's reading, and be prepared to discuss strengths as well as possible revisions. Although I left it up to my students to negotiate the ethics and logistics of peer review, I exempted them from a crucial part of the process—the development of a set of reading heuristics.

While I do not consider my original approach to peer review a total failure, I do recognize the flaws inherent in it. I also realize how important it is for me as a teacher to take a moment to examine my own assumptions and goals for peer review *before* creating classroom activities. That kind of examination, however, cannot stop there. It is vital to engage my students in a discussion about their concerns, goals, anxieties, and ideas related to peer review. In this way, we can co-construct an approach that is more fluid and flexible—one capable of responding to their ever-changing rhetorical goals. In this way, we can get closer to a community, to a communal ethic of trusting one another like that of the forestry students.

Works Cited

Berlin, James A. *Rhetoric and Reality: Writing Instruction in American Colleges, 1900–1985*. Carbondale: Southern Illinois UP, 1987.

Faigley, Lester. "Nonacademic Writing: The Social Perspective." *Writing in Nonacademic Settings*. Ed. Lee Odell and Dixie Goswami. New York: Guilford, 1985. 231–48.

Odell, Lee. "Beyond the Text: Relations between Writing and Social Context." *Writing in Nonacademic Settings*. Ed. Lee Odell and Dixie Goswami. New York: Guilford, 1985. 249–80.

Using Group Conferences to Respond to Essays in Progress

SUSAN K. MILLER

Mesa Community College

Although Susan Miller describes strategies for encouraging peers to respond to classmates' writing, she also discusses strategies for melding peers' responses with a teacher's responses. This can be difficult to orchestrate because student writers often privilege the comments and questions offered by the person assigning the course grade.

When I began teaching first-year composition as a teaching assistant, one of my biggest challenges was encouraging students to respond to each other's writing in helpful, constructive ways that would facilitate revision. I also found that once they had written responses to each other, they were often reluctant to revise according to what other students suggested, although they would listen to what I said about their essays. I wanted to combine the benefits of peer response (Brooke, Mirtz, and Evans 3) and teacher response (Harris 5), so I began conducting group conferences on work in progress, a strategy originally introduced to me by Greg Glau.

Responding to work in progress not only helps authors see their writing through another's eyes, but it also helps readers see their own writing in a new way. Erika Lindemann claims that a class where students discuss their work in progress "enables students to see themselves as real writers and readers, engaged with others in using language to shape communities" (34). I wanted my students to see themselves as part of a writing community, negotiating meaning (Gere 73–74). I also wanted to create an environment in which all students would be encouraged to participate, in which they would still feel ownership over their own writing, and in which they would be exposed to the writing of others. I find that carefully constructed group conferences meet these goals.

I conduct group conferences by having students bring in first drafts of their essays and then distributing copies of that first draft to the other members of their writing group (usually two to three other people). If the class meets in a computer-mediated classroom, I usually have them send their essays by e-mail or post them to an asynchronous discussion forum. They read each other's essays as a homework assignment and write responses based on questions I have given them in class. Finally, we meet at a scheduled conference time to discuss the drafts together, looking at each student's essay in turn. Everyone (including the teacher) must say one thing he or she thinks each author did well and one thing each author could work on in a revision. The author is always given a chance to clarify or ask questions, and then we go around the circle and say what we will revise before the next class. Students give their written responses to the authors to help in their revisions, and they are all expected to bring revised second drafts to the next class period.

As we go around the circle and share our comments, we often find that we have similar ideas. The confidence level in the classroom rises as students realize that many of their suggestions are the same as the teacher's. They begin to acknowledge that their peers have helpful, constructive comments to offer. At the end of the semester, several students always comment that group conferences were the most useful part of the class; they realized that we could all help each other in the process of writing.

Group conferences have helped me with the challenges mentioned earlier. They give students a framework for offering their comments, so that they have a model for writing helpful suggestions that will facilitate revision. In addition, they hear the comments of other students and the teacher about the same essays, clarifying for them what was expected in the assignment while providing additional examples of the kinds of comments they could make. Although most students are still reluctant to offer their suggestions in front of the whole group at first, their comments are usually confirmed by the others in the group, either by students saying things like, "Yeah, I noticed that, too," or by other students making similar comments during their turns. Authors are always given the choice of using the comments they find the most helpful—nobody is required to change everything suggested to them.

The day students bring their first drafts to class, I give them the following instructions:

Group Conference Instructions

1. *Read the essay thoroughly and critically.* As you read, consider whether the author has fulfilled the essay assignment.

2. *Read through the questions we discussed and practiced answering in class* (usually questions I have given them in class or questions from a text). Write *at least* one page in response to these questions for the author.

3. *Be certain to pay equal attention to things the author did well and places in which the author could improve the essay.* Try to phrase your response so that it gives specific help, so the author has an idea of what to revise. Try to write a response that you would like to receive—one that gives praise and also suggests places to begin rewriting.

4. *Finally, remember that this is the most exciting step in the writing process.* This is when we get to see our writing through the eyes of our audience, a luxury we often don't have when we hand in writing for an assignment or send it out to be published. Come to conferences with an open mind; be prepared to listen to your peers' comments, and be ready to share constructive comments of your own.

I always give them questions to respond to in step 2 that we have already discussed in class (and often they have written the questions themselves). Ideally, we would have spent a class period prior to this one answering the questions together for an essay we have all read. This process helps students feel comfortable as they answer the questions for each other, because they have seen an example of what I expect them to do.

The following draft of an essay by one of my students, Lynn, along with group conference comments from her classmate Nancy and from me, provide an example of how this process works. Lynn wrote an essay about an event that was significant in her life, a rock-climbing trip that she took shortly after arriving at college. Her first draft follows:

A Remembered Event 1

"I can't believe I survived after the three days" that was the first thing I said on Thursday morning, the day we were doing back from the trip. I went to a rock climbing with my teacher and friends last spring. I hadn't done rock climbing before and I was not good in any of the sports. I was really scared and I thought the trip was going to be long for me, but instead, it was a wonderful experience. Kayo is one of my good friends. We decided to go on that trip together. Both of us were beginners. We were all scared and couldn't believe we just sign up for a rock climbing trip. A week before the trip, we when to the library and borrowed a lot of rock climbing magazines. We were looking at the pictures and day dreaming. We were dreaming about being one of them, even we knew it's impossible. We were climbing up and down the bathroom door, tables. . . .

We left the school in the Monday morning. There were seven other girls went with us. On the way to the rock climbing jam, we didn't really talk to each other. As soon as we got to the Jam, we started to help each other out, we started to talk. The jam was really big that had six climbing well in the middle. There were made for different levels of people. It took me a long time to find the right size shoes for me and to put them on. The shoes were tight on me, they weren't comfortable to wear.

When I was walking, I couldn't walk too fast because the sticky thing in the bottom of the shoes. On the wall, there were things stick out from the wall that we could use to climb. I started with the easiest one on the walls. It wasn't hard. I tried the harder one, then another one. When I was climbing, my friends would watch me and tell me what's to do. The second day, we went out to a real climbing place a lot of big rocks. The teacher taught us the right way to climb. We were learning fast. People were helping each other again, then, we got closer to each other. The third was the best day in the whole trip. We took a long hike in to a mountain. We were walking with our equipment , lunch, water. . . . It wasn't an easy hike with all those things.

Finally, we got there. We put sunscreen on because the sun was really strong at that time. Susan the teacher and other two girls went to set the climbing equipment up. There were two of them. One was a easy one the other was harder. We took turns went up the easy one. I made it the first time. It was easy so not a big deal. The fun part is the harder one. It was a tall one with a slid patter and smooth surface. Some of the people went up there easily because they had been climbing before. It was my turn. It wasn't hard at the beginning but on the half way, I could started feel the wind blowing, I couldn't find any thing for my right hand to hang on, then I couldn't find any space for my foot. I almost cried. My friends were telling me where to put my hands and feet, but I just couldn't find any way to do it. Suddenly I herded Susan said "Lynn, you are doing great, just keep going, you are safe up there." I felt much better.

But still, my legs were shaking. I decide to try one more time see if I could go any further. Then I did. I made it all the way up there. I stood there for one minute just look at the view. The fifteen minutes I was climbing I felt like one year. The view was really beautiful.

I didn't think the trip could be so fun for me. I went all way up there when most of them didn't make it. Other then that, I met a lot of friends. After I came back from the trip, I felt stronger. That was a good thing for me to do.

Lynn's first draft gives us the chronology of what happened, but she doesn't provide the reader with specific details. Several of the students in her conference group asked her questions about the details of her story, demonstrating to Lynn that she had to consider her audience as she wrote her story. Nancy, a fellow student in Lynn's conference group, made the following comments to Lynn about her first draft:

To Lynn,

I think it's a well-told story. I think the climax of this story is when you were trying to climb up the harder wall on the third day. It was described minutely, so I could imagine you climbing up the wall easily. I, however, can't understand some basic things and the significance. I want to know more abut the rock climbing and the trip. What is rock climbing? (What kind of equipment does it need? Where can you do it?) Why did you and your friend decide to go on the trip? Was it a tour of many clubs? How did you know that? Did you practice something before leaving for the trip? Where, when and to whom did you say, "I can't believe I survived after the three days."?

I think most of the story is described vividly, but you need to describe how you felt on each day. If you add them, the story will be more vivid and more autobiographical. What did you feel after you experienced the rock climbing for the first time? What was the sticky thing in the bottom of your shoes? Did it affect your climbing? What did you think when you saw the real climbing place? Did you feel excited at night of the second day or before you tried the harder wall? "After I came [back] from the trip, I felt stronger." I think this sentence means how important the trip was for you, so it will be better if you add more information about the feeling or the life. After the trip, did this experience affect your life? If so, how? The organization of your story is so nice, I think. The beginning arouses my curiosity and lets me want to read it. You should describe the second day more minutely. And add your feeling or opinion to the ending.

Nancy helped Lynn start the revision process by asking specific questions about details in the story. She asked about details of the trip, how Lynn felt at different times, and she asked for more description of parts that she didn't understand or that she thought were underdeveloped. All students don't naturally ask questions about the essay in their written comments, so I model this technique in class when we practice responding before the first group conference. To encourage them to use questions in their responses, I demonstrate how much easier it is to start revising when we have specific questions to answer. Nancy did not comment on the mechanics or overall organization of Lynn's essay because I emphasize that we are looking at the content of the essay in the first draft. We conduct a workshop on editing toward the end of the writing process, and at that time we look at mechanics, organization, and overall clarity.

When I commented on Lynn's first draft, I asked about several details that Nancy mentioned. We both asked for more information about the car trip on the way home, Lynn's introduction to the story. In addition, we wanted to know more about the events on the third day—the main focus of the trip. We both asked specific questions about how she felt and what she saw on that day, and Nancy asked for more information about the other days, too. My comments also focus on specific things that I like in Lynn's essay:

Lynn,

I'm impressed with the fact that you went rock climbing! It's a very challenging and dangerous sport, and you should be very proud of your accomplishment! I love to go hiking, and I can relate to your excitement at finally reaching the top. I am a little scared of rock climbing, however, so I admire your courage.

I really liked how you started the essay in the car on the

way home. It's almost as if you started at the end and then went back . . . a "flashback." Can you tell us more at the very beginning about how you felt on the way home? Were your muscles sore? Were you tired? Were you happy that you went, even though you didn't think you could do it? Did you feel like you would ever go again? You don't have to give us a lot of detail there, but I just wanted to know more about how you felt . . . what your emotions were.

In the middle part of your essay, you give some details about each of the three days of the trip. I was wondering if you could focus on Day 3. It seemed like that was the most exciting and challenging day. Can you give us more details about that day? How did you feel as you climbed? Where did you put your feet and your hands? Who was in front of you and who was behind you? Were you roped to your instructor? Were you scared? Did you ever look down? These kinds of details will help us to imagine the climb as if we were there.

Finally, I wondered if you could go back to the car scene that you have in the introduction at the end of the story. This would provide a frame for your essay that would help to conclude it. Just an idea . . . perhaps you can think of an even better way to end it.

Good job, Lynn! I look forward to reading your revision.

Lynn used Nancy's and my responses, along with the comments from the other students in her group, to revise her draft. Everyone asked for more description of the third day, so Lynn focused on that part of the essay in her revision. The varied sets of comments she received from her group members helped her to look at her draft through several sets of eyes, and then she chose the suggestions she found most important to start her revision. In the draft that follows, Lynn has included more details about her trip, including large-scale revisions such as a more complete description of her climb on the third day and smaller explanations such as describing the purpose of the sticky substance on the bottom of her shoes:

Rock Climbing

"I can't believe I survived after the three days." That was the first thing I said on Thursday morning, the day we were coming back from the trip. I went rock climbing with my teacher and friends that week. I hadn't done rock climbing before and I was not good in any sports. I was really scared, and I thought the trip was going to be long for me, but instead, it was a wonderful experience.

Kayo is one of my good friends. We decided to go on that trip together. Both of us were beginners. We were all scared and couldn't believe we just signed up for a rock-climbing trip. A week before the trip, we went to the library and borrowed a lot of rock climbing magazines. We were looking at the pictures and day dreaming. We were dreaming about being one of the rock climbers, even though we knew it was impossible. We were climbing up and down the bathroom door and tables.

We left the school on Monday morning. There were seven other girls who went with us. On the way to the rock climbing jam, we didn't really talk to each other. As soon as we got to the jam, we started to talk and help each other out. The jam was really big, and had six climbing walls in the middle. They were made for different levels of people. It took me a long time to find the right size shoes for me and to put them on. When I was walking, I couldn't walk too fast because the bottom of the shoes were sticky to help me climb. On the wall, there were things sticking out from the wall that we could use to climb. I started with the easiest wall. It wasn't hard. I tried the harder one, then another one. When I was climbing, my friends would watch me and tell me what to do.

The second day, we went out to a real climbing place, which had a lot of big rocks. The teacher taught us the right way to climb. We were learning fast. People were helping each other again, and, we got closer to each other.

The third day was the last and best day in the whole trip. We walked for almost one hour. Finally, we got to the bottom of the wash. It was such a beautiful place. There were two big walls on our left and right side. The rocks were red just like the sun on top of us. We almost forgot to put sunscreen on because of the beautiful scenery. We all sat on a big rock for lunch. The lunch was only some cold sandwiches I made that morning, but, I thought that was the best thing I had ever eaten because I was so hungry by the time. After the lunch, our teacher Susan who was also a very good climber went another way to set up the ropes. After that, we started to take turns climbing.

Brook had been rock climbing for several years, so she went up first. All of us were watching her. She was so good that she didn't even need to think. We weren't surprised when she made it. She came back down and told us how beautiful the view was on the top. After her, I watched several people climb. The beginning part was easy, but it got harder at one point. Most of the people gave up right at that point.

It was mine turn to go up. I put the harness on and took several steps forward. When I was climbing, I felt it was different from what I saw. It was much harder to do by myself. I put my hand on, then feet. Very fast, I was in the middle of the wall. I got to the hard part where almost everyone stops at. I looked down; I couldn't see people's faces because I was so high. The wind started blowing and my legs started shaking. I couldn't move either of my legs. I started yelling for help: "God, I am so scared what should I do! Somebody help me!"

People down there just tried to calm me down. I could hear people saying:

"Lynn, you are doing good, just put your right hand in that crack and put your foot into that hold."

I took a big deep breath and decided to move on again. I put my right hand in a crack so I could push my self up. But when I put my right hand in the little space, I felt something just pinch my hand. That hurt, but I couldn't let my hand go. Until I pulled myself up, I realized my hand was on a cactus. The next step was even harder. I got to put my balance on my left leg. It wasn't an easy thing for a beginner to do. I tried to put my weight on my left leg, but I felt like I wasn't going to stay on any more. My arms started shaking not only that, my throat was so dries that I couldn't even say anything. I was stuck. I didn't know what to do.

" Maybe I should just give up right here."

These words kept coming up to my head. When I was just going to give up, I heard Susan say, "Lynn, you are doing good. Try to go further if you can. You are doing just fine."

After I heard that, I felt much better. I took another deep breath, I found another crack that I could hang on to. Then, I tried the best I could. I was up. I just did the hardest part and the rest was easy. I just kept going, try to find place to put my hands and feet. Suddenly, I heard people clapping. Then I realized I was on the top of the wall. I made it! My legs and arms were still shaking though. I looked around. The wind was blowing, but I felt good. I was on the top for a minute to just enjoy the view and the happiness. I could see the top of the mountains and the world.

On the way back, all of us were in the van singing because every inch of our bodies was so sore that couldn't we move anything except our mouths. We were singing and talking as loud as we could because we were so happy. All of us were glad we went on this wonderful trip together. Not only learned how to rock climb, I also got some great friends and a good memory.

Although Lynn revised her essay further after her second draft, she was pleased with the description of her climb in her revision, and she began to realize the importance of having a real audience read her writing. The group conference helped Lynn by providing her with a forum for discussing those comments openly before revising. In addition, the conference helped Nancy by providing her with a model for writing comments to the author and giving her the opportunity to listen to other comments about the same draft.

Works Cited

Brooke, Robert, Ruth Mirtz, and Rick Evans. *Small Groups in Writing Workshops: Invitations to a Writer's Life.* Urbana, IL: NCTE, 1994.

Gere, Anne Ruggles. *Writing Groups: History, Theory, and Implications*. Carbondale: Southern Illinois UP, 1987.

Harris, Muriel. *Teaching One-to-One: The Writing Conference*. Urbana, IL: NCTE, 1986.

Lindemann, Erika. *A Rhetoric for Writing Teachers*. 3rd ed. New York: Oxford UP, 1995.

A Possible Sequence of Peer-Group Responses to a Student's Emerging Text—Autobiographical Essay

DUANE ROEN

Arizona State University

In the following article, Duane Roen presents a sequence of activities designed to help students deepen their engagement with each other while refining emerging pieces of writing

Day 1: The writer brings to class a list of five or six possible autobiographical moments. In small groups, peers ask questions of the following kinds:

How much does the writer know and care about each moment?

What seems to be the personal importance of each moment?

How well can the writer develop this topic?

What makes the event memorable?

What kinds of details can the writer recall?

To what extent is the event steeped in pathos?

Goal: To help the writer find an appropriate autobiographical topic for the essay.

Day 2: The writer brings to class a list of details about one autobiographical moment. In small groups, peers ask questions and offer comments of the following kinds:

What do you think is the personal importance of this event?

How obvious is the importance?

What is the significance of this detail?

What other sensory details can you recall?

What is a _____?

Goals: To help the writer generate further details and reflect further on personal importance. To help the writer narrow or broaden the focus.

Day 3: Discuss a published essay using some of the criteria listed earlier (day 1 and day 2) to evaluate its effectiveness.

Goal: To help students see how the basic features can work in a remembered-event essay.

Day 4: The writer brings to class a partial or full draft of the *narrative* of the autobiographical moment. In small groups, peers comment on or ask:

I identify with _____ in what you've drafted.

I like _____ in what you've drafted.

What is a _____ ?

How would you describe the purpose of the _____ that you mention?

What did you do/think/feel when _____ did _____ ?

Now what do you think is the significance of this event?

Goal: To develop the narrative further. To contemplate personal importance.

Day 5: The writer brings to class a full draft of the narrative and explanation of its personal importance. In small groups, peers comment on or ask:

How have you made the explanation of personal importance more than what is obvious to anyone reading this essay?

Why did you separate the explanation of personal importance from the narrative? or

Why did you integrate the explanation of personal importance and the narrative?

Goal: To sharpen the statement of significance.

Day 6: The writer brings to class a revision of the essay, one that reflects previous peer responses. In class, peers ask or comment:

How have you used or not used previous peer responses in this revision?

Why?

I identify with _____ in this version.

I like the way that you've done _____ in this version.

Goal: To encourage the writer to use peers' responses more fully.

Day 7: The writer brings to class a fully revised version of the essay, one that is ready for editing. In class, two peers read and suggest ways to edit the essay's surface features—punctuation, syntax, word choice, spelling, and the like.

Goal: To help the writer edit surface features.

Day 8: The writer brings to class a revised and edited version of the essay. In class, the writer reflects on the act of composing this essay.

Goals: To better understand composing as a social-epistemic activity. To begin or continue the work of constructing the course portfolio.

Possible Sequence of Peer Responses to Developing Arguments

Note: On any given day, you might be doing other activities in class.

Day 1: The writer brings to class a list of several possible topic areas. In small groups, peers ask questions and offer comments of the following kinds:

What kind(s)/degree of investment do you have in each of these topics?

What do you want to learn about each of these topics?

What do you already know about each of these topics?

How could you work with each of these topics across four papers?

What kinds of sources will you need to explore as you work with each of these topics?

What views do you hold about each of these topics?

What makes each of these an arguable topic?

If you pose each of these topics as a problem, what are possible solutions?

Goal: To help the writer see the challenges and opportunities of each potential topic.

Day 2: Having chosen a topic, the writer brings to class elaborated written responses to the questions from day 1. In small groups, peers offer the following questions and comments:

How have you altered your position on this topic since you began investigating it?

What would it take for you to reverse your position on this topic?

What kinds of research do you need to do to learn about other positions on this issue?

What has brought you to your current position on this topic?

What do you need to do to strengthen your ethos as you argue for your position?

What kinds of emotions (pathos) does this topic evoke in people?

Goal: To help the writer better understand his or her position on the topic.

Day 3: The writer brings to class a list of appeals that support his or her position on the topic. In small groups, peers brainstorm counterarguments for each appeal that the writer presents. Peers also brainstorm counterarguments for appeals that the writer has not yet generated.

Goal: To help the writer see other perspectives on the topic more fully; they need to be addressed.

Day 4: The writer brings to class lists of written responses to the counterarguments raised on day 3. In small groups, peers help the writer decide how to develop each response to counterarguments: acknowledge, concede, and/or refute. Peers will also discuss needed research for supporting counterarguments.

Goal: To help the writer understand how to address other perspectives on the topic effectively.

Day 5: Discuss an argumentative essay using any criteria from above (days 1–4) to evaluate its effectiveness.

Goal: To help students see how the basic features can work in an essay arguing a position.

Day 6: The writer brings to class a partial or full draft of the position essay. He or she has labeled each of the following parts that appear in the draft:

1. *exordium* (introduction): where the writer gains attention and/or establishes

2. credibility

3. *narratio* (narration): background or context for the argument

4. *propositio* (proposition): thesis or major claim

5. *partitio* (partition): delineation of the steps to be followed in the case

6. *confirmatio* (confirmation): proof and evidence in support of the thesis/claim

7. *confutatio* (confutation): refutation of opposition viewpoint

8. *digressio* (digression): related points

9. *peroratio* (peroration): conclusion and/or call for action

In small groups, peers offer the following kinds of questions and comments:

You've acknowledged that counterargument, but you may need to concede that point or refute it.

Are there any counterarguments you might concede?

You may need to qualify your major thesis a bit more to read something like this: " . . . "

What do you think would be the effect of reorganizing the essay around refutation, given that you have so much to refute?

What support do you have for that assertion?

What documentation do you have for that support?

You cite a known left-wing/right-wing political journal here. You might use a more neutral source instead.

You use *The National Enquirer* to support your assertion about George W. Bush. You might look at the following indexes to find more reliable, even scholarly, sources. (These indexes will vary, depending on the holdings of your school library.)

Goal: To help the writer see the gaps.

Day 7: The writer brings to class a full draft of the position essay. In small groups, peers might use any criteria above (days 1–6) to evaluate the full draft. Peers might also repeat the conversation from day 6.

Day 8: The writer brings to class a revised version of the full paper. In small groups, peers focus on the ways in which the writer has quoted and documented sources.

Day 9: The writer brings to class a revised version in which he or she has attended to the use of sources. In small groups, peers do round-robin editing of the writer's revised position paper.

Day 10: The writer brings the polished version of the position paper to submit to you. At the beginning of class, the writer reflects on the process of composing the position paper. This written reflection will serve as invention material for the portfolio later in the course. It may also serve to make the transition to the next paper in the course.

CHAPTER 9

RESPONDING TO IN-PROCESS WORK TO PROMOTE REVISION

Whereas the previous chapter focused on peer responses, this chapter focuses on teacher responses. Although getting peers to do this work helps everyone in the classroom (writers, peers, and teacher), teachers can also respond to in-process work. Some essays include response strategies that encourage writers to be responsible for their writing—as opposed to thinking that teachers are responsible. Then Jasna Shannon and Rebecca Jackson address a key support system that writing instructors at many universities enjoy—the local writing center. Their essays explain the role that such centers can play in providing individualized assistance and responses to student writing in progress.

Less Is More in Response to Student Writing

Clyde Moneyhun
University of Delaware

Moving away from numerous "corrections" toward a more pared-down style, Clyde Moneyhun outlines a rationale and method for rethinking traditional responses to student writing.

Response to student writing, especially written response, might be the issue I've spent the most time thinking about and working on during my twenty-year career as a writing teacher. My methods have run the gamut from maximal to minimal, from massive and minute "correcting" in red pen to not reading certain drafts at all.

At first I corrected because that's what my teachers had done to my writing (though not so massively or minutely) and because that's what supervisors expected of me. One early mentor insisted that I use the correction symbols from the inside cover of the huge hardback rhetoric we were required to use: "mm" for "misplaced modifier" sticks in my head. These were the bad old days of "current traditional" pedagogy, with eleven essays in fifteen weeks and no revisions (except for grammar). I spent an average of forty-five minutes on each paper. Little of that effort seemed to help students improve their writing. I sometimes wish I could do a blanket mailing to people I taught during my first couple of years to apologize for what amounted to student abuse.

It wasn't long, fortunately, before the winds of change blew across the field, and teaching writing as a process required us to find new ways to respond to student writing. The May 1982 issue of *College Composition and Communication* turned my world around. In "Responding to Student Writing," Nancy Sommers documented "the appropriation of the text by the teacher," showing me how I'd done more to confuse and intimidate my students than help them. I saw that I was reacting to every draft, whether it was early or late, in the same way, with "rubber-stamp" comments that didn't respond in any real way to what was actually on the page. In the same issue, Brannon and Knoblauch raised the stakes in "On Students' Right to Their Own Texts," framing the issue almost as an ethical one. My rubber-stamp comments were most often a willful misreading and mis-understanding of students' intentions, informed as they were by my inner vision of the perfect paper, not by any real engagement with what they had written. Another early essay that meant a lot to me was Elaine Lees's "Evaluating Student Writing," which helped me move away from correcting toward posing questions to students that put more of the writing decisions in their hands.

I still ask new teachers to read these essays in the graduate writing pedagogy course I teach, along with other classic research on the subject, especially the essays in Lawson, Ryan, and Winterowd's *Encountering Student Texts,* which challenge us to place our reading of student texts on a continuum with all our acts of reading, and to complicate our view of what student writ-ers might "intend," what student texts might "mean," and what reader roles we might be playing consciously or unconsciously. My graduate students typically resist the ways in which process-centered pedagogy forces a new style of response from us, at least until they are a semester or two into their teaching, when (they come back to tell me) it all starts to make sense.

The specific lesson I preach is that "less is more" in response to student writing. Over the years, I've shifted my emphasis from an intensive, extensive, one-on-one relationship with individual students in my response comments to the creation of an environ-ment in which students can work on their writing intensively, with my comments as only one of the forces that help create their texts. I try to structure good readings, make good assignments, set up good student-student interaction, have good one-on-one time with students myself (especially outside the classroom), and generally keep everybody on track through the many, many drafts that are produced at various paces. Most of all, I try to set it all up and then get out of the way, dipping in now and then with minimal response.

The specific content of the comments is not terribly original. First, I try to make the right kind of response at the right time. On early drafts, I comment on global issues such as choice of topic, orientation toward topic, and focus of topic. Later, I'm on the alert for how the topic is presented, with what points in what order, with what supporting ideas and information, for what purposes, for what audience. Still later, we turn our attention to style and, finally, mechanics. Second, I try to remain flexible about the stage the particular draft might be at, not insisting on attention to mechanics just because the paper is in its fourth or fifth draft when it still needs work on more fundamental issues. Third, I try to remain open to the student's intentions for the text and try to avoid imposing my own. In my comments, I am more likely to ask a question than make a specific suggestion; if I make suggestions, I might list three mutually exclusive directions the paper might go in and ask the student to choose one or invent a fourth. Fourth, all my comments are formative rather than summative, always pointing forward to the possibilities of the next draft rather than backward to the infelicities of the present draft. My comments on "final" drafts often begin, "If you had more time to work on this . . . ."

I think my strong point is the discipline I bring to the response process. I comment on only one aspect of writing (or at most two) on any draft, and then only briefly and with as much concision as possible. Rather than overwhelm students with response, I try to point to the one most basic issue that needs attention at that point in the process, and I do it draft after draft after draft. My most minimal comment goes on the draft that has made no progress other than a few commas and verb tense changes: I refer the student to my previous comments and offer the opportunity of another rewrite. In the end, in spite of the number of drafts, I spend no more time on response to student writing than I did in the bad old current-traditional days, maybe even less.

One implication of the "less is more" method is the sheer number of drafts it asks students to write—in my classes usually five or six or more. Some students resist this process, especially at the beginning, preferring instead that I comment on "everything that's wrong" so they can "correct" it all in one shot. I stick to my method patiently, though, and usually see a shift in attitude among enough of the students to convince me that it works. The majority eventually takes advantage of my "open rewrite" policy, soliciting comments they know will be minimal but might also be helpful. I take this as evidence that they have taken a step toward writing in the ways that Sommers tells us professional writers do. In addition, students often write on end-of-semester evaluations that I "really listen" to them, that I'm open to their ideas, and that I respect them, and I take this to be a nice by-product of the "less is more" method.

Works Cited

Brannon, Lil, and C. H. Knoblauch. "On Students' Right to Their Own Texts: A Model of Teacher Response." *College Composition and Communication* 33 (1982): 157–66.

Lawson, Bruce, Susan Sterr Ryan, and W. Ross Winterowd, eds. *Encountering Student Texts: Interpretative Issues in Reading Student Writing.* Urbana, IL: NCTE, 1989.

Lees, Elaine O. "Evaluating Student Writing." *College Composition and Communication* 30 (1979): 370–74.

Sommers, Nancy. "Responding to Student Writing." *College Composition and Communication* 33 (1982): 148–56.

One Dimension of Response to Student Writing: How Students Construct Their Critics

CAROL RUTZ
Carleton College

Carol Rutz describes how she designed a study to help her assess students' fascinating assumptions about teacher responses to their writing.

Response to student writing at all levels, K–graduate school, is an active research site for composition theorists. I was introduced to this area of inquiry in a composition research methods course taught at the University of Minnesota by Chris Anson, who is well known for his investigations into teacher response.

At that time, I was teaching my third composition course. I had entered the Minnesota Ph.D. program with no previous teaching experience, although I had done a great deal of training, workshopping, and public speaking. The transfer to teaching was easier than I expected, with one important exception: responding to student work. Our courses used a draft-and-revise model—the usual mode—and I was conscientiously responding to drafts as well as final papers. In addition, students read each other's work and commented on drafts. In theory, student writers would benefit from having several readers actively comment on their work.

By that third course, I was beginning to notice that students sometimes revised according to the advice they received from me. Sometimes they ignored it. I thought I understood the role of power in students' choices: they were more likely to "obey" the person who wielded the grade book than they were a fellow student who crossed out commas in no particular pattern. Where content was an issue, students seemed to give more weight to my comments than to peer comments for at least two reasons: (1) I was doing the grading and would notice if they took my advice, and (2) I presumably had more experience and could offer them suggestions that peers might overlook. And for those students who rejected my advice—well, the reasons could range widely, from stubbornness on their part to ghastly handwriting on mine.

Since then, I have learned from my students and from the response literature that many more factors affect students' revision processes. (See the Further Reading list.) I also take note of warnings by Straub and others to avoid taking over student texts. But at that time, I wondered if students would respond to anonymous criticism. In the absence of the critic's credentials, such as "instructor" or "peer," would students take the content of criticism seriously?

Study Using Anonymous Criticism

To test the effectiveness of anonymous criticism, I recruited six students, five men and one woman, from my business writing class to help me with a pilot research project. All of the volunteers were juniors, although their ages ranged from twenty to forty. Borrowing techniques from social psychology, I gave the six volunteers a cover story. I asked them to write 500-word position papers on any topic of their choice. I told them their papers would be given without their names to two composition instructors, who would write out comments for them. I would then interview them as they read and reacted to the two sets of comments. Throughout, I stressed that neither the writers nor the readers would be identified. All of the students granted written permission for me to use their work in my research.

Students completed the 500-word papers on time, and I scheduled interviews with them a few days later to give readers time to write the comments. I explained that the readers would be commenting on content, not grammar, spelling, or mechanics. I have excerpted one of the papers below, along with the reader commentary and interview transcript.

"George" wrote on challenges faced by children in single-parent families (first and last paragraphs):

> A lack of love, family values, and money are just some of the challenges that children born out of wedlock must overcome. Today's society delivers the message that single parents families are not only acceptable but also fashionable. As a child raised in by a single parent, I have experienced some of the challenges that these children face and believe that society must promote the traditional family structure of two parents. . . .
>
> American society cries sexist and outrage at the belief of supporting the traditional family structure of two parents. One only need to look as far as Dan Quayle's speech which talked about Murphy Brown to see this. Society needs to look

at two missed factors. First, as I was raised by my father, I know that not all single parents are mothers. This disqualifies the belief the traditional family supporters are denouncing female's rights. Secondly, it is true that some single parents can raise children better on their own, but as a whole, a child can receive more attention, learn more values, and receive more money from two parent families. The adults in American must stop seeking their own civil liberties and protect those of their children.

Reader X commented:

> From your first sentence, I thought you were going to talk about illegitimate children. By the end of the first paragraph, I thought *you* were an illegitimate child. Then at the end of the paper, you say you were raised by your father. So what's the story? Does your personal situation have something to do with the paper? If it does, you better be clear about what your situation is! I don't know what you are comparing to what—or if you are just whining.
>
> You identify some advantages that kids from two-parent families have: love, family values, money. I think you also claim that children of single parents have these things too, but not enough. It's simple math, right? Two of everything is better than one. Two income-producing parents can give their precious baby more—more in the sense of material goodies—than a single parent can. You seem to discount very quickly the kind of parents a kid is better off without. You read about them in the paper every day: abusers, drug addicts, you name it.
>
> What surprised me about this paper is your fuss about the single parent who works hard and therefore can't make it to the school play or whatever because of exhaustion. Would you rather be in a welfare family? Think about it. I don't know your situation (since you really didn't explain it), so I can't say much. But if you are in college and getting a good education, there are some pretty good things going on in your life. Give your dad a break and lay off Murphy Brown.

Reader Y commented:

You raise a lot of difficult issues here, and if they are operating in your own life, it must be really tough to write about them for a paper in a composition class. Your thesis statement refers to three "challenges" (lack of love, family values, and money) that are treated in separate paragraphs in the essay. You give a perspective on the child's experience that is painful, but valuable. I gather that you have problems with day care as a substitute for parenting and you seem to be critical of the single parent who pursues a career. Do you have any advice for parents? What should they do differently?

On the issue of family values, I was haunted by the image of all the child loses by having only one parent. Are you suggesting that the noncustodial parent always be involved? What if the parent is dead or lives in another state? What can the custodial parent do to transmit the values of the other parent's traditions? Are grandparents one avenue?

Finally, you talk about the financial effects of a one-parent income. This is certainly a difficult problem. As you know, there are many single parents, especially women, who are unable to support their families and must turn to government assistance. Yet many of these same single parents are devoted to their children and do the best they can for them. You express with heart-breaking understatement the deprivation that children experience. What can single parents do differently?

I can understand why you would be critical of a woman who would purposely have a child by herself with no intention of involving the child's father in parenting. Your statement that adults should be less selfish and protect their children's rights makes sense—support it carefully.

If I were revising this paper, I think I would start with the ideas in the final paragraph. Then you could use your personal experience to support your argument. Otherwise, you are vulnerable to the charge of "sweeping generalization." You make a lot of claims without statistics or specific examples to back them up—except for your own experience.

George's responses to my interview questions:

INTERVIEWER: What is your initial reaction to the comments from reader X?

GEORGE: (Laughter.) What do I think? If this was graded, I'd be pretty angry. This isn't proactive. If I got this back on a paper, I'd think, "What is the point of writing anything else?" It's easy to anger the person reading it. I think working with this teacher, you wouldn't feel you'd go to them with any questions.

INTERVIEWER: Reader Y?

GEORGE: (Laughter.) Much more open and questioning. More feedback. Still contains some of the same things, but said in a different way. It's what my current comp teacher does: "Good start, now work on *this*." I could relate better to a teacher like this because they seem open to ideas.

INTERVIEWER: If you could talk with either reader in person, which would you choose: X? Y? Both?

GEORGE: Both. X is negative, but I'd go in. It's not really about the paper—you'd find it easy to get angry. I'd end up writing to fit where I thought the teacher was coming from. I'd suppress what I want to write about. It wouldn't be a very fruitful conversation. More subjective. For Y, I could actually go in and talk about something concrete—more objective, more clear-cut guidelines.

INTERVIEWER: Do you have a sense of either reader's gender? If so, what are the cues?

GEORGE: X—either way, could be a woman, but I think it's a man. Y—woman. Her last three paragraphs all talk about women as single parents—it's not defensive or offensive, it's presented in a neutral fashion.

INTERVIEWER: Any other comments?

GEORGE: Y sparks questions and ideas. I feel like talking about the paper. There is a team level of communication. X—if I got this person, I'd think, "I'm going to drop this class!" It's frustrating to deal with a person like that—too hierarchic.

Interview Results

Reader X offers quite negative, almost abusive response, and George, like the other students in the study, reacts angrily. His initial laughter seems to me, as an interviewer, an indication of just how startled he is to be confronted so harshly. George seems to feel personally attacked and hopeless about working out an understanding with this reader.

Reader Y addresses many of the same features in the essay, but Y does so with a softer tone, which makes the reader seem more approachable. George says as much, when he notes that the comments contain "some of the same things, but said in a different way."

When asked if they would want to discuss the feedback with either X or Y, most of the students were eager to talk with Y and nervous about talking with X. Nevertheless, George, like the others, wanted to straighten out the negative reader's perceptions, even if he felt bound to revise the paper in compliance with the teacher's point of view.

I asked each of the students to speculate about the gender of each reader, and four of six tended to think of the brutal reader as male and the more nurturing reader as female. Even before I posed the question, some of them used masculine pronouns for reader X and feminine pronouns for reader Y.

Observations

The most telling observation for me is that my initial query about the impact of anonymous criticism is simply a nonissue. All of the students in the sample took the criticism seriously. All of them wanted to talk with critics, especially the negative critic. They felt misunderstood and misjudged; they wanted to get things straight with that person.

What I found most dramatic was the students' construction of these anonymous readers. Students not only assigned gender to the critics, but they also began to script the conversations they imagined having with these people. In other words, they invented teacher-student relationships, using models from their experience and the critics' words. It seems safe to conclude that a critic's actual words give students cues to gender and attitudes that students instinctively use to develop a constructed "other" with whom they prepare to engage in dialogue.

As George's responses show, the negative critic is assigned a hostile, impatient, male persona who would be inclined to argue with a student, offering accusations rather than helpful writing advice. The kinder, gentler critic is assigned a supportive, constructive, female persona who would be personally approachable and more specific in formulating writing advice.

There was one important deviation from this pattern. The one black student in the sample, a man from Texas, assigned gender to his critics as George did. He, however, appreciated the negative (male) critic's directness and scoffed at the constructive (female) critic's gentleness: "Minnesota people can't take a knife in the heart, but it doesn't bother me. She could have given it to me straight." I would like to do a larger study to determine whether racial or regional factors would generate more of this kind of response from students.

I found the speculation on gender particularly interesting because I had invented both sets of responses. Only one student, a man age thirty-nine, identified both critics as female. In keeping with the cover story, I did not reveal my authorship of the commentaries.

Whichever style of commentary the students preferred, they clearly wanted the critique to continue as a dialogue between themselves as writers and these critics who were maddeningly beyond their reach. Those of us who ponder reviewers' comments on grant proposals and journal submissions can sympathize.

In my own classroom, I have found that having done this study, my responses are affected. Especially at the beginning of a term I am vigilant about the relational cues I may communicate to students. Do I invite dialogue? Do I credit and enlarge on peer comments? Do I intimidate? Dismiss? Insult? Challenge? Praise? And so on. Sometimes I seem to get it right, and the student finds my commentary helpful. Sometimes I blow it and guess wrong about the kind of written dialogue I can sustain with a particular student. I'll keep working on it.

For the record, please note that my informal pilot study is not meant to endorse either of the response styles represented by readers X and Y: X is too harsh and Y is too manipulative for my taste. The sources below point all of us, new and experienced teachers, to research and reporting that examine response to student writing in many dimensions.

Further Reading

Anson, Chris M., ed. *Writing and Response: Theory, Practice, and Research.* Urbana, IL: NCTE, 1989.

Connors, Robert J. "Teaching and Learning as a Man." *College English* 58 (1996): 137–57.

Connors, Robert J., and Andrea A. Lunsford. "Teachers' Rhetorical Comments on Student Papers." *College Composition and Communication* 44 (1993): 200–223.

Lawson, Bruce, Susan Sterr Ryan, and W. Ross Winterowd, eds. *Encountering Student Texts: Interpretive Issues in Reading Student Writing.* Urbana, IL: NCTE, 1989.

Nystrand, Martin. "Sharing Words: The Effects of Readers on Developing Writers." *Written Communication* 7 (1990): 3–24.

Prior, Paul. "Contextualizing Writing and Response in a Graduate Seminar." *Written Communication* 8 (1991): 267–310.

———. "Tracing Authoritative and Internally Persuasive Discourses: A Case Study of Response, Revision, and Disciplinary Enculturation." *Research in the Teaching of English* 29 (1995): 288–325.

Smith, Summer. "The Genre of the End Comment: Conventions in Teacher Responses to Student Writing." *College Composition and Communication* 48 (1997): 249–68.

Sommers, Nancy. "Responding to Student Writing." *College Composition and Communication* 33 (1982): 148–56.

Straub, Richard. "The Concept of Control in Teacher Response: Defining the Varieties of 'Directive' and 'Facilitative' Commentary." *College Composition and Communication* 47 (1996): 223–51.

———. "Students' Reactions to Teacher Comments: An Exploratory Study." *Research in the Teaching of English* 31 (1997): 91–116.

Straub, Richard, and Ronald F. Lunsford. *Twelve Readers Reading: Responding to College Student Writing.* Cresskill, NJ: Hampton, 1995.

Tobin, Lad. "Car Wrecks, Baseball Caps, and Man-to-Man Defense: The Personal Narratives of Adolescent Males." *College English* 58 (1996): 158–75.

———. *Writing Relationships: What Really Happens in the Composition Class.* Portsmouth, NH: Boynton/Cook Heinemann, 1993.

Ziv, Nina D. "The Effect of Teacher Comments on the Writing of Four College Freshmen." *New Directions in Composition Research.* Ed. Richard Beach and Lillian S. Bridwell. New York: Guilford, 1984. 362–80.

Another Kind of Teacher-Student Talk: Conversational Responding and Revising

SETH L. KAHN

Syracuse University

Seth Kahn explains why he utilizes conversational responses to student writing, and shares sample student work to illustrate how these responses function to engage students in deep, global revision of their writing.

My purpose here is to advocate a method of responding to student writing, a method called "conversational" responding. Conversational responses differ from more traditional responses; specifically, their tone and their goals are geared toward helping students think more about what they're saying than about how to correct errors or evaluate their work. To make my case, I've divided this discussion into three sections: a discussion of conversational response theory; a demonstration I have developed based on the work of a former student; and some ideas about how teachers can use conversational responding no matter what kind of writing course they might be teaching.

Introduction to Conversational Response

Teachers know the look of fear that appears on students' faces when they start to hand back written assignments. Even assignments that aren't graded seem to generate a "deer-in-the-headlights" gaze, as if students are silently praying that we won't run over them, spilling ink, slashes, circles, commas, semicolons inserted and deleted, "AWKs," "Frag.s," and so on all over their fragile egos. The body of composition lore would have it that students react this way because their high school teachers have spent years hacking up their writing, writing only complaints and attacks in the margins, and providing no global commentary except a grade. My own high school education certainly fits this picture. I can't recall a single high school writing course that encouraged revising or rewriting papers; why would my teachers have spent time offering suggestions for improving an essay when they weren't offering to read them again?

My story is certainly not unique. Fortunately, since the advent of process pedagogies, compositionists have been developing ways of responding to student writing that actually help students revise. One of the key moves, which developed out of process theory's attention to the act of writing instead of to the products of writing, was a turn away from mechanics. Instead, responders began to attend more deeply to matters of content and organization, asking students to look again at their ideas rather than their presentation. This turn has generated a variety of response styles, many of which involve two primary techniques: questions (à la the Socratic method); and reader response comments, which provide students a playback of the responder's reactions to the writing, ideally as an "authentic" member of an audience. The style I have found most useful for me and my students is called conversational responding.

In a 1996 *Rhetoric Review* article, "Teacher Response as Conversation: More Than Casual Talk, an Exploration," Richard Straub outlines three principles that characterize teacher responses as "conversational." Straub's study is an analytical close reading of six sets of responses to the same essay from prominent composition teachers. His analysis proceeds by looking for features that invite students to reconsider their thinking, without directly telling them what and how to revise. Claiming influences from the work of Nancy Sommers, Lil Brannon and C. H. Knoblauch, Chris Anson, Nina Ziv, and others, and deriving from his reading of these six sets of responses, Straub names these three characteristics of conversational response:

1. They [responders] create an informal, spoken voice, using everyday language. Straub explains:

   They talk with the student rather than talk to him or speak down at him. At its most elemental level, of course, achieving a conversational style of response means just this: getting the gestures, tone of voice, and sense of speech in one's written comments. As Danis notes, picturing response as a conversation "does for us as teachers what our advice about picturing an audience is meant to do for our students: it concretizes the awareness that we're communicating with someone" (19). ("Teacher Response" 380)

2. They tie their commentary back to the student's own language on the page, in text-specific comments ("Teacher Response" 380), or, in Nancy Sommers's phrase, they are "anchored in the particulars of the students' texts" (152).

3. They focus on the writer's evolving meanings and play back their way of understanding the text. Having noted that two of the responders don't really respond this way, Straub explains, "they all focus on what the writer has to say and engage him in a discussion of his ideas and purposes . . . . All four of these teachers go out of their way to understand and appreciate the writer's intentions and to play back their way of interpreting the text." ("Teacher Response" 380–81)

In the past three years, I've worked extensively with this formulation of conversational response. During this time, however, I've come to understand that responding conversationally calls for developing more than a particular kind of comment on student papers. Granted, the interaction between student writer and writing teacher that happens in writing and responding constitutes a significant portion of the conversation about writing in any composition course; in my classes, I would say that this portion of the conversation has been upwards of 75 percent of the talking we've done about specific pieces of student writing. But it seems to me that there are also at least three other significant portions of the conversation that speak directly to what the writing students do: (1) revisions that take up or ignore teacher commentary; (2) classroom talk about student writing that may or may not have been produced in the particular course; and (3) whatever conversations students are, will be, or have been involved in about writing outside of a particular writing course. A more detailed notion of conversational response helps account for these other elements of the writing-course conversation.

A Demonstration

Perhaps a look at the conversation that occurred across part of a semester between a student and me would illustrate the method. This particular student, Star, took a research-paper course in which students wrote two descriptive/analytical essays, with six short exploratory pieces in between. The focus of the course was on fieldwork and ethnographic writing. After doing the first essay, which concentrated on observation and description, the students spent six weeks doing fieldwork, writing an exploratory essay each week responding to prompts I had given them in advance. I provided detailed written responses to four of the six exploratory pieces; on the last two exploratories, I asked only for peer responses. Once they had completed the sequence of exploratory writings, students wrote two drafts of an ethnographic essay; all written responses to the first draft were from peers. In between the fieldwork and the drafting of their last papers, we spent a week talking about different styles of writing ethnographies, using extensive samples I'd collected from previous semesters.

The original impetus in my choosing Star for this illustration is that she is unique in my teaching experience—a student whose writing consistently called on me to prompt her to say less. Each of the seven pieces of her writing I kept from that semester (fall 1997) is longer than the announced page goal. The first draft of her ethnography (which I won't discuss because I didn't respond in writing to it) was eleven single-spaced pages—my goal for the class was seven to ten double-spaced pages. A more important factor in selecting Star is that she almost never spoke in class unless I called on her specifically. In conferences she was obedient, almost to the point of being a problem; she would only ask for help after I told her that I wouldn't lead the conversation, and even then it was an effort to get her to speak. Her reticence to speak allows me to focus more sharply on the written interactions we had. The final factor that makes her work useful to generate examples from is the subject of her ethnography—a local hip-hop group, which represented a subculture that most members of our class were interested in but didn't know much about.

What I wanted to know as I looked at Star's work was how likely she was to take up different kinds of comments, and just as important, how likely she was to revise according to what I'd intended. My responses can be broken down into three general types (please keep in mind that all of my responses, regardless of the issues they raise, are formulated according to Straub's criteria): (1) requests for additions, i.e., more information or more explanation (e.g., "What did he say then?" or "Can you explain what they meant by that?"); (2) suggested deletions (e.g., "Do we need to know so much about what they were wearing?"); and (3) reader-response comments that don't suggest anything in particular (e.g., "That's really interesting," or "Cool"). I should note again that there was some pressure on her to cut down the final paper substantially, which almost certainly accounts for some of her deletions. After crunching the numbers (which I won't recount in detail here), I saw a pattern emerging: about two-thirds of the time, Star made a revision of some kind based on a comment. Quite frankly, given the number of odd reader-response comments I typically make as I read, I was happy to see that about one-third of the time she didn't feel obligated to revise simply because I'd made a mark. Certainly, it seems that Star usually responded directly to my comments. I consider myself a fairly directive responder, so I was pleased that over a quarter of the time she responded in a way that was different from what I'd expected or suggested. If I ignore the reader-response comments that didn't suggest any particular revision, I find that about four-fifths of the time Star made her revisions according to the kinds of responses I'd given her. Still, about one-fifth of the time she made her own decisions regardless of what she thought I was asking for.

There are several factors to be considered that might have changed the results substantially. First, as I noted earlier, Star's first draft of the ethnography was much longer than the assignment allowed; therefore, it seems likely that at least some of her deletions and ignoring of my comments are a function of that rather than of my comments. Second, I'm assuming that she interpreted my comments in the way I intended them, although there's no way for me to know that for sure. Third, I don't have copies of her exploratory essays that went through peer response, so I don't know how many of my comments were confirmed or contradicted by classmates. What's important here isn't necessarily the weight of the specific numbers that emerged from the research but that Star seemed to engage in conversations with me about her writing by writing more, which is exactly what I'd hoped for.

Even if the data cannot be tortured to admit to statistical significance, it still seems likely that Star's overall willingness to comply with my comments makes a significant point. No matter what her motives and perceptions behind the ways she addressed my comments, the fact that she fairly faithfully attended to them suggests that she was using her writing as a way of talking with me about the subject. She had a lot to say about her research, and I had a lot to say about her writing about her research. Fortunately, it seems that my comments helped her find more, or at least more clear, things to say. Since she didn't participate actively in classroom discussions, it seems reasonable to believe that her writing was her forum.

With these overall results in mind, let me provide some specific examples of types of responses and some of Star's revisions that I believe took up those responses. Easiest to spot are the additions and deletions; here's a sequence of additions and deletions arising from the first sentence of her first exploratory writing:

Star's Exploratory One: The name of the rap group is Seeds of Wisdom.

Seth: Do you know what the name means?

Star's Exploratory Three: The name of the group is Seeds of Wisdom. That stands for the Trinity of Knowledge or The Holy Trinity. Knowledge, wisdom and understanding make up The Holy Trinity. Knowledge is how to do something. Wisdom is learning from experience. Understanding is connecting knowledge and wisdom to make predictions and apply them to your life. Each member of the group represents an element of The Holy Trinity. A seed is the origin of all things and beginnings of life. It is the first step in growth. Growth equals progression and evolution. Life itself is a constant state of flux and change. Change comes from learning from your experiences and adapting to new ones. Through their music they plant seeds of new ideas in people's minds. A seed is also a symbol for the cycle of life. A seed grows, produces fruit or a flower, decays, dies, and returns to the Earth to nourish new life. Their music is like seed because it is constantly changing and growing. It produces new ideas and inspires others to continue the process. I think their name is a representation of life itself, its cycle and its purpose. The group's name was influenced by: Taoism, Egyptian religion, science, and the structure of animal societies.

I made three responses at various points in this new paragraph. To the sentence, "Each member of the group represents an element of The Holy Trinity," I asked, "Which is which?" The segment from "Growth equals . . . its cycle and its purpose" drew the comment, "This is some pretty philosophical stuff. Is this how they want people to react to them?" At the end of the paragraph, I noted, "Good. I wondered about that."

The next time Star took up this issue was in the final paper. Her last version of this particular paragraph is:

The name of their rap group is Seeds of Wisdom. That stands for the Trinity of Knowledge or the Holy Trinity. Knowledge, wisdom, and understanding make up The Holy Trinity.

Knowledge is how to do something. Wisdom is learning from experience. Understanding is connecting knowledge and wisdom to make predictions and apply them to your life. Each member of the group represents an element of The Holy Trinity as a seed. A seed is the origin of all things. Taoism, Egyptian religion, science, and the structure in animal societies influenced the group's name. "Seeds" is an acronym for something, they wouldn't tell me what for.

What makes this exchange interesting from my (the responder's) point of view is the amount of revision that develops from a very simple comment. By the time Star was working on the last draft of the last paper, she seems to have realized that the length of my comments was not necessarily proportional to the space she needed to devote to revising. In fact, the first of my three comments on the paragraph in Exploratory Three, asking which member of the group represented which element of the Trinity, garnered a full-page description of each band member, explaining not only their connections to the terms of the Trinity, but also their professional goals, goals as college students, and philosophical divergences among them that would ultimately constitute the most interesting work in the paper.

Of course, not every short response on my part generated this kind of revision. When I discovered in Exploratory Two that the hip-hop group worked at the campus radio station, I wanted Star to describe some of the physical details of the station. It seemed important to me to help her see that the kinds of posters, stickers, and other decorations in the space might tell her important things about how Seeds of Wisdom fit into the radio station community. In class, I had done an exercise in which students observed every physical detail they could in a short time, and the following passage from Star's exploratory piece seems to be her attempt to emulate that exercise in her own site:

The room was roughly an eight by twelve foot triangle. It had two doors, one on each end of one of the longer walls. There was a bookcase of CD's that sat between the two doors. The bookcase took up half the height of the wall. The walls were painted gold. They were covered with stickers and graffiti. . . . There were three tables arranged in the shape of a C. They were against the wall opposite the bookcase. They took up most of the space in the room. The tables held turntables and a switch board with lots of lights and buttons. . . . Several panels were missing from the ceiling. They exposed the network of cables that powered the broadcast.

I made three responses to this paragraph—two requests for additions and one that questioned the relevance of some of her details. In the final draft, none of the details or explanation I was hoping for appeared, although, as noted before, that may be because the first draft of the ethnography was nearly twice as long as requested. The wealth of physical detail about the layout of the station was cut.

This example also allows me to make a point about the way conversational response can connect to the larger goals of a course. In this instance, especially in Star's case, one of my major pedagogical goals was teaching students how to select details to include in an essay. One of the reasons I teach ethnography (primary field research resulting in a descriptive essay) is that it foregrounds this goal—students collect and generate far more material than they could include in a single paper. I spend a couple of class periods in any given course explaining the rationale behind this goal, which is to say, in short, that the expertise gained by fieldwork requires far more extensive knowledge of the site than readers need. Therefore, even though my responses to Star's exploratory writings often asked her to think about more details or explanations, I certainly never intended for her to address every one of my responses in her texts. While other responders might think Star had simply ignored their comments, I believe that Star chose not to address the issues I raised in these comments because she ultimately decided that her focus needed to be elsewhere, a decision supported by the larger conversation that constituted the daily meetings of the class.

Of course, a teacher has to be extremely careful to make the connection between classroom talk and conversational responses. I have had a few experiences with students who blurred the dis-

tinction between rethinking their ideas and revising their writing—one example illustrates this particularly clearly. As a part of
my class routine, I gave students about thirty minutes a week
during the ethnography just to talk out loud to everybody else
about their work—problems, interesting things they were finding, comparisons to other projects, venting, and so on. One student was very talkative, and I noticed after a couple of weeks
that he spent much of his talking time in class addressing issues I
had raised in my comments on his exploratories. He would answer my questions or tell me I'd misunderstood something. What
I discovered when I read the last draft of his ethnography was
disturbing: he hadn't addressed in the paper any of the issues
he'd raised in class. There was enough effort in the paper to indicate that he hadn't just blown it off, so I had no idea how to
explain this. But, if I'm right about the notion that revision is
part of the larger classroom conversation, then I may have an
answer: maybe because he'd addressed my comments aloud, he
believed that he didn't have to do it again.

Pitfalls like this one are possible, in fact likely, in any course—
I mention it only to highlight the need to make sure that the
conversation takes place in students' writing in addition to (not
instead of) in the classroom. Conversational response, to the extent that it creates an extended dialogue between writers and
responders, echoes James Moffett in *Teaching the Universe of
Discourse:*

> One of the unique qualities of dialogue is that the interlocutors
> build on each other's sentence constructions. A conversation is
> verbal collaboration. Each party borrows words and phrases and
> structures from the other, recombines them, adds to them, and
> elaborates them. An exchange may consist of several kinds of
> operations, or rather, co-operations, such as question-answer,
> parry-thrust, and statement-emendation. (72–73)

Moffett makes this point in the midst of discussion about using
talk in the writing classroom (in fact in any classroom), which
leads fairly logically to the idea that responding to writing *in*
writing is particularly productive when it continues and emu-
lates the kind of talk that happens face to face.

Specific Suggestions

As I noted earlier, the key to conversational responding is to think of it as part of the larger conversation about writing that constitutes a writing course. Responses are the teacher's place to have a dialogue with individual students about their own texts and ideas, and that dialogue should work with the classroom talk that happens every day to help students think more about their writing. The easiest way to think about specific suggestions is to return to Straub's three elements described earlier, using those as a framework within which to outline possibilities.

1. Create an informal, spoken voice using everyday language.
As simple as this piece of advice sounds, it may actually take more practice to get used to than any of the others. The goal is to sound as much like your everyday spoken voice as possible, which, depending on the kinds of comments you've gotten in your writing career, may feel counterintuitive at first. Just keep in mind that you aren't likely to say "Awk" or "Frag" in the classroom every day, and that those terms mean as little on paper as they would spoken. One of the underlying principles of conversational responding is that it encourages you to speak the same language your students do—in other words, not to use lingo that may not mean anything to them. Along the same lines, using an informal voice humanizes the responses; the teacher's responses come from another living person whom the students ideally trust, rather than from a grammar police officer. So, for example, instead of simply marking a passage "Unclear" in the margin, you might say, "I'm not following you. Are you saying that . . . ?" Or, instead of saying "Good," you might say, "Very interesting. I needed to know that."

As you begin to develop an informal response voice, you'll likely find yourself spending considerable time at first; since you may feel like you're just talking with the writer on paper, the temptation is to say everything that pops into your head. Learn to resist that temptation. Keep in mind that you don't have to address every question or problem at once, just as you shouldn't expect your students to be able to address every issue at once.

Because conversational responses often assume the form of complete sentences or questions, your responses will already look longer than many students are accustomed to; no matter how many times you explain that more of your ink doesn't indicate more problems for them, students will probably be shocked when they see the amount of writing you do on their papers. As a matter of habit, I show students a sample essay with responses before I give anything back to them, just so they have some idea what to expect.

2. Tie commentary back to the student's own language on the page, in text-specific comments.

This element is important to your responding for a number of reasons. First, it shows the students that you've read carefully and paid attention to particular ways they've said things. Second, it allows you to comment on specific pieces of the text; depending on what kind of revision you're after, you might find that students will pursue what to them seem like off-hand sentences to a degree they wouldn't have thought possible without some prompting. Finally, attaching your comments to specific pieces of their text helps writers retain a sense of authorship because you're showing respect for their text.

There are a number of ways you can go about anchoring your comments in specific places, depending on your personal preference. I tend to make lots of marginal responses and write very short end comments. Making marginal responses allows me to place my comments immediately next to the text I'm responding to so that students can immediately see what inspired the comment. I'll either bracket off passages or underline specific segments in order to show specifically what text draws the response. Some responders believe more strongly than others that they shouldn't make any marks whatsoever in the text; Frank O'Hare, for example, numbers passages and then writes his corresponding comments on a separate sheet of paper (Straub and Lunsford 13). Other responders rely more heavily than I do on end comments. Whereas I try to limit my end comments to between two and three sentences (because I do so many margin notes), some responders rewrite or quote extensively from the

student texts in order to discuss revision strategies or suggestions. Wherever you choose to locate your responses (in the text,
in the margins, at the end of the text, etc.), the key point is to
make sure you refer to specific language that students use in their
work. So, for example, you might say, "I like the emphasis of
saying 'They were more than just a little confused,' rather than
only saying, 'They were confused.'"

**3. Focus on the writer's evolving meanings and play back their
way of understanding the text.**
This element is certainly the most conceptually difficult of the
three. In a nutshell, the goal is to show students that you respect
their goal of discovering/creating meaning (depending on your
epistemological bent) in their writing. To accomplish this goal,
your responses should ask questions or make assertions that encourage them to think more deeply about the issues they're raising. That depth may come from providing more details, or
explaining a concept more completely, or naming an idea more
sharply, or any number of other sources. Or it may result in the
student's deleting an idea entirely in favor of emphasizing a different aspect of the work. Over the span of a term or semester,
your part of the conversation consists of asking for more and
more thinking about what needs to be said and what doesn't,
while the student's part of the conversation consists of writing
either more or less about the given idea (or ignoring your feedback altogether, which isn't necessarily a problem as long as you
can tell they've thought about it).

The notion of playing back your understanding of the text
for students is an integral part of this conversation. Most, if not
all, writers have experienced that moment when a reader has
reacted to something they said that wasn't quite what they meant.
Playback responses show students how we are reading their texts,
not as assessors, but as readers. Done well, playback responses
affirm students when they've made the point they're after, and
cue them that they aren't quite making the point they thought
they were when they need to know that. Playback also lets them
know that different readers respond differently to the same texts.

Although these responses are the most difficult to get a handle
on conceptually, you'll find that they're not necessarily more com-

plicated on paper. In Star's work, for example, I often made simple responses that turned her back into her thinking: "Can you make a guess at what that symbolizes?"; "What do you make of that?"; "Does this have anything to do with their future plans?"; and so on. Similarly, I played back my understandings at various points with comments such as, "I see. So they don't always get along so well," and "So you think Randy is the real leader even though he says he isn't"; I'm always especially careful to make sure these comments are clearly attached to the text that draws them. The responses don't have to be long to be useful. For those of you who want to do fewer margin notes and longer end comments, the end comment provides a space for more extended playback, where you might try to capture a text's meaning, purpose, or thesis in a sentence or two so the student can gauge how effectively he or she has made a point. One useful trick is to make playback comments at particularly confusing points in a passage, trying to slightly misstate what you think the writer is after; while this move is a bit manipulative, it functions to demonstrate the potential for misreading the writer's intention. A writer, we hope, will be more likely revise a passage more aggressively in the face of evidence that the point has been missed entirely.

In order to help students understand the role of playback responses in their revisions, I would suggest having them practice that kind of response in their peer workshop sessions. I usually limit responses in peer groups to playback for the first couple of sessions, until I'm comfortable with the postures they take toward each other (not too critical, not too accepting) and we can move on to more detailed kinds of feedback. Having them make interpretive statements on each other's texts helps them react more constructively to those comments on their own texts, a claim that probably holds true for most kinds of feedback.

4. Miscellaneous thoughts and advice.

Notably absent from the discussion of conversational response is attention to matters of correctness. A little common sense will tell you that writing "You need to take this comma out" and drawing a circle around the offending mark probably isn't worth the extra work, when simply marking out the extra comma would make the point more quickly and clearly. There's a reason I haven't addressed correctness in this discussion—given my goals as a teacher, correctness tends to be a low priority for most of my students. There are almost always issues in every student's writing that seem more important to address. Even when I work with students who are ready and interested in attending to mechanical problems or issues, I try to approach these lessons within the framework that the course-long conversation has established. In other words, rather than correcting mistakes for students, I ask margin questions such as, "What's different about this sentence if you use a semicolon instead of a comma in the middle?" Although the end result may be the same (changing the comma to a semicolon), hopefully the question encourages the student at least to think about the issue instead of simply changing the mark because I said so. The idea is to help students think through mechanical issues because they need to, rather than to ask them to memorize and apply rules to text that may well disappear as they revise their work.

Another issue, which I mentioned almost tangentially earlier, is the effect of conversational response on peer groups. Although I never could have predicted this, my experience indicates that students who engage in conversational response and revision with me have a much better time with peer workshopping than students to whom I've responded differently. Maybe it's because I've gotten better at teaching workshopping methods, but I think the response style is at least a factor. It stands to reason that once students realize they don't have to command the specialized lexicon of writing teachers to give each other productive feedback, they become more comfortable with the process of asking questions and playing back interpretations of their classmates' work.

Finally, although getting into the habit of conceiving any given set of responses as only a small part of a much larger conversation may take a while, once you can let yourself believe that, you'll find that the pressure to solve every problem with every draft of every paper is substantially reduced. Not only will you have other drafts of the same or other papers to work with, but also you can always take up the conversation in the classroom or in conferences. In other words, this model of conversational response blurs the boundaries between written and oral feedback, between interpersonal/dialogic conversation and classroom-wide discussion, and between teacher-as-grader and teacher-as-collaborator, allowing you to work with a variety of students in a variety of ways.

Concluding Ideas

Keep in mind that I have described only one particular version of the conversational responding model; what makes this model most interesting to me, however, is its applicability to a number of different pedagogies and assignments. Just remember that what you're doing is talking to students about their texts and about the ideas, contexts, and problems that weave in and around their texts. The tone you adopt is up to you, as long as it's consistent with your classroom tone: students shouldn't be hearing a voice on paper that they don't hear in person. As a final note, I should make the point that conversational responding also provides you with one of the most useful and challenging opportunities you'll face as a writing teacher—to learn to praise what students do well and explain why you're praising them. In my experience, one of the most difficult elements of response (whether teacher or peer) is being able to tell a writer why something is good. In a conversational mode, you'll find that you need to discover ways to explain not only what's wrong, but also what's right. Your students will thank you for it.

Suggested Further Readings

If you're interested in seeing Straub's model of conversational response in its extended form, I suggest reading the complete text of "Teacher Response as Conversation." I have taken up only the first half of his argument here; in the second half, Straub contends that conversational responding works to extend the exploratory nature of writing by turning students back into their thought processes, rather than pointing them to specific textual revisions. In a related piece, "The Concept of Control in Teacher Response: Defining the Varieties of 'Directive' and 'Facilitative' Commentary" (1996), Straub examines teacher comments for their various degrees of directivity; in other words, he tries to determine how much control comments take over the revisions students do. His final argument, in short, is that certain kinds and levels of directivity are fine as long as the responder doesn't take over the writing process from the writer.

Perhaps the most in-depth study of response to date is *Twelve Readers Reading* (1995), coauthored by Straub and Ronald Lunsford. Straub and Lunsford collected responses to a common set of student essays from twelve prominent composition scholars, and analyzed their responses for attention to global versus local issues (i.e., structure, logic versus sentence-level problems), degrees of direction versus facilitation, and so on. Each responder who participated in the study provides an explanation of his or her goals for responding. What's especially interesting about this book for new teachers is that readers get to see twelve very different response styles to the same student essays, a vision that not only reinforces the notion that different readers read in very different ways, but, more important, provides a broad spectrum of models and ideas from which to develop a personal style.

Although Straub's work has been particularly influential on my own theories of responding, other scholars and theorists have done important work in the area. I couldn't possibly list all the extant work on response, but in the Further Reading list I've compiled a few that I have found particularly useful.

Works Cited

Moffett, James. *Teaching the Universe of Discourse*. Boston: Houghton Mifflin, 1968.

Sommers, Nancy. "Responding to Student Writing." *College Composition and Communication* 33 (1982): 148–56.

Straub, Richard. "The Concept of Control in Teacher Response: Defining the Varieties of 'Directive' and 'Facilitative' Commentary." *College Composition and Communication* 47 (1996): 223–51.

———. "Teacher Response as Conversation: More Than Casual Talk, an Exploration." *Rhetoric Review* 14 (1996): 374–98.

Straub, Richard, and Ronald F. Lunsford. *Twelve Readers Reading:*

Responding to College Student Writing. Cresskill, NJ: Hampton, 1995.

Further Reading

Anson, Chris, ed. *Writing and Response: Theory, Practice, and Research.* Urbana, IL: NCTE, 1989.

Brannon, Lil, and C. H. Knoblauch. "On Students' Right to Their Own Texts: A Model of Teacher Response." *College Composition and Communication* 33 (1982): 157–66.

Connors, Robert J., and Andrea A. Lunsford. "Teachers' Rhetorical Comments on Student Papers." *College Composition and Communication* 44 (1993): 200–223.

Smith, Summer. "The Genre of the End Comment: Conventions in Teacher Responses to Student Writing." *College Composition and Communication* 48 (1997): 249–68.

Ziv, Nina. "The Effects of Teacher Comments on the Writing of Four College Freshmen." *New Directions in Composition Research.* Ed. Richard Beach and Lillian S. Bridwell. New York: Guilford, 1984. 362–80.

Guidelines for Responding to Student Writing

RICHARD STRAUB
Florida State University

Richard Straub initiates a discussion of basic principles teachers can follow in order to maximize the effectiveness of their responses to student writing.

Offering advice about responding to student writing is like offering advice about playing chess. You can learn how each piece moves, a number of gambits, and some general strategies. But the game has to be played—and learned—on the board, amid a hundred shifting factors. The moves you make depend on the board in front of you, the ground you want to hold or seize. It's only after you've played a while—only after you've gotten an idea of all the choices and the way contingency must be reckoned with at every turn—that you're in a position to really learn the game. Learning how to respond is a bit like learning to use your pawns wisely or knowing when to put your queen into play. You try to follow certain principles. You look for certain keys. You watch for certain warnings. In this piece, I offer a fairly detailed set of strategies for responding, with the aim of helping both new and experienced teachers get some bearings on how they might best respond to their students' writing. I offer advice not only about making comments, but also about situating comments within the larger work of the writing classroom.

Teacher response, I am assuming here, is integral to effective writing instruction—as important as any other activity or responsibility we take up as writing teachers. The comments we make instantiate what we really value in student writing. They offer an opportunity to make the key concepts of the class more meaningful to students, and they enable us to give substance to the claims we make about their roles as writers, our roles as teachers, and the work of writing. If we claim to be facilitators in the classroom, our comments should be noticeably encouraging and helpful. If we claim to give students practice in making their own choices and developing their authority as writers, our comments should allow them room to decide which comments they take up and which they pass up in revision. If we claim to emphasize the content and thought of writing, our comments should deal mostly with the author's ideas.

Running through all of the following advice is the belief that careful, thoughtful commentary can make a real difference in the immediate and long-term development of student writers. Never mind claims that teacher commentary doesn't make a difference. Never mind the easy skepticism that students don't even read the comments; all they're interested in is the grade. Give students sincere, well-designed comments, comments that provide thoughtful feedback about what they have to say (not just how they say it or whether it's correct) and how they might work on their writing, in a classroom that is charged with a belief that students can learn to write better, and they will read the comments, appreciate them, and get something out of them—if not on the next draft, then on the next paper, or on the one after that, or perhaps when they write again next semester.

Bringing the Class into Your Responses

1. Response begins with the course description. It begins with the assignment and the work in class. It begins with your values and expectations. It begins with what the students write. You read the writing, but you read the writing both as a reader and with the reader in mind. You read with an eye to the assignment, to the work you've done in class, and to the work you hope to accomplish. You read with an eye to the writer in the text and the student behind the writing. Before you even pick up the pen or open a file, much about how you'll respond has already been determined. So it makes sense as you invent the class, day by day, in the assignments, the lessons, the class discussions, and the things you say about writing, that you also consider how these choices will ultimately come to bear on the way you read and respond to what your students write—and how your responses, in turn, might help you shape your instruction.

2. Before you start to read a set of papers (optimally, even as you put together the assignment and talk with students about the writing they are to do), consider the aims of the writing. Try to get a sense of what you are looking to accomplish with this writing right now, in the short term, and over time, in the long term. What do you want to accomplish through your reading and your comments? What is the one thing, above all others, you'd like these comments to do? How does what you are looking for here mesh with what you have been working on or what you intend to work on in the class? Decide what your main focus will be—and what you will generally *not* deal with in these papers.

3. Decide how long you'll take with each paper—and how many you'd like to have finished in an hour or two. Do all you can to stick to the plan. You may not be able to keep up, but you've got a goal in mind.

4. Once you start actually looking at the papers, you have two choices: reviewing the paper first before you make any responses, or responding as you read the first time through. Both options have their strengths and drawbacks. The first method: Read the paper over once quickly and select the focuses of your response. Put a line next to key passages and jot down a list of your concerns as you go. Then, after you've gone through the paper, decide your major points, work up a general strategy, and compose your response. This might seem at first to take more time, but it probably ends up being more efficient since it allows you to focus better when you comment on the paper. The second method: Just comment as you read the first time through the paper, and cast your comments in terms of a reader's moment-by-moment responses. Whenever something strikes you as worthy of a comment (based, if you're smart, on priorities you've established), you write it down. This method is riskier: it can take a lot of time, it can lead to some erasing and recanting, and it can easily lead to commentary that ranges far and wide and that fails to provide adequate direction to the writer. But it does provide an opportunity to respond more fully to specific passages (and, when it is well done, perhaps greater guidance and stronger control).

Viewing Response as an Exchange

1. Look to engage students in an inquiry into their subject by treating what they have to say seriously and encouraging them, in turn, to take their own ideas seriously. Turn your comments into a conversation with students, a real dialogue that encourages them to read the comments and respond to your responses. Write out your comments, especially the most

important ones, in full statements. Short, cryptic comments, abbreviations, and a lot of editorial symbols may too readily be taken as the hasty marks of an editor or critic . . . or the pouncing corrections of a teacher. Fuller comments help create an exchange between reader and writer, teacher and student. They dramatize how you are reading and making sense of the text, and they construct you as someone who is intent on helping them improve their writing.

2. Write your comments as much as you can in nontechnical terms, tying the comment to specific concerns in the writing and using the language of the student's text. The goal here, again, is to enact an exchange. The more you address the content of the writing, tie your talk to the student's language, and refer to specific issues and passages in the writing, the more likely you are to engage the student and bring him or her into a discussion.

3. Try to link your comments to the key terms of the larger classroom conversation. It's important to establish a vocabulary for talking about writing—one that may well go beyond the language students bring into the course. Yet, at the same time, keep this talk grounded in your students' own writing.

4. Add follow-up comments that explain, elaborate on, or illustrate your primary comments. Comments that explain other comments will be construed as help.

Responding as Selecting

1. Focus your commentary on no more than two or three concerns in a set of comments, making sure that your comments reflect your priorities and advance the goals of the course. Students do best when they can work on a couple areas of writing at a time.

2. There's no need to address every instance of a problem—or, for that matter, every success. Select key instances and

build your response on them. Leave the rest for the student to identify and work out on his or her own.

3. Don't overwhelm the writer with comments. Look to address five to ten passages per paper. Look to write somewhere between twelve to twenty-five comments (i.e., statements) per paper, including margin and end comments. It's not the number of comments that distinguish informed teachers' responses from those of uninformed teachers; it's what you do in the comments you provide. Instead of being comprehensive, try to cover less ground and be more effective with what you do take up.

4. Be respectful of the student's space: be careful about crossing through sentences or writing indiscriminately between the lines of the text. You expect students to be neat and orderly; try to do so yourself.

5. Look for ways to limit what you take up and try to accomplish in a given set of comments. Not every paper you read needs to be commented on extensively—or, for that matter, commented on to the same extent. Write more comments on papers that seem more open to fruitful revision. Write more comments for students who need more help or students you want to challenge to do even better work.

Focusing on First Things First

1. Emphasize matters of content, focus, organization, and purpose. Work on these concerns until the writing achieves a reasonable level of maturity. If you're working on early drafts or even immature final drafts, feel free to deal exclusively with matters of content and development. There is no sense in getting into shaping and refining a paper that has nothing yet to say.

2. Address local matters in detail only after the writing is doing more or less what it sets out to do in content, focus, and organization. Unless you have good reason, don't emphasize matters of correctness either too early in the drafting of a paper or too early in the course. Asking students to serve several masters can lead only to their serving none of them well.

3. Employ minimal marking for errors: punctuation, grammar, spelling, and other local conventions. Instead of marking and explaining every error, just put a tick mark in the margin next to the line where the error occurs. Leave it up to the student to locate and correct the error. Have students meet with you if they have trouble, or check their work after they've had a chance to make corrections. (Another option: when you return the papers with your comments, hold a fifteen-minute workshop in which students find and correct the errors you've minimally marked in the margins.)

4. Keep an eye always on the next work to be done: the next draft, the next paper, the next issue of writing that the class or this student writer will take up. Make comments that are geared toward improvement, not simply the assessment of a finished text.

5. Experiment with ways of focusing your comments on certain issues at certain times in the course. Sequence your comments across the semester, taking up issues that are most important to you at the start of the course and adding other areas as you go. On early papers, for example, present only positive comments or restrict yourself to commenting only on the content and development of student writing. On some papers or some drafts, just deal with the voice and tone of the writing. On final drafts late in the semester, abandon work on developing the content and focus exclusively on sentence structure or the pacing within paragraphs.

Shaping Your Comments to the Larger Context of Writing

1. Read the student's text in terms of its (stated or assigned) rhetorical context. Does the writer construct a persona that is appropriate to the occasion? How well does the writing address the intended audience? Does it achieve the purposes it sets out to achieve?

2. Tie your talk on the page to the work you've been doing in class and to your immediate and long-terms goals. Use the key terms of the class in your responses—again, to give them local habitation and a name.

3. Decide how closely you are going to hold students to following the exact demands of the assignment, or how much room you are going to allow them to develop their own topics and their own purposes in their own ways.

4. Shape your comments according to the needs of the individual student. It's not the paper in front of us, after all, that we're teaching. Work on what the student would do best to work on.

Creating Relationships through the Way You Frame Your Comments

1. Learn the uses of both directive and facilitative forms of commentary. Without criticism and calls for changes, there would be less direction in your responses. Without comments that play back the text, ask questions, provide reader responses, and offer explanations, there would be less help and encouragement in your commentary.

2. Take advantage of the many uses of praise: to recognize a job well done, to teach a principle, to underscore successful strategies, and to encourage students to continue working

on their writing. Use praise in one area or in one passage to build confidence for tackling others. Write at least as many praise comments as criticisms. Be supportive and encouraging. Yet also be demanding. Look to move students, wherever they are now in their development as writers, forward.

3. Frame your comments in forms that modulate the control you exert over students' writing. Instead of relying on commands, shape your calls for changes in the form of advice. Instead of using only direct criticism, present some of your criticisms as qualified evaluations or reader responses, forms that highlight the subjective or contingent nature of commentary. Ask questions—real, open questions, not simply questions that disguise a criticism or command. Too many directive comments can close down interaction and take away the authority a writer needs in order to develop as an author, a writer with something to say. Students do best when they are involved in an exchange, not in a battle of wills. More than a critic pointing out problems or an editor dictating changes to be made, construct yourself in the role of a reader, a guide, a helpful teacher, a challenging mentor, or some kind of coach.

4. Try to make at least occasional use of comments that simply play back your reading of the student's text, without overtly evaluating, questioning, or advising the student about the writing. Comments that provide your interpretations will let the writer know how the writing is being understood. They will also let the student know you are reading the writing first of all for its meaning.

5. Fit your comments to your own strengths and style as a teacher, and along the way look to add to your strengths as a responder. No one way of responding will work, or work the same way, for every student. It is necessary, then, to develop a repertoire of responding strategies to meet the demands of different students and different settings.

RESPONDING TO IN-PROCESS WORK TO PROMOTE REVISION

On Marginal Comments and End Comments

There is no necessary difference between putting comments in the margins or in a separate response in endnotes and letters. Marginal comments allow for greater immediacy and specificity. They allow you to deal directly with specific issues in relation to specific passages. They also lend a ready concreteness to your responses. End comments encourage you to provide a fuller context for your comments and to carry on a fuller discussion about them. They also give you a chance to lend some perspective to the various issues you raise in the margins.

In end comments, generally speaking, start with praise or a general overview of what you see the student doing in the writing. Direct the student's attention to your key concerns. Elaborate and explain your comments and tie them back to the student's text. Try to make your end comments somehow complement your marginal comments. The endnote may highlight and elaborate the key marginal comments. It may focus on one key area that is addressed in the margins. It may take up areas that are not treated in the marginal comments but that you now want to focus on. The overriding idea here, as in response in general, is to find ways to involve students in an exchange about their writing, with the aim of leading them to work further on developing themselves as writers.

Integrating Responses into the Class

1. As teachers, we show what we value by spending time on it in class. If all we do after we've spent hours making comments is hand the papers back in a rush at the end of a class while students are packing their books away, we make the statement that the comments are not important, that they are not to be taken seriously. We allow the comments to be seen as a matter of course: students write papers and hand them in, the teacher comments on the papers and hands them back, we all move on to the next paper, checking another thing off the list of things to do. Develop a different habit. Whenever you're about to hand papers with your comments

back to students, take time to talk about the responses you've made. Indicate any important patterns you've seen in their papers, note the key concerns of your responses, and discuss the purposes behind your comments. Let students know what they are to do with the comments now they are in their hands.

2. Make response a two-way street—or, better yet, a free-flowing highway. When the students hand in their papers, encourage them to direct your attention, in a separate note attached to their writing, to special concerns they have about the writing. Read the paper in light of these concerns, or use them in discussing your own responses to the paper. At different times in the course have students react to your responses, identifying any questions or confusions they might have and pointing out those they find most and least useful.

3. Concentrate most of your work with response in the first half of the course. Gradually have students take on greater responsibility for responding to one another's papers. The more students see you modeling your own ways of reading, evaluating, and responding to writing, the more adept they will be when it comes time for them to respond to one another's writing. The more you put into your responses early in the course, the more you will be able to establish a firm foundation for your work to come, and the more you can rely on students to provide useful feedback to one another's writing later on.

4. Make self-evaluation a part of the course: Have students periodically evaluate their own strengths, progress, and areas for improvement as writers. Such work will lead them to develop a keener sense of what you are looking for, and what they might look for, in their writing.

These, then, are some principles to follow, some guidelines to help you find your way. Ultimately, of course, if responding is indeed like playing chess, you finally have to develop a feel for it on your own. Discover your own strengths. Find your own best strategies. Develop your own style. The best comments, finally, do not focus on one area or another. They do not provide just a little criticism or a lot of help. They are not directive or facilitative. The best comments take on what is most important in this paper, for this student, at this time. They encourage students to look back on their choices and consider their options. They pursue. They apply pressure. They offer incentive. They teach. And they challenge the student to make the next move.

Why Student Conferences Are Important

MICHAEL STANCLIFF
Arizona State University

Michael Stancliff addresses the key role that individually discussing evolving drafts with students plays in his teaching.

Conferencing with students is central to my pedagogy. Like many of my colleagues, I believe that writing practices and difficulties are highly individualized, and that the only way to effectively address this broad range of issues is to provide each student writer with a chance to bend your ear. Also, I find that students almost always appreciate this direct access, which is so rare in large universities especially. It is my hope that students come to understand that I take their concerns as writers seriously. In this way, conferencing often encourages a greater sense of collaboration and trust in the class as a whole.

Each semester I try to schedule an individual conference with each student and a group conference during which I meet with a workshop group. In each case, I hold the conferences while writing projects are in draft stage. I think it is important in the individual conferences, however, to give students a chance to discuss any classroom issues they deem important. Regularly, I get incredibly important feedback about my teaching during these conferences.

I recommend considerable preparation for the conferences. Take time in class to decide what the conference agenda will be. When conferences are organized around students' drafts, I require them to articulate their own criteria for response, to read one another's papers ahead of time outside of class, and to make extensive written comments. Often, I will add criteria for peer readers to consider. When we meet, each student receives my comments and those of her or his group members. Students report that this range of responses is very helpful, and I am struck again and again by the excellence of the advice peer readers provide when they are given the time and encouraged to respond in depth. Students also report that the experience of reading their peers' writing helps them to think more critically about their own writing.

Aside from these "official" conferences, I recommend holding as many office hours as possible and encouraging students to attend frequently. Much of the best work I do happens when students take advantage of this forum.

Expanding the Uses of Writing Centers

JASNA R. SHANNON
College of the Holy Cross

Jasna Shannon's article describes how writing centers can function collaboratively with faculty to reinforce and support students' development as writers on many levels.

Researchers have long alerted us to the fact that writing centers "were established to serve needs that traditional writing programs did not meet" (Hilgers and Marsella 232). According to Hilgers and Marsella, "many writing centers function exclusively by providing services not provided by the traditional curriculum, as havens in which writers edit, format, and print their finished products" (236).

Most writing centers are seen as remedial centers for struggling writers. A common misconception is that only poor writers should go to the writing center because they need all the help they can get. Students have also recognized this notion and become leery of the stigma that follows them to the center. Unfortunately, as a result many students make an effort to avoid going to the writing center unless absolutely necessary (and often as the last minute solution that is supposed to fix all their writing problems). Needless to say, given this perception, the image and reputation of writing centers will tarnish and send the wrong message to the college community.

But writing centers can and should be much more. Even though weaker writers most often seek the help of a tutor in an undergraduate writing center, strong writers may benefit most from collaborative engagement with other strong writers who work in the center. Colleges should strive to create centers that are rich, creative environments that attract and engage the strongest writers and remove the stigma associated with the traditional remedial image of writing centers. This can be achieved through careful selection and training of the writing center staff and through effective communication with faculty and students.

Tutor Selection and Training

One of the key issues in creating a rich environment where strong writers want to associate and engage in dialogue with other strong writers, and where communication and collaboration take place, is selecting and training the writing center staff. A successful writing center needs tutors who are able to provide a coaching function—that is, serve as collaborators who engage in discussion about writing. The emphasis here is on collaboration and engaging the student in dialogue. The tutor becomes a resource to help students expand and improve their writing strategies, among other things.

Tutors can be selected in many different ways. At my institution, I try to involve the faculty in helping me find qualified and interested students who would be strong candidates for writing center tutors. I also try to recruit students from a variety of majors (not only English) in order to provide a rich environment in the center, to show students that they don't have to be English majors to be strong writers, and to emphasize the importance of writing throughout the disciplines.

One resource I use in training undergraduate student tutors is Emily Meyer and Louise Smith's *The Practical Tutor*. This resource alerts tutors to various problems they frequently face in writing centers. The emphasis in *The Practical Tutor* is on collaboration between the tutor and the student. The book provides a large array of sample dialogues that illustrate how to formulate questions that will help students grow as writers, instead of merely showing them how to "fix" their sentences and essays. Furthermore, the emphasis is on first presenting the various aspects of composing and forming concepts and then shifting the focus to surface errors.

At my institution, prospective tutors take a semester-long training course (Composition Theory and Pedagogy) for which they earn full credit. In this course, students learn firsthand about collaborative learning through exercises and journal assignments, role-playing techniques, and discussion. Before they start interning in the writing center halfway through the semester, I provide a short handout outlining and summarizing the key points Meyer and Smith offer tutors, in order to facilitate the learning experience and better serve the students' needs.

1. Meeting the writer and establishing trust

    ◆ Identify writer's problems.

    ◆ Remain objective and neutral.

    ◆ Establish clear objectives for tutoring session and explain tutor's function.

        a. look for patterns of error and focus on the most serious
        b. avoid rewriting student papers

2. Promoting dialogue and communication through collaboration

    ◆ Ask open-ended questions and listen; let the student lead the discussion.

◆ Encourage the student to reflect on his or her work and find answers/solutions; avoid giving the answers.

3. Questions to consider as you read student papers

◆ What is the assignment and does the paper adequately meet the assignment requirements? (Consider how well the student understands the assignment.)

◆ What point(s) does the paper make? Is the thesis evident/clear? Is the student able to rephrase what the paper is about or state what he or she wants to say in the paper?

◆ Is the introduction effective?

◆ Is the paper logically organized and presented? Do the points made in the paper logically lead to the student's conclusion?

◆ Are all the points supported well and effectively? Are the sources documented correctly in the documentation style appropriate for the course?

◆ Are the transitions between ideas effective and appropriate? Are the ideas related clearly and smoothly? Has the student thought about audience?

◆ Is the conclusion effective? Does the student merely summarize the main points?

◆ Are the sentences varied and grammatically correct? Is the word choice varied? Is the tone appropriate and consistent?

◆ Does the paper show depth of thought, sophistication, and complexity, and does it reflect the assignment adequately (Meyer and Smith Chapter 1)?

Communication and Collaboration with Faculty

In many schools, communication between tutors and students is kept confidential; that is, the faculty member usually doesn't know when his or her students visit the writing center, nor what took place during the tutoring session. At my institution, however, the faculty not only want to know when their students visit the writing center, but they also encourage them to do so, and they want to know what occurs during each tutoring session. Here is where communication between faculty and the writing center becomes crucial. Not only will this communication help publicize the writing center widely, but it will also establish a strong rapport with faculty.

One of the first communications between faculty and the writing center at my institution is a letter the head tutors (a group of four or five tutors who have additional administrative responsibilities) send to all faculty informing them about the writing center and the services it provides. They also encourage the faculty to invite a tutor to visit their classes to explain to their students how the writing center operates, what it can provide for them, and what they can expect from a tutoring session. As the director of the writing center, I also send a letter to all faculty at the beginning of the year to provide basic information about and main objectives of the writing center (e.g., that the writing center helps students discuss assignments, brainstorm ideas, organize and write drafts, rethink and revise second drafts or returned papers, improve their clarity and organization as well as style and diction; I also explain the role of tutors as a resource to help students expand and improve their writing strategies, etc.). I encourage faculty to take advantage of "special assignments," in which a tutor is assigned specifically to their class or to an individual student who will work with the same tutor on a regular basis. Such a letter to faculty provides practical as well as promotional information about the writing center, and it also promotes communication between the writing center and the faculty. The writing center is there to work with the faculty to promote and strengthen student writing.

In addition to these letters and class visits to introduce and remind the faculty of this important resource, tutors also keep online records of their tutoring sessions, which are then printed and mailed to the faculty member. In this manner, faculty members know which of their students visited the writing center and what the tutor worked on with the student during the session. For special assignment tutoring, there is more communication between the tutor and faculty member in order to better serve the needs of the class or the assigned student.

Faculty are also encouraged and therefore willing to contact the director of the writing center about specific problems a student has in order to better serve the student's needs. This kind of communication not only shows the faculty member's concern with the student's writing problems, but also helps the writing center tutors know what specific problems they need to focus on in their sessions with the student.

One of the important ways faculty can help is to identify the students who could really benefit from the writing center. At times it is the better student writers, those who are making solid and above-average grades, who could truly benefit from engaging in dialogue with a writing tutor and make progress in their writing style or diction. In other words, better writers can also benefit from engaging in dialogue about writing and writing strategies, as well as add to the stimulating and rich environment the writing centers strive to achieve. Needless to say, such an environment can only benefit other students seeking help.

Writing centers are and should be seen as places where students of all levels and writing skills can congregate to seek additional help and support in order to become better writers, where tutors act as sounding boards and listen and encourage without being judgmental, and where together they can engage in productive dialogue about writing.

Works Cited

Hilgers, Thomas L., and Joy Marsella. *Making Your Writing Program Work: A Guide to Good Practices.* Newbury Park, CA: Sage, 1992.

Meyer, Emily, and Louise Z. Smith. *The Practical Tutor.* New York: Oxford UP, 1987.

Writing Center Consultations

REBECCA L. JACKSON
New Mexico State University

Rebecca Jackson outlines some of the benefits writing centers provide students and teachers, particularly when they are utilized and presented appropriately.

Like student-teacher conferences, writing center consultations (or tutorials) provide students with highly individualized, supportive, one-to-one assistance with all aspects of writing, from planning and brainstorming to drafting and revision. For your students, however, the shift in audience from teacher to consultant may make all the difference. No matter how supportive, nonevaluative, and facilitative you might be during conferences with your students, you are still their teacher, an authority figure charged to evaluate their work and assign it a grade. They feel compelled (and who can blame them!) to agree with our suggestions, to follow our advice, to let us take the lead. With consultants, students feel freer to engage in "real" conversation; to start, stop, back up, and start again; and to agree, disagree, and negotiate. Through this dialogic process—a process that is difficult, if not impossible, to achieve fully in student-teacher conferences—students acquire the self-critical skills they need to become more effective writers and revisers.

That said, let's look more closely at writing centers themselves, at where they're located, how they might be set up, and what kinds of services they provide. Individual writing centers come in an array of shapes, sizes, forms, and configurations and are situated within an equally wide variety of departmental or institutional "homes." Writing centers may be staffed by undergraduate peer consultants, graduate student tutors, faculty consultants, or some combination of these groups. Consultants (sometimes called "tutors," "advisors," or "assistants") may also come from very similar or very different disciplinary backgrounds: writing centers may be staffed by individuals who have or are working on degrees in English, or they may be staffed by individuals who are completing or have completed degrees from across the disciplines. Some writing centers work on an appointment basis; others observe a drop-in schedule. Some work with students in hour-long sessions; others are firmly committed to thirty-minute consultations. And while many writing centers are housed in departments of English, still others can be found in administrative buildings and college and university libraries, or as components of larger "learning centers," sites providing assistance in a variety of areas—math, history, or time management, for example—with writing being just one of these.

Local realities aside, writing centers are largely united in their mission to provide one-on-one writing assistance for all writers—novice or experienced, undergraduate student or faculty member—at any stage in the writing process, and to provide a safe, nonevaluative, firmly student-centered environment in which writers meet with writing consultants to converse about writing. Okay, so what do writing centers look and sound like in action? Perhaps the easiest and best way to discover an answer to this question is to spend some time in your own writing center observing and listening to consultants and students as they interact. Writing centers typically buzz with activity: you'll see pairs of consultants and students working side by side at desks or tables or in front of computer screens. Together, they may be brainstorming ideas for a paper not yet written, discussing a rough draft, looking through a handbook for rules about documentation, or talking about ways to develop a paragraph, construct an effective thesis, or write a powerful introduction. You'll hear consultants ask questions, provide reader feedback, exclaim over well-written passages, and model rhetorical strategies. And you'll hear students respond, ask questions of their own, experiment with rhetorical strategies, clarify important points, and propose solutions. Writing centers provide what writers need most: "talk in all its forms" (North 443), conversations that take place *during* the writing process and at specific points of need rather than after the writing is "finished," turned in, and graded. Stephen North offers perhaps the most well-known articulation of this idea:

> Nearly everyone who writes likes—and needs—to talk about his or her writing, preferably to someone who will really listen, who knows how to listen, and who knows how to talk about writing too. Maybe in a perfect world, all writers would have their own ready auditor, . . . [someone] who would not only listen but draw them out, ask them questions they would not think to ask themselves. A writing center is an institutional response to this need. (440)

Above all, writing centers are sites of student-centered learning. Writing centers insist that students accept full responsibility for their writing, that they retain "ownership" of their work. This stance requires that students, rather than consultants, determine the focus for consulting sessions and that students collaborate actively and fully with consultants to solve the writing challenges they face. Consultants are not responsible for fixing or writing or editing students' papers. Instead, their mission is to help students understand how to write, revise, edit, and "fix" their *own* work more effectively. As Jeff Brooks explains, "a student who comes to the writing center and passively receives knowledge from a tutor will not be any closer to his own paper than he was when he walked in. He may leave with an improved paper, but he will not have learned much" (84).

Of course, the ultimate goal of the writing center conference is to move writers toward greater independence and self-sufficiency, to help them acquire the skills, processes, and habits of mind more experienced writers possess. Stephen North puts it this way: "In a writing center the object is to make sure that writers, and not necessarily their texts, are what get changed by instruction. Our job is to produce better writers, not better writing" (438).

As a teacher of writing, it's crucial that you know what writing centers do and how they go about doing it—their practices and methods. But it's equally important to know *why* they do what they do, or to phrase it a bit differently, what it is about writing center practices that make them so valuable to student writers. Writing centers provide what writers need most:

- ◆ intervention in the writing process
- ◆ feedback and dialogue
- ◆ experience with writing
- ◆ a safe, nonthreatening environment

Let's look at each of these individually. First, writing centers intervene in the writer's process. This intervention is crucial, especially for novice or inexperienced writers who may believe that the hard work of writing resides in drafting and editing, not in revising. As an experienced writer, you know that good, effective, powerful writing requires that the writer engage fully in the writing process: planning, drafting, talking, planning some more, drafting some more, getting response and feedback, revising, revising,

revising, and editing. But knowing this and telling your students that every stage in the writing process is important is much different from having the actual time you'd need to consult with your students at each of these stages. This is why the writing center is so valuable; it affords your students the opportunity to talk with an experienced reader at *any* and *every* stage in the writing process, but particularly in the crucial early and middle stages. A writer may meet with a consultant to talk out plans for an upcoming paper assignment—to explore possibilities for addressing the assignment and/or options for arranging ideas. Some writers may seek help understanding particular assignments, while others may want to work on creating outlines, developing important ideas, or constructing effective introductions. Writing centers give students the opportunity to work actively and at their own pace on those stages in the writing process that teachers may only have enough class time to discuss briefly.

Second, writing centers offer writers feedback on their work and engage them in conversations about their writing. These activities are important for several reasons. When consultants offer face-to-face feedback or response to a writer's work, they reinforce the idea that we write to connect with particular audiences, to enter or participate in the community conversations we value most. Feedback lets writers know where they've met their audience's expectations, where they've confused readers, where they've bored readers, where they need additional information, or where they've failed to consider alternative viewpoints. Reader response is particularly valuable for inexperienced writers who tend to compose "associatively"; that is, without a keen or conscious awareness of the information readers need to make sense of the writer's text. As Meyer and Smith explain, inexperienced writers "leave out crucial information," producing "elliptical" prose (28). In Linda Flower's terms, their writing is "writer based" rather than "reader based."

In their face-to-face conversations with consultants, students are able to practice the kinds of internal conversations that experienced writers have with their "other selves" (Meyer and Smith 28). These other selves, or inner monitors, collaborate with experienced writers as they compose—questioning, evaluating, considering, suggesting—helping them to write pieces that are sophisticated, complex, and complete. Inexperienced writers *have* an inner monitor; they simply aren't as adept at either cultivating or listening to it. Writing center consultants seek to change this situation through collaboration, by asking thoughtful questions and modeling an experienced writer's behavior—in short, by "stand[ing] in as the inexperienced writer's questioning self" (Meyer and Smith 28). In this way, writing center consultants help students develop their capacity for internal conversation. Meyer and Smith explain this process clearly: "The writer hears and responds to the kinds of questions he should be asking himself. The conversation provides practice that will help him internalize dialogic linguistic structures and thereby develop his critical faculties" (28).

Equally important, writing centers recognize that writers learn to write by writing, not by hearing lectures about writing or completing grammar exercises. Learning theorists tell us that we learn best through experience and active participation, that learning itself is not a matter of receiving information passively, but of involving ourselves fully in the process of learning (Bruner). In their emphasis on student responsibility, ownership, dialogue, and practice with writing, writing centers reflect and reinforce these ideas.

Last, writing centers work because they offer writers a safe, nonevaluative context in which to experiment with their writing. The logic goes something like this: the greater the student's degree of security and trust, the better his or her relationship with the writing center consultant; the better the relationship with the consultant, the better their collaborative interaction; the better their interaction, the better the student's learning (Tiberius). Writing center consultants aren't in the business of evaluating or judging students. Instead, they are fellow writers, people who understand well the complexities and challenges of writing. It is in the context of such writing center relationships that student writers thrive.

Okay, you now know what a writing center is, what writing centers do, and why their work is so valuable. So what can you do to prepare your students for productive writing center consultations? The following tips will help ensure that your students use the writing center as fully and effectively as possible:

Familiarize yourself with the writing center and its policies. Find out where the writing center is located; what its hours of operation are; whether it works with students by appointment only, drop-in only, or some combination of the two; what procedures students should follow to make appointments; what kinds of writing resources are available to students and faculty; what the writing center's policies are for such things as editing, failing to show up for an appointment, being late for an appointment, or providing summaries of students' visits to instructors; whether the writing center has a Web site and/or online writing lab (OWL); what the writing center's mission statement is. The list of things to know is potentially endless. The larger point is to acquire as much information as possible about your writing center's particular ways of doing things. The writing center I direct, for example, is located in the Department of English. We operate on an appointment-only basis, although students are welcome to drop in to see a consultant immediately if slots are available. Students sign up with consultants for hour-long sessions and are aware that the writing center may cancel their appointment and give it to another student if they are more than ten minutes late. Knowing your writing center's policies and guidelines will allow you to address your students' questions about the writing center confidently, accurately, and specifically. This is important. Experience has taught me that students lose interest in the writing center and what it might do for them when their teachers can't answer basic questions about the center's hours of operation or what kinds of services it provides. Left to find this information out for themselves, students tend to dismiss the writing center altogether as "too much trouble." In addition, being able to talk intelligently about your writing center sends students the message that the writing center is important to you, that you value what it does. This goes a long way toward dispelling the myth that writing centers are sites of punishment and remediation.

Spend some time in the writing center. Once you have the basics down, spend some time becoming familiar with the space itself. Walk around the room; imagine you are a student entering the writing center for the first time. Is there a receptionist's desk? If so, is this where students sign in? If not, where *do* students sign in? Where do tutorials take place? How are consultation areas arranged? The goal here is to try to understand the writing center experience from a student's or "outsider's" perspective. Writing centers can be intimidating places, especially to someone who's never visited one and who might have misconceptions about what writing centers are about and who they're for. Students will feel much more comfortable in the writing center if you've spent some time talking with them about what they can expect—who will greet them, what kinds of forms they'll be asked to fill out, where they'll probably sit, and what activities they might engage in.

Get to know the writing center director and consultants. Talk with the director about his or her visions for the center, what the director is trying to accomplish currently, and what directions the center would like to move in. Tell the director about your own visions for the writing center, the ways you imagine the writing center might help you become a better teacher and your students better writers. Chat informally with several of the writing center's consultants, perhaps asking them about their experiences as consultants, what they like most about consulting, what things cause frustration. You might even ask them to talk about what they wish instructors would do or refrain from doing, things that generally hinder or help the consultation along. The goal here is to establish a working partnership with the center's director and consultants, to create a climate in which directors, consultants, and instructors feel comfortable talking with one another freely about assignments, expectations, the needs of particular students, strategies for assisting students, and other important issues.

Provide the writing center with all course materials related to writing. This might include copies of your syllabus, copies of your assignments, evaluation criteria, or any information or handout you think writing center consultants could use to help your students with the writing they do for your class. Talk with your students about the writing center on the first day of class and frequently throughout the semester. Writing centers emphasize that collaboration is a normal and necessary part of the writing process for all writers. As teachers, you reinforce this idea when you talk about the writing center on the first day of classes, as just one of the many stages in the writing process you expect them, as writers, to engage in. Talking about collaboration as a fundamental part of the writing process also encourages students to use the writing center *during* the process rather than after their paper is written. As most of us who work in writing centers understand, consultations are most helpful during the brainstorming, drafting, and revising stages of the writer's process. Arrange for a writing center orientation.

Writing centers offer different kinds of orientation services: consultants or the director may visit individual classes and provide ten- to fifteen-minute writing center introductions, or they may invite classes to the writing center itself for an inhouse orientation. If you have a choice, arrange for an inhouse writing center orientation. This gives your students the opportunity to see where the center is located and what it looks like, as well as hear about the kinds of services it offers. If an inhouse orientation is unavailable, request that a consultant speak with your class about the writing center. Ask questions during the visit and encourage your students to do the same. Request a mock consultation. Ask a writing center consultant to model an effective consultation for your class.

Many students are afraid of writing centers. They don't know what to expect; they don't know what is expected of them. Seeing a mock writing center consultation is one of the best ways to alleviate your students' anxieties about writing center consultations and to prepare them for a productive session of their own. This last point is especially important. Consultants at the writing center I direct complain most frequently about students who arrive for sessions unprepared—without copies of the assignment, without notes or drafts, without any real sense of what they would like to accomplish in the session. Mock consultations allow consultants to dramatize what it means to be prepared. Compare writing center consultations to the professional writing process. Discuss the writing center consultation as an enactment of the professional writing process. I've found that one of the best ways to dispel myths about writing center work and actually get students into the writing center several times over the semester is to compare the writing center consultation to the collaboration between a professional writer and his or her colleagues, editors, and readers. I explain, for example, that I always solicit my colleagues' feedback on various drafts of the pieces I plan to send out for publication. I emphasize that the collaborative process continues even after I send the piece out, that editors send my article to peers in my field who then offer revision suggestions for publication. This is the form of professional academic conversation, a process similar to the face-to-face collaboration students and consultants engage in during their writing center consultations. Discussing the writing center consultation as an enactment of the professional writing process works to alter students' misconceptions that "real" writers don't need critical feedback on their work.

Ask your students to talk about their writing center experiences. Students are a writing center's best, most powerful advocates. When students hear that their peers have gone to the writing center and have had positive experiences, they feel more comfortable making that leap themselves. Ask students in your classes who have visited the writing center to talk about their experiences. Give them time to be specific and to answer any questions their peers might have. Help students get ready for writing center consultations. Spend class time helping students identify questions or areas of focus for upcoming writing center sessions. This helps ensure that the consulting session is spent working on the student's writing and not on figuring out what the focus of the session should be. Consider the pros and cons of requiring/referring students to visit the writing center.

Requiring students to visit the writing center can take a variety of forms. Some faculty refer individual students to the writing center when they think the student needs or would benefit from additional work on his or her writing. Some may mandate writing center visits as a condition for receiving a passing grade in the course; others may "strongly suggest," but not require, that the student work with a writing center consultant throughout the semester. Generally, writing center folk oppose these kinds of referrals: first, referrals reinforce the stereotype that writing centers are for "problem" writers only, that they are sites of remediation. In a study of writing center referrals and their effects on students, Gary Olson discovered that "if the student believes that being sent to the center is punitive, the chances are good that the student's reaction will be hostile" (160). Consultants know all too well how difficult, almost impossible, it can be to work with students who are angry or indifferent. Most tutors would prefer to spend time working with students who *want* to work on their writing. Olson explains that individual referrals are most effective when the instructor "speak[s] with the student personally . . . and explain[s] that the writing center is not a place for 'basket cases,' but a place where students can seek professional help for common problems" (169). Bell and Stutts agree, noting that faculty "should encourage students to visit the center (not threaten them with the possibility in a detention-like way), and offer them positive reinforcement when they go" (5).

Many instructors have turned to the classwide mandatory writing center visit as an alternative to individual referral. These instructors require that every student visit the writing center a set number of times each semester. Like Bell and Stutts, many instructors view required writing center visits as a way of getting students into the center and transforming them into "enthusiastic advocates" (5). Bell and Stutts point out that another advantage of a classwide visit policy is that it "doesn't stigmatize the struggling writers in the class as can individual referrals" (5). Wendy Bishop argues that a required first visit tells students that "the writing center is resource for all writers and should be used by them to enhance their writing throughout their university careers" (38).

Those who oppose the use of individual referrals and even classwide mandatory visits argue that while requiring students to work in the writing center may sound like a good idea—it *does* get students into the writing center—it really does more harm than good. Bell concedes that her mandatory visits "were not as successful as [she] had hoped. Students often waited until the last minute to sign up for required consultations and then made it clear that they didn't really want to be there." The situation, Bell concludes, left tutors "overburden[ed] and frustrat[ed]" (Bell and Stutts 6). I was recently forced to address this issue in my own writing center: consultants became increasingly upset when students who had been required to visit the writing center showed up in hordes just two or three days prior to an important deadline. Consultants felt used and overworked. In consultation after consultation, they found themselves trying desperately to work productively with students whose only concern was that the consultant "sign the paper to show that I've been here." Consultants felt strongly that their time would have been much better spent working with the many students who had been turned away from the writing center because the schedule was booked.

My advice is this: Carefully weigh the advantages and disadvantages of requiring individuals and/or entire classes to work in the writing center *before* you make your final decision. If you *do* decide that classwide visits are worth a try, make sure to consult with your writing center's director beforehand. He or she will be able to tell you whether the writing center has enough tutors and time slots to accommodate such requests (imagine how many students would need appointments if even five people in your department required entire classes to visit the writing center during the semester!) and, if it can, what times during the semester are likely to be especially busy and/or slow.

I'd like to leave you with one final, yet very important idea: used fully, writing centers can play as powerful a role in your own development as a teacher of writing as it can in your students' development as writers. For teachers, writing centers can be rich sites of learning and research. Spend time in a writing center as a consultant, as an interested observer, or as a language researcher, and you'll discover the ways in which the writing center can transform your teaching philosophies and practices. My own is a story of conversion: I learned to teach writing not by reading composition theory (although this helped), not by engaging in discussions about pedagogy (although this helped too), and certainly not by standing in front of a classroom talking about writing to the masses. I learned to teach writing by working slowly and methodically with individual writers, writers who had signed up to work with me for thirty to forty minutes at a time in a writing center. And what did I learn? I learned most about individual writing processes—how different writers tackle writing projects, where they struggle, how they struggle, and the role that praise and dialogue and thoughtful questions play in assisting them in their attempts to make meaning with words. Writing center work made me a better listener, a more sympathetic reader, and a facilitator of learning rather than a director.

Working and/or observing in the writing center, you'll see students wrestling with poorly conceived assignments, struggling with writing, and trying to manage deeply held insecurities about their abilities and potential. Through this experience, you'll likely become better at creating assignments that work, better at understanding your students' frustration, and better at working with your students individually in conferences of your own. You'll come to better understand the instrumental role that conversation can play in helping students overcome the challenges they face. Valerie Balester says it best: "The writing center should be the place . . . where writing is not only critiqued but also discussed, produced, researched and enjoyed" (170).

Encourage your students to discover, use, and enjoy the writing center at your institution, and discover, use, and enjoy the writing center yourself!

Works Cited

Balester, Valerie. "Revising the 'Statement': On the Work of Writing Centers." *College Composition and Communication* 43 (1992): 167–71.

Bell, Barbara, and Robert Stutts. "The Road to Hell Is Paved with Good Intentions: The Effects of Mandatory Writing Center Visits on Student and Tutor Attitudes." *Writing Lab Newsletter* 22.1 (1997): 5–7.

Bishop, Wendy. "Bring Writers to the Center: Some Survey Results, Surmises, and Suggestions." *Writing Center Journal* 10.2 (1990): 31–41.

Brooks, Jeff. "Minimalist Tutoring: Making the Student Do All the Work." *The St. Martin's Sourcebook for Writing Tutors*. Ed. Christina Murphy and Steve Sherwood. New York: St. Martin's, 1995.

Bruner, Jerome S. *Toward a Theory of Instruction*. Cambridge: Belknap/ Harvard UP, 1966.

Flower, Linda. "Writer-Based Prose: A Cognitive Basis for Writing Problems." *College English* 41 (1979): 19–37.

Meyer, Emily, and Louise Z. Smith. *The Practical Tutor*. New York: Oxford UP, 1987.

North, Stephen M. "The Idea of a Writing Center." College English 46 (1984): 433–46.

Olson, Gary A. "The Problem of Attitudes in Writing Center Relationships." *Writing Centers: Theory and Administration*. Ed. Gary Olson. Urbana, IL: NCTE, 1984. 155–69.

Tiberius, Richard G. "The Why of Teacher/Student Relationships." *Teaching Effectiveness: Toward the Best in the Academy* 6.1 (1994– 1995): 1–2.

CHAPTER 10

RESPONDING TO AND EVALUATING POLISHED WRITING

O ffering strategies for responding to writing that students consider fully polished, this chapter is designed to help teachers decide when and how to encourage students to do yet one more round of revising content or editing surface features. It should also help teachers decide when enough is enough—when the exigencies of the semester don't permit another round or when the student can't muster the energy to revise and/or edit again. How can a teacher's comments help the student understand what he or she has and has not accomplished with the project? How might the student reflect on the project in the course portfolio? How can a teacher's comments help the student understand the grade on the paper?

Developing Rubrics for Instruction and Evaluation

Chris M. Anson and Deanna P. Dannels
North Carolina State University

These authors illustrate how rubrics may be designed and implemented to facilitate students' understanding of the evaluative processes teachers use when assessing their writing.

Of all our many responsibilities as teachers of writing and communication, evaluating students' work is certainly one of the most difficult and time consuming. The process of reading and judging students' work can be confusing, contradictory, and subjective. While we may know a good piece of writing when we see one, it is often hard for us to come to grips with our expectations, specifying exactly what we mean by "effective style," or "coherent organization," or "insightfulness." And while these uncertainties may be veiled behind our authority, our students daily hold us accountable to clarity of expectations in their own confessions of ignorance or requests to please explain "what we want" in an assignment.

In depth and helpfulness, no method can replace a full-fledged response to a student's paper. Sitting next to a writer and working through a draft, asking questions for clarification, offering reader-based response, or prompting ideas for revision not only models the collaborative processes that writers experience in countless professional settings, but also gives students the language and intellectual framework for responding to their own and other writers' work. What we "value" in good writing for a particular occasion takes the form of constructive critique, not just judgment.

In most teaching situations, of course, we don't always have the time to consult extensively with each student: even in a class of twenty, thorough individual conferences can take up to two full days. With adequate preparation, peer groups can provide students with ample, helpful response, even if it is of a less refined and expert nature than what might come from a teacher.

But even if the peer groups use revision prompts to guide their discussions, in most academic settings the teacher will still read and judge students' work, arriving at a grade or other type of final assessment. How, then, can we turn this responsibility to evaluate students' work back into our classroom instruction, creating formative assessment strategies from what are often only final, summative judgments?

For many kinds of writing and speaking assignments, the use of evaluative rubrics can ease the often bewildering process of measuring a student's work and also help the entire class to begin applying important rhetorical, textual, or presentational principles to their work. In this essay, we suggest some ways you can design evaluative rubrics for student work and, by introducing and explaining those rubrics to students before they begin an assignment, increase students' application of standards for judgment to their ongoing projects.

Rubrics: What Are They?

Rubrics come in many forms; at their simplest, they are evaluative scales based on categories that usually derive from expectations for a genre, assignment, or performance. If you were to develop a rubric for an upcoming experience at a trendy restaurant, for example, you could divide that experience into several categories, each weighted on a simple scale (see Figure 10.1). A visit to Chez Pierre's Bistro may yield an excellent rating for service, food, and ambiance, but the meal may not be worth the exorbitant price.

The specific "cells" of your evaluation reflect individual qualities, a distinction which increases the fairness and explicitness of your judgment; but when taken together, these cells also give an overall assessment: Chez Pierre's is excellent, but its high prices draw down an otherwise stellar rating.

Note also that these four categories are more complicated than they seem (categories almost always are). "Service" is really a container for several more specific characteristics: the way diners are greeted at the door, the promptness of responses to requests, the attention to detail, the demeanor of the waitpersons,

	poor	average	good	excellent
service				
food				
ambiance				
value				

FIGURE 10.1

and so on. Essential to rubrics is knowing what a category means at its richest, most complex, and most specific.

The categories themselves may also suggest differential values depending on the purpose and context of the evaluation. For diners who eat at trendy or expensive restaurants, perhaps the cost is less important than the quality of the food or service. Assigning weights to each category can add depth and complexity to the rubric while also creating a fairer evaluative tool: just as the quality of food at a chic restaurant may be more important than price, the sophistication or insightfulness of ideas in a student's journal entry may be more important than how many words he or she has misspelled.

Almost anything that can be valued can be placed into a rubric. For written and spoken discourse, such valued characteristics can come from several sources, leading to somewhat different kinds of rubrics. *Course-specific rubrics* are commonly handed out with syllabi. Because they cover all the artifacts produced in a course, they tend to be very general and are not always useful for students beyond setting the broad parameters of a grading scheme. The following excerpt from a course-specific rubric explains to students what it means to get a B on any paper in the course:

> **B:** This paper goes beyond the routine response to the assignment. The thesis or viewpoint reflects thoughtfulness and balance. The development of the focus is careful and accurate. The organization is clear, coherent, and well suited to the paper's purpose and audience. The voice and tone are appropriate, consistent, and effective. For the most part, the style is clear, smooth, and free of distracting errors in usage, grammar, and mechanics.

There may be some very minor lapses in some area (such as attention to detail, stylistic sophistication, or an effective conclusion), but these will not, taken together, seriously compromise the writer's credibility and the paper's overall strengths. The B paper is strong overall, but not outstanding.

Discipline- and genre-specific rubrics tap into the conventions and formats of various fields and kinds of discourse. A lab report in a mechanical engineering class will follow entirely different conventions from an APA-style review of the literature on a topic in a social psychology course. At their best, evaluative rubrics clarify such conventions and help students understand what is expected of them in particular fields or kinds of written or spoken discourse. In an evaluative rubric for a large final project in a history course, for example, the "focus" or "thesis" (one of six characteristics to be judged) is glossed with specific reference to the principles of writing in history:

Introduction and Focus or Thesis
(Provides succinct and clear picture of the project, the historical event(s) to be explored; adequately explains the importance of gaining new knowledge of this area/place in historical work)   Strong   Average   Weak

Assignment- and outcome-specific rubrics are specific to an assignment or an expected learning outcome and can be helpful in focusing students' attention on certain characteristics or strategies you want them to learn. In a course on writing about literature, for example, a professor has developed a rubric that balances the application of particular "lenses" for interpretation with the quality of the writing. The students briefly study six or seven interpretive approaches (reader-response theory, New Criticism, psychoanalytic and feminist approaches, and so on). As students learn about these approaches, they apply them to poems or short stories and write "interpretive sketches"—brief, unrevised papers somewhat more formal than freewrites or journal entries but less formal than standard essays.

The professor who teaches this course has developed his rubric with his students over time. In each new section of the course, he works through the rubric with the students, handing out drafts of sketches he has gained permission to use from previous students. After two or three sample sketches, the students begin to understand both the nature of the interpretive sketch as a course-specific genre and the sorts of textual and intellectual qualities that separate a good sketch from a poor one.

application of critical method	5	4	3	2	1
insightfulness/sophistication	5	4	3	2	1
general coherence of response	5	4	3	2	1
surface quality (given expected mid-level of formality)	5	4	3	2	1

As students practice applying the rubric to sample sketches, they learn how to distinguish between a 5 and a 4 on "insightfulness" or between a 3 and a 2 on "surface quality." Because the sketches are informal, single-draft papers, this teacher grades them in increments of five. Each value is multiplied by five, yielding one hundred possible points. The sketches themselves have a lower weighted value than formal papers in the overall grading scheme for the course (5 percent each, or 25 percent of the final grade for a total of five sketches).

Designing Rubrics for Writing Assignments

Carefully designed rubrics for evaluation can't be assembled quickly, and in most cases they are improved by trial and error. As you read students' writing, you'll refine your assignment and the work you do in class to develop it; along with these changes, your rubric will also have to develop because it is inextricably tied to your instruction.

To develop a rubric for a writing assignment, you might find the following process helpful:

1. Begin with an assignment that leads to a final text that you then evaluate, formally or informally, as part of a student's grade. What's the goal of the assignment? How is it woven

into the fabric of your course? What are students supposed to learn or practice by virtue of the assignment?

2. List any *processes and/or intellectual activities* the writing assignment will require. These will be directly connected to your purpose for giving the assignment. For example: "In this particular ethnographically based paper, the student carefully observes the context and analyzes its cultural or social characteristics"; "The student will find two conflicting accounts of the same historical event by doing appropriate library research"; "For the literature review, the student needs to read and understand at least six studies on the topic and then synthesize them."

3. Now describe the textual *evidence* that will show that the student has engaged in the process(es): "The first part of the ethnography will adequately describe the various contexts (physical, social, etc.) of the chosen group"; "The two conflicting accounts will be described in the paper, and there will be citations included at the end indicating the sources the student consulted"; "The literature review will include references to at least six works and they must be on a specific topic or specific aspect of a topic; synthesis of these works will be shown in the student's awareness of the studies' conclusions, and there will be a concluding statement summarizing what the studies show about the topic collectively and what still needs to be known."

4. List any specific textual features or characteristics of the paper you expect in addition to the characteristics you described in step 3. For example: "This paper must conform to MLA style in all respects, including the use of references"; "The literature review should include an introduction specifying the topic being addressed; a section synthesizing the studies; and a conclusion summing up what is known from the research and what still needs to be known ('implications' or 'further research')"; "The ethnography must show a balance between inference and observation. Typically, this means that interpretive statements will be accompanied by (preced-

ing or following) some more representational account of the context."

5. From your lists, now try to describe characteristics of "strong," "average," and "weak" papers for this assignment: "The strong paper will show clear organization using the format of literature reviews; the first part will establish the domain or focus of the works to be reviewed; the second part will include discussions of each work, though the organization may be linear or conceptual; the third part will provide a general conclusion; and the fourth part will suggest unanswered questions not addressed in the works discussed. The paper will also . . . ."

6. Try to tie the descriptions to your grading standards. Do you need more categories? Remember that the greater the number of categories, the more complex and time-consuming your grading.

7. Now prepare two documents for students: a simple rubric with the main categories you'll use in your assessment of their work, and the descriptive characteristics you drafted in step 5. Try editing your language so that you address students directly: "Your literature review should show that you've worked through the principles of structure we will have discussed in class (chronological, topical, oppositional, etc.) and that your choice is clearly tied to the nature of the topic you've chosen to research."

As you design the two documents in step 7, keep the main rubric simple (this is the one you'll use to evaluate students' work at the end), but give the descriptive characteristics as much detail and complexity as you wish. By the time you evaluate students' work, you and the students should be clear about what each of the categories in the main rubric means and what it contains or implies. In a long research paper, for example, you may want students to work on everything from broad structural issues to the correct form of ellipses in quoted material. If you develop a rubric with too many features, or if the features are too specific, you may end up spending much more time than you want when you comment on or evaluate each paper.

Instead, look for broad categories that you can then make more complex internally. Use "quality of source work" to encompass several aspects of students' research and writing, including their summaries of outside sources or their use of MLA style. Each broad category then becomes a label for a kind of holistic reading within its boundaries—a reading based on your descriptive criteria. A student may have done really well at integrating outside sources into his or her own treatment of a topic but not paid much attention to citation style. The strength of the former will pull up your judgment while the weakness of the latter pulls it back down, but you can reach an overall judgment of the category more quickly than if you were to look through the paper again and again for one specific characteristic at a time.

Remember that the rubric itself may seem simple on the surface—four characteristics with three or four rating categories. The key is to spend considerable time in class talking about the rubric and everything contained in each category.

Using Rubrics

Ideally, a well-crafted rubric can drive some or much of what you do in class to help students work through an assignment. Evaluation becomes both a goal or outcome and a way of helping students work on their projects.

Give your rubric to the students before they start an assignment. If students don't know how you'll evaluate the product of their work, they can't use your evaluation productively. Giving students an evaluative rubric before they begin to work on a project helps guide them during the various stages of its production. A simple rubric for a problem-solution paper, for example, might include the characteristic "appropriateness of problem." Inappropriate problems might include those that are not really problems, or problems that are too general or ill defined, or problems too easily solved by simple actions. By showing this one aspect of evaluation to students, by talking through it and offering examples of successful and unsuccessful problems, you are helping students in the planning stages of their writing ("Choose an appropriate problem"). You're also helping them in the drafting and revising stages, especially if they meet with other students in small revision groups ("Is my problem appropriate for this task?"). Ideally, your rubric should match or reflect any guides you give to students to prompt their revisions of drafts.

Explicitly link the rubric to your goals. In a classroom setting, an evaluative rubric should be explicitly tied to your educational goals. This will usually mean foregrounding some aspects of a written text and backgrounding others. If you want students to practice incorporating more details into their writing, you might craft a brief, informal assignment involving the description of a place or scene. A rubric for such an assignment would highlight the quality of description but perhaps deemphasize, for the moment, the sophistication of the essay's structure (most descriptions being organizationally static or linear). Because details may be the main or only goal of the task, your rubric can "unpack" what you mean by description and present several more specific evaluative dimensions on a simple scale:

Rubric for Quality of Description

use of descriptive language	1	2	3
appropriateness of details	1	2	3
variety of details	1	2	3

Use models to teach the characteristics of the rubric. Successful writers have internalized dozens of evaluative principles, which they apply while drafting and revising their work or planning and delivering an oral presentation. As writers read through a draft, these tacit principles become activated in the context of a word, sentence, or entire section; the writer worries about how his or her audience will respond, or ponders whether an argument seems too strident or one-sided. Rubrics offer you and your students a more explicit way to work with such principles and questions.

Students often find it difficult or impossible to translate our vague criteria ("the paper should be coherent," "avoid too many generalizations") into specific textual choices. Each of the dimensions of the rubric for "description," for example, would require some discussion and modeling in class. "Variety of details," for example, could mean attention to different *kinds* of details, a balance of details from the various senses, or details that range around a scene, from focal point to perimeter. Or it could mean some combination of these things.

To be most effective, rubrics need to develop from actual writing and should be applied to writing in progress. After developing or presenting a rubric, ask students to look at a draft of a paper and apply the rubric to it, justifying their judgments with specific references to the text. As they work through such drafts, using the rubric to provide lenses into certain characteristics of the text or genre they are reading and writing, they will begin to internalize the rubric's principles. Later, in working on their own papers, they can tap into these principles as they make wise decisions about the direction and nature of their writing.

Designing and Using Rubrics for Speaking Assignments

For the writing teacher, speaking assignments can be difficult to evaluate because we are not always trained as teachers of small- or large-group communication, nor are we always accustomed to making judgments about work in "real time." With the increasing emphasis on speaking in many writing programs, however, it's worth thinking about how evaluative rubrics can be used in the service of students' oral performance.

In one upper-level writing course, for example, a teacher gives students the option of designing and delivering a presentation to the class and substituting this project for one of the five main papers in the course. Students must give a written plan to the teacher for feedback before delivering the presentation. This plan is based in part on the evaluative rubric the teacher gives the class during the first week of the course:

Evaluation of Presentations

1. *Intellectual Content.* How well researched, informative, and interesting was the material? How carefully selected was it, given the probable mass of information surrounding the topic? 25 percent   Assessment: __

2. *Planning, Timing, and Orchestration.* How carefully planned and executed was the session? How much attention to sequence, timing, and related issues was reflected in the session? 25 percent   Assessment: __

3. *Method.* How engaging and appropriate were the methods used during the session (discussion, group work, lecture, overhead transparencies or use of media, illustration, etc.)? How carefully integrated were these methods with the content of the session? 25 percent   Assessment: __

4. *Deportment.* This is an all-purpose category that relates to the actual delivery of the session by its member(s). Carefully planned sessions will usually lead to a kind of professionalism in delivery. If presenters are scattered, lose their place in a mound of disorganized notes, forget what they are supposed to do, etc., then the session will be compromised. 25 percent Assessment: __

Students learn more about each of the four categories in this assessment throughout the process of designing and developing their presentation: in class discussion, in small-group work, in consultation with the teacher, and in the final assessment of their session (which includes written commentary). "Timing and orchestration" alone, for example, are covered in additional handouts discussed in class:

Coordinate the timing of your session carefully. Time is tricky; if you don't script out your session, you may find that there's not enough time to do all you wanted to. Activities usually take longer than you think. If you put us into groups, we can't do much in less than ten minutes. If we write, give us at least four to five minutes. Think carefully about what you're asking us to do in the time you give us. If you lead a discussion, remember that we can't delve into the issues in just a few minutes. As you craft your agenda, think in blocks of time: "provide background on topic— five minutes; run small-group activity—ten minutes; follow up— ten minutes," etc. Then practice the session with a clock ticking.

In addition to the principles for designing rubrics for writing assignments, consider the following questions when creating a rubric for evaluating students' oral presentations:

1. How will you group and weight items—according to a possible flow of the actual presentation? Or according to the elements of research in the assignment? How will you group issues of content or coverage in relation to delivery?

2. How will you word the items? Remember that the goal is to be able to *use* this instrument in real time and that you're providing it to students as a guide. Language that is action oriented and describes what the student should be doing (or saying) is probably going to work best.

3. How will you select and anchor your scales? Some teachers use 10-point scales; others use a "+/–" scheme. Still others use categories such as "good," "weak," and so on that carry particular grading values. In thinking about your scales, you'll want to consider whether to allow for a middle point (for example, 5- and 7-point scales have middle points 3 and 4, respectively); a 10-point scale does not have a middle point. While this issue may seem trivial, remember that any degrees of difference on a scale or in a set of categories should be meaningful and should lead to consistency of evaluation. If you can meaningfully talk about the differences between a 4 and a 5 on a 5-point scale for the category of "organization" but not between a 6 and a 7 on a 7-point scale, then you probably want to use a 5-point scale. You will also want to think about decision making in real time. A 10-point scale presents you with a range of ten decisions.

4. How will your scale translate into the grading or evaluation scheme used on your campus? Some teachers shy away from 5-point scales because students implicitly translate the scale into an A–F framework. They then interpret the numerical assignments in terms of that framework, even though the numbers may mean something different.

After designing your evaluative rubric for students' oral performance, you'll need to decide how to use it. Some teachers, for example, assess students' performances in real time. This is perhaps the most authentic way to grade oral discourse because you're making judgments as you experience them. All other ways of grading oral performance involve considering some artifact of the performance, such as an outline, a tape, the notes you've taken during a session, and the like. In particular, consider the following strategies: the teacher who uses the rubric reproduced earlier takes copious notes during the session, bracketing evaluative thoughts along the way, and then writes a lengthy response to the student later using the notes as a guide.

Grading students' oral performances takes practice. Trust your instincts, but remember to keep track of new ideas that come to you about "quality" that you haven't fully articulated in class or in your rubric. Some of these new ideas will come to you as students give their presentations.

If you make comments to yourself during the presentation, it helps to develop a shorthand so that you're not missing important parts of the presentation as you're writing down your thoughts. A common problem for many students comes from trying to explain complicated information verbally, without the help of a bulleted list on the board, a handout, or an overhead transparency. One teacher uses the bracketed note [OH/HO?] to mean "maybe it would have been helpful to have some of this on an overhead or handout?"

When it comes time to give a student an assessment, you can do so during a conference or in written form. For the latter, it helps to balance written and numeric feedback. Make sure that if you're assigning middle-of-the-road numbers for a student, your comments also identify areas of improvement. Students find it confusing if they get points equivalent to a C but the comments are all positive. Similarly, if you're assigning high numbers for a performance, suggest some areas for improvement in addition to offering praise (for example, suggest some ways that a strong performance could be improved for an even more demanding context such as a business setting or important conference). Finally, *rely on the rubric*. Your students have had it all along; focus your commentary on those features you've discussed, modeled, and explored in class.

Enlisting the Cooperation of Students in the Design of Rubrics

Evaluation is often something we do alone and impose on our students well after they have completed their work. Even when we spend time developing rubrics and explaining them to students before they begin a project, the students themselves often have no opportunity to participate in the evaluative process.

Beyond sharing criteria with students, there is a sometimes even more productive method for helping students learn about and work with standards for speaking and writing. In this method, you introduce a particular assignment and discuss the genre or form it will yield. After introducing the assignment, your goal is to have the *students* to come up with a list of specific features or characteristics that would describe a "good" piece of writing in that genre or a good oral performance. This takes some work—often it helps to form small groups. It also may take some samples of both successful and unsuccessful papers responding to the same or a similar assignment.

Large-group discussion then focuses on creating a list or a description of a successful project—the start of a rubric for evaluation. You can intervene and ask questions if you think certain areas are not being covered. The list may be done on a board or overhead, but it's crucial for you to copy down the items before you leave the class. Then, at home, work up a handout that incorporates the students' self-generated standards, and hand it out to the students during the next class. Continue to refine the standards in class, explaining that they will be the same ones you'll use as a reader-grader of the students' work. Later, when you read their papers, refer to the group-generated description often.

As we have seen, rubrics can offer you and your students an excellent way to be specific about the qualities we judge in a piece of writing or an oral performance. As a generative tool, they help students measure their ongoing work against clear outcomes and expectations. As an evaluative tool, they help you know what you're looking for, and they help students see the relationship between your assessment and what they've produced. For some assignments or projects, of course, rubrics may be inappropriate, and there may be occasions when you want to allow and encourage unrestricted, impressionistic kinds of response to students' work. If used too mechanically, rubrics can also yield formulaic responses to formulaic tasks.

As you design and use rubrics, remember that you should adapt the principle of evaluation to your specific assignment, course, discipline, and learning context. Just as it takes hard work and plenty of revision for students to produce a piece of writing or design a talk, your evaluative methods themselves will demand continuous scrutiny, reflection, and evaluation.

What Makes Writing "Good"?/ What Makes a "Good" Writer?

RUTH OVERMAN FISCHER
George Mason University

Ruth Fisher debunks the notion of "good" writing as a myth and explores the damaging potential of that myth in the first-year composition class.

Those of us who write and/or teach writing often take for granted just how "natural" using written language to convey thought seems to be. We forget how our years of engaged reading, writing, and overall language use have helped us acquire the competencies necessary to produce an effective piece of writing. We may even have succumbed to the myth that there is an entity called "good writing" and even that there are naturally "good" writers. (And when we find ourselves in the midst of people who see these myths as truths, as I recently did on a listserv exchange, the lively discussion that ensues produces a list of characteristics so abstract that they tend to be meaningless.)

The danger in succumbing to such myths for us as writing teachers is that we can erroneously assume that the students in our first-year composition classes either have these "good" skills or not and either are "good" writers or not for any occasion. Either of these assumptions sets us up to do a great disservice to these students. What makes a piece of writing "good"—actually a more accurate term would be "effective"—is highly contextual.

This context is made up of mutually influential aspects beginning with the rhetorical situation, which in turn calls for the appropriate genre and its linguistic expectations, which in turn creates a space for the subject matter under consideration. How well students understand and have experienced each of these aspects contributes to their production of a particular piece of effective writing. Since one of our potential strengths as writing teachers is a reflection on our own writing practice, let's look at how we, at various levels of consciousness, approach a particular writing task with an eye toward these aspects.

One of the first questions we have to ask as writers is what the rhetorical situation requires. What is the purpose of the writing task? What is the subject matter that prompted the task? Who makes up the audience and what do they know and/or believe about this subject matter? As a writer, what is my relationship to the audience?

Our next concern deals with the genre appropriate to shape the particular piece of writing. Currently in the field of composition, genre is seen as a highly complex construct, which can be viewed from sociocognitive and political perspectives as well as disciplinary and structural ones.[1] Regardless of the perspective, however, we ask ourselves certain questions: What kinds of format does this genre require? What kinds of vocabulary/jargon and sentence structure are expected? Should sentences be simple or complex? Or are bulleted phrases allowed or even expected? Should active or passive voice be used? Can I use the pronoun "I"? What kinds of argument are expected or even acceptable? Or figurative language? How competent am I in the use of these linguistic structures?

And then we have to consider how well we understand the subject matter that forms the heart of our writing project. Are we comfortable with the subject matter, and do we feel free to write with some kind of authority? Or are we still in the process of coming to an understanding of it?

Our ability to address each of these questions and our ability to put our answers into practice contribute to how "good" or effective our written products will eventually be deemed by our ultimate evaluators, our audience. The more experience we have had with a particular rhetorical situation and its consequent genres and related linguistic expectations and subject matter, the greater the repertoire on which we can draw. And if we think back to how we became successful writers in a particular rhetorical situation, we can probably recall a situated "give and take" between our readers (be they peers, editors, or professors) and ourselves, helping us acquire a sense of the genre.

Applying this self-reflection to our work as writing teachers, we recognize that learning to write effectively is a developmental process spanning one's writing career. And within this overall development is the development of a particular piece of writing within a particular context. And so when we consider our first-year composition students who come to us with a variety of writing experiences and training (as well as their own favored kinds of intelligences and learning/personality styles), we realize that both writers and writing need context to become "good."

Note

1. I recognize that these perspectives do not exist in isolation from each other. Each of the following sources, however, seems to focus on the perspective mentioned. For a sociocognitive perspective, see Carol Berkenkotter and Thomas N. Huckin, *Genre Knowledge in Disciplinary Communication: Cognition, Culture, Power* (Hillsdale, NJ: Erlbaum, 1995); for political perspectives, see Wendy Bishop and Hans Ostrom, eds., *Genre and Writing: Issues, Arguments, Alternatives* (Portsmouth, NH: Boynton/Cook-Heinemann, 1997) and Bill Cope and Mary Kalantzis, ed., *The Powers of Literacy: A Genre Approach to Teaching Writing* (Pittsburgh: University of Pittsburgh Press, 1993); for a disciplinary perspective, see Aviva Freedman and Peter Medway, eds., *Learning and Teaching Genre* (Portsmouth, NH: Boynton/Cook, 1994); for a structural perspective, see John Swales, *Genre Analysis: English in Academic and Research Settings* (New York: Cambridge University Press, 1990).

Contexts and Criteria for Evaluating Student Writing

JANE E. HINDMAN
San Diego State University

Emphasizing the centrality of grading to any teacher's activities and philosophy, Jane Hindman provides a theoretical background for various approaches to grading, and then outlines several specific strategies for refining those approaches.

Of all your responsibilities as a composition instructor, evaluating student writing occupies most of your time and has the furthest-reaching material effects. Though you may spend lots of hours preparing for class, conferencing with your students, and actually teaching, chances are you'll spend many more grading. Though we instructors often place the highest value on the methods and content of our classrooms—be they critical pedagogy and Marxist interpretations of Clinton's impeachment trials, or traditional grammar drills and a New Critical reading of *Paradise Lost*—the grades that we assign our students are the only concrete, as well as the most valuable, cultural capital that our teaching creates. As Evan Watkins says in his analysis of what transformative effect our teaching actually has in our culture,

> you don't report to the registrar that [your student learned] . . . a revolutionary fusion of contradictory ethical claims. . . . You report that 60239 got a 3.8 in Engl 322, which in turn, in a couple of years, is then circulated to the personnel office at [for instance] Boeing as 60239's prospective employer. (18)

As a general rule, though, new instructors spend much less time training to be graders than training to be facilitators in the classroom. In fact, you may be wondering why you need to learn how to grade at all, for you may think you know how already. In the teacher-training courses I've taught, most fledgling teachers have initially imagined that grading is a skill they already have, that—as former English majors and/or good writers themselves—they can "naturally" evaluate essays. After all, they reason, they've received enough comments on their own papers, right? They know how the process goes, and good writing is obvious: we all know it when we see it, so it should be pretty easy to figure out how to evaluate it.

Would that it were that simple. In actuality, and as a visit to any norming session[1] comprised of instructors from across a campus will demonstrate, few university faculty agree on what good writing looks like. In fact, it's highly unusual when faculty from other departments *do* agree with the criteria for good writing that we in composition espouse. Even within our own departments (and within your group of new writing instructors, perhaps), commanding debates flourish about issues such as which factors should have the highest priority in determining a grade—grammar or content; whether a five-paragraph essay signals proficiency or a lack of critical thinking skills that necessitates developmental writing work; how many aural/oral confusions should be "allowed" in a passing essay; how much "credit" a student should get for taking risks in his or her argument. These sometimes heated discussions are the rule rather than the exception.

Why do people disagree so much about what constitutes good writing? And considering that no department yet has been able to find the definitive resolution to these debates, what are *you* going to do to be a consistent and fair evaluator, especially if students try to argue with you over grades? (And believe me, they will.) How can you feel confident that your grades and/or your guidance to students about how to improve the quality of their writing are not "just" subjective interpretations? If your supervisor or department chair reviews your grading practices, how can you be sure that your evaluations will be sanctioned, that you are fulfilling the goals of the writing program, the department, and the institution that employs you?

My advice is to integrate the following tenet into your composition theory and practice: *"Good" is a rhetorical term whose application and definition depends on its context.* In other words, evaluations of writing are always relative because they're contextually determined. As a matter of fact, the power of *any* specific use of language depends on its context, regardless of whether the "power" is judged to be sublime (to use a literary term), "felicitous" (to borrow from speech act theory), appropriate, pornographic, persuasive, humorous, disgusting, satisfactory, bland, or "awesome, dude."

What does this tenet mean with respect to your efforts to learn how to evaluate student writing? The perhaps bad news is that you'll have to disabuse yourself of the notion that there are universal standards for good writing, that if we just look hard enough and argue long enough we'll uncover those standards once and for all. The necessity to let go of that notion may seem commonplace to you, especially if you're a proponent of postmodern theory and/or Foucault's discussions of the order of discourse. On the other hand, you may be someone who thinks that not supporting the belief in inherent qualities of good writing is virtual heresy. Regardless of your predisposition, in practice understanding and internalizing the context-dependent nature of writing evaluation can be difficult.

Imagine, for instance, that the person sitting beside you in a holistic grading exam session believes that spelling errors are the mark of illiteracy and so wants to give the lowest score possible to the very same essay that you found outstanding because of its well-developed discussion of the sexist implications in the weapons imagery of *Die Hard 2*. It often seems "obvious" to us writing instructors that idea development is more important than spelling, that organization supersedes mechanics as a criterion for quality writing. But, like the definition and arrangement of all criteria for evaluation, the privileging of those characteristics depends on their context.

Lest you think we're dangerously close to the slippery slope of solipsism, let me reassure you that there is some good news: *mediating the context(s) within which you evaluate will ensure that your practices are fair, consistent, and authorized.* In other words, if you understand and internalize the purpose(s) of each specific evaluation process you participate in, as well as the criteria developed for judging that specific writing task, then you will have sufficiently evaluated the context. As a result, your applications of "good" (or "mediocre," or "excellent," and so on) will be not merely haphazard nor "subjective" (to you alone); rather, your scores or grades will be consistent (with the purpose and criteria of that context) and systemic (i.e., relative to the system within which you're evaluating).

To return to our example of the "spelling = illiteracy" person sitting beside you in the norming session, if the leader of the session has provided graders with a rubric for evaluation, then you can refer to that description to adjudge the disagreement between you about which to privilege in the *Die Hard 2* essay—the development of the claims about sexism, or the spelling of the essay. Chances are that the ensuing discussion will expand not just in topic (from spelling to "grammar" and from idea development to "content" and "thinking") but also in number of speakers. Such discussions are an integral aspect of the process by which grading session participants come to agreement about the purposes and criteria specific to each grading context. If the leader of an evaluation session does not provide a rubric, then the debate about spelling and development provides you and the other graders with the opportunity to decide between yourselves what criteria you should consider when you read the papers you're charged with scoring.

On the other hand, if and when you yourself are the person with sole responsibility for grading students' writing (as you probably will be when you teach your own sections of composition), then your fairness and consistency depend in large part on your careful determination of your purposes and criteria for evaluating. Many writing programs assist instructors by prescribing general purposes for writing (and therefore for the evaluation of) individual assignments and criteria for grading. These clarifications maintain consistency across different sections of the same course and supply individual teachers with the written description of the "what you want in this paper" that students often ask for. In addition, programmatic criteria for grading offer new and experienced instructors with the materials they need to best understand the institutional goals that inform their specific classroom contexts. In the context of individual assignments (or sometimes in lieu of any stated programmatic goals for composition courses), many instructors negotiate with their students the criteria for grading essays. Such a process makes explicit for students *and* the instructor what expectations and standards will be adjudicating their evaluations.

But enough talk. It's in the actual doing that these complicated, contextually dependent meanings become clearer. So not to worry if what I've said so far seems abstract or confusing. The exercises that follow are intended to illustrate in practice what I've just theorized. If you have a leader directing your training, he or she should be able to supply the sample student papers you need and oversee your group discussions. But even if you are not a member of an organized teacher-training program, if you and at least two or three other new teachers can find some sample student essays and complete these activities, you will develop a good understanding of the following:

- assumptions about good writing that you and others currently have

- instances of specific writing practices that demonstrate your (and others') assumptions

- revisions to your assumptions that you want to make

- assumptions about good writing explicitly or implicitly required in your institutional context(s)

- descriptions of the criteria for good writing that facilitate students' understanding

- variety of purposes for evaluating student writing

- variety of methods of writing evaluation and the purposes they best serve

- variety of contexts within which composition instructors evaluate student writing

Good luck, and happy grading.

Activities

Part One—Taking Placement Exams, Defining Criteria

INDIVIDUAL WORK

1. Diagnostic Writing (30 minutes). Write a response to the prompt you are given. (Trainers or groups—see Appendix I if your program can't supply a sample essay placement exam prompt.) Be

sure to save your essay, as you will refer to it again after several other activities.

2. Metacognitive Writing about Diagnostic Writing (30 minutes). Write about the process of writing the in-class diagnostic essay. What strategies did you use to be successful on the exam? For instance, which aspects of the writing process (invention/ freewriting, planning, organizing, drafting, revising, proofreading) did you most attend to? Which did you ignore? Did you make conscious decisions about how to divide your time? If so, on what basis did you make those decisions? Did you maintain those decisions or change your mind later? If you didn't consciously make such decisions, why not? What choices would you make again during an in-class writing situation? Which choices would you change?

3. Defining Good Writing. Make a list or write a description of what you think constitutes good writing. What are the characteristics of mediocre writing? Of definitely bad writing? Now write about how you have formulated these opinions about writing. Whose attitudes have you adopted and whose are you rejecting? In what circumstances would you change your mind about what constitutes good writing? Which characteristics of good writing are immutable?

Group Work

1. First, share your criteria for good writing with each other. On what points (if any) do you agree? On which do you most forcefully disagree? Decide between group members which criteria you want to represent the group's consensus. If applicable, repeat this process within the large group. When all groups have reached an agreement, make an official list of those criteria.

2. Now, evaluate each criterion's usefulness:

   ◆ What type(s) of writing will it best measure? (For instance, what writing tasks does it best assess: proficiency writing exams that receive a holistic pass/fail grade, placement exams that determine the appropriate level of composition instruction for individual students, formal research papers that receive a letter grade, rough drafts that will be revised later, journal writing that demonstrates students' engagement with their reading assignments, in-class timed writing essays, take-home essay tests? Is it intended to assess developmental writing rather than advanced composition and/or any other level(s) of writing? Should it be?)

- ◆ How specifically does it articulate the characteristics of good writing? Will students be able to understand the terminology it uses? For instance, does it rely on a COIK (clear only if known) explanation of development or organization?

- ◆ Is each level of quality uniquely defined? Are highest, middle, and lowest levels demarcated with specific descriptions? Are the middle and lower categories explained in their own right, or are they defined only in opposition to the highest category?

- ◆ What other aspects of the criterion need to be considered?

- ◆ Discuss what you have learned about the most effective methods for constructing and evaluating criteria for grading.

Part Two—Holistically Scoring Placement Exams

INDIVIDUAL WORK

1. Holistically score student placement exams.

   - ◆ Read several examples of essays that incoming first-year students wrote—preferably in response to the same prompt.

   - ◆ Read "A Rubric for Freshman Placement Essay Evaluations."

   - ◆ Reread and assign a score to six to eight different student essays. (Trainers or groups—see Appendix II for how to choose these essays.) Make brief notes to remind yourself which characteristics of each essay evoked the score you assign so that you can discuss your choices with the group.

2. Compare and contrast your group's collaborative criteria for "good" with "A Rubric for Freshman Placement Essay Evaluations." In what ways are your group's views ignored or undermined? *What specific purpose is this evaluation of placement exams and its rubric meant to serve?* In what contexts might the exam and the criteria given in this rubric not apply? In what ways are the rubric's descriptions vague or fuzzy? What difficulties might a new English instructor have with internalizing the criteria assigned by the rubric? Would your group's criteria improve the instructor's ability to internalize or not?

GROUP WORK

1. Referring to the six to eight essays you scored on your own, stage a norming session in which you discuss your scores with

each other. (Refer to Appendix II if you don't have a supervisor who can conduct the session.) Keep track of how much fluctuation you see between your scores and others'.

2. After the norming session, discuss these issues: Which readers are usually high or low? What seems to be the explanation for that tendency? Which persuasive points during the norming session most convince you about another evaluator's point of view? What points of your own seem the most persuasive? What most annoys you about other people's view of writing? Why do you suppose that particular thing annoys you?

3. In a large group, grade ten to twenty more essays after the norming discussion. How consistent were you as a group? How "normalized" were you as an individual?

4. Discuss as a group what the session has taught you about evaluating placement exams.

5. *Optional:* Anonymously grade two of your peers' essays (also anonymous) that they wrote to the prompt. Ask the trainer or your fellow students to return all essays to the original owners. Review your essay and reflect on the ones you evaluated. Did you and/or your colleagues perform as well as you expected? What (if anything) does your performance and/or theirs tell you about the effectiveness of timed writing assignments in assessing writing proficiency?

Review together the metacognitive writing you each did about your process of writing to the prompt. What clues does that writing provide about the strategies most effective in timed writing settings? How do those "clues" translate into strategies you'll teach your students?

Part Three—Responding in Writing to Student Essays

INDIVIDUAL WORK

1. Read about various ways to evaluate student writing. For instance, look at the chapter titled "Responding to Student Writing" in Erika Lindemann's *A Rhetoric for Writing Teachers.*

2. Write about what you see as the differences between holistic grading and responding in writing to student essays. What different strategies must an instructor employ in each context? How would a wise writer's strategies change according to the method by which he or she will be evaluated?

3. Letter-grade students' final drafts for a first-year composition class.

   ◆ Read three to five student essays provided.

   ◆ Assign a letter grade and comment on each as if you were responding to the student who wrote the essay.

   ◆ Be prepared to share your comments in class.

GROUP WORK

1. Individually record in writing the criteria you used for assigning a letter grade to the student essays you read. Then discuss the criteria you each used. Is there any agreement? Where? What criteria are most contested among you?

2. Compare your grades on the three to five essays you evaluated.

   ◆ Consider the agreement/disagreement in assessment and then compare that disparity with the agreement/disagreement on criteria. What, if anything, is significant about the relationship between the two?

   ◆ Now review the written comments that different instructors make. What different purposes inform their comments? For instance, are instructors writing to improve the student's next essay, to justify the grade they assign, to motive the student to keep trying, to engage the student in further thinking about the ideas discussed in the essay? Which of these reasons for commenting seems most useful to you? Why?

3. If your trainer and/or the writing program offers criteria for evaluating student essays, refer now to that. If not, decide between yourselves and record which criteria you'll be using to comment on the student essays written for the first formal assignment you'll be grading.

4. Using the criteria you've been given or that your group has developed, grade and respond to three more samples of student essays written in a context similar to that of the first formal assignment you'll actually be grading. Compare your grades and comments this time around to the ones you made before you discussed the criteria. Have the grades and/or the flavor of the comments changed? How? What purposes do the changes serve? Do they make grading more effective and/or more consistent? In what ways?

Part Four—Evaluating Rubrics

INDIVIDUAL WORK

1. In addition to the rubric supplied by the writing program you'll be teaching in or the one created by your group, collect at least two rubrics for grading first-year composition essays. If your writing program cannot supply you with these additional examples, you could check Web sites or books about writing assessment. (Some large writing programs make public their criteria for evaluation of student compositions; the University of Arizona, for instance, has published many editions of *A Student's Guide to First-Year Composition*, which usually includes a rubric for evaluating student essays.)

2. Write about the different ways these rubrics operate. Do the criteria contribute to your ease of grading and/or to the students' understanding of what and how they should write? In what ways are the rubrics' descriptions vague or fuzzy? Which rubric most undermines and/or supports your views of what constitutes good writing? Which of the rubrics you've encountered would best accommodate a new English instructor's efforts to internalize the criteria assigned by the rubric? Why? Which system would you most like to be graded under? Why?

GROUP WORK

Discuss each of your individual appraisals of these various rubrics. (Refer again to the list for evaluating criteria in Part 1.) Compare them to the one you'll actually be using when you grade students' essays. Is yours explained as clearly as it could be? If not—and if it is a version required by your program—how will you explain or supplement it so that your students will best understand how to shape their writing? *What views of writing inform the rubric you will use?* Which specific features of the rubric(s) reveal its perspective on writing and the writing process?

Part Five—Writing Responses to Drafts, Evaluating Response Methods

INDIVIDUAL WORK

1. Read Edward White's article "Post-Structural Literary Criticism and the Response to Student Writing" and Peter Elbow's article

"Ranking, Evaluating, and Liking."

2. Respond in writing to these sets of questions:

♦ White claims that ETS developed holistic scoring as a way to produce consistent test scores and thus to decrease the unfairness inherent in previous grading situations (291). Do you agree with White's belief that the holistic scoring method improves fairness and promotes a sense of community among English teachers? Why or why not?

♦ Summarize (or cite) one point Elbow makes that you support wholeheartedly and explain why you agree with his view, *or,* do the same about a point you disagree strongly with. Describe how you might successfully apply one of Elbow's ideas or suggestions to a classroom, *or,* describe what disaster (or mere problem) you think would probably result from your using another of Elbow's suggestions.

♦ White claims that "the simple fact is that the definition of textuality and the reader's role in developing the meaning of a text that we find in recent literary theory happens to describe with uncanny accuracy our experience of responding with professional care to the writing our students produce for us" (289). Elbow advises us to learn to "see potential goodness underneath badness," to "read closely and carefully enough to show the student little bits of *proto*-organization or *sort of* clarity in what they've already written" (202). Analyze and explain how this suggestion supports or contradicts (or both) White's viewpoints about the ways we read student writing.

3. Review your comments on the papers you read for Part 3—Responding in Writing to Student Essays. Imagine now that the student essays are rough drafts that you will return and from which students will develop their final, graded versions. Considering that new context and what you've read in Elbow's and White's essays, reexamine and renew your earlier comments on those essays. How and why have you changed (or not) those earlier comments? How does responding to a student's draft differ from responding to a final version?

Group Work

1. Discuss your responses to the two essays, in particular your perspectives on the similarities (or lack thereof) in White's notions

of teachers "developing the meaning of a text" (289) and Elbow's notions of "proto-organization or sort of clarity" (202).

2. Discuss the ways that each of you in the group changed your comments when you were responding to a draft rather than to the final version of a student's paper. List the differences in strategies you find most useful for responding to rough drafts and for responding to final versions of student essays. If applicable, share your list with the large group and then revise a large list that reflects all groups' perspectives.

Part Six—Synthesizing Possibilities

INDIVIDUAL WORK

1. Read Brook Horvath's article "The Components of Written Response." Write in response to the following:

   ◆ Describe at least two ways that reading Horvath's article motivates you to revise (or shape for the first time) your beliefs about responding to student writing.

   ◆ List at least four different purposes for evaluating student writing and four different methods of evaluating. Now write about which methods work best in conjunction with which purposes. Be sure to explain your reasons.

GROUP WORK

1. Discuss and come to some consensus about integrating methods for responding to student writing with the purposes of evaluating individual assignments. Also discuss these other important issues related to evaluating student writing:

   ◆ What other aspects (besides criteria and purpose for assessment) of the context for evaluating student writing are salient? How do those other aspects affect the criteria for grading and/or the purpose(s) for evaluating an assignment?

   ◆ What strategies can individual instructors use to align predetermined and prescribed criteria with their purpose(s) for evaluation in a specific writing context? How can they align a predetermined purpose for evaluating student writing with their own (or with a group's negotiated) criteria for the assignment? How can they teach students to strategize in these same ways? Should they teach them such strategies?

Writing Assignment—Evaluating Student Writing

The purpose of this paper is to facilitate your *synthesis* and *critique* of the various methods you've considered for assessing and evaluating student writing. In some way or another, you should demonstrate that you've read, analyzed, and thought about the materials. You might use this paper to formulate and defend your philosophy about grading papers or to analyze the ramifications of using a particular system. Whatever the claim you want to make, the argument of your paper should be based on your response to the different modes of assessment and evaluation of student writing that you've examined.

What you're being asked to do is construct a context—a writing assignment and purpose—as well as a method for evaluating the written product. Explain how the method you chose to evaluate the writing is the most effective for the specific context, task, and goal you've constructed, or your essay could be a response to at least two different modes of assessment and evaluation of student writing. You could compare the two grading systems you've practiced or compare the benefits and drawbacks of holistic grading with those of other ways to respond to student writing. You could also compare two or more of the published writers' viewpoints on assessing student writing.

Regardless of your choice for approach, you'll need to do more than simply summarize the method(s) or view(s) of evaluation. *Take a position about a preference for a particular method of evaluation.* Based on what you've read and experienced during this unit and from your other experiences as a writer and student (and teacher), what method of evaluation do you promote? What makes that method preferable? *In what context is the particular method effective and why?*

Suggested criteria for evaluation:

Content: Does your essay demonstrate that you have read and used the materials you've discussed as a class? Are you contributing additional insight and reflection to the body of knowledge that you've built through group activities? Do you rely on overgeneralizations or personal declarations (e.g., "Students learn better if they get feedback") to support your points, or do you use specific examples from the texts or from other research as support? Do you use enough examples from the student essays and/or the other texts you've read to support your argument?

Organization: Are the details (examples) of your essay arranged in the order that will most convince readers that your claim is true and sustain their interest? Are like ideas chunked together? Have you logically connected one idea to the next *and* explicitly signaled just what those logical connections are? Have you given enough signposts so that the reader can easily see the "map" of your essay?

Expression: Is the language of the essay easily accessible to the readers, concrete, and appropriate to your purpose? Do you avoid unnecessary formality, mixed metaphors, and stilted sentence structures and phrasing?

Mechanics: Are grammar problems infrequent and minor enough that they don't impede readers' understanding of your text?

Appendix I

Prompts for Thirty-Minute Timed Writing Essays

These samples are similar to those often used to place students in writing programs or to assess their writing skills.

1. Choose a specific event or situation from your elementary school years. It might involve school, home, or some other aspect of your life that you remember. It might be a single moment or an event that happened over time. The event or situation should be one that was important to you. Discuss it and then put it in perspective through mature reflection.

2. Certain things are not taught in the classroom, such as how to get along with others, how to rely on yourself, or how to manage money. Describe something you learned outside of school and how you learned it, and discuss its importance in your life.

3. "Don't ever slam the door, you might want to go back." This quote considers the issue of "burning one's bridges." Have you ever left a situation unpleasantly and then later wished you had handled things differently? Discuss the result and explain how it affected you later, or if, on the other hand, you have managed to keep all your "doors open," discuss how you accomplished this, and explain how it has affected your life.

4. Begin your essay with the following sentence (copy it into your essay): *The women's rights movement has made great strides toward the goal of equal treatment for men and women.* Select one of the following sentences as the second sentence of your essay (copy the sentence of your choice into your essay immediately following the first sentence):

   a. But we still have important work to do before our society can be considered nonsexist.

   b. In fact, we must be careful not to infringe on the rights of men in our attempt to compensate women.

   c. Unless we make changes in language, however, our culture will remain biased in favor of men.

   Complete your essay.

Appendix II

Norming Session

If you're new to norming, you'll get the best results if you can persuade someone experienced to run the session for you. If your particular program doesn't give placement exams or upper-division writing exams and thus doesn't have people practiced in running norming sessions, perhaps someone in the testing office at your university is familiar with holistic grading. If, however, you have no choice but to run the session yourself, try these procedures. To prepare for the session:

1. Choose at least seven or eight student essays as samples. The samples should have been written to the same prompt or for the same assignment that your graders will be evaluating. (In the best scenario, the sample essay and the essays to be graded are written to the same prompt that the graders and you wrote to in the first activity, "Taking Placement Exams.") The number of sample student essays you will need varies, depending on the system for grading you're using. You'll need at least one representative essay for the highest, the lowest, and the middle scores

of the rubric you'll be using during your grading session. For instance, if you have a 4-point system, choose an essay that is *without doubt* (or as close to that as you can get) a 1, another that's a clear 4, and then a 3 or a 2. (One of the ways to be sure about scoring is to get experienced graders to help you decide which essay is an "absolute" 4 and so on.) You also need to have at least one essay that stirs up controversy, an essay that evokes a wide range of scores from different readers. If you can find what's called a "1/4 split" (meaning that from two different readers the same essay received a score of 4 from one reader and a 1 from the other), then you've got a great example of a "controversial" essay; a 3/1 split is the next best bet. And, finally, you need a couple of essays that mark the middle range of your rubric; these I'll refer to later as your "neutral" essays.

2. Make copies of all essays for all your graders. (They're assigned to read these in Part 2, Individual Work, step 1.)

3. Make copies of the prompt or the writing assignment for all your graders.

4. Make copies of the evaluation criteria for all your graders.

To conduct the session:

1. Ask all graders to read the criteria for grading and the prompt or writing assignment carefully.

2. Ask graders to reread the "high," "middle," and "low" essays. Don't tell them which is which. Don't even announce that you're presenting a range of essays. Just ask them to read and score "these three essays."

3. When they've finished, decide which of the three essays you'll discuss first (probably the "high" one) and ask each person to announce his or her score to the group. Don't discuss these scores yet; just record them on the board or make a note to yourself and ask the graders to do the same.

4. Ask the most experienced grader (and/or the person[s] whose score coincided with the one you intended to represent) to explain his or her reasons for assigning that particular score. *Require the grader to use specific aspects of the student text and of the rubric to support the reasons for assigning a particular score.*

5. Ask for discussion between the group members about their various scores. If the person whose score is most "off" the one you intended to represent is willing, ask him or her to explain the score. At this point, all group members can and should discuss

their individual explanations for their scores. *Require the grad-ers to use specific aspects of the student texts and of the rubric to explain their reasons for assigning a particular score.*

6. You—especially if you are or seem to be an authority figure to the other group members—would probably do best not to offer an opinion about which score is "right." If, however, group members' conversation gets overly heated or their debates can-not be resolved, you can mediate their discussion by calling on the people with the most experience and/or whose scores seem most reasonable to you. Don't let individuals overgeneralize about writing or criteria; insist that they refer to the specific rubric for this context and to some specific features of the student text(s) they're discussing. If none of these plans work to mediate de-bates or if you don't know for sure just who the experienced people are, then simply move on to another essay. *The point of this session is for group members to norm themselves, not for you to get them to conform to what you or one other group member thinks.*

7. Repeat this process (steps 3–6) with the "lowest" essay and then with the "middle" one. If necessary, offer other essays for the group to read that you think are examples of the score(s) about which the group members seem to have the most trouble agree-ing.

8. Repeat this reading-discussing process with one of the "neutral" essays. If a relative consensus is reached (say, for instance, only two or three of ten people continue to disagree with a score, and their disagreement is a number away), then ask the group to read and score the sample essays that you chose as examples of split scores. Again, don't tell graders why you're giving them this particular example, just ask them to read and score it. Again, begin the discussion by asking for scores from all graders and then for comments by graders you deem reliable. Permit the group to discuss their variances.

9. When graders and you feel satisfied that you have discussed their individual points of view, give them the last "neutral" essay(s) to read and score. If, after sharing their scores, you have no splits in the scores, you're now "normalized"—i.e., you're ready to begin an actual grading process and should have relatively reliable consistency among the scores graders assign. If, how-ever, you still have drastic splits (the widest possible range of

scores are assigned to the same essay), then my directions have probably been fairly worthless and you're probably going to need the assistance of a trained professional. Sorry.

Note

1. A *norming session* is a preparatory portion of a group's process of evaluating writing. In the session, graders review the criteria for scoring, often called a *rubric;* they then read samples of the type of writing they'll be evaluating, individually assign a score to each sample, and finally discuss their individual scores with each other. The purpose of the norming session is to calibrate scores among the group members so that as much consensus as possible results when these group members individually evaluate the essays they'll be scoring. These evaluators and their trainers (if they are leading the norming session) use the group discussion about the sample scores to inform members about and persuade each other of specific interpretations of the rubric and of the characteristics of particular writing samples.

Works Cited

Elbow, Peter. "Ranking, Evaluating, and Liking: Sorting Out Three Forms of Judgment." *College English* 55 (1993): 187–206.

Horvath, Brook K. "The Components of Written Response: A Practical Synthesis of Current Views." *Rhetoric Review* 2 (1984): 136–56. Rpt. in *The Writing Teacher's Sourcebook*. 2nd ed. Ed. Gary Tate and Edward P. J. Corbett. New York: Oxford UP, 1988.

Lindemann, Erika. *A Rhetoric for Writing Teachers*. 3rd ed. New York: Oxford UP, 1995.

Watkins, Evan. *Work Time: English Departments and the Circulation of Cultural Value*. Stanford: Stanford UP, 1989.

White, Edward M. "Post-Structural Literary Criticism and the Response to Student Writing." *College Composition and Communication* 35 (1984): 186–95. Rpt. in *The Writing Teacher's Sourcebook*. 2nd ed. Ed. Gary Tate and Edward P. J. Corbett. New York: Oxford UP, 1988. 285–93.

Portfolio Standards for English 101

DOUGLAS D. HESSE

Illinois State University

The following portfolio grading guide was prepared for use by English 101 faculty. It was approved by the department Writing Committee and is being shared with English 101 students to help them understand levels of performance in the course.

Unlike individual paper grading, portfolio evaluation involves judging a collection of texts written by a writer. The grade reflects an overall assessment of the writer's ability to produce varied kinds of texts, not an average of grades on individual papers. Raters will choose the description that best fits the portfolio. In other words, not all of the criteria in a selected grade range may apply to a given set of papers, but that cluster of criteria more accurately describes the portfolio than any other. Feedback to student portfolios will usually consist of some indication to the students of how their work measures against these various criteria, plus a few sentences of written response to the portfolio as a whole. Individual papers are not marked.

The "A" Portfolio

"A" portfolios demonstrate the writer's skillful ability to perform in a variety of rhetorical situations. "A" portfolios suggest that the writer will be able to adroitly handle nearly any task an undergraduate student writer might encounter, in both academic and public forums. The papers, the drafting materials, and, most important, the reflective introduction demonstrate the writer's sense of his or her development through the semester, his or her ability to reflect analytically and critically on his or her writing, and the relations among works submitted in the portfolio.

Individual works in "A" portfolios tend consistently to be appropriate to their intended audiences, audiences who are characterized as well read or knowledgeable on the topics and ideas addressed. These readers would often be struck by the freshness of ideas, strategies, perspective, or expression in the work. Writers are usually able to bridge knowledge or opinion gaps between themselves and their readers and effectively create a context for the writing.

The quality of thought in "A" portfolios is generally ambitious and mature. Not only is the writer able to state claims or ideas clearly and effectively, but also he or she is generally able to provide support and discuss warrants for those claims in a manner that reflects the complexity of issues and yet still takes a plausible position. Not only is the writer able to describe phenomena or events clearly and effectively, but also he or she is able to analyze and interpret their possible meanings, going beyond the obvious. "A" writers usually have a keen eye for detail. Individual works are most often characterized by an effective texture of general and specific ideas or by such compelling specific ideas or accounts that generalizations are implicit.

Through allusions, interpretive strategies, and stylistic sophistication, "A" portfolios often suggest that their authors read or have read widely, not only materials assigned for courses but also a variety of public texts: newspapers, magazines, and books. These writers are able to incorporate ideas and insights gained from reading into their texts, sometimes critically, sometimes generatively, sometimes as support or illustration of ideas. This is not to suggest, however, that all works in portfolios must be documented. Indeed, reference to outside sources in many papers would be contrived, inappropriate, and undesirable.

"A" portfolios frequently show how their writers are able to draw on personal experience and direct observations of the world around them. They are able to connect these experiences and observations to readings or to new situations. Their writing often displays analogical or metaphorical thinking.

"A" portfolios may show frequent evidence of the writer's ability to make conceptual or global revisions—wide-ranging changes at the idea level—as well as local revisions—changes that affect meaning primarily in sentences and paragraphs. The writer is often able to use the entire range of revision operations: addition, subtraction, transposition. The writer is frequently able to use teacher and peer response generatively, moving beyond a single, narrow comment to revise other aspects of the paper—or to initiate revisions on her or his own.

"A" portfolios are generally marked by a range of sophisticated stylistic features appropriate to a given writing situation, perhaps including sentences of various types and lengths (especially cumulative and other subordinated structures), striking word choices that are appropriate to the situation of the paper, and the effective use of metaphor and analogy, often extended. Papers often reflect a distinctive voice. The opening strategies of "A" papers are generally creative and engaging, the conclusions more than simple restatements of preceding ideas.

"A" portfolios, although not necessarily perfect, are virtually free of the kinds of errors that compromise the effectiveness of the piece, and have virtually no stigmatized errors.

"A" portfolios are neatly printed and organized as described in "Guidelines for Turning in Portfolios."

Incomplete portfolios may not be graded "A."

The "B" Portfolio

"B" portfolios generally suggest the writer's skillful ability to perform in a variety of rhetorical situations, though a few areas may not be as strong as others. "B" portfolios suggest that the writer will be able successfully to handle nearly any task an undergraduate student writer might encounter, in both academic and public forums. The papers, the drafting materials, and, most important, the reflective introduction suggest progress toward the writer's becoming conversant with his or her development, toward an ability to reflect analytically and critically on his or her writing, and toward understanding the relations among works submitted in the portfolio.

Individual works in "B" portfolios are usually appropriate to their intended audiences, audiences who are characterized as well read or knowledgeable on the topics and ideas addressed. "B" portfolios may be less ambitious in their choice of intended topics or audience, or may be less sophisticated in they way they address their readers than "A" portfolios. "B" writers are often able to bridge knowledge or opinion gaps between themselves and their readers and to create a plausible context for the writing.

The quality of thought in "B" portfolios is often ambitious and mature. Not only is the writer able to state claims or ideas clearly and effectively, but also he or she is frequently able to provide support and discuss warrants for those claims in a manner that frequently reflects the complexity of issues. Not only is the writer able to describe phenomena or events clearly and effectively, but also he or she is generally able to analyze and interpret their meaning. Individual works are often characterized by an effective texture of general and specific ideas.

Through allusions, interpretive strategies, and stylistic sophistication, "B" portfolios suggest that their authors read widely, not only materials assigned for courses but also a variety of public texts: newspapers, magazines, and books. These writers are able to incorporate ideas and insights from reading into their texts, sometimes critically, sometimes generatively, sometimes as support or illustration of ideas, although this is often done less fluently or facilely than in "A" portfolios. This is not to suggest, however, that all works must be documented. Indeed, reference to outside sources in many papers would be contrived, inappropriate, and undesirable.

"B" portfolios occasionally show how their writers are able to draw on personal experience and observations of the world around them. They suggest that their writers are able to connect experience and direct observations to readings or to new situations. Occasionally, their writing may display analogical or metaphorical thinking.

"B" portfolios show occasional evidence of the writer's ability to make conceptual or global revision (or frequent evidence of such revisions that are not always fully successful). They show the writer's ability to make effective local revisions and to use a variety of revision strategies. The writer is sometimes able to use teacher and peer response generatively, moving beyond a single, narrow comment to revise other aspects of the paper.

"B" portfolios display a variety of sophisticated stylistic features, including sentences of various types and lengths (perhaps including cumulative and other subordinated structures), word choices that are appropriate to the rhetorical situation of the paper, and the occasional use of metaphor and analogy, though sometimes these features may not be fully controlled or appropriate. There is frequently a distinctive voice to the papers, although this may be uneven. The opening strategies of "B" papers are creative and engaging, the conclusions more than simple restatements of preceding ideas.

"B" portfolios, although not necessarily perfect, are virtually free of the kinds of errors that compromise the rhetorical effectiveness of the piece, and have virtually no stigmatized errors.

"B" portfolios are neatly printed and organized as described in "Guidelines for Turning in Portfolios."

Incomplete portfolios may not be graded "B."

The C Portfolio

"C" portfolios demonstrate the writer's ability to perform competently in a variety of rhetorical situations, perhaps even showing skills in some writings. The set of papers, the drafting materials, and, most important, the writer's reflective introduction suggest progress toward the writer's becoming conversant with his or her development, toward an ability to reflect analytically and critically on his or her writing, and toward understanding the relations among works submitted in the portfolio. "C" writers, however, may not be nearly as perceptive as "B" writers in making connections between projects, in discussing and illustrating general tendencies in their writing, or in critically analyzing their drafting processes. These portfolios may seem to be more compilations of isolated works than at least partially connected wholes. Again, the reflective introduction will be most useful in making this judgment.

Writing in "C" portfolios adequately addresses knowledge and attitudes of peers. While this writing may often successfully address a well-read and knowledgeable outside audience, the context and occasion for the writing tend to be confined more to the classroom situation itself.

The quality of thought in "C" portfolios is competent and sometimes compelling, though often standard or familiar. Not only is the writer able to state claims or ideas clearly and effectively, but also he or she is able to provide support and discuss warrants for those claims, although the complexities of the issues involved may be suggested rather than fully treated—or perhaps dealt with very little. Not only is the writer able to describe phenomena or events clearly and effectively, but also he or she is able to analyze and interpret their meaning, although the interpretations may be obvious or sometimes perfunctory. Individual works are often characterized by a texture of general and specific elements, but paraphrase and repetition may often take the place of development. Papers may be developed more by partition or addition, in the mode of the five-paragraph theme, rather than by logical or organic development of a central idea.

"C" portfolios demonstrate the writer's ability to read course materials critically and analytically and to incorporate ideas from reading into his or her texts. There may be some suggestions of the writer's facility with outside readings, but they may not be well integrated into papers, used rather in a more cut-and-paste fashion than a more organic one.

"C" writers may be able to draw on personal experience and observations of the world around them and connect these to readings or to new situations. The connections, however, may not be as fully integrated, explored, or subtle as in "B" portfolios.

"C" portfolios demonstrate the writer's ability to make local revisions, perhaps with one dominant strategy (addition, for example). While these portfolios may suggest the writer's ability to make global revisions, this ability is not clearly demonstrated. Revisions are frequently tied narrowly to specific comments made by the teacher or peers; the writer is less clearly a self-starter when it comes to revision than the "A" or "B" student.

"C" portfolios display a reasonable range of stylistic features, although sentences tend to be of a fairly uniform type (usually subject-verb-complement) and sentence length is mostly a function of coordination rather than subordination. There is infrequent use of metaphor and analogy. The voice of these papers is perhaps generic, competent but largely indistinct from other student prose. The opening strategies of writings in "C" portfolios may rely fairly directly on the assignment sheets or use some version of a funnel strategy. Conclusions tend to summarize the preceding ideas.

"C" portfolios are virtually free of the kinds of errors that compromise the rhetorical effectiveness of the piece, and they have few stigmatized errors and no consistent patterns of stigmatized errors.

"C" portfolios are neatly printed and organized as described in "Guidelines for Turning in Portfolios."

Incomplete portfolios may not be graded "C."

The "D" Portfolio

"D" portfolios suggest the writer's inability to write competently in several rhetorical situations. Writers of "D" portfolio work will likely have difficulty in other college or public writing situations. The set of papers, the drafting materials, and, most important, the writer's reflective introduction suggest that the writer is not fairly conversant with his or her development as a writer and is fairly unable to reflect analytically and critically on his or her writing. These portfolios generally seem to be more compilations of isolated works than partially connected wholes.

While the writing is sometimes appropriate to an audience that is knowledgeable on the topics and ideas addressed, frequently the writer assumes less—or more—of his or her readers than is appropriate. There are considerable knowledge or opinion gaps between the writer and his or her reader, and the context for the writing is usually limited to the classroom assignments themselves.

The quality of thought in "D" portfolios is frequently stock or perfunctory. The writer may be able to state claims or ideas clearly but is able to provide only minimal support and discuss virtually no warrants for that support. The writer may be able to describe phenomena or events clearly, but his or her interpretations may be obvious or perfunctory. While works may sometimes display a texture of general and specific elements, paraphrase and repetition may often take the place of development. "D" portfolios may contain papers that are consistently shorter than is needed to successfully engage the tasks.

"D" portfolios suggest their authors' difficulties in reading course materials critically and analytically. These writers may have some difficulty summarizing complex ideas. Or they may be able to summarize but unable to respond critically or interpretively. They incorporate ideas from reading into their texts in ways that are frequently not well integrated, in more of a cut-and-paste fashion than an organic one.

"D" portfolios suggest the writer's ability to make local revisions, but these are often infrequent or do not substantially improve the paper from draft to draft. Revisions may take the form primarily of proofreading or direct responses only to the teacher's or peers' comments.

"D" portfolios may display a narrow range of stylistic features, with most sentences of a fairly uniform type. The result may be an overly predictable text, at levels all the way from the sentence, to paragraphs, to openings and closings.

"D" portfolios may display some of the kinds of errors that compromise the rhetorical effectiveness of individual works and may have some stigmatized errors, even a pattern of one such error.

"D" portfolios may not be neatly printed, or they may not be neatly organized as described in "Guidelines for Turning in Portfolios."

"D" portfolios may be incomplete.

The "F" Portfolio

"F" portfolios demonstrate the writer's inability to write competently in various aims (persuasive, explanatory, and narrative), although the writer may be better in some than in others; writers of "F" portfolio work will have difficulty in most writing situations. The set of papers, the drafting materials, and, most important, the writer's reflective introduction generally indicate that the writer is not conversant with his or her development as a writer and that he or she is unable to reflect analytically and critically on his or her writing. These portfolios generally seem to be more compilations of isolated works than at least partially connected wholes.

The writing is almost never appropriate to an audience that is knowledgeable on the topics and ideas addressed; the writer assumes less—or more—of his or her readers than is appropriate, expecting readers to fill in all the gaps, to make all the connections, and automatically agree with the writer's perspective.

The quality of thought in "F" portfolios is perfunctory, obvious, or unclear. The writer may offer claims or ideas but be unable to provide much support. The writer may be able to describe phenomena or events but be unable to analyze or interpret them. Paraphrase and repetition often take the place of development. "F" portfolios may contain papers that are consistently shorter than is needed to successfully engage the tasks.

"F" portfolios demonstrate their authors' difficulties in reading course materials critically and analytically. These writers may have considerable difficulty summarizing complex ideas. They are unable to respond critically or interpretively. They incorporate ideas from reading into their texts in a cut-and-paste fashion rather than a more organic one.

"F" portfolios show relatively little evidence of revision, and what is there is frequently done at the sentence level or narrowly in response to a teacher's comment.

"F" portfolios may display the kinds of errors that compromise the rhetorical effectiveness of individual works; they may have patterns of stigmatized errors.

"F" portfolios may not be neatly printed, or they may not be neatly organized as described in "Guidelines for Turning in Portfolios."

"F" portfolios may be incomplete.

English 101 Final Portfolio Cover Sheet and Checklist, Spring 1999

Please provide the following information, which will help make sure you submit all the appropriate materials with your final portfolio. Turn this sheet in with your final portfolio. Thank you.

Name_____Social Security Number_____
Instructor and Section Number_____

Local Address and Phone:

_____

Permanent Address:

_____

I. A check on the right numbers and kinds of works
____This portfolio contains a total of 20–30 pages.
____This portfolio contains a reflective introduction (Part I, Course Guide, p. 8).
____This portfolio contains at least 17 pages of revised writing from the course, appx. 5000–7500 words (Part II, p.8).
____The writings in Part II consist of at least 4 but not more than 8 papers.
Note: It's acceptable to list a paper in more than one category below:
One persuasive paper in the portfolio is titled:
One paper that has analysis or critique as its primary aim is titled:
One paper that makes substantial use of readings is titled:
____This portfolio contains an analysis of writing done for another course and a copy of that paper (Part III, p. 8).

II. A check of format for the portfolio
____I have included drafts for each paper. These are arranged exactly as described in step 3 on page 11 of the English 101 Course Guide. I understand that the Writing Program strongly urges me to keep a photocopy.
____I have provided an electronic second copy of the portfolio exactly as described step 7 on page 11.
____I have turned in all materials in a two-pocket folder. On the outside of the folder is the information requested in step 9 on page 11 of the Course Guide. I understand that I can pick up my portfolio from my teacher at the beginning of next semester.

III. Permission: Choosing to give or withhold permission will not affect your grade in any way. Report any concerns or irregularities to the director of Writing Programs or the program ombudsperson.
    I give my permission to the English Department to reproduce writings from this portfolio in future editions of Language and Composition I Course Guide: ____yes ___no

I give permission to my instructor or to the English department to reproduce or otherwise use my writings for teacher training or research purposes. This includes permission to quote from my work in published articles or books. I understand that I will not be identified in any way, that my participation is completely voluntary, and that I may withdraw my permission, in writing, at any time. ___yes ___no

IV. Certification

The works submitted in this portfolio do not violate the plagiarism policy stated in the Course Guide. I understand that plagiarism will result in an F for the course.

_____

(signed)   (date)

Handling the Confrontative Conference

RUTH OVERMAN FISCHER
George Mason University

Ruth Fischer provides guidelines for making the most of individual conferences with confrontational writing students.

Conferencing with students on their writing in process is the hallmark of a process-oriented pedagogy, regardless of genre. Providing formative feedback presents teachers with the opportunity not only to help students in shaping their writing along the lines of the assignment, but also to get a sense of how a student learns and what kind of support a student needs in order to do well. These formative conferences can be pleasant, if not downright enjoyable.

But there comes the day when we have to provide a summative evaluation of a piece of writing. We have to assign The Grade. Students who tell us they "always got A's" on their writing in high school—and even those who don't—can respond with a range of emotions when they see that first C or whatever grade lower than expected. After all, they did the assignment, so they should get an A.

And perhaps in the midst of their various manifestations of angst, plagued by your own concerns that you have been too easy or too hard, you are feeling nervous about having to give grades at all. Students are asking to meet with you about their grades. And you find yourself faced with what might be called the Confrontative Conference. What follows is a way to set up a productive interaction with your students.

1. Set up an appointment for sometime after class in your office. Students upset about a grade usually cannot listen effectively. And when they appear on the attack, it's difficult for the teacher to respond appropriately without sounding defensive. So don't try to deal with these students in the moment in class. Schedule an appointment and ask them to read over their paper, your comments, and the assignment before they meet with you. You might even ask them to write a note to you explaining how they think they have met the requirements of the assignment and why they should have received a better grade. The time between getting the paper with its unacceptable grade and sitting down to discuss the paper allows students to calm down and gives you a chance to gather your thoughts.

2. Construct a good assignment in which the expectations are clearly stated and you have clear expectations in mind. Actually, in terms of the overall assignment, this step precedes the first one. Constructing an assignment with clearly articulated expectations is one of the best ways to ensure a solid understanding of the assignment on all sides of the desk. Not only do you need to be clear about what you want students to try to do, but also you need to provide students with a frame for their writing. In addition, in-class discussion of the assignment provides a context for

one-to-one conferences. Discuss these expectations with the students and draw them into the evaluation process by asking them to help you construct criteria.

3. Set a positive tone for the conference. When the student comes in for the conference, greet her or him in a friendly manner. Ask the student how she or he is doing and how other classes are going, and extend other basic greetings. Invite her or him to sit down where you and the student can look at the draft together, preferably side by side with the draft in the common space between you.

4. Get down to the business at hand. To initiate the businesslike part of the conference, ask what you can do for the student and then validate whatever feelings pour out, if expressed, but don't get sucked into these feelings. Ask the student to explain the expectations of the assignment to you and to show you how she or he thinks the paper met them. Use your class-generated list of criteria as a common focus of your discussion about the paper. Remember that your concerns are most likely about the quality of the writing and the development of your student as a writer, and so you'd like the student to understand in what ways the paper has not met the criteria, allowing the student to learn from these mistakes. The student's major concern is most likely The Grade, so what she or he would like is for you to raise the grade. Resist grade changes on the spot. Instead, ask the student what she or he would change in the next draft, if it is your policy to allow an additional draft, or if not, how she or he might use what she or he has learned in the writing of subsequent papers. Keep in mind that students have an ongoing subtext in your class, so what you allow for one student, you should allow for all students.

5. End the conference politely but firmly. When you think the conference has stopped being productive, end the conference politely. Shift back to more global comments about an upcoming assignment or campus event to signal that the business part of the conference is over. If the student remains unhappy and will not be rewriting the paper, validate that feeling but let her or him

know that you have to end the conference. Keep calm and remember that you are helping students become acculturated to a new environment in which they will have to learn effective ways of negotiation—as such, you are providing a useful service to the university community at large!

Establishing Weighted Criteria for Evaluating Writing

KAREN VAUGHT-ALEXANDER
Portland State University

Karen Vaught-Alexander provides some essay guidelines she uses to evaluate student writing, excerpted from her English 191 class.

Evaluation Sheet: English 191 Final Essay

In-Class Literary Analysis

Name_____Grade_____

I._____ x12 =_____

II._____x 8 = _____

Note: Compliments or suggestions for improvement will use criteria outlined below, as well as my usual reference to the Troyka # system and individual comments or questions as appropriate, given your individual writing improvement action plan.

I. Content and Development: Interesting and Insightful
(a) Clear and explicit connection of literary elements such as plot,

conflict, symbol, etc. in thesis and body paragraphs; interesting and insightful analysis

(b) Well-selected examples and quotes to prove thesis, showing "deep" textual reading and organized "literary" thinking—i.e., analysis; synthesis; connections between meaning and literary elements employed

(c) Relevant, if not perspicacious, references to text, rather than retelling of literary work

(d) Techniques of academic writing, used effectively and freshly, especially introductions, conclusions, paragraphing, transitions, etc.

All Criteria Met	Most Criteria Met	Some Met	Few Met	None Met
5	4	3	2	1

II. <u>MLA Citations and Editing & Proofing</u> (Attach your final improvement checklist with strategies used for this assignment, as well as your planning notes.)

(a) Text citations correctly use MLA (author/page) system; also author tags, "blends," only especially felicitous quotations, quote "lead-ins" with correct punctuation, documenting of paraphrases and summaries. I should be able to read and know which are your thinking and ideas and which ideas are from a source.

(b) Grammar and usage effectively edited

(c) Mechanics and spelling: sentence punctuation patterns, especially homonym misspellings, common mechanical knowledge such as use of apostrophe, colon, etc.

(d) FYC stylistic competence demonstrated: i.e., FYC conciseness, academic voice, and word choice, inclusive language, variety and emphasis, etc.

All Criteria Met	Most Criteria Met	Some Met	Few Met	None Met
5	4	3	2	1

CHAPTER 11

TEACHING WRITING WITH TECHNOLOGY

EDITED BY SUSAN K. MILLER
Mesa Community College

The purpose of this chapter is to encourage teachers to consider the choices they need to make about using technology in writing instruction. The contributors to this chapter represent a wide range of experience in computer-mediated classrooms, including instructors who have been using and researching the use of technology in the writing classroom for years and those who are just making the transition to the electronic classroom. Our goal is to provide a variety of perspectives in this emerging area of writing instruction and research, and to facilitate the discovery and critical analysis of the possibilities of teaching writing with technology.

In an effort to reach this goal, this chapter encourages teachers to ask the following kinds of questions: How can I best prepare myself for using these tools in my teaching? How do such tools transform/modify/mediate/alter literate practices? How can I help students decide when and how to use current electronic technologies? How do electronic literacies change the nature of texts? How can I assess the use of technology in the writing classroom?

We start with an overview and impressions of teaching with technology and then move on to suggestions for the computer-mediated classroom, offering practical suggestions and activities the authors have used in their own classrooms, from strategies for facilitating collaboration to Web-based writing assignments. The contributions represent a wide range of theoretical perspectives on the use of technology in the writing classroom.

Overviews and Impressions of Teaching with Technology

Overcoming the Unknown

Adelheid Thieme
Arizona State University

Adelheid Thieme was asked to write this part of the chapter because she has worked diligently to overcome lack of experience with technology. Her story demonstrates that a composition teacher can learn to use current electronic technologies in a relatively short time.

In 1989 I entered the graduate program in English at Arizona State University. Since I grew up at a time when personal computers did not yet exist, I did not have the opportunity to develop computer skills at a young age. At the beginning of the graduate program, my lack of computer expertise was not a major problem. Typing the relatively short term papers for my classes was time consuming and required a lot of concentration, but it was a manageable task. When I started working on my dissertation, however, I realized how useful computer knowledge would be, even if it were limited to simple word processing. Yet I was sure I was unable to learn even the most basic computer functions. If it had not been for an eye-opening experience, I might never have found the motivation to overcome my computer anxiety.

One evening I was invited to a birthday party for one of my friends in the English department. My doctoral adviser and several fellow students were at the party, too. I was enjoying myself until the conversation turned to computers. My fellow students, who were much younger than I, shared how they used computers in their studies. They also discussed the ever-increasing importance of computer literacy and the significant role that computers would play in research and in the teaching of writing. Listening to them, I realized I was unable not only to comprehend the computer jargon they used, but also to eventually teach composition in an electronic classroom. It dawned on me that I would not be competitive on the job market. My doctoral adviser must have read my mind, for he asked me, "So, when are you going to give it a try?" Still reluctant, I responded lightly, "Well, I guess you cannot teach an old dog new tricks." For a split second, there was silence. My doctoral adviser gave me a disapproving look. Then one of my fellow students remarked jokingly, "That depends on the type of dog." As I drove home that night, I decided that I would never again feel embarrassed because of my lack of computer skills. I would prove to myself that I could do it.

Fortunately, over the next years I met many people who gave me a lot of help and encouragement. My doctoral adviser offered to teach me the basic elements of WordPerfect. After the initial session with him, I worked independently through a tutorial. My efforts paid off as I went through multiple drafts of my dissertation. When the assistant director of composition offered an introduction to Pine e-mail, I forced myself to register for the workshop. I quickly learned to use Pine. E-mailing my students was so much more efficient than calling, and I began to appreciate my new skills. Shortly after that, when the department announced a workshop for teaching composition in an electronic classroom, I already felt confident that I would be able to practice computer-assisted instruction.

In the fall of 1997, I was given the opportunity to teach English 101 in a computer lab. At the beginning of the semester, I spent many hours in the computer classroom, practicing each step of the computer functions the students would use. If unforeseen problems arose, I still had to rely on the help of a student who was majoring in computer science. But I did not feel bad about it. It was a give-and-take situation. That same semester, I taught myself PowerPoint and learned to search the Internet. I also participated in an electronic forum discussion with my service-learning students. This past summer, I learned the basics of HTML and designed my own professional Web site.

Over the years, my step-by-step approach has served me well. Starting out with relatively easy computer functions, I have gradually expanded my knowledge and will continue to do so. I now incorporate computer-related assignments into all of my composition classes and encourage my students to work on becoming computer literate. I hope they will enjoy it as much as I do.

Asynchronous Online Teaching

DONALD WOLFF

Eastern Oregon University

Donald Wolff discusses the value of asynchronous online teaching in his institutional setting and outlines the types of challenges and benefits to expect when creating and maintaining online courses.

For several years now I have been teaching a number of online courses that don't meet face to face. My computer conferencing courses are asynchronous, meaning the students are not all online at the same time. Not only do we not meet face to face, but also we are almost never working at the same time, seldom trading comments in real time by means of chat rooms or other simultaneous exchanges.

Teaching by means of asynchronous computer conferencing is a good match for my teaching style because all work is done in writing—a good thing in itself—and I prefer a method through which I can be sure I have the students' attention. I have never been good at creating truly effective small-group interactions, and when I am lecturing I always wonder what my students are thinking, especially those in the back row whose attention I can't seem to hold. But I know I have the students' full attention when they are online because otherwise they wouldn't *be* online. Also, one of my strengths as a teacher and one of the aspects of teaching I most enjoy is one-on-one dialogue, either about ideas or their presentation in writing, about global and sentence-level issues. Asynchronous computer conferencing allows me to focus directly on individual student concerns, simultaneously teaching to the class as a whole as they witness my exchanges with their cohorts. This also encourages students to respond to one another—they can hardly resist.

It is important to reflect in this way on your own teaching preferences in order to determine if online teaching is a good fit with your teaching style and pedagogy. In addition, my institution greatly values this kind of teaching because it reaches students who are place-bound—who for one reason or another cannot make it to the campus for their courses. This makes a lot of sense in rural Oregon—our service region is 40,000 square miles, an area larger than Pennsylvania. And that's just eastern Oregon. My courses are in demand throughout the state; I have students who live on the Oregon coast 500 miles away and on the Idaho border 150 miles in the opposite direction and many points in between. And while distance education makes sense in rural Oregon, it is growing in popularity nationwide, even worldwide, for a variety of reasons, not the least of which is students' desire to further their education while concurrently working and raising a family. More and more campus courses employ listservs to generate student discussion.

Different modalities match different teachers—asynchronous computer conferencing isn't for every teacher, just as it isn't for every student. While that's true of all our pedagogies and the ideologies they represent, it's still important to determine if online teaching will suit you. Reflection has become a central feature of composition, if not of English studies in general, and careful reflection on your own teaching practices will enable you to determine if asynchronous teaching is a good fit with your pedagogy. There are a number of important issues to consider—student profiles, workload, course organization, dialogical exchange, the faceless intimacy engendered by online exchanges, sentence-level work, tutoring, and politics as usual. What follows, then, are my reflections on what has become central to my teaching—working with distant students exclusively through asynchronous computer conferencing. And although I focus on the asynchronous environment, you will no doubt see applications to teaching in a computer classroom and even to using listservs to support traditional face-to-face campus courses. These reflections may prove useful to you as you think about what you want to teach and how you want to go about it.

Background and Student Profiles

Eastern Oregon University has been recognized nationally as a leader in distance education, and so it came as no surprise that my dean asked me to develop an online course. There is great demand for these courses off-campus as a large number of place-bound students seek their degrees. That was the administration's interest in requesting the course, and it was difficult to say no to my dean before I had tenure. But since there was a pronounced need for the course, the administration granted my request that it be counted as "inload"—that is, as part of my regular teaching load, an important point when considering workload issues. If I taught it as an "overload," I would be paid extra for it, but for me time is more valuable than money. The way I teach, with an intensive writing emphasis, leaves no time for overload, even if there is money to be made.

But I already had an interest in doing an online course. As a composition specialist and coordinator of writing across the curriculum, I wanted to see what would happen if one of my courses was conducted *entirely* in writing. As a proponent of writing-to-learn, I wanted to see if it would be more effective to have students do all their course work in writing. In the end, I can't claim with certainty that they learn more this way, but I know *I* do. And most of what I learn about is what they're thinking—I know exactly how students regard the issues we discuss and their level of conceptual understanding, and I can pay extraordinary attention to individuals and our dialogue. I enjoy asynchronous teaching because everything happens in writing, so I know more precisely than in face-to-face classes what each student is thinking about the issues we discuss. I know the students better because the medium encourages a kind of faceless intimacy, which makes me a better teacher.

The students enjoy the convenience because they are spread all over Oregon, from the Pacific Coast to the Idaho border and many points in between. These online courses work extremely well for independent learners who must also balance the demands of other courses, family, and work. They are *very* grateful for the opportunity, and there is a rich exchange among them when things are going well, as they do most of the time.

Workload and Individual Attention

I enjoy teaching online because I can teach any time of day or night, and my distance-learning students feel the same way. I enjoy it because there is no student sitting in the back row whose attention I must worry about—if students are online, they're paying attention. I enjoy it because, after initial time-consuming, front-end preparation for the course, once the course is up and running I can focus all my energies, including what I used to dedicate to class preparation each day, to responding to individual students. The entire cohort group witnesses these responses, so that I simultaneously teach the group while addressing the specific concerns of an individual. Such individual attention grounds our discussions in the students' reality.

I've never understood why these courses are profitable for the university, since I limit enrollment to fifteen. I simply couldn't respond to more incoming messages, as I have each student submit three short formal pieces each week. That's forty-five messages a week for a single course, plus all the optional queries and comments, of which there are a substantial number. Then there are the responses to the responses and sometimes responses to those last responses as well. Still, this quarter I'm not taking any papers home. In contrast, my on-campus, face-to-face sections enroll forty-five students or more. In these, for a single course I might read 135 pages a week for ten weeks, plus 225 pages of finals. While I can answer all queries verbally, I always have a stack of forty-five brief papers (one to two pages) to read and evaluate. But there is no way I could handle forty-five students online. The electronic classroom makes an extraordinary demand on my time and energy—a not altogether healthy one on my eyes, wrists, and lower back. You really have to prefer trading stacks of papers for stacks of electronic bulletin board messages.

Course Organization and Politics (as Usual)

The software I use, First Class, designates the place where messages are actually posted as "subconferences," as opposed to the
"conference" that houses the various subconferences. These, together with e-mail, constitute the course itself. I focus each week
on each course text through a minilecture posted to the
subconference dedicated to that particular textbook. If there are
three textbooks, for example, then there will be three
subconferences, with three minilectures to be composed for each
one, each week. These minilectures tend to become set pieces,
effectively freezing one's discourse and ideas. I had to get used to
this. My classroom style is predicated on as much student involvement as possible, and lecturing does not come naturally to
me. Even when lecturing, I am alert to student questions and will
pick up on the slightest gesture or quizzical look to depart from
prepared notes in order to pursue an issue about which even a
single student might have a question. Minilectures posted to an
online subconference would seem to belie this student-centered
approach. But the minilectures force me to focus more sharply,
something students no doubt appreciate since I tend toward the
highly discursive. Meanwhile, the time and energy I save *not* preparing for a class lecture or activity can be channeled into responding to individual students.

Asynchronous computer conferencing also suits my obses-
sion with organization. The courses are composed of a set of
subconferences dedicated to various aspects of the course. Usually I have two or three texts for each course, so there is a
subconference for each one. I post minilectures that focus on
important parts of the books we're studying at that point in the
syllabus, and I post study questions. The study guide questions
require formal responses of 250 words, which I have students
submit through e-mail so that when I respond, summative comments remain confidential. At some point, students will often
request that the study guide responses be posted to the whole
group so that they can see what their cohorts have to say. Grading these public responses creates a little more work for me, but
it's well worth not only the high standard the best students set

for the rest of the class, but also the advantage of having students express concepts even more effectively than I can. Students can also ask me questions about statements in my minilectures, although they seldom do.

In addition to the subconferences on each text, I hold a class discussion conference during which students can raise issues related to our subject but not directly addressed in our textbooks or my minilectures. Although participation in this conference is optional, it often sees the most dialogical exchanges, and one soon discovers the wealth of knowledge and experience available from the students themselves. This is especially true of older, more experienced students, who are hungry for the critical exchanges enabled by the medium.

I also establish a more informal "café" conference and encourage students to get to know each other there by exchanging information about their personal lives, which I model by telling about my two young children and my extracurricular interests, which seem to match up exceptionally well with the children's. In one course I create a subconference called "Café Grammatique," and rather pride myself on being able to get the word *grammatique* into each student's lexicon. But the real importance of the forum is that it allows students to get to know each other better in a class where they never meet face to face. The cafés leaven the anonymity.

Being especially interested in reflective practice and assessment, I always establish an evaluation subconference. There I periodically ask students how things are going and more pointed questions about not only the course but also working in an asynchronous environment. This allows me to monitor the course itself and to make adjustments while the course is still in process—which research indicates is the best way to make use of student evaluation. It also allows me to collect qualitative data for research purposes. In fact, I believe online courses are a particularly rich field for research.

I usually establish a technical assistance subconference in which I encourage students to help one another navigate the myriad requirements of working online, so confusing to the uninitiated. I warn students, however, to think of me as an ineffective last resort. I use a Macintosh, so I am completely incapable of assisting all those PC users. Luckily our technology personnel, who work with many distant students, are effective and responsive. Furthermore, I insist that the software I use be extremely user-friendly for me, so that my knowledge of the enabling systems can be kept at the absolute simplest and minimum—just like the students'. I insist that the technology come to me. Solving technical problems is the worst use of my time—it's not what I know best, nor does it play to my strengths as a teacher. Fortunately there are systems even I can use effectively, such as First Class and Web Course in a Box.

As you can see, asynchronous online teaching involves a lot of organization. One of my courses has eight subconferences. Add to that the minilectures I have to prepare, and you can see that a great deal of time is required initially to set up each course. Most online instructors don't go to such lengths to set up their courses—don't obsessively create so many subconferences—but they all report that a great deal of time and effort goes into developing their courses. It's an important point to consider before committing to this approach. At our institution, small grants are available for developing online courses, which the administration wants to encourage.

It should be noted that many faculty from across the curriculum oppose the development of a substantial number of distance courses, feeling that they draw resources away from campus programs. It is best to consider these political dimensions to the decision to teach online. While the administration usually supports the creation of such courses, evaluation of them is still in the developmental stage. Furthermore, since summative evaluation of teaching for professional review purposes often rests primarily with program or department faculty, especially in the all important initial stages, some of those faculty will actively resist this new pedagogy, as they do many of the new pedagogies initiated by composition programs. As with any student-centered approach—and online teaching can lead to a more completely student-centered pedagogy than almost all face-to-face approaches—it is sometimes difficult for evaluators to perceive that teaching is actually occurring since so much of the teacher's knowledge is embedded in structures that appear "natural" or are "transparent," as with the course organization outlined earlier. For the time being, at least, online pedagogy is at the cutting edge of university instruction; it is important to keep in mind that not all faculty welcome it and not all administrators understand the amount of time, energy, and expertise it requires.

Dialogical Discourse and Analytical Prose

Asynchronous courses enhance analytical discourse. That is, the quality and depth of student-to-student and student-to-teacher exchanges are higher than in face-to-face classes. It is in fact a *better* medium for focusing on content, on the exchange of ideas, on dialogue and dialogical thinking, than face-to-face classroom discussion, as you may know from participation in a professional listserv. While some believe computer conferencing encourages a focus on surface features rather than ideas, just the opposite has been my experience. Computer conferencing greatly facilitates response to ideas rather than surface features, in part because it is so clumsy at allowing the instructor and tutor to address sentence-level issues—there are no margins to write in. If you set it up well and have the right kind of students, more people participate in the online discussions of ideas and issues than in classroom discussions. That's one of the things I like most about computer conferencing—you hear from everyone, including and especially those quiet but intelligent students who like to think before they speak. Another advantage is that those who speak most often in a classroom but have little of substance to contribute become just another voice instead of the dominant one. In fact, in surveys I've conducted in my courses, one of the things my students like most is the chance to think before they "speak." I have to slap myself on the forehead with the palm of my hand and say, "They like to *think* before they speak. What a great idea! I wish I'd thought of it." Thus, dialogical academic analysis is not only possible in an online environment but is actually facilitated by it.

One of the reasons for the more vibrant dialogical exchange in my online courses is that computer exchanges exist somewhere between formal writing and speech. That increased informality, plus the chance to think before speaking, in addition to the egalitarian effect of a medium that reduces the impression of teacher authority, added to the willingness to be more forthright in a faceless medium where one can truly fashion a self—all contribute to greater and more pointed exchange of ideas, views, and opinions. The trick, of course, is showing students how to move all of that valuable discussion into an analytical, reader-based, formal prose. But that's always the trick in first-year composition. (Another trick is remaining civil in an online environment, but I haven't seen any flaming in my courses.)

Faceless Intimacy and the Play of Presence

Perhaps I'm just not adept at generating efficacious exchanges in the classroom. Many teachers are, and I fully expect that that capacity readily transfers to the virtual medium. Anxiety about that transfer, however, is common for those who are married to actual as opposed to virtual reality, for those who like their voices embodied rather than disembodied. Nevertheless, such teachers will most likely find that they get to know their students as well if not better than in face-to-face classes, which is one reason that many on-campus courses now include participatory listservs for the express purpose of dialogical exchange.

The students who don't do well in asynchronous computer conferencing courses are more dependent on face-to-face contact and feel disoriented and unmoored in the online environment. They need the structure of a physical place to contain their wandering attention, to keep their faces toward the teacher in the front of the room. In my experience—and I've been teaching online courses for several years now—they are usually average or below-average students, whatever the venue. Online courses don't work so well for less independent students or for underprepared students who are less academically literate (who report a paucity of reading and writing experience and fail to display intellectual curiosity). Still, many of the students who do well in the electronic environment nevertheless report that they would prefer traditional, face-to-face classes if they were not place-bound. There's something in us that loves the appearance of presence.

Sentence-Level Work and the Virtual Voice

It is true that online instruction can focus too readily on surface features, but I've experienced the opposite problem—that it is extremely difficult to get students to work on surface features in a virtual environment. In fact, the major task in online courses is not generating analytical discourse, but helping students recognize the importance of editing when submitting formal work, or recognizing error patterns and coming up with editing strategies. Most of the exchanges in my courses are informal, a discourse somewhere between talking and speaking, a virtual voice, in which many of the conventions have limited value if full participation is to be encouraged:

> such writing looks something like this. the conventions just get in the way of faster typing and we begin to see just how nonessential most mechanics are. online exchanges actually facilitate just this kind of rapid writing and response from a very specific audience. its one of the reasons we enjoy our email so much. some online instructors I know don't ask students to submit formal work to the computer conference. instead they have them fax their papers in, where the instructor has a chance to read hard copy, write in the margins, and fax the papers b9ck for further revision.

I have resisted the use of faxes and snail mail in my courses, preferring that *all* work be done online, since anything that arrives in my mailbox tends to get put aside until the end of the quarter, much too late for any formative purpose. So the challenge for me is to be clear about when students must submit carefully edited work and when they can write more informally, as in my example. It is not difficult to be clear about these expectations—it is easy to indicate when formal writing is required (when, where, and how formal assignments are submitted) and when there is greater emphasis on the exchange of ideas. But it *is* sometimes difficult for the students to switch back and forth and to figure out where to send what, what to submit to electronic conferences for the sake of discussion and what to submit privately through e-mail to be graded. And it is difficult, once formal work is submitted, to address sentence-level errors because the instructor does not have margins to write in or the opportunity to sit down with the students and interpret the marginal comment or editorial correction. Most sentence-level errors need *a lot* of explanation because the students are completely unfamiliar with the conventions. For this reason, the "rules" themselves and the handbooks that house them have limited value in enabling students to learn to correct their own errors, without teacher or tutor intervention. Of course, this is only a problem if the instructor wants to make a point of requiring formal, edited work, at least part of the time.

I have addressed this problem in a couple of ways. First, I am very clear about when carefully edited prose is required. Second, I limit the places where I address sentence-level problems. I might, for example, include weekly sentence-combining exercises for which I take off a point for every error. The exercises are brief, so I can efficiently pinpoint the nature of the mechanical problem and have the time to explain the error or invite the writer to seek an explanation. Third, I employ an expert online tutor, who addresses global issues first and then turns her attention to sentence-level issues. The difficulty of tutoring writers on sentence-level problems points up the difficulties that online teaching faces in this regard and highlights the advantage of teaching online for the purpose of exchanging ideas rather than instruction in the conventions of formal English.

Tutoring

My efforts to help students improve their formal, academic writing are ably supported by an expert tutor here at Eastern, Judy Cornish. She reports that tutoring online is much more difficult than face to face because she has no visual or aural clues—no one sitting next to her, no face or barely audible inflections she can use to gauge the writer's understanding. (Dependence on such cues is often a source of anxiety about teaching online—some teachers are as dependent on face-to-face contact as some students.) And there is an additional problem—it is difficult to get students to submit their work far enough ahead of time to give the tutor a chance to respond and the writer a chance to revise, and then to have another round or two of responding and revising before the students turn in a final draft. That's what it takes to address consistent error patterns or lack of facility with the complex sentence structures and precise phrasing that effective academic analysis requires.

Coda: The Future of Grammar

The problems with addressing sentence-level errors indicate one of the challenges facing instructors who want to require not only intellectual engagement in online courses but also formal academic prose. Presently, teaching asynchronously does not facilitate such attention to error. It may well be that standards for grammatical correctness will change because of the nature of online exchanges and because of the influence of what's known as "global English," the influence of nonstandard forms from languages and dialects that employ English as a lingua franca. American English is in fact becoming the international lingua franca, with the result that nonstandard oral usage is finding its way more and more often into formal writing, as you may know from working with international students or surfing the Net. Online exchanges, including asynchronous computer conferencing courses from across the curriculum, may make some grammatical conventions of formal, edited, academic English less important. After all, fewer and fewer professors fuss over the who/whom distinction.

I have wanted for some time to establish a sophomore-level Applied Grammar Workshop to be taught in a computer-aided instruction (CAI) classroom. Students would bring in final drafts of papers they were working on, or, if they weren't working on any papers, I would assign some. We would load a paper into the network so that a copy would appear on each student's screen or on a large screen at the front of the classroom. Then we would run the paper through the grammar checker, discuss each error it highlighted, and decide if the grammar checker was correct. (Most of the time my grammar checker signals problems that are stylistic in nature rather than strictly grammatical. In fact, it is wrong most of the time.) We would do that for paper after paper, week after week. By the end of the term, students would have seen most of the grammar problems they and their cohorts produce in their writing and be so familiar with them that they would be able to intelligently choose whether to follow the advice of their grammar checker.

This plan demonstrates one of the advantages CAI classrooms have over asynchronous online tutoring. But I suspect the point is not too distant when such an arrangement will be available to all online environments, at which point composition teachers will be able to address the full range of issues they confront when teaching writing or other subjects online asynchronously.

Work Cited

Cornish, Judy. "The Virtual Tutor: An Exploration of the Difference between Online and In-Person Tutoring." Unpublished paper, 1999.

SUGGESTIONS FOR THE
COMPUTER-MEDIATED CLASSROOM

Class Peer Review in a Computer-Mediated Classroom: Using Classroom Projection Capabilities and E-mail Messages

LAURA L. BUSH
Arizona State University

Laura Bush provides a rationale and detailed set of instructions for using technology to share students' evolving drafts in whole-group peer-review sessions.

Objectives

- ◆ To analyze a student writer's draft as a class.
- ◆ To suggest revisions and compliment a student on successful aspects of a written draft.
- ◆ To model peer review within a large writing group using technology.

Theory and Teaching Benefits

In *Writing Groups: History, Theory, and Implications* (1987), Anne Ruggles Gere argues that writing groups "provide tangible evidence that writing involves human interaction as well as solitary inscription" (3). This theoretical shift in teaching composition as accomplished through "individual effort" by a "solo performer" to teaching composition as taking place within a social interaction supports the desirability and benefits of class peer review, especially in a well-designed computer-mediated classroom. As Gere explains, "Collaboration ameliorates alienation by reorienting writers toward their readers" (68).

A computer-mediated classroom facilitates collaborative class peer review especially well because all class members have immediate and ready access to one student's draft without making too many arrangements beforehand and without student writers being required to make multiple hard copies that waste paper and time. I use class peer review one to two periods before students will be reviewing each other's papers as writing partners. Using this method of analyzing a student paper as a class before writing partner peer-review day allows me to:

- reiterate important aspects of the writing assignment

- answer questions that many students may have but not be asking

- model peer review

- offer substantive feedback on a few student drafts

- reinforce the need for multiple drafts, revision, and editing

- demonstrate the multiple ways each student could fulfill the assignment

- demonstrate uses for improving writing using technology

Class peer review creates an immediate public audience for students who are willing to share their work with the entire class for critique. The sense of a wider reading audience usually motivates students to produce an even finer draft than they would have if I, their teacher, were going to be the only reader. Because peer-review feedback frequently gives multiple voice to particular strengths or weaknesses in a draft, the method shows student writers that I am not the only reader who was either entertained or confused at particular points in a draft.

Such a large collaborative experience for students who are willing to share with the class often turns into a reward because they receive many detailed written suggestions for improvement and a pat on the back for specific aspects of the draft that the class deemed successful. Moreover, this method illustrates the real needs of an audience and demonstrates the difference between reader-based and writer-based composition.

Teaching Method

1. *Preparing for Volunteers:* One period before class peer-review day, remind students that you will be asking for one or two volunteers to share a draft of their paper on disk. Explain that their writing will be projected for everyone to read and critique simultaneously. (In a fifty-minute class period, you should be able to review one student's draft well. To review two drafts well, you will need a seventy-five-minute class period.)

2. *Projecting the Draft:* On the day of class peer review, load the draft onto a computer that has projection capabilities. Increase the font size of the draft so that class members can read the text of the draft throughout the room.

3. *Reiterating the Writing Assignment:* Remind students about key aspects of the writing assignment. Ideally, these aspects could be quickly reviewed in a PowerPoint slide or even a word-processed list projected on the screen.

4. *Writing Peer-Review E-mail Messages:* Ask all students in the class to begin an e-mail message to the student whose draft you will be reviewing. Make sure the student reviewers send a copy of the e-mail message to you. Also make sure they type the same wording in the subject line so that you and the student writer can easily sort the peer-review messages from the rest of your e-mail. The subject line could read, for example, "Jane's draft #1."

5. *Prepping Student Reviewers:* Tell students that you want them merely to listen and read along as the student writer reads his or her paper aloud. After this first reading, you will

ask them to type their first impressions. Then tell students that you will ask the student writer to read through the draft again before they will need to give more specific feedback.

6. *Reading the Paper Aloud:* Ask the student writer to stand before the class and read the draft aloud. As the teacher, you can operate the computer and scroll through the paper, freeing the student writer from concerns with the technology.

7. *Offering Written First Impressions:* Once the student writer is finished reading, ask class members to freewrite their first impressions of the draft in their e-mail messages to the writer. Do not encourage any verbal feedback yet. This is the time for each peer reviewer to offer individual written first impressions. Do not allow the writer to make verbal comments to the class about the draft either.

8. *Reading the Paper Aloud Again:* Now ask the student writer to read the draft a second time, slowly. Instruct class members to type quick notes to themselves in the e-mail message about what they are noticing or about the responses they may want to expand on after the second reading.

9. *Offering Written Feedback:* After the student finishes reading the paper aloud a second time, ask peer reviewers to describe the strengths of the draft in their e-mail message to the writer. Guide the peer reviewers to discuss how the student writer may be fulfilling specific aspects of the assignment or engaging them as readers. You may even ask them to answer specific questions about the draft. Pause to give peer reviewers time to think and type their messages. Then ask peer reviewers to address areas of the paper that need improvement, especially based on the criteria for the writing assignment. Pause to give peer reviewers time to think and type their messages. Ask student reviewers to send the e-mail messages.

10. *Discussing the Draft Aloud:* When the peer reviewers have sent their e-mail messages, allow the student writer to explain what he or she believes to be the strengths of the draft and what he or she would like to do to improve it.

Then direct a class discussion about the draft. Ask students to summarize the content of their e-mail messages to the writer, verbally praising the draft's strengths and asking questions or examining areas of the draft that need revision. You may now verbally offer your own impressions of the draft, making additional suggestions for improvement. In general, class members' impressions and suggestions will cover much of your own; however, this is not always the case. You may need or want to zero in on particular aspects of the draft, depending on the needs of your class at the time.

Asking students to write their responses to the draft before they discuss it verbally forces them to think through and articulate their responses more thoroughly than they might if you were to discuss the draft only verbally. It also provides the writer with a written record of class members' responses. Having a class discussion after writing the e-mail messages provides the student writer an opportunity to discuss the draft and may also help him or her understand class members' e-mail messages later.

I often write an e-mail message to the student writer after class, thanking the student for sharing the draft and summarizing my own responses and suggestions. I used to write responses to students along with the class peer reviewers, but I found that I had difficulty writing my own response, directing the students, and operating the classroom technology all at once.

Work Cited

Gere, Anne Ruggles. *Writing Groups: History, Theory, and Implications.* Carbondale: Southern Illinois UP, 1987.

Web Page "Place" Assignment and Analysis Assignment

PATRICIA R. WEBB-PETERSON
Arizona State University

Patricia Webb-Peterson's "place" assignment requires students to become critically aware of the rhetorics of space. It also encourages a thorough engagement with considerations of purpose and audience as students coauthor Web pages designed to describe the sites they investigate.

The assignment described and illustrated below was designed for a second-semester composition course that fulfilled a university requirement. Although it was a 100-level class, the majority of the students in the class were sophomores and juniors. The theme of the course was persuasive writing, and I devised a syllabus around the theme of place as rhetorical strategy. This particular assignment was the capstone assignment (the last one they completed and the one the other assignments built up to); it requires that students collaboratively create a Web page that introduces first-year students to the important places of the University of Illinois campus. Unlike official university pages, this site was intended to give an insider's view of these places. Our goal was to help new students feel comfortable and at home on their campus. I broke the class up into six groups of four and assigned each group an area of campus. They were to research the areas (by using the Web, observing activity patterns, interviewing, researching the history of the buildings, etc.), decide which buildings and areas were important to new students, collaboratively write descriptions of the buildings and areas, and then present their finished descriptions to the entire class for evaluation and revision suggestions. Once each group finished its sections, we evaluated the descriptions as a whole class and then decided how we wanted to present the information online.

This discussion of how to present descriptions of place on our Web page opened up many useful avenues of inquiry. Students began to realize how different writing situations require different writing practices and that there is not only one correct way to write for all situations. They began to see that the purpose of the class was not to teach them how to write once and for all but to illustrate that writing is contextually situated, socially defined, and interactionally executed. Far from writing alone in their studies, students were required to negotiate with each other during each phase of the writing process. One particularly interesting discussion highlighting the kinds of negotiations they had to make focused on the concept of voice. Questions raised during this session included the following: Should the Web document appear to be written in one voice, or should it include multiple voices? Who exactly should be responsible for this document? How should the authors of this text be identified? Should the page adopt a purely informative tone, or could it also be persuasive? All of these questions led them back to issues of purpose and audience, two important topics that are often hard to explain in concrete ways in the classroom-sponsored writing situation. I had tried in previous semesters to encourage students to write for a specific audience, but this discussion was by far the most engaged conversation about audience I had ever had with students. That they were familiar with the medium in which they were going be to writing—the Web—and that they had critically analyzed its component parts, its focus, its possibilities and limits, prepared them to have an in-depth discussion about how to write for this audience. The Web as a fairly new technology certainly opened up a conversation about audience and grounded it in specific, concrete space—students could point to exactly where their work was going to be published and used, and they had clearly and specifically defined their audience.

Because students had a conception of not only who was actually going to be reading this but also why it was important for them to be writing this text, this particular class discussion was quite rich. In subsequent discussions about audience and shaping our page to meet our audience's needs and expectations (which may or may not be the same), students began to collaboratively explain why this writing task was important. When they were first-year students here, they had no clue what all the buildings on campus housed, and they often heard terms thrown around—

e.g., the Orange, the Six Pack—but did not know where those places were, what they were used for, or the campus lore about them. By including these things in their descriptions on the Web page, my students were providing first-year students with information that they themselves wished they had had. They were sharing their expertise about this place with those who were inexperienced but desperately wanted to fit in.[1] Thus, it was clear that the writing they were doing was intended for an audience other than the instructor and that they were constructing goals that related to broader audiences. They were more vocal about how to present this information once they recognized its importance to themselves and to their audience. They also knew that their writing was going to be published—that others besides me would read it. And that seemed to encourage them to assume an accountability toward it that I have not always seen students assume. I have not been able to achieve these kinds of discussions in classes where I taught only the essay.

Following is the actual assignment sheet I gave students. It outlines the resources they should use and how this assignment fits with previous assignments.

Web Page Place Assignment

We have been pursuing the theme of space/place and how the physical and symbolic aspects of certain spaces shape our interactions there. We have also looked at the connection between bodies and cities—how cities shape what our bodies are allowed to do, how bodies shape the construction and maintenance of cities. A key focus has been on subjectivity—our sense of self as defined through our interactions with others and with our environment.

Now I am asking you to turn your critical eye to a very familiar space—that of the University of Illinois. The goal of this unit is for us, as a class, to collaboratively produce a documented Web page which maps out the important spaces that make this university what it is. Each group of two (and one group of three) will be responsible for researching a particular area of campus, finding the different places there, analyzing the space as a whole, and drawing conclusions about the interactions between the physical space, the symbolic space, and the bodies that inhabit and use that space. Once each group has researched its specific area, we will as a class create a Web site that combines all the individual groups' findings. The intended audience for the Web site is first-year students, but as we have found this semester, we can't always control who will "hit" our page.

Writing assignments will be as follows:

◆ reviews of three new places each week by the group

◆ evaluation of group members and your own contribution, weekly

◆ proposal

◆ weekly summaries of work accomplished

◆ audience analysis (interviews, etc.)

◆ first draft of site

◆ Web sites that you want your booklet linked to

◆ potential graphics

◆ peer revisions of your booklet (you need to solicit these responses)

◆ final draft

Description of Analysis Assignment

After the actual construction of the page, I asked my students to write an analysis paper in which they reflected on the process of describing the space of the university in this format. What had been left out? What dominant view of the university had we presented? How might other groups view this university differently? How had their positioning as insiders—students who had access to most of the spaces on campus (though some students had a problem gaining access to some buildings and had to gain access through other people)—shaped what they wrote? The two key articles we had read during the semester[2] had not only presented places, but also had critiqued the stories behind the places, explaining how the shape of the places excluded certain people while inviting others in. In what way did our descriptions of the places on campus replicate that bias? Did we find the campus to be a public space? A private one? And how was this reflected in our descriptions? In what ways did our descriptions—which were, in a way, meant to promote a favorable view of the campus—hide some of the social, political, and cultural aspects of the university? In what ways could we have incorporated those aspects into our page? Who is the author of this page? How will people who hit our page know who the author is? What different ideas of authorship does the construction of this page suggest? This paper encouraged students to think critically about the project they had just completed and to examine not only what they learned about the topic, but also what they learned about writing.

The actual paper description I gave my students is as follows:

Rhetoric 143
Individual Analysis Paper: U of I Unit
Paper Length: 3–5 pages
Grade: 15% of your grade

This paper will require you to reflect on the U of I Web site assignment—i.e., the process of describing the space of the university. The two key articles we have read during the semester not only presented places, but also critiqued the representation of places, questioned the assumptions made about certain places, and explained how the shape of the places excluded certain people while inviting others in. The previous assignment—the Web site of the U of I—asked you to describe places, but it did not ask you to critically reflect on how we undertook that assignment. This paper asks you to critically reflect on that process, using the articles (Zukin and Grosz), our class discussions, your group project describing one section of U of I, your classmates' U of I projects, and any Web sites that apply.

Questions to guide your writing/thinking:

◆ In our descriptions of the U of I as a place, what got left out?

◆ What dominant view of the university did we present?

◆ How might other groups (other than our class—inside and outside of the university) view this university differently?

◆ How did your positioning as insiders—students who have access to most of the spaces on campus—shape what you wrote?

◆ Did you have a difficult time accessing certain buildings? Why do you think this was? How did your research into these places change (or not) your perception of the university's accessibility?

◆ Zukin highlights that certain places are constructed to invite certain people in and to keep others out. How did our descriptions of the university replicate this bias?

◆ Was the campus a public or private space? A combination? In what ways did our descriptions—which were, in a way, meant to promote a favorable view of the campus—hide some of the social, political, and cultural aspects/struggles/inequalities of the university?

◆ In what way could we have incorporated these left-out elements into our page? (the left-out elements that you identified in the previous question)?

◆ Who is the author of this page?

◆ How will people who hit our page know who the author is? What different ideas of authorship does the construction of this page suggest?

Notes

1. This was the students' perception of their audience, which they drew from their own experience as first-year students.

2. We read Sharon Zukin's "Whose Culture? Whose City?" and Elizabeth Grosz's "Bodies-Cities."

Using the Web to Enhance Students' Critical Literacy Skills

SIBYLLE GRUBER
Northern Arizona University

Sibylle Gruber has designed the following assignment to engage students in critical evaluation and production of hypertext documents.

In recent years, teachers at all levels have been encouraged to participate in the "technological revolution" as it relates to their teaching practices. Teachers who are interested in providing students with new venues for knowledge acquisition, however, are deterred by the onslaught of information and the many practical, methodological, and pedagogical issues left unanswered. Basic questions relate to the creation of Web pages for specific courses and specific course goals, introducing students to various aspects of the Web, finding and linking to relevant sites, and integrating the virtual environment successfully into the face-to-face environment of the classroom.

The Web can create realities that are in constant motion and that are not limited by the linearity and monologic discourse often attributed to conventional texts. Accordingly, users of the Web can move beyond current perceptions of textuality toward the more dynamic and collaborative forms of writing and reading preferred by many teachers and students. As a consequence, the Web allows for exploring diverse forms of literacy practices emphasized in many educational institutions. Hypermedia texts can help students be actively involved with a constantly changing text. In its ideal form, hypertextual discourse can enhance innovative teaching practices that promote student participation in the learning process. In other words, the Web can furnish teachers and students with innovative tools for supporting already existing educational goals such as involving students in the learning process, using collaboration as a teaching and learning strategy, and creating a space for active learning, exploration, and innovation.

The exercises are intended to help students and teachers see the Web not only as a rapidly expanding information source, but also as a place that can support an accessible and engaging curriculum by foregrounding new ways of approaching knowledge. In many cases, authors and audiences of hypermedia are encouraged to transform established perceptions of writing and reading practices, and to create a writing space that can provide more flexibility than traditional print texts.

The exercises also show that teaching students how to use and create hypertexts does not present an entirely new approach to texts and to teaching. Instead, hypertext applications in classroom situations enhance many already existing educational practices—from teaching writing as a process to increasing audience awareness—by combining newness with familiarity. Teachers, for example, can use these exercise to support students' often nonlinear composing processes. Students can be encouraged to conduct research on the Web, select and gather important data, brainstorm and organize their ideas, decide what to include in their drafts, and experiment with new ways of presenting information. These activities can move students from passive to active learners, encouraging them to explore and evaluate new concepts and new ideas. At the same time, students can learn how to apply their newly acquired skills to already existing frameworks within their fields of inquiry. For example, once they realize that research on the Web can be fun *and* instructive, they might also engage more actively in offline research.

By using these exercises, teachers and students can explore the new possibilities of hypertexts, and teachers can create an engaging curriculum that allows students to move between different layers of texts, visual presentations, and sound. And, because hypermedia texts move beyond words on the screen to incorporate audio and visual elements, teachers can explore the definition and meaning of *text* with their students, establishing new criteria for acceptable communication.

The exercises included here can be used by any undergraduate or graduate class that integrates computer-mediated communication into the curriculum. Specifically, I used a series of prompts intended to move students from analyzing Web pages, to actually creating their own pages, to evaluating their performance as well as the performance of their peers. I wanted to get them used to thinking critically about the Web and its possible functions. I also wanted to make sure they were aware of the possibilities of the Web as a resource and as a tool for presenting themselves online. I started the exercises by asking them to analyze a Web site, went on to get them into groups for working on a class Web page with various internal and external links, and then asked them to evaluate the group's performance. The specific topics for these prompts could vary widely. The ones I used were geared toward "academic culture" since that was the general topic for the class.

Analyzing Material on the Web

For this project, you need to explore specific sites on the Web. As we all know, not all information posted online is equally reliable, valuable, and useful. To increase your critical reading and thinking skills, and to expand your analytical skills to being critical about sources on the Web, I printed out some Web addresses for you to look at and analyze.

What I would like you to do:

1. Get together in groups of three.

2. Surf the Web using three to four of the addresses I listed below.

3. Analyze their value for educational purposes. Here are some (it's not an inclusive list) questions you can consider when analyzing the Web pages:

   ◆ What does the Web page look like (layout)?

   ◆ What do you think is the purpose of this page?

   ◆ Who is the audience for this Web page?

   ◆ Did the creator(s) of this page achieve the purpose?

   ◆ Is it easy/difficult for you to find your way around?

   ◆ Does it link to important other sites?

   ◆ What do the different sites have in common? What's different?

   ◆ What features do you like the best? What appealed to you?

   ◆ What features do you like the least?

   ◆ What suggestions do you have for improving these pages?

4. Write down your findings and bring them to class tomorrow.

5. Here are the links from which you can choose: [include links geared toward the general topic of the class]

**Constructing a Web Page for English 105:
Presenting Ourselves Online**

Next week (Monday through Wednesday) you will be working in groups to hammer out the procedures for creating our own Web page, what you would like to present, and how you would like to do this. The groups are listed below. It might be a good idea to exchange phone numbers and e-mail addresses.

Working on this project should provide you with these opportunities:

- learn how to collaborate

- increase your knowledge about a topic of your choice

- connect your writing experiences with "real" uses in a real-world setting

- address real audiences

- increase your analytical/critical thinking skills

- increase your audience's awareness of issues important to you

When you put together this page, make sure you know who you want your primary audience to be, what the purpose of this page is going to be, and what language you think is appropriate for this Web page. Language in this respect also includes graphics, pictures, background—everything that your readers will see/ read when they look at this page.

Before you put together this group project, you might want to go back to some of the Web sites you've already explored to see how others approached the creation of their Web sites.

Here are some issues to consider:

- What do you want the focus of your site to be? (This addresses issues of audience and purpose.)

- What do you want your audience to know after visiting your site?

- How do you want to draw their attention to your site?

- What kinds of links do you consider important?

◆ What kinds of visual aid/layout would you want for your Web site?

And on an organizational level:

Since you will receive a grade as a group, you'll have to figure out various organizational matters: How do you want to work as a group? How often do you want to meet? Do you want to divide the responsibilities among the group members? How are you going to ensure that everybody is doing his or her share? How will you report on your progress? Are you going to do a peer evaluation?

You will be working in your groups from Monday through Wednesday instead of regular class meetings. On Thursday, we'll get together in class again, and each group will report what they have been working on.

Groups [list groups]:

Progress Report: Presenting Ourselves Online

To ensure that all participants in the various groups contribute to our class Web page, each of you will need to fill out a progress report. In this report, you can tell me how many times you met, who was present/absent, who provided constructive feedback, who was present but didn't really contribute much, how decisions were made, and what comments you would like to make about your group members.

What to include:

◆ Meetings (number of times you met, who was present/absent)

◆ Summary of what you discussed/accomplished during each meeting

- ◆ Discussion of group dynamics

- ◆ Comments you would like to make about the group project

- ◆ On a scale from 1 (excellent) to 5 (poor), evaluate your group's performance (as a group)

- ◆ On a scale from 1 (excellent) to 5 (poor), evaluate each participant's performance:

  1. your own:

  2.

  3.

  4.

Working in an Electronic Classroom

Julia V. Gousseva
University of Arizona

The three assignments designed by Julia Gousseva utilize Connect.Net software to initiate collaborative work and discussion that addresses online and traditional materials.

Following are descriptions of three assignments I used with my first-year composition students in a networked classroom (we used Connect.Net software[1]). The assignments are a collaborative rhetorical analysis of an essay, a collaborative rhetorical analysis of Web sites, and an example of an anonymous online discussion assignment. Some of the students' end-of-semester comments illustrate their engagement with these technologies:

I liked the anonymity involved with Connect.Net. It allowed the more timid students to express their opinions with more confidence. The only thing that concerned me with Connect.Net is the amount of information that is passed through a particular time because some points can get lost. However, this process made it easier to divide the work among the people in collaborative groups. Connect.Net made it easier to see the requirements for an "A" paper since the other papers are readily available.

What I liked about the collaborative work in the classroom and the COH lab is that I was exposed to many different ideas and opinions. It is because of these variations in beliefs that I have been able to open my own mind a bit more. I know that people may believe and think differently than me. That is okay. What I have noticed, however, is that there are some people that can be opinionated about many topics of discussion. I don't think they realize that there is more than just one type of thinking in this world. Also, it is because of this standpoint that some people are afraid to speak up in class. They are afraid that someone will refute their statement and embarrass them.

Connect.Net made writing collaborative papers easier. Instead of having to schedule a meeting time, it was very convenient to be able to work and communicate during your own time in your own home.

I enjoyed getting to know other people really well in my class. This class has caused us to become good friends in the process of helping each other to complete the assignment. I like that in collaborative projects the work is not entirely up to you to complete; it is divided evenly between the people in the group. I think group work also helps you to grow and stretch yourself and your own boundaries and learn how to deal and work and cooperate with someone. You also begin to see things from another person's perspective. And you really begin to understand the assignments better because you aren't just looking at it from just one viewpoint but three or four. However, I disliked that one of my group members decided to do the vast majority of all the work every time we had a group assignment and didn't really seem to want anyone else's help because they wanted to present their idea, and the way they wanted it. I disliked that sometimes it got really hectic and hairy when it came to the communication and clarification process of what we were supposed to be accomplishing for this assignment. I would have liked to have found a better way to cooperate and collaborate.

Connect.Net made it easier to write collaborative papers because we could read each other's work and then comment on how we could make it better. This helped us to improve the quality of our work. It was easy to divide our work for the rhetorical analysis because we just took all the points and split them into three equal parts. Then we went back and changed what did not sound good together. Sometimes, however, it was hard to make sure that everyone would do their own part, sometimes one person would do more work than another but we made up for it in the next papers.

A Brief Theoretical Explanation of Collaborative Writing Assignments in an Electronic Classroom

Collaborative writing is not a new concept. Historically, collaborative writing groups have existed since at least 1728 and have proven to be an effective tool for improving essay quality and the intellectual level of the participants. In 1728, Benjamin Franklin became one of the initiators of mutual improvement societies, "groups of people outside academic institutions who shared their interest in enhancing intellect but had to rely on themselves to create opportunities for fostering it" (Gere 32). Although the various mutual improvement societies differed, they shared many common features—the main one being a considerable interest in writing.

Asynchronous interactive writing, in dialogue journals, letters, computer conferencing, and electronic mail, has been implemented effectively in educational settings since the early 1980s. This activity helps the students "establish a written 'dialogue' with the instructor about a topic of their choice, providing a very specific audience/reader and a purpose for communication" (Gonzalez-Bueno 57), thus making the assignment more meaningful for the students.

Synchronous (real-time) written interaction in the writing classroom has been used since at least 1985, when the first major effort to implement real-time communication in a composition classroom was undertaken at Gallaudet University. Trent Batson, the director of ENFI (English Networks for Interaction), argues that computer networks can promote the best aspects of current process-oriented, student-centered approaches to teaching writing as: (1) a social act, rather than a solitary act, (2) a process rather than a product, and (3) a collaborative effort among students and the teacher.

The introduction of computer-mediated communication (CMC) into the classroom has affected both our perception and the practice of second-language (L2) writing. CMC facilitates L2 students' written interaction and collaboration among themselves, with the teacher, and with the native speakers of the target language. CMC can help the students work at their own pace and provide the less fluent students with an equal chance at participation in discussions. In the CMC classroom, "more students are producing more language" (Phinney 151), so there is more opportunity for L2 practice. The effectiveness of CMC in the classroom, however, ultimately depends on how we, as teachers and researchers, adapt the technology to meet our educational goals, and on how we adapt our teaching practices to "meet the demands of electronic writing spaces" (Hawisher 96).

Assignment: Rhetorical Analysis of a Collaborative Essay

Write a comprehensive rhetorical analysis of the essay of your choice. Remember to discuss the writer's persona, audiences and intentions as reflected in the essay, as well as the rhetorical strategies (including the three appeals) used. Your essay should do (but not be limited to) the following:

1. *Briefly* summarize the message your text is trying to convey to the readers.

2. Derive the writer's intended purpose from textual evidence (use quotations from the essay to support your assertions).

3. Describe the characteristics of the target audience.

4. Describe the various strategies and appeals the author uses to achieve his or her purpose(s) and use examples from the text to illustrate the various appeals.

5. Evaluate how appropriate and/or effective the strategies the author is using are in convincing this particular audience.

For more specific suggestions applicable to each group, please see my comments on the final draft of the Web site project.

Assignment: Rhetorical Analysis of Web Sites (collaborative)

This assignment requires you to work in your small group to find any *five Web sites* and do a rhetorical analysis of these sites.

Criteria for analysis include general rhetorical analysis issues as well as specific questions pertaining to Web sites. Following are some of the specific questions/issues to consider when analyzing Web sites (you can also check the "Evaluating Web pages for relevance" site at http://www.slu.edu/departments/english/research/rcont01.html):

1. General evaluation criteria: purpose and audience

   ◆ Purpose: (a) Is the site intended to be educational or entertaining? How can you tell? Explain. (b) Is the site meant to be informational or promotional? Why? Explain. (c) Why was this site created?

   ◆ Audience: (a) What does the author assume the user already knows about the topic of the site? What makes you think so? (b) Who is the intended audience for this site: general user, professional audience, etc.? Why do you think so?

2. Evaluating the authority/credibility of a Web site

   ◆ Who is the author: Is the author an authority in the field? What are the author's qualifications? Does anything in the Web site suggest that the author has a bias or a special interest?

   ◆ Who is the site's host/sponsor:

      a. If the host is a periodical publication (journal, magazine, newspaper), it should have an International Standard Serial Number (ISSN). If it doesn't, it may be "home-grown" and may have less authority.

      b. If the host is an independent service provider, check the organization's homepage for:

     i. an available address/phone number—if it doesn't have it, it is probably not a credible source

    ii. the organization's statement of purpose or list of objectives, to see if there are any special interests they may seek to promote in the sites they sponsor

    iii. the date of the last update

3. Graphics, colors, and special effects: how do they help the author of the Web site create his or her persona (the image of him- or herself the author wants the readers to imagine), and what message do they convey to the users?

The format for the paper could be that of an extended annotated bibliography, i.e., a list of Web sites (complete with http addresses and titles), in which each Web site address is followed by a two- to three-paragraph annotation. The annotation should provide brief information about the purpose, audience, and rhetorical features of the Web site (see above guidelines).

Assignment: Genetics or Society: What Causes Crime?

Today we will try a different format for discussion: you will be working in groups of four to five people. None of these people will be the ones you usually work with, AND the discussion will be anonymous. I will be joining your groups as the discussion progresses (also anonymously). Using the <u>comments</u> feature, discuss the following quotes from this week's readings with your group. Please remember that our general question for today is whether crime is determined by biological or social factors, and try to address this question in your discussion. Can you think of ways to refute the following statements? What are some of the potential dangers in the biological explanation of crime? In the social explanation?

From *Are Criminals Made or Born?*
". . . Crime . . . has a foundation that is at least in part biological. The average man is more aggressive than the average woman in all known societies and . . . the sex difference is present in infancy well before evidence of sex-role socialization by adults, and similar sex differences turn up in many of our biological relatives—monkeys and apes. Human aggression has been directly tied to sex hormones, in experiments on athletes engaging in competitive sports and on prisoners known for violent and domineering behavior" (Selzer 3, p. 874).

"The most compelling evidence of biological factors comes from . . . studies of twins. Identical twins are more likely to have similar criminal records than fraternal twins" (Selzer 3, p. 875).

"Studies of adopted children . . . show that the biological family history contributes substantially to the adoptees' likelihood of breaking the law" (Selzer 3, p. 876).

"Starting with studies in the early 1930s, the average offender in broad samples has consistently scored 91 to 93 on IQ tests for which the general population's score is 100. The typical offender does worse on the verbal items of intelligence tests than on the nonverbal items but is usually below average on both" (Selzer 3, p. 876).

"For some repeat offenders, the predisposition to criminality may be more a matter of temperament than intelligence. Impulsiveness, insensitivity to social mores, a lack of deep and enduring emotional attachments to others and an appetite for danger are among the temperamental characteristics of high-rate offenders" (Selzer 3, p. 878).

"A chemical treatment of the predisposition is a realistic possibility" (Selzer 3, p. 880).

From "Address to the Prisoners in the Cook County Jail":
"I do not believe that people are in jail because they deserve to

be. They are in jail simply because they cannot avoid it on account of circumstances which are entirely beyond their control and for which they are in no way responsible" (Selzer 2, p. 862).

"There ought to be no jails; and if it were not for the fact that people on the outside are so grasping and heartless in their dealings with the people on the inside, there would be no such institution as jails" (Selzer 2, p. 863).

"I think that all of this had nothing to do with right conduct. . . . [N]ine tenths of you are in jail because you did not have a good lawyer and, of course, you did not have a good lawyer because you did not have enough money to pay a good lawyer. There is no very great danger of a rich man going to jail" (Selzer 2, p. 865).

"This crime is born, not because people are bad . . . but because they see a chance to get some money out of it" (Selzer 2, p. 867).

"The only way in the world to abolish crime and criminals is to abolish the big ones and the little ones together. Make fair conditions of life. Give men a chance to live. Abolish the right of private ownership of land, abolish monopoly . . . " (Selzer 2, p. 872).

From "Why Aren't There More Women Murderers?"
"Fewer than 3% of serial killers are female, according to FBI statistics. No one knows why this disparity exists, although many researchers believe that differences in brain chemistry may be the primary reason why men are so much more violent than women" (Selzer 1, p. 895).

"Burgess and other forensic experts believe that there are sharp differences between men and women's brain chemistry, and that those differences are accentuated by cultural differences in the way males and females are raised" (Selzer 1, p. 896).

Note

1. Connect.Net is software that turns a word-processing package into a networked environment that allows for online discussions, collaborative revisions, and class management.

Works Cited

Batson, Trent. "The ENFI Project: A Networked Classroom Approach to Writing Instruction." *Academic Computing* 2.5 (1988): 55–56.

Gere, Anne Ruggles. *Writing Groups: History, Theory and Implications.* Carbondale: Southern Illinois UP, 1987.

Gonzalez-Bueno, Manuela. "The Effects of Electronic Mail on Spanish L2 discourse." *Language Learning & Technology* 1.2 (1998): 55–70.

Hawisher, Gail E. "Electronic Meetings of the Minds: Research, Electronic Conferences, and Composition Studies." *Re-imagining Computers and Composition: Teaching and Research in the Virtual Age.* Ed. Gail E. Hawisher and Paul LeBlanc. Portsmouth, NH: Boynton/Cook, 1992. 81–101.

Phinney, Marianne. "Exploring the Virtual World: Computers in the Second Language Writing Classroom." *The Power of CALL.* Ed. Martha C. Pennington. Houston: Athelstan, 1996. 137–53.

Assignment Sources

Bass, Alison. "Why Aren't There More Women Murderers?" Selzer 1: 894–99.

Darrow, Clarence. "Address to the Prisoners in the Cook County Jail." Selzer 2: 862–72.

Herrnstein, Richard J., and James Q. Wilson. "Are Criminals Made or Born?" Selzer 3: 872–82.

Selzer, Jack, ed. *Conversations: Readings for Writing,* 3rd ed. Boston: Allyn and Bacon, 1997.

Teaching Composition with International Students in an Electronic Classroom

VIKTORIJA TODOROVSKA
Arizona State University

This section provides ideas for using technology in an ESL writing context. In an ESL classroom, the teacher must consider issues of second-language acquisition when determining how to use technology to teach writing.

The following activities were designed for use in an English 108 class taught in a networked classroom. English 108 is a class for foreign students that focuses on doing research and writing argument papers. Teaching this class in a networked classroom gives students the opportunity to become more proficient at doing research on the Web in addition to the more traditional types of research; students participate in a number of group activities in class that ask them to do research on the Web and identify sources on a particular topic, evaluate those sources, and extract the information they need to construct their arguments. In addition, the fact that this is a networked classroom enables students to workshop their papers in class, engage the teacher in a one-on-one conference about their papers, as well as share their papers with their peers and thus receive and give feedback.

In addition to using word-processing software and engaging in Internet research, the students in a networked classroom participate in synchronous and asynchronous discussions (either in groups or as a class). These discussions range from chats on readings to brainstorming sessions, from comments on evolving drafts to suggestions for strategies to help construct a more effective argument. The online discussions provide more students with greater opportunities to express their opinions and to consult the records of those discussions at any point for ideas. The following are samples of activities that illustrate how technology may be incorporated into writing instruction.

The first activity is an evaluation paper assignment. Since the class is being taught in a computer classroom and the students do a great deal of their research online, the assignment asks them to choose a Web site and evaluate it for the quality of its information. This assignment gives the instructor a chance to initiate a discussion of the criteria used to evaluate Web sites and how those criteria are similar and/or different from the criteria used to evaluate other types of sources (primarily print ones). Thus, it helps students realize that not all information on the Web is accurate, and it teaches them to locate good online sources.

Assignment 1: Evaluating a Web Site

The first paper assignment in this class asks you to evaluate a Web site. By now you should have done a fair amount of research on the Web and decided on a site to evaluate. The site can be of either personal or professional interest to you. It is important that you choose a site you're interested in because that will make the process of writing the paper a great deal more enjoyable.

Evaluations express judgments about particular things or matters. However, the judgment expressed in an evaluation needs to be supported by reasons and examples. Remember that in order to write an effective evaluation you need to choose a well-defined subject that you will present to your readers. Also, you need to make a claim about this subject (in our case, the subject is the Web site you're evaluating). You need to support the claim that you're making with evidence and examples in order to persuade your readers that you know what you're talking about and that your judgment is sound. You can also support your claim by comparing the Web site you chose to other similar Web sites and establishing its advantages or disadvantages. Your judgment and the argument proceeding from it need to be based on well-defined and accepted standards (the criteria for evaluating Web sources that we developed in class).

The paper should be no less than 500 words and should incorporate all the elements of evaluations mentioned above.

The next activity is a series of questions used to help students generate material for their papers. Students often struggle when trying to decide what to write about and what kinds of information to include in their papers. This activity helps them explore the topic from a number of different points of view and generate most of the material they will later incorporate in their papers. It also helps them think of issues they might not have thought about and generate counterarguments that might otherwise be hard to see.

Answer the following questions in as much detail as you can. This will help you write your paper:

1. Identify your subject clearly so that even people who have never heard about it can understand what it is. This means that you have to provide the URL and title for the Web site you are evaluating and describe it for your readers. Remember that your readers will not be familiar with this Web site, so you need to be very specific when you are identifying it.

2. What is your thesis for this paper? What is the claim you are making about the Web site you are evaluating? Try to state this claim as concisely and clearly as you can.

3. Give at least five reasons you will use to support your claim in this paper.

4. Give as much support as you can for the five reasons you just listed.

5. List all the positive features of the Web site you are evaluating and explain why you consider these things to be positive features. Use the criteria that we generated in class yesterday.

6. List all the negative characteristics of the Web site that you are aware of. Why do you consider these characteristics negative?

7. How are you going to deal with the negative features of this Web site? How are your going to explain them? How will they affect the claim you are making?

8. Who are your readers? Be specific. What can you assume about them? What are they likely to know about this Web site (if anything)? What other similar Web sites might they be familiar with? Are they likely to agree or disagree with your claim and the reasons for it? Why?

9. What is your purpose for evaluating this Web site? What do you want your readers to learn from this paper? Be specific.

10. List at least two other Web sites that are similar to the one you're evaluating.

11. How is the Web site you are evaluating similar or different from these two Web sites? Compare and contrast them in detail and explain how this is significant for the Web site you are evaluating.

Approaches to Using Computer Technology When You Don't Teach in an Electronic Classroom

Arizona State University

Timothy Ray addresses possibilities for using technology in writing instruction while still teaching in a "traditional" classroom. The piece both provides ideas for teachers without access to a computer-mediated classroom and suggests ways to begin using technology critically before making the transition into an electronic classroom.

One of the most difficult—if not *the* most difficult—aspects of utilizing computer technology in a first-year composition classroom is gaining access to the technology in the first place. As anyone who teaches in the first-year composition classroom is aware, computerized classroom facilities are at a premium on most college campuses. Even when facilities are dedicated for use exclusively by writing courses, there can be considerable competition for computerized classrooms, particularly when dozens of sections of the same course are offered—as in the case of first-year composition—and only a limited number of those sections can be accommodated by the available resources. Add to that the fact that administrative decisions about who gets to teach in a computerized classroom typically are made on the basis of previous experience teaching in a computerized environment or on the basis of successful completion of formalized training or course work in computers and composition, and you have a situation in which many instructors eager to incorporate computers into their writing pedagogy find themselves having to improvise in their efforts to do so.

Of course, many other instructors, for any number of very good reasons, prefer to teach in noncomputerized classrooms and to utilize computer technology as a means of supplementing their teaching in that environment. Either way—whether instructors have chosen to teach in conventional classroom settings or have found themselves accepting the fact that they won't be assigned to a computerized classroom—there are numerous ways that writing instructors can incorporate computer technology into their teaching in a noncomputerized environment.

I found this out for myself firsthand as a doctoral student at Bowling Green State University. Because the first two years of my assistantship were in the form of a graduate editorship for a journal in the College of Education, I was not able to teach in the composition program until my third year. And because of the high demand for the limited number of opportunities to teach in the program's computerized classroom, instructors were assigned to that classroom on the basis of their previous teaching experience, both in computerized classrooms and in conventional classrooms. Because my chances of being assigned to the computerized classroom were slim, and because I was trying to present myself professionally as a computers and composition specialist, I resolved not only to focus my course work intensively on computers and composition pedagogy, but also to become as resourceful as possible in incorporating computer technology into my conventional composition classroom once I started teaching. That experience has continued to influence my desire professionally to work back and forth, both physically and reflectively, between teaching in computerized classrooms and teaching in conventional classrooms supplemented by computer technology.

E-mail

As many people who have taught in a noncomputerized environment have quickly discovered, one of the easiest ways of using computer technology to supplement a conventional classroom is through the use of e-mail outside of class. This can take many forms, of which instructor-student interaction, student-student interaction, and whole-class interaction are the most obvious.

Instructor-Student Interaction

Rather than publicizing office hours, an office phone number, or even a home phone number, instructors seem to be increasingly inclined to publicize their e-mail addresses as their preferred mode of contact with students outside of class, posting their e-mail addresses prominently on their course syllabi. This method of communication with students has both advantages and disadvantages for both instructors and students, and can be utilized in a number of ways. One of the more obvious ways this means of communication can be employed is through one-to-one contact with students who wish to discuss daily assignments, reading assignments, and essay assignments. Students can ask questions, get clarification on assignments easily, and even send copies of their essays as e-mail attachments on dates they are due or even in advance.

One disadvantage of using e-mail to interact with students is that, as Hawisher and Moran have noted ("Electronic Mail and the Writing Instructor"), such a constant availability to students can create additional work for instructors (what they call "telework") and can raise student expectations that you will be available at all hours. Because of this tendency for overwork and for expectations of constant availability, it is advisable to caution students that you may not respond immediately or even before the next class to their messages, and to set limits on when you will be available online and in what time frame students should expect a response. For instance, while I could be almost constantly available online both when I'm in my office and at home, I make a habit of disconnecting from the network on a regular basis so that (a) I can get more work done on other projects and (b) I can have a life away from work. Further, I tell my students that I cannot guarantee that I will respond to an e-mail they have sent to me within twelve hours of class, even though I regularly do respond to e-mail sent to me as late as an hour before class. Just as often, however, I walk into class and tell a student, "Sorry I didn't get back to you on your e-mail," and they almost always respond with "Oh, that's okay," or something along those lines, and then go on to tell me what they did about their problem in lieu of my response.

Another potential disadvantage to interacting with students through e-mail is that the ease with which students can attach a copy of their essay to their e-mail builds in a resulting expectation that you will be able to respond to their tentative draft or intermediate draft as readily and as thoroughly as you might a final draft or even a required rough draft. I handle this situation the same way I do hard copies of drafts: I tell students that I can't possibly respond to everyone's drafts other than at those times when I collect drafts from everyone, so unless they can direct me to a specific part of their essay or a specific concern they have about their intermediate draft, then I won't respond to it. Whether teaching in a computerized or a conventional classroom, I always require that students turn in a hard copy of their evaluated drafts because of the potential for electronic copies to get "lost in the ether" in transmission and because I'm not always sitting at a computer when I find some unscheduled time to respond to student drafts. At the same time, while I require hard copies of evaluated drafts, I also encourage (but do not require) students to submit an electronic copy of their evaluated drafts, along with a release statement, so that I can accumulate drafts of student essays to use anonymously for scholarly and teaching purposes.

Many instructors and students feel that they get to know each other better through the use of e-mail than they would otherwise, and this helps break down barriers between students and instructors. On the other hand, one of my dissertation committee members, who happened to teach in the complex field of computer science, told me that the more he made himself available to students through e-mail, the less they took advantage of his ample office hours, the less he felt that he really knew his students on an individual basis, and the more his teaching evaluations suffered as a result. So e-mail outside of class can at times be a double-edged sword for both instructors and students.

Student-Student Interaction

Even when meeting in a noncomputerized classroom, composition instructors can utilize student-to-student e-mail exchanges for several purposes, including responding to readings and to each other's drafts. Either purpose can be achieved by pairing students into "e-mail buddies" or by setting up e-mail distribution lists that constitute several students (and possibly the instructor as an observer of the distribution list activities or of the e-mail buddy system, if the instructor's e-mail address is included in the "cc" portion of the e-mail header). Using e-mail to put students in pairs or peer-response groups for responding to readings or to essay drafts that are included as e-mail attachments encourages notions of collaboration, social construction, and audience awareness. Making sure that you are included in the "cc" line of the header helps provide oversight, not only to make sure that students are performing the peer response assignment, but also to bring material generated from such discussions back into the classroom for discussion by the class as a whole. In addition to the assigned e-mail exchanges, unassigned interactions between students can be valuable for students who want to catch up on assignments they missed because of absences, for brainstorming assignments with others, and for creating a sense of community in the classroom. To encourage and facilitate such unassigned interactions, I require students to have an e-mail account by the end of the first week of class, and during the second week of class I distribute a class e-mail address sign-in sheet (with optional phone numbers), which I then reproduce and distribute to the entire class.

Whole-Class Interactions

Probably one of the most common ways to bring computer technology into a conventional classroom is through the creation of a class e-mail listserv. A listserv uses an e-mail list processing system provided by most university e-mail servers to distribute e-mail messages contributed by any subscriber to the list to the rest of the subscribers to the list. Whether teaching in a computerized or a noncomputerized classroom, I have always created listservs for each of my classes and required students to subscribe to the list. I reinforce this requirement by creating various assignments to be carried out over the list, so any student who doesn't subscribe loses points for not having completed those assignments.

Listservs can be used for a variety of purposes in a first-year composition classroom, the most obvious overarching statement about their application being that they enable classroom discussions to be extended beyond the classroom walls and beyond the standard class meeting times. A common assignment utilizing a class listserv requires students to post to the class listserv their responses to a reading or to an in-class activity and then respond to one or more of their peers' responses in order to generate ongoing discussion on the list. This has some rather practical ramifications such as ensuring that students have read the readings or done the activity or assignment, but it's also particularly useful in a first-year writing classroom in helping students to formulate their ideas and arguments in writing, in making them aware of an audience of their peers, in generating much more discussion than can usually be encapsulated in class, in encouraging reflective and thoughtful responses instead of spur-of-the-moment responses delivered orally in class, and in generating text that can be brought back into class for a whole-class discussion or even a text/discourse analysis.

Because such a class would not normally meet in a comput-

erized classroom, and because not all students have online capabilities from home, I would encourage giving students more time
than just the next class period to complete such an assignment.
Since accessibility is still an issue, instructors need to provide the
greatest amount of fairness to the greatest number of students
for online assignments.

Another possible assignment involving class listservs asks students to post their possible essay topics along with their reasons
for why they might want to write about each one, and then to
respond to each other's topic choices to help them decide which
topic sounds most promising for the essay assignment. Such an
assignment invites a greater variety of responses than might be
generated during an in-class small-group activity. Of course, you
should try to make sure that every student gets a response, either
by assigning students to respond to at least two or three of their
peers, or assigning students to respond to someone they haven't
responded to before, or by writing responses to students whose
postings don't receive any responses from the rest of the class.
This type of activity can also be used for interview questions,
research questions, and the like.

Because usually anyone with an e-mail address can subscribe
to a listserv, another possible pedagogical application of a listserv
is inviting outside experts, "guest speakers," or authors of works
that are being read in class to participate in the listserv discussion. Such experiences further heighten students' awareness of
outside audiences and the challenges of writing for a more public
audience than just you or their peers. Yet another benefit of
listservs is the ability to link two or more classes for specific discussions or even for the entire term (see Harris and Wambeam).
Particularly when classes are separated by great distances, students are forced to consider geographical, cultural, and political
differences and the subjectivity of ideas, opinions, and knowledge.

Although a number of assignments can be carried out by
means of a class listserv, I feel that one of the greatest benefits of
such a list is the growing sense of community within the classroom that a list fosters. To facilitate this process, I try not to set
strict parameters on what types of activities should be allowed or
disallowed on the list. Instead, I spend at least one class period

near the beginning of the semester introducing students to the subject of "netiquette"—etiquette on the Internet—and encourage them to set some ground rules between themselves for how the list should function aside from the required assignments conducted over the list. I have found that most students appreciate the occasional off-topic postings, including jokes, stories, interesting Web sites, and so on; such off-topic discussions seem to give students a sense of ownership of the list and contribute to community formation. When things do go awry on the list and a "flame war" erupts or possibly objectionable material is posted, I find it best, as Laurie George suggests, to bring the online discussion back into a face-to-face environment for discussion.

Finally, although students seem to be all too familiar with the possibility of conducting research on the World Wide Web, they should also be reminded of the possibilities of conducting research by e-mail, such as through one-on-one contact with experts on the topic they are researching or through participation in listservs and Usenet newsgroups devoted to their topic. My own view of e-mail shifted, from seeing it primarily as a communications medium to seeing it also as a research tool, when I posted a question about something I was researching to a scholarly listserv and received numerous responses directed to me, and when I witnessed how my inquiry had spawned a lively thread of discussion on the list in the process. While the challenge with the Web is to limit the number of sources from the Web that students want to cite in their works cited lists, the challenge with e-mail seems to be to encourage students to include at least one e-mail correspondence in their works cited lists.

The World Wide Web

And speaking of the Web, there are a number of ways that the Web can be incorporated into a conventional first-year composition classroom as well. Probably the most obvious is allowing or encouraging students to use sources from the Web in their essays—something students usually bring up first and that requires very little, if any, encouragement. Less obvious, however, is the strategy of encouraging students to conduct research *about* the

Web. Whether I'm teaching in a computerized or a conventional first-year composition classroom, I usually turn to the Web when it's time to have students write evaluative essays or critiques; I assign them an essay evaluating what makes a good Web site on whatever topic they have chosen, or critiquing the effectiveness of a Web site in putting forth an argument about a particular topic. In undertaking this assignment, we usually spend a day in class discussing some of the conventions of Web sites, what makes a good Web site in general, how Web sites differ according to their purpose (inform, entertain, persuade, etc.), and how to evaluate Web sites for reliability, accuracy, currency, and other factors that can be important when using Web sites for research in general or for this assignment in particular. For the last part of this discussion, I distribute a list of helpful Web sites that have been prepared by various reference librarians across the country who have concerned themselves with helping students learn how to evaluate Web sites for research purposes.

I also create a class homepage for every class I teach, regardless of whether it is offered in a conventional or an electronic classroom, and I accumulate helpful resources for students and post them there. My class homepages also detail the class schedule and requirements, just in case students lose their syllabus and need to find out what's happening in class. In addition, I encourage students to either give me copies of their essays on disk or post them to their own Web space so that I can link to them from the class Web page for their peers, friends, and family members to view, although most practitioners in this area agree that links to students' essays should be password protected to guard against plagiarism.

The Web site evaluation assignment is almost impossible to complete without actually scheduling time in an available computer lab or computerized classroom, and I would encourage those instructors who are interested in doing this type of assignment to research the availability of computer labs on campus and what their reservation procedures and policies are. While some schools allow instructors to reserve computer labs for classes, others do not. In case of the latter, I think it's important to remember that classes normally scheduled in computerized classrooms do not necessarily need to meet in a computerized environment every time, so instructors who normally hold class in a conventional classroom but who want to teach two or three classes in a computerized classroom should seek out their colleagues who teach in computerized classrooms and ask them at least a couple of weeks in advance if they would be willing to switch classrooms from time to time.

Conclusion

These are just some of the more obvious ways that instructors who teach in noncomputerized classrooms can incorporate computer technology into their teaching and, in effect, have the best of both worlds. Indeed, between the extremes of a totally computerized composition classroom (or a class that meets totally online) and a composition class completely devoid of computer technology, the real "happy medium" in every sense of the phrase may be the class that meets in a conventional classroom but is supplemented with a class listserv, a class homepage, and online activities, assignments, and research. So it shouldn't come as a surprise to anyone that instructors who have taught in both computerized and noncomputerized classrooms may prefer the noncomputerized classroom that is supplemented with computer technology outside the classroom.

Works Cited

George, E. Laurie. "Taking Women Professors Seriously: Female Authority in the Computerized Classroom." Spec. issue of *Computers and Composition* 7 (1990): 45–52.

Harris, Leslie D., and Cynthia A. Wambeam. "The Internet-Based Composition Classroom: A Study in Pedagogy." *Computers and Composition* 13 (1996): 353–71.

Hawisher, Gail E., and Charles Moran. "Electronic Mail and the Writing Instructor." *College English* 55 (1993): 627–43.

Further Reading

Cooper, Marilyn M., and Cynthia L. Selfe. "Computer Conferences and Learning: Authority, Resistance, and Internally Persuasive Discourse." *College English* 52 (1990): 847–69.

Eldred, Janet. "Pedagogy in the Computer-Networked Classroom." *Computers and Composition* 8 (1991): 47–61.

Faigley, Lester. "The Achieved Utopia of the Networked Classroom." *Fragments of Rationality: Postmodernity and the Subject of Composition.* Pittsburgh: U of Pittsburgh P, 1992.

Gruber, Sibylle. "Re: Ways We Contribute: Students, Instructors, and Pedagogies in the Computer-Mediated Writing Classroom." *Computers and Composition* 12 (1995): 61–78.

Hawisher, Gail E. "Electronic Meetings of the Minds: Research, Electronic Conferences, and Composition Studies" *Re-Imagining Computers and Composition: Teaching and Research in the Virtual Age.* Ed. Gail E. Hawisher and Paul LeBlanc. Portsmouth, NH: Boynton/Cook, 1992. 81–101.

Hawisher, Gail E., and Cynthia L. Selfe. "The Rhetoric of Technology and the Electronic Writing Class." *College Composition and Communication* 42 (1991): 55–64.

Janangelo, Joseph. "Technopower and Technoppression: Some Abuses of Power and Control in Computer-Assisted Writing Environments." *Computers and Composition* 9.1 (1991): 47–64.

Knupfer, Nancy Nelson. "Teachers and Educational Computing: Changing Roles and Changing Pedagogy." *Computers in Education: Social, Political, and Historical Perspectives.* Ed. Robert Muffoletto and Nancy Nelson Knupfer. Creskill, NJ: Hampton, 1993. 163–79.

Regan, Alison. "'Type Normal Like the Rest of Us': Writing, Power, and Homophobia in the Networked Composition Classroom." *Computers and Composition* 10.4 (1993): 11–23.

Romano, Susan. "The Egalitarianism Narrative: Whose Story? Which Yardstick?" *Computers and Composition* 10.3 (1993): 5–28.

Selfe, Cynthia L. "The Humanization of Computers: Forget Technology, Remember Literacy." *English Journal* 77 (1988): 69–71.

Takayoshi, Pamela. "Building New Networks from the Old: Women's Experiences with Electronic Communications." *Computers and Composition* 11.1 (1994): 21–35.

Warshauer, Susan Claire. "Rethinking Teacher Authority to Counteract Homophobic Prejudice in the Networked Classroom: A Model of Teacher Response and Overview of Classroom Methods." *Computers and Composition* 12.1 (1995): 97–111.

CHAPTER 12

CONSTRUCTING A TEACHING PORTFOLIO

This chapter describes the possible contents of teaching portfolios: teaching philosophies, annotated syllabi, annotated assignment prompts, syntheses of course evaluations, supervisors' class visit reports, students' in-process papers with the teacher's written responses, annotated lesson plans, and the like. The contributions include discussions of the functions of teaching portfolios for graduate students, tenure-track faculty, tenured faculty, and adjunct faculty. They also include some sample materials from teachers. It may seem odd to include a chapter on teaching portfolios in a book such as this, but the subject is an important one because teachers need to begin constructing teaching portfolios during the first year of teaching—not the year they apply for jobs, not the year they are considered for tenure, not the first time they encounter posttenure review. Beginning this work the first year of teaching helps teachers become the kinds of reflective practitioners that Donald Schön describes in *Educating the Reflective Practitioner.*

Teaching-Portfolio Potential and Concerns: A Brief Review

CAMILLE NEWTON

University of Louisville

Camille Newton traces the recent history of teaching portfolio use and addresses the advantages of constructing portfolios for new teachers, as well as some of the concerns commonly associated with portfolio evaluation.

The interest in and use of teaching portfolios have grown significantly in the past ten years. Peter Seldin estimates that between the years 1990 and 1997 (the span between the publication of the first and second editions of his influential text *The Teaching Portfolio: A Practical Guide to Improved Performance and Promotion/Tenure Decisions*), the number of U.S. universities using teaching portfolios jumped from a modest ten to as many as one thousand institutions (2). Patricia Hutchings notes that the 1991 American Association of Higher Education monograph *The Teaching Portfolio: Capturing the Scholarship in Teaching* is one of the most popular AAHE publications in recent years (1). And Carrie Shively Leverenz and Amy Goodburn note that the number of articles about teaching portfolios in the ERIC database jumped from a first reference in 1991 to over thirty in 1996 (15). This startling growth in teaching portfolio use and interest may be attributed in large part to the ability of teaching portfolios to address recent calls by educators, politicians, and concerned citizens for greater emphasis on the documentation of teaching improvement and excellence. Politicians, parents, and students want "proof" that money being spent on higher education is producing results. Proponents contend that teaching portfolios can be used to document for such audiences that teachers are meeting educational objectives. For many teacher educators, and for faculty and administrators charged with hiring and tenure/promotion decisions, teaching portfolios offer rich portraits of the teaching practices of those teachers they are expected to mentor and/or evaluate. Finally, teaching portfolios offer teachers the responsibility and opportunity to explore and display their teaching practices for purposes of development and evaluation. Through such uses, advocates contend, teaching is documented and accorded the attention, respect, and value it deserves but has not always received in higher education.

Teaching portfolios have gained acceptance and recognition in part because they can be modified and adapted to the contextual needs of the institutions and individuals using them. Indeed, Russell Edgerton, Patricia Hutchings, and Kathleen Quinlan contend that "there is no single thing called 'a teaching portfolio'; neither the concept nor its practice is all figured out" (3). Despite their flexibility, however, teaching portfolios may be generally defined as a teacher's selective collection of reflective narratives and the teaching documents that illustrate or support such reflections (possibly including, for instance, syllabi, assignments, and responses to student texts). The contents of the reflections, and the documents included as support, vary according to the purpose and audience of the teaching portfolio, but they are always more than a haphazard collection of papers. The collection ideally represents the best work of the teacher, and it documents the teacher's achievements and development in a variety of settings over a significant period of time. The teaching portfolio may be used by new or experienced teachers entering the job market, by teachers seeking promotion or tenure, by teachers pursuing awards or other recognition for teaching excellence, and by all of the above who are working to develop and improve teaching performance.

Because of their flexibility and the variety of uses teaching portfolios might serve, it seems most practical to provide here both the general assumptions that support and encourage teaching portfolio use and the recent concerns being voiced about teaching portfolios, so that new teachers of writing may use the practical suggestions and assignments in this chapter in careful and informed ways.

Teaching portfolios are lauded for their ability to contribute to teachers' development and to present more contextual information about teachers and their teaching for evaluators. Donald Schön contends that the best teacher education programs do not focus exclusively on the transmission of theoretical knowledge, but instead focus on methods that allow new teachers to operate "in action"—to help them learn to deal productively with the "messy practice" of teaching. Schön recommends that teacher educators help teachers find ways to reflect on a teaching situation and its features—and their actions in the situation—in order to explore their actions and the knowledge they used to act. Such education in reflective practice, Schön contends, can help teachers evaluate their teaching decisions and the assumptions that inform them and give them the ability to use such knowledge "in action" in future teaching contexts.

What Schön advocates and describes is the type of reflective practice that developmentally focused teaching portfolios ideally produce. In teaching portfolios, teachers are encouraged to examine their specific actions within the context of classroom situations, to reflect on their decisions, and to explore their development in light of their teaching experience and professional development activities. Patricia Hutchings notes that the very process of constructing a teaching portfolio contributes to a teacher's development and learning (3). She quotes one teacher with whom she worked as acknowledging, "I never realized why I do [a particular activity] in my classroom until I did the portfolio" (4; brackets in original). Robert P. Yagelski asserts that teaching portfolios were an essential component for helping preservice English teachers with whom he worked to practice critical reflection about their teaching experiences. Chris Anson believes that teaching portfolios can encourage reflective practice, and in an early article asserts that such reflection is enhanced by a collaborative portfolio program and teachers' subsequent awareness of an audience:

> Through the imagined eyes of a colleague or administrator, the college teacher now rethinks the overly dictatorial tone in her course syllabi. Anticipating the scrutiny of a hiring committee looking at his portfolio, the recent Ph.D. wonders whether his sample assignment seems clear enough to demonstrate his best work. Knowing she will soon be sharing her comments on student papers with her peer teaching team, the instructor at a community college begins reflecting on her style of response. The various audiences invited into these teachers' portfolios inspire them to think in more principled ways about how their teaching

> materials are written, and this process leads to revision, new
> thought, and new actions where perhaps otherwise there would
> be little change. (188–89)

Teaching portfolios are valued for their potential to encourage
reflective practice and to help teachers develop a critical awareness of their teaching practices. Ideally such critical reflection
helps teachers to develop, refine, and share successful practices
with a community of teachers committed to teaching development and excellence.

In addition to these developmental benefits, administrators
and teacher educators value teaching portfolios for their contribution to the evaluation and professionalization of teaching.
Evaluating teaching is a challenging endeavor; experts acknowledge that traditional measures of teaching success such as student evaluations and classroom observation reports often do not
provide sufficient information on which to base award, hiring,
promotion, or tenure decisions. Teaching portfolios can help to
provide more contextual information for such purposes:

> Through portfolios, faculty can present evidence and reflection
> about their teaching in ways that keep this evidence and reflec-
> tion *connected* to the particulars of what is being taught to whom
> under what conditions. . . . [F]aculty can arrange and "anno-
> tate" these pictures in ways that document an overall approach
> to teaching. . . . In this sense, portfolios constitute a considerable
> advance over the practice of classroom visits by an outside ob-
> server. . . . When maintained over several semesters, the portfolio
> can even allow a look at the gradual unfolding of expertise in a
> way that no other method makes possible. (Edgerton, Hutchings,
> and Quinlan 4–5)

Such teaching-portfolio "documentation" arguably contributes
to a view of teaching as a scholarly activity—it is akin to the
documentation of publications and presentations on a résumé
that is traditionally deemed "scholarship" in higher education.
Ideally, through use of teaching portfolios, teachers have more
opportunity to shape and participate in the terms and methods
of their evaluation, and teaching may be documented and evaluated as a scholarly endeavor.

In addition to positive reports, teaching portfolios are also the focus of some recent critical examination. The common practice of using teaching portfolios for both developmental and evaluative purposes has generated some questions and calls for further evaluation of and research into teaching-portfolio use. In his generally positive article about using teaching portfolios "as vehicles for . . . growth and reflection" with preservice English teachers, Yagelski acknowledges that some students felt frustrated in their attempts to reconcile the ideally developmental portfolio process with the grade they would receive for the products they produced (258). Pearl R. Paulson and F. Leon Paulson note that the teachers constructing portfolios for their classes discovered "that the need to tailor a portfolio [to an audience that may be judgmental in varying degrees] was influenced by how much personal risk could result were they to bare their own perspectives" (289). Chris Anson, in a presentation at the 1998 Conference on College Composition and Communication, expressed some concern about how much the consequences of evaluation might negatively affect the developmental potential of teaching-portfolio use for some teachers. And Carrie Shively Leverenz and Amy Goodburn are concerned that the very professionalization of teaching that teaching portfolios promote may direct new teachers' focus too early in their careers away from learning about teaching and practicing teaching, instead encouraging them to focus on the production of scholarship about teaching. Leverenz and Goodburn suggest that such a focus contributes to what they see as a troubling emphasis on teaching professionalization rather than on teaching professionalism.

Despite such concerns and need for further research, teaching portfolios are increasingly put to use for their potential to encourage reflective practice and to contribute contextually rich information for evaluation purposes. Teaching portfolios are routinely required for graduate school and job applications, for promotion and tenure files, and for ongoing professional development purposes. New teachers of writing may be asked to prepare a teaching portfolio for any or all of these situations. A knowledge of the rationale for teaching-portfolio use, a thorough understanding of the audience for and purpose of the portfolio they are producing, and the practical suggestions and information in this chapter may prove a useful place to begin such teaching-portfolio preparation.

Works Cited

Anson, Chris. "Portfolios for Teachers: Writing Our Way to Reflective Practice." *New Directions in Portfolio Assessment: Reflective Practice, Critical Theory, and Large-Scale Scoring.* Ed. Laurel Black, Donald A. Daiker, Jeffrey Sommers, and Gail Stygal. Portsmouth, NH: Boynton/Cook, 1994. 185–200.

Edgerton, Russell, Patricia Hutchings, and Kathleen Quinlan. *The Teaching Portfolio: Capturing the Scholarship in Teaching.* Washington, DC: AAHE, 1991.

Hutchings, Patricia. Introduction. *Campus Use of the Teaching Portfolio: Twenty-Five Profiles.* Ed. Erin Anderson. Washington, DC: AAHE, 1993. 1–6.

Leverenz, Carrie Shively, and Amy Goodburn. "Professionalizing TA Training: Commitment to Teaching or Rhetorical Response to Market Crisis?" *WPA: Writing Program Administration* 22.1-2 (1998): 9–32.

Paulson, Pearl R., and F. Leon Paulson. "A Different Understanding." *Situating Portfolios: Four Perspectives.* Ed. Kathleen Blake Yancey and Irwin Weiser. Logan: Utah State UP, 1997. 293–304.

Schön, Donald A. *Educating the Reflective Practitioner: Toward a New Design for Teaching and Learning in the Professions.* San Francisco: Jossey-Bass, 1987.

Seldin, Peter. *The Teaching Portfolio: A Practical Guide to Improved Performance and Promotion/Tenure Decisions.* 2nd ed. Bolton, MA: Anker, 1997.

Yagelski, Robert P. "Portfolios as a Way to Encourage Reflective Practice among Preservice English Teachers." *Situating Portfolios: Four Perspectives.* Ed. Kathleen Blake Yancey and Irwin Weiser. Logan: Utah State UP, 1997. 225–43.

Yancey, Kathleen Blake, and Irwin Weiser, eds. *Situating Portfolios: Four Perspectives.* Logan: Utah State UP, 1997.

Thinking about Your Teaching Portfolio

C. BETH BURCH

State University of New York, Binghamton

Beth Burch provides some simple and practical guidelines for new instructors to follow when beginning to construct a teaching portfolio.

A teaching portfolio can help you display the aspects of your teaching, secure promotion within your department, or gain a new teaching position. Preparing a teaching portfolio also helps you be more conscious of your strengths and weaknesses. Here are some thinking points for planning your portfolio:

1. Collect. It's important to collect a wide variety of material by saving a copy of everything related to your teaching each semester—book orders, class lists, syllabi, assignment sheets, lesson plans, rubrics, memos. You may find it helpful to reserve a drawer where you can save copies of documents. Then at the end of a semester, clean out the drawer, gather and order the materials, and file them in a folder specifically marked for each course (complete with section number, specific course name, and date). Keep full course records; you may need the information later.

2. Select. Before you select material for your teaching portfolio, consider the rhetorical task that lies before you. You are going to prepare a many-faceted document that will, in effect, persuade its audience to consider your teaching positively. You are preparing a persuasive piece! Your teaching portfolio may persuade readers to move you to the next level of pay, land you a position mentoring other instructors, earn you a teaching award, or induce someone to invite you to an interview for a new position. The portfolio may be the only view that departmental administrators have of your teaching abilities. Given these considerations, it's important to be aware of your audience and your purpose.

Your Audience. Who will read your teaching portfolio? Will just one person read it? Or will your portfolio be read and evaluated by a committee? Will readers be familiar with terms specific to your university and your department? (Course names are, for instance, more meaningful than course numbers; if your teaching portfolio says you taught English 112, but your reader does not know what English 112 is, then you haven't been thoughtful of that reader.) How many portfolios will readers evaluate? Consider all possible readers. Follow directions. Choose representative samples of your work. Keep the length manageable—twenty pages maximum. Use terms your readers will know.

Your Purpose. Why are you submitting this portfolio? Are you trying to persuade readers that you should be allowed to teach a new and perhaps more difficult course? Is your purpose to get a raise? Do you want an interview? What kind of teaching personality do you want to project? What you include in your teaching portfolio should reflect your purpose and fit the requirements or guidelines set for portfolios as well. Determine what you should show readers to accomplish your purpose—and then resist the impulse to throw in more.

Selection of items for the portfolio is easier if you consider what aspects of teaching you want to address or emphasize. These aspects for emphasis will vary according to your audiences and purposes. Generally, though, consider these ways that your teaching talents are manifested:

PRESENTATION. The way you present information to your class and conduct yourself in front of your class is what many people first think of when teaching is mentioned. How can you demonstrate your skills in presenting materials? What would be necessary for a stranger to get a sense of your in-class behavior—of your style? What kind of documents can convey this information?

Consider these: a lesson plan that articulates a clear sequence of activities; observation reports by a supervisor, by a discriminating colleague (you can learn a lot from watching your peers teach), or by a professor or colleague from another department on campus; teaching evaluations (synthesized and excerpted) from your students; a ten-minute video of you in action. If you include a video, consider that your audience may not want to take the time to view it or may not have a videotape player handy.

CURRICULUM. What you choose to teach and how you organize material for teaching is another important aspect of teaching. How can you demonstrate that you choose and arrange materials wisely? How can you articulate the underlying theory of your teaching? How can you persuade readers that you provide a rich array of opportunities for thinking, reading, and writing?

Consider these: syllabus; brief unit plan; lesson plan; assignment sheet; invention guide, writers' group handout, or portfolio rubric; reading or reference list.

INTERPERSONAL CONNECTIONS. How do you conduct yourself with other people, including your students and your supervisor(s)? Departments value folks who can get along, who make their intentions clear, and who communicate well. How can you show your communication abilities and demonstrate your commitment to the department as well as to your students?

Consider these: copies of business memos (book orders, room requests, meeting announcements, etc.); copies of letters of recommendation written for students or colleagues; teaching observation reports written for others; memos to students about excessive absences or other course details; comments on students' work; details of committee work or other service to the department.

DEVELOPMENT. How can you demonstrate your growth as a teacher? How can you show your increasing sophistication and understanding of what and how you teach? How can you show readers that you are a restless intellect, that you continue to learn and to improve your teaching?

Consider these: reflective notes to yourself, perhaps a series of excerpted journal entries; reflective pieces for each major section of the portfolio; a reflective letter analyzing a teaching experience or lesson that was especially fruitful—or that went awry; a descriptive, reflective overview of your portfolio; a statement of teaching philosophy. Reflection— what transforms a collection of material into a portfolio— unites and explains portfolio components.

3. Reflect. Reflection is easiest if you do it as you go along. You might find it useful to establish a habit of regularly writing to yourself about your teaching experiences. You don't have to write every day, certainly, but notes written at strategic course junctures (e.g., after your students have drafted a major assignment, at midterm, after portfolio evaluation, after an observation, at the end of the course) can help you take stock. This way, you establish a reflective habit of mind that will serve you well as you prepare the portfolio for presentation.

4. Present. Be especially mindful of your readers as you present your teaching portfolio (audience and purpose again!). Include a table of contents keyed to numbered pages or color-coded sections. Arrange materials in a logical, organized way. Label everything. Assume that any reader may not be clear about your duties, course numbers, or expectations for your students. Keep the portfolio manageable: portfolio readers typically read many portfolios and rarely have leisure to sift through long documents. Be professional: use clean, heavyweight paper and a laser printer; avoid mixing more than two fonts; proofread carefully. Remember to put your name on the outside of the portfolio, on both the spine and the front of the portfolio, so that it can be easily identified.

You're ready now to start creating your teaching portfolio: happy teaching, thinking, and writing!

A Philosophy of Teaching: Backseat Driving

RENEE T. THOMAS

University of Illinois at Urbana-Champaign

As she notes here, Renee Thomas is a new teacher. Her phi-losophy statement demonstrates, though, that she has reflected on her teaching in useful ways. It can also be found on her Web site: http://www.english.uiuc.edu/405/Thomas/philosophy. htm.

Even though I have taught writing for only one semester, I do feel that I can claim to have a philosophy of teaching. It is certainly half-baked, if that much, but it is informed by much of the read-ing I have encountered this semester as well as by my experiences with my Rhetoric 105 class and what I have learned through trying to mesh those two forces. But before I can describe my philosophy of teaching, I feel I must describe my philosophy of writing, simply because that is what I teach.

On the first day of the professional seminar for teaching rheto-ric, Paul Prior asked us to draw our conceptions of writing. I was only too happy to do this because somewhere along the way in college I did begin to form an image of what writing is to me. It is essentially this: a series of decisions and choices, much like those we make when we drive—without a map—somewhere we have never been before. So, on that first day of class, I drew a system of roads, some of which connected and some of which didn't, some leading to the big happy finished piece of writing on the horizon, and some leading off toward Never-Never Land, or K-Mart, or even, perhaps, hell.

Clearly, the writer is the driver. She may choose the road to hell just to see what's there. She may go to K-Mart for something she needs, or only to look around. She may travel to Never-Never Land and find that all the answers are hidden there, or that it is all a myth, and Never-Never Land is just another town peopled mostly with grown-ups who think they are children.

There is something to see and learn down every road. It is perhaps tempting to say therefore that it doesn't matter which road a writer takes, so long as she learns something. But I think it does matter, it matters very much, and it is the pressure of choosing, in those few panicked moments in the middle of an intersection, that make writing such difficult work.

This is what I believe.

I believe lecturing is by and large a waste of time in a writing class. To learn how to write, students must do it. They must get behind the wheel and make the decisions and choices, figure out what to do when they get lost or run out of gas, and see which roads are the smoothest. This is not to say that as a teacher I shouldn't talk to my students and help them see things they might not see. There is information to be given about writing; there are some rules of thumb—spelling things correctly, for instance, usually goes over well, and so does using clear thesis statements and referring to people by their last names. These kinds of things are important for students to know, and once they are said, they are said. But knowing what a thesis statement is and actually writing one are not the same at all; in fact, I would go so far as to say that until students try to write a thesis statement, they don't know what one is.

So I believe in talk rather than lecture. Talking with my students, not at them, and trying to get them to talk to each other, not just near each other, is a way of forming a classroom community. Like any other, this community is made up of different people with different views and, frankly, different levels of intelligence or development. Talk is the lifeblood of the community; it can lay bare some of those differences and allow them to be used. Talking is good for students because it makes them articulate their thoughts, which is what they need to do when they write as well. And listening is good for students because it allows them to step outside of their own worldviews for a moment. What I'm saying is that talking and listening make students think and ensure that they are intellectually—as well as physically—present in the classroom community. And I must be there as well, as part of that community. In a sense, I define the boundaries of it—I assign the reading and the papers, and I shape the talk sometimes too. But because I am in this particular position in the community, my attitude and persona are extremely important. It is essential that I foster a comfortable environment in the classroom so that students are not intimidated by me, so that they don't speak for my ears only, but for themselves. One of the easiest ways to do this is to be frank and honest with them at all times, to make the reasons behind the reading and writing assignments explicit. I also think it's important that we have fun sometimes, and laugh, and let ourselves be ourselves when we have discussions. I don't just ask for students' thoughts and opinions; I give my own, with the acknowledgment that my thoughts are not necessarily the "right" thoughts—they are just mine.

I believe in constant dialogue between students and me. They write journals every week, and I write back to them, commenting only on their thoughts, never on their language or mechanics (see Elbow). I encourage them to e-mail me whenever they have questions or concerns. This is a neat trick, because—whoops!—they have to write e-mail, and when they do they have a specific audience (me), a point to make, and a form to follow. I think these relatively one-on-one forms of student-teacher dialogue are important because through them I am able to get to know my students better, and vice versa. I get to see other, less polished and less formal pieces of their writing besides their papers. I don't think it's a coincidence that frequently I saw better writing in the journals than in the papers, on the levels of both thought and sentences.

Which brings me to another belief: I believe in as much student autonomy as possible. Students can surprise themselves with their own abilities when they are given the freedom to choose (there it is again) what they want to write about (see Atwell). It makes no sense, no sense at all, for me to take away possible roads and eliminate much of the work that is writing by giving them topics and telling them what to learn. I believe that in order for students to become writers, they have to struggle with the decisions and choices. They are responsible for what they say and how they say it; I am not, or at least I don't believe I should be. I am only there to help them see what kinds of choices they have.

Finally, I believe it is possible to help students think and develop writing skills at the same time. That's what all the reading, talking, listening, and writing are about. So while I will never get in the driver's seat, I can travel with my students on their writing journeys for a semester. My role, as I see it, is that of the backseat driver, because sometimes you can see better from there than from behind the wheel, and sometimes you even hold the map. If my students ask for directions, I'll provide them, but always with the knowledge that it's not my choice or decision—it's not my paper, my thoughts, or my life.

Works Cited

Atwell, Nancie. "Everyone Sits at a Big Desk: Discovering Topics for Writing." *Reclaiming the Classroom: Teacher Research as an Agency for Change.* Ed. Dixie Goswami and Peter R. Stillman. Upper Montclair, NJ: Boynton/Cook, 1987. 178–86.

Elbow, Peter. "Ranking, Evaluating, and Liking: Sorting Out Three Forms of Judgment." *College English* 55 (1993): 187–206.

Statement of Teaching Philosophy

AMY D'ANTONIO
Arizona State University

When Amy D'Antonio, a Ph.D. student specializing in Romantic poetry, composed this teaching philosophy, she was just finishing her first semester of teaching first-year composition. Her training in Romantic poetry is readily evident in this statement—from the initial sentence on. But she also demonstrates here that she is working to integrate rhetorical theory into her perspective.

In studying the writers of the British Romantic movement—that is, the movement in which our modern conception of "author" began to be formulated—I have had the opportunity to consider a variety of statements on the purposes of writing and on the position and responsibility of the writer. Considering that Fleming's survey of the past and design for the future of rhetorical education reveal that, in its most historical and most promising sense, the study of rhetoric is "aimed at the moral and intellectual development of the student" (172), Shelley's articulation of the natures of writing and writer offers a sound foundation on which to build a method of teaching designed to encourage such student development. In "A Defense of Poetry," Shelley implicates the principle of love with moral and intellectual development achieved through writing:

> The great secret of morals is Love; or a going out of our own nature, and an identification of ourselves with the beautiful which exists in thought, action, or person, not our own. A man, to be greatly good, must imagine intensely and comprehensively; he must put himself in the place of another and of many others; the pains and pleasures of his species must become his own. The great instrument of moral good is the imagination; and poetry administers to the effect by acting upon the cause. (Reiman 487–88)[1]

In the rhetoric classroom, I encourage such "going out of our own nature" through the construction of a community based on interidentification among its members. In their writing, my students learn to think and to communicate by putting themselves "in the place of another and of many others" through their responsibility to the living audience of their peers. In their reading, my students develop "an identification of [themselves] with the beautiful which exists in thought, action, or person, not [their] own" through their responses to each other's writing.

I consider my role in the community not that of an instructor, but rather that of a reminder. I find that I must continually refresh students' sense of responsibility for each other's moral and intellectual development. I accomplish my reminding not only by declining authority, but also by actively allocating it to the students themselves. When we discuss progress on writing assignments, for example, I always ask first what successes students have had, then what difficulties they are experiencing. The students are then in the position to give and receive advice and share writing strategies among themselves. Such continual peer teaching prepares my students for their final portfolio assignment, for which they assemble materials by which to assess the intellectual and moral development they have achieved through their writing and reading. In an oral presentation followed by discussion of the portfolio project to an audience of both familiar and unknown instructors and students, they prove their ability to communicate to both known and unknown audiences. Additionally, they sympathize with each other's successes and difficulties, offer authoritative advice and encouragement, and, through such imaginative sympathy, develop and articulate insights into their relationships, through their writing and reading, with each other. Thus, "the pains and pleasures of [their] species . . . become [their] own."

Note

1. Since Shelley considers artists and inventors of all kinds to be poets, and since he explicitly states that "the distinction between poets and prose writers is a vulgar error" (Reiman 484), I find his insight here applicable to student compositions, rather than to metered language exclusively.

Works Cited

Fleming, David. "Rhetoric as a Course of Study." *College English* 61 (1998): 169–91.

Reiman, Donald H., and Sharon B. Powers, eds. *Shelley's Poetry and Prose: Authoritative Texts, Criticism*. New York: Norton, 1977.

Reflection on Teaching

NEIL A. WALDROP

Arizona State University

Neil Waldrop, who was finishing his first semester of teaching college-level composition when he wrote this reflection, is fairly candid about his successes and failures as a new teacher. He also thinks forward to what he plans to do in the future.

I have typed copies of each lesson plan from this semester, my first ever as an instructor. These plans, and the progression they suggest from day one until the last, indicate clearly the philosophy under which I operated this year: be prepared. I felt that the only way to overcome my initial nervousness was to have a plan for everything, and then a backup plan for each of those when things went awry, as they often did. I learned early on, however, that there is no accounting ahead of time for the dynamics of a classroom. I know from my own experience as a student that the syllabus exists more as a guideline than as a hard-and-fast rule. Knowing this ahead of time alleviated some of the pressure and anxiety I felt going into teaching. I felt I owed it to myself, however, to pack my daily lesson plans in the beginning of the semester with more activities than time would allow.

This system of overpreparation eliminated the possibility for "down time"—the time I most dreaded before stepping in front of a class for the first time. "What would happen if I stood in front of these people and had nothing to say?" I thought. The very idea horrified me. Surprisingly, one situation that did not bother me was the one in which a student asked me a question for which I didn't have an adequate answer. I have learned in graduate school that it is perfectly acceptable for an instructor to answer a question with, "I don't have an answer to that. I'll check on it and get back to you next time." I used this reply and met with only favorable responses—except for the time I forgot to write down the question and thus neglected to search for an answer. I heard about that one for a week.

Following the first unit, I relaxed somewhat regarding class preparation. I felt that after one unit I had a pretty good idea what I would need to prepare for each of the very different class personalities: For my 1:40 class, I would need a minimum of material since there were a number of active participants in that class. For my 3:15 class, a bunch of sleepers, I needed to prepare more material to keep the class lively and focused. I waited all semester for the "flip-flop" of class personalities that experienced instructors had spoken of, but it never happened.

My in-class demeanor changed as the semester progressed. As I became more comfortable standing in front of the class, I trusted myself more to wing it, to go in the direction the class led itself. From the beginning, though, I subscribed to the philosophy that the class belonged to the students and I was there merely to facilitate discussion and provide guidance. The students (not all of them, but some of the lesser dedicated ones) had trouble accepting this idea; many fixated on the fact that I would be grading their papers and assessing their "abilities" as writers.

My goal was to emphasize process, and to do this I often made references to my own works in progress. My intention was to get the students to focus more on coming to class and discussing the readings and their writing, and not on the final draft they were to hand in for evaluation. I noticed that as the semester progressed, fewer and fewer students attempted more and various invention activities; most stuck to the "shotgun" draft theory. My attempts to collect invention work for homework, or to get the students to respond to peers' emerging writing, did not work as well as I had hoped. I attribute this to my lack of experience, personally and professionally, with writing as a process. I found myself empathizing with the students who did little invention work beyond the "find an appropriate topic" work.

While I recognize the value of the process philosophy, at times my inexperience made it easier for me to fall back on more familiar philosophical territory. This, I believe, harmed those students who were not inclined to do the invention work on their own. Those students who did the invention work, who were often also those who came to my office hours to discuss such work, did better on average than their peers who discounted invention material.

During my first semester of teaching, I learned how to develop a productive and engaging classroom rapport without (completely) losing sight of the tasks at hand. Now that my anxiety over classroom instruction has disappeared, I hope to devote the bulk of my time to constructing and implementing useful and creative strategies for in-class work. It is in this area that I feel I need to improve the most, and it is here that I will begin thinking for my next semester of teaching.

Statement of Teaching Philosophy

JENNIFER A. MILLER
Arizona State University

Jennifer Miller's philosophy demonstrates concerns that are unique to her role as an ESL instructor; as such, she is especially attentive to her students' need to develop increasing autonomy.

Regardless of the academic setting and students' needs, I view teaching as a means of allowing students to teach themselves and of providing them with an opportunity to reach their own potential. As an ESL/EFL teacher, my ultimate goal is to provide students with an environment that allows them to emerge as communicatively competent speakers of English. These students ultimately hope to master the syntax, phonology, and morphology of the English language. Although I hope that I help motivate students and give them the necessary input they need in order to reach this goal, ultimately, through the time and effort they spend with in-class activities and homework, they learn by themselves. While I do my part in providing the information, these students choose to teach themselves, for without their efforts mine too would be futile. This is a constant in all fields of teaching, and proved itself to me while I was teaching English 101 this past semester. Although these students' goals and needs were quite different from those of the students I have had in the past, these students also taught themselves. As their teacher, I attempted to enable their self-education by presenting activities, encouraging discussions, and assigning readings in interesting ways, but again, these students had to emerge as writers on their own. All forms of growth stemmed from within the students—I merely provided an atmosphere that encouraged this growth. Indeed, as an instructor in both ESL and EFL settings, I am not an untouchable authority, but rather a moderator. Through the assumption of the role of moderator, I facilitate my students' growth. In the various academic settings I am a part of, I strive to employ this tenet in my teaching practices. Contexts vary for each individual, so I attempt to organize all activities around the students in order to encourage them to find within themselves and each other that which they need to grow. As an ESL/EFL instructor, I employ such a methodology by providing a situation in which students are given adequate time to view their peers' work and to receive feedback on their work as well. In an ESL/EFL class with twenty students and one teacher, this is a necessity—were I simply to lecture, valuable time that is needed to practice the language would be lost.

The most successful learning situations in my classroom are motivated by peer discussion and modeling. As a writing instructor, this methodology has remained consistent: I view myself as a facilitator. Students seem to grow the most from working amongst their peers and responding to one another's thoughts. They are allowed a great amount of time to share their reflections, ideas, and writing, which perpetuates the learning process. With group work, in-class presentations, peer review, and invention work, I find that my students encourage and enable growth not only among themselves, but also for me. This growth has taken the form of bettering my teaching practices and techniques and improving my skills as a writer, reader, and critical thinker. By providing an atmosphere that allowed a dialogic relationship to emerge between and among my students and me, I learned which teaching practices worked best and which needed to be reconstructed and/or modified. I find myself employing techniques in my own scholastic work that I first presented to my students and that proved successful. In the past, I was less of a process-oriented writer—I would often (as many of my students once did) simply write a final draft of a paper the day before it was due. Now I am much more aware of the need to organize carefully before drafting—and this realization is due to the experiences with my students this past semester.

Teaching Philosophy

Laura L. Nutten
Arizona State University

Laura Nutten, an experienced teaching associate and a graduate student in literature, explains how theory informs her practice. Further, she makes connections between her teaching in composition and in literature.

From my first introduction to theories of pedagogy, I have been attracted to the ideas of Paulo Freire, David Bartholomae ("Inventing," "Writing," and with Petrosky, *Ways of Reading*), and Benjamin Bloom. As a result, my approach to teaching and my understanding of my roles and responsibilities as a teacher are, I believe, strongly influenced by these three individuals.

Further, since the goals of the many courses I teach vary, and the needs of my students are not static, I have found that a willingness to be flexible, to adjust my approach to meet those changing demands, is essential.

Though my teaching is probably not as "hands off" as Freire's "problem posing" approach, which asks instructors to step back, turn over the authority in the classroom to the students, and make them the centers of discovery and knowledge, I do try to direct my students toward the path of self-discovery as much as possible. I am aware, however, that not all students respond well to that approach and need a little more direct instruction for learning to occur. Further, I firmly believe that some things must be taught. In a writing classroom, for example, I think it is my responsibility to teach students what an introduction, body, and conclusion are and to teach them what grammar is. I also feel a responsibility to teach them the differences between and interactions among various rhetorical modes such as narrative, analysis, argument, and so forth. This information is imperative to their success not only in the writing classroom but outside of it as well, both in other classes and in their future careers. But once I have explained what these things are, I enjoy turning the discussion back over to my students to let them discuss and discover why these things are important and why they should learn how to use them. Such student-led discussions are invaluable for empowering students—for helping them feel that the class is their class and that they have some say in how things are done, what they will learn, and how the course material is of value to them. Student-led discussions are also an opportunity for me to learn. Based on the content and tone of the discussions, I can often assess whether students have successfully processed the information and concepts introduced to them. In a basic writing class I taught last semester, for example, I had assigned as homework some reading from the textbook about various rhetorical modes. I spent the first fifteen minutes or so of the class going over the reading. Then I broke the class into groups and asked each group to prepare a brief presentation on one of the modes. As I moved around the classroom, I noticed that the group preparing the presentation on classification was not talking much. After a brief interaction with them, I discovered that no one in the group was really clear yet on what classification was. We turned to the book, looked up a few things together, discussed a couple of examples, and suddenly the light dawned. One of the students took over and explained to the rest of the group what she understood classification to be, using her own example. Her explanation helped the others in the group to understand, and their group presentation, in turn, helped the rest of the class. Had I not broken the students into groups and asked them to discuss the material on their own, I might not have learned there was a lack of understanding until it turned up in their drafts.

I also see student-led discussions as a way for both the students and myself to learn about other social, cultural, and racial groups. Indeed, embedded in my teaching philosophy is a deep awareness and appreciation of the diversity found at the university. I consider the wide range of voices in my classrooms stimulating and exciting, and often make use of it to quicken students' critical thinking skills. I think it is important to let all students in my class have a voice, to express how their personal experiences affect what they know, what they have learned, and how they perceive social and educational issues. Often, the classroom is the only place many of these students interact with members of different cultural and racial groups, so it is important to use the classroom as an opportunity to build bridges of understanding. Exploring a public issue, a community problem, or a piece of literature from a number of perspectives is an excellent way to do this. An added benefit is that students learn to engage issues, problems, and literatures with a wider focus, to take the perspectives of others into account, and to think critically about their own beliefs and reasons for holding them.

Though my students' beliefs may be different from my own, and the reasons they have for seeking an education vary tremendously, I recognize and appreciate that most students have the same expectations for my class—to improve their English-language skills. To that end, I am not afraid to challenge my students, to set the bar high, while giving them the skills to meet the challenge (I think Bartholomae's influence on my pedagogy is evident here). For example, I often assign Paulo Freire's "The Banking Concept of Education" as the first reading assignment in my first-year composition course. Though the students sometimes find this difficult reading, they are also able to relate to what Freire coins "the banking concept" of education—wherein instructors see their students as passive, empty vessels waiting to be filled—because most of the students have had this type of experience sometime during their educational careers. I use the article to begin the critical thinking process, to get the students thinking about how they have been taught in the past and about what they should expect from my class—very few "deposit"-type lectures and a lot of group discussions, student-led discussions, and self-discovery. I want them to understand from the get-go that I consider my first responsibility as their instructor to be teaching them how to teach themselves—in other words, that I will challenge them to take responsibility for their own education.

For some students, this challenge may be intimidating at first. My training and experience, however, have prepared me to work well with these students. Though both my M.A. and Ph.D. are in English literature, I have taken many rhetoric, composition, and linguistics courses, including composition theory (Problems in English), writing for teachers of English (Advanced Expository Writing), American English (Language Differences), rhetorical theory (Stylistics), and history of the English language (Studies of the English Language). I have continued my professional development by organizing and attending a variety of workshops geared toward pedagogy, in both the composition classroom and the literature classroom. Among these were two workshops which provided specialized training for teaching in a computer classroom, training I have subsequently used to teach three computer-aided first-year composition classes. Further, I have always viewed my research as a means of augmenting my teaching and continually look for ways to bring the discoveries I have made into my classroom. These educational experiences have given me the tools to reach students who may be struggling. I have successfully taught many basic writing courses and have worked with illiterate adults through Literacy Volunteers of America. I approach both settings with the same basic philosophy I bring to my more advanced classes—I invite the students to reach a bit, to challenge themselves, while I help them recognize and believe they can do the work. These students, not surprisingly, usually need a little extra help coming to that recognition—their confidence in their academic skills is often limited. To help, I generally design each step in my lesson plans to target one type of learner (e.g., the innovative learner, the analytic learner, the commonsense learner, and the dynamic learner), and I think students of all types gain by the progression. Students are challenged at some levels, while they gain confidence as they master the level geared toward them. Thus, there is a built-in reward system. More specifically, as I reflect on my actual teaching process, it is apparent that the progression through most of my lesson plans parallels the hierarchy set forth in Bloom's taxonomy. I begin by helping students find meaning in the course material by connecting the material to concrete experiences and examining and analyzing those experiences. Some sort of demonstration here to generate interest works well, as does asking students to share their own personal experiences. I might, for example, come into class and lecture for a bit, without letting the students participate at all—e.g., overdo "I'm the expert here" attitude (very uncharacteristic of me—they know something is up)—then explain to the students that I had just illustrated the banking concept of education. Or I might ask students to share their past educational experiences—both experiences they have enjoyed and those they have not. The idea is to get students anxiously anticipating the information that will follow, to make them want to learn it for some specific purpose.

Next, I "teach" the new material to my students. New concepts and/or information are presented to the students in an organized and sequenced way. This is where concepts are defined and illustrated—e.g., given order. To continue with the earlier example, I would go over Freire's article with them closely, paragraph by paragraph, and help them make sense of it (in a literature class, I would take this same sort of an approach with whatever new text they had read for class). We would define terms, discuss concepts, and dissect problematic ideas. This step can happen in the classroom, as an informal lecture or class discussion, or outside of class time with reading, videos, audiotapes, and so forth (depending on the nature of the new material). These first two steps seem to coincide with Bloom's levels of knowledge and comprehension. Students are exposed to the information; process it by means of small-group discussions, in-class activities, whole-class discussions, and journal writing; and store it for later use.

Once they have learned the new information "in theory," students are asked to work with the material in practice. This is a time to experiment, to see what happens when material is worked first within a given structure, then outside of it. Bloom's levels of application and analysis come into play here. Students are asked to apply general principles to specific, practical situations, and the outcomes of these applications encourage students to look at how the different parts of the equation fit together. Again, I use group discussions and activities, class discussions, and journal assignments to get them thinking about and working with the material. I often ask my students, for example, to come up with a list of responsibilities for me as their instructor and themselves as students based on the Freire article and our discussions concerning it. Then we use that list as a contract of sorts for the rest of the semester.

Next, students are asked to create something new, both conceptually and structurally, out of the "givens." They get to synthesize all the information gathered through presentation and experiment and make something of their own with it. These are their formal writing assignments. To continue with the Freire example, I would ask students to write an essay about what education means to them. They would be asked to reference their own personal experiences, invited to agree or disagree with Freire, and encouraged to come up with their own definitions, philosophies, and goals. I encourage interaction and group work at this stage as well, so that students can learn to recognize the difference between ideological dead ends and freeways by discussing and debating with other students. During these discussions, students will often challenge each other to remember material presented earlier in the course. In peer-review groups, for example, students will often look for their peers' essays to include skills taught/learned over the course of the semester, not just the last few weeks. They often point out to each other when these things are missing. This is a great help to me because students become aware of the absences and often fix them before I see the drafts. Further, helping their peers helps all of the students solidify more fully the material in their own minds.

Finally, I prompt all of my students to reflect on why they have made certain choices about what to include or leave out of their formal essays, why they have organized material in a particular way, and why they have developed their particular writing processes. In a sense, I invite the students to teach themselves by paying attention to what they do when they write and why they do it in that particular way. These last steps also parallel Bloom's taxonomy, integrating both synthesis and evaluation.

This progression of introducing and processing new information encourages students of all sorts to engage the material with confidence. While my teaching style is challenging, I am always accessible and supportive. I meet regularly with my students one on one to keep in touch with them and to assess how well they are grasping the course materials. I encourage students to drop by my office at any time to talk about their progress in the course or just to chat. These meetings give me the opportunity to get to know my students (which I enjoy), and they let students get to know me too (which I think they enjoy). I am a dedicated and accomplished teacher, and, because I always put the needs of my students first and go out of my way to help them whenever possible, I believe I am well liked. Having this kind of a relationship with my students is important to my pedagogy because without their trust I cannot as effectively help them to learn.

Works Cited

Bartholomae, David. "Inventing the University." *When a Writer Can't Write: Studies in Writer's Block and Other Composing-Process Problems*. Ed. Mike Rose. New York: Guilford, 1985. 134–65.

———. "Writing on the Margins: The Concept of Literacy in Higher Education." *A Sourcebook for Basic Writing Teachers*. Ed. Teresa Enos. New York: Random, 1987. 63–83.

Bartholomae, David, and Anthony Petrosky. *Ways of Reading: An Anthology for Writers*. 3rd ed. Boston: Bedford, 1993.

Bloom, Benjamin. *Taxonomy of Educational Objectives: The Classification of Educational Goals*. New York: McKay, 1969.

Freire, Paulo. *Pedagogy of the Oppressed*. New York: Continuum, 1981.

Chapter 13

Teaching Matters of Grammar, Usage, and Style

The chapter begins with Keith Rhodes, who provides a context for discussing the teaching of grammar and usage. Other contributors then describe various methods they use to incorporate the teaching of grammar and mechanics in order to develop students' style. Analyzing literary texts, using sentence-combining and sentence-expanding exercises, and evaluating sentence structure can all be useful in building on students' abilities to write with clarity and style.

A Cautionary Introduction

KEITH RHODES

Missouri Western State College

*Keith Rhodes's introduction sets the stage for this chapter by
discussing key issues in what is often one of the most polemical
aspects of writing instruction, the teaching of grammar.*

Most writing teachers, myself included, do include lessons on
usage, grammar, and correctness in their own composition courses.
Indeed, many writing teachers—again, myself included—will read
this section more eagerly than they will read any other in this
collection. Even so, we should feel ambivalent at best about the
wisdom of including such a section in a book of this kind.

The reasons may seem simply political. The general public
views first-year college composition as by rights mainly a grammar course. Many who hold that view may have only a foggy
idea of what they mean by "grammar." But whatever grammar
is, most everybody is for it, and most everybody is fairly convinced that it can be taught directly and simply by anyone deserving of a bachelor's degree in English. So long as that perception
stands, the still-emerging discipline of composition will never get
a chance to do the full range of good that such a discipline could
do. College composition programs will be underfunded; they will
be undervalued; they will be caught up in "administrivia"; they
will be blamed for every real or perceived flaw in student writing. Any help this section might offer us as classroom teachers
could be overwhelmed by the harm it does in maintaining this
powerfully destructive myth. We should mind the first law of
holes: When you find yourself in a hole, the first thing you should
do is stop digging. In reality, the average first-year composition
course is already much more deeply mired in a grammar pit than
it ought to be; thus, we ought to shift our focus openly and point-
edly to other facets of writing, even to the point of eschewing
public mention of things remotely like grammar lessons.

If that sounds like radical politics taken to the extreme, we
need only focus on the other side of the balance: exactly what
good do we accomplish when we do focus on correct language?

The very existence of this section implies to the general public, even if indirectly, that there is such a thing as "good grammar teaching." We have little if any explicit evidence for that implicit claim, regardless of what definition of *grammar* anyone might choose. Certainly, that claim is not supported by the combination of extensive research and sophisticated theorizing supporting the opposing claim: that grammatical work of any kind is overrated at best and possibly counterproductive. Public supporters of grammar lessons typically satisfy themselves by picking at that opposing record, presuming that if grammar lessons cannot be proven ineffective, by default we ought to resort to them. The political and historical sources of that highly suspect presumption are complex and have been discussed fully elsewhere (Daniels; Connors). The argument really need not be that involved, however. Once we level the scales and look at the general weight of the evidence (Hillocks; Braddock, Lloyd-Jones, and Schoer; Holden), the most likely hypothesis is that students get little advantage out of anything remotely like grammar lessons. Ultimately, that suspect presumption in favor of grammar lessons turns out to be the most "substantial" point in favor of any sort of concerted work on grammar, usage, and correctness.

Supporters of work that the general public would call "basic grammar" often seek further support in auspiciously titled books by Rei Noguchi *(Grammar and the Teaching of Writing)*, Susan Hunter and Ray Wallace *(The Place of Grammar in Writing Instruction)*, and Constance Weaver *(Teaching Grammar in Context)*. But little in that canonical troika offers any real support for grammar lessons, as those who read beyond the titles will find. Noguchi carefully and openly conditions an extended hypothesis about grammar teaching on this unproven, highly unlikely assumption: "If grammar is potentially transferable to style, and if [ineffective grammar teaching and learning] are negated in some way, then formal instruction in grammar can be of help in the area of style" (12). We should note that this is essentially the same logical formula by which wishes become horses. Hunter and Wallace collect articles that largely explore what else grammar study might be good for other than improving usage in student writing. Weaver's astute devaluation of grammar-based teaching actually belies the title of her book in the most common, public understanding of her terms—though of course "insiders" quickly get her point about enhancing written style and correctness through methods other than grammar lessons. In the end, it is difficult to remain both accurate and charitable in characterizing the resort to these works as support for grammar lessons.

The ultimate fallback argument for grammar lessons is that if we do not teach grammar, we do not care about student success in the "real world." To the contrary, a focus on grammar still has much more to do with an elite, hothouse English-class unreality than with any "real" world results. The reality is that no grammar lesson of any kind has ever been shown to create real-world success. Even the more enlightened sort of turn to enhancing grammatical writing has produced at best a highly speculative and anecdotal record. Thus, those who actually attend to and care about the "real world" of student success should be among the most resistant to grammar lessons.

To abandon grammar lessons is not to abandon successful, effective writing—admittedly, a point some opponents of grammar lessons need to heed more carefully. All writing teachers should aim for a powerful transformation of the meaning-making and communicative abilities of our students, but we rarely get enough support to do this as well as we could. But part of why the discipline of composition teaching does not get enough support is that a powerful public identification of "composition" with "grammar" obscures the very concept of fully "disciplined" composition. We would sacrifice little for much if we would work hard to disconnect that identification. There would be value in that disconnection if the efforts to improve the correctness of student writing were only as innovative and informed as those we find in better composition classrooms. Thus, it may well be that this section of this book is just another variant of a siren song, luring us once more onto the rocks.

Of course, I cannot resist reading this section any more than most of you can. Most of us love grammar, love both the elegance of its rules when they work and the sublime moments when meaning pushes through the breaks in them. With guilty pleasure, I will most likely try everything here, dreaming a gambler's dream of the perfect system for beating the odds. Like nearly all writing teachers, I know viscerally that something in the argument against grammar rings hollow, that some day we will find a way back to a language about language that can support better writing. Maybe that way leads through here. Still, we must consider carefully what this eternally springing hope is costing us along the way. To the extent that, like Weaver, most of us are seeking more grammatical writing through means that bear no relationship to the grammar lessons of old, we should at least consider a rhetoric of titling and explanation that does not sustain the myth of composition as mainly work on "grammar" (or its euphemisms). We should consider carefully whether it might not have been possible to disperse every good suggestion that follows to sections bearing aggressively rhetorical titles, as would have been possible with nearly every article in Hunter and Wallace's collection. In sum, we should read on, but dialogically, alert to what our very attention communicates.

Works Cited

Braddock, Richard, Richard Lloyd-Jones, and Lowell Schoer. *Research in Written Composition*. Urbana, IL: NCTE, 1963.

Connors, Robert J. "Grammar in American College Composition: An Historical Overview." *The Territory of Language: Linguistics, Stylistics, and the Teaching of Composition*. Ed. Donald McQuade. 2nd ed. Carbondale: Southern Illinois UP, 1986. 3–22.

Daniels, Harvey A. *Famous Last Words: The American Language Crisis Reconsidered*. Carbondale: Southern Illinois UP, 1983.

Hillocks, George. *Research on Written Composition: New Directions for Teaching*. New York: NCRE/Urbana, IL: NCTE, 1986.

Holden, Michael. "Effectiveness of Two Approaches to Teaching Writing in Improving Students' Knowledge of English Grammar." ERIC, 1994. ED 366 006.

Hunter, Susan, and Ray Wallace, eds. *The Place of Grammar in Writing Instruction: Past, Present, Future*. Portsmouth, NH: Heinemann, 1995.

Noguchi, Rei R. *Grammar and the Teaching of Writing: Limits and Possibilities*. Urbana, IL: NCTE, 1991.

Weaver, Constance. *Teaching Grammar in Context*. Portsmouth, NH: Boynton/Cook, 1996.

And the Question Is This—"What Lessons Can We, as Writers, Take from This Reading for Our Own Writing?"

ELIZABETH HODGES

Virginia Commonwealth University

Elizabeth Hodges shows how conducting detailed analyses of the mechanics and grammar in literary texts can be useful in developing students' writing skills.

As teachers of writing, we have to have some working definition of what writing is, as well as some working sense of who our students are as writers. My sense of my students is that they are largely unpracticed writers and readers. I define writing as a craft, not an art, because a craft is something one can develop and an art seems to be the gift of only a few lucky individuals, unattainable to most. This definition has helped me learn how to use readings to teach writing, as well as how to come up with a sensible response to those students and composition theorists who question the place of professional writing in a composition class. I perceive my students as unpracticed because I believe that most of them can become competent crafters of writing if they work to develop their abilities as writers and readers. A lot goes into such development, but it mostly comes down to learning crucial lessons about writing at points when one can make use of—apply—those lessons in one's own practice. A major source of lessons that I find tremendously powerful is the readings we discuss in class. Some might respond to that statement by saying, "But where's the news? We have traditionally used readings, read*ers*, to teach writing. Readings serve as models." This may be true—but models of what, and how do we get the lessons of those models to transfer?

Readings can serve as models of modes, though teaching modes has, happily, lost the dominance it once held in writing classrooms. Readings can serve as rhetorical models, which emphasize the communicative nature of writing, specifically the role of audience in writing, but as Peter Elbow argues in "Closing My Eyes as I Speak," sometimes the need to consider audience gets in the way of writing as thinking (50). Audience invoked too soon can cramp a writer's style, a writer's craft. From my perspective, I want my students to focus on themselves as writers, on their habits, their craft, their subjects, from their angles, for their own reasons. Readings can also serve as models of the range of possible results within a genre, thus opening students' eyes to possibilities and freeing them from the narrow scope of written shapes to which most of them are accustomed. For me, then, key words are *options, possibilities, choices,* and *crafts.* As Ann Berthoff wrote many years ago, "Composing involves the writer in making choices all along the way and thus has social and political implications: we aren't free unless we know how to choose" (22). To teach students that they have options to consider and choices to make, I use readings.

By the time my students enter my first-year college writing classroom, a lot has gone on to dissuade them from seeing themselves as writers, and a lot has gone on that has created them as passive readers—readers who do not interact aesthetically with what they read. They read to decode, to get meaning. When I ask how many *hear* a voice in texts when they read, rarely do I see any raised hands. And because they are not caught up in the conversations writers are seeking to hold with them as readers, they are bored and resistant. It's hard enough for them to get meaning, much less anything like writing lessons. So when I tell them that there are writing lessons in everything we will read for the semester, in their own writing as well as in that of the professionals who fill our reader, they are bemused. When I tell them they will learn to read like writers (in order to write like readers), they roll their eyes. And then we begin.

I think that to make my point here I will focus on a few passages that share lessons about sentences, pointing as I go to other lessons as well. Remember, the operative question is, "What lessons can we, as writers, take from this reading for our own writing?"

Scenario 1

We are reading Langston Hughes's often anthologized "Salvation." To get the text off the page, several of us take turns reading the following passage aloud:

> My aunt told me that when you were saved you saw a light, and something happened to you inside! And Jesus came into your life! And God was with you from then on! She said you could see and hear and feel Jesus in your soul. I believed her. I have heard a great many old people say the same thing and it seemed to me they ought to know. So I sat there calmly in the hot, crowded church, waiting for Jesus to come to me. (17)

"What do we hear?" we ask ourselves after several readings. Most agree that it is hard to read this passage aloud without hearing the voice of an excited child. We push further and agree that the voice is child*like,* not child*ish.* I talk a bit about the distinction between the two and how it can be easy to slip into a childish voice when we try to recreate our child selves. So how does Hughes's writing evoke that excited, childlike voice? What lessons can we learn here that will help render childhood experiences effectively? I ask the class to make observations about the writing—about sentences, words, punctuation—that might add up to the voice we hear.

Four of Hughes's seven sentences are short and simple. They read fast. Breathless. Even his three longer sentences are written so that they read in short units, sustaining breathlessness. In sentence one, the units are: "My aunt told me that when you are saved you saw a light" and "and something happened to you inside!" Sentence six ("I have heard . . .") contains two relatively short independent clauses connected by *and.* Aloud, sentence seven breaks into two short parts between the clause ("So I sat there calmly in the hot, crowded church") and ("waiting for Jesus to come to me"). But short units alone don't evoke the child. My students observe that Hughes begins two sentences with *and* and that he uses *and* six times in this paragraph. Some observe that past teachers they've had would correct that. So why has he used *and* so much? Why has he opted to write, "you could see and hear and feel Jesus" rather than using a comma instead of the first *and*? They come up with answers. Repeating *and* six times in this paragraph not only helps establish the fast, breathless pace, but when it begins the sentences, it also truly imitates the way children talk when they are excited, using *and* to hold the floor, going on, gushing, breathless. Students note that with the exclamation points, the simple language, and Hughes's making clear that he understood that he would experience the light and the coming of Jesus as something concrete, the illusion of the child is complete.

We return to the question of what makes the voice childlike and not childish and determine that the answer lies in the fact that Hughes does not overrely on this voice. The preceding paragraph sets the intellectual and situational contexts, using a range of sentence structures and length, many more sophisticated, more adult, often containing the reflection of the adult Hughes. The paragraph I've quoted sets up the child's emotional context. The following paragraph carries us into the church, with rich description catching the sounds of the preacher and his flock. But in the passage quoted here, we hear and sense the child Hughes was, believing and naive. We need no more and no less of this voice for him to make his point. The voice is childlike because it contrasts with his more adult voice in the rest of the essay.

Scenario 2

Short sentences and sentence units are not just the domain of the child. We are reading Judy Ruiz's "Oranges and Sweet Sister Boy," an essay rich with lessons about how to keep thematic threads alive, how to tell or weave stories within a larger narrative, and how to make metaphors work for us. In paragraphs one and two, we meet the speaker:

> I am sleeping, hard, when the telephone rings. It's my brother, and he's calling to say that he is now my sister. I feel something fry a little, deep behind my eyes. Knowing how sometimes dreams get mixed up with not-dreams, I decide to do a reality test at once. "Let me get a cigarette," I say, knowing that if I reach for a

Marlboro and it turns into a trombone or a snake or anything
else on the way to my lips that I'm out there in the large world of
dreams.

The cigarette stays a cigarette. I light it. I ask my brother to
run that stuff by me again. (225)

Ruiz's voice is that of an adult, wakened abruptly to news
that trips her up. No child is speaking here. My students describe
her further as "sort of tough," "worldly," "cool." There is a jerki-
ness to the rhythm of the prose in this passage that reflects Ruiz's
content. Her use of short sentences or short units within sentences mimics the phase-by-phase process she experiences when
awakened by the phone from deep sleep and given news that is
difficult to hear. One student comments that there is also a sort
of "jazz" to the rhythm, observing that maybe that's why she
sounds cool to us. Another points out that the persona her voice
evokes has to do with "simple words, some slang, some cool
images."

When we read this aloud, some of the first readers do not
pay attention to the commas in the first sentence, and one student who volunteers points that out and reads to emphasize the
effect of the commas, many of which are optional. This raises a
useful question about the effect of commas and another question
about why, since the commas are optional, Ruiz chose to include
them. I ask, "What do commas do anyway?" My students have
answers—not in terms of comma rules, but something more like
comma sense. "They flag us to pause," "like yield signs," and
when "fencing" off one word, they suggest we "read it by itself."
"They call attention to parts of sentences." "Like paragraph in-
dentations say 'a change is coming.'"

We talk about how the sentences would differ, how the voice
might differ, if Ruiz had chosen *not* to use commas where she
has, and that leads us to diction. What if she had used not *hard*
but *deeply*. *Hard* sounds like what it means; the *d* at the end
stops us momentarily, but significantly, as we read. We cannot
slur from *hard* into *when* as we could from the softer *deeply* into
when.

When I ask my students to describe Ruiz's voice, they imagine her as tough, cool, and calm because of what she tells us
about herself. She smokes Marlboros. In the face of the news she

gets, she doesn't rush into things. She takes a moment "to chill." She uses informal phrases such as "a reality test," "fry a little, deep behind my eyes" (which reminds some students of those antidrug commercials, "This is your brain on drugs"), and "run that stuff by me again." Stuff. All of these elements create the scene and her persona. Her toughness of voice is in the terseness of her presentation of content. It reads choppily because of the sentences, and the one sentence that is longer and more fluent suggests that Ruiz might have experience with the fine line that sometimes exists between dreams and reality—that sentence raises the same question about her use of *or* that we asked about Hughes's use of *and*. Why does she use *or* between "a trombone" and "a snake" where she could have placed a comma? In fact, where has she not put commas that she could have, and what would be the effect of their presence in her sentences as opposed to the effect of their absence?

If I sound like I'm going too far with this attention to detail, let me say in my defense that my students love this, and they quickly catch on. They learn lessons about what goes into written style; they learn lessons about the rhetoric of punctuation, about the wiles of diction, about uses of italics for organizational purposes (see, for example, Judith Ortiz Cofer's "Silent Dancing" as well as Ruiz's "Oranges and Sweet Sister Boy"). In Langston Hughes's "Salvation," we pause at a passage of dialogue and students generate observations and, yes, some rules for punctuating and indenting direct discourse. Even lessons in documentation, particularly how to interpret it and the logic of it, abound in readings.

Scenario 3

We are reading Barry Lopez's "Stone Horse," which offers a dramatic change from the shorter sentences we've looked at in Ruiz and Hughes.

> The deserts of southern California, the high, relatively cooler and wetter Mojave and the hotter, dryer Sonoran to the south of it, carry the signatures of many cultures. Prehistoric rock drawings

in the Mojave's Coso Range, probably the greatest concentration of petroglyphs in North America, are at least three thousand
years old. Big game hunting cultures that flourished six or seven
thousand years before that are known from broken spear tips,
choppers, and burins left scattered along the shores of great Pleis-
tocene lakes, long since evaporated. Weapons and tools discovered at China Lake may be thirty thousand years old; and worked
stone from a quarry in the Calico Mountains is, some argue,
evidence that human beings were here more than two hundred
thousand years ago. (1–2)

Reading this passage aloud, my students struggle and get frustrated. "Bor—ing," they say. "Sounds like a history book." "It's
hard to read." But why? "Because of the words." "Lots of names
I don't know." "The sentences." So I ask them to tell me about
the sentences, and they struggle to do so until I ask a classic and
familiar question: where are the subject and the verb in each sentence? *This* is a question they can answer from long practice, but
answering it in this context lets them begin to talk about how
much Lopez has imbedded into the sentences and then to observe that the sentences are actually all structured quite similarly
and that that actually creates a rhythm that is smooth and lull-
ing. They begin to hear the voice as similar to the voices in PBS
documentaries. It's "formal," "knowledgeable," "like a teacher,"
and, yes, "bor—ing." I ask them to find two places in their next
drafts where sentences like this would suit and to try to imitate
what Lopez is doing. We talk a bit about whether we actually
need to know the places and entities Lopez mentions, and we
decide not. He is either going to go further and teach us about
these things or he is mentioning them to be concrete—perhaps,
one student adds, "because they sound dramatic. Documentaries
always sound dramatic."

The usefulness of Lopez's essay is that it is divided into three
sections and each has a different predominant voice. In order to
call students' attention to this (and to give them hope in case
they find the first paragraph off-putting), I read the first sentences of each section:

1. The deserts of southern California, the high, relatively cooler
   and wetter Mojave, and the hotter, dryer Sonoran to the south
   of it, carry the signatures of many cultures. (1)

2. A BLM archeologist told me, with understandable reluctance, where to find the intaglio. (5)

3. A short distance away I stopped the car in the middle of the road to make a few notes. (14)

I ask them to note, as they read the entire piece, elements in the writing that create these different voices, as well as to consider as they read why Lopez has divided the essay into sections and why he has shifted voice from section to section. Another essay that invites the same questions, and very productively so, is Richard Selzer's "Lessons from the Art."

The essays I have discussed here are often anthologized, though I have documented them from their original sources. But any good collection of readings offers a rich variety of writers who can become our co-teachers in the classroom if we ask students to pay attention to how the mechanics and grammar influence the meaning of the writing.

Some final thoughts about teaching writing and reading for writing lessons: a major challenge for teachers of writing is making sure that writing is the subject matter of their courses. While textbooks with advice for inexperienced writers abound, students are often unable to relate that advice to their own texts, just as they often can't relate to texts that provide prescriptive rules for grammar and mechanics, and in both cases, the vocabulary that such texts use can be more troublesome than not. Students don't understand what that vocabulary means in any applicable way: while the steps for writing processes or the rules for correctness might be familiar to students, acting those steps out in authentic ways and applying those rules to their own writing does not come naturally. They often have not had opportunities to experience writing as a craft, and that is what they need to experience in order to evolve beyond the nonwriters they believe themselves to be. Likewise, composition readers can either help make writing the subject of the writing classroom, or they can help us avoid talking about writing in more than general ways. The fact is, talk about writing in ways that help students learn about writing and themselves as writers is a difficult discourse for many teachers to develop, perhaps because it demands that we name the specifics of writing differently than we have been trained to do—not using the vocabulary of grammar and mechanics, of rhetorical modes, or of literary analysis, but a vocabulary of craft that shows the dynamic connection between the written word and its effect on the making of meaning. I have found that while this vocabulary certainly incorporates terms we teachers of writing and writers have long used, it does so in ways that make their meaning vital. I have found, too, that this vocabulary of craft is very much made up of contributions from students and thus varies from course to course, semester to semester, as much as my students vary. But because they learn to take active roles in developing our vocabulary of craft, in naming the traits they are learning to see in what they read, they better understand our discussions about writing and are much more likely to act on that understanding in their own writing.

Works Cited

Berthoff, Ann E. *The Making of Meaning: Metaphors, Models, and Maxims for Writing Teachers.* Portsmouth, NH: Boynton/Cook, 1981.

Cofer, Judith Ortiz. "Silent Dancing." *Silent Dancing: A Partial Remembrance of a Puerto Rican Childhood.* Houston: Arte Publico, 1990. 87–98.

Elbow, Peter. "Closing My Eyes as I Speak: An Argument for Ignoring Audience." *College English* 49 (1987): 50–69.

Hughes, Langston. "Salvation." *The Big Sea.* New York: Farrar, Straus, and Giroux, 1968. 17–19.

Lopez, Barry. "Stone Horse." *Crossing Open Ground.* New York: Vintage, 1989. 1–18.

Ruiz, Judy. "Oranges and Sweet Sister Boy." *The Best American Essays 1989.* Ed. Geoffrey Wolff and Robert Atwan. New York: Ticknor, 1989. 225–33.

Selzer, Richard. "Lessons from the Art." *Mortal Lessons: Notes on the Art of Surgery.* New York: Simon & Schuster, 1976. 37–48.

Empowering Sentences

NICHOLAS J. KAROLIDES

University of Wisconsin–River Falls

Nicholas Karolides explains how he uses sentence-combining and sentence-expanding exercises to help students discover ways to enhance the content and structure of their writing.

Analysis of first-year students' compositions often reveals a poverty of content and a paucity of sophisticated structures. Too many student writers have not achieved the level of maturation of structure identified by Kellogg Hunt in his research into the developmental patterns of syntactic structure of the sentences of schoolchildren. While insufficiency of content development may seem divorced from structural immaturity, they are potentially linked. Immature sentences are often barren, devoid of clarifying detail, exploratory thought, or nuances of description—devoid of specification. Such details added to a sentence can fertilize its basic thought. Francis Christensen and Bonniejean Christensen put it this way: "The teacher can use the idea of levels of structure to urge the student to add further details to what he has already produced, so that the structure itself becomes an aid to discovery" (24).

The premise of this essay—and the activities illustrated—is that there is a connection between content and structures, that form and function can come together meaningfully and expressively. When I have taught first-year composition, I have used sentence-combining and sentence-expanding principles and practices to foster this connection and to advance both the development of thought in and through writing and the concomitant dexterity with and control of structure.

Sentence combining emerged as a method of English classroom instruction in the mid-1970s on the heels of Frank O'Hare's research with seventh-grade students. His intent was to measure whether "sentence combining practice that was in no way dependent on the students' formal knowledge of transformational grammar would increase the normal rate of growth of syntactic maturity in the students' free writing" (35). Over a period of eight months, the experimental group completed nineteen lessons on sentence-combining techniques and practice. Subsequently, both the experimental and the control group wrote a variety of compositions, matched-paired samplings (pre- and postexperiment) that were evaluated by eight experienced English teachers.

Here are two sample exercises, lessons 8 and 20, respectively:

A.   As soon as he got to the Pearly Gates, Joe told St. Peter SOME-THING had never occurred to him.

The tires on his Jaguar might decay. (IT-THAT)

B.   As soon as he got to the Pearly Gates, Joe told St. Peter it had never occurred to him that the tires on his Jaguar might decay.

A.   SOMETHING irritated Albert.

The mechanic examined the carburetor carefully. ('S + LY + EXAMINATION)

Albert asked SOMETHING. (WHO)

SOMETHING would take so long. (HOW LONG)

He completes SOMETHING. (IT - FOR - TO)

He inspects the whole car. ('S + INSPECTION + OF)

B.   The mechanic's careful examination of the carburetor irritated Albert, who asked how long it would take for him to complete his inspection of the whole car.

The results were phenomenal: the experimental group experienced "highly significant growth" and "highly significant superiority" over the control group on all six factors; "the experimental group wrote well beyond the syntactic maturity level typical of eighth graders and, on five of the six factors of syntactic maturity, their scores were similar to those of twelfth graders" (66).

This study was replicated by other researchers with similar results. One of these researchers, Elray Pedersen, has written that sentence-combining practice improves semantic fluency—attending to, storing, and expressing more meaning in sentences;

conceptual fluency—competent formulation and expression of ideas and generalizations; logical fluency—use of appropriate words and sentences to define relationships among words and sentences; and grammatical fluency—structurally correct and free from spelling, punctuation, and mechanical errors. How and why these last two occur is not clear, but evidence of all of them is present in the studies.

Frank O'Hare's method of engaging students in sentence combining, obviously successful with seventh graders, seems stilted and stiff to me, given both my interactive teaching style and the nature of college students. I prefer a more open approach in which the writers decide how and what to combine rather than following the dictates of cues. My purposes reach beyond teaching familiarity with a range of structures and practicing them so as to habituate them. In addition, my goals are to cause students to recognize the several ways a group of base clauses can be combined, to consider these in relation to meaning, and to examine the influence of the selected combining words and strategies in eliciting these variances. An extension of this is the goal of understanding the repercussion of uniting one thought with another or two in terms of the interrelationships created and evoking direction of the thought. I want to make students more conscious of words and word order as they create nuances of meaning.

Each sentence-combining exercise consists of groups of sentences without cues. (I have used selections from William Strong's texts *[Sentence Combining* and *Sentence Combining and Paragraph Building]*; my own creations, sometimes from paragraphs in novels or essays; and student paragraphs. Also, Bonniejean Christensen provides explanations, sentences, prompts, and strategies in *The Christensen Method: Text and Workbook*.) Here is a sample from William Strong:

1.1. The quarterback crouched low.
1.2. The crouch was behind the center.
1.3. The quarterback glanced down the line.
1.4. The glancing was left and right.
1.5. The quarterback barked his signals.
1.6. The barking was sharp.

    1.7.   The quarterback took the snap.

    1.8.   The quarterback dropped straight back.

    1.9.   The ball was tucked against his thigh.

There are usually from three to ten groups of such sentences in one exercise, varying in difficulty.

My instructions are simple: all major ideas and words must be maintained; forms of words may be changed; articles, prepositions, and the like may be omitted; combining words may be added; and combining strategies may be created. (It rarely takes more than one or two exercises for students to know what to do.) While the students are processing the exercise, I meander about the room, looking over shoulders, noting which sentence group is emerging with many variations and unique constructions. A selection of these is written on the board by the authors. Generally, this part takes about fifteen minutes.

The key discussion occurs after the students have had an opportunity to examine the sentences. The focus is on meaning—variant meanings and nuances of meaning—and causes of the differences—word selection, word order. In this vein, we consider when one variant might be chosen over another. Important to this discussion is the identification of combining words and tactics, particularly those that have not previously made appearances. Its author is asked to comment about the why and how of its use. I call attention to the novelty, uniqueness, and level of sophistication of these sentences.

Applying these lessons to their own writings is, of course, the critical next stage. I use revision procedures—individual and peer critiquing—to focus on sentence strengthening—and original writing. I provide objects or identify situations, for example, for one or two paragraphs of practice.

My sense of these proceedings is that the students react to them as language puzzles. After realizing there is a purpose to the exercises, for the most part they respond with thoughtful energy. They learn from each other, so that after one of them, perhaps a more mature writer using a familiar form, stumbles on something, others tend to try it. This scenario is more effective in promoting responses and "copying" than my illustrating the combining tactics on the board would be.

Francis Christensen and Bonniejean Christensen approach the analysis and development of the sentence (and the paragraph) from a quite different direction. In contrast to sentence combining, they advocate sentence expanding (my term) in their *Notes toward a New Rhetoric*. They base this advocacy on their close inductive study of contemporary prose to establish rhetorical principles and to ascertain the structures of the sentences of the selected distinguished professional writers.

With regard to sentence structures, the Christensens' research reveals that "our faith in the subordinate clause and the complex sentence is misplaced and that we should concentrate on the sentence modifiers, or free modifiers" (xiii). Further, school grammars are confusing and misleading in the grammatical classification of sentences as simple, compound, and complex, asserting that the last is more mature than the others because it has a subordinate clause. A simple sentence, its base clause extended by free modifiers, can project complexity of thought; its construction requires mature writing skill. They note that this Hemingway sentence would be identified as "simple" by school grammars and rhetoric:

> George was coming down in the telemark position, kneeling, one leg forward and bent, the other trailing, his sticks hanging like some insect's thin legs, kicking up puffs of snow, and finally the whole kneeling, trailing figure coming around in a beautiful right curve, crouching, the legs shot forward and back, the body leaning out against the swing, the sticks accenting the curve like points of light, all in a wild cloud of snow.

The Christensens' "generative rhetoric" of a sentence concentrates on the cumulative sentence:

> The rhythm of good modern prose comes about equally from the multiple-tracking of coordinate constituents and the downshifting and backtracking of free modifiers. But the first comes naturally; the other [the cumulative sentence] needs coaxing along. (24)

The cumulative sentence is dynamic. It generates ideas by adding free modifiers primarily, but not limited to, the back of the sentence after the base clause, thus accumulating information as it develops. It contrasts sharply with the periodic sentence, promoted by traditional rhetoric; in this type, the sentence is front-loaded, saving the base clause for the end. The cumulative sentence is the structure of choice by twentieth-century writers of literary merit.

Four principles were identified through the Christensens' research: addition, direction of modification or movement, levels of generality or levels of abstraction, and texture.

Addition (a structural principle): Meaning emerges in a sentence from what you add to it—that is, the qualifiers added to substantiate the noun and the verb. "The noun, the verb, and the main clause serve merely as the base on which meaning will rise . . . . The modifier is the essential part of any sentence" (John Erskine, qtd. in Christensen and Christensen 26).

Direction of modification or direction of movement (a structural principle): The main clause advances the discussion. If it is preceded by a sentence modifier, which moves forward the modifier, the modifier anticipates the main clause, defining it in advance; if it is followed by sentence modifiers, which move the thought backward, they clarify, specify, or exemplify the main clause. The latter is the more usual pattern in contemporary prose. (The Christensens' exclude restrictive modifiers from their discussion; the position of the modifiers in the sentence is obligatory; their overuse is lifeless and "tone deaf.")

Levels of generality or levels of abstraction (a structural principle): The additions shift to a lower level of abstraction or generality. (These terms confuse my students; I substitute the word *specification,* which helps them understand the application of the principle.) The additions may all be at the same level (a two-level cumulative sentence) or on several levels (a multilevel cumulative sentence). See later examples.

Texture (a stylistic principle): The density or quantity of additions affects the quality of the prose. Ideally, the degree of density should relate to the pace of the text; variety of texture is a mark of effective prose.

My purposes in applying the Christensens' principles are, first, to promote cognizance of the potential and structure of the cumulative sentence and to advance the students' ability to construct them. Concomitantly, I want to hone their observation skills of language and the world—to see their surroundings with zoom-lens eyes, thus causing them to refine and particularize their written texts. By providing access to this sentence strategy, I wish to raise consciousness of language and thought, the consideration and reconsideration of their words, images, and ideas.

To develop understanding of the addition principle and initiate practice, I opt for a dynamic, student-interactive approach. A lecture and demonstration or workbook format won't do, especially for this motivational lesson. We build sentences, individually and together, and assess what meanings we interpret from them as we proceed.

I start with the barest of base clauses, a subject and a predicate: "He smiled." Then I add, "to himself," and then, "as he ran." After the original and each addition, I ask essentially the same questions: "What do we know from these words?" and "What don't we know?" As you would expect, the responses are minimal, quite denotative; the last word sparks some guesses.

In this first lesson, I introduce verb clusters, specifically, the participial phrase; it appears to be the easiest for first-year students to start with. (If I have preceded sentence-expanding exercises with sentence combining, it will be familiar.) My instructions are simple: "Using 'He smiled to himself as he ran' as a base clause, add a participial phrase—a phrase that begins with an "ing" word—to it." Then, I ask for volunteer sentences and put them on the board. There is no hesitation; they seem, indeed, eager to report their variations. Typical examples include:

anticipating seeing his girlfriend

hearing the shouts from the stands

imagining the surprise of his parents

I add to these my addition, chosen deliberately to propose a dramatic shift in venue: "clutching the string of pearls in his hand." The class is invariably intrigued by this unexpected turn; it leads readily to a discussion of the information—setting, activity, age—established or interpreted from the additions.

One more addition solidifies the cognitive and practical outcomes of this exercise. I ask them to add a second participial phrase to any one of the student sentences and also to mine. Here are some examples:

The race: leaning forward to break the tape with his chest
breathing evenly before the last spurt

The pearls: crunching the broken glass with his boots
ducking sideways into the alley

I add mine: shouting, "Mommy, Mommy, I found them! I
found them!"

The lesson concludes—or another lesson begins, if time runs out—with a discussion of Irwin Shaw's original sentence from "The Eighty-Yard Run":

> He smiled a little to himself as he ran, holding the ball lightly in front of him with his two hands, his knees pumping high, his hips twisting in the almost girlish run of a back in a broken field.

I lean the discussion toward the kinds of information—details—that Shaw provides to create the vision of this football player's action. Invariably, someone calls attention to the surprise of Shaw's detail—"almost girlish run." We talk about the impact of the surprise, the accuracy and preciseness of the image, and the value of the detail. In another lesson, I use this sentence to introduce the absolute phrase.

This opening exercise serves as a segue to others: practice with the verb cluster addition, including the sharpening of its details, language, and rhythms; introduction of other types of free modifiers and their practice. Part of the learning program involves peer-critiquing activities to spotlight sentences in students' own writing for revision attention. (This phase goes a long way toward ensuring that "revision" is much more than "correcting" errors.)

Three other free modifier types of additions are useful to teach: noun clusters, adjective clusters, and absolute phrases.

Noun cluster: a cluster of words consisting of a noun head and its modifiers forming a structural unit; e.g., "a blur of TV voices in the background," "a rapid intake of breath."

Adjective cluster: a cluster of words consisting of an adjective head with its modifiers forming a structural unit; e.g., "svelte in black silk and diamonds," "flamboyant as flamingos."

Absolute phrase: a condensed sentence that has been transformed into a phrase by omitting a (helping) verb or by changing the verb into a participle, e.g., "her feet at right angles," "his mouth trembling." (See also the previously quoted Irwin Shaw sentence.)

As the students progress, three other features need attention, that is, the three other principles. Direction of movement is easily understood and applied, there being but three positions for additions—before, in the middle, and after the base clause. The levels-of-abstraction (specification) principle is more difficult to comprehend. Christensen and Christensen provide numerous examples of the two-level sentence in a diagram format; these help students see the structures and the possibilities. Several of their examples suffice here:

Two-level sentences:

1. The jockeys sat bowed and relaxed,

    2. moving a little at the waist with the movement of their horses. (VC)

                                      KATHERINE ANNE PORTER

1. He could sail for hours,

    2. searching the blanched grasses below him with his telescopic eyes, (VC)

    2. gaining height against the wind, (VC)

    2. descending in mile-long, gently declining swoops when he curved and rode back, (VC)

    2. never beating a wing. (VC)

                                      WILLIAM VAN TILBURG CLARK

Multilevel sentences:

1. He dipped his hands in the dichloride solution and shook them,

2. a quick shake, (NC)

   3. fingers down, (Abs)

      4. like the fingers of a pianist above the keys. (PP)

                                SINCLAIR LEWIS

2. Calico-coated, (AC)

2. small-bodied, (AC)

   3. with delicate legs and pink faces in which their mismatched eyes rolled wild and subdued, (PP)

1. they huddled,

   2. gaudy motionless and alert, (A + A)

   2. wild as deer, (AC)

   2. deadly as rattlesnakes, (AC)

   2. quiet as doves. (AC)

                      WILLIAM FAULKNER

With all this attention to sentence expanding, there is some tendency for students to overindulge; their sentences may become cumbersome. The texture is too rich, weighted down with too many additions. In addition to precautionary statements, exercises in style in relation to purpose are necessary. Models of good writing, illustrating the ebb and flow of rich and spare sentences and changes to suit pace and tone, are useful, as are peer critiquing and read-aloud strategies.

In my experiences teaching first-year composition, I have found a curriculum including sentence-combining and sentence-expanding activities to be meritorious, in conjunction with teaching other composing principles; my students' writing improved. I contrast these experiences with previous efforts and results. Empowering students' sentences empowers them as writers.

Works Cited

Christensen, Bonniejean. *The Christensen Method: Text and Workbook.* New York: Harper, 1979.

Christensen, Francis, and Bonniejean Christensen. *Notes toward a New Rhetoric: Nine Essays for Teachers*. 2nd ed. New York: Harper, 1978.

Hunt, Kellogg W. "Early Blooming and Late Blooming Syntactic Structures." *Evaluating Writing: Describing, Measuring, Judging*. Ed. Charles R. Cooper and Lee Odell. Urbana, IL: NCTE, 1977. 91–104.

O'Hare, Frank. *Sentence Combining: Improving Student Writing without Formal Grammar Instruction*. Urbana, IL: NCTE, 1973.

Pedersen, Elray. "Frontiers of Sentence Combining Research." ERIC, 1979. ED 178 909.

Strong, William. *Sentence Combining: A Composing Book*. 2nd ed. New York: Random, 1983.

———. *Sentence Combining and Paragraph Building*. New York: Random, 1981.

Teaching Style

KAREN VAUGHT-ALEXANDER
Portland State University

Karen Vaught-Alexander links lessons in mechanics and grammar with issues of clarity in her teaching of writing.

Working with meaning and style interests my students more than working with grammar and mechanics. The intentional use of style for emphasis of ideas, for readability and visual impact, and for conciseness is often a new idea for student writers who view grammar and mechanics as "correctness." This fruitful approach provides the least proficient as well as the most proficient writers with ways to self-assess and improve writing for particular contexts. Writers find themselves looking at "writing errors" as opportunities to rethink and say more purposefully what they intend. The following is a set of activities I provide to my students in order to work toward clarity in their writing.

Creating Readability and Emphasis for Your Ideas

Modern English is a Subject-Verb-Object (SVO) language, its basic written unit the independent clause (IC) or sentence. When we read, we read for key ideas in the main IC. Initial or final placement creates the most emphasis, while middle placement of ideas in dependent clauses (DCs) can still be visually emphasized, with details and less important points modifying the IC with words or phrases.

Emphasizing Your Ideas for Maximum Readability and Meaning

Do you unintentionally deemphasize key ideas and emphasize minor details when you write? Do you communicate your intended meaning to your reader? To unlock the power of the English sentence, you need to be able to name and recognize key syntax and punctuation choices. Admittedly, we draw much of our ability to write from our stored reading and writing textual experiences. To use those "intuitions" productively, however, college writers need a motivating context for writing improvement and a long-term focus on that improvement.

Analyzing Your Writing for Stylistic Choices

In the Center with a WA (writing assistant), or on your own, analyze a final draft of your own writing. Using a yellow highlighter, highlight your complete sentences or ICs. Then, with another color of highlighter, look for your use of DCs. Bracket in ink all conjunctions, coordinating and subordinating. Then analyze your style, setting improvement goals through these questions and the information on the back of this page.

◆   Does your academic or professional writing context have particular syntax preferences? Is there a favored diction and voice? Those determine appropriate style choices (i.e., passive voice for a more "objective science" voice or a thesis statement such as "This paper will . . ." or "I will prove that . . .").

◆ Do you have your most important idea in your ICs? Or do you have "empty" ICs such as "it is a fact that" and hide your key point in the "that" clause?

◆ Are the next most important ideas in DCs? Essential or nonessential?

◆ Are the least significant ideas in modifying phrases and words?

◆ Do you choose coordinating and subordinating "connectors" accurately? (Note: Although in conversation "and" and "but" are frequently used, writing requires more accurate, less repetitious, conjunctions.)

◆ Do you use a variety of sentence lengths and types? Do you begin sentences with the same structures or words?

◆ Do you have sentences that need "combining" for clear idea relationships?

◆ Do you choose verbs for maximum meaning, or do you overuse the verb "to be" and bog down your syntax with unneeded modifiers?

◆ Do you save time in your writing process to revise for readability and style? Do you bring your paper to a WA for input on style and other writing goals?

Emphasis in English Syntax
Here is the hierarchy of emphasis for English sentence structures:

Independent clause	Most Important Ideas
Dependent clause	>>
Modifying phrase	>>
Modifying word	Least Important Ideas

In sentence combining, you may reduce three or four sentences to one or two, as you place ideas into structures equivalent to their degree of importance. Experienced and proficient writers have a "mature syntax and diction" in which style reinforces meaning. Ursula Le Guin calls this connection between meaning and style the "craft" of writing.

Coordination and Subordination

The *subject slot of the IC* highlights a key focus, i.e., (1) *relationships among ideas* can be emphasized through conscious use of coordination and subordination; and (2) *conscious use of coordination and subordination* can emphasize idea relationships. Your intended meaning and your writing context determine whether (1) or (2) would be a better choice.

Equal or similar emphasis of ideas	IC—IC.
	IC. IC.
	IC; IC.
	IC, coordinating conjunction IC.
	IC: IC. (1st IC generalization: 2nd example)
Dependent or subordinate ideas	DC, IC.
	IC DC. (If nonrestrictive DC, use ", DC.")
Modifying specific ideas or details	Introductory phrase or word, IC.
	S, modifier or nonrestrictive DCs, VO.
	IC, participial phrase.
	IC: vertical or horizontal listing.

Visual Emphasis for Readability

White space, one-sentence transition paragraphs, and short SVO sentences all create emphasis and readability. (Note: While too many short SVO sentences can make your writing "telegraphic," academic or professional writing contexts will help you determine appropriateness.) Punctuation can also signal visual emphasis of key ideas.

Dash —	Most visual emphasis
End marks ? ! .	>>
Colon :	>>
Semicolon ;	>>
Comma (with coordination)	Least visual emphasis

Emphasis through Variety

If overused, any style technique can become ineffective, i.e., the dash or too many sentences repeating the same parallel structure. Look at your writing with an eye for variety in the following stylistic choices:

◆ Sentence length

◆ Sentence type (simple, compound, complex, or compound-complex)

◆ Placement and punctuation of DCs and modifiers

◆ Punctuation choices

◆ Other style options (parallelism, ellipsis, listings, dashes, inversion, etc.)

◆ Connector or relationship words or phrases

Parallel Structures

EMILY GOLSON
University of Northern Colorado

Emily Golson shares some exercises she uses to help students understand how parallel structure affects the rhythm and clarity of their prose.

One of the most commonly overlooked units of writing is the sentence, and one of the most fundamental concepts in sentence construction is the use of parallel structure. "Parallel structure," proclaims Robert Walker, "is the most common and fundamental of rhetorical figures" (108). When taught as style, parallel structure forms the basis for a number of rhetorical devices that improve rhythm, balance, and meaning. When taught as grammar, parallel structure often increases students' understanding of the basic elements of sentence structure. Parallel structure also forms the basis for much of Christensen's generative approach to language. Its importance is such that it should be emphasized in every course. The following explanations and exercises address the needs of basic and intermediate writers and have been used in ESL and traditional classrooms, as well as composition instructor training.

My parents don't understand me. They think I am immature and have dumb things to say. For example, when I want to take the car or go see a friend, my father complained that I don't do my homework, and discusses how the last time I took the car I was late getting home. He is constantly judging me both by what I say and my reactions. It doesn't matter if he is happy or is mad, he just likes to pick a fight. Not only yelling at me, but he criticizes me for what I do. My mother just goes along with him. Sometimes I think that it is easier for her to say no than to worry about what will happen if she says yes to me. Both think that I either obey them or get punished. What do they know about growing up and how to get the car? If I were my mother and she was me. If I were my parents and they were me, I would be more understanding about my problems, the dreams I have and know that I really want to talk to them.

This paragraph, written by a sixteen-year-old, lacks parallelism. The writer has a lot to say but is unable to cast equal or parallel ideas in parallel form. Parallelism can occur with nouns and verbs, as well as with phrases and clauses. The simplest parallels occur in strings of nouns, adjectives, verbs, verb phrases, and phrases linked by commas or the coordinate conjunctions *and, but, nor,* and *or.* Study the following sentences.

Nouns

// The city,   She wants to be // a lawyer or

    the country,   a nurse.//

    and the mountains //are

    all pleasant

The city, the country, and the mountains are all pleasant

She wants to be a lawyer or a nurse.

Adjectives

The // tired,   The // tall,

    sleepy,   slender,

    hungry //child   beautiful //woman fell

    finally found a   on the ice.

    home.

The tired, sleepy, hungry child finally found a home.

The tall, slender, beautiful woman fell on the ice.

Verbs

He // ran,   The car // pulled in,

    tripped,   pulled out,

and fell// on the way to class.   and sped away from //the

                         parking lot.

// Having studied,

    having slept well,

and   having had a good breakfast, //he

was ready for the test.

He ran, tripped, and fell on the way to class.

The car pulled in, pulled out, and sped away from the

parking lot.

Having studied, having slept well, and having had a

good breakfast, he was ready for the test.

Verbals

Nancy likes// <u>to swim,</u>   Bob// <u>neither smokes</u>

<u>to fish,</u>   <u>nor drinks.</u>

but not   <u>to hike.//</u>

Nancy likes <u>to swim, to fish,</u> but not <u>to hike.</u>

Bob <u>neither smokes nor drinks.</u>

Prepositional phrases (at, in, by, for, on, against, toward, under, beneath, below, between, among . . .)

He felt her presence // <u>in the sun,</u>   The book was // <u>in the</u>
<u>in the moon,</u>   <u>living room,</u>

<u>in the wind,</u>   <u>on the table,</u>

and   <u>in all things.</u>   <u>under</u> the tablecloth.//

He felt her presence <u>in the sun, in the moon, in the wind,</u> and <u>in all things.</u>

The book was <u>in the living room, on the table, under the tablecloth.</u>

Noun phrases

// <u>The study of history,</u>

<u>the study of geography,</u>

and   <u>the study of physics//</u> are essential to understanding today's world.//

<u>The study of history, the study of geography,</u> and <u>the study of physics</u> are essential to understanding today's world.

Subordinate structures

The same principles of parallelism may be applied to subordinate clauses in complex structures. (Common subordinators are after, although, so, as if, as long as, as though, because, before, even though, how, if, in order that, once provided that, since so that, then, though unless, until, when whenever, where wherever, whether, while.)

Conditional clauses

> // <u>If you study,</u>
>> <u>if you sleep well,</u>

and   <u>if you have a good breakfast,</u> // you will be ready for the test.

<u>If you study, if you sleep well,</u> and <u>if you have</u> a good breakfast, you will be ready for the test.

Cause and effect clauses

She went to the game // <u>because she liked basketball,</u>
>> <u>because she wanted the school to win,</u>

and   <u>because she had a crush on the star player.//</u>

> // <u>Even though it was a school day,</u>
>> <u>even though the meet was far from the campus,</u>

and <u>even though a chilly rain was falling,</u> // hundreds turned out for the race.

She went to the game <u>because she liked basketball, because she wanted the school to win, and because she had a crush on the star player.</u>

<u>Even though it was a school day, even though the meet was far from the campus, and even though a chilly rain was falling,</u> hundreds turned out for the race.

Temporal clauses

> //<u>Once you have gotten your pencils</u>
and <u>once you have read the instructions,</u>// you may begin.

<u>Once you have gotten your pencils and once you have read the instructions,</u> you may begin.

Exercise 1: Combine the given sentences into one concise sentence containing parallel structure.

1. The road was narrow. The road was steep. The road was muddy.

2. I should have finished my homework. I should have cleaned up my room.

3. I like to become acquainted with the people of other countries. I like to become acquainted with the places in other countries. I like to become acquainted with the customs of other countries.

4. He stared at me for a long time. He never said a word.

5. A calculator makes it easy to figure gas mileage. A calculator makes it easy to figure sales taxes. A calculator makes it easy to figure your bank balance.

6. The boy was old enough to work. The boy was old enough to earn some money.

7. He preferred to play baseball. He preferred to play video games.

8. I dislike living in the city because of the air pollution. I dislike living in the city because of the crime. I dislike living in the city because of the traffic.

Paired Conjunctions

The most commonly paired conjunctions are both . . . and, not only . . . but also, either . . . or, neither . . . nor, and whether . . . or. The general rule is that structures following each conjunction should be parallel.

> We evaluate a response to an assignment
> both <u>for its eloquence</u>
> and <u>for its accuracy.</u>

> We evaluate a response to an assignment both <u>for its eloquence and for its accuracy.</u>

> We evaluate a response to an assignment for both its <u>eloquence</u> and <u>accuracy.</u>

Either <u>they do the work</u>   Whether <u>drunk</u>
   or <u>they fail the class.</u>   or <u>sober</u>, he liked to
                                              pick a fight.

Either <u>they do the work</u> or <u>they fail the class.</u>

Whether <u>drunk</u> or <u>sober</u>, he liked to pick a fight.

When the subjects following each conjunction change, problems with verb tenses can occur. Study the following examples:

Both <u>John</u> and <u>Henry</u> are here.	Two subjects connected by both . . . and take a plural verb.
Not only <u>John</u> but also <u>Henry</u> is here.	When two subjects are connected by not
Not only <u>John</u> but the <u>twins</u> are here.	only . . . but also, either . . . or, or neither . . . nor, the subject that is
Not only the <u>twins</u> but <u>John</u> is here.	closest to the verb determines whether the verb is singular or plural.

Notice the parallel structure in the following examples. The same grammatical form should follow each word or pair.

The outing will take both <u>time</u> and <u>money</u>.

Yesterday it not only <u>rained</u> but <u>snowed</u>.

I'll take either <u>chemistry</u> or <u>physics</u> next term.

The movie was neither <u>fun</u> nor <u>accurate</u>.

Exercise 2: Combine the following into sentences that contain parallel structures. Use appropriate paired conjunctions (both . . . and, not only . . . but also, either . . . or, neither . . . nor, whether . . . or).

1. He does not have a book. He does not have a pen. (He has neither book nor pen.)

2. Bob likes skiing. Mary likes skiing.

3. You can have a soda. You can have lemonade.

4. The grocery store does not have the magazine I need. The library does not have the magazine I need.

5. Bob was absent today. Mary was absent today.

6. Pam did not tell her mother about her problems. Shirley and Jane did not tell their mothers about their problems.

7. She wants to go out with John, or she wants to go out with Ben.

8. We can eat here or we can go out.

Exercise 3: Rewrite the paragraph at the beginning of this lesson using parallel structure. Parallel structures often make good generating devices, allowing the writer to create a more accurate description or analysis of the subject at hand. For example, rather than saying the tall girl entered the room, a writer might say the silly, tall, blond girl entered the room.

Exercise 4: Divide into groups. Create several examples of parallel structures in noun form, adjective form, and verb and verbal forms. Next, create several examples of parallel structures using different phrases and clauses. Finally, create parallel structures using paired conjunctions.

Bonus: Winston Weathers, in "The Rhetoric of the Series," claims that "a two-part series creates an aura of certainty, a three-part series creates the believable and logical, and a four-part series suggests the human, the emotional, the inexplicable" (96). Experiment with numbers of nouns, verbs, clauses, etc. in your series and explain how the number affects the meaning, tone, or mood of your sentence.

Parallel structure and style

It is possible to write very long sentences using various types of parallel structures. When this begins to occur, it is best to vary your sentence length by summarizing the meaning of a long sentence in a short sentence. Read the following imitation of a paragraph by Virginia Woolf.

But while we think about our parents and review their values, we are aware, and our siblings are partly responsible for this consciousness, of a sweet yet not wholly innocent child in the background. Our childhood selves are always there. It is true that this child says nothing, but our adult selves can feel a young presence, in the living room, at the dinner table, in the bedroom, recording important moments, cataloguing them, attempting to interpret the incidents that began occurring somewhere around the age of three. We see our younger selves as rather sensitive, rather naive, rather malicious human beings, with a taste for adventure, music, sports or education. Brief infatuations are also a little to our liking. Thus, with each recurring memory, the awareness comes, incisive, startling, haunting, imploring us to laugh, to cry, to shout, to accuse, to forgive. We do our best. We work very hard in the school of insight, but the effort is too exacting. We halt halfway through the twisted halls of memory. Perspectives shift; moments transform; lives go on. Eventually, we put our memories away and attempt to enjoy the moment, rising with a smile at the beginning of each new day, enjoying the simple pleasure of sun and wind. In the end, we forget.

Our children take up our cause as they sort through how we, their parents, influenced their lives. . . .

Exercise 5: Circle all parallel structures. Underline the simple sentences, sentences that consist of subject, verb, complement. For purposes of this exercise, semicolons mark the boundaries of simple sentences. Now read the simple sentences aloud. How do they complement the longer sentences? What do the long, cumulative sentences do?

Exercise 6: Contemporary writers often use parallel structure to highlight the dramatic quality of events, giving added resonance to a piece. Read the memorial to the Challenger *crew written by Lance Morrow for* Time *magazine (Morrow, Lance. Time. 10 February 1986: 23). Write a similar piece about someone that you lost. What did that person symbolize? Did he or she have faults as well as weaknesses? Try to include as many parallel structures as you can.*

Works Cited

Christensen, Francis. "The Generative Rhetoric of the Sentence." *Rhetoric and Composition: A Sourcebook for Teachers*. Ed. Richard L. Graves. Rochelle Park, NJ: Hayden, 1976. 129–38.

Walker, Robert L. "The Common Writer: A Case for Parallel Structure." *Rhetoric and Composition: A Sourcebook for Teachers*. Ed. Richard L. Graves. Rochelle Park, NJ: Hayden, 1976. 102–9.

Weathers, Winston. "The Rhetoric of the Series." *Rhetoric and Composition: A Sourcebook for Teachers*. Ed. Richard L. Graves. Rochelle Park, NJ: Hayden, 1976. 95–101.

Sector Analysis

PATRICIA LICKLIDER
John Jay College—CUNY

Patricia Licklider devises some strategies for enhancing the quality of students' sentences. By turning statements into questions, students unravel the grammatical structures of phrases.

Background: Sector Analysis

The main focus of a first-year writing course, especially if its members do not write well, should be on writing, from brainstorming, to drafting, to revising, to editing. Throughout this process, writers should be sharing their writing with one another and their instructor and should be receiving feedback on it. The second focus should be on reading: the students should read both their own writing and other, more complex texts. These activities help familiarize students with the demands of written, as opposed to spoken, English.

Both these foci have been shown to improve student writing more than working only on individual sentences or on grammar lessons (see Patrick Hartwell's attack on the teaching of grammar as a way to improve student writing, as well as Constance Weaver's more recent advice).

Yet when students come to editing their work, writing instructors may find that the students need to learn something about sentence boundaries and other features of standard written English (SWE) in order to make their own writing standard. How do instructors give them the information they need without taking too much time away from writing and reading? What strategies for manipulating sentences and other features of SWE are most efficient for students to learn and to use as they edit their writing? While grammar instruction by itself, taught through textbook exercises and divorced from particular pieces of student writing, does not usually help students edit their own writing, some grammar instruction can be helpful to student writers if it occurs only (1) as needed, (2) within the context of a student's writing, and (3) in strategies that are easy to remember and use. Finally, whenever possible such instruction should build on the language skills students already possess. One sequence of such strategies that I have been teaching for many years is an adaptation of a form of sentence analysis developed years ago by Robert Allen at Teachers College, Columbia University. He called it sector analysis, and, though it's almost forty years old now, its essentials are not difficult to learn or remember since it was found to be simple enough for fifth graders to learn and use, and it builds on students' ability to speak English. Sector analysis helps them both to check their sentences quickly for completeness and, if necessary, to check other matters, such as whether their subjects and verbs agree.

Allen's system is tagmemic; that is, it divides and orders the parts of a sentence according to their function and position in the sentence. These parts can then be reordered or revised at will. Allen saw sector analysis as helping students write more mature and varied sentences. Louis Milic suggests using it as a way to teach college writers about their own and other writers' styles. I have also used it as a window into style in an advanced composition course. But I have used it primarily for helping students find and fix fragments and errors in subject-verb agreement. For a detailed description of sector analysis, see Allen's *English Grammars and English Grammar* and *The Verb System of Present-Day American English*. Together with Rita Pompian and Doris Allen, he also produced a textbook called *Working Sentences*, where I first learned about sector analysis. I made use of parts of Allen's system in my own textbook *At Your Command: A Basic English Workbook*.

In the instructor's guide to his textbook, Allen discusses the distinction between oral and written English and the fact that many remedial students are unfamiliar with the demands of SWE and may have seldom or never studied grammar formally. They "know" English syntax and semantics already because they know how to speak the language, but they usually cannot articulate what they know in the terms of formal grammatical analysis. If such students were familiarized with the conventions of SWE, he says, they could reproduce them in their own sentences. I do not agree with Allen that remedial students can best improve their writing by focusing on individual sentences as they compose. But I do find his kind of analysis useful for some students to learn when they are editing. Thus, what I provide here is a very abbreviated form of Allen's work, the form in which I present it to students whose command of sentence boundaries or of subject-verb agreement in SWE is uncertain.

Sector Analysis: Step One

Every declarative sentence in English can be turned into a question that can be answered with a yes or a no. This fact can be used to check on the grammaticality of student-produced sentences. I start by showing students how this statement-into-question works with simple sentences, usually culled from the students' own writing. I tell them to turn the sentence into a question that can be answered yes or no without changing anything else in the sentence, not its tense or the position of its words, and without adding or deleting any words either. If the students can do so, they know that the original sentence is grammatically complete. If they cannot, then the sentence is probably a fragment, and, as they try to turn it into a question, they will find themselves correcting it. Restating the "corrected" sentence as a statement is one way of correcting the fragment. Another way is to join the fragment to the sentence preceding or following it, depending on what the writer wants to say. I begin with simple sentences containing a form of the verb "to be," for example:

True success is not just about making money.→

Is true success not just about making money?

The students can conclude that the original sentence has been properly punctuated with a period.

Because I can gain promotions within the company.→

This *cannot* be made into a valid English question without removing "because" or adding more words. Often, students will automatically remove "because" as they try to resay the "sentence" as a question, thereby changing the original dependent clause into an independent sentence:

Can I gain promotions within the company?

Sector Analysis: Step Two

Once students can successfully manipulate such simple sentences, I move them on to simple sentences that contain no part of the verb "to be." At this point, I tell them that the only words they may add to a sentence when turning it into a yes/no question are *do, does,* or *did.* If the verb is in the past tense, they should use *did;* if it's in the present tense, they should use *does* for verbs with an -*s* ending or *do* for those with no ending. It helps students remember which of these three auxiliary verbs to use if they think of *did* as taking its -*d* ending from the verb if it has one, and *does* as taking the -*s* ending from the verb if it has one. (Incidentally, the use of *does/do* to turn statements into questions is also useful for students who have trouble making their subjects and verbs agree. Such students can practice using/not using the -*s* ending by changing a series of simple sentences into yes/no questions.)

The legislators voted to end debate after three days of wrangling. + did

Did the legislators vote to end debate after three days of wrangling?

The new law tests the limits of free speech. + does

Does the new law test the limits of free speech?

The courts have the final say on the constitutionality of this law. + do

Do the courts have the final say on the constitutionality of this law?

Sector Analysis: Step Three

If I see that a student often writes dependent clauses as complete sentences, I may proceed to the last part of this strategy to illustrate the punctuation of complex sentences. First, I briefly introduce the notion of dependent clauses and how they change simple sentences into complex ones. The students and I have probably already done some of this work when turning simple sentences into yes/no questions because some of the supposedly simple sentences were really dependent clauses separated from their independent clauses. (I introduce the idea of simple/complex sentences wherever it first arises.) I illustrate the movability of many dependent clauses: they can be placed at the start of a sentence, at its end, or sometimes even in the middle. After students have become familiar with a list of adverbial conjunctions, i.e., words that start dependent clauses, they practice writing complex sentences and moving the dependent clauses to different positions in the same sentence. Then we go back to turning sentences into yes/no questions, first moving any dependent clause appearing at the beginning of a sentence to the sentence's end.

Before the Supreme Court agrees to hear a case, it must be tried in lower courts.

→ A case must be tried in lower courts before the Supreme Court agrees to hear it.

→ Must a case be tried in lower courts before the Supreme Court agrees to hear it?

Although the bill would raise the minimum wage, labor unions are against it.

→ Labor unions are against the bill, although it would raise the minimum wage.

→ Are labor unions against the bill, although it would raise the minimum wage?

Afterword

I teach students the simplest strategies first. Only when these fail do I move on to a more complex strategy. Before teaching students how to use the method I've just described, for example, I find out if they can find fragments simply by reading a passage aloud. Sometimes, simply helping students learn to pay close attention to their own voices as they read is all they need in order to "hear" the periods and commas they have naturally produced in their speech. If they cannot "hear" periods and commas, I move on to the strategy of yes/no questions.

Also, I seldom teach grammar to an entire class since usually only some students need help with a particular grammatical concept. Rather, I work with students one on one or in small groups. Thus, I can provide as much or as little information as individual students need to use a proofreading strategy effectively. Occasionally, I may "go public" with a grammatical concept if it has ramifications that everyone in a class would find useful.

As with most instruction in grammatical concepts, each step of this fragment-finding strategy opens to scrutiny another seemingly unrelated grammatical concept. Thus, the turning of simple sentences into yes/no questions raises the concept of subject-verb agreement as well as the use of the *-ed* ending on regular, but not irregular, verbs. And the added steps for testing the grammaticality of complex sentences and dependent clauses raise not only the concept of complex sentences (how they function, why a writer might use them, and so on), but also the fact that pronouns can be used only after the nouns to which they refer (in the two examples of complex sentences earlier, a noun and a pronoun switch places when we reposition the dependent clause). Sometimes, if I see that students also need help with this other grammatical feature that arises, I take advantage of its sudden appearance to provide instruction on this feature as well. The trick, however, is not to overload students with more information than they can handle at one session. One strategy at a time. (Now demonstrate that the preceding sentence is really a fragment!)

Works Cited

Allen, Robert L. *English Grammars and English Grammar.* New York: Scribner, 1972.

———. *The Verb System of Present-Day American English.* The Hague, Neth.: Mouton, 1966.

Allen, Robert L., Rita Pompian, and Doris Allen. *Working Sentences.* New York: Crowell, 1975.

Hartwell, Patrick. "Grammar, Grammars, and the Teaching of Grammar." *College English* 47 (1985): 105–27.

Licklider, Patricia. *At Your Command: A Basic English Workbook.* 2nd ed. Boston: Little, Brown, 1983.

Milic, Louis. "Composition via Stylistics." *Linguistics, Stylistics, and the Teaching of Composition.* Ed. Donald McQuade. Akron: University of Akron, 1979. 91–102.

Weaver, Constance. *Teaching Grammar in Context.* Portsmouth, NH: Boynton/Cook, 1996.

Encouraging Editing

EDWARD A. KEARNS

University of Northern Colorado

Often, teachers mark the errors in students' essays, thereby taking responsibility for proofreading their prose. Edward Kearns's suggestions for editing students' writing encourage students to assume responsibility for developing their own proofreading skills.

The suggestions that follow build on Richard Haswell's "Minimal Marking" and pertain primarily to the proofreading or editing stage of writing. The premise is simple: students will not develop their own strategies and skills in proofreading if teachers edit their manuscripts for them by, for example, circling misspellings, supplying missing commas, or correcting faults in agreement. Instead, students must learn about their own writing styles and their own most common errors so that they can develop individualized strategies in proofreading their work. Therefore, careful, accurate analysis of word- and sentence-level faults must include successes as well as mistakes. Yes, the paper contains 15 misspellings, but it also contains 485 correct spellings. How do we account for that? Are there types of words or letter combinations that produce most of the writer's errors? Yes, the paper contains seven sentence fragments and five run-on sentences, but it also contains thirty complete sentences. How do we account for that? Has the writer attempted a variety of complex, compound, and compound/complex sentences? Does the problem have to do with his or her lack of understanding of what complete sentences are, or is the writer simply uncertain or ignorant about punctuation options? Certainly, attention to successes provides opportunities for praise and positive reinforcement, but more importantly, it is essential to ensuring accurate assessment and effective learning. The following steps aim at that learning.

For faults that are clearly identifiable and for which specific remedies are needed, such as spelling, missing commas, or agreement problems:

1. Do not mark the errors directly; rather, place check marks in the margins corresponding with the errors. (A given line may have more than one check mark.)

2. Require the writer to find and correct the errors; when in doubt, the writer should write a (?) beside the check mark.

3. Review each error with the writer in conference, looking for patterns. Some mistakes will be simple oversights; the student knows the correct form but missed it in proofreading. Others, however, will reflect uncertainty or ignorance—e.g., inconsistent use of apostrophes, repeated errors in subject-verb agreement, a scattering of comma splices. Most students make a few mistakes frequently rather than many different kinds of mistakes.

4. Call attention to the patterns; many students will be relieved to discover that the numerous check marks actually refer to only a few errors.

5. Analyze and discuss the faults in grammar and punctuation in conjunction with positive, successful elements; for example, "You have a nice style—your work shows sentence variety and you frequently use introductory elements (phrases and clauses); you simply need to be consistent in using commas to attach them to the main clauses."

6. Ask the writer for various ways to correct errors (e.g., correcting comma splices), or suggest some if the writer becomes stymied. Require the writer to make choices.

In sentences containing problems that may be corrected in a variety of ways (e.g., awkward phrasing, missing words, vague pronoun references, sentence fragments, etc.):

1. Underline or [bracket] the sentence or a portion of it.

2. Ask the writer to see if he or she can find the problem and solve it.

3. In conference, discuss the revision or, if the writer has been unable to find and solve the problem, have him or her read the sentence aloud (this may involve repeated readings).

4. Consider various ways to rewrite the sentence, then have the student make a choice.

These diagnostic strategies help direct writers toward personal proofreading strategies. Some writers, for example, may be unaware of what they sound like or they may proofread much too quickly; such writers, perhaps, should read their papers aloud to themselves or to roommates, at least for a while. Other writers may need to watch for particular constructions—not avoid them—and practice correct forms of punctuation.

This personalized approach to proofreading and editing reinforces the idea that conventions (grammar, spelling, punctuation) can serve as tools for making meaning and developing style, rather than as external rules to be memorized. As such, it is also inherently self-motivating. Finally, and especially through conferencing, the process may reveal undiagnosed disabilities such as dyslexia.

Work Cited

Haswell, Richard H. "Minimal Marking." *College English* 45 (1983): 600–604.

CHAPTER 14

TEACHING RESEARCH SKILLS

Chapter 13 examined the connections between writing and grammar, usage, and style; we now turn to explore the role of research in writing. Why should writing teachers teach research skills? What should students know about conducting effective research? How do teachers construct interesting research assignments for students? Chapter 14 provides some possible answers.

First-Year Composition as an Introduction to Academic Discourse

M. J. Braun and Sarah Prineas

University of Arizona

This essay is a revision of material that originally appeared in
A Student's Guide to First-Year Composition, *20th ed., edited*
by Sarah Prineas, Lori Church, and Adrian Wurr (Edina, MN:
Burgess, 1999). Thanks to Burgess Publishing for permission
to reprint this material.

A Background for Instructors

From the inception of the composition course in the late nine-teenth century, composition instructors and the professoriate at large have assumed that a student would emerge from first-year composition prepared to write for all academic purposes, with little regard for whether the course's content included instruction in academic conventions. Only in the last thirty years of compo-sition studies, however, have scholars attempted to identify what these conventions are. This work spawned debates over the wis-dom of teaching what came to be called academic discourse. Al-though the debate has been far reaching, its terms have coalesced around three issues: the advisability of teaching students aca-demic discourse (scholars have argued that first-year students do not need this type of instruction); the ethics of teaching academic discourse (scholars have argued that academic discourse repro-duces hegemonic power relations that suppress the voices of op-pressed groups); and the very existence of such a genre (scholars have argued that academic conventions are more dependent on disciplinary than academic concerns). As a result of these chal-lenges, few composition scholars now write unproblematically about academic discourse; in fact, most discussions about the need to prepare students to write for the university have been relegated to scholarly work on writing across the disciplines. But through all of this, the expectations of many composition pro-grams and the professoriate at large have never strayed far from the now century-old assumption that once students leave their first-year composition course, they will be better able to write in any future course they take.

As graduate associate teachers in the Department of English at the University of Arizona, we participated in a two-year pilot study to redesign the first-year composition course, English 101, so that it would better prepare students to read and write for academic purposes. But we did not want the new design to jettison a widely recognized strength of the course: introducing students to rhetorical analysis. Rhetorical analysis, as defined in the University of Arizona's *A Student's Guide to First-Year Composition,* is a method of judging the effectiveness of a writer's choices by analyzing the purpose, audience, and context of a text, its arguments, claims, and assumptions, and its appeals using the Aristotelian categories of ethos, pathos and logos. We emerged from the two-year study conceiving of the course as one in which students are asked to investigate the rhetoric of scholarship by offering them a chance to engage in what David Bartholomae has called "an academic project." Like Bartholomae's, our purpose for teaching academic discourse is not gatekeeping—that is, guarding the hallowed halls of academe from the barbarous hordes. Rather, our purpose is to arm young scholars with the frameworks they will need to be able to assess scholarship critically, even from their nonexpert positions within the university.

In the following slightly edited excerpt from *A Student's Guide to First-Year Composition,* we invite students to enter the world of scholarly research in the way scholars do. We use Bartholomae's distinction between the novice and the expert scholar to help students segue from high school to university standards of research. We define these two sets of standards by identifying the following distinctions: purpose of research, generating a topic, method of inquiry, and evaluation of sources. We begin by introducing the students to the master trope for the process of engaging in an academic project—the Burkian parlor.

Suggested Reading

Bartholomae, David. *Facts, Artifacts and Counterfacts: Theory and Method for a Reading and Writing Course.* Upper Montclair, NJ: Boynton/Cook, 1986.

———. "Interchanges: Response." *College Composition and Communication* 46 (1995): 84–87.

———. "Writing with Teachers: A Conversation with Peter Elbow." *College Composition and Communication* 46 (1995): 62–71.

Bizzell, Patricia. *Academic Discourse and Critical Consciousness*. Pittsburgh: U of Pittsburgh P, 1992.

Bridwell-Bowles, Lillian. "Discourse and Diversity: Experimental Writing within the Academy." *College Composition and Communication* 43 (1992): 349–68.

———. "Freedom, Form, Function: Varieties of Academic Discourse." *College Composition and Communication* 46 (1995): 46–61

Elbow, Peter. "Being a Writer vs. Being an Academic: A Conflict in Goals." *College Composition and Communication* 46 (1995): 72–83.

———. "Interchanges: Response." *College Composition and Communication* 46 (1995): 87–92.

———. *Writing without Teachers*. New York: Oxford UP, 1973.

Geisler, Cheryl. "Exploring Academic Literacy: An Experiment in Composing." *College Composition and Communication* 43 (1992): 39–54.

The Process of Research: Joining the Conversation

Why Do University Scholars Research?

University scholars not only make knowledge accessible to each new generation entering higher education, but they also work at developing new lines of inquiry and producing new knowledge in their various fields of study. This activity is known as scholarly research, and the ways of thinking, speaking, and writing that emerge from the act of research are often referred to as academic discourse. In *The Philosophy of Literary Form*, Kenneth Burke uses the metaphor of conversation to describe academic discourse:

> Imagine that you enter a parlor. You come late. When you arrive, others have long preceded you, and they are engaged in a heated

discussion, too heated for them to pause and tell you exactly what it is about. In fact, the discussion had already begun long before any of them got there, so that no one present is qualified to retrace for you all the steps that had gone before. You listen for a while, until you decide that you have caught the tenor of the argument; then you put in your oar. Someone answers; you answer him; another comes to your defense; another aligns himself against you, to either the embarrassment or gratification of your opponent, depending upon the quality of your ally's assistance. However, the discussion is interminable. The hour grows late, you must depart. And you do depart, with the discussion still vigorously in progress. (110–11)

Because these academic conversations have been going on, as Burke says, "interminably," a scholar cannot expect to join them until she has done some research. Once the scholar has situated herself in the ongoing conversation through research and reading, she will be ready to become an active "speaker" in that conversation. In order to produce new knowledge, she considers what has been left out of the academic conversation. She asks, "What questions need to be raised? What arguments need to be made? What issues have been left unexamined?" Once she has found such a site for further argument, the scholar continues her research. Most scholars pursue a particular line of inquiry throughout their lives. Over the years, they develop theories about the phenomena they have researched, resulting in the production of new knowledge. This knowledge is often developed in opposition to previously held theories.

Because the scholar conducts research in this way, her work follows certain conventions. For example, she will cite authoritative sources to give her own work academic *ethos,* or credibility, in the eyes of scholarly readers. Second, she conducts research in order to sustain the conversation within her own work so that the other voices who have spoken on her issue can be heard speaking within her own work. Because sustaining this conversation is so important to scholars, they also value proper citation format for quotations and paraphrasing and always include an accurate record of sources—a bibliography or works cited. By including citations and a bibliography, the scholar makes it possible for the next person who picks up the conversation to become well informed on the issue by going back and studying the works cited.

How Do Scholars Decide upon a Topic?

Before starting research, it is important to be aware that in the university scholars choose topics that have relevance to the academic community. Topics for research do not begin and end with unexamined personal biases, because scholars expect to have their assumptions challenged by the academic conversations in their disciplines. For students at the university, topics arise from class discussions and from class readings—from any class, not just English composition. Beginning scholars and researchers need to become aware of the conflicts in their classrooms: What issues are under debate? What are scholars arguing about? What terms do different groups define in different ways? For example, English majors become aware that there is extensive debate about the "canon," or the list of texts considered by some scholars to be "authentic" literature. Some scholars insist that the traditionally assigned texts by revered authors—Chaucer, Shakespeare, Milton, Johnson, Dickens, or T. S. Eliot—must remain required materials. Other scholars working from different theories and assumptions call attention to the fact that the authors just mentioned represent a limited literary tradition that privileges the work of middle- and upper-class European males and insist that the canon must be expanded to include works previously not considered to be literature because of the gender, sexual orientation, religion, or ethnic or racial background of its authors. A novice scholar, for example, might explore the canon debate, analyze the arguments put forth by each player in the debate, and conclude by making an informed argument. Here's another example: In the medical field, nursing students and professors may be concerned about the issue of euthanasia and the role they should play as professionals within that debate. Other disciplines have other hot issues about which scholars argue. These are the sites where established assumptions have been called into question, and these questions are up for debate.

What Research Methods Do Scholars Use?

Less experienced researchers who are just entering the scholarly conversation should be careful not to jump to hasty conclusions, because they need to follow their research where it leads. That way they can leave their options open, allowing possibilities for new arguments to arise from the research. Often, novice researchers have been taught to find bits and pieces of texts that will fit smoothly into the argument they already want to make, glancing quickly through articles, circling only those quotations which support their previously determined position, and dismissing views which contradict their own. They may not consider the possibility that they might want to revise their original argument because the issue has broader implications than they had realized.

Experienced researchers approach research as a necessary step *before* participating in the scholarly conversations occurring in their disciplines. They realize the need to read first, to keep an open mind as they read, and to revise their original assumptions in the face of new knowledge. They recognize the complexity of issues and thus do not claim to have simple answers to complicated problems. Scholars generally respect opposing views because they know that issues can be approached in varied ways and that one can learn a great deal from other approaches, even those that challenge one's own assumptions. Experienced researchers keep careful track of their sources and evidence because they know they may have to give a careful accounting of their evidence if their conclusions or reasoning is challenged. Finally, scholars are aware that research takes time; they do not expect to complete their research in one trip to the library.

For example, as English 101 student Guy Natale began working on his academic project, he decided that as an aerospace and mechanical engineering major he wanted to research the military's use of unmanned aerial vehicles. Unlike most novice researchers, though, Natale did not begin his research with a set thesis in mind. As his instructor relates,

> While conducting his research Guy stumbled upon a topic that needed to be pursued further. Most of Guy's research in the beginning of the assignment centered on finding out how unmanned aerial vehicles (UAVs) are made and what they are used for, but as he slowly became an expert on UAVs, he realized that he did not approve of their potential use as weapons-bearing vehicles in warfare. Guy did not come upon this argument in a professional journal or read it in the newspaper; instead he developed his

ideas about the ethical use of UAVs in conjunction with his research. At the time he wrote this essay, these little, computer-
controlled crafts were not being used to deliver missiles, but Guy
could sense that this would be the next step. He proceeded to
research and write a position paper that had a complex purpose:
the goal was to take a stand against using unmanned aerial vehicles as weapon delivery systems and also to reaffirm the hor-
rific nature of war by pointing out some of humanity's past
mistakes.

Defining a Topic

Once students have begun to identify an area of inquiry—say,
for example, the canon debate in English literature, or the euthanasia controversy among health professionals—it is time for them
to learn more about the history of the issue, the players involved
in the debate, and the kinds of arguments that are being deployed
in the debate. The best way to go about this is to begin by visiting
the library's computerized catalog of holdings. The first search
through this database will be most effective if students approach
the task with the attitude that they are engaging in play—they
are exploring, searching for useful terms, following promising
leads, getting ready to enter the stacks where the books and journals are waiting for them. After they've written down some call
numbers, they will be ready to explore the library to track down
the sources themselves. When they get to the stacks and find the
book they were searching for, they should sit down right there
and leaf through the book. They check the table of contents, the
index, and the bibliography. They evaluate the chapter or essay
titles, skim the introduction and conclusion, and figure out what
type of source they have in front of them. They decide right there
whether the book might be useful. If it is, they take a look at the
shelf where they found that book and examine some of the nearby
texts. By browsing the stacks and exploring texts in this way,
they begin to get a feel for the debate they are researching. Possibly, certain names will appear several times—these are the players in the debate, the people engaged in the continuing argument.
After checking the publication dates of each text, they begin to
get a sense of the history of the debate. After reading a few introductions, the positions (rather than rhetorical choices) of those
involved in the debate will become more evident.

Evaluating Sources

As scholars assemble research material, they are aware that there is a hierarchy of credibility among sources. This section analyzes the difference between scholarly and nonscholarly texts.

WHAT IS A SCHOLARLY TEXT?

A scholarly text is distinguished by the fact that the author makes evident in the text that he or she is making an argument as part of a continuing conversation. The author does so through literature reviews, bibliographies or works cited, footnotes or endnotes, and indexes. In other words, scholarly texts make the other voices—the voices of scholars who have previously written or spoken about the issue—"heard" and therefore present in the text. In nonscholarly texts, usually only the voice of the author can be heard.

Some examples of scholarly texts can include the following:

Singly and collaboratively authored books: These scholarly texts contribute something that has not been argued before in a scholarly conversation. These new arguments always build on knowledge that came before: sometimes they take an oppositional stance to that previous knowledge; sometimes they examine previously unconsidered aspects of the argument. Scholarly books are most often published by university, not commercial, presses. Books are published only after they have undergone a rigorous review process. A panel reviews the book to ensure that the author has a thorough understanding of the scope of the scholarly conversation; however, the panel does not evaluate the veracity of the argument. Scholarly works that have undergone this review process are considered credible sources among academics. Be aware that some books may seem to follow these scholarly conventions, yet their credibility is nonexistent in the academic community. For example, in *The Bell Curve: Intelligence and Class Structure in American Life* by Richard J. Herrnstein and Charles A. Murray, the authors argue that intelligence levels, not environmental circumstances, poverty, or lack of education, explain many of our social problems.

In making their argument, the authors assert that intelligence is biologically, not environmentally, determined, and based on their data, they find that blacks are less intelligent than whites or Asians. The book *seems* to follow academic conventions, is written by two Harvard professors, is well documented, and acknowledges the theories on which the authors rely. Yet despite its semblance of credibility, as soon as the book came out scholars across the country, including scholars from Harvard, began to make academic arguments against it, questioning its use of evidence, the authors' manipulation of data, and the authors' suspect conclusions. Geneticists, biologists, and social scientists have challenged the book's premises, pointing out that the authors never clearly define "race," and, referring to the body of knowledge in their various disciplines, arguing the premise that race is in fact socially constructed. According to academic standards, *The Bell Curve* may seem to be a credible text; however, experts in many fields have rigorously questioned its "truth."

One thing to remember when reading scholarly texts is that the introductory chapter usually presents a concise overview of the author's central argument. The introduction often contains a literature review (a review of the major voices in the conversation whose purpose is to review and then problematize what has been said before).

Journal articles: An academic journal, by definition, contains articles relevant to a specific discipline. Journal articles, authored singly or collaboratively, do the same work as a book, in the sense that they are scholarly texts that present an argument and participate in the scholarly conversation. Before an article can be published in an academic journal, it must be refereed, which means that it has been reviewed by a panel of scholars expert in that field. The panel reviews the article to ensure that the author has a thorough understanding of the scope of the conversation; however, the panel does not evaluate the veracity of the argument. Note that while journals are usually found in hard-copy format, they are increasingly appearing in online format. An example of a journal article is R. G. Newby and D. E. Newby's "'The Bell Curve'— Another Chapter in the Continuing Political Economy of Racism," which appeared in *American Behavioral Scientist* in 1995. The authors critique Herrnstein and Murray's *The Bell Curve: Intelligence and Class Structure in American Life* as part of their argument about the role that intellectuals have played in different historical periods in producing knowledge about intelligence and race. They argue that such pseudoscientific arguments about race arise under certain political and economic conditions. Therefore, for Newby and Newby, Herrnstein and Murray's "data" are less important than the political and economic conditions in which their book was produced.

Anthologies: Anthologies are collections of scholarly writings about a common subject. The materials published in anthologies are edited by scholars in a field. The articles republished in anthologies usually appeared first in academic journals or at academic conferences. Anthologies have a theme; all of the articles address some specific topic within the field. *Current Problems in Sociobiology* is an example of an anthology of academic papers presented at a conference at Cambridge University in 1980. The theme of this particular anthology, obviously, revolves around problems facing scholars engaged in sociobiological research.

What Is a Textbook?

While scholarly work seeks to produce new knowledge, textbooks construct a canon of knowledge, in the sense that they present previously theorized knowledge as information that is "true" without interrogating that "truth." In other words, textbooks do not employ the conventions of scholarly writing, because scholars always interrogate "truths." Because a textbook usually presents knowledge as, essentially, dead information, the conversation ends. At the same time, textbooks often come out in new editions in order to update the knowledge contained within, as the conversations have continued.

What Is a Nonacademic Text?

Nonscholarly texts are intended for a general, or popular, audience. While scholarly texts make evident their participation in a conversation, nonacademic texts derive their authority from a huge range of sources—from scholarly work, to received knowledge, to ideology. In this sense, nonacademic texts are problematic because the theoretical assumptions in the texts are less evident and require a more actively analytical and knowledgeable reader. One problem with nonacademic sources is that novice readers lack the analytical skills to recognize whether the theoretical assumptions underlying the text are credible, sometimes to the extent that anything that appears in print may seem credible. In nonscholarly texts, only the voice of the author is heard, while other voices—the voices of scholars who have previously written or spoken about the issue—are usually not present in the text. In academic texts, the voices of other participants in the conversation can be heard.

Singly and collaboratively authored books. These nonacademic texts don't make a scholarly argument; their theoretical assumptions are either unexamined or buried. For example, in *You Just Don't Understand: Women and Men in Conversation,* author Deborah Tannen, writing for a popular audience, argues that men's and women's conversational styles differ. In this book, she presents numerous examples from men's and women's speech to illustrate her point; however, Tannen does not explicitly refer to the large body of linguistic theory which informs her analysis. In her scholarly work on the same subject, *Gender and Discourse,* Tannen supports her method of analysis by citing the linguistic theory that informs it. Nonacademic texts pose a problem more for the uninformed than the informed reader because those readers who are, in this case, unfamiliar with linguistics are unaware of the author's knowledge of linguistics itself and her standing as a scholar in that field. A reader unfamiliar with conventions of academic texts has no way of knowing if a book by Deborah Tannen on gender and conversation is more credible than a book by Oprah Winfrey on the same subject.

Oprah Winfrey might have interesting things to say about the differences in men's and women's conversational styles, but her observations would not be based on accepted linguistic theory or current research, but rather on passively received ideas. For example, according to linguistic theory, gender differences in conversational styles are explained as socially, not biologically, contingent. On the other hand, a nonlinguist may recognize that there are gender differences in conversation styles but attribute these differences to testosterone rather than the social roles men and women play.

Anthologies. Nonacademic anthologies are collections of popular rather than scholarly writings about a common subject. The materials published in popular anthologies are not necessarily edited by scholars and usually appeared first in popular sources such as books, newspapers, or magazines. An example of a nonacademic anthology is *The Bell Curve Wars: Race, Intelligence, and the Future of America*, edited by Steven Fraser, containing articles written by scholars for a popular audience. The anthology contains many articles arguing against the claims made by sociologists Herrnstein and Murray in *The Bell Curve: Intelligence and Class Structure in American Life*, including articles by biologist Stephen Jay Gould and literary theorist Henry Louis Gates Jr. These articles are not scholarly in that Gould, for example, does not write for an audience of biologists, but for a more general audience interested in the debate.

Magazines may seem to provide current information, but they are generally not considered by scholars to be reliable sources. Often, they do not acknowledge their sources, as scholars do, and they are usually not aimed at an academic audience. Magazine articles may even be authored by someone not trained to speak on the subject. For example, a magazine reporter has been trained in journalism, not the subject about which he or she is writing.

Newspapers. Newspaper articles have the same limitations for scholarly use as magazine articles. Reporters, rather than scholars, usually but not always write the articles. Because sources for newspaper articles are unacknowledged, there is no way of knowing what sources are informing a reporter's version of events.

Web pages. In the hierarchy of credibility, Web pages are less credible than print or hard-copy texts for a variety of reasons: anyone (not necessarily an "expert" or scholar) can publish a Web page; Web pages are ephemeral (that is, they can be revised without warning, unlike print sources); sometimes the organizations that publish Web pages can construct the site in such a way that it seems "official" and credible, when in fact it is not. In addition, the Web itself was originally developed by the military and adopted for commercial purposes. Therefore, the format and content of the Web may serve hidden purposes outside of scholarly inquiry. Recently, some scholarly journals have begun to publish on the Web and follow all of the conventions of hard-copy journals.

Works Cited

Burke, Kenneth. *The Philosophy of Literary Form.* Baton Rouge: Louisiana State UP, 1941.

Current Problems in Sociobiology. Ed. King's College Sociobiology Group. New York: Cambridge UP, 1982.

Fraser, Steven, ed. *The Bell Curve Wars: Race, Intelligence, and the Future of America.* New York: Basic, 1995.

Herrnstein, Richard J., and Charles A. Murray. *The Bell Curve: Intelligence and Class Structure in American Life.* New York: Free, 1994.

Newby, Robert, and Diane Newby. "'The Bell Curve'—Another Chapter in the Continuing Political Economy of Racism." *American Behavioral Scientist* 39 (1995): 12–24.

Tannen, Deborah. *You Just Don't Understand: Women and Men in Conversation.* New York: Morrow, 1990.

Teaching Research Skills in the First-Year Composition Class

MARK GELLIS

Kettering University

In this piece, Mark Gellis provides some basic guidelines for teaching research skills, answering many common questions students and teachers have on the subject.

The research paper is probably the least favorite assignment for many taking, and teaching, first-year composition. It is also an assignment that can demand an enormous amount of time and labor on the part of both students and teachers, often to no good purpose. We need look no further than our own experience or the experiences of our colleagues to see how much trouble students and teachers often have with research and research papers. What I hope to do in this essay is provide some guidelines for teachers who need to teach the research paper. There will be little in the way of theory here. Rather, this is a practical discussion based on my years of experience as a teacher and designed to answer what I have found to be the most common questions asked by new teachers about this subject. In other words, here is the Teaching Research Papers FAQ.

First things first: *Why is research the province of writing? Why should we bother with teaching research skills?* The natural response of some composition teachers asked to teach research papers is to ask whether it is our job to teach research skills. After all, we do not teach fact finding; we teach writing. Is not fact finding the province of librarians or faculty in specific disciplines? The reality of the situation, however, is that librarians usually do little more than help students find specific sources. They simply do not have time to teach our students research skills on a one-to-one basis. Library tours can be helpful in introducing students to the available resources in a particular library, but we should not assume that students actually learn how to do research by listening to someone else. They must do it for themselves to truly learn it. Furthermore, faculties in other disciplines frequently provide students with little or no instruction on the specifics of research in those disciplines.

It might be worth adding a "commonsense" answer to this question: it is difficult to write if you lack information, and unless you are writing about yourself, you will probably have to do some research to complete any writing project. We might as well teach these two skills together. Since common sense is rarely sufficient to prove anything in academic circles, I shall continue this line of reasoning by citing from authority. Aristotle clearly identifies rhetoric, the discipline within which composition, technical writing, and similar fields are contained, as involving both artistic and nonartistic proofs (37). Nonartistic proofs are external evidence, including witness testimony and laws; in effect, rhetoric is divided between arguments generated by the rhetor and external evidence that must be discovered. Research, therefore, is part of rhetoric and within the province of the composition class.

Teaching research skills is necessary. Teaching research skills is part of the tradition and responsibility of our discipline. So there.

What are my educational goals for the research paper segment of first-year composition? This is an important step, but one we frequently overlook. The reason for this mistake is fairly simple. Unlike people preparing to teach in K–12 systems, we are not often required to take courses in education, educational psychology, or educational administration. We have been taught how to analyze literature and we have been taught what heuristics are, but many universities that allow students to pay their way through graduate school by teaching lower-division courses have done little to make sure these graduate instructors have any real background as educators. To be blunt, they have dropped the ball, either because they themselves do not know how (the blind leading the blind) or because they think it will be too expensive to teach graduate instructors what they will eventually figure out anyway. Meanwhile, our students and our discipline suffer because of our lack of knowledge, training, and experience.

There is no time here to provide a complete introduction to educational theory, but I can at least discuss a few key concepts such as goals and outcomes. Goals should be distinguished from outcomes. While different educational experts disagree about the specific meanings of these terms, for the purpose of my discussion I will treat a *goal* as something you hope to accomplish with a class or an assignment and an *outcome* as some measurable evidence that proves you have reached your goal. Thus, teaching students how to do research is a goal; students producing researched papers that show they know how to find the information they need is an outcome.

All assignments should be based in goals and outcomes. Before you ask a student to do an assignment, you should figure out the underlying reasons for doing that assignment in the first place and then figure out how you are going to assess whether the student has learned what you want him or her to learn. Erika Lindemann's *A Rhetoric for Writing Teachers* covers these issues to an extent, and her observations may prove useful.

I believe that one of the problems teachers have with research papers is that teachers do not understand why they are teaching them. Unless teachers define the goals of a project for themselves, they can neither explain those goals to students nor correct assignments that are flawed because their goals are unclear or unsound. If you do not understand what an assignment can or should accomplish for your students, the assignment will frequently become a dull and mechanical exercise that benefits no one.

Specific goals and outcomes will vary from class to class, from teacher to teacher, and from assignment to assignment. Some of my research-related goals, for example, are as follows:

- Students will know how to define a feasible research project.

- Students will know how to find experts on a particular subject.

- Students will know how to contact experts by phone or e-mail.

- Students will know how to conduct an interview.

- Students will know how to analyze data gathered in an interview, identifying trends and distinguishing points based on their significance.

- ◆ Students will know how to find and use advanced reference works such as *Ward's Business Directory,* the *Encyclopedia of Associations,* and the *United States Government Manual.*

- ◆ Students will know how to find printed sources on a particular subject.

- ◆ Students will know how to distinguish between and evaluate various kinds of printed sources such as books, scholarly journals, trade journals, government publications, corporate publications, popular magazines, and newspapers.

- ◆ Students will know how to incorporate researched material into a paper in a stylistically effective manner.

- ◆ Students will know how to document sources, both internally and in a bibliography, using APA format.

These are, of course, only suggestions. For a while, I taught rhetorical criticism as an alternative to the traditional research paper. In this case, my goals changed substantially. In addition to some of the goals listed above, I wanted the following:

- ◆ Students should be able to research historical and biographical sources.

- ◆ Students should be able to identify specific ethical, logical, and emotional appeals.

- ◆ Students should be able to assess the effectiveness of an argument.

(By the way, students had mixed feelings about rhetorical criticism. Some liked it a lot, often because it was a clearly defined project that allowed them to examine subjects outside of their academic discipline, but others found it irrelevant to their personal and professional goals and despised the project.)

The important thing to remember is that you can evaluate any assignment by asking what educational goals it will fulfill and what educational outcomes will be used to measure its effectiveness. In addition, you can save yourself a great deal of time when planning assignments by identifying your pedagogical goals first and then building assignments around them.

How do I help students define research projects? One of the most interesting things about teaching research is that you can achieve many of the same pedagogical goals with a wide variety of projects. You can teach library research methods, critical thinking, evaluation of sources, report writing, and evaluation and revision with papers on George Washington, ecological disasters, twentieth-century poets, or dog breeding.

Your first decision is fundamental. You may either allow students to write about anything or you can select a range of topics for them to examine and choose from. The first alternative has the advantage that students are likely to write about subjects that interest them; this increases the likelihood that they will be motivated to do their best work and thus learn more from the project. The main disadvantages are that without some guiding structure, many students will not know what to write about. An added disadvantage is that you may have to read a large number of papers on topics that either do not interest you (e.g., painting military miniatures) or that actively repulse you.

Limiting the research paper topic gives you more control over what students are working on, may reduce the risk of plagiarism, allows you to use class lectures to cover material that will be relevant to all students working on these projects, and provides students who need more structure with clear guidelines about what they should be writing about and how they should approach the topic. The main drawback is that some students may not be interested in the topic and will produce poor work due to weak motivation. For this reason, if teachers decide to limit the topics for a research paper, they must clearly define for themselves and their students their reasons for doing so. Students will usually accept limitations on research projects (some welcome the limitations because it is one less decision they have to make) as long as the projects have some relevance to themselves and what they understand to be the general goals of the course.

Whether the range of topics is broad or narrow, unless you want to assign a specific question to students (this is good if you need to punish them for something, but not for much else), they have to come up with an actual topic. Here are some guidelines for helping them choose:

◆ Students learn more when they are interested in the subject. Furthermore, students often have greater interest in a project when they do not already know everything about the topic, because they are researching for themselves as well as for their audiences. With this in mind, it makes sense to tell students to begin with general subjects they find interesting (e.g., British history) but to choose specific subjects about which they still have questions (e.g., the events leading up to the Armada of 1588).

◆ Students are often motivated when their research will actually affect others. Assignments for which they are writing for real audiences and only being graded by the teacher are often far more motivating and effective than those that are purely academic.

◆ Students can rely on their own networks for projects. This works in a couple of ways. First, if we combine this idea with the last two points, we have a terrific heuristic for finding research projects. Students can list the various groups to which they belong (e.g., family, school, hometown, special interest groups, etc.) and identify the problems or questions facing those groups. This gives them a list of research topics that have relevance to them and the potential to affect others. In addition, it is a useful method for turning general research questions into specific ones. Any general issue can be made more specific by exploring how it affects a particular community or group. Students who are interested in eliminating teenage smoking, for example, do not have to write a research paper for "the general public," but can write a paper directed specifically to the school board in their hometown (which would allow them to draw on concrete details that are both familiar and relevant to their audience).

◆ When in doubt, have them solve a problem. Problem-solution papers have a simple and easily understood structure (introduce the paper, explain the problem, describe and defend the solution, and close by summing up and urging the readers to act) and have the advantage that many students will be motivated by the opportunity to help others.

◆ Define a research question. One of the most important aspects of a successful research project is that the researcher understands the questions he or she is trying to answer. As Janice Lauer and colleagues have pointed out (1991), one of the most important factors in creating a successful writing process is to clearly define a question that will guide the student's inquiry. The purpose of a research paper is, after all, to answer a question or solve a problem for an audience. While the question or problem may evolve during the course of the research process, students should not go forward with a project until they can clearly articulate an initial version of the question they are trying to answer or the problem they are trying to solve.

What kind of research is acceptable for a first-year composition class? This is up to you. It depends on the goals and outcomes you have determined for the course. I allow students to use a lot of primary sources because most of my students are engineers and a great deal of their real-life fact finding consists of calling people on the phone and asking them what something is or how it is done. Other people feel uncomfortable with this approach and focus more on library research. The main areas of research you will have to decide on are as follows:

◆ Traditional library research. Library sources are usually referred to as secondary sources because the researcher is reporting what others have discovered. Most people do not have trouble with this one. Students go to the library to read books, scholarly journals, government reports, videos, and so on. The biggest problem you will have here is that most students do not yet know how to tell the difference between, say, an article on heart disease in *Time* and an article on heart disease in the *Journal of Cardiopulmonary Rehabilitation*. In addition, a lot of them think that copying an article out of an encyclopedia is doing research.

◆ Primary research. Here, students find information by conducting surveys, interviews, or even experiments. Primary research can be exciting for students. It is also similar to a lot of the research they will do as professionals in business (and it is important to remember that the vast majority of our students will not be English majors and will not grow up to be teachers; we need to keep this in mind when we develop courses, write textbooks, and so on). Primary research is also difficult at times. Students have to identify subjects or sources. They have to develop questions. They have to actually conduct the surveys or interviews. All these tasks are skills in and of themselves. Two final problems with primary research are (1) it may not be necessary (if someone else has already done this research and published an article on it, there is no need for students to reinvent the wheel), and (2) the allure of primary research can blind students to the wealth of information available through other sources.

- ◆ Internet research. Internet research combines aspects of library research and primary research. It is discussed in more detail in later sections.

I know how to find information on Dickens, but my student needs to find information on the Airborne Laser System and I do not even know what that is. How do I help students find the information they need? What is the research process? What should my students do? There is no research process. It is like the writing process. It is different for each person. A general template that students can follow, however, is this:

1. Define your research question. [This has been discussed already.]

2. Identify and screen sources. Before you can dive deeply into any one source, you should develop a working bibliography, first developing a large list of potential sources and then narrowing that list down on the basis of the reliability of the source (is it any good?) and its relevance to the question at hand (even if it is any good, does it relate to *my* project?).

3. Read relevant and reliable sources, taking copious notes. At this point, additional sources may end up being cut from the list of sources actually used on the basis of relevance or reliability. Often, you can't know the value of a source to your project until you have studied the source. In addition to photocopying important sections or quotes, by the way, it is often useful to summarize sources in your own words while you are reading them; this way, the information is fresh in your mind and the source is close by so you can check for accuracy once you have completed your summary.

4. If need be, identify and interview experts to answer questions raised or left unanswered by printed sources. [Teacher: Robert Berkman covers this process in detail in *Find It Fast*.]

5. Evaluate progress and, if need be, go back and do more research. Research is recursive. You may find after you have done some research that you still have questions that need to be answered or that the question you have been trying to answer is not the question you really need to answer.

6. Write the report. [This activity is covered in a later section of this essay.]

7. By the way, you can find some information on the Airborne Laser System at http://www.airbornelaser.com.

How can I keep my students on track? Long reports constitute a hidden danger for many students. Because they are long projects, often spaced out over several weeks, some students who do well otherwise fall behind and end up doing a poor or even a failing job.

I find that borrowing a technique from industry is helpful. First, students should submit proposals in writing (hard copy or by e-mail) in which they explain what they want to do for their research project and why. (This can be graded or used as a diagnostic essay.) Students should also submit, in writing (hard copy or by e-mail), at least one working bibliography and one progress report before any draft is submitted. This way you can make sure that most of them have a good topic to begin with, have found good sources fairly early in the research process, and are not going to try to research and write the entire paper the night before it is due. Some students will get off track or cheat regardless, but these short assignments will be useful in keeping most of them on track.

A related assignment I use is to have students give short oral presentations in class on concepts related to the research paper. Often they will summarize a chapter of the textbook or handbook for the class, or describe one or more research resources available in the library. I find that this is often more useful than lecturing on these subjects myself because the students must learn the material in order to develop a presentation on it. In addition, if students make mistakes or leave out material during their presentations, I can fill in the gaps (usually at a later time so I do not embarrass the student who gave the presentation); in some cases, drawing attention to material in this way makes it more memorable for students.

Should I let my students do research on the Internet? Why? What special problems does Internet-related research create? I believe it is a mistake to tell students they cannot do some of their research on the Internet. The Internet provides rapid access to a wide range of sources and materials. It often allows easy access to library catalogs at your own institution and at other nearby ones, even when the library itself may be closed. It is also often the easiest way to access experts since e-mail addresses are sometimes easier to find (or guess) than telephone or fax numbers. In fact, it can be a useful assignment to have students contact experts by e-mail and ask them a question about a topic of interest to the students. At the same time, here are some cautions I pass on about using the Internet:

- Students who are comfortable with the Internet sometimes use only the Internet. As a result, they will often miss the best sources for their papers. At the college level, my solution is simply to tell them they are responsible for determining if they have enough information. They are, after all, adults. It also helps to provide a few concrete examples of how much is still not on the Internet.

- Unlike books and magazines, for which the information must usually pass through an editorial screening before it is released to the public, quality control on the Internet is far more erratic. This is actually a good thing since it makes the Internet a richer and more dynamic medium. At the same time, students can be taken in by slick Web pages produced by people who do not really know what they are talking about but who understand online design well enough to look like they know what they are talking about. We discuss this issue in more detail in class when I talk about evaluating sources in general.

- Since the Internet is so new, the standards for citing online resources are still being ironed out. Even though excellent guides such as Li and Crane's *Electronic Styles* are available, there is often confusion about how to cite a particular source. This means you should be prepared to spend extra time in class and in conferences on how such sources should be cited, both internally and in the bibliography.

My students do not understand the difference between Time *and the* Journal of Cardiopulmonary Rehabilitation. *What do I tell them about periodical sources?* Periodicals are called periodicals because they are published periodically (instead of just once, like a book). *Ulrich's International Guide to Periodicals* lists more than 100,000 of them. The general categories are as follows:

- newspapers
- popular magazines
- trade journals
- scholarly journals

Newspapers are daily, semiweekly, or weekly publications that cover and comment on current events, either locally or in general. They are read by people who are interested in these topics or who need up-to-date information on them to complete their professional responsibilities. Newspapers vary in quality, but readers can generally rely on the *New York Times* and the *Wall Street Journal* to provide accurate and detailed coverage of current events. (It is also easy to find out what they covered because both newspapers publish indexes.) In addition, local newspapers (and, even better, the journalists who write for them) are some of the best available sources on local events and recent local history.

Popular magazines are usually published weekly, biweekly, monthly, or quarterly. They are generally published for people who are interested in certain topics and those who may find the information useful but who do not need the information to complete professional responsibilities. They are useful because they can provide overviews of subjects and explanations of technical subjects in lay terms, but they should not be relied on exclusively.

Trade journals are magazines written for professionals in specific fields. Their content usually consists of information that is needed or will be useful, rather than information that is interesting in its own right. If you are looking for serious and pragmatic discussions of a topic, look here, but be prepared for the fact that these journals are written for professionals rather than the general public.

Scholarly journals are periodicals intended for scientists and university faculty. These journals usually discuss theoretical or critical aspects of a field that will be interesting or useful but usually not immediately needed for completing professional responsibilities. If you are looking for theoretical, philosophical, or scientific examinations of a subject, look here, but be prepared for the fact that these are not written for the general public.

It is also useful to remember that in addition to books and periodicals, other printed sources may prove valuable to your students. The most important of these will be government and corporate publications.

My students have found some sources, but they are not sure whether they are any good. Are there any systems for evaluating sources? There are actually a number of systems for doing this, but I like the CARS system developed by Robert Harris, which is available at http://www.virtualsalt.com/evalu8it.htm. I strongly recommend that you read his discussion in full, but briefly, what Harris says is that there are four basic criteria for researched information:

- credibility
- accuracy
- reasonableness
- support

A source is credible when there is reason to find it trustworthy, such as the author's credentials, the reputation of the publisher, evidence of quality control (e.g., journals with blind peer review of articles), and so forth.

Here we have one of the great dangers of using the Internet for research. It is extremely easy to create Web pages that have a slick, published look, regardless of whether the author actually knows anything about the subject. It may not always be possible, for example, to determine if the person who has created the *Locust Resource Page* is an entomologist, a pastor with a theological interest in locusts but no formal training in their biology, or a fifth grader putting her class project on grasshoppers on the Web because she thinks bugs are cool.

My recommendation for solving this problem is to tell students they cannot use anonymous Internet-based sources; authors must identify themselves and their credentials (or affiliation) in the Web page. By effectively limiting Web pages to those that can be identified as having been produced by experts in industry, academia, or government, or official Web pages of corporations, research centers, universities, government agencies, and other organizations, you eliminate many of the problems with reliability created by using Internet sources.

A source is accurate when it is current, sufficiently detailed and accurate in its coverage of the subject, and so on. Accuracy is, of course, relative. A source that is too old or too general in its discussion of the topic may not be inaccurate, but it may not be accurate enough to be useful.

A source is reasonable when it examines its subject fairly, in a balanced and objective manner, sometimes by considering alternate points of view. Logical fallacies, conflict of interest, obvious bias, or an overly emotional tone can be signs that a source is not reasonable.

A source is supported when its information can be corroborated, often by having the author list his or her sources or provide documentation or contact information.

A source that meets these four criteria is probably reliable; a source that cannot meet these four criteria may still be reliable, but the writer should treat it with suspicion, expect that audiences will do so too, and probably find other sources that corroborate its information before using it in the paper.

The textbook I am using does not really explain how to write a research paper. How do you write a research paper? How is a researched report different from an essay? Perhaps because they understand how varied writing is, many textbook writers do not want to give a fixed format for the research paper. For many first-year students, however, having some kind of basic structure they can rely on or use as a springboard can be valuable. One of the best descriptions of report writing I have ever read is in Paul Anderson's *Technical Writing: A Reader-Centered Approach*. Anderson relies on two basic concepts that I consider valuable for almost any writing situation:

1. Most writers produce documents that belong to existing genres such as reports, proposals, autobiographical essays, etc., and most of these genres employ one or more templates that provide guidelines for composition.

2. Generic templates are generally based on the questions that audiences want answered by a communication. The specific questions are genre specific because each genre tends to serve one or more specific communication purpose.

All proposals, for example, are effectively asking for permission (and often support) to do something. The audience wants to know what you want to do, why you want to do it, what problem your project is going to solve, how your project will benefit them, how you plan to do it, how much it is going to cost, and so forth.

Anderson describes a basic template for a report, reminding us that a researched report has at least one and sometimes two goals: it is always an informative document; it is also sometimes a persuasive one, particularly if the writer is obliged to make final recommendations. It differs from an essay in that it usually focuses on the topic rather than the writer (which is often the focus of an essay). It is also meant for readers who need the information, whether or not they would seek it out to read during their leisure time. As a result, the style should be direct and straightforward; while there is often need for document design, there is usually little room for stylistic artistry. The audience of a report cares about the information and what it means to them; they are far less concerned about being engaged philosophically, aesthetically, or emotionally (although if a report has a persuasive goal, it is often necessary to appeal to their values and concerns). They usually do not care at all about what the subject means to the writer. I strongly urge people to read Anderson's more detailed account, but briefly, he says that a researched report should contain the following parts:

- *Introduction.* The introduction tells readers what they are going to get out of this report. It answers the questions, "Why should I read this report? What am I going to get out of it?" It can briefly explain the topic and the need to understand it, forecast the overall organization, and even list the main conclusions that will be discussed in detail in the rest of the report.

- *Methods.* The methods section explains how the report was researched. It can cover methods and specific sources. This builds the writer's credibility since it shows that the facts are reliable, and it provides a service for the reader, who may wish to do similar research and now has a model to follow.

- *Facts.* The findings section is often the longest section of the report. It explains what the writer found out about the topic that may be relevant to the reader. In a lab report, this would be the raw data before it is interpreted.

- *Discussion.* Here, the writer interprets the facts, looking for patterns or relationships between them.

- *Conclusions.* The conclusions section goes beyond simply interpreting the facts and explains how these findings are significant to the reader. In many cases, it is reasonable to combine the discussion and conclusions sections.

◆ *Recommendations.* Not all reports need a recommendations section, but the last question readers often ask is, "What should we do now?" If the report allows the writer not only to draw conclusions about the topic but also to suggest future action to readers, this is the place to do it. It is important to distinguish between a conclusion, which is a statement about a topic, and a recommendation, which is a suggestion for action or belief made to a reader.

In some cases, students may combine sections. It is sometimes easier, for example, to build a report around its conclusions, dividing the main body of the report by topic and beginning each section with a topic sentence whose claim is then supported by the data that would otherwise be placed in a separate facts section.

I know how to teach MLA (or APA) format, but my students want to know why they should cite their sources in the first place. What do I tell them? While few students openly ask this question, a lot of them are probably thinking it. It is not such a ridiculous question, either. To scholars who have spent years teaching and grappling with such issues as credibility, evidence, audience reaction, ethics, and intellectual property, it makes perfect sense to clearly identify where you got your information. To an eighteen-year-old who is taking your class only because it is required, these things may not be self-evident. I believe there are three basic reasons for citing sources: credibility, convenience, and courtesy.

◆ *Credibility.* This is probably the easiest one to sell. People often want to know not only where you got your information but also who provided it so that they can judge the quality of your information. And failure to identify sources means there is no guarantee you are not just making up things, or, more likely, that you are sloppy in your fact finding and perhaps sloppy in your thinking. This is the same cruel logic we find with writers who are judged because of surface-level errors. The ideas may still be good, but if they misspell the evidence, no one takes them seriously. If writers cannot even identify which sources they used, how can we trust them to have understood those sources or reported accurately what they said?

♦ *Convenience.* This is not as easy to sell but easy to explain. Sometimes people will be involved in similar projects and will want to use your sources. Why make them work harder than they have to?

♦ *Courtesy.* This last point is less obvious to students but sometimes makes a big impact on them. I ask them how they would feel if they helped someone out on a research project and that person took all the credit for it, maybe even claiming that they had come up with ideas that the students had actually generated. I ask them how they would feel even if it were an accident, such as sloppy reporting on the writer's part during research. Most of them say they would not like it much. "So don't do it to someone else," I tell them. I also draw on the philosopher Hillel, who, asked about the meaning of the Torah, once said that it was quite simple: "That which is hateful to you, do not do to your fellow man. That is the whole Torah; the rest is commentary." This is a good ethical principle in general, but one that is also helpful, I think, when it comes to explaining the reasons for citing sources.

I would like a reference I can turn to. Any recommendations? You should run, not walk, to purchase the most recent edition of Robert Berkman's *Find It Fast.* This is probably the best book available on doing research. *The Craft of Research,* by Booth, Colomb, and Williams, will also prove valuable. Ellen Metter's *The Writer's Ultimate Research Guide,* although oriented toward writers of fiction, is also useful because it describes a large number of sources. If you are interested in business-related research or competitive intelligence, Leonard Fuld's *The New Competitor Intelligence* and John McGonagle Jr. and Carolyn M. Vella's *Outsmarting the Competition* will prove useful. Finally, for the muckrakers in your class, Steve Weinberg's *The Reporter's Handbook* and Dennis King's *Get the Facts on Anyone* are good starting points for investigations and investigative reporting.

Works Cited

Anderson, Paul V. *Technical Writing: A Reader-Centered Approach*. 4th ed. New York: Harcourt Brace, 1999.

Aristotle. *On Rhetoric: A Theory of Civic Discourse*. Trans. George Kennedy. New York: Oxford UP, 1991

Berkman, Robert I. *Find It Fast: How to Uncover Expert Information on Any Subject*. 4th ed. New York: HarperPerennial, 1997.

Booth, Wayne C., Greg G. Colomb, and Joseph M. Williams. *The Craft of Research*. Chicago: U of Chicago P, 1995.

Fuld, Leonard M. *The New Competitor Intelligence: The Complete Resource for Finding, Analyzing, and Using Information about Your Competitors*. New York: Wiley, 1995.

Harris, R. *Evaluating Internet Research Sources*. 17 Nov. 1997 (visited 17 Mar. 1999) <http://www.virtualsalt.com/evalu8it.htm>.

King, Dennis. *Get the Facts on Anyone*. 2nd ed. New York: Macmillan, 1995.

Lauer, Janice, Gene Montague, Andrea Lunsford, and Janet Emig. *Four Worlds of Writing*. 3rd ed. New York: HarperCollins, 1991.

Li, Xia, and Nancy B. Crane. *Electronic Styles: A Handbook for Citing Electronic Information*. 2nd ed. Medford, NJ: Information Today, 1996.

Lindemann, Erika. *A Rhetoric for Writing Teachers*. 2nd ed. New York: Oxford UP, 1987.

McGonagle, John J. Jr., and Carolyn M. Vella. *Outsmarting the Competition: Practical Approaches to Finding and Using Competitive Information*. Naperville, IL: Sourcebooks, 1990.

Metter, Ellen. *The Writer's Ultimate Research Guide*. Cincinnati: Writer's Digest, 1995.

Weinberg, Steve. *The Reporter's Handbook: An Investigator's Guide to Documents and Techniques*. 3rd ed. New York: St. Martins, 1996.

Situating Research: Writing Research Proposals in First-Year Composition

JOYCE A. SIMUTIS
The University of Scranton

Joyce Simutis incorporates the use of human participants in her approach to teaching the research paper, a move that broadens the context of her students' awareness of audience.

The first-year research paper takes students on a library expedition to find, read, summarize, and analyze sources. On completion of multiple notecards or other helpful devices, students are then prepared to synthesize the information they've found, taking a new stance—or at least a stance new to them. Although this standard assignment works well in many classes, it generally relegates the research paper to the classroom community. But there are other ways to approach this assignment, ways that promote situating student writing within a broader university context. To provide that context for student writing, the lesson described in this section encourages students to write a research proposal that seeks approval from the University of Scranton's Institutional Review Board for a research project. This project requires that teachers and students alike seek assistance from multiple campus resources. It requires ingenuity, interpersonal communication, and rhetorical strategies from all writers. But it also reveals the wonder and satisfaction that come from discovering new findings and accomplishing a research goal. It is an assignment that *matters* to students.

Rationale and Aims

Assigning a human subjects research project in first-year composition follows sound pedagogical theories. First, it provides "contexts *for*" text production as well as contexts for the "*use of*" those texts (Chin 446–47). It requires that students work at a steady pace to complete their writing rather than allowing them to write a paper at the last minute. (See Nelson for a discussion of how students trivialize assignments by writing them right before they are due.) It encourages social interaction outside of the classroom, an interaction that Elaine Chin notes affects the composition process (476). In other words, conducting research involving other individuals provides a situated context for and gives meaning to the writing process. It also integrates writers and readers in a sociocultural context of text production. This integration helps students become familiar with writing in the university. Gaining this familiarity, Barbara Rogoff contends, defines development (11–18).

The multiple goals of the research project enable students to better understand the sociocultural context. The assignment extends the contexts and audience for writing and research outside the classroom. It gives students the hands-on experience and motivation to answer questions that are meaningful to them. It makes students accountable for what they write because their writing has consequences for them. Their writing determines whether they can continue their research.

Procedure

Advocates of situated learning such as Jean Lave and Etienne Wenger suggest that "learning is an integral and inseparable aspect of social practice" (31). That is, people learn by becoming practitioners within a culture. As Allan Collins, John Seely Brown, and Susan E. Newman contend, "Apprentices learn these methods [for carrying out tasks] through a combination of what Lave calls observation, coaching, and practice, or what we, from the teacher's point of view, call modeling, coaching, and fading" (455–56). Using this terminology of modeling-coaching-fading becomes helpful as we design tasks for first-year composition students. It is especially useful for the research proposal because all writers—teacher and students—make the same investment in the process. That process consists of submitting a coherent rationale and plan for research involving human subjects to the Institutional Review Board (IRB). This process is necessary for any research involving individuals outside of the immediate classroom.

For students to conduct research, the teacher's first task is to gain approval for the class projects that do not need full IRB approval. The teacher's proposal provides a model that students can respond to and edit before they begin writing their own proposals. In addition to writing the proposal, the teacher will also fill out the application for research approval and discuss any relevant reports or regulations stipulated by the IRB. This second discussion cautions students about the possible risks of human research and the reasons why human subjects are protected, especially vulnerable groups such as small children or students under the age of eighteen. It also helps students think about the risks involved in influencing others through language and the benefits of replicating research studies, encouraging them to question what they accept as "fact."

As students begin their own application and research process, the teacher can then coach them, having been through the process him- or herself. That coaching may require discussions of rhetorical questions, types of research, how to write rationales and procedures sections, how to gain consent, how to structure surveys or interviews, and how to observe a setting to provide "thick description" (Geertz 6). While many teachers would not attempt such research in traditional first-year classrooms, the enthusiasm of students and their continued persistence to gain approval far outweigh the problems in teaching such challenging formats.

The process began for my classes at the University of Scranton during a semester focused on the topic of "learning." In the early weeks of the semester, students read essays on learning from experience, learning through diversity, and learning new ways to think about intelligence, curricula, and classrooms. When the students' first papers argued for motivation and hands-on experience in the classroom, we began our journey through the research process. Students asked questions important to them: How does sleep deprivation affect students' work habits? Students are given appropriate time-management techniques in their first-year seminar, but how do they really schedule their time? How do colors affect our memory? Does the gender of the professor affect students' learning? How does the school's physical environment affect learning? The students planned research to answer their questions and wrote proposals to conduct surveys, observations, and short experiments, using the process described below.

Students first fill out the IRB application, which calls for their proposals. If the IRB forms are online, students will need only to complete the application. First-year students with even minimal computer experience are able to either print the forms from the site or download the forms and fill in pertinent information. Filling in the application becomes another learning experience as students begin to see that the Review Board must consider all aspects of research, protecting subjects from drugs, food additives, injections, and other potentially harmful procedures.

Once students have drafted their proposals, the teacher coaches them through the revision process, often discussing the rhetorical context of the proposal. If their proposals must be reviewed by the full board, students must understand the implications of all aspects of their study. During the first round of revision, the teacher gives feedback on what the studies will find, how responses are determined by the ways in which questions are asked, and how researchers' biases and assumptions show up in their questions.

If the teacher acts as the board of review for studies that do not require full IRB approval, his or her standards must be as specific as those of the IRB. That is, the teacher must relate his or her concerns about the rationale for the research (why students choose to use human subjects or participants), what assumptions underlie the questions asked of subjects or participants, and how the study will help the student researcher answer his or her question. Students who submit their proposals to the IRB will also benefit by having others read and respond to their proposals in advance of submitting it. At the University of Scranton, the director of research services has been invaluable in reading student proposals and noting parts of the experiment or research that the board will reject. If the board asks for revisions, their suggestions are specific and relate to the problems that could arise from conducting the study as currently written. Suggestions by those outside the classroom situate the student proposal in ways that matter, in ways that have consequences for both students and the university.

Once student proposals are accepted, the next step—conducting the study—becomes students' responsibility. The teacher fades from the process but continues to provide feedback and advice when necessary. Class discussions center on what students are finding, how their findings relate to or dispute the studies they have read to date, and which data they might use as evidence to support their tentative claims.

Research can be written as a research report, or evidence from students' studies can be incorporated into the research paper itself. During this time, the class can discuss several issues: (1) what counts as evidence, (2) which pieces of evidence might be most valuable, (3) how their evidence either relates to or contradicts the information they find in the literature, (4) which claims they can make and which they cannot support, and (5) how their findings add to our body of knowledge. Since evidence is often one of the most difficult aspects of writing student research papers, this discussion helps students understand how to present evidence that will be meaningful to their readers.

In the classroom context, student writers are more concerned with writing for their teacher and classmates than for an external audience. But when applying for research permission, students become aware of multiple aspects of writing. They see that what they write affects what they are permitted to do. They see that the structure of their research plans influences their readers. They come to understand that how they present their procedures matters to readers. They soon realize the need to write in a timely manner in order to gain permission and still do the research before they must write the research paper. And they learn that they must write coherent proposals to get their research accepted.

Risks

As with any writing assignment, the process of constructing research proposals and conducting research has its own share of problems. Knowing some of these will help you determine whether the value of the task is worth overcoming the difficulties. So first

I discuss some of those problems and then I suggest strategies for completing the process successfully.

Possibly the most difficult task for students is revising long after they think the proposal should be finished. When the IRB makes suggestions for revision, students often see it as a sign that they should abandon the project. For example, when D. K., a student proposing to teach a lesson in a first-grade class, was asked to revise her proposal by the IRB and given specific suggestions for doing so, she asked me several times if she should abandon her research topic and choose another project. The Review Board was concerned that her lack of expertise might influence the children's understanding of a lesson so they gave her several suggestions for revision. She saw this as a rejection of her proposal altogether. Revision in this sense is seen as discouragement rather than as a way to rethink the procedures. But revising research projects becomes a way for students to work out the difficulties not only in the proposal but also in the project design itself. It becomes a way for them to reevaluate what they hope to prove by conducting their study and why their study is important.

A second difficulty in this assignment is the time factor in completing the proposal, project, and research paper. Obtaining IRB approval requires attending to deadlines, waiting for the board to meet and discuss the proposals, and revising the proposal before approval is granted. This must be scheduled so that students have the opportunity to conduct their research and use their data for their own research paper. The proposal is only one step in the process, and they cannot wait until the last minute to complete the work. Students working with populations at risk, especially children, will possibly need more time to see their proposal through the review and revision processes. They will need encouragement and guidance through what might seem like an endless process, but they will come to a fuller understanding of the revision process.

A third set of problems arises from the limitations of student research and their understanding of the problems with their research instruments. Some first-year students show characteristics of William Perry's dualistic learner or the received knower that Mary Field Belenky, Blythe McVicker Clinchy, Nancy Rule Goldberger, and Jill Mattuck Tarule describe in *Women's Ways of Knowing* (35–51), and these students may have difficulty understanding why they should question any research. They may also find it difficult to understand why their questions are biased or unnecessary to their research. At this point, the class should examine its own biases and assumptions about research and its purposes. When discussion focuses on biases and assumptions, teachers and students may reflect on the rhetorical purposes and audiences for their writing, reflections that are often missing in first-year composition.

Benefits

Even though problems are highlighted during the proposal project, the process also has benefits that may not be found in the traditional research assignment. Students learn to follow explicit directions, or their proposals will not be accepted. Submitting the proposal to readers outside the classroom enables students to get feedback from multiple audiences. These audiences read from multiple perspectives, examining the proposals for problems that students would not need to consider in a classroom context.

By participating in proposal writing, students enter into the conversations of the academy in unexpected ways. They become more than participants in class—they become active members of a research community and problem solvers in their own right. They explore questions of consequence to them. This exploration, as Collins, Brown, and Newman remind us, is a necessary part of the learning process: "Exploration involves pushing students into a mode of problem solving on their own. Forcing them to do exploration is critical, if they are to learn how to frame questions or problems that are interesting and that they can solve" (483).

Teachers benefit in unexpected ways as well. They learn progressively more about the issues students bring to the table, and they also receive interesting texts to read. The process proves effective for everyone involved because it includes sharing the workload. "Most of the effective [educational] programs . . . involve socially shared intellectual work, and they are organized around joint accomplishment of tasks, so that elements of the skill take on meaning in the context of the whole" (Resnick 13).

Strategies for Success

Key factors in ensuring success for this assignment are preparation and planning:

◆ Develop a good working relationship with the staff of the Office of Research Services or the equivalent at your school. This relationship is critical to understanding the thinking of the Institutional Review Board or its equivalent at your school. Ask staff members to comment on your application and give you suggestions for revision. Complete those revisions as soon as possible.

◆ Study the IRB forms, either in hard copy or online, and teach students to go through them step by step, adding comments to clarify what they should and should not do in their studies.

◆ Read and study all materials required by the IRB.

◆ Help students understand what the IRB requires.

◆ Use your application as a model for students and suggest ways they can revise that model to fit their own studies.

◆ Complete any revisions suggested by the IRB and return the forms as soon as possible.

◆ Use a procedure similar to that of the IRB when accepting or rejecting student proposals that do not require full board approval (e.g., studies involving other college students on campus). This stresses to students the importance of reading, writing, and thinking through their procedures as they solve their particular problems. It also becomes a way to discuss the need for revision not as punishment but rather as a way to rethink the proposal. It is a way for students to strengthen their authority, to prove that their study is credible, trustworthy, valid, and reliable.

◆ Enjoy collaborating with your students. The research proposal gives teachers and students alike a sense of accomplishment and pride in writing.

Works Cited

Belenky, Mary Field, Blythe McVicker Clinchy, Nancy Rule Goldberger, and Jill Mattuck Tarule. *Women's Ways of Knowing: The Development of Self, Voice, and Mind.* New York: Basic, 1986.

Chin, Elaine. "Redefining 'Context' in Research on Writing." *Written Communication* 11 (1994): 445–82.

Collins Allan, John Seely Brown, and Susan E. Newman. "Cognitive Apprenticeship: Teaching the Crafts of Reading, Writing, and Mathematics." *Knowing, Learning, and Instruction: Essays in Honor of Robert Glaser.* Ed. Lauren B. Resnick. Hillsdale, NJ: Erlbaum, 1989. 453–94.

Geertz, Clifford. *The Interpretation of Cultures.* New York: Basic, 1973.

Lave, Jean, and Etienne Wenger. *Situated Learning: Legitimate Peripheral Participation.* Cambridge: Cambridge UP, 1991.

Nelson, Jennie. "This Was an Easy Assignment: Examining How Students Interpret Academic Writing Tasks." *Research in the Teaching of English* 24 (1990): 362–96.

Perry, William G. Jr. *Forms of Intellectual and Ethical Development in the College Years.* New York: Holt, Rinehart and Winston, 1970.

Resnick, Lauren B. Introduction. *Knowing, Learning, and Instruction: Essays in Honor of Robert Glaser.* Ed. Lauren B. Resnick. Hillsdale, NJ: Erlbaum, 1989. 1–24.

Rogoff, Barbara. *Apprenticeship in Thinking: Cognitive Development in Social Context.* New York: Oxford UP, 1990.

An Assignment for Encouraging Research

JEANNE GUNNER

Santa Clara University

*The assignment described in the following article weds the ac-
tivities of research with the reading of literature.*

I developed this assignment for the second of a required two-
course first-year sequence. As director of our writing program,
I'm pushing to break down some calcified notions of research-
based writing—such as its "advanced" nature and so restriction
to the second-quarter course; the idea that research means library-based research only; and that the goal of such writing
projects is to teach discrete "skills." The following assignment is
an attempt to start using research, especially traditional library
research, in ways that illustrate the rhetorical and social issues
that I believe ought to be invoked.

Composition and Rhetoric II, Winter 1998

Gunner
Project 2: Historical Evaluation (due Friday, 2/13; 5 pp.)

Chinua Achebe's *Things Fall Apart* depicts Ibo culture in a particular historical period—the end of the nineteenth century. As
one of the few African works commonly read in the U.S. curriculum, it serves for many of us as the major source of information
about (one aspect of) African culture and its interaction with
European forces. But how reliable is the text as a source of historical information? Is its depiction a valid illustration of the Ibo
values of the time (as Okonkwo exemplifies them, for example,
or of the role of women in the culture, or of the culture's religious

practices)? Is its depiction of early colonial practices and purposes accurate (its depiction of missionary methods, for example,
or of attitudes toward converts)? Because the text is a piece of
imaginative literature, not a primary historical document, we need
to consider its validity as a source of information on such topics.
In this project, you are asked to do this evaluative research.

To conduct this inquiry, you'll need to engage in library-based
research (as opposed to other methods, such as empirical or ethnographic, though you may end up consulting empirical or ethnographic works). You can then consider Achebe's work in the
context of the information you gather. Focus on one cultural or
historical issue (the role of women, for example, or the mission-
aries' conversion methods, or some other issue—the choice is
yours). Read broadly on the topic, taking notes on all sources
consulted. Develop your argument about the text's validity in
relation to your chosen topic, citing the sources that most clearly
help you establish or limit the credibility of Achebe's text.

Your argument, then, will be a statement on the text's historical worth, tested by means of your research on one cultural
or historical aspect of the text. Consider how you will need to
build your argument: this "essay" is really about establishing
authority for your claim, which you'll need to do by gathering a
variety of convincing sources that you can use to support your
judgment. You'll need to cite multiple sources even as you assert
your own voice authoritatively. The writing challenge in this
project, therefore, is stylistic as much as logical.

<u>Grading criteria</u>:
fully developed thesis
logically progressive structure
effective citation use
breadth of research
correct documentation conventions
syntactic variation
stylistic punctuation use
recursive style

Citing Ourselves: Students as Specialists and Scholars

DONNA REISS

Tidewater Community College

Donna Reiss's lesson weaves students' voices into the discourse of their research projects.

To actively enter the world of scholarship before they undertake their required major research project, and to learn the importance of accurate integration and documentation of sources, students in my first-year writing classes cite their classmates as authorities in at least one of their shorter papers. After sharing their preliminary writings about a text or topic in an electronic forum (for example, e-mail, Daedalus InterChange, Norton Connect, or a threaded Web discussion), students have at hand a "published" text by another student in the class. As they draft their papers, they include in their support at least one quotation and at least one paraphrase from at least one classmate. They prepare a works cited listing that includes the classmate.

To ensure that every student has an opportunity to be cited, I team the students in pairs or in groups of three. Occasionally students say they have difficulty making their classmates' comments fit the purposes of their papers; however, they collaborate in their writing groups to find a way to do so coherently. This process gives students practice with the courtesies and conventions of documentation of sources, as well as with collaborative writing and editing.

For example, following several computer conferences in which students collaborated on a discussion of Theodore Roethke's poem "I Knew a Woman," Tim F. included the following passage in his final paper, "Mortal and Eternal Love Is Bridged by Death: An Explication of the Poem 'I Knew a Woman'":

Death and eternal life tie into the poem upon close inspection. "Of her choice virtues only gods should speak" leads the reader to believe that the woman is already deceased, although alive in the heavens somewhere. Another indication that the woman is deceased comes in the fourth stanza, "Let seed be grass, and grass turn into hay." The woman starts as seed then blossoms into grass and finally dies as she turns to hay, as noted by Mark N. The speaker expects to pursue his love via the bridge of death when he states, "What's freedom for? To know eternity." To discover eternity one must be free. The freedom the speaker is expecting is the releasing of his soul from his body through death, and crossing into eternal love with the woman he adores.

Mark N. is cited as a scholar along with the literary critics Tim found through his research, and Tim includes Mark's computer message as a citation in his final works cited listing:

N., Mark. Daedalus InterChange Conference "Roethke." English 112-04, Tidewater Community College, Summer 1995.

This activity invites first-year writing students to take seriously their own thinking and writing as well as that of their peers. They demonstrate the kind of collaboration and practice at scholarship described by Kenneth Bruffee as "interdependence," of the kind their professors practice in their own scholarly communities.

Work Cited

Bruffee, Kenneth A. *Collaborative Learning: Higher Education, Interdependence, and the Authority of Knowledge.* Baltimore: Johns Hopkins UP, 1993.

INDEX

EDITORS

Susan K. Miller is a doctoral candidate in rhetoric, composition, and linguistics at Arizona State University. She has taught first-year writing at universities and community colleges since 1996. Currently, she is a full-time faculty member in English and English as a second language at Mesa Community College in Arizona. Her research interests include teaching writing with technology, especially distance learning technology, and second-language writing.

Veronica Pantoja is a doctoral student in rhetoric and composition at Arizona State University, where she has served as a teaching associate in the English department and research associate in ASU's Center for Learning and Teaching Excellence. She taught and tutored writing at Del Mar College and Texas A&M University–Corpus Christi, and earned an M.A. in English from Texas A&M University–Corpus Christi in 1997 before coming to Arizona. Her research interests include computer-mediated teaching and learning, composition studies, and faculty development.

Duane Roen, professor of English at Arizona State University, performed duties as director of composition for four years before assuming his current job of directing ASU's Center for Learning and Teaching Excellence (www.asu.edu/clte). Prior to that, he directed the Writing Program at Syracuse University, as well as the graduate program in rhetoric, composition, and the teaching of English at the University of Arizona. Early in his career, he taught high school English in New Richmond, Wisconsin, before deciding to complete a doctorate at the University of Minnesota. In addition to more than 140 articles, chapters, and conference papers, Roen has published the following books: *Composing Our Lives in Rhetoric and Composition: Stories about the Growth of a Discipline* (with Theresa Enos and Stuart Brown); *The Writer's Toolbox* (with Stuart Brown and Bob Mittan); *A Sense of Audience in Written Discourse* (with Gesa Kirsch); *Becoming Expert: Writing and*

Learning Across the Disciplines (with Stuart Brown and Bob Mittan); and *Richness in Writing: Empowering ESL Students* (with the late Donna Johnson).

Eric Waggoner received his Ph.D. in American literature from Arizona State University in 2001. He has taught at West Virginia Wesleyan College and in the composition and literature departments at Arizona State University. He has contributed articles to several academic publications including *Hemingway Review, A/B: The Journal of Autobiographical Criticism,* and the *Dictionary of Literary Biography.* Waggoner is also a freelance writer, editor, and journalist, and is a regular contributor to the Phoenix *New Times.* His research and teaching interests include technical and professional writing as well as contemporary U.S. literature and cultural studies. He is currently teaching at Marshall University in Huntington, West Virginia.

Lauren Yena is a doctoral student in rhetoric and composition at Arizona State University. Before coming to Arizona, she spent five years teaching courses in composition, American literature, and English as a second language at universities and community colleges in Florida, Rhode Island, and Gothenburg, Sweden. In 1997 she earned an M.A. in literature from the University of Florida. Her current interests include computer-mediated composition and pedagogy, classical and contemporary rhetorical theory, and issues surrounding the needs of nontraditional student populations.

This book was typeset in Sabon by Electronic Imaging.
Typefaces used on the cover include Slimbach and Palatino.
The book was printed on White 50-lb. Williamsburg
Offset Smooth paper by Versa Press.